D1422758

World History of Warfare

CHRISTON I. ARCHER,
JOHN R. FERRIS,
HOLGER H. HERWIG, AND
TIMOTHY H. E. TRAVERS

CASSELL

Cassell
Wellington House, 125 Strand
London WC2R OBB

British Library Cataloging-in-Publication Data
A catalogue record for this book is available from the British Library

ISBN 0-304-36352-9

Printed and bound in USA

CONTENTS

ILLUSTRATIONS

MAPS

PREFACE

This book is both an introduction to the history of world warfare and a reinterpretation of that history. It does not simply repeat what other texts have argued but offers fresh views on the troubled past of our world. Similarly, the text does not aim to offer either an operations approach to warfare or a war and society emphasis exclusively but seeks to include both. Hence, the text should be of value to both students and the general reading public with an interest in military history. In addition, the authors have made a special effort to include non-Western material in the text, since almost all histories of warfare up to now have tended to be mainly Western in their approach or have even been predominantly restricted to European military history. The text also gives more weight to the earlier periods of military history, which normally either do not appear at all or are given little attention. Further, because the four authors each deal with different time periods and evidence, the chapters demonstrate the research and methods of each author and contain different emphases. Hence, the book does not follow the stereotyped textbook approach but reflects each author's own fresh insights and conclusions.

Any attempt to write a world history of warfare must focus on certain themes in order to organize the mass of material that exists. Emphasis on these areas varies from chapter to chapter according to available evidence and the nature of the material. The intent of each chapter is to illustrate these themes: first, the *idea of war*, meaning the attitude of a particular age toward warfare; the *experience of total war* in each era, that is, how war influenced the society of a particular period; the *impact of technology* on warfare in each age, focusing on changes in warfare; the *nature of armies*, considering the way armies are structured and organized in every era of warfare; and the *experience of the soldier*, that is, how individual soldiers actually experienced the warfare of their time. Finally, each chapter presents a case study of a specific battle or engagement that gives the reader a concrete example of what happened, how it happened, and why the event occurred at a particular time and place. Generally, these case studies illustrate the most significant battle or engagement of the period.

Another basic idea underlies the previously mentioned themes: the concept of change. The authors emphasize the importance of change in warfare, whether through technical invention or through tactical or strategic innovation. What did or did not change and why? By focusing on the significant changes in warfare and on the above-mentioned themes, the authors hope this unconventional text and reinterpretation of a world history of warfare will offer new light on the age-old human struggle for survival and conquest.

WORLD HISTORY OF WARFARE

INTRODUCTION
The Origins of Warfare

The origins of warfare lie shrouded in mystery. It seems very likely, though, that the weapons and preconditions for conflict, which certainly preceded warfare chronologically, initially emerged out of groups engaged in hunting. Bands of nomadic hunters clearly needed to cooperate in order to hunt, and by the Paleolithic age (from about two million years ago until the close of the last ice age, around 13,000 B.C.) groups were hunting with spears and by the Neolithic period (8000–4000 B.C.) were using the bow and arrow and the sling. Daggers also became available for dispatching wounded animals. However, Paleolithic cemeteries in Egypt reveal spear and flint arrowhead injuries likely to have been produced by raiding and ambushes, while cave paintings at the beginning of the Neolithic period show a more organized form of warfare. The well-known Neolithic cave painting from Morella la Villa in Spain unmistakably shows a battle between two small groups of archers. Nevertheless, organized conflict between large groups of humans, as opposed to conflict between individuals or sporadic raids and ambushes, was probably not a common occurrence. It may be, in fact, that the only traces of the link between hunting and warfare that can now be reliably detected are the combined hunting-military rituals of the Royal Hunt at the dawn of Sumerian history (c. 3000 B.C.) or the Royal Hunt of the Shang dynasty in China (c. 1765–1027 B.C.) or the "Great Hunting Game" of the Western Chou dynasty in China (c. 1027–771 B.C.). As an early Western Chou poem about the changing seasons declares,

> In the days of the Second [month, February] is the Great Meet;
> Practice for deeds of war.

However, since organized aggression does not seem to have been biologically programmed into early man, there must have been specific reasons for the development of warfare. One widely accepted possibility is that warfare emerged at the point of transition between wandering hunter-gatherer bands and the settlement of some groups into settled village life (perhaps around 6500 B.C. in western Asia). The occasion for the emergence of conflict in this case would have been the accumulation of surpluses of food and goods in the newly settled villages that became worth stealing by the roving groups of hunter-gatherers. This explanation is possible, although looting implies a modern concept of "economic man" that may not have been a strong Paleolithic or Neolithic motivation.

Alternatively, it could be argued that organized warfare had quite late and rather specific origins initiated by the competition for land in conjunction with population growth. Thus, in Europe about four to five thousand years ago, early colonizing Neolithic farmers moving into the area came into conflict with Mesolithic foragers and built ditches to keep the foragers out. Similarly, villages in northern Mesopotamia in the late Neolithic period, such as the Samara culture, built defensive walls and ditches, presumably for protection against attack, just at the point in time when these villages were expanding and competing for fertile land. Later, the people of the Lungshan culture of northern China (c. 3000–2000 B.C.) protected their settled, farming villages against attack with earthen walls and long, deep ditches because of population pressure on diminishing farming land, which no longer permitted the previous wasteful slash and burn methods of cultivation. Population growth, therefore, produced the splitting of larger Lungshan villages into numerous satellite villages, creating competition for land, which in turn created conflict among villages and between those who maintained the slash and burn methods and those who farmed identifiable fields contiguous with settled villages.

But a sense of territory did develop among some later societies when population growth, rising agricultural production, and the increasing complexity of societies produced cities with elaborate walled defenses and citadels, somewhere between 3500 and 3200 B.C. in Mesopotamia. In this context, it was thought that the inhabitants of the city of Jericho, further south in the Jordan valley, had built the first recorded defensive fortifications in history, perhaps around 7000 B.C. But archaeologists now consider that Jericho's 1.6-meter-thick walls and 8.5-meter-wide and 2-meter-deep moat actually were constructed to ward off flooding. Thus,

Jericho does not undermine the case for the development of defensive fortifications in cities only in the 3500–3200 B.C. period. In fact, early cities probably existed as much to assert dominance over the farming villages of the surrounding area as to provide defenses against external aggression, which may explain the growth of cities in other areas, such as the cities of Mohenjo Daro and Harappa of the Indus valley civilization of India (c. 3200–1600 B.C.). In the case of these two Indian cities, fortifications were confined to the citadels while the lower parts of the city were not protected by walls, suggesting that the primary function of the citadel was to affirm domestic authority rather than defeat besieging forces.

Military aspects of society become clearer with written history, beginning with the Sumerian culture around 3200 B.C. These linguistically mixed people settled around lower Mesopotamia, between the Tigris and Euphrates Rivers. Originally, there were a number of city-states, such as Kish, Uruk, Ur, and Lagash, that feuded against each other and seemingly contained relatively democratic political structures that elected a religious king figure. Pressure from the nearby Elamite kingdom seems to have produced dynastic states and the parallel transition from heroic to institutionalized, or structured, warfare. Two of the most important and earliest representations of warfare, the Standard of Ur (2500 B.C.) and the Stele of the Vultures of Lagash (2460 B.C.), show kings leading their people in battle. The sense of discipline and commitment of these followers, revealed by the military formations employed, is strongly conveyed. More importantly, these two pictorial representations of warfare, one a wall panel and the other a limestone stele, show the style of war in the middle of the third millennium B.C.

The Standard of Ur style of war provided a combination of chariots and infantry spearmen in relatively close formation. In the lower register, the chariots are really battle cars or wagons, since they are four wheeled, with solid wooden wheels, and are drawn by four animals with long ears, which are not horses but are either Asiatic "half asses" or mules. These animals have a neck harness and are controlled by single lines through a rein ring on a single yoke to nose rings, which suggest the origins of the chariot as a bovine-drawn farm cart or sledge. The battle cars are quite small and narrow, with room only for two men—the driver and a spearman or javelin thrower. The spearman stands directly behind the driver and holds onto him, which is necessary because the sides are

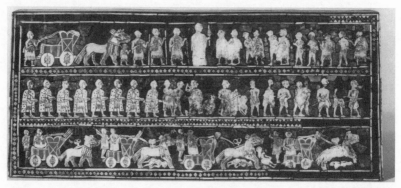

Fig. Stele of Standard of Ur, c. 2500 B.C. Sumerian warfare, showing a combined arms force of spearmen and chariots. BL WA 121201. (c) Copyright The British Museum.

low or nonexistent while the front of the battle car has a high breastwork to protect and provide support for the driver. There is a quiver of javelins to the front and side of each car.

The function of this battle car is debatable because the position of the spearman or javelin thrower behind the driver would make for difficult throwing except to the flanks. A charge toward a massed enemy would have been difficult not only because of the reluctance of the animals to move into or over obstacles (in the panel the existence of bodies under the animals symbolizes either a battlefield or the defeat of the enemy) but also because the lack of a swivel front axle made for a wide and awkward turning circle. Moreover, in one chariot the rear warrior is shown carrying a battle axe, indicating the necessity to step off the chariot to fight at close quarters. Indeed, the spear or javelin throwers behind the driver seem to stand on a rear step rather than inside the chariot.

It seems likely that this Sumerian battle car ran along the front or sides of an enemy force while javelins or spears were thrown. Additionally, the chariot would chase the retreating enemy or bring high-ranking officers to the battlefield, who would then dismount to fight. No doubt the battle car acted as a psychological weapon as well, especially if the enemy did not possess such a weapon, as this particular scene suggests. It is significant in this respect that the royal war chariot at the top left has higher sides and appears as a more formidable vehicle. Meanwhile, the infantry spearmen in the middle register are all dressed in similar studded cloaks and wear metal helmets. The suggestion of a phalanx, or tight infantry formation, is strongly indicated by their overlapping spears. They probably carry daggers under their cloaks, and the royal guard in the top register carry axes as well as spears. Overall, it can be suggested that this Sumerian army was a well-disciplined and cohesive force, relying on an early battle car maneuver to create gaps in a particular area of the enemy line, which would then be exploited by the weight and discipline of the tightly structured formation of the spearmen. These would advance and thrust their spears in unison to provide maximum impact on the enemy and, at the same time, maximum protection for each spearman.

It is remarkable that only forty or fifty years later, the art of war had apparently moved very considerably along the lines suggested in the Standard of Ur panel. In the Stele of the Vultures (c. 2460 B.C.)— a victory monument to the clash between the city-states of Lagash and Umma—the infantry formation of Eannatum, king of Lagash, has become even tighter. Indeed, it is a fully developed phalanx, not to be seen again until the Greek hoplite phalanx some 1800 years later. The top panel shows a column of metal-helmeted soldiers advancing in six files, with large rectangular shields locked together and long, heavy spears held firmly in two hands. They are led by King Eannatum himself, who carries a sickle sword in his right hand and probably a similar long spear in the other. He wears a long "field dress" slung over one shoulder and reaching almost to his feet, and his soldiers wear a lesser version— possibly some form of leather armor in strips. In the lower panel, the king in his chariot leads his army in triumph, and now the soldiers have their long spears and socketed axes slung over their shoulders. The king again holds a spear and a sickle sword and, in the front of the chariot, has a quiver of javelins ready for throwing as well as a battle axe. Just visible behind the king seems to be the hand of either a protective spearman or the chariot driver. Since both of the king's hands are occupied with weapons and the reins do not seem to be tied around his waist, there must have been a driver.

Due to the obliteration of much of the stele, it is impossible to fully reconstruct the style of war of Lagash, but clearly the close order infantry phalanx was the centerpiece of the attack. Probably it was preceded by a javelin throwing chariot action, and it may be that the chariots were accompanied by and formed a unit with a formation of light infantry. This may be deduced from the lower panel, where the king's chariot is accompanied by a structured formation of light infantry without shields, who carry both long spears and axes. Perhaps they are the royal guard, but they are certainly different from the heavy phalanx. It seems reasonable to assume, therefore, that following the mobile action of chariots and light infantry, the heavy phalanx went to work and, like the hoplites centuries later, simply pushed their way into the enemy ranks by the sheer weight and discipline of their locked shields and steady advance. The disorganized enemy was then finished off by the chariots and light infantry.

The Lagash army was evidently a formidable force. It was probably a standing army and served the expansionist policies of the Lagash dynasty (2570–2342 B.C.), which sought to control the trade routes to the Arabian Gulf and the Mediterranean. The weapons employed in Sumeria had not varied much for some one thousand years—the spear, the axe, the dagger, and the javelins of the chariot, while the sickle sword was probably more ceremonial than useful, since bronze could not yet be made hard enough to increase the length and therefore the utility of the weapon. Notable in their absence from the Standard of Ur and the Stele of the Vultures are the bow, the sling, and the mace. Apart from the possibility of simple absence due to damage or the whim of the artist, it seems that the mace had been offset by the metal helmet and replaced by the piercing axe. The sling required considerable training and perhaps, too, was offset by the helmet and the shield. However, despite its absence in the two steles, it is known that the single-arc, or stave, bow was in use at least by 3000 B.C. in Mesopotamia. This weapon was one of the oldest used in the hunt and in war, but it was not until the development of the composite bow by the time of the Akkadian expansion, including the defeat of Lagash and indeed the conquest of the whole area between the Arabian Gulf and the Mediterranean by Sargon the Great (2334–2279 B.C.) and his successors, that the bow came to be the dominant weapon of the battlefield.

The powerful Lagash system of war was defeated by the new style of the Akkadian army of Sargon. Sargon advanced from the north, partly because the Sumerian arable lands were starting to suffer from serious salinization problems by around 2350 B.C., which led to loss of fertility and economic decline. But Sargon's army was also more effective than that of Lagash because it included long-range archers, likely using the composite bow. The earliest certain representation of the composite bow occurs in the victory stele of Naram-Sin (2254–2218 B.C.), but such a complex weapon requires a considerable period of development, and an earlier Sargon victory stele (now attributed to the beginning of the reign of Sargon's son, Rimus [2278–2270 B.C.])

shows what appears to be a composite bow in action. Therefore, it seems likely that Sargon possessed this weapon, and it seems to have proved irresistible.

The composite bow was formed of wood, animal horns, animal tendons and sinews, and glue. As these substances were glued or bound together, and, before the string was attached, the bow was structured so that the two arms bent away from the body of the bow, thus creating great tension. The effective range of the bow was 250 to 300 yards.

The Akkadian army, as portrayed in the victory steles of Sargon/ Rimus and Naram-Sin, reveal a lightly armored three corps army of archers, axe bearers, and spearmen. Chariots are not shown in either stele and are not in use in Naram-Sin's better-preserved stele because this depicts mountain warfare, perhaps against the Elamites. Nevertheless, a later Babylonian poem, "The Curse of Agade," refers to Naram-Sin's chariots, and they probably existed even if they were largely ceremonial. In any case, Sargon's army (who fought thirty-four battles) evidently relied primarily on light infantry and the coordination of the three arms, with the composite bow archers as the most important element. With this army, Sargon created a large empire stretching from the Mediterranean to the Arabian Gulf, where he "washed his weapons" in a ritual celebration of his victories. The strategy of this expansion, like that of his predecessors and successors, was to protect the Akkadian monopoly of trade routes and to acquire raw materials such as cedar, tin, and silver. But again, like the Mesopotamian empire builders before him, Sargon and his Akkadian successors had great trouble in policing their distant lands, despite the innovation of appointing governors and the creation of the office of the high priestess of the moon-god at Ur as a royal sinecure and a centralizing religion.

Through internal strife as much as external invasion, the Akkadian empire crumbled by 2154 B.C. Later, it rose again as part of a homogenized Akkadian-Sumerian culture, under the title of the Third Dynasty of Ur (2112–2004 B.C.). This dynasty was noteworthy for attempting to stem the tide of invasions of Amorites and Elamites by building an incredible wall, 270 kilometers in length, that also cut across the Tigris and Euphrates Rivers, but to no avail: the city of Ur was besieged, the walls were breached, the city itself was devastated, and the last king of Ur was led away to captivity in Elam. Besides noting that the defenses of Ur were no protection, a Sumerian poem gives a sense of warfare at the time:

Dead men, not potsherds,
Covered the approaches,
The walls were gaping,
the high gates, the roads,
were piled with dead.
In the side streets, where feasting crowds would gather,
Scattered they lay.
In all the streets and roadways bodies lay.
In open fields that used to fill with dancers,
they lay in heaps.
The country's blood now filled its holes,
like metal in a mould;
Bodies dissolved—like fat left in the sun.

I. WARFARE OF THE ANCIENT EMPIRES

Egypt, Assyria, Persia, India, and China each viewed war according to the particular internal circumstances, economics, geography, and external threats they experienced at different times. Egypt, for example, faced the challenge of external threats such as the Hittites, the Hyksos, and the Sea Peoples; Assyria had the need to control trade routes and obtain minerals; Persia developed large armies and, under Xerxes, invaded Greece; India experienced a largely indigenous warfare; and China fought the wars of unification. Each civilization was profoundly influenced by warfare, although conflict was often localized. Armies (and maritime forces) became structured and less chaotic, but the success in warfare of these ancient empires was due to innovation, administration, and inspired leadership as much as to the development of particular weapons, metals, or armies. Of particular importance was the willingness of empires to learn from their neighbors and to adapt. This might be called "innovation on the periphery." The experience of the ordinary soldier was not usually remembered, although occasionally individual stories emerge.

Egypt

In Egypt the Old Kingdom (c. 2770–2200 B.C.), which united Upper (southern) and Lower (northern) Egypt, had come to an end, beset by economic and climatic problems and by the emergence of powerful provincial nobles who wrested central leadership away from the ruling pharaohs. These difficulties were worsened by internal bandits and by invasions of desert peoples. But around 2050 B.C., centralized rule in Thebes (Upper Egypt) was restored, and the progressive age of the Middle Kingdom (c. 2050–1560 B.C.) ensued.

Under the pharaohs of the Middle Kingdom, an integrated military force existed, composed of heavy infantry armed with spears and carrying large, wide shields, supported by light infantry armed with small shields, axes, daggers, stabbing spears, and javelins. The most important of these weapons were the spears and the axes. The Egyptians themselves do not seem to have developed a force of archers until the later stages of the Middle Kingdom period but relied on recruited Nubian archers. Nor were chariots used at this time. Egypt had natural geographical defenses—the Mediterranean to the north, the Red Sea to the east, and desert to the west—which meant that the most the country initially had to deal with were desert tribes and the Nubians to the south, and they could be controlled sufficiently by means of a relatively simple infantry-based standing army, as described above.

Yet changes started to filter into Egypt. It has been suggested that the Middle Kingdom employed a forward defensive strategy. This strategy required raids into the Palestine area and perhaps as far north as the Orontes River; it also required the building of a series of forts in the northeast along the Suez isthmus line and a defense-in-depth system of fortresses between the first and second cataracts of the Nile. A mobile, disciplined army capable of defending forts and undertaking siege warfare was required for this type of system. Hence, Egyptian archers who were not Nubians began to appear, because siege warfare required long-range weapons to keep defenders off the walls while breaches were made in the defenses. Perhaps originally the bow was the weapon of the Egyptian nobility, but by the close of the Middle Kingdom period the double-convex bow as well as the single-arc bow were in common use.

In addition, a forerunner of the battering ram, a very important weapon, made its appearance in the Egyptian army around 1900 B.C. According to a wall painting from Beni-hasan showing the siege of a desert fort by the Egyptians, a rudimentary ram consisting of a long, metal-tipped pole operated by three soldiers from within a sheltered hut now appears. Judging by the similarity of the clothing of the archers on both sides, this may be a Nubian fort, but in any case, the painting reveals that the ram apparently developed from a prizing weapon, originally a lengthy spear or pike that sought to lever apart the building blocks or gates of a city or fort. It is interesting that this prizing weapon and the more modern style of battering ram, using weight and momentum for effect, are shown simultaneously in a siege conducted by King Ashurnasirpal of Assyria (883–859 B.C.) because it means that the original prizing weapon was still useful, as indeed the Romans discovered later. However, judging by the glacis built to defend cities against battering rams and their necessary ramps, the ram existed in other societies, perhaps as early as the twenty-fifth century B.C.

The Middle Kingdom, like its predecessor, began to run into internal troubles from about 1786 to 1560 B.C. Over a lengthy period of time, Semitic peoples from the Palestine area (probably Canaanites) began infiltrating into the Delta area of Egypt, and gradually these people took over the running of the pharaonic government. Accompanying these groups were more mobile warriors, fanning out to capture cities in the eastern Delta. Between 1672 and 1649 B.C., a local warlord named Salatis seized Memphis and founded a regional empire based on the stronghold of Avernis. The Egyptians referred to the leaders of these Semitic people as "Hikau khasut," or "Rulers of Desert Uplands," later corrupted to "Hyksos." It should be emphasized that the Hyksos did not lay waste to northern Egypt in a single devastating invasion, which for a long time was the accepted interpretation. Rather, this was a gradual takeover of the Delta area. Similarly, in the South nomadic Nubian tribes gradually infiltrated into Upper Egypt. The fortress defense-in-depth system collapsed, with nomads taking over the ruins but accepting the suzerainty of the Hyksos in the north.

Although there is still debate on the subject, it does not appear that the Hyksos overwhelmed northern Egypt with the chariot. Rather, the weakened state of the defenses of the Delta area was the prime cause of the Hyksos' more gradual success, although it is possible that the Hyksos may have had access to the composite bow. The Egyptians probably encountered the chariot first in their Asian expeditions, since the Asiatic origin of the chariot in Egypt is attested by the different woods used in construction, by the Canaanite names for parts of the chariot, and by the use of Asiatics to drive and maintain at least some of the chariots. In fact, the chariot seems to have emerged around 1700 B.C. and perhaps originated in Armenia. Nevertheless, by the time of the Egyptian war of liberation against the Hyksos around 1600 B.C., a wide range of new weapons had been introduced from western Asia, including the (small) horse, the horse-drawn chariot, scale armor, the composite bow, bronze weapons, and new designs for daggers and swords. It is also possible that the Hyksos or other Asiatics from further north introduced new methods of defending fortresses by building a smooth glacis (to prevent rams and siege towers from approaching the walls), which have a battered stone base and massive angled gateways. As for the army, toward the end of the Hyksos period it was possible for chariots, foot soldiers, and archers to fight together (the Egyptian chariot normally had a crew of driver and archer), while horses were also used for reconnaissance and messages. In later Egyptian reliefs at Karnak and elsewhere, the pharaoh is frequently shown in his chariot, which, psychologically at least, was seen as a key weapon. Moreover, the chariot was a far more functional vehicle than it had been before, with spoked rather than solid wheels, a rear axle, horses controlled by bits, and an archer with the composite bow on board.

The life of the Egyptian soldier was likely to be either routine or very tough when on campaign. An Egyptian exercise book, entitled *Be a Scribe*, that deliberately portrays the life of the soldier as unpleasant nevertheless gives some idea of what military service could be like: "He is called up for Syria. He may not rest. There are no clothes, no sandals. His march is uphill through mountains. He drinks water every third day; it is smelly and tastes of salt. His body is ravaged by illness. The enemy comes and life recedes from him. He is told, 'Quick forward, valiant soldier! Win for yourself a good name!' He does not know what he is about. His body is weak, his legs fail him. If he leaps and joins the deserters, all his people are imprisoned. He dies on the edge of the desert, and there is none to perpetuate his name."

Despite the mention of the ever present desert for the unfortunate soldier, much warfare in Egypt was actually maritime, given the presence of the Nile and the Delta. For example, Kamose, an early Theban Egyptian leader of the revolt against the Hyksos, gives an idea of the experience of war under these conditions: "I fared downstream [i.e., from Thebes in the south toward the north] in might to overthrow the Asiatics . . . my brave army in front of me like a breath of fire, troops of Medjay [Nubian mercenaries] aloft upon our cabins to spy out the Setyu [Asiatics] and to destroy their places. East and West were in possession of their fat and the army was supplied with things everywhere."

Arriving in front of the stronghold of an Egyptian collaborator with the Hyksos, located near Hermopolis, which was Kamose's target, he continues: "I spent the night in my ship, my heart happy. When the earth became light, I was upon him as it were a hawk. The time of perfuming the mouth came [midday meal], and I overthrew him, I razed his wall, I slew his people and I caused his wife to go down to the river bank. My soldiers were like lions with their prey, with serfs, cattle, milk, fat, and honey, dividing up their possessions."

Kamose next sortied toward the Hyksos' fortress at Avaris, and the first Egyptian mention of chariots is contained in his victory stele: "I will seize the chariot teams." However, Kamose did not live to see the final defeat of the Hyksos; this was left to his successor, Amosis (c. 1552–1524 B.C.), who eventually captured the Hyksos capital of Avaris. Yet Amosis apparently had trouble gaining the victory, for the siege was a long one, seemingly because Avaris was defended by canals as well as walls. Thus, a naval victory was necessary before the walls could be approached. After this, Avaris was captured. Amosis then made an important move, advancing into Palestine to besiege a town called Sharuhen. Although this siege took three years (indicating that Amosis was unable to breach the walls and therefore had to starve out the inhabitants), Amosis had established an important new Egyptian "forward" policy, a policy of imperial expansion, with the objective, initially at least, of eliminating the incursions of Asiatics and Nubians into Egypt by defeating them in their homelands. Thus, Egypt became a more aggressive and militarized society that sought to subdue the peoples of Palestine, Syria, Canaan, Anatolia, and Lebanon as well as those of Libya to the west and Nubia and the gold rich kingdom of Kush (Ethiopia) to the south.

Not only did Amosis initiate a new imperialism, but because of his victories on the battlefield, he also created a new image of the pharaoh as a national hero—a warrior-god leading a professional army of chariot warriors. Henceforth pharaohs would launch numerous campaigns to maintain their empire. Tuthmosis III (1490–1436 B.C.), for example, fought no less than seventeen campaigns over a period of twenty years against the Mitanni in Palestine and Syria. Additionally, it was necessary to develop alliances among the shifting peoples of western Asia in order to try and maintain control as well as establish garrison towns at crucial geographic points. For logistical reasons, however, it was impossible to permanently pacify the western Asia region, and from about 1350 B.C., the Hittites in the area of Syria became a growing threat to the Egyptian state.

Sethos I (1309–1291 B.C.) campaigned vigorously against the Hittites and managed to capture the town of Kadesh, but his overall campaign was not decisive. It was left to his son Ramses II (ruled 1279–1213 B.C.) to conclude the war against the Hittites. Indeed, for the first ten years of his reign, Ramses focused his energies almost entirely on the Hittite problem.

Battle Scene: Kadesh

In late April 1274 B.C., the New Kingdom army of Ramses II set forth
to locate and defeat the Hittite army in its own region of Syria and so
began probably the most celebrated campaign of ancient Egypt. It is
also, however, a much debated campaign, and some historians believe
the plentiful temple reliefs depicting the campaign are purely symbolic
and do not represent the "real" campaign at all. In fact, one historian
believes that a large-scale battle did not take place at all and that the
major event of the campaign was a number of Ramses' soldiers being
executed by Ramses himself as punishment for cowardice. With these
reservations in mind, the Kadesh campaign can be portrayed.

At this time, the army of the pharaohs was a well-structured force
of divisions of some 5,000 men, each division bearing names such as
Amon and Ra (later named "Mighty of Bows" and "Plentiful of Valor,"
respectively). These divisions were composed of twenty companies of
250 men each, with their own standard-bearing company commanders.
Each company was then subdivided into platoons of 50 men each, led by
"the great ones of the fifty."

The pharaoh acted as army commander when he was in the field,
while his vizier played a vital role as war minister. The generals on campaign, such as divisional commanders and the chariot commander (often one of the pharaoh's sons), formed an army council advising the
pharaoh. The army was composed of heavy infantry, who wore no armor but carried spears, shields, battle axes, and swords (the spear being
the chief weapon), and archers, who carried their own shields as well as
the composite bow, a quiver for arrows, and a personal weapon, such
as a dagger. Many archers were chariot-borne, and each light chariot
contained a driver and one archer per light chariot. Their task was to
pick off the enemy at a distance and allow the heavy infantry to fight at
close range. Logistically, for this long-range campaign, there was also a
well-organized commissariat of baggage carts pulled by oxen, donkeys
carrying supplies, mobile field equipment to water and feed the chariot
horses, and resupply from ships along the coastal route.

Ramses set forth with an infantry army of four divisions—Amon,
Ra, Ptah, and Sutekh—plus chariots and a royal advance guard. The
force numbered at least twenty thousand men. According to a number of
sources, Ramses first marched along the coastline for logistical reasons,
then turned inland and reached the small town of Shabtuna, where a ford
crossed the Orontes River. At this place, two desert Bedouin (Shasu),

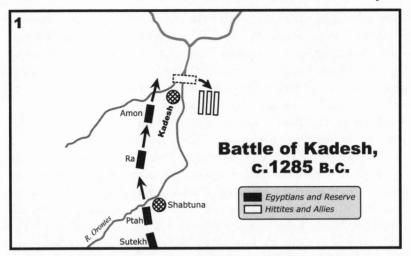

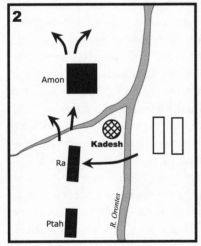

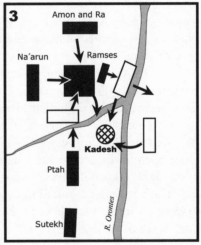

Map 1.1

sent secretly by the Hittite leader Muwatallis, falsely informed Ramses that the Hittites were far to the north, near Aleppo. This caused Ramses to cross the ford with the Amon division, followed at some distance by the Ra division, but the other two divisions did not cross the ford. Moreover, the false information caused Ramses "not to draw up for fighting him [Muwatallis], to battle with the wretched foe of Hatti [Hittites]." This means that Ramses did not form his men into close battle order but continued to march with his divisions in a long-drawn-out line.

When Ramses was about seven miles from the major town and fortress of Kadesh, Muwatallis withdrew his army to the northeast of Kadesh to conceal his presence. Ramses continued on in blissful ignorance of the Hittites and set up camp to the northwest of Kadesh with the Amon division. Since Ramses was well acquainted with the principles of warfare, he then either went out himself with his guard to see that the area was secure or sent out scouts. These scouts, or the guard, apparently captured two Hittite scouts, who were brought to Ramses and tortured. They eventually were forced to admit: "See the wretched foe of Hatti is stationed together with many countries [i.e., allies]. . . . They are equipped with infantry and chariotry, bearing their weapons, more numerous are they than the sands of the shore. See, they are standing, drawn up for battle behind Kadesh the deceitful."

For Ramses this was a nasty shock. But the events that immediately followed this startling piece of information have, until very recently, been open to dispute because the sources available to historians have been highly embellished accounts—written as poetry or carved as temple reliefs at Karnak, Abu Simbel, and elsewhere, together with an inscribed record on the reliefs. In these reliefs the pharaoh, Ramses, naturally emerges as a major hero. But new research, of a linguistic nature, has been able to identify parts of an original military daybook account (which is reliable for the first part of the battle), upon which the Egyptian scribe was later to embellish a rhetorical and literary account praising the actions of Ramses.

It appears that after the two Hittite scouts confessed, Ramses did have sufficient time to call together the army commanders at hand. There was no conference, as is usually assumed, because the action to be taken was obvious. Ramses urgently sent a horse messenger plus his vizier in a chariot to the south to hasten the arrival of the nearest division, Ra, and, further to the south, that of Ptah. These messages got through before the Hittites attacked so that an important section from the daybook states: "Then the infantry and the chariotry of his majesty were discomfited before them when going northward to where his majesty was." This means that the division of Ra and the accompanying chariot force had already started north to help Ramses before the Hittite assault, but they were prevented from reaching Ramses because the Hittites must have already moved between Ramses and his army to the south. According to the daybook, however, the Hittites did not just split the Egyptian army in half, but "they cut through the division of Ra in its middle, while they were marching without knowing." One final reliable daybook entry is puzzling: "They crossed over the ford [which is to the] south of Kadesh." Whether "they" refers to the last two Egyptian divisions hurrying across the ford at Shabtuna or to the Hittite chariots crossing south of Kadesh to launch an attack is uncertain.

The sources from this point until the end of the battle are once more less reliable poetry and inscriptions. Nevertheless, some deductions can be made. Since it is known that the Ra division was apparently not able to help Ramses, it seems the Hittite chariot attack, with twenty-five hundred chariots, actually was two-pronged: one driving south to attack the division of Ra, probably cutting it in half, and the other turning north to attack Ramses' camp and the division of Amon. This neatly separated the Egyptian army into two halves. According to the less reliable poetic source, the southern half of the newly divided Ra division was thrown into confusion, while the northern half ran into Ramses' camp and frightened both themselves and the Amon division into panicked flight. The Hittite chariots then penetrated Ramses' defended camp, at which point Ramses is supposed to have mounted his chariot and single-handedly fought off the Hittites: "I [Ramses] charged all countries [i.e., the Hittites and all their allies], while I was alone, my infantry and my chariotry having forsaken me. Not one among them stood to turn about [i.e., turned around to help Ramses]." All this seems highly unlikely given the light Egyptian chariot and the surrounding force of twenty-five hundred Hittite chariots. Although the heavier Hittite chariots carried three men, two of whom were allies and only one Hittite (suggesting that the Hittites did not fully trust their allies), they were only armed with thrusting spears. Therefore, despite the obvious propaganda in favor of Ramses, it does seem possible that Ramses showed leadership in collecting together his royal guard and whatever chariots were available and then counterattacking by riding up and down the front and flanks of the Hittites, using the long-range composite bows to keep the Hittites at a distance. Ramses apparently attacked the extreme right of the Hittite line and drove this group into the Orontes River.

This maneuver was sufficient to keep the Hittite chariotry unbalanced. Additionally, many Hittites and allies gave up their chance of a decisive victory by getting off their chariots and plundering Ramses' camp. Meanwhile, Muwatallis hesitated to commit his very large force of infantry to the battle, still on the right bank of the Orontes, perhaps because they were vulnerable to the long-range Egyptian bows or because Muwatallis was still uncertain as to the flow of the battle. But at this critical point, a relieving Egyptian force arrived from the west (not the south). This force had almost certainly been summoned at the same time as Ramses had sent out his urgent messages for help to the south and was composed of Na'arun (young men), said to be recruits from the coastal region of Amor. It is also quite possible that this was a flanking formation, guarding Ramses' left (west) flank, while the Egyptian right flank would have been protected by the Orontes River. In any case, this new force slaughtered the Hittites in Ramses' camp. Then Ramses and his royal guard, plus the new arrivals, together with the remains of the Amon and Ra divisions rallied to attack the Hittite chariots blocking the southern Egyptian divisions. Muwatallis replied by sending another one thousand chariots from his reserve but still no infantry. Then Ramses' vizier arrived with the Ptah division and attacked the Hittites from the rear. Thus, the Hittite chariots were encircled from the south and the north, and the rest of the Hittite army retired inside the fortress of Kadesh. The battle being effectively over, Ramses is reported as victoriously viewing the defeated captives from his chariot as well as watching his officers throwing down in front of him the severed hands of the slain Hittites and allies, a traditional Egyptian method of celebrating victory and counting the enemy dead.

Yet Ramses did not take the fortress of Kadesh, probably because his forces were logistically unprepared to besiege the town and perhaps because his army was in poorer shape than he admitted. Indeed, tablets from the Hittite capital of Boghazkoy claim that the battle of Kadesh was actually a Hittite victory. According to these tablets, Ramses was forced to retire to the south, while the country of Amor was conquered by Muwatallis. Reading between the lines, it does appear that Ramses' army was forced to make a strategic retreat, although Ramses himself may have helped stave off defeat at a critical juncture. Ultimately, Ramses managed to survive the battle of Kadesh because he received information about the Hittites' intentions before they attacked, giving him just enough time to call in reinforcements. Additionally, Ramses' army had superior weapons: the composite bow and more maneuverable chariots versus the heavy Hittite chariots armed only with short-range thrusting spears. These advantages probably kept the Hittites at bay long enough for reinforcements to arrive.

Ramses fought several more campaigns against the Hittites in the area of Syria and Palestine without result, and stalemate set in. A sensible peace treaty with the Hittites ensued as well as marriage with the eldest daughter of the Hittite king and even joint Egyptian-Hittite military training. No doubt this was partly because Egypt was conscious of threats from the Libyans in the northwest as well as the Nubians to the south. From the Hittite point of view, the peace treaty was also opportune since they needed to deal with a new power emerging in the north—Assyria. Similarly, the Hittites renewed a peace treaty with the Kassites, who were also afraid of the Assyrians.

Ramses II was succeeded by other able pharaohs, especially Ramses III (1182–1151 B.C.). Following Ramses III there were less competent rulers, Egyptian creativity declined, and eventually the Egyptian empire could not be held against revolts and social corruption from within and attacks from without. These attacks came from groups like the mixed "Sea Peoples" (perhaps from western Anatolia, around 1200 B.C.), from Libyans (from the mid-tenth century to the end of the eighth century B.C.), from Kushites (from around 750 until 670 B.C., and ultimately from the Persians (in 525 B.C.), who absorbed Egypt into their empire. Among those who invaded, defeated, and ruled the Egyptians between 671 B.C. and 663 B.C. was the same aggressive power that had frightened the Hittites—the Assyrians. Ironically, however, this late-Assyrian intervention in Egypt overextended Assyrian power and seems to have precipitated the destruction of the Assyrian empire some fifty years later. However, all this was in the future when, in the fourteenth century B.C., a series of capable rulers transformed the city of Ashur on the Tigris into a growing power.

Assyrians

Assyria derived its name from Ashur, which as a city-state was originally subject to Babylon. Assyrian rulers such as Assur-uballit I (1365–1330 B.C.) occasionally managed to impose some control over Babylon, and in the thirteenth century B.C., the Assyrian king Tukulti-Ninurta I (1244–1208 B.C.) actually sacked Babylon and captured its ruler, reporting: "[I] trod with my feet upon his lordly neck as though it were a footstool. Bound I brought him as a captive into the presence of Assur, my lord. Thus I became lord of Sumer and Akkad in its entirety [i.e., the lower Tigris and Euphrates Valley] and fixed the boundary of my land as the Lower Sea [i.e., the Persian Gulf] in the east."

There was method in Tukulti's military efforts, for Assyrian strategy was to remain fixed for almost all the period of Assyrian supremacy. The strategy was, first, to control the profitable trade routes to the east and west, and second, to obtain access to mineral sources (tin, silver, and later iron), which tended to lie north of Assyria. This was important because Assyria, and Mesopotamia generally, lacked mineral resources. Thus, the powerful and energetic Tiglath-Pileser I (1115–1077 B.C.), among his many campaigns, used his chariot-based army to extend his rule through northern Syria to the trading lands of the Mediterranean. However, toward the end of Tiglath's reign, there came the first of the invasions of Aramean tribes from the western desert, which brought about a decline of 150 years in Assyrian fortunes. But in the ninth century B.C., a succession of aggressive Assyrian kings emerged who engaged in extensive military campaigns. Prominent among these were Assurnasirpal II (883–859 B.C.) and his son, Shalmeneser III (858–824 B.C.). They were to be followed by another group of prominent military rulers from the mid-eighth century B.C.—such as Tiglath-Pileser III (744–728 B.C.), Sargon II (721–705 B.C.), Sennacherib (704–681 B.C.), and Assurbanipal (668–627 B.C.).

Turning to the ninth century B.C., Assurnasirpal II and Shalmeneser were especially successful in expanding the Assyrian empire along trade routes as well as making secure the boundaries of Assyria just beyond the Tigris and Euphrates Rivers. This was especially the case to the east and north, where the mountains harbored unfriendly Aramean and Urartu tribes. At the time of Assurnasirpal II and his immediate successors, the formidable Assyrian army was well organized in its infantry and siege arms, but the mobile arm was in transition. The infantry was formed into two main groups: the spearmen and the archers. The former were the shock troops of Assyria, heavy infantry wearing a long coat of mail and a helmet and carrying a lengthy iron-tipped spear, a relatively small shield, and an iron sword. These troops were organized for hand-to-hand fighting. However, the main power of the Assyrians appeared to be their archers. These men were armed with an advanced composite bow and a sword and also wore armor. Protecting the archers from their opponents generally required shield bearers, who stood beside the archer shielding him, forming an archer pair. When this was the case, the archers wore less heavy armor. Standing behind the archers, but only from the mid-eighth century B.C. onward, were slingers, who were particularly useful at sieges in directing high-angle fire. These were undoubtedly captured units or auxiliaries, since this was not an Assyrian tradition. It is also of interest that the Assyrians employed many eunuchs in their army, often as officers, recognizable in sculptures by their beardless faces.

The siege arrangements of the Assyrian army were well developed, for a great deal of Assyrian warfare, if not the majority, was not open-order battle but sieges of the forts and towns of rebelling or resisting tribes and minor kingdoms. The Assyrians under Assurnasirpal II employed a mobile, armored ram with an iron point shaped like an axe blade. A mobile assault tower carrying archers accompanied the ram. There were also miners capable of tunneling under walls and armored sappers who prized away at the foundations of walls and gates with pikes and spears. Meanwhile, archer pairs were employed in keeping defenders' heads down, while scaling ladders were placed against the walls. Shock spearmen, carrying shields upraised to protect them from arrows and rocks, used the ladders to scale the walls. Identifiable by their headdresses, these shock troops were from the royal guard and always led the assault. The combined assault of archers and royal guard was normally, but not always, sufficient to cause the swift defeat of the defenders.

During the reign of Assurnasirpal II, the mobile force of the Assyrians was composed of chariots. These carried a driver and an archer and were drawn by two horses, with a third horse—an outrigger—as a spare. However, the outrigger experiment was later dropped. The driver carried a spear for defense, and the chariot also contained an axe and a shield slung at the back. These chariots were, like the Egyptian models, used for fast, flanking maneuvers, harassing the enemy, and pursuit rather than shock, since they were not capable of breaking through enemy ranks. Later on, Assyrian chariots became heavier and higher, carrying four men—the driver, an archer, and two shield bearers—drawn by four horses, and designed more as a mobile platform for archers. This heavy chariot was apparently developed first in northern Syria and then adopted by the Assyrians.

Fig. 1.1. Assyrians at siege warfare, attacking a town in Egypt. From Ashurbanipal's palace, c. 645 B.C. BL WA 124928. (c) Copyright The British Museum.

Finally, Assurnasirpal II's army saw, for the first time, the creation of cavalry. His cavalry was composed of pairs, one horseman holding the reins of the second horseman who was actually an archer. The two-man team that originally occupied the Assyrian chariot simply moved forward onto the backs of two horses in front of the chariot, creating the evolution from chariot to cavalry. But at this stage, cavalry and chariots operated together. Eventually, under Sargon II (721–705 B.C.), with the assistance of new reins and bits, the cavalryman as a mounted archer began to ride independently, and a separate Assyrian cavalry force was created. Subsequently, cavalry lancers also developed, for pursuit and for harrying isolated enemy groups.

This was a significant revolution in warfare. It can be charted chronologically by the Assyrian records of captured or donated chariots and cavalry, which show a changing preference. Hence, at Qarqar in 853 B.C., Shalmaneser III captured horses and chariots in a one-to-one ratio, that is, one cavalry unit worked with one chariot team. But in 831 B.C. in Damascus, the ratio reverted back to three to one in favor of chariots. Then in 790 B.C., Shamshi-Adad V attacked Babylon and captured chariots and cavalry in a one-to-two ratio. Finally, some eighty years later, in 709 B.C., Sargon II gave chariots and cavalry to the governor of Babylon in the ratio of one to ten, meaning, cavalry were more useful than chariots by a factor of ten. These ratios were confirmed by the capture or supply to Sargon II's army of fifty chariots, two hundred cavalry, and three hundred soldiers from Carchemish and two hundred chariots and six hundred cavalry from Hamath. (The exception was Samaria, which relied exclusively on chariots, and so Sargon II simply placed fifty Samarian chariots in his army as a single unit with a Samarian commander.) Thus, by the late eighth century B.C., cavalry had replaced chariots as the favored arm. Mounted archers were an established force in warfare, assisted by a new reining system, new bits with more braking power, a more comfortable saddlecloth, new breeds of imported horses, and foreign experts (Urartu for cavalry, while Nubia and Samaria still provided chariot expertise). It was the emergence of this cavalry arm that forced the shift of Assyrian chariot use toward the heavier, more specialized archer platform, as can be seen in seventh-century-B.C. wall carvings. This was because the previous chariot role of opening the battle by swift maneuvers along the front and sides of the enemy formation had been usurped by the cavalry.

What made the Assyrian army so successful? It was not the development of the new iron technology around 1200 B.C., as often argued. Because of its initial rarity, iron had a prestige value, and only the Assyrian kings used iron weapons. But even when iron was commonly available, bronze weapons continued to be used. When iron weapons did become more widespread, they were still seen only as a substitute for bronze. That is, when iron technology became widely known, iron replaced bronze mainly because bronze was scarcer. Finally, iron had a greater impact on agricultural and craft tools than on weapons. Although the Assyrian army did use iron weapons, they were not a critical factor in establishing Assyrian supremacy.

If not metallurgy, then what? It appears the most important reason for Assyrian success was that Assyrian rulers were progressive in importing, incorporating, and improving military ideas, expertise, and weapons from neighboring and often hostile societies. For example, they used foreign military experts, mercenaries, horses, chariotry, cavalry, and the composite bow. The Assyrians also learned from and incorporated into their army whole units of auxiliary troops of those societies they had defeated. These units both reinforced the Assyrian army and introduced new ideas. This borrowing and adapting took place not just in warfare but also in other areas; for example, the Assyrians learned how to make water tunnels from Palestine and Syria.

The next most important reason for the success of the Assyrian army was that the Assyrians proved very clever at organizing an integrated army, which dovetailed shock, missile, mobile, and siege troops (infantry, archers and slingers, chariots, cavalry, and siege engineers) into a single effective force. The core of the army were the archers and the spearmen, supported and made more effective by the actions of the mobile arm. All this came about through trial and error, as can be seen in the way in which the Assyrians experimented with different shields and armor for their infantry, in the development and changing roles for their cavalry and chariots, and in the changing types of ram used, from heavy and cumbersome to the lighter and more mobile models of Sennacherib. In other words, the Assyrians were open to innovation and change, largely because of the stimulation of the continuing integration of conquered peoples from different societies into their army.

The Assyrians also quickly learned the value of propaganda in preventing rebellion within their empire and in encouraging hostile tribes or kingdoms to surrender. Thus, the Assyrian army and society tried to present themselves as both irresistible and terrible. Recently, it has been argued that much of this "terror" propaganda was exaggerated and that it did not represent what actually happened, since the wall carvings of various Assyrian kings in their palaces show only victories and never defeats. Even so, the measured, personal tone of kings like Assurnasirpal II when recording his treatment of defeated rebellious groups, such as Ahia-baba and his city, must have given potential rebels pause for thought: "I erected a pillar opposite his [Ahia-baba's] city gate, all the chiefs who had revolted I flayed, with their skins I covered the pillar, some in the midst I walled up, others on the pillar on stakes I impaled, still others I arranged around the pillar on stakes. Many within the borders I flayed, with their skins I covered the walls. As for the chieftains and royal officers who had rebelled, I cut off their members."

Meanwhile, the unfortunate Ahia-baba was taken to Nineveh, where he was flayed and his skin spread upon the wall of Nineveh. When recording the capture of another city, Assurnasirpal II stated in the same personalized fashion: "I cut off their heads, I burned them with fire, a pile of living men and of heads over against the city gate I set up, men I impaled on stakes, the city I destroyed, I turned it into mounds and ruined heaps, the young men and maidens in the fire I burned."

Even if not always true, the declaration of this terror treatment of those who rebelled (as opposed to those who were conquered or who submitted) was sufficient to prevent a certain amount of resistance, except in periods of Assyrian weakness. No doubt this also must have helped the Assyrian army when approaching rebellious towns or fortresses, particularly because of the well-known Assyrian treatment of the kings or leaders of revolts. Thus, under Assurbanipal, the rebel lord of the desert Bedouins, one Yatha, when he sought forgiveness in Nineveh, found his cheeks and jaw bones pierced, a rope inserted, and the rest of him chained like a dog and set to guard the gate of Nineveh. When Assurbanipal tired of this, he had Yatha pull his chariot, along with three other deposed leaders. Besides these punishments, the Assyrians also followed the policy of deporting conquered or potentially awkward populations to opposite ends of the empire, just as Ramses II had done in Egypt. This, too, must have made the task of the Assyrian army easier in traveling across or subduing fractious areas.

Another important reason for the success of the Assyrian army was the administration of the empire that lay behind it. The empire was divided into provinces, each with a governor who answered directly to the king. Distant provinces were run by vassal kings. A bureaucracy and civil service grew up, the latter often staffed by eunuchs. (These sometimes became too powerful, and it seems Sennacherib was forced to destroy their power when he acquired the throne.) Labor and military service were regulated and provided by each province, with feudal land tenure providing the basis for military service, although by Tiglath-Pileser III's time (745–727 B.C.), the beginning of a standing army had been established. This able monarch reorganized the provinces, reintroduced an effective imperial government, and created a system of posting stages for rapid communication across his large empire. The careful effectiveness of such a central government can be seen in the detailed provision of horses for the Assyrian army. This has always been a problem for armies with cavalry and other horse needs, since horses do not appear by themselves. Thus, by the early seventh century B.C. each Assyrian province typically contained two important "horse officials" called "musakisus," who continually traveled their provinces seeking horses for the king and who wrote reports directly to him. One officer, in charge of the royal stables near Nineveh, wrote daily "horse reports" directly to the king, often requesting decisions about what to do with animal drafts. Around one hundred horses arrived per day in Nineveh from all parts of the empire. If such care was taken with horse supply, it is evident that equal care would be taken with running all parts of the Assyrian empire and army. Without this attention to detail, just as in the later Roman army, military efficiency and success could not have come about.

Finally, even behind the administration of the empire, lay the strategy of the Assyrians, which provided the empire with sufficient funds to maintain both army and empire. Something has already been mentioned concerning trade routes, but it is useful to look specifically at how one Assyrian king set about the problem. Shalmaneser III (858–824 B.C.), like the other Assyrian kings, did not set out to expand his empire in random fashion but consciously sought to control supplies and trade routes. Shalmaneser III achieved good relations with Babylon because that state controlled trade routes to the south and the Persian Gulf, making it essential to expand west and east. The area to the west provided the best sources of iron and silver, and it was there that the Assyrian king focused his military campaigns. Therefore, Shalmaneser III fought three separate campaigns in the area of Qarqar, in 849, 848, and 845 B.C.. Then, Jehu of Israel submitted in 841 B.C., meaning that Shalmaneser III had conquered Hamath in Syria and thus controlled the trade routes through central Syria to Asia Minor and also the Mediterranean. Turning to the east, Shalmaneser conducted campaigns in the Zagros mountains because that area dominated trade routes to the east (e.g., routes for tin from Afghanistan), and he also forced tribute from Gilzam in northeast Iran because Gilzam supplied horses for the Assyrian chariots. So significant were the eastern and western locations of Shalmaneser III's campaigns that when these campaigns were commemorated—on his Nineveh bronze gates, on steles, on the Warka vase, on the Black Obelisk, and on his throne base—they were commemorated according to geographical groupings rather than chronologically.

As a conclusion to the Assyrian style of war, it is useful to look at a campaign conducted and fully reported by Sargon II in 714 B.C. This ruler moved his palace to Khorsabad, further to the north, and seems to have extensively occupied himself with northern campaigns against the Haldian and Urartu peoples between the Van and Urmia Lakes and to the east of Lake Urmia. In the latter case, this was partly to protect trade routes through what is now modern Tabriz, toward the Caspian Sea. The overall campaign, however, aimed at restoring the Urartu to obedience, at looting all the many villages and towns in the region, and, judging by the tribute brought in, at obtaining animals—fast horses, mules, and camels—for the Assyrian army. This was a mountainous region, and Sargon II had to abandon all chariots except his own (which was carried when it could not advance), and he relied instead on cavalry, archers, spearmen, and engineers. A baggage train of camels and mules provided logistics, and a type of light ram that could be dismantled was carried along. At one point Sargon had to use his engineers to break open the rocks with their bronze axes in order to make a road so that the army could advance at all. Sargon also related how he besieged the double-walled fortress of Parda by running one ram up the steep road to the gates and then making a causeway for a second ram while his engineers, archers, and spearmen helped to take the fortress.

Later, Sargon learned that the Haldian tribe, under its leader Rusash, was offering resistance by drawing up an army in the open. Sargon therefore made a lightning dash to attack them with only his cavalry, probably because they were not a formidable obstacle. Sargon's account, although overstressing his leadership skills, has the ring of truth:

> The unhappy troops of Assur [Assyria], who had marched by a distant route, were moaning and exhausted. They had traversed many mighty mountains, whose ascent and descent were difficult, and they had changed their appearance. Their fatigue I did not soothe, water for their thirst I did not pour out. I did not set up my camp, I did not fortify the wall of my camp. I did not send my warriors forth, I did not collect my army, those who were at my right or my left did not return to my side, I did not look back, I did not use the greater part of my troops, I did not raise my eyes. With my chariot alone and with the cavalry who march at my side, who never leave my side in a hostile and unfriendly land . . . like a mighty javelin I fell upon Rusash, his destruction I accomplished, I routed him. The bodies of his warriors like malt I brewed. His warriors who bore the bow and the lance before his feet, the confidence of his army, I slaughtered. Two hundred and fifty of the royal seed, his governors, his officials, and his cavalry in my hands I took and I broke his battle-line. I shut him up prisoner in his camp, and his horses trained to the yoke [i.e., chariot horses], with javelins and arrows I destroyed under him. To save his life his chariot he abandoned, he mounted a mare, and before his troops he fled.

Fleeing did not help Rusash, since Sargon continues complacently: "Rusash feared the report of my mighty arms, and like a bird of the glen who flees before the eagle his heart trembled. As a man who has poured forth blood, he left . . . his royal city, like one fleeing the hunter he reached the flank of his mountain. As a woman in travail, he laid himself down on a couch, food and water he refused, an incurable disease he inflicted upon himself."

Sargon's account shows that the sudden Assyrian cavalry charge was sufficient to break the Haldians, who then rapidly retreated into their fortified camp. By this time the Assyrian archers and spearmen had evidently arrived, and they attacked the camp, destroying the Haldian chariots and their horses. Then Rusash fled, and when all hope was gone, he poisoned himself. Sargon replaced him as ruler, exacted labor dues from the Haldians, carted off huge booty, and took away able-bodied men for military service.

Sargon then continued on with his subjugation of the mountain tribes of the north. But the borders and trade routes of Assyria continued to give trouble, and Sargon soon had to stem the revolts of both Elamites and Chaldeans. Sargon met an obscure death when his camp was attacked in 705 B.C.—apparently his elite body guard had allowed itself to be caught napping while on campaign against a minor king on the eastern border of Assyria. However, in his lifetime, Sargon perfected the creation of a standing army through native levies and through the incorporation of large numbers of foreign troops. Sargon also developed the royal guard, composed of the Companions, the nobility of Assyria, and the troops "of his feet"—one thousand picked soldiers so-called because they served close to the king.

Despite the accession of capable rulers after Sargon, especially his son Sennacherib and Assurbanipal the scholar, Assyria started to flounder. Part of the problem was the power of Babylon to the south, always aided and abetted by its allies the Elamites and Chaldeans. Babylon had been destroyed, flooded, and turned into "a meadow" by Sennacherib, but the city again revolted in 652 B.C. Assurbanipal commenced a siege in 650 B.C., but Babylon only surrendered in 648 B.C. because of starvation. Obviously Assurbanipal had been unable to reduce the city in any other way. The ruler of Babylon threw himself into the sacred flames of his palace, Assyrians looted the city, and the rebel leaders were given short shrift as recorded by Assurbanipal: "I tore out their tongues and defeated them completely. The others, alive, I smashed with the very same statutes of protective deities with which they had smashed my own grandfather Sennacherib—finally a belated burial sacrifice for his soul. [Sennacherib had been assassinated in Babylon, supposedly under the gaze of these same statues.] I fed their corpses, cut into small pieces, to the dogs, pigs, zibu-birds, vultures, the birds of the sky and to the fish of the ocean."

Assurbanipal obviously thought he had dealt with Babylon. But on his death, the city once more asserted independence, and in 612 B.C. a coalition of Babylonians, Medes, and Scythians besieged and destroyed Nineveh, the Assyrian capital. The Assyrian empire fell apart, never to rise again, despite the feeble efforts of one or two successors to the throne. Assyria had overextended itself in its seventh-century Egyptian campaigns, could never finally deal with Babylon either through conciliation or destruction, had increasing trouble maintaining distant Assyrian provinces created by ninth- and eighth-century campaigns in order to protect trade routes for minerals and timber, and had weakened itself through incessant attempts to subdue the mountain kingdom of Urartu and other states to the north and west. The system of provincial self-government under delegated governors or rulers, which had permitted the growth of Assyrian power, could not be sustained because the empire had grown too large to be controlled. Ultimately, Assyria had been too successful militarily and had overexpanded.

The Persians

The leading force that helped to destroy Nineveh was the army of the Medes, led by their king Kyaxeres. The Medes had unified around the second quarter of the seventh century B.C. and created a small empire that extended from south of the Caspian Sea toward the Black Sea and embraced the southern Zagros Mountains. According to Herodotus, the Greek historian, Kyaxeres is said to have remodeled the Median army into an effective force by separating out the arms of spearmen, archers, and cavalry, who were previously mixed up together. Whether or not this happened, the Median army was successful, and at some point in the seventh century the Persians joined forces with the Medes as junior partners.

The Persians were a society of obscure origin, who first settled in two or three areas and then in the Iranian land to the east of the Persian Gulf. The first great Persian ruler was Cyrus the Great (560/59–530 B.C.). According to Herodotus, Cyrus lived a charmed life as a youth. The story goes that the Median king of the time, Astyages, married off his daughter to a Persian noble, and they produced a son named Cyrus. But Astyages dreamt that this grandson would supplant him, so Astyages gave Cyrus to his trusted general Harpagos, to dispose of. However, the scheming Harpagos substituted the stillborn son of a herdsman for Cyrus, and Cyrus was then brought up by the herdsman's family in northern Media. At a young age, Cyrus's behavior of playing at being king brought him to Astyages's attention, who then realized that Cyrus was actually his own grandson. Astyages allowed Cyrus to live but punished Harpagos by serving up his own son to him at dinner. Understandably, Harpagos became angry but bided his time and then incited Cyrus to revolt, and in due course Cyrus defeated Astyages, whose army may have mutinied against him. The date and nature of this victory are uncertain, but, while the rest of Herodotus's story may not be true, Cyrus did take over the crown from Astyages sometime between 554 and 550 B.C.

Cyrus did not have to create a kingdom; he had one ready-made in the small Median empire. But his further conquests showed him to be an unusually capable military leader as well as an astute administrator. In the latter role, Cyrus borrowed from Median institutions, and he created a diverse empire. He achieved this by offering peace, clemency, and friendship to most of those that he either conquered or won over by other means. Thus, local religions and priests were honored, local officials were retained wherever possible, and everyday life was left undisturbed. Cyrus appointed governors, known as satraps, to each province, although they were not necessarily Persians. However, the power of the governor was counterbalanced by the appointment of a treasurer and a garrison commander to each capital city, directly responsible to the king, and there was an annual visit by a royal inspector, the "King's Eye." Each province provided tribute according to past tradition. Army commanders likewise did not have to be Persian, and Cyrus and his successors were generous in giving grants of land to local as well as to Persian soldiers. These then were obliged to provide chariotry, cavalry, and bowmen, according to the status of the fief-holder. Cyrus was generally seen as a liberator and welcomed by many in the provinces he incorporated into his empire. For example, the Jews hailed Cyrus as some kind of Messiah, and the temple in Jerusalem was rebuilt. Thus, his empire survived on toleration.

There is some dispute in regard to the composition of Cyrus's army. Xenophon, the Greek soldier and writer, claimed that Cyrus's army originally consisted of one thousand "peers," ten thousand light infantry, ten thousand slingers, ten thousand bowmen, and no cavalry. But Xenophon's knowledge is suspect, and carvings at Susa and Persepolis show infantry armed with both bows and spears, as well as the king's chariot and, in front of the chariot, some enigmatic barebacked horses. In front of these horses are grooms carrying whips and what look like saddlecloths, suggesting an elite or emerging cavalry force. Additionally, Herodotus says that Persians were taught three things only: "to use the bow, to ride a horse and to speak the truth." No doubt the Medes, and in turn the Persians, would have learned of the benefits of cavalry from their contacts with Assyria.

It seems, however, that Cyrus did commence with a purely infantry force, probably due to an initial lack of horses. But after 539 B.C., Cyrus looked to the east to continue his campaigns, and there a cavalry force was necessary. Not trusting the Medes, who did use cavalry, Cyrus developed his own force, which became the best cavalry of any army before the arrival of Alexander the Great. Indeed, this cavalry came to be the dominant arm of the Persian army. The cavalry employed different methods: horse archers could circle the enemy and fire in volleys of arrows, the cavalry could hurl javelins into the enemy mass, or heavier cavalry could use spears and swords at close range. But the original strength of Cyrus's army would have been in its archer pairs, called *sparabara* (a composite bow archer defended by a shield bearer), combined with close order spearmen, who also carried a dagger and wore light leather armor. The royal guard, however, were armed with lengthy spears as well as the bow, and troops are shown in wall reliefs as carrying both a short spear and a composite bow. The archer and spearman combination seems to have become the norm, and instead of having a shield bearer, the archer would plant a large wicker shield in the ground and then fire arrows from behind this defense. The army, led by an obviously ingenious commander, became mobile and adaptable, supported by some chariotry and later by the cavalry.

Cyrus's ingenuity was displayed during his swift invasion of Lydia. In this campaign, the Lydian commander, Croesus, attempted to stem Cyrus's advance with his cavalry, taking advantage of Cyrus's lack of cavalry, but was out-generalled when Cyrus brought up camels. The smell of these beasts was enough to stampede Croesus's cavalry. Cyrus then found himself up against the walled defenses of the main Lydian city of Sardis. Cyrus did not have the siege skills to take Sardis, and eventually he would have been forced to retire, except that one day a Lydian defender was observed to drop his helmet, climb down the walls to retrieve it, and then climb back up again. A select group of Persians was therefore detailed to follow the soldier's route up the wall, which they did, and the city was taken. However, Croesus was treated with kindness, and Lydia became a Persian province.

A similar story of ingenuity concerns the capture of the city of Babylon in 539 B.C. This city had been thoroughly repaired and its defenses made formidable by its earlier Chaldean ruler, Nebuchadrezzar II (604–562 B.C.), with outer and inner walls and defenses covering the Euphrates River. But the present incumbent, Nabonidus, was far from popular due to excessive religious zeal, and Cyrus was a master of propaganda in presenting himself as the prospective liberator of Babylon. There are two versions of the taking of Babylon—one states that after capturing other centers in Babylonia, a rebel leader, Ugbaru, led a Persian force into the city without a battle. The other story comes from Herodotus, who relates that Cyrus found the walls of Babylon impregnable and so had the Euphrates River diverted in order that Persian troops could secretly enter along the dry river bed, underneath the fortifications. Possibly this last version is a corruption of Cyrus's later irrigation projects in the area. Either way, the citizens of Babylon did not resist unduly, and Herodotus claims that "Owing to the vast size of the place, the inhabitants of the central parts . . . long after the outer portions of the town were taken, knew nothing of what had chanced, but as they were engaged in a festival, continued dancing and reveling until they learned the capture but too certainly." In any case, Cyrus entered Babylon in triumph. Branches were placed in front of him, and, forbidding looting, he proclaimed peace to all men, the continuation of Babylon's priesthood and religious institutions, and even claimed to have compensated those who had suffered under Nabonidus. Cyrus appointed his own governor but left the civilian administration intact. Then in 538 B.C. Cyrus made his son, Cambyses, king of Babylon, a post that Cambyses did not fill with distinction and so had to be removed.

With the eastern half of his empire under control, Cyrus ventured far to the east, possibly as far as modern Afghanistan. Finally, in 530 B.C., Cyrus reappointed Cambyses as king of Babylon and left for an expedition against a rebel Bactrian tribe in distant central Asia. Here Cyrus tried a typically clever ruse, for, according to Herodotus, he crossed the Jaxartes River and set a trap for the tribe by leaving his undefended camp full of wine and food. The camp was plundered, and Cyrus was easily able to dispose of one of the three divisions sent against him. But the other two divisions of the tribe under their queen, Tomyris, attacked

Cyrus. The battle was drawn-out, first fought at a distance by cavalry and archers behind their wicker shields and then at close range, where the Bactrian tribe prevailed and Cyrus was wounded. Cyrus's wound festered, and he died. Cyrus may have had logistical problems in this distant campaign, and his forces would have been reduced in numbers, especially as Cambyses, who had accompanied Cyrus as far as the Jaxartes, was sent home, presumably taking some part of the army with him. Tomyris then apparently used Cyrus's skull for a drinking cup in celebration, if Herodotus is correct.

It appears that Cyrus built his empire as much by political acumen and propaganda as by military means. In addition, Cyrus benefited considerably from the political vacuum created by the end of the Assyrian empire. The Assyrians had already eliminated the powerful Elamites between 646 and 640 B.C., leaving only the unpopular Babylonian city-state and the Medes, with whom Cyrus initially allied. Cyrus's original army of archer-spearmen does seem unusual, but it was well led and could rely on Median experience and traditions as well as lessons learned from contact with Assyrians and Elamites. The secret of Cyrus the Great's army, however, was the high quality of archery and the skilled use of the spear, both derived from considerable training and pride in their use. Cyrus also began the process of incorporating provincial forces to supplement the core Persians and Medes, and thus he initiated the Persian emphasis on size as the ultimate guarantee of success. It is notable, however, that the conquered provinces were soon forbidden to give military training to their young men, in order to prevent rebellion. Instead such training was provided once these levies were in the Persian army.

Cyrus was succeeded by Cambyses, who invaded Egypt in 525 B.C. with a large force of mounted archers. This was sufficient to defeat the Egyptians at Pelusium, to the east of the Delta. Cambyses has received a bad name from Herodotus, as a tyrant, but was a reasonably able army commander. However, he did not live long, dying in 522 B.C. when he contracted blood poisoning after accidentally stabbing himself in the thigh with his own sword as he mounted his horse. His successor, Darius I, proved to be an extremely capable administrator, organizing such matters as roads, coinage, and taxation. In particular, he reorganized the Persian Empire into twenty satrapies, each giving a fixed tribute, adjusted for ability to pay. Governors of satraps were responsible for both military and civilian affairs. There was a standing army and strong garrisons at frontier posts, but each satrapy was also supposed to supply levies in the event of a major campaign. In this case, there were certain marshalling points in the empire for bringing levies together and channeling the men and material of the vast empire. The empire under Darius I extended to include the lower Hindush (Indus) Valley to the west and in the east the Skudra and Scythians, around the Black Sea.

The Persian army possessed an inner core of the "Ten Thousand Immortals" (so-called because the unit was never allowed to fall under this number). At the center of the elite Immortals were the two royal household regiments, the first being the royal guards—one thousand archer-spearmen, carrying a composite bow and quiver slung over the left shoulder and a seven-foot-long spear held in both hands, with a golden apple on the butt, which rested on the toe of the shoe. The other household regiment consisted of one thousand archer-spear cavalry, which are not shown in wall carvings. The remainder of the Immortals were infantry archer-spearmen, the difference being that the front ranks of the Immortals carried only a six-foot-long spear and shields, to provide a solid barrier behind which the archers could launch massive flights of arrows. The archers also carried a broad sword for personal protection. According to Herodotus, the Persian army as a whole was built up in a decimal manner, with squads of ten, companies of one hundred, regiments of one thousand, and divisions of ten thousand. The highest unit was a corps, of which there were six, giving an army strength, at least on paper, of sixty thousand. Finally, according to Herodotus, there were twenty-nine infantry "armies" drawn from all the satrapies of Persia, giving an overall potential Persian strength of 1.74 million men, not counting the Immortals and what must have been an immense baggage train. Of course, this was an impossible number, invented by Herodotus. The doctor Ctesias, with Persian sources, gives the number of troops as eight hundred thousand, and even this must be too large. Whatever the number, it was evidently a very large army.

Of the twenty-nine "armies," six came from Persia and the old provinces of the Median empire and were composed of heavy infantry wearing armor and carrying bow and spear, club and sword, and shields for the front ranks. Another series of armies were effective light infantry soldiers with various side weapons, such as Bactrian and Scythians armed with bows and either short spears or a form of axe. A further ten armies were light infantry from all over the empire according to tribal origin. The majority of these light infantry did not wear armor and simply carried spears and javelins. The final seven armies were light infantry archers of bewildering variety, such as Indians, Nubians, and Sarangians from southern Afghanistan. There were seven armies of cavalry also. These were either the traditional Persian archer-spearmen (really infantry converted to cavalry) or genuine archer-horsemen from Bactria, Paricania, the Caspian area, and India. The Persian cavalry seems not to have employed shock tactics but, rather, a flanking, harassing, and pursuit role, riding up close to the enemy line and firing arrows or javelins before wheeling away again. There was also an Arab dromedary corps and a strange group of eight thousand Sagartians, who carried lassoes and daggers. Possibly this last group tried to entangle the legs of horses and men with their lassoes before finishing off the task with the dagger. Scythed chariots were reported in use but without conspicuous success—indeed the age of the chariot had really drawn to an end—even though the Persian army continued to use chariots in an attempt to disrupt the enemy line at the beginning of a battle.

Against poorly organized or primitive forces, this huge Persian army was successful. But the Persian army was really a conglomeration of levies from across the vast empire, each infantry army fighting according to its own native tradition, and thus there was an important lack of integration and cohesion among the infantry units. Only the Immortals, and the six armies of heavy infantry, of Persian and Median background, usually fighting in the center of the line, provided a secure hinge for the army. This lack of integration also applied to the cavalry but to a lesser extent since their role in any case required a degree of independent action. Moreover, only the Persians could field a cavalry strength of seven armies, hence this unique ability was sufficient for most campaigns. One other important attribute characterizes the Persian attitude to warfare, namely, the inclination to "gigantism," which means that logistics were extremely important, in fact so important that the ability to put a huge army into the field seems to have become an end in itself. All in all, the Persians relied on their traditional archer-spearmen, on their cavalry, and on their commissariat and saw no reason to change and innovate as the Assyrians had done.

This attitude eventually got the Persians into trouble when they met Greek hoplite (heavy infantry) forces, who had developed a style of warfare of their own. The Persian Empire reached its zenith at the time that Darius turned his attention to the Greek mainland, drawn in as a result of internal Athenian politics and an attempt to extend Persian influence into Athens. A revolt by the Ionian colonies in 499 B.C., supported by Athens, stimulated the Persian decision to intervene. After one abortive expedition in 492 B.C., Darius sent another army, supported by six hundred ships (fighting triremes and transports—see next chapter for naval warfare), in 490 B.C.. Eventually, the fleet landed at Marathon, and the army disembarked. Here the Persian army of fifteen thousand outnumbered the eleven thousand Athenian and Plataean hoplites, and for a space of some eight days there was stalemate, with neither side willing to attack. Then, after hearing of the victory of part of their army to the north, at Eretria, the Persian generals decided to end the standoff by moving directly to Athens by sea and started embarking the Persian cavalry. While the Persians were engaged in this awkward maneuver, the Athenians decided to attack quickly.

Knowing that their shields and armor were invulnerable to Persian arrows except at very short range, the Athenians charged in at the run in order to cut down the time period during which they were vulnerable to arrows. Once at close range, the heavier Athenian bronze armor, helmets, bronze reinforced round shields, and long thrusting spears proved more efficient than the iron "fish scale" tunic armor, wicker shields, and shorter spears of the Persian army. Brushing aside the two light infantry wings of the Persians, the Athenians then rolled up the Persian heavy infantry center, which had held its own until this point. The Persian army then broke and fled for their ships, most of which were able to get away.

The outcome of this battle for the Persians was simply an annoyance, but for the Athenians it was a psychological victory proving that the much vaunted Persian army could be beaten. Yet, neither Darius nor the Persian army commanders learned much from Marathon, or if they did, change proved too difficult to implement in the diverse and sometimes incompatible units of the vast Persian army. Nevertheless, when Darius died in 486 B.C., his successor, Xerxes, began to plan an immense invasion of the Greek mainland. In many ways, the logistical aspects of this invasion are the most interesting. Clearly, when the full Persian force went into action, as in Xerxes' invasion of Greece in 480 B.C., the logistical problems must have been immense. Not only were the numbers of men involved truly staggering, but the Persians, addicted to gigantism, allowed a train of attendants and hangers-on to accompany the army, compounding the problem even more. Just to take the case of the Immortals, it seems that they were permitted numerous concubines and attendants who traveled in carriages, and the Immortals were also supplied with select food and supplies that had to be carried on camels and other beasts.

Herodotus gives the size of Xerxes' land army at an extraordinary 1.7 million men before further additions, not counting the maritime portion of more than six hundred triremes and another two thousand or more smaller support craft. Herodotus's figures for the land army are impossible, and several historians have attempted to arrive at more realistic figures. Persian sources give a figure of 800,000, but this, too, seems far too high. Alexander the Great found he could not travel with many more than 50,000 men, although Xerxes' objective was nearer, at the edge of his empire, and he had much greater resources to call upon. Moreover, Xerxes had spent several years preparing the expedition. If one accepts that there were twenty-nine corps, or armies, present at 10,000 men each, plus the Immortals, a figure of 300,000 for the Persian army is reached. Even this figure is difficult to accept for logistical reasons, and it seems more likely that the real figure was somewhere around 170,000 men, comprising sixteen armies of 10,000 men each, plus 10,000 Immortals.

Whatever figure is chosen, it was clearly the largest army the world had seen up to that time, and the invasion could not have been logistically possible unless the army was supplied by sea. Herodotus reports that the Persian army traveled along the coast in order to keep in constant touch with the grain supply ships, which were protected by the fleet. It is often forgotten that the fleet would also have needed the protection of the land army. The triremes and other ships were light craft carrying large numbers of rowers with no room for supplies and needed to land frequently take on water or wine and food. Unless the land army was there to protect the fleet at its frequent stops, the invasion could not have continued.

Additionally, Persian logistics were solved by setting up supply dumps ahead of the army, by populated areas along the line of march being forced to feed the multitude, and by the creation of a large baggage train composed of camels and sumpter beasts. Xerxes also took care to march at harvest time in order to make use of this food, and, judging by Herodotus's account, the march was so planned that, for example, between Doriscus and Acanthus, the army divided into three sections so that each section did not compete with the others for forage and water.

But one section always remained marching along the coast to have access to supplies from the ships and to protect the fleet.

The army crossed the Hellespont on two constructed pontoon-style bridges, according to Herodotus, taking seven days and nights to cross, which certainly indicates a very large force. The army then traveled along the coast to Doriscos, where it was counted by the curious expedient of herding each mass of soldiers into a fenced-in area that could just contain ten thousand soldiers when squeezed closely together. After the counting, the army proceeded to Acanthus, marching along the coast. But from Acanthus, the army had to march inland across the Chalcidice Peninsula to reach Therma. In order to do this, the army evidently had to load up the camels and sumpter beasts with sufficient food supplies for the trip across land, and Herodotus reports that lions attacked the camels along the way. When the army reached Therma, Herodotus claims that it spread along the coast as far as the Haliacmon River, presumably to obtain supplies from the fleet, to obtain water, and to forage without the competition of too many soldiers in one area. Similarly, the fleet would have replenished their food and water supplies from a number of different places. From Therma, the fleet sailed south along the coast toward Magnesian territory, as usual ahead of the army. Herodotus was so impressed with the logistical problems of the Persian army that he wrote: "I am not at all surprised that the water of the rivers was found too scant for the army in some instances; rather it is a marvel to me how the provisions did not fail, when the numbers were so great. For I find on calculation that if each man consumed no more than a choenix of grain a day, there must have been used daily by the army 110,340 medimni [160,000 bushels], and this without counting what was eaten by the women, the eunuchs, the sumpter beasts, and the hounds [that followed the army]."

Of course, Herodotus believed the army to be much larger than it actually was, but his comment is apt; the logistics must have been a nightmare. The problem became worse with the storm that hit the Persian fleet near Cape Sepias. The storm was followed by a series of indecisive naval conflicts at Artemisium, with the Persians probably getting the better of it. But in adding together the results of the storm and the naval battles, Herodotus maintains: "As for the number of the provision craft and other merchant ships which perished, it was beyond count." This obviously exaggerates, but there were no more than about 350 Persian ships left, which had two consequences: the Persian fleet could no longer automatically count on naval superiority and, logistically, Xerxes could not afford to be held up as he headed south toward Athenian territory.

Unfortunately for Xerxes, a holdup is exactly what happened when his army arrived at the famous pass at Thermopylae. Here the huge Persian army was checked by a small force of Spartans under Leonidas, plus some Greek allies. After waiting for a short time to see if the Greeks would retreat, Xerxes attacked the narrow pass, which was perhaps only fifty yards wide. The Spartans held out for three days, despite attacks by the Immortals. Herodotus describes the action: "The two armies [were] fighting in a narrow space, and the barbarians [Persians] using shorter spears than the Greeks, and having no advantage from their numbers. The [Spartans] fought in a way worthy of note, and showed themselves far more skillful . . . often turning their backs and making as though they were all flying away, on which the barbarians would rush after them with much noise and shouting, when the Spartans would wheel round and face their pursuers, in this way destroying vast numbers of the enemy."

Xerxes was in despair, but a Greek, hoping for a reward, told the king of a mountainous route around the pass. The Persian army secretly ascended the pass at night, and although the feet of the soldiers shuffled the leaves on the ground so that the noise alerted the Greek sentries, the Persian army could not be not halted. Leonidas's force was outflanked, and the next day the Persian army was able to surround the Spartans, who meanwhile had sent their Greek allies away to save lives. Leonidas and his Spartans fought to the last, but it is of interest that Herodotus says of the remaining Spartans that although "the spears of the greater number were all shivered . . . with their swords they hewed down the ranks of the Persians." In other words, even without spears, the Greek heavy infantry was superior to their Persian counterparts. The Persian army then resumed its march toward the city of Athens. The city and the Acropolis fell easily, since the defending force was small and most of its inhabitants had fled. But the Athenian commander, Themistocles, recognizing that the vulnerability of the Persian army was actually its supporting fleet, managed to entice the Persian fleet into the narrow bay at Salamis. Here, in September 480 B.C., one of the most famous sea battles of ancient history took place, under the eyes of Xerxes, who watched from a golden throne overlooking the straits.

Essentially, the Greek fleet enticed their opponents into the narrow straits of Salamis. Herodotus states that the Greek allies sailed with 380 ships, while the Persians possessed some 350. Other sources give the advantage to the Persian fleet by some 40 ships. In any case, the Greek strategy was to draw the Persian ships into the straits and use the narrow waters to their advantage. The space was made even narrower by the little island of Psyttalia, on which the Persians had silently landed an infantry force at night so that they might capture stragglers and provide sanctuary for their own men. The Greeks backed water to entice the Persian fleet even further into the limited space and then turned about and attacked the Persian ships, which were led principally by the Phoenicians and the Ionians, who were Persian allies. Apparently the Greeks maintained their line, while the Persian fleet fell into confusion, perhaps because of a morning swell that ran counter to their direction or because of a breeze that affected the higher Phoenician ships more severely. Herodotus states that since "the Greeks fought in order and kept their line, while the barbarians [Persians] were in confusion and had no plan in anything that they did, the issue of the battle could scarce be other than it was."

The confusion was also increased by the Persian ships in the rear, who, feeling the eyes of Xerxes on them, pressed forward and got entangled with their comrades ahead of them. When the front line Persian ships tried to flee, they got even more entangled with the ships behind that were still pressing forward. This is the case, for example, with the one vessel of the Persian fleet commanded by a woman, Artemisia, which simply sank the nearest Persian ship in order to escape. Once the ships locked beaks, the fight was transformed into a land battle, in which the Greek hoplites, who had been embarked on the Greek ships, were clearly dominant. In fact, this naval battle became a matter of close-range infantry fighting. For example, Herodotus tells the story of a Persian ship, a Greek Samothracian trireme, that had sunk an Athenian ship but that was crippled in turn. But the Samothracians "were expert with the javelin, and aimed their weapons so well that they cleared the deck of the vessel that had disabled their own, after which they sprang on board and took it."

Furthermore, not all of the Persian fleet was involved in the battle, and so the Persians could not bring their full force to bear. Thus, the large Egyptian contingent was notably absent, possibly guarding the western Megara exit to the straits. The Persian fleet had lost some two hundred ships; the Greeks, around forty. Many of the men manning the Persian squadrons were also lost, since as Herodotus says, "they did not know how to swim," and all of the Persian infantry on the island of Psyttalia were also slain. Xerxes was in serious trouble, for the fleet upon which his land army depended for supplies was forced to retreat to Phalerum "and there sheltered themselves under the protection of the land army." In other words, the fleet was defeated and could no longer guarantee grain for the Persian army. Winter was approaching, and the Persians were forced to retreat to Asia Minor. But Xerxes was unwilling to accept a total, humiliating defeat, and so one-third of his army was left to winter in Thessaly. This force included the Immortals, presumably supplied with food by local resources and ready to resume campaigning in the spring. However, Greek sources tell of a headlong retreat by the remaining two-thirds of the army, not so much out of fear but because of lack of food. Once again, Herodotus tells the story: "In five and forty days he [Xerxes and army] reached the place of passage [the Hellespont], where he arrived with scarce a fraction . . . of his former army. All along their line of march . . . his soldiers seized and devoured whatever food they could find belonging to the inhabitants; while if no grain was to be found, they gathered the grass that grew in the fields, and stripped the trees, whether cultivated or wild, alike of their bark and of their leaves, and so fed themselves. They left nothing anywhere, so hard were they pressed by hunger."

Xerxes' retreating army was helped by the fact that the harvest was in and some grain must have been available. They also had the fleet, which wintered over in Samos, to protect the Ionian Islands. Without these supply ships, there was literally no way to feed the army except by foraging. Herodotus does not mention the baggage train, but in any case there was no food for the animals to carry. If the march took only forty-five days, clearly the army was moving fast, in forced marches, to minimize the lack of supplies, a trick that Alexander the Great later used. Only at Abydos, at the end of their journey, were there sufficient provisions, undoubtedly provided by the Persian administration through advance warning of the sorry state of the army. Disease and dysentery, the soldiers' curse, also attacked the army, and the sick had to be left behind in the care of local cities. It must have been a pathetic army that finally reached Sardis. However, Xerxes was unwilling to admit defeat, and the great resources of the Persian Empire enabled him to reinforce his troops in Thessaly in 479 B.C. There, in late summer, a confused battle, with mistakes on both sides, took place at Plataea. Despite the superior Persian cavalry, the Persian army had still not learned to properly integrate foot and horse, and once more the Greek hoplites proved battle winners. With this defeat, the Persian threat to the Greek mainland vanished forever.

From then on, the Persian Empire began a slow decline. Egypt successfully revolted in 405 B.C. and was not reconquered until 343 B.C. through the use of mercenaries. By 400 B.C., the feudal system, which sustained the army, was in decay, and the army that faced Alexander the Great in the 330s B.C., although still very large and heavily reliant on cavalry and chariots, was no longer effective against an outstanding general and a carefully structured Macedonian army. In fact, for much of the fourth century B.C., the Persian kings had only been able to crush revolts in the empire and achieve military success by paying mercenaries, usually Greek. However, it has been argued that a Persian military commander, Megabyzus, between the 480s and 450s B.C., was the first to integrate Greek (infantry) hoplites with barbarian (Persian) cavalry. It is also the case that, despite an overall Persian decline, a number of innovations were introduced in the fourth century B.C., particularly heavy infantry and heavy cavalry. Thus, by 401 B.C., when Cyrus the Younger attempted to oust his elder brother from the throne, he used Greek hoplites as the centerpiece of his army but surrounded them with a cavalry corps as a protective screen. In this way, the great problem of the Persian army, the lack of good heavy infantry, was remedied, and when added to the traditional Persian cavalry, it formed the basis for future armies for several centuries. Yet this was only a first step, for it was also necessary to integrate further arms into such an army to make it adaptable, such as light infantry, slingers, archers, skirmishers, and both heavy and light cavalry. In other words, the central core of the army, the heavy infantry phalanx, had to be integrated with a variety of other arms to make the whole army flexible enough for tactical maneuverability on the battlefield. This is what Philip and Alexander of Macedon were able to achieve.

India

In 515 B.C., Darius completed the eastward expansion of the Persian Empire with his invasion of India. There the Persian army found that the Indians fought according to ideas that would later be used in medieval Europe. That is, the Indians put together a form of the future medieval "lance," a tactical unit composed of elephants, chariots, cavalry, and infantry. Later, Alexander the Great was to invade the Indus Valley and achieve a celebrated victory at the Hydaspes in 326 B.C. What was the military state of the Indian civilization that the Persians and Greeks encountered, and did this civilization possess unique military features? According to archaeological excavations, there was an initial farming culture as early as the sixth millennium B.C. in the Indus Valley and in the Baluchistan Uplands to the east. Following this, there developed a mature indigenous Indus Valley civilization or tradition between about 2600 B.C. and 1300 B.C.. This civilization was based on agriculture but was primarily urban in focus, with some seventy urban centers so far discovered. There were extensive trade links with Mesopotamia between roughly 2300 and 2000 B.C., and the major sites so far excavated—for example, Harappa and Mohenjo-Daro—reveal cities with some thirty-five to forty thousand inhabitants.

Harappa and Mohenjo-Daro were fortified, the most prominent feature being a central citadel, which seems to have been built with the aim of reinforcing domestic authority rather than defeating external aggressors. Numerous bronze and copper spears, axes, daggers, short swords, and arrowheads have been found. It is argued that these do not reflect weapons for war but are tools or hunting weapons. However, several mace heads were also found, along with a large number of small and large baked clay missiles, presumably either sling shots or for throwing and probably used for raiding or local feuds. Finally, at Mohenjo-Daro a number of scattered skeletons have been found in positions that suggest simultaneous, and in some cases violent, death. But recent archaeology suggests that there was no Aryan invasion between 1900 B.C. and 600 B.C. as previously thought. Instead, the Indus Valley civilization slowly decayed over a long period as a result of internal factors and perhaps a series of Indus River floods.

Following the Indus Valley civilization was the Vedic age (c. 1500–1000 B.C.), so-called because of the four sacred "books" known as Vedas. These were not written down until centuries later but were composed over a period of time stretching from the beginning of the second millennium B.C. until around 1000 B.C. and were passed on orally. At this time, the horse and the chariot are mentioned. The chariot had been in common use from around 1700 B.C. in the Near East, and it is frequently referred to in the Rig Veda, where Indra's two bay horses and his chariot do much damage: "mounter of the chariot at the neighing of his two bay horses—Indra is the shatterer of even the steadfast." Indra apparently conquered many minor princes or kings with the chariot: "These twice ten kings of men . . . you [Indra] cast down with your ill-falling chariot wheel, O famous one, along with their sixty thousand and ninety-nine [men]." Armor, composed of bronze, is also frequently referred to, no doubt used only by the chariot elite. But clearly the bow is the principal weapon: "With our bow we would win cows, with our bow the match, with our bow we would win fierce battles. Our bow causes the enemy's dislike of us: with our bow we would win all the regions." There is also some discussion of iron weapons, which would indicate a later date for some of the Rig Veda hymns, since iron was only introduced in India around 800 B.C. Thus: "The one [arrow] that is smeared with poison, has the head of a stag [made from antlers] and whose tip is iron."

In regard to chariot warfare, the Rig Veda shows that the chariot carried two men, a driver on the right and a warrior on the left. Presumably the latter was armed as an archer, and the chariot probably also carried spears or javelins. The foot soldiers, following the chariot with its banners, probably fought in tribal or village groups and were variously armed with bows, axes, short swords, and slings but did not have armor, shields, or helmets. No doubt this style of warfare was a fairly disorganized affair.

Following the Vedic period was the Epic age (c. 1000–500 B.C.), so-called because, once again, information comes to a considerable extent from vast epics such as the Ramayana and the Mahabharata. Like the Vedas, these epics were composed over centuries. The Mahabharata, the most useful epic for military historians, refers at one point to an actual battle fought near Delhi around 1400 B.C., but it was not, in fact, actually written down until sometime between 400 B.C. and A.D. 200. The Mahabharata signals a change in Indian warfare, since from about the seventh or sixth century B.C., the traditional four-fold Indian army appears.

The four-fold army was composed of the four arms of chariots, elephants, cavalry, and infantry. Interestingly enough, the army was structured according to a strict ratio of 1 chariot, 1 elephant, 3 horses (cavalry), and 5 foot soldiers. This unit was multiplied by three to get the next higher unit and so on, thus, for example, a gulma, or "thicket," consisted of 9 chariots, 9 elephants, 27 horses, and 45 foot soldiers. Ultimately a full-strength army consisted of 21,870 chariots, 21,870 elephants, 65,610 horses, and 109,350 foot soldiers. As in other cultures, the chariot went through various stages, sometimes containing as many as 6 men, as alleged in Alexander's Hydaspes battle, and sometimes only

3, but the focus was on the chariot as a platform for archers and for slingers of various weapons, such as darts. Originally of great importance, the chariot gradually lost significance but held on longer than in the West, in fact until the arrival of Scythian tribes in India in the early centuries A.D., who showed what cavalry could do. Nevertheless, the original significance of the chariot is seen in the many admiring references to it in the Mahabharata; for example, in one battle the hero king is surrounded and overwhelmed by enemy chariots: "The warriors could be seen by the hundreds of thousands making intricate maneuvers with their chariots on the battlefield. With their sparkling diadems and chaplets, sparkling armor and banners, and sparkling ornaments they brought joy to my heart. But with all my showers of arrows . . . I could not overcome them, rather did they overcome me. As I was being pressed closely by the many masters of arms who were experienced at warring, I began to feel pain in the great battle."

In this period the elephant carried three archers and a driver, but later it carried even more. Despite problems in battle and prodigious difficulties in providing the beasts with sufficient food and water, elephants became psychologically important to Indian armies and remained in use as late as the eighteenth century A.D. Elephants also needed part of the infantry force to protect them, since they were very vulnerable to attack by enemy infantry. Lines from the Mahabharata illustrate this: "Bhima [a warrior hero] did not stagger, but clubbed, in the vanguard of the . . . [enemy] army, an elephant with its mahout and fourteen footmen." These footmen were obviously the protective force for each elephant. Similarly, "Nakula [another hero] was seen leaping from his chariot, brandishing his sword, and he scattered like seeds the heads of the men who guarded the elephants' legs. Sahadeva [yet another hero] engaged the elephant warriors [those on top of the elephant] on [from] his chariot and toppled them with iron spikes [a throwing weapon] like peacocks from trees." In the same battle, Nakula demonstrated the vulnerability of elephants, for when he was set upon by an elephant, he wielded his sword and shield, and "closed in on the animal and hacked off its trunk and tusks at the root. With a loud wail the elephant, which wore rings on its feet, fell with lowered head to the ground, shattering its mahouts."

The next arm was the cavalry, who were originally lancers, carrying two lances and a shield, but by the first century A.D., under the influence of the Scythians, they had become horse archers. This change apparently was not a great success and faded away. Cavalry are barely mentioned in the Mahabharata; no royal figure rides a horse, and the horse is decidedly inferior to the chariot arm. As in other countries, the cavalry in India seems to be a late development, although by the time of Alexander's entry into India, the cavalry was well established and eventually would replace the chariot.

Looking lastly at the infantrymen, it seems that these were predominantly archers, although some carried javelins instead. They all carried a broad sword and shield for self-defense, wielding the sword with both hands at close range. The most striking feature of the archers was their bow, which can only be described as an early form of longbow. According to the Macedonian Nearchus, "The foot-soldiers carry a bow made of equal length with the man who bears it. This they rest upon the ground, and pressing against it with their left foot, thus discharge the arrow having drawn the string far backwards: for the shaft they use is little short of being three yards long, and there is nothing which can resist an Indian archer's shot—neither shield nor breast-plate, nor any stronger defense if such there be. In their left hand they carry bucklers made of undressed ox-hide."

This four-fold army appears somewhat unwieldy, partly because the chariots and cavalry would perform much the same function and partly because the elephant was an awkward arm to fit into any army. A good way of looking at the integration of this force is to look at their order of battle against Alexander the Great at the battle of the Hydaspes in June 326 B.C. Porus, the local ruler, who led the Indian army against Alexander, organized his forces so that his 85 elephants were lined up in front of the army at fifteen-meter intervals. These gaps were so that the Indian infantry could protect the elephants and also allow infantry charges, in cooperation with the elephants. Moreover, Porus knew that the horses of Alexander's cavalry would not face the elephants, since they were afraid of the beasts. Behind the elephants were the infantry, about 20,000 strong, extending beyond the elephant line. The 2,000-odd cavalry were deployed on the two wings, and in front of them was a screen of some 240 chariots.

Porus's plan was to use the elephants to scare off Alexander's cavalry, then pin Alexander's infantry with his own, and use the elephants, cavalry, and chariots to attack the flanks and rear of Alexander's army. It was a reasonable plan, but things did not work out as planned, for

Alexander realized that it was necessary first to eliminate the Indian cavalry. This he achieved by loading up his right wing with almost all his cavalry and launching a mass attack, which attracted most of the Indian cavalry. Alexander had previously detached one cavalry force under Coenus that circled around behind the Indian army and thus trapped the majority of the Indian cavalry in an encirclement. Alexander also had an important technical advantage in his one thousand horse archers, using this unit to initially harass and disorganize the Indian cavalry. The Indian cavalry were either destroyed or moved in under the protection of the elephants. Then Alexander's light infantry were able to deal with the elephants with javelins and by opening gaps as required when the elephants charged. Finally, the heavy Macedonian phalanx moved forward, crowding the elephants and infantry into a confused mass with the aid of their long spears, the *sarisae*. Eventually the Indian infantry broke through the cordon and fled.

It is of interest that Porus's army really relied on the elephants as their crucial weapon. Porus himself rode an elephant and not a horse, and it seems that the Indian cavalry were outnumbered and not a very effective force. Heavy rains the day of the battle undermined the Indian chariots, which could not maneuver on the muddy ground, and in the account of the battle by the historian Arrian, there is no mention at all of the chariots in the fighting. The rain also prevented the Indian archers from gaining a proper purchase on the slippery ground for their unique method of firing arrows. Finally, the Indians did not possess horse archers, and this arm was very important at the start of the battle. All in all, it can be seen that Alexander used the right tactics and had a much more cohesive force on the field. Porus, on the other hand, was out-generalled, and the Indian cavalry did not maneuver well or cooperate usefully with the other arms. In addition, the Indian chariots were already an anachronism against a disciplined and organized force, as the Persian Darius had found out earlier at the battle of Gaugamela against Alexander.

However, Alexander's influence on the structure of the Indian army was small. After Alexander's departure, the army of the liberator and empire builder Chandra Gupta Maurya still used the traditional fourfold army of old. The difference was that Chandra Gupta maintained a standing army of large proportions, said to number six hundred thousand infantry, thirty thousand cavalry, nine thousand elephants, and an undetermined number of chariots. On the other hand, Chandra Gupta had observed Macedonian tactics, and he was able to defeat Seleucus, Alexander's successor in Syria and Persia.

Chandra Gupta's army was supported by a severe land tax, and the whole state (which comprised most of north India) was run in a bureaucratic and harsh manner, including the death penalty for infractions of the royal decrees, frequently through the administration of poison. There was also an elaborate system of spies at all social levels, for Chandra Gupta feared sedition and assassination so that he changed his sleeping quarters every night. It is clear that Chandra Gupta's success was based on efficient administration, for he established a war office of thirty members, who ran six boards, comprising five members each. These boards were the infantry, the cavalry, the war chariots, the elephantry, the admiralty (to prevent pirate raids), and the transport commissariat and army service. This last board ran the bullock train, which provided all logistics to the army, as well as "servants who beat the drum, and others who carry gongs; grooms also for the horses, and engineers and their assistants. To the sound of the gong they send out foragers to bring in grass, and by a system of rewards and punishments ensure the work being done with dispatch and safety." Chandra Gupta sounds similar to Cyrus the Great in his establishment of an army, roads, garrisons, forts, a bureaucracy, a taxation system, and an efficient administration to run a large empire.

Chandra Gupta's most illustrious descendant was his grandson Ashoka, who ruled between 273 and 232 B.C. and enlarged the empire to include almost all of India, except for the extreme south. But after one particularly bloody campaign, Ashoka renounced war, became a follower of Buddha, espoused vegetarianism, and maintained his empire through negotiation and diplomacy. Although no democrat, Ashoka improved life for his subjects but neglected his army. This neglect, after his death, was part of the reason for the fall of the Maurya dynasty in 184 B.C., which occurred when the last ruler was murdered by his army commander.

The Indian army system differed from that of the Near Eastern systems in its four-fold structure, but India did have contacts with the outside world that influenced their military organization, for example, the introduction of the horse and the chariot. Yet the other great power of the Far East, China, really produced an indigenous approach to war that proved significantly different from other systems.

China

The earliest dynasty that is well documented in China is that of the Shang, which flourished from the eighteenth to the eleventh century B.C. There is debate on the dating of this dynasty, and there are excavations of earlier pounded wall (hang-t'u) enclosures dating back more than four thousand years. The Shang was a farming culture based on the plains surrounding the middle Yalu (Yellow) River valley, although towns had developed, such as the late Shang capital at An Yang, and trade was carried on with regions to the south. Particularly notable was the bronze metal working of this civilization, which reached a very high level. However, to the north and west and on the east coast, there were nomadic tribes with which the Shang both warred and traded while a complex military system was developed by the Shang.

Nevertheless, the primary reason for Shang warfare was not so much the need to defend against nomads as the need to gather prisoners of war in order to use them as sacrifices. Thus, Shang oracle bone records show that on one occasion 300 prisoners were sacrificed for ancestor worship, while 600 victims were sacrificed for the construction of a single house at Hsiao-t'un, and another 164 were put to death to accompany one individual into the tomb. Sometimes prisoners would be put to death shortly after the end of a campaign. Thus, after one expedition, an inscription reads: "The eighth day (hsin-hai), 2,656 men were chastised [i.e., executed] with the halberd [a form of long-handled axe]." This scale of sacrifice obviously required a good deal of raiding of neighboring states, and the Shang were thus frequently at war.

Shang rulers maintained a standing army, and a system of military units supplied men for warfare as required. This system was based on the *tsu*, or patrilineal clan, which provided one hundred men per clan for the army, while the king himself and his princes and consorts also headed up several *tsu*. Through this system, armies from one thousand up to around ten thousand men could be put into the field. The structure of the Shang army was of infantry, archers, and chariots. The infantry and archers comprised squads of ten men each, formed into three companies of one hundred men each, of the left, center, and right, which produced one regiment of three hundred men. Ten regiments produced a larger unit of three thousand men. In regard to the chariot force, five chariots formed one squadron, and five squadrons formed one chariot company. Each chariot carried three men: the soldier standing on the right was an archer with a composite bow; in the middle was the driver; and on the left was the driver's protector, carrying a large shield and a bronze halberd. The chariot itself has been reconstructed accurately from the excavation of several chariots and horses ritually buried in Shang tombs, and it is apparent that the chariot was already an advanced type, with multispoked wheels and normally drawn by two horses. This suggests that the chariot was not indigenous, and it was in fact introduced into China between 1500 and 1300 B.C., probably from Transcaucasia, where multispoked wheel chariots were then in use.

A picture of Shang warfare is hard to reconstruct, but a burial at Hsiao-t'un apparently represents a structured fighting force. There are five groups buried, with the center of the force being a squadron of five chariots with their three man crews. A unit of 25 men, including 4 non-commissioned officers (NCOs) and 1 officer, is buried near the chariots and obviously functioned as the tactical allies and protectors of the chariots. These would be foot soldiers, probably armed with halberds, carrying small shields, and wearing leather armor. To the right and ahead of the chariots is a group of 125 foot soldiers, including 25 officers and NCOs. These might be a mixture of archers, armed with composite bows and wearing leather armor, and the previously described foot soldiers. (The only other weapon carried by all the warriors is a small knife or dagger.) To the right again and by himself is a single individual, perhaps the commander of the infantry and archer forces, and behind the chariots is a scattered group of humans and animals. Possibly these are prisoners of war and captured horses. If this burial structure is accurate, it would show a ratio of infantry and archers to chariots of thirty to one, and two separate but interconnected tactical units on the field—that of the chariots and foot soldiers and that of the mixed archers and foot soldiers. The central chariot of the squadron would be the command center for the entire force. According to this burial, the Shang approach to battle would be with the left, center, and right units of infantry and archers in front and the chariots and foot soldiers in the rear. This arrangement, however, is the reverse of chariot-led armies in other cultures and so may not be accurate.

Shang civilization was eventually overtaken by a neighboring state named Chou, which flourished from around 1100 B.C. until 256 B.C., when the Ch'in state destroyed the last vestiges of the Chou dynasty. The Shang were first defeated by the Western Chou state, which existed from about 1100 B.C. to 771 B.C., and in turn the Eastern Chou ruled from 771 to 256 B.C. (including the Warring States period of 453–221

B.C.). The Shang defeat was not a sudden affair, but it is normally dated to the battle of Mu-yeh, which took place somewhere between 1122 and 1027 B.C. The battle lasted for one day, from dawn to dusk, but seems to have been won by King Wu of Chou with some ease. There are no descriptions of the battle, but the Chou style of warfare apparently differed from that of the Shang in that King Wu allegedly led an army that was more infantry-oriented.

The Chou army consisted of three hundred war chariots and three thousand "tiger [royal guard] warriors" (evidently infantry), plus troops sent by eight other states. These other states were primarily mountainous states that could have only supplied infantry, as infantry was the most useful arm in such territory. It seems then that the infantry-geared Chou army was more flexible than the Shang and was able to maneuver more easily on the battlefield. It was also the case that the Chou army was much better armed. The halberd was strengthened and improved, a bronze sword was introduced, and Chou armor was converted from leather to bronze. There was a bronze helmet, bronze greaves, and bronze plates were attached to the back and chest of the warrior. Bronze may also have been added to the shield. The bow and the chariot remained much the same in both armies, although the Chou chariot was a more versatile vehicle and eventually added two outrider horses to make a four-horse chariot. But the Chou technical superiority of bronze armor and swords was quite sufficient to win the battle by itself and is similar to the same superiority achieved by the classical Greek hoplite force.

Not only did the Chou win through better tactics and armaments, and perhaps through internal Shang discontent, but their overall strategy was also more intelligent. Since Chou was a small state, it followed a policy of forming alliances with states and culture groups that eventually surrounded the more powerful Shang, which the Chou reinforced with military camps facing their enemy. Then, while the Shang were involved with a rebellious tribe along their eastern border, the Chou took advantage and made inroads on the western edge of the Shang state. Thus, the defeat of the Shang involved a lengthy period of time, and the battle of Mu-yeh was simply the culmination of much preparation. The following centuries under Chou domination do not reveal much change in warfare until the sixth century B.C.. Before this, Chou armies simply grew in size and number, with six (Chou) armies of the west, based on the six Chou regions; eight (old Shang) armies of the east, garrisoned at Ch'eng-chou; and another six (Yang) armies of the southeast. If all recruits were called up, the six Chou armies amounted to seventy-five thousand men in total. Logistics were supplied by ox drawn wagons, a formidable bureaucracy grew up to administer such large armies, and a form of feudalism developed as a means of controlling local regions and guaranteeing peace and order. But the Chou still fought with chariots and surrounding infantry in a traditional manner.

The Chou chariot still contained the same three noblemen as in Shang times, but the chariot was surrounded by four infantry platoons: one in front, one behind, and one on each side. Drums and bells were used for communication, and the banners on the commander's chariot acted as a rallying point. If lowered, for example, the banners signaled the retreat. At night the chariots would form a barricade around the marching camp, one behind the other, except for the north and south gates, which were created by facing two chariots toward one another and lacing their raised poles together. In the morning of a potential battle, the commanding general consulted his tortoise shell oracle, analyzed dreams and omens, and if favorable, the camp prepared for war. If these divinations were unfavorable, the army waited for another day or moved to a better location. If the order for battle was eventually given, the officers organized their formations and symbolically mounted their chariots. Then the officers dismounted and, accompanied by their halberdiers, went to hear the general's orders and speech of encouragement. The chariots were then remounted, but only briefly, for once again the officers dismounted in order to join in the prayer.

Finally, the army was ready for combat and either remained on the defensive or advanced to the attack. If the former, acts of bravado and provocation by individuals might draw the enemy to rash assault. If the latter, the general's drum gave the order to advance, which was repeated by the drums of each contingent. The army surged forward, with leadership, momentum, and morale more important than tactics or strategy. The chariot forces exchanged courtly messages with their opponents and engaged in separate challenges and combats. A general melee ensued. Afterward there was feasting for the victors on the enemy's food stores, possibly some human sacrifices ("blood for the drums"), and cutting off the left ear as a body count or as a symbol of subjugation. It is difficult to judge how often this ritualized style of combat gave way to more pragmatic concerns, but at least at the battle of Ch'eng-pu in 632 B.C., Duke Wen, commander of the Chin forces, put into operation a cunning strategy.

Before the battle of Ch'eng-pu began, Duke Wen received the customary challenge from his opponent, the commander of the state of Ch'u: "I beg to try my strength with your lordship's men, while you lean upon your chariot-rail and watch." Duke Wen responded confidently: "Let me trouble you, sir, to tell two or three of your nobles, 'Look well to your chariots, reverence your lord's affairs, for I shall see you at the crack of dawn.'" In fact, Duke Wen had scouted his opponent well, and, realizing that Ch'u's best troops were in the center, he ordered his own center to pin those troops, while his right wing pretended to flee, thus enticing the enemy left wing forward. Then chariots were instructed to drag tree branches through the dust to create confusion on that wing so that Duke Wen's men could turn around and take their opposite number by surprise. Meanwhile, part of Duke Wen's center also detached to help surround the Ch'u left wing. Then Duke Wen's left army loaded up with chariots and managed to put to flight the Ch'u right wing, leaving the Ch'u center vulnerable. Victory was assured for Duke Wen, many prisoners and chariots were taken, and the commander of the Ch'u forces committed suicide, at which Duke Wen exclaimed: "There is nothing more to poison my joy!" The battle plan of Duke Wen has a Napoleonic touch, and it may be that earlier Chou warfare was also less ritualized and formal than is generally believed; certainly this is the case toward the end of the Chou period. But already by the sixth century B.C. important changes were taking place.

A certain professionalization began emerging in Chinese warfare, parallel to a centralization that was taking place in the various states of China. Thus, one Wu Ch'en in 584 B.C. undertook a military mission to the southern state of Wu, teaching that army how to use arms and how to fight in formation. This indicates a move toward an accepted structure of warfare at this time. The same state of Wu and the neighboring state of Yueh both located on the fringes of central China in the lake and marshland regions of the lower Yangtze River, were the first to fully emphasize infantry since the geography of their area prevented effective chariot use. In somewhat similar fashion, the border areas of the Chin state were obliged to create infantry forces in 541 B.C. to combat the Wu-chung barbarians from the mountains, who only fought on foot. In this particular campaign, the Chin general organized an encirclement tactic that was quite similar to Hannibal's future battle of Cannae. The state of Cheng in eastern Honan followed suit in forming infantry formations, and by around 500 B.C. infantry generally had reduced the centuries-long dependence on the chariot.

This entailed a new view of warfare in which much larger infantry armies were possible. At the same time the larger infantry armies needed discipline, order, and efficiency, and a new type of recruit, the soldier-peasant, helped to devalue the old aristocratic concepts of honor and ritual. The chariot did not disappear at once and even maintained an equivalence with cavalry (mounted archers) into the third century B.C.. But the increasing dominance of the infantry, and subsequently the introduction of mounted archers, undercut the elitist, ritualized style of warfare of the Shang and the Chou, which had found in the chariot a sufficiently complex and expensive weapon to support that aristocratic experience.

Clearly, a full scale military revolution was in progress, undoubtedly stimulated by the decline of the Chou state and by the onset of the period of the Warring States, between 481 and 221 B.C.. Between 460 and 200 B.C., professional generals fought for land and resources in a "rational" manner, and, a sure sign of a military revolution, a large-scale literature of military handbooks was created, the most famous being Sun-tzu's *Art of War*, dated to somewhere between 400 and 320 B.C.. Very significant military innovations also took place, for the introduction of large scale infantry forces was followed by the remarkable Chinese invention of the crossbow around 475 B.C.. This was followed by the use of the catapult at about the same time and the introduction of mounted archers in 307 B.C. In this last case, the king of Chao explicitly borrowed the idea of mounted archers, and their style of dress, from the horse nomads of the northwest.

The Chao and other Chinese states, however, could not match the horse skills of the nomads, and so they tended to rely more on the crossbow and on the construction of defensive walls against the nomads, beginning in the fifth century B.C. These walls in later centuries were connected to produce a continuous defense line two thousand miles long, thus forming the origin of the Great Wall of China. Siege warfare also developed from the fifth to the third centuries, with sieges lasting sometimes as long as three years against walled cities. Movable towers, scaling ladders with wheels, earth ramparts, tunnels and mines, and bellows to blow smoke along enemy tunnels were all used. Warfare on a large scale also called for an increase in agricultural production to feed the new armies, creating the need for irrigation. Therefore, canals were dug, starting in the fifth century B.C. Thus, the kingdom of Wu built a lengthy canal linking the Yangtze to the Huai River in 486 B.C. and another from the Huai to the rivers of south Shantung. Not by coincidence, the state of Wu was one of the first to create an army of foot soldiers. Rivers and canals had to be defended too, and the same king of Chao who had imitated the mounted archers of the barbarians also called for boats and oars, which he did not yet have, to defend the Yangtze and other rivers.

Naval warfare thus achieved some attention at this time, although China was late in developing maritime skills and land war was always more significant in the period before the Ming accession (1368 B.C.). This was partly because of China's traditional inward-looking stance, stemming from the land war struggles of the various states for dominance, partly because of China's necessary focus on defense against barbarian steppe tribes (including the later Mongols), and partly because the inland waterways were seen primarily as means of transporting land armies and supplies. Thus, the state of Wu, because of its geographical location, used the Yangtze River to convey its army in ships to attack the state of Ch'u in 506 B.C. and then sent a fleet of soldiers northward to raid the state of Ch'i in 486 B.C.

Maritime warfare of the time can only be visualized through scenes on an unusually decorated Hu wine vessel, dating from the late sixth to the fifth century B.C. and excavated in 1965 in Szechwan province. The scenes show two boats with high prows and sterns being rowed at some speed by figures with oars, who are on a lower deck, but who are standing up to row. The figures on the upper deck are warriors armed with the conventional land weapons of the time—spears, halberds, swords, and shields—but there are no archers on board. Banners are flying, and a drummer at the stern is signaling the attack and encouraging his comrades. Only the two lead warriors in each boat are fighting each other, with swords, but one warrior has also been thrown into the water. Essentially this is land warfare transferred to water. It reveals that the boats did not ram each other but were instead brought together at speed. A general melee ensued in which the longer-range halberds and spears would have been effective. It may be, however, that the lead warrior in each boat was critical to the success of the venture, for they are armed differently, with swords and shields rather than spears and halberds, and thus there may still be an element of ritualized individual combat involved. Coincidentally, the same wine vessel also shows scenes of siege warfare, where a group of soldiers is scaling the walls of a fortification either by ladder or ramp. Curiously, only the defenders seem to possess bows, while the attackers have the usual weapons of spears, shields, swords, and halberds, except for one figure who seems to be trying to undermine the walls. In both naval and land scenes, all the warriors are wearing headdresses, and an accepted form of combat appeared to be to seize one's opponent by the hair and pull him to the ground before dispatching him.

The period of the Warring States witnessed battles on a vast scale, with armies allegedly reaching figures as high as six hundred thousand. These were fought according to cunning and "rationality" but also with greater brutality. Reportedly, the victorious Ch'in army in 260 B.C. first of all killed fifty thousand Chao soldiers in one battle, and then massacred the four hundred thousand survivors. On several other occasions dikes were deliberately breached, drowning large numbers of innocent civilians as well as soldiers. However, the intensification of warfare also produced one powerful state, the Ch'in, which eventually defeated the six main competing states—the Ch'i, Yen, Chao, Han, Wei, and Ch'u— one by one, and in 221 B.C. the Ch'in finally achieved a momentous event, the unification of China through the elimination of all rivals. The ruler of the Ch'in, Shih Huang Ti, was later called the first emperor of China because of this feat, and his dynasty (221–207 B.C.), though brief and violent, marked a turning point in Chinese history.

In terms of warfare, Shih Huang Ti conscripted young peasant soldiers according to a quota system and opened his army to promotion according to merit. Hence, one Fan Sui rose to the rank of general even though he came from the rival state of Wei. It was in fact Fan Sui who developed the Ch'in strategy of making alliances with distant states while conquering neighboring states. Nevertheless, failure in battle or refusal to carry out orders was not tolerated, and even the most successful Ch'in general, Bai Qi, was demoted and executed after thirty-five years of service for refusing to lead what he considered a hopeless expedition. Parallel with this strict military organization, Shih Huang Ti built a network of canals and military roads, centralized the administration and bureaucracy so that it was nonhereditary and responsible to himself personally, abolished serfdom, promoted agriculture, exacted heavy taxes, standardized weights and measurements, unified the Chinese system of writing, built and connected defensive walls that ran for two thousand miles, and conscripted labor in vast numbers. In particular, Shih Huang Ti's abolition of feudalism meant the resettlement of noble landowners and the creation of the peasant farmer-soldier as the foundation of the economic and military power of the state. Shih Huang Ti remarked: "If the whole world has suffered from unceasing warfare, this is the fault of feudal lords and kings. Thanks to my ancestors, the Empire has been pacified for the first time. If I restored feudal holdings, war would return. Then peace would never be found!"

The first emperor of China in actuality created a militarized society, not unlike that of the Frederick the Great of Prussia many centuries later. But in his later years the emperor became paranoid, attempted to burn all the books in his kingdom except for medical texts, executed 460 scholars, and searched obsessively for the elixir of immortality. He did not succeed in this search, and in 210 B.C., the emperor died. But for some years before his death, Shih Huang Ti had conscripted 700,000 laborers to build an underground mausoleum, covering an area of twenty-one square miles, which included not only the first emperor's tomb but also an entire buried terracotta army. Parts of this tomb and the army were excavated in the early 1970s and provide excellent specimens of the weapons, dress, ranks, and structure of the successful Ch'in forces. The organization of the buried army follows the accepted structure of the day: "long-range crossbows in front, halberds behind; bows are the outer layer, halberds and shields the inner; skilled soldiers and strong bows on the flanks." The emperor's army is buried in three pits. Pit one contains the core of the army—some 6,000 soldiers. The great majority of the infantry are arranged in nine long columns, four abreast, and are composed of lightly armored infantry carrying spears or halberds and swords. Leading them are a vanguard of 200 unarmored bowmen and crossbowmen. Six command chariots stand just behind the vanguard, and these are protected by three infantry squads with long spears. On the flanks of the infantry are two long ranks of armored archers, and, to protect the rear of this huge infantry phalanx, there are three lines of armored infantry.

Pit two contains fourteen hundred men, divided into four groups. A vanguard of archers and spearmen lead two groups, one a mixture of cavalry (mounted archers) and chariots, the other a mixture of chariots and armored infantry. The last group contains a formation of sixty-four chariots. Of interest here is the fact that chariots and cavalry are about equal in number, with the cavalry around the periphery and the chariots in the middle, associated with protective infantry. This strongly suggests that the Ch'in army had not yet fully adapted to cavalry, but nevertheless pit two was obviously the mobile independent force, attached to the main infantry, which was the real striking force of the army. Finally, pit three contained the headquarters unit, with the commander in chief's war chariot, guarded by sixty-eight infantry, who all stand at least six feet two inches in height. There is a fourth pit, but it is empty, suggesting that work was abandoned before completion. Very likely, pit four would have been another cavalry-chariot unit, matching the main infantry force but on the opposite side. Thus, mobile forces would have operated on both wings of the infantry.

Altogether this entire army numbered some eight thousand men, and the key feature that emerges is that this army, largely composed of infantry, was light and mobile. None of the soldiers wore helmets, and most were lightly armored. It was adapted to offensive warfare, rapid attack, and quick maneuver and was obviously not designed to win through sheer weight and size. Instead, the idea was to quickly close with the enemy so that the foot soldiers could get to work. Although iron weapons were available, they did not replace bronze weapons until the Han dynasty (202 B.C.–A.D.221). The mobile aspect of the army was in transition (possibly the shortage of horses was critical), and the cavalry did not gain dominance in Chinese armies until the Han had to face larger numbers of mounted archer barbarians. Nor did archers constitute a large part of the Ch'in army. Instead the buried terracotta army was overwhelmingly an infantry force.

With the fall of the Ch'in dynasty, the new Han dynasty mounted a program of military and commercial expansion that greatly extended China's borders into central Asia, as well as to the south and into Korea. But the roots of this expansion had come from the centralized and militarized society of the Ch'in, which formed a critical turning point in the history of China. In turn, the unification of China by Shih Huang Ti was made possible by the military revolution that had already taken place during the Warring States period.

The military successes of the ancient empires outlined in this chapter were mainly achieved not so much by particular armies or weapons or by advances in bronze or iron but through administration, organization, economic capabilities, and leadership. Yet, beyond even these essential foundations, one can point to the ability of societies and empires such as the Egyptians, Assyrians, and Chinese to borrow and learn ideas, techniques, and innovations from their neighbors and to incorporate these into their own armies. This process may be called innovation on the periphery and was aided by the great irruption and migration of nomad peoples from central Asia and western Asia starting around 2000 B.C. and continuing for at least a millennium. Pastoral peoples, such as the Amorites, Hurrians, Kassites, Hittites, Hyksos, Aryans, or the Hsiun Nu barbarians on the Chinese borders, appeared to innovate more easily and compelled the most successful empires to change, learn, and adapt. Yet even the greatest empires of the ancient world did not survive forever, as the history of the classical empires of Greece and Rome testify.

Suggested Reading

Origins of Warfare and General Studies of Ancient Warfare
The best discussion of the origins of warfare, stressing the warlike nature of mankind, is Lawrence Keeley, *War Before Civilization* (Oxford, 1996). See also Raymond Kelly, *Warless Societies and the Origin of War* (Ann Arbor MI, 2001). Recent reliable overviews of ancient warfare can be found in Arther Ferrill, *The Origins of War* (London, 1985); Gen. Sir John Hackett, ed., *A History of War in the Ancient World* (London, 1989); and Richard Humble, *Warfare in the Ancient World* (London, 1980). Very useful for an analysis of the much maligned chariot and its evolution is M. A. Littauer and J. H. Crouwel, *Wheeled Vehicles and Ridden Animals in the Ancient Near East* (Leiden, 1979). An evaluation of the major ancient empires is in J. N. Postgate, *The First Empires* (Oxford, 1977). For a brief look at ancient maritime history with some interesting ideas, see Chester Starr, *The Influence of Sea Power on Ancient History* (New York, 1989). Extremely useful in its specialized area and containing excellent visual material, although a little outdated, is Yigael Yadin, *The Art of Warfare in Biblical Lands*, 2 vols. (Jerusalem, 1963).

Egypt
Information about ancient Egypt is readily available. Among general histories are Cyril Aldred, *The Egyptians*, rev. ed. (London, 1984), and Bruce Trigger et al., *Ancient Egypt: A Social History* (London, 1983). Essential documents, inscriptions, and interpretations of sculptures concerning Egyptian warfare are included in James Breasted, *Ancient Records of Egypt*, 5 vols. (Chicago, 1906); Sir Alan Gardiner, *The Kadesh Inscriptions of Rameses II* (Oxford, 1960); and Kenneth Kitchen, *Ramesside Inscriptions: Historical and Biographical*, 5 vols. (Oxford, 1968–78). The structure of the New Kingdom army is found in Alan Schulman, *Military Rank, Title and Organization in the Egyptian New Kingdom* (Berlin, 1964). Important for a linguistic analysis of Egyptian documents concerning the battle of Kadesh are Anthony Spalinger, *Aspects of the Military Documents of the Ancient Egyptians* (New Haven, 1982), and, more recently, H. Goedicke, ed., *Perspectives*

on the Battle of Kadesh (Baltimore, 1985), and Ian Shaw's chapter in Alan Loyd, ed., *Battle in Antiquity* (London, 1996). A discussion of the impact of the Hyksos on Egypt can be found in John Van Seters, *The Hyksos: A New Investigation* (New Haven, 1966). Similarly, a balanced overview of the confusion surrounding the Sea Peoples and their impact on Egypt is N. K. Sandars, *The Sea Peoples: Warriors of the Ancient Mediterranean, 1250–1150* B.C., rev. ed. (London, 1985).

Assyria

Surprisingly, literature on Assyrian warfare is rather limited, but a good place to start is the relevant chapters in William Hallo and William Simpson, *The Ancient Near East: A History* (San Diego, 1971), and in Georges Roux, *Ancient Iraq* 3rd Penguin ed. (London, 1992). Useful also are some sections in A. T. Olmstead, *History of Assyria* (New York, 1923), and selected articles from the journal *Iraq*. Since Assyrian sculptures are well preserved and tell us much about warfare, useful books are R. D. Barnett, *Sculptures from the North Palace of Ashurbanipal* (London, 1976); R. D. Barnett and M. Falkner, *The Sculptures of Tiglath-Pileser III* (London, 1962); and Julian Reade, *Assyrian Sculpture* (London, 1983). Convenient material is gathered in D. D. Luckenbill, *Ancient Records of Assyria and Babylonia* (Chicago, 1926; New York, 1968). A balanced overview of the place of Babylon in Assyrian history is found in Joan Oates, *Babylon* (London, 1979).

Persia

There is not an abundant military historiography on ancient Persia. One essential primary source, although requiring a skeptical approach, is Herodotus, *The Histories*. The size of Xerxes' army in 480 B.C. is explored by T. C. Young in *Iranica Antiqua*, vol. 15 (1980). Some attention is paid to the military aspects of Persia in A. R. Burn, *Persia and the Greeks: the Defence of the West c. 546–478* B.C., 2nd ed. (Palo Alto, 1984); the Cambridge *History of Iran, Volume 2: The Median and Achaemenian Periods* (Cambridge, 1984); J. M. Cook, *The Persian Empire* (New York, 1983); and Richard Frye, *The History of Ancient Iran* (Munich, 1984). An older but occasionally rewarding overview is A. T. Olmstead, *History of the Persian Empire* (Chicago, 1948).

India

By and large, the historiography of Indian warfare is rather poor. The best book on the subject, apart from a strange flight of fancy concerning ancient aerial warfare, is V. R. R. Dikshitar, *War in Ancient India* (Madras, 1948). Also useful on many details is Sarva Daman Singh, *Ancient Indian Warfare* (Delhi, 1965, 1989). Other books, which basically follow one another without the benefit of original research, are Lt. Col. H. C. Kar, *Military History of India* (Calcutta, 1980); B. K. Majumdar, *The Military System in Ancient India* (Calcutta, 1955, 1960); and

Maj. G. Sharma, *Indian Army Through the Ages* (Bombay, 1966). Sir Mortimer Wheeler, *The Indus Civilization*, 3rd ed. (Cambridge, 1968), provides a somewhat outdated archaeologist's perspective. Most recent, is the valuable text by Jonathan Kenoyer, *Ancient Cities of the Indus Valley Civilization* (Oxford, 1998), which rejects the idea of an Aryan invasion. Essential primary sources include *The Rig Veda*, *Mahabharata*, and the *Puranas*, also J. W. McCrindle, *Ancient India as described by Megasthenes and Arrian* (London, 1926). Finally, a basic introduction to India is Stanley Wolpert, *A New History Of India* (New York, 1977).

China

There is little information on ancient Chinese warfare in English, apart from books concerning Huang-ti and his terracotta army. It is necessary, therefore, to turn to the accounts of art historians and archaeologists such as Kwang-Chih Chang, *Shang Civilization* (New Haven, 1980); Wen Fong, ed., *The Great Bronze Age of China* (New York, 1980); and Cho-Yun Hsu and Kathryn Linduff, *Western Chou Civilization* (New Haven, 1988). Regarding Huang-ti, see Arthur Cotterell, *The First Emperor of China* (London, 1981), and R. W. L. Guisso and Catherine Pagani with David Miller, *The First Emperor of China* (Toronto, 1989). General accounts of ancient Chinese society, with some military material, include Jacques Gernet, *Ancient China, from the beginnings to the Empire*, trans. R. Rudorff (Berkeley, 1968), and Henri Maspero, *China in Antiquity*, trans. Frank Kierman (University of Massachusetts, 1978). An exception to the dearth of material on Chinese warfare, although dealing overwhelmingly with later periods, is Frank Kierman and John Fairbank, eds., *Chinese Ways in Warfare* (Cambridge, 1974), and now Hans van de Ven, ed., *Warfare in Chinese History* (Leiden, 2001). Finally, a rather difficult discussion of the impact of barbarians on China is in Jaroslav Prusek, *Chinese Statelets and the Northern Barbarians in the period 1400–300 B.C.* (New York, 1971).

2. WAR AND SOCIETY IN THE CLASSICAL WEST
450 B.C. to A.D. 450

Julius Caesar said that two things created power—soldiers and money—and that they depended upon one another: "For it was by proper maintenance . . . that armies were kept together, and this maintenance was secured by arms; and in case either one of them were lacking, the other also would be overthrown at the same time." The military importance of men and money varied over the classical period. "Men" meant that part of any population that fought, excluding minors, women, foreigners, and slaves. In Greece, Athens alone had more than twenty thousand citizen soldiers, from a population of five hundred thousand people, while the two great land powers, Thebes and Sparta, never mustered more than ten thousand. The largest allied armies of Greece rarely possessed even fifteen thousand soldiers and never more than forty-five thousand. Greek forces did not serve for long. Conversely, Carthage and the Hellenistic empires—the Seleucid kingdom, master of most of the Middle East, and Ptolemaic Egypt—maintained one hundred thousand soldiers for years on end, while Republican Rome had 350,000 legionaries. This growth in armed strength stemmed from politics. Greek states were small and distrusted their neighbors. Macedonia, the Hellenistic kingdoms, and Carthage all became greater than Greece because they were politically more skillful and able to control territories such as Spain, North Africa, and the Balkans. In turn, they were outmatched by Rome, whose political and administrative capacity stood supreme in antiquity.

Sparta and Macedonia provide extreme examples of the difference between the size of a population and its army and of the strategic consequences of political and social structures. Spartan society rested on three groups—Spartiates, citizens; *perioeci*, noncitizen freemen who served in the army; and the enslaved bulk of the population, the helots. Spartiate society centered on the army. In peace and in war, Spartiates ate and lived with their comrades in military messes. They were defined by birth and wealth—their status vanished if they could not pay high mess bills. The Spartiates, a small part of the population, could devote their lives to war but only because they lived off their helots. Sparta rested on the edge of a volcano. Any serious defeat anywhere might produce a helot revolt, which would threaten the economic basis of many Spartiates and the social structure of Sparta. In order to avoid this fate, Sparta created a ruthless state that ruled through terror. Every year Sparta declared war on its helots. A special section of soldiers permanently policed the helots and killed all and any dangerous ones. During its worst days of the Peloponnesian War (432–404 B.C.), Sparta asked helots to volunteer for military service in return for their freedom, and these serfs were murdered immediately, because nothing threatened Sparta more than helots who would accept such an offer.

Spartan society was savage and inefficient. It produced very good soldiers in very small numbers. At the Battle of Platea in 479 B.C., Sparta's army included 5,000 Spartiates and 5,000 *perioeci*. By 371 B.C., only 1,500 Spartiates remained—controlling 5,000 armed *perioeci*, 250,000 helots and 4 million Greeks. By normal Greek standards, in 371 B.C. Sparta should have had 30,000 infantrymen. It had just 6,500. This deficit stemmed not from battle losses but Spartan society. Over the centuries, property slowly fell into fewer and fewer hands, especially following victory over Athens in the Peloponnesian War. Hence, fewer males could remain Spartiates, while those born into the status but deprived of it became another source of unrest. Spartiates also reduced the number of their children to maintain the status of the survivors. Diplomatic strength countered some of this demographic weakness. Between 530 and 370 B.C., through its control of the Peloponnesian League, Sparta dominated its neighbors and usually raised the largest army in Greece. Spartans rarely made up even 33 percent of the Peloponnesian host, sometimes just 10 percent of it. Their allies' strength made up for their own weakness. Nonetheless, demographic weakness often made Sparta take the greatest risk of all: to free and arm helots. Spartan policy was paralyzed for several years in the 420s and the 360s B.C. simply because the enemy held one hundred Spartiate prisoners. By killing just four hundred Spartiates at the Battle of Leuctra, (371 B.C.), Thebes shattered Spartan power forever. The entry of Thebes's army into the Peloponnese sparked an immediate rising against Sparta of helots, *perioeci*, disenfranchised Spartiates, and old allies. Local states formed an

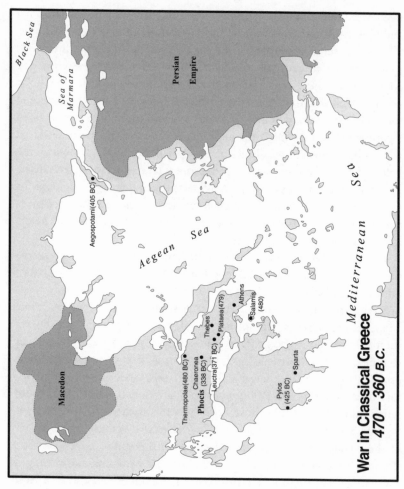

War in Classical Greece
470 – 360 B.C.

Black Sea

Sea of
Marmara

Persian
Empire

Aegean Sea

Mediterranean Sea

Aegospotami(405 BC)

Macedon

Thermopolae(480 BC)
Chaeronea
(338 BC)
Phocis
Thebes
Leuctra(371 BC)
Plataea(479)
Athens
Salamis
(480)
Sparta
Pylos
(425 BC)

Map 2.1

anti-Spartan coalition and destroyed the Peloponnesian League. Thebes liberated many helots, which simultaneously weakened Sparta and left a permanent enemy on its frontiers.

Conversely, in 360 B.C. an invasion from the north almost smashed the populous but politically fragmented kingdom of Macedonia and brought a new monarch, Philip II, to the throne. His subjects, confronting annihilation, gave this king great support. He used that opportunity with skill, establishing a strong government and increasing Macedonia's territory and wealth. Through diplomacy, he made neighbors into allies, who provided him with fifteen thousand soldiers. Through politics, Philip turned the Macedonian nobility from a threat into his officers and cavalry. He brought their children to his court, where they became his servants, and their parents, hostages. He granted aristocrats holdings on conquered lands and ennobled foreigners in order to counterbalance the old elite. By 338 B.C. Macedonia had over 1.5 million people—far and away the largest population of any Hellenic state. Philip raised the strength of the Macedonian army from ten thousand men in 358 B.C. to thirty-five thousand in 338 B.C.—four times the size of the Theban levy and thirty times the number of Spartiates. He controlled virtually as many soldiers as all of Greece. Soon he controlled all of Greece.

Money was needed to maintain fleets and mercenaries and to keep citizen armies in the field for more than a few weeks. During the fifth century B.C., Athens alone in Greece had a large supply of money, although Persia was far wealthier. In 432 B.C. Athens had a reserve of sixty-five hundred talents and an annual income of six hundred talents. This was essential to its sea power: as ever, navies were a rich man's weapon. At that time, a trireme cost one-half talent to build; one hundred talents were required to keep sixty triremes and their crews at sea for eight months. During the first decade of the Peloponnesian War, Athens could afford to maintain a large fleet, repair battle damage, and recruit mercenary oarsmen to augment its citizen seamen. Its enemies could not do so, and their fleets soon wasted away. In the last decade of the war, however, the balance of financial and maritime power turned. With its population declining, Athens could maintain the quality and quantity of its navy only by hiring more mercenary oarsmen, which it could no longer afford to do. Its reserves had declined to fifteen hundred talents and its income decreased by half. Simultaneously, bankrolled by Persia, the Peloponnesian League built large fleets, replaced battle dam-

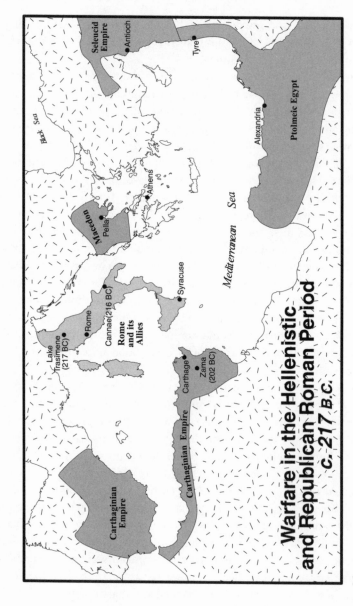

Warfare in the Hellenistic
and Republican Roman Period
c. 217 B.C.

Black Sea

Seleucid
Empire

Antioch

Tyre

Ptolmeic Egypt

Alexandria

Macedon

Pella

Athens

Mediterranean   Sea

Syracuse

Rome

Cannae(216 BC)

**Rome
and its
Allies**

Lake
Trasimene
(217 BC)

Carthage

Zama
(202 BC)

Carthaginian Empire

**Carthaginian
Empire**

Map 2.2

age, hired trained oarsmen to stiffen its amateur crews, and challenged Athens at sea. Athens sank these fleets several times over, but its enemies always rebuilt them. When the Athenian navy was smashed in 405 B.C.— by surprise, while its men were ashore eating lunch at Aegospotami in the Bosphorus—the war was over.

During the next fifty years, all Greek states were impoverished. In order to subsidize wars at home, Sparta and Thebes sometimes sold their national armies as mercenaries abroad. Sparta was financially too puny to maintain the empire it sought to force on Hellas, let alone the war it launched against Persia in 396 B.C. Persian money destroyed this threat and again revolutionized Greek politics. It built a Greek fleet that sank Sparta's navy, which Persia had subsidized a decade before to smash Athens's empire. When Sparta could not afford to replace its navy, its maritime empire vanished while its enemies in Greece, subsidized by Persia, rose up in arms. Greek poverty was the trump suit for Persian diplomacy. Between 412 and 368 B.C., Persian silver continually avenged Salamis. Persia became the overlord of Greece because it could give any city the money needed to overawe the rest.

Subsequently, some Greek states became far wealthier. During the 350s B.C., the small city of Phocis looted 10,000 talents from the shrines at Delphi. This means of finance let Phocis maintain twenty thousand mercenaries—equal in numbers to the largest Hellenic federation—and fight half of Greece for several years. Philip II had an annual income of 2,500 talents, where his Athenian enemies had only 400, much of which went to welfare. Athenian commanders routinely had to raise pay for their forces through piracy or by selling their men as mercenaries or farmhands. Philip had no such distractions. His treasury maintained the largest army in Hellas, and it allowed him to concentrate solely on conquest and the bribery of statesmen throughout Greece. He fought Greeks and he bought Greece. The Hellenistic kings were far wealthier even than Philip. Through captured Persian treasuries, Alexander the Great maintained a reserve of 180,000 talents—twenty-eight times larger than Athens had done a century before. His successors, the *diadochi*, controlled the territories and resources both of Greece and Persia. They routinely held treasuries of 5,000 and 8,000 talents, annual incomes of up to 11,000 talents, and standing armies of fifty thousand men.

Money and mercenaries led to a swelling of armed strength. A wealthy state could raise a professional force larger than any citizen army and of equal or superior quality. Many Hellenistic states possessed such wealth, and silver pulled ahead of citizens as a source of military power. By 260 B.C., however, the balance between men and money shifted again. As the quality of many Hellenistic armies and the wealth of their governments fell, the military significance of a citizen host rose again. In particular, Roman economic and demographic resources were no greater than those of its rivals but were tapped with greater efficiency. Macedonia retained a good citizen army, but little larger than in Philip II's day, while other Hellenistic states recruited their armies from tiny fractions of their populations. Carthage's citizens served as soldiers or sailors only in emergencies, and its empire was loosely organized. It relied on mercenaries, often of superb quality but rarely more than one hundred thousand men strong. The Seleucid and Ptolemaic armies were less good and less large. The Seleucid army consisted of Macedonian farmer-soldiers and light infantry and cavalry drawn from ethnic minorities, but it did not recruit soldiers from its largest population groups in Syria and Iraq, fearing the political risks. While Egyptians did serve alongside Macedonians in the Ptolemaic phalanx, its quality fell. Conversely, Rome routinely conscripted 10 to 30 percent of its menfolk for years on end and maintained armies two or three times larger than the greatest Hellenistic ones. It triumphed through quantity as much as quality. During the First Punic War its citizen population declined by 20 percent, or fifty thousand men—more citizens than Carthage possessed. In 226 B.C. Rome and its Italian allies had one million citizens of military age; Macedonia had eighty thousand.

As the size and cost of classical armies changed, so did their composition and tactics. Between 1200 and 750 B.C., Greek battles were Homeric in nature. Soldiers clashed in loose bodies of unarmored swordsmen, beginning with missile bombardments and finishing with single combat between warrior-aristocrats. Javelins and long swords were the main weapons; men carried flimsy cowhide shields. By 750 B.C., however, Greek soldiers began to fight in phalanxes, tight formations of armored spearmen, to wear bronze armor and helmets, together weighing fifty pounds, and to adopt the *hoplon* (from which hoplites take their name), a bowl-like wooden shield three feet in diameter and sixteen pounds in weight, often covered with a light sheet of bronze. Initially, hoplites carried both a javelin and a thrusting spear seven feet long and stood in loose ranks alongside unarmored men. Soon light troops left the phalanx while hoplites abandoned the javelin. These developments changed the nature of battle. Hoplites were too clumsy to move or fight as skirmishers. Their helmets blocked vision to the side. After about thirty minutes of battle, physical exhaustion crippled their ability to hold their equipment, let alone use it. Their spears were not particularly effective for individual combat, while the *hoplon* was too small to defend its bearer if he stood alone. Both spear and shield, however, were well suited for collective defense by men in a tight phalanx. Homeric heroes were praised for their individual skill as warriors, and hoplites were praised for their contribution to the spear line as a whole. Proverbially, hoplites carried breastplates for themselves and shields for their comrades.

The change of military systems in societies where men had to pay for their own arms reflected a political revolution; perhaps it sparked one. A hoplite's equipment was expensive, and horses were even more so. One ancient observer, Aristotle, argued that a military system relying on cavalry would favor rule by a wealthy few, one centering on hoplites would produce a wide oligarchy of small landowners, while one emphasizing light troops and sailors would lead to democracy. Homeric warfare was suited to societies dominated by a few aristocratic warriors. The rise of the hoplite system coincided with the destruction of aristocratic dominance, the expansion of franchises, and the rise of equality between citizens. In all states wealthy men served as cavalry. Only in Athens did many citizens serve neither as hoplites or horsemen, because its central tool of war was a navy manned by trained citizen oarsmen, who were regularly paid by the state. Free but disenfranchised Greeks were not trusted to play a major role in war—this would risk a revolution. One hoplite was as good a citizen and soldier as another. Each had to fight for all if the whole were to survive. The phalanx was the citizenry in arms. This collective military service was a fundamental means—one of few outside of religious ceremonies—to reinforce the bonds of citizenship within Greek states.

For political, social, and economic reasons, these were amateur armies. They did not fight long or often. Farmer citizens could not campaign away from their crops for more than a few weeks time, and cities could rarely pay to feed them for long periods of time. Many states encouraged gymnastic exercises to prepare men for individual combat, but few maintained elite trained units. To do so would threaten equality between hoplites and provoke political danger. Trained bands would have to be raised from a part of the citizenry, usually wealthier men who did not have to work for their daily bread and who might turn military superiority to their political advantage. Since most hoplites were amateurs, professionals had major advantages, which explains Sparta's long pre-eminence within Greece.

Hoplite hosts were always threatened by the danger of panic. They were held together not so much by training as by social bonds—the fear of being thought a coward, the desire to save a friend. A Roman military writer, Onasander, held that hoplites had fought best with brother "in rank beside brother, friend beside friend, lover beside lover." Institutionalized homosexuality linked the greatest of hoplites—the Spartiates and the "Sacred Band" of Thebes. Every Spartiate adolescent became the lover of an older man, while the Sacred Band consisted of pairs of lovers, one called the "chariot" and the other the "crew," stationed one behind the other in battle. For such soldiers, to flee the fight was to betray not just comrades but lovers. And they did not run. Most Spartiates at any defeat stood and died in the wreck. In its only failure on the field, at the Battle of Chaironeia in 338 B.C., the Sacred Band fell to a man.

Between 490 and 338 B.C., on a flat and narrow field hoplites could smash any other infantry on earth as well as cavalry without stirrups or bowmen whose arrows reached only one hundred yards and could not penetrate a *hoplon*. At Platea massed ranks of Persian archers bombarded ten thousand Spartan hoplites for three hours and killed but ninety-one of them. The Spartan charge killed thousands of Persians in three minutes. Hoplites were less effective in rough or open country, where a shield wall would break or be outflanked. Light infantry, cavalry, or archers often annihilated hoplites in such terrain. Persian forces, invariably outclassed on battlefields in Greece, also defeated every hoplite invasion of the interior of Asia Minor. In everything except heavy infantry, the Persian army actually was better than Greek ones.

Hoplites usually adopted a formation eight men deep, each man a yard from his neighbors on all sides. The best soldiers stood first in a file, serving, the Greek writer Asclepiodotus wrote, as "the cutting edge of the sword," and last to hold the rest steady and shove them like a blade into the belly of the enemy's phalanx. These solid walls of shields bristling with spears advanced toward one another and charged when they stood a few hundred feet apart. In the process, part of a phalanx often outpaced the rest, threatening their solidity. As the Greek soldier Xenophon wrote of the Battle of Cunaxa in 401 B.C., "The Greeks sang the paean and began to move forward against the enemy. As they advanced, part of the phalanx surged forward in front of the rest and the part that was left behind began to advance at the double. At the same time they all raised a shout like the shout of 'Eleleu' which people make to the War God, and then they were all running forward. But the Persians, even before they were in range of the arrows, wavered and ran away. Then certainly the Greeks pressed on the pursuit vigorously, but they shouted out to each other not to run, but to follow up the enemy without breaking rank."

Sometimes a charge settled a battle. Spartan hoplites, dressed in scarlet with the bronze facing of their shields polished to a dazzle, moved at a disciplined pace to the sound of flutes where other armies rushed. Their fearsome advance often made enemies break on the spot. When enemies did not retreat, the two phalanxes collided like linebackers. Shields shattered, spears broke, men were knocked off their feet, trodden underfoot, and suffocated in a melee a few hours or a few minutes long.

The tactical aim was to break the integrity of the hostile phalanx, which would make the enemy drop its shields and run. The front rows of each phalanx shoved their shields together, smashing the enemy's *hoplons* and wrecking its strength. The first three ranks of soldiers also thrust their spears over or under enemy shields, aiming for flesh rather than armor. Spears were held underhand as the phalanxes charged but thrust overhand for greater accuracy in the melee. Genitals and necks were favored targets. As the Spartan poet Tyrtaios put it, "No, no, let him take a wide stance and stand up strongly against them, digging both heels in the ground, biting his lips with his teeth, covering thighs and legs beneath, his chest and his shoulders under the hollowed-out protection of his broad shield, while in his right hand he brandishes the powerful war-spear and shakes terribly the crest high above his helm." Members of the remaining five rows of the phalanx leaned forward on their shields, pushing their first row into the enemy line. They replaced fallen comrades and butchered enemy wounded underfoot.

Before the Persian invasion, Greek battles were ritualized. Hoplites could fight only by mutual consent, while any army that stayed behind its walls was invulnerable. Defenders did not have to fight in order to prevent the devastation of their crops, and, in their short campaigning seasons, attackers could not damage agriculture enough to starve entire populations. Simple means existed to block invasion or avoid battle. Light infantry could hamper or prevent the movement of hoplites across mountain passes, while phalanxes would not attack hoplites standing behind natural obstacles such as a stream. That would break their shield wall. But hoplites did not adopt such means to avoid battle—they did not use strategy to increase their chances for victory. They viewed war as a game fought by accepted rules, a ritual of manhood. When first viewing a catapult, the Spartan king Archidamos said "By Herekles! the valour of a man is no more." Battles not between phalanxes but picked champions sometimes settled wars of this era. Similarly, reliance on light infantry would threaten the military—and political—supremacy of hoplites. Instead, two phalanxes met by mutual consent on a fair field and fought it out. This approach was rational in social if not in strategic terms. Such wars would be short and would not disrupt the rhythm of agriculture. Nor were they particularly costly. When the losers dropped their heavy shields and fled, they could easily outpace the victors. Only some in the first ranks might be stabbed in the back before they fled. Yet the victor's aim was not annihilation but to prove their manhood and to conquer a minor piece of territory, which victory itself had already done. In proof they erected a battlefield monument, and the losers requested permission to bury their slain, a fundamental religious duty, thus recognizing their defeat and ending the war. Even states that routinely lost by these rules continued to play by them. Conversely, when Greeks fought non-Hellenic peoples who were not part of this customary style of war, they pursued genocide, seeking to destroy their enemies to a man and enslave their people.

Strategy emerged in Greece during the Persian invasion. Greeks, facing an enemy that neither fought by nor could be defeated by Hellenic rituals, either had to lose their independence or change their way of warfare to think strategically. This was most successfully done by the Athenian leader Themistocles. He realized that the Persian force rested on a complex symbiosis between army and navy. Only seaborne supplies could provision their army, while Persian sailors had to land in the shelter of their soldiers to sleep. Persian warships were more skilled at maneuver than Greeks but carried fewer marines; Hellenic crews could capture any Persian ship they boarded. Thus, Themistocles lured the enemy into narrow waters at Salamis, where all Persian strengths were divided and Greek ones multiplied. The Persian fleet was smashed: without supplies, most of their army had to return to Asia, and the remnant were annihilated at Platea. Themistocles had stumbled on the essence of strategy: use the enemy's weakness so to smash its strength. Over the next century, the role of ritual declined and that of strategy rose in Greek warfare. Customary restraints collapsed. Helpless Hellenic prisoners were butchered in their thousands; rotting enemy bodies were used as diplomatic bargaining chips; campaigns became longer and more complex. Armies operated semipermanently in the field, often from fortifications built in hostile territory, and thus could completely devastate their enemies' crops. Some defenders did face a choice between bread or battle. States constructed frontier fortification systems; their enemies responded with deep surprise drives from unexpected directions through weakly guarded passes.

Hoplite tactics were stereotyped; hence, even minor changes produced major successes. All hoplites could maneuver in one way before a battle began, by outflanking their foe. Only Spartans and Thebans could do more. Spartans conducted feigned withdrawals, opened and closed their ranks during combat, and exploited one fundamental factor in hoplite psychology. Hoplites instinctively veered toward their right as they advanced, each sheltering his exposed spear arm within his neighbor's shield. Spartans deliberately exaggerated this move, concentrating their mass against the enemy left flank, which could most easily be enveloped, and then using their superiority in discipline and maneuver to wheel as a line and strike the enemy's center on its unprotected side. Varying with the circumstances, Spartans placed their most dependable or expendable troops on their own exposed left flank, to pay the butcher's bill and pin the enemy down. "Spartans," the historian Thucydides wrote, "fight their battles long and stubbornly, standing their ground until they rout their foes, but when they have routed them their pursuits are brief and only for a short distance." Sparta would not risk high losses or a reversal of fortune by breaking the shield wall. Even when virtually all of Sparta's allies ran away, the enemy failed to reorganize before Spartans turned inward and demolished them.

This simple tactic, successful for so long because Greek armies were so primitive, could easily be countered. During the 370s and 360s B.C., Theban phalanxes did so by adopting a dense and oblique formation up to fifty ranks deep, led by the Sacred Band. They deliberately and counterintuitively held back the right edge of their line and threw their weight to the left, so striking the Spartan right flank long before the rest of the fronts collided. These tactics were a form of politics by other means. Thebes consciously avoided battle with Sparta's allies. Its forces swung like a hammer against the right flank of Spartan-led phalanxes— precisely against a massively outnumbered and quickly overwhelmed body of Spartiates. Before most members of either phalanx met, the fight was already over.

Between 430 and 350 B.C., Greek tactics gradually became more sophisticated. Spartan and Theban phalanxes pursued more elaborate maneuvers than hoplites had done before. Generals experimented with night marches, ambushes, surprise attacks with part of their forces before either phalanx had fully formed up, and the use of other arms. Cavalry delayed the advance of hoplites, pursued defeated enemies, and served as a reserve in battle. Peltasts—lightly armored soldiers carrying short swords and javelins—used the rough country landscape to harass and sometimes smash hoplites.

It was from this era of experimentation that Philip II of Macedeon produced a new style of warfare. His army came from a Homeric society, with tactics beyond those of the hoplites. His soldiers were his subjects, not citizens, drawn from a scattered peasant population rather than one urban center. They were bound by loyalty to a charismatic monarch who led them in battle and awarded them land and by a corporate sense of Macedonian nationality. The army was the people—over the next centuries in all the Macedonian kingdoms, the army tried traitors and appointed kings.

Philip created heavy infantry different from and superior to hoplites. They fought in a phalanx eight to sixteen men deep, depending on circumstances and the enemy. Their armor was light because Macedonians could not afford a hoplite's equipment, but in compensation they used a longer pike, the fourteen-foot-long *sarissa*. Since both hands were needed to wield a *sarissa*, Macedonian phalangists carried only a small shield attached to one arm.

The Macedonians had the advantage of first strike of spear against hoplites. The first five ranks of a Macedonian phalanx could bring their pikes to bear on the foe, while the remainder served as reserves to replace fallen comrades or waved their *sarissas* in the air so to block enemy arrows overhead. Phalangists invariably kept hoplites at bay and frequently destroyed them before Greeks could get to close quarters, where heavier armor, better shields, and more flexible spears would provide a decisive advantage. All phalangists were better trained than most hoplites while the three-thousand-man elite corps of *hypaspists* reached Spartiate standards. Phalangists could function on narrow plains and in broken country, against both hoplites and the lighter, less disciplined but more mobile forces of the Balkans and Persia.

Into this mix Philip added *peltasts*, archers, light cavalry, and heavy lancers. The latter could break Persian infantry head-on. They could not charge an unbroken hoplite spearline, but they could threaten a flank and annihilate a wavering enemy. The Macedonian army was the first in the ancient west to integrate specialized forces with different strengths and weaknesses into one combined arms system—to reach the Assyrian standard. Philip and his officers could also control reserves, especially the cavalry, when battle began and attack targets of opportunity such as a suddenly exposed part of the enemy line. At Chaironeia in 338 B.C., for example, Philip confronted a Theban and Athenian front anchored by two impenetrable obstacles. He broke that position by having part of his phalanx feign a withdrawal. Athenian hoplites surged forward and opened a gap in their lines through which Macedonian cavalry immediately charged, striking into the flank and rear of the divided Greek phalanx, which phalangists smashed from the front. Philip was an innovator in tactics and also a great strategist. His operations were marked by fast, deep, and unexpected drives, the outflanking of fortified zones, the concentration of all his forces against enemies rendered divided and unready by his diplomacy, and the expansion of the campaigning season from six to nine months.

Phillip's son Alexander the Great used his father's army, tactical system, and strategic style to revolutionize the classical world and its warfare. Greeks rarely fought beyond Greece, Sicily, and the Aegean coast of Asia. Philip operated only in Europe, south of the Danube. Between 334 and 325 B.C., however, Alexander campaigned seventeen thousand miles from the Balkans through Asia Minor to Egypt, central Asia, India, and back again. He was a drunkard, a megalomaniac—he thought himself the son of God, imitated the actions of Achilles, and intended to conquer the world, which was somewhat larger than he realized—and a master strategist. His initial weakness, for example, lay at sea. He could not match the Persian fleet, which might support his enemies in Greece, nor could he trust any Hellenic navy to keep Persia at bay, so Alexander defeated the enemy's fleet on land. His army seized every Persian naval base in the Mediterranean Sea before it advanced east to the heart of the Persian Empire. He defended his base by capturing the enemy's means to threaten it. From Alexander onward, classical generals thought in terms of continents.

Again, the Persians were weaker in heavy infantry but stronger in all other arms than Greeks. They could not defeat a phalanx through a frontal assault but could harass it with light troops and envelop it with cavalry. So Alexander's archers kept Persian bowmen away from the phalanx that, one flank protected by an impenetrable obstacle or by cavalry and light infantry, pinned down most of the enemy. Meanwhile, the *hypaspists* and most of the cavalry attacked any weak spot that emerged on the enemy's other flank, particularly as the foe moved to envelop Alexander's army. His cavalry breached the line, the *hypaspists* widened the gap, the two wheeled inward to hammer the Persian host on the anvil of the phalanx, and a terrible cavalry pursuit converted defeat to destruction. Even at the nearest run of Alexander's battles—Gaugamela in 331 B.C., when a numerically superior Persian army simultaneously threatened to envelop both Macedonian flanks and penetrated a gap in its center—Alexander's divided army held together. *Hypaspists* and horsemen smashed the Persian left and Alexander, turning to view the whole battlefield, flung his cavalry around the enemy's line and crushed the enemy from behind.

In his last years, Alexander merged Macedonian and Asian soldiers and their military systems, producing the Hellenistic style of war. Armies under the command of his successors (the *diadochi*) moved like lightning, exploiting surprise and forced marches to concentrate mass against an unready foe, using every advantage possible in terrain, timing, and tactics. They fought in self-contained wings, each capable of independent action. The phalanx dominated the center of the battlefield and won the battle against inferior infantry. When footmen of equal caliber engaged, decision stemmed from cavalry operating on the flank. During the great *diadochi* wars, engagements between rival phalanxes were rare and cavalry usually produced victory. Commanders applied every trick in the book of generalship; in fact, they wrote it.

No one added more pages to this volume than the greatest exponent of the Hellenistic style of war, Hannibal Barca, in the greatest of classical conflicts. In two wars with Rome, the mercantile city of Carthage exhibited military skill and resolution to match the most warlike of ancient states. During and after the First Punic War (264–241 B.C.), Rome seized Sardinia and Sicily from its old ally Carthage. These conquests, combined with Roman naval superiority, left Rome free to strike any Punic possession while blocking any Carthaginian maritime riposte at Italy. Carthage, desperately vulnerable to further aggression, sought to strengthen itself by expanding its empire in North Africa and Spain. This effort was dominated by the Barca family, whose members swore never to become "friends" (i.e., vassals) of Rome. But that was Rome's intention. Its renewed attempts to cripple Carthage caused the Second

Punic War (218–201 B.C.). Rome expected to win quickly, easily, and completely by invading Spain and Carthage simultaneously. Hannibal, the Punic commander in Spain, spoiled these plans. His army marched eight hundred miles from southern Spain to northern Italy, feeding itself in the midst of wild terrain and evading attacks by Romans and local peoples. The surprise onslaught forced Rome to abandon most of its offensive plans and thus defended Carthage. For the next fifteen years, 33 percent of Carthage's army tied down 75 percent of Roman forces and in Italy, making the enemy pay the price of war.

Hannibal crossed the Alps with twenty-six thousand men, losing the same number on the way. In Italy he acquired twenty-five thousand Gallic allies, whom he used in the bloodiest parts of the battle line to tie down Romans and save his veterans. This force challenged an army of over one hundred thousand soldiers. Yet from 217 to 216 B.C. Hannibal's soldiers marched five hundred miles through the heart of Roman territory to southern Italy, smashing en route three armies that equaled or exceeded their own size. This stemmed from tactical finesse. At the Battle of the Trebbia, for example, Hannibal feigned incompetence so to lure an arrogant enemy to rashness. As a result, the foe advanced across rough country and a cold river, becoming cold, hungry, and exhausted while Hannibal's men rested and ate a hot meal. As the battle began, each of his skirmishers matched two Romans—they defeated the light Roman troops and then withdrew to fight the legionnaires on his flanks. Gauls took the Roman thrust in the center. Although legionnaires broke through them, this took time and blood. Meanwhile, Hannibal's veterans held his wings steady to serve as the pivots for envelopment of the enemy. His cavalry crushed the Roman horsemen on both flanks and, together with two thousand Punic soldiers concealed in ambush, smashed the legionnaires from the side and rear.

Several months later, by devastating fat Italian farmland, Hannibal lured another army to destruction. On a misty day, overconfident Romans rushed the only Carthaginians they could see, a few heavy infantrymen blocking a narrow mountain road. Suddenly Hannibal's cavalry struck their rear, his missile troops bombarded the long narrow column of legionnaires, and his skirmishers and Gauls smashed down a slope and drove its fragments to drown in Lake Trasimene. At Cannae, Hannibal virtually defeated the enemy by means of its own strength. His infantry was outnumbered two to one but his cavalry was superior. He drew up his army like a kettle, with a bulge facing out to attract a Roman attack.

Within that bulge, in a thin line, he placed his expendable Gallic allies and his skilled Spanish swordsmen, intended to fall back slowly under Roman pressure. On their flanks, in two oblique lines leaning inward like a fan, he placed his phalangists. On the far left his Numidian light horsemen tied down greater numbers of mounted Romans; on the right his heavy cavalry outnumbered their counterparts. As legionnaires advanced, they reversed the shape of Hannibal's kettle and trapped themselves in it. They pushed Gauls and Spaniards back to form a solid line of swords. Suddenly, on both sides phalangists turned inward and a dense line of seven-foot spears pinned the Romans on both sides of the kettle. His heavy cavalry smashed the Roman cavalry on the right and rode behind their lines to break the mounted Italians on the left. The Numidians pursued the fleeing horsemen while the Carthaginian cavalry turned to slam shut the lid on the most celebrated massacre in military history.

Over the next decade, facing the largest army on earth, cut off from reinforcements, continually and grossly outnumbered, and in hostile country, Hannibal fought across southern Italy. He smashed several more Roman armies and never lost his cunning. This was true even in his last battle against Rome, and the only one he lost. Outside Carthage at Zama in 202 B.C., Hannibal skillfully used the inferior part of his forces, the Carthaginian militia, to absorb the enemy's thrust and wreck Roman cohesion, and then he held all the legionnaires in check with his grossly outnumbered veterans. Had he possessed superiority in cavalry, Zama would have been another Cannae: but he did not. Rome ultimately won. Carthage was less strong, Rome more resolute, and numbers and nerve determined victory in this prolonged struggle of attrition. No matter its losses, Rome routinely fielded two hundred thousand good citizen soldiers. At best, the Punic army never exceeded seventy-five thousand excellent mercenaries and as many more half-loyal tribal auxiliaries or half-trained citizen levies. Their performance veered between the extraordinary and the incompetent. The best Carthaginians defeated any Romans, but the rest were beaten by average Italians. Carthage never had the means to destroy Rome, nor did the greatest efforts it could muster crush Rome's empire in southern Italy, Sicily, and Sardinia. During the three years after Cannae, Carthage placed one hundred thousand men in these theaters against two hundred thousand legionnaires and a superior Roman fleet. Rome took more damage than any other classical society, and it never gave up. Carthage, conversely, could not take Roman punishment. It could inflict a Cannae but not survive one. Slowly, over fifteen years, Roman forces numerically no greater than local Punic garrisons, and sometimes smaller, wrecked its empire. In both Spain and Africa, one great defeat was enough to wreck Carthage's hold over its subjects. Once crippled, Carthage could never recover.

The effort needed to defeat Carthage set Rome on the path to master the Hellenistic world. Republican Roman citizen soldiers exceeded Greek ones in quantity, quality, tactics, and command. They were conscripts, serving for years on end, practicing daily with their weapons and as units. The aristocratic and popular elements of Roman society were integrated in a remarkably stable political system. More of the population served in the levy than in most Greek states. Although soldiers paid for their own arms, legions found use for unarmored soldiers, allowing even small peasants to fight. Only the poorest of freemen escaped service. The Italian allies also provided legions. Each legion included seven officers and sixty centurions, noncommissioned officers drawn from tested soldiers. All Romans fought like samurai. As the Greek historian Polybius put it, they regarded "their one supreme duty not to flee or leave the ranks." Defeated Romans were expected never to surrender or be captured but, instead, to die with all their wounds on the front or to commit suicide. They generally met these expectations because of ferocious discipline. The penalty for the infraction of regulations on campaign was death. Misbehaving units were "decimated"—one-tenth of their personnel, selected by lot, were publicly flogged to death to encourage the others.

The Republican army had an elaborate structure. Legions, forty-two hundred men strong, had four groups of footmen—twelve hundred *velites*, unarmored javelin throwing skirmishers; twelve hundred *hastati* and twelve hundred *principes*, with sword, armor, and two javelins; and six hundred *trieri*, heavily armored soldiers with a seven-foot thrusting spear. While *velites* and *trieri* were similar to *peltasts* and hoplites, no state except Carthage had forces like the *hastati* or the *principi*. Most Hellenistic infantry relied on the pike. They also carried short swords but were untrained in their use. Soldiers stood shoulder to shoulder, each in an area one yard square, their power lying not in single skill but in mass solidity. Only 33 percent of phalangists actively fought at any one time and they could never be relieved. The rest stood packed within range of enemy missiles, steadily becoming exhausted. Legionnaires, conversely, relied primarily on sword and javelin and were trained to fight at close range. Against phalangists, twenty feet determined life or death—whether *sarissa* or sword was master. Either fifteen spearheads thrust at every legionnaire in the front row, unable to retaliate, or Roman steel slashed at men holding tiny shields, caught midway between dropping pikes and drawing swords. Legionnaires functioned both in units and as individuals, with spaces between men and formations. As battles began, the *velites* harassed the enemy and then withdrew to the rear. Legions stood in three lines, one hundred yards apart. Each line was divided into maniples of 120 soldiers, who formed a small phalanx, 20 men wide and six deep. Lines and maniples could maneuver independently or collectively. Each legionnaire had up to five square yards in which to move, fight, or strike a target of opportunity. Over two-thirds of the men in a legion always rested outside the killing zone, while those in battle were relatively fresh. When they grew tired, soldiers could be relieved by their comrades in the maniple, or the entire first line could withdraw behind the second. The third line, the *trieri* supported by velites, served as a final reserve or a rallying point.

This organization was superior to most Hellenistic ones. Between 198 and 169 B.C., Macedonian and Seleucid phalangists, coming from wealthy states, were heavily armored and carried twenty-one-foot *sarissas*. They scared and often smashed legions in open territory, but they were far less mobile than in Philip II's day and desperately vulnerable in broken country. Ultimately, the Romans exploited their superior mobility on rough ground to avoid the pike-hedge, to reach close range, and to annihilate the muscle-bound phalangists. At the Battle of Cynosephalae in 197 B.C., for example, a Macedonian phalanx on the right drove legions downhill while Romans routed *peltasts* and disorganized phalangists on the left. Rome won because, on his own initiative, an officer at the rear of the left led twenty-five hundred legionnaires across rough terrain to hit sixteen thousand phalangists from behind before they turned about.

The flexible phalanxes of Hannibal and the *diadochi* Pyrrhus of Epirus, conversely, were as maneuverable, better-trained, and fought with the same grim determination as legions. They incorporated Roman elements such as maniples and the three line formation and usually defeated larger Roman armies. Hannibal's infantry integrated skirmishers, swordsmen, and phalangists more effectively than legions did and, beyond that, used missile troops. Even at Zama, his veterans held a greater Roman force at bay until, finally, Numidian cavalry allied to Rome won the day. The Republican legion was no better than the phalanx at its best, nor was heavy infantry the only component of warfare. Rome's great weakness was its mediocre cavalry. It defeated Carthage in Africa and the Seleucids in Asia only because local allies provided horsemen, and then the Romans fought like *diadochi*, winning with cavalry on the flanks. Rome's real edge was not in quality but quantity. In 279 B.C. Pyrrhus invaded Italy and smashed a Roman army but remarked, "Another such victory will ruin me." He could not replace losses like the one suffered against Rome. Hannibal killed or captured over one hundred thousand Roman and allied soldiers between 218 and 216 B.C. He killed another one hundred thousand over the next decade, as large a bag as any commander in antiquity, but even he could not slaughter all the hordes of Rome.

More exotic forces also fought in classical battles, usually with little effect. Persians attacked Alexander with scythed chariots as did Seleucids against Rome, without much success. Conversely, when first used against an army, elephants often were a battle winning tool. Victory at Ipsus in 301 B.C., the most important of the *diadochi* battles, was decided when the cavalry of Antigonus the One-Eyed would not approach a line of elephants that blocked their return to a battlefield where his phalanx was annihilated. In 255 B.C., just outside Carthage, elephants crushed legionnaires standing in an unusually deep formation, which were then overrun by a Punic phalanx from the front and cavalry from the side. This denied Rome a decisive victory in the First Punic War. However, experienced forces could easily counter elephants. When their feet were impaled by spikes or their mahouts shot, elephants often ran amok through their own lines. In general, they damaged their own side more than the enemy. Hellenistic armies often used catapults on the battlefield but rarely with consequence because of their low rate of fire and mobility. They were most useful covering assaults on beaches and riverbanks, slowing advances up passes, or bolstering prepared positions. In 353 B.C., for example, Macedonian forces were lured into a valley and then ambushed by catapults. The Phocian infantry immediately charged the disordered Macedonians, inflicting the only battlefield defeat ever suffered by Philip II.

Classical armies rarely fought at night, partly from a belief that night attacks were cowardly but primarily because formation could not be maintained in the dark. This problem wrecked the Athenian army when it launched such an attack as a last gamble outside the walls of Syracuse in 413 B.C. As Thucydides wrote, "Once the original confusion had taken place, many parts of the army ended by falling upon each other, friend against friend and citizen against citizen, not only causing panic among themselves, but actually fighting hand to hand." Similarly, both sides lost control of their men during a chaotic night battle at Cremona during the Roman civil war of A.D. 69. The Flavian and Vitellian armies wore the same uniforms, held the same weapons, learned each other's watchwords, and captured and carried each other's standards confusing friend and foe. The battle ended in the morning, as a result of exhaustion and rumor. One Flavian legion, manned by sun-worshippers, turned to cheer the rising of the sun. Concluding that friends must be arriving, other Flavians surged forward while for the same reason the Vitellians ran away.

Ancient states knew the topography of western and southern Europe, North Africa, and the Middle East. Yet knowledge marched hand in hand with ignorance. Alexander the Great, an avid student of geography, thought the world ended on a line between the Ural mountains and the Bay of Bengal. Augustus Caesar underestimated the size of Germany by one-third, which shaped his disastrous attempt to conquer it. News marched more quickly than men. Horse or semaphore relays transmitted information one hundred miles per day. In the same space of time, hoplites moved ten miles, Hellenistic and Roman armies fifteen, while fleets traveled fifty-five to eighty miles. Sailing from Rome to the northern coast of Syria took 50 days, to walk there, 125, and men marched only where they could be fed. Classical supply systems were no better than those of Assyria and often worse. Greek armies, accompanied by a host of camp followers, usually ran out of food within a month. Philip II revolutionized this situation. He reduced the number of his camp followers, and he trained Macedonians to carry most of their own equipment and to march faster than Greeks. This had major strategic consequences. Thirty-five thousand Macedonians could march four hundred miles on the same amount of food that took twenty thousand hoplites three hundred miles. Philip also improved his baggage train. He replaced oxen with horses, which carried the same weight three times as far on half the forage. Alexander the Great's logistic system fed sixty-five thousand soldiers and their horses over a distance of thousands of miles for years on end. Three hundred forty horse drawn carts were needed to carry the 511,000 pounds of grain and forage these forces consumed each day. Roman armies too minimized the requirements of soldiers on campaign and maximized weight in their packs.

The lethality of ancient combat varied widely. In hoplite battles, on average victors lost 5 percent and losers 14 percent of their strength. Conversely, combat between the *diadochi* was often bloodless. In their many battles between 303 and 281 B.C., only seventeen thousand soldiers were killed. Generally 1 to 10 percent of the victors and 30 to 50 percent of the vanquished died in Hellenistic and Republican Roman battles. Most casualties were inflicted when an army broke, and they were especially high when one was trapped. At Cannae only ten thousand of eighty thousand Roman soldiers escaped death or capture. Virtually none survived the ambush at Lake Trasimene. Close combat between armored and unarmored soldiers, hoplites and phalangists against Persians, Romans against Germans or Gauls, produced one-sided massacres. At sea, victors generally lost 5 percent of their fleet and the defeated, 30 percent but often 50 to 100 percent of it. Prisoners were usually enslaved but sometimes freed or executed. For citizen armies, defeat often meant genocide—the death of every male and the destruction of their people. The populations of cities taken by storm were invariably annihilated or enslaved.

Classical warfare centered as much on the control of territory through fortifications and their capture as on pitched battles. The Peloponnesian War, for example, was slow and costly—a prolonged siege—because cities were hard to take. By constructing walls to its port, the inland city of Athens established unbreakable contact with the sea. Athens refused to come out when superior enemies ravaged its territories—it could not be forced either to fight or starve. Athens was invulnerable on land and free to concentrate its energies at sea. So long as its fleet ruled the Aegean Sea, Athens could draw food and finance to continue the war. It used fortified bases in hostile territory to threaten the enemy. In particular, through a walled port at Pylos, on the Spartan coast, it subverted Sparta's hold over its helots. That nightmare, and the fact that Athens captured 120 Spartiates on Pylos, pinned Sparta on defense, leaving Athens free to attack Sparta's allies elsewhere. Sparta later returned the favor. It maintained a fort near Athens that permanently threatened that city and prevented it from using its farmland. This tied down troops, forced Athens to rely entirely on imported foodstuffs, and gave Sparta's navy the opportunity to cut Athens's throat through blockade.

Subsequently, forts served as centers of power along the roads and frontiers of the *diadochi* empires. Seleucid power in Asia rested on fortifications, garrisoned by Macedonians, that controlled the local countryside. In Greece, citadels were built within already walled cities. Their purpose was not to defend a city but to dominate it. Macedonian power in Greece rested on garrisoned fortifications in the major cities along the choke points of communications. They provided immediate support to Macedonia's allies and ensured that whenever necessary its troops could march through Greece instead of having to fight through it.

The sophistication and the success of siege craft varied widely, according to the supplies and strength of both sides and the ingenuity of commanders and engineers. Many states were ineffective besiegers, for which they paid heavily. Before 400 B.C., Greek sieges were invariably slow and primitive. They turned on one question—whether the besieged starved or lost their nerve before the besiegers did. When cities fell quickly, the cause was treachery or surprise. Between 460 and 350 B.C., Greeks required years to capture towns of just a few thousand people, defended by nine-feet-thick and fifteen-feet-high masonry walls. Tactics involved little more than circumvallation—encircling a position through entrenchments—assaults up siege ramps (mounds of earth piled against city walls) and attack on gates with fire and battering rams, occasionally protected by a "tortoise" of shields resting on a frame. This stemmed from military culture. Hoplites would not pay the casualties needed to take a city by storm nor use tools like siege ladders or battering rams which required them to set aside the *hoplon*.

Between 400 and 390 B.C. in Sicily, however, Greeks and Carthaginians revolutionized siege craft and the art of war. They devised new tactics and technology, such as the earliest form of *ballistai*, the traction catapult, a crossbow with a range of 250 yards. Greeks and Carthaginians assaulted walls and gates with overwhelming numbers of mercenaries, tortoises, and wheeled siege towers. Catapults from the ground and archers from towers suppressed the defending fire. Assault troops charged parapets across the drawbridges of towers, miners sapped beneath walls, iron rams stove in gates, and human wave attacks were thrown through breaches and up ramps or ladders. During that decade almost every city in Sicily fell to siege—more than in the entire Greek world over the previous century and in weeks rather than years. Quick decisive victories could be achieved against the enemy's centers of power. Greeks and Carthaginians stormed alternately from one side of Sicily to the other at a time when campaigns in Greece stalled before any wall. This decade also featured the first known application of high-technology to warfare. The traction catapult was invented in 399 B.C.

when Dionysius, the tyrant of Syracuse, hired the leading engineers of Greece specifically to create instruments of war. Over the following centuries, classical engineering remained an arm of war. Technology has followed that cue ever since.

The fourth century B.C. was a golden age of siege craft, without which the successes of Macedonia would have been impossible. Philip II built an admirable corps of engineers, which conducted research alongside sieges. They produced new weapons using the principle of torsion, which stored energy through the twisting of hair and suddenly released it to fire an object. These included catapults and "ram-tortoises," battering rams mounted on protected carriers. Philip's siege train included mobile towers 120 feet tall. It is unclear whether he achieved great success through sieges, but he did better than any other Greek city had done. He seized several cities rapidly and even his failures were sensational. This may have led his neighbors to accept his hegemony. In any case, Philip's engineers served his son well. Alexander occupied the entire Asian coast of the Mediterranean Sea in eighteen months and launched several great sieges against major centers. So to batter a city from all angles, he placed *ballistai* on ships, on moles constructed from the mainland and on earthworks fifty feet tall. Breaches were made at several sections of a wall; massive artillery barrages and infantry assaults from all angles divided the garrison. When attacking the island city of Tyre, bombardment vessels covered the attack of infantrymen carried on board special landing craft. Alexander's engineers took every city his armies assaulted, usually within a few weeks or months. His successes would have been impossible had sieges been as slow as a century before. Despite his genius on the battlefield, Alexander, without his engineers, could never have demolished Persia cheaply and quickly.

The success of siege craft soon declined, because defensive techniques improved. *Ballistai* worked for the besieged as well as the besieger. Siege works and catapults had to be deployed within range of defending fire. Catapults penetrated shields but not walls and shot burning arrows or huge stones into wooden equipment four hundred yards away. Only armored towers could survive such pounding. Alexander's siege of Tyre lasted six months, because catapults and sallies delayed the attacker and once destroyed all his siege works. Between 214 and 212 B.C., Rome took three years to capture Syracuse, defended by the great engineer Archimedes. After ships were sunk and towers were shattered, Romans became so frightened that they abandoned active measures and simply starved the city out. As defensive techniques improved, sieges again became slow and costly affairs, conducted with greater sophistication but no more success than in the Peloponnesian War. Great armies again spent months taking a town and years capturing a city. Hannibal bestrode the battlefield like Alexander but his sieges were less successful. After Cannae, the war in Italy turned on the defense of and attack on walled towns, and here Hannibal could not master Rome: the limitations to his siege craft reduced him from menace to nuisance. Hannibal was Alexander without engineers.

Imperial Rome was the ancient master of the making and taking of fortifications. It maintained a high standard of military engineering and sophisticated equipment. Each legion carried ten large catapults and forty-five *carroballistai*, large crossbows with crews of two to ten men. Romans built siege ramps 675 feet long and 275 feet high, topped with stone platforms 75 feet high or towers six stories high, 30 feet square, and 5 feet thick, covered by anchor chain to deflect catapult bolts. Soldiers advanced toward cities in trenches or armored galleries and ripped walls apart with crowbars. During the siege of A.D. 70, Romans attacked the walls of Jerusalem with three towers, armored and eighty feet tall. At the base, rams smashed walls and gates, and, above, men charged the parapets or were lifted by cranes while catapults and archers on the top platforms fired at the garrison below. Miners sapped and 180 catapults hammered the walls, throwing fifty-pound stones a distance of five hundred yards. Soldiers in tortoise formation (shields held interlocked over the heads) charged into breaches. From the second century B.C. to the fall of the Roman Empire, however, the role of sieges within the strategy of the Mediterranean world declined because of the Roman peace. Besieged cities during civil wars tended not to fight to the death. Even for Rome, sieges against determined defenders in Spain, Carthage, and Israel took years to complete.

Ancient warships were long and narrow oared vessels. Triremes, the dominant naval type between 530 and 322 B.C., were 120 feet long and 15 feet wide. For three hundred years after the *diadochi* smashed Athens's navy in 322 B.C., larger vessels of varying sizes dominated the seas. These "polyremes" often had twice the dimensions of triremes. Quinqueremes, for example, were 26 feet wide and 180 feet long. After 31 B.C. the Roman Empire, undisputed master of the Mediterranean, relied on cheaper warships—triremes or smaller. Triremes usually carried crews of two hundred men, and quinqueremes carried crews of three hundred men.

Their sailors and marines were free men, invariably citizens, while their oarsmen were usually citizens, allies, or mercenaries, though slaves were used when manpower was short. During peacetime, for example, most Athenian oarsmen were citizens. By the last years of the Peloponnesian War, however, only 10 percent were citizens, 25 percent were slaves, and the remainder mercenaries. Slaves rowed alongside free men and rarely in chains; they often were freed en masse before or after combat. Fighting had too much status to be done primarily by slaves.

Only wealthy powers could maintain great navies and then only with private help. Even the two great sea powers of antiquity, Athens and Rhodes, relied on their captains personally to pay for the maintenance of their vessels. Forced loans from citizens financed the Ptolemaic navy and the Roman fleet that finally won the First Punic War in 241 B.C. Naval construction required the greatest economic activity of antiquity—large numbers of dockyards, ship sheds, shipwrights, and work crews with unimpeded access to huge supplies of timber and tar. Oarsmen were expensive and required constant practice to row with a unified rhythm. Athens never had more than 170 triremes with thirty-one thousand men at sea, and Rhodes had only 33 percent of that strength. Rome and the great Hellenistic kingdoms never had more than 280 polyremes with ninety-two thousand men. Only Athens and Rhodes always maintained sizable navies in fighting trim. After smashing Rome's fleet in 249 B.C., Carthage decommissioned its own fleet—in the middle of a war—which allowed Rome to turn the tables eight years later. After constructing the greatest fleets of antiquity, the *diadochi* empires let them rot after 250 B.C.; Rome soon did the same. Between 167 and 67 B.C., Rome ruled the Mediterranean, but pirates routinely ravaged the Italian coast.

Naval battles occurred close to coasts—warships were even captured by soldiers attacking from beaches. Fleets advanced in line abreast, often in two echelons. One wing might be drawn up on the coast, the largest vessels gripping the center like a phalanx and the fastest ones sweeping like cavalry on the far wing. Each warship stood two oars' length from its neighbor to the side or more, depending on seamanship. Archers and *ballistai* raked decks, wrecking defenses and the rhythm of oarsmen. Ships sailed over men in the water while marines speared ship-wrecked sailors like fish. Their tactics centered on boarding and ramming. Warships were both fighting platforms and torpedoes. Ramming, conducted by the bronze beak on a prow, took three forms: *antiproroi*, or bow smashing bow; *diekplous*, or "breaking the line," sailing between enemy ships and wheeling to strike their bows, sides, or banks of oars; and *periplous*, outflanking warships and striking them from side or rear. Ramming, sometimes conducted at twenty-five miles per hour, relied on the skill of sailors and boarding on the strength of marines. Greek triremes carried 20 to 40 marines, Roman quinqueremes carried 120 marines. Grappling irons pinned vessels together or were cut away. Arrows and javelins swept decks, pikes drove defenders from the sides, and marines leapt aboard with sword and axe.

Navies combined these tactics. They rarely relied on just one and then only because of a discrepancy in seamanship. During the 420s B.C. Athenians so outclassed their enemies that they could avoid boarding; in the 250s Romans could win through no other means. Triremes relied equally on ramming and boarding. Polyremes, slower and carrying more marines, emphasized boarding and mass above seamanship and the ram. Neither tactic was absolutely dominant. Ramming was hard to execute in enclosed waters or against an enemy that maintained disciplined order. It was most successful where room for maneuver existed and the enemy was disorganized. As the great Athenian admiral Phormio said, "Lack of sea room is a disadvantage for a small, experienced and fast squadron fighting with many badly managed ships. One cannot sail up in the proper way to make an attack by ramming, unless one has a good long view of the enemy ahead, nor can one back away at the right moment if one is hard pressed oneself; it is impossible also to sail through the enemy's line and then wheel back on him—which are the right tactics for a fleet which has the superior seamanship. Instead of all this, one would be compelled to fight a naval action as though it were a battle on land, and under those circumstances the side with the greater number of ships has the advantage."

Classical navies were as innovative as any in history. Fire ships, loaded with wood and pitch, annihilated fleets at anchor. Bowmen crammed on small boats fired mass volleys at warships. Reinforced bows helped one side conduct *antiproroi* against another; iron-shod beams bolstered hulls against all kinds of ramming. Catapults fired grappling hooks or jars containing snakes at warships just as battles began. Such innovations turned the tide of battles and sometimes of wars. Rome won the First Punic War largely because of the "claw." These boarding bridges, thirty-six feet long and four feet wide, were dropped on warships attempting a *diekplous* and were crossed by Roman marines. This negated superior

Carthaginian seamanship and let Rome fight at sea as if on land. In 190 B.C., conversely, "fire baskets" dropped by light Rhodians warships overcame Seleucid polyremes closing to board. The Seleucids flinched away and exposed themselves to Rhodian rams.

Command of the seas did not exist in the classical era. Crews had to land every evening to sleep, and fleets did not move during the winter or cross the high seas. These coasting navies ran risks in sailing just three hundred miles from a friendly port. For such reasons Rome lost 440 quinqueremes and between 20,000 and 130,000 men to storms during the First Punic War. These factors also explain ancient maritime strategy. Between 475 and 414 B.C., for example, Athens controlled the largest and best navy in the Aegean Sea and almost every port there. It had an excellent chance to intercept in open waters any hostile fleets operating between Cyprus, the Peloponnese, and the Dardanelles. Enemy warships found it hard to sail in that area, let alone fight there. This let Athens design warships and tactics that exploited all its skills at maneuver and avoided its enemies' strength at boarding. At their peak Athenian squadrons were virtually unbeatable—they once defeated a Peloponnesian fleet five times greater in size. Sparta began to win at sea only when Persia subsidized its navy, while that of Athens was crippled because of disastrous losses suffered in the attempt to conquer Sicily. Sparta used these opportunities to break into the Aegean Sea and shatter the foundations of Athenian sea power and strategy. Sparta seized ports and acquired the ability to evade Athenian triremes on open water. This crippled Athenian finances and its base network and forced it to defend all of its maritime empire at once, especially the Dardenelles, through which flowed vital imports of food. This forced Athens to fight where its enemies wanted, in narrow waters, which negated its superiority in maneuver.

Fleets might blockade a port but never a coast. They could damage trade but not destroy it. Sea power guaranteed that one could ship troops and invade coasts and that one might intercept enemy vessels trying to do so but it could never absolutely prevent an inferior enemy from using the seas. Despite Roman naval superiority, during the Second Punic War Carthage shipped sixty thousand soldiers from Africa and Spain to Italy, Sicily, and Sardinia—it once sailed ten thousand men directly from Gibraltar to Genoa. Superior enemy fleets did not keep Roman armies from crossing the Adriatic Sea during the civil wars of the 30s and 40s B.C. Yet classical sea power sometimes worked in a classical fashion. Between 218 and 167 B.C., maritime supremacy let Rome invade Spain, Africa, Greece, and Asia Minor and maintain large expeditionary forces overseas for years on end. Fear of Roman sea power forced Hannibal to invade Italy by elephant rather than by ship—Rome's navy sank half of his army. During its wars against Macedonia in the 190s and the 160s B.C., sea power let Rome advance from several sides at once, to threaten every port under Macedonian control, and to tie down much of its army in coast defense.

Citizen forces, even the best of them, had an odd sense of discipline. In 368 B.C. when their elected officers led their men to disaster in Thessaly, Theban troops voted them out of office on the spot and called on Epaminondas, then serving in the ranks, to take command and save their lives. In 168 B.C. the Roman general Aemilius Paullus complained that his men acted "as though they were all commanders," by continually giving him unsolicited advice on tactics. Professional fighting forces also had unusual social relationships, particularly because families and possessions moved with their menfolk. This shaped some of the oddest campaigns in history. The *diadochi* armies could launch daring attacks across hundreds of miles of wilderness and execute fine maneuvers on the field of battle. Yet when they clashed, one side almost always surrendered or betrayed its master, usually because its own families and goods had been seized by the enemy. Many battles were decided by raids on the enemy's baggage—cavalry achieved more through this means than heroic charges. Seleucid armies routinely marched with thousands of cooks, whores, and huge trains of goods, including gold tableware. As the classical historian Justin wrote, during their disastrous campaign against Parthia in 129 B.C., the Seleucid army seemed to be marching to dinner rather than to battle. When their baggage was captured, Seleucid armies collapsed. Yet this was not so much a characteristic of Hellenistic armies as of professional ones. During an ambush in 54 B.C., even some of Julius Caesar's veterans broke ranks in order to save their plunder and so lost their lives. In A.D. 89 one Roman general led two legions to revolt by seizing their savings bank and with it their loyalties.

As hoplite battles began, commanders often stood behind the phalanx, seeking to observe tactical opportunities and to use them. At the crisis of the battle, however, when hoplites began to weary and waver, commanders influenced their men by example. They moved to the front of the spear-line, inspiring their soldiers to glory or to death. Classical commanders often engaged in personal combat, culminating with one beheading the other. How better to break an army, especially one with little training, than by waving its leader's head on a pole above the fray? Romans called armor stripped by one general from another after single combat, "The Noblest Spoils." During the fifth and fourth centuries B.C., most commanders and senior officers of a vanquished phalanx fell in that action. Before 222 B.C., every Spartan king who was defeated in battle died on that field.

Danger existed even for successful generals. The great Theban commanders Epaminondas and Pelopidas both died as their armies triumphed. Following Pelopidas's death and his men's victory, in a scene almost out of Homer, his Thessalian friends flocked to his body, still wearing their armor, their wounds unattended, shearing their hair and their horse's manes in grief, piling before his body spoils taken from the enemy. Alexander the Great led his Household Cavalry into battle, twice by charging directly at the Persian Emperor. He often was the first through the breached walls of a besieged city.

During the Hellenistic and Roman periods, tactics were more sophisticated, soldiers better trained, and their commanders had greater control over their forces during battle. Many beaten commanders ran away so to fight another day. Yet the older pattern of command often recurred. At the Battle of Raphia in 217 B.C., the Egyptian monarch Ptolemy IV stood in the forefront of a phalanx whose morale was shaky. A decade later Hannibal's brother Hasdrubal launched a suicide charge on Roman forces once he knew that his forces had lost. Polybius praised this action as the epitome of generalship. George S. Patton expressed the same sentiment twenty-three hundred years later: "THERE IS NOTHING MORE PATHETIC AND FUTILE THAN A GENERAL WHO LIVES LONG TO EXPLAIN A DEFEAT."

War was a religious act to classical societies. Armies conducted sacrifices at all stages of a campaign, even on the battlefield with the enemy a few hundred yards away. They were accompanied by seers whose duty, like intelligence personnel in modern armies, was to foresee the outcome of operations. Generals were bound by custom and opinion to consult their seers before taking actions, though they could override them or find other interpretations for omens. For this purpose, some commanders learned the techniques of augury. Many generals were cynics—as Julius Caesar once said, "The omens will be as favorable as I wish them to be"—but more were believers. Spartan armies never moved during holy days. Alexander the Great ignored his lieutenants but sometimes accepted the advice of his seer, Aristandros. The two men spent the night before Gaugamela offering sacrifices. As that battle began Aristandros, wearing white coat and golden headband, shouted to Alexander's soldiers that an eagle flying straight toward the enemy was an omen of victory from the gods. Rome credited many defeats to errors in ritual. The cause for one catastrophe at sea in 249 B.C. was thought to be angry gods, when the consul Claudius Pulcher, infuriated because the sacred chickens would not offer a favorable omen by eating the food placed before them, had them thrown overboard with these words, "If they will not eat, let them drink!"

In Carthage, Republican Rome and many Greek states, generals were elected as much for political as for professional reasons. Success or failure in battle directly shaped politics and vice versa. If a great soldier was not elected as a general, he could not lead and might serve under an incompetent. Again, generals sometimes were appointed to difficult commands simply in order to wreck their political position. Unsuccessful Greek generals were exiled or executed; Carthaginians were crucified. When in 406 B.C. Athens's fleet won a great victory but left many citizens to drown, Athens executed its victorious admirals. Not coincidently, one year later its fleet was badly led and entirely sunk. In Republican Rome, conversely, beaten commanders less frequently lost their political position—defeat was blamed not on aristocratic incompetence but on their soldiers or the gods. Only a defeated commander who betrayed the dignity of Rome through cowardice or surrender suffered disgrace. Even Terentius Varro, crushed at Cannae, was praised and given other important commands because he "did not despair of the Republic" but instead rallied the survivors to fight again. So to maintain civil supremacy and to prevent the rise of overmighty commanders, states often sent several generals to control the same army—command literally switched between them on alternate days. Spartan generals were accompanied by commissions of elders, sometimes empowered to override their battlefield commands. Only when facing disaster would Republican Rome let one man, a "dictator," command all its armies.

This approach could create confusion. Hannibal defeated several armies by exploiting differences between their generals. Yet such controls were also fundamental to the constitutions these armies were intended to uphold. When they collapsed, so did the Roman Republic. Legionnaires traditionally were conscripted for short campaigns in Italy. Rome did not conscript the poorest of freemen—the *capite censi*—into the army, fearing the political consequences. This system collapsed in the first century B.C., a victim of its own success. The economic consequences of conquest increased the size of the *capite censi* while Roman armies campaigned for years on end far from Italy. This destroyed a soldier's civil livelihood, and he could only recover it by receiving a sizable bonus on discharge. Generals also began to recruit volunteers from the *capite censi*—precisely those men most likely to face such economic problems and to see a solution to them in military service. They could serve because soldiers no longer paid for their own equipment, the hallmark of a classical citizen army, but received it from the state. Increasingly soldiers became professional volunteers rather than citizen conscripts and their relationship with the state changed. They became a caste apart from civilians. Generals personally paid their men and acted as their agents with the state in negotiating discharge bonuses. Soldiers became loyal to their commander rather than Rome and regarded the armies of other generals as rivals. Commanders used their men as mercenaries in coups d'état and civil wars. Ultimately, this led to the destruction of the Republic and the formation of an empire by the adopted son of Julius Caesar, Augustus.

Case Study: The Imperial Roman Army

Augustus created the army of Imperial Rome, the greatest bureaucracy of antiquity—it filled out forms in quadruplicate. This, as much as anything, caused Rome's victories. Augustus established an army of 150,000 legionnaires, specialized heavy infantry and combat engineers, supported by 150,000 auxiliaries with complementary skills. Half the auxiliaries were cavalry, ranging from armored lancers to horse archers. Each of these 300,000 men consumed a pint of wine each day and one-third of a ton of corn each year. The army was the largest manufacturer and employer in the empire, maintaining weapons factories, artillery ranges, office blocks, and spas.

Detailed routines governed training and operations. Recruits were admitted into legions only after documenting that they were Roman citizens, providing referees, undergoing a medical exam, and meeting minimum standards for age, intelligence, eyesight, and height (five feet ten inches)—only in the last desperate years of the empire did these standards fall. Units kept files on each soldier, a personnel bureau in Rome held the records on every officer and centurion. Commanders continually monitored the bureaucratic machine. Every day officers in-

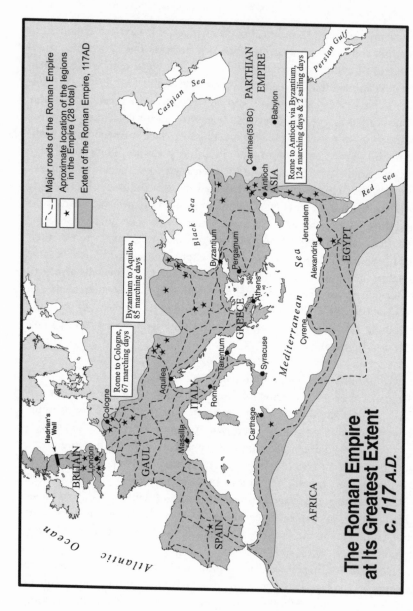

Major roads of the Roman Empire

Aproximate location of the legions in the Empire (28 total)

Extent of the Roman Empire, 117AD

Caspian Sea

PARTHIAN EMPIRE

Carrhae(53 BC)

●Babylon

Persian Gulf

Black Sea

Byzantium

Pergamum

Antioch

ASIA

Red Sea

Rome to Antioch via Byzantium, 124 marching days & 2 sailing days

Byzantium to Aquilea, 85 marching days

Rome to Cologne, 67 marching days

Athens

GREECE

Jerusalem

Mediterranean Sea

Cyrene

Alexandria

EGYPT

Cologne

Aquilea

ITALY

Rome

Tarentum

Syracuse

Carthage

Massilia

GAUL

Hadrian's Wall

BRITAIN

London

SPAIN

AFRICA

Atlantic Ocean

The Roman Empire at Its Greatest Extent
C. 117 A.D.

Map 2-3

spected their men and sampled food to prevent quartermasters from cheating, generals checked the packs of their soldiers on campaign and threw unauthorized equipment away, and emperors inspected units and forts on the frontier.

Augustus's system rested on a meticulous balance between dangers. External threats would swamp a small army; a large one would wreck the economy and increase the risk of coups d'état. His system worked for 250 years, and it cost as much as the empire could bear. Nonetheless, this created permanent stress. In order to pay campaign costs the emperor Marcus Aurelius once had to sell his private belongings at public auction. The army became a professional and Imperial force, no longer a citizen or Roman one to avoid the chaos that military forces under private control had wreaked on the late Republic. Soldiers, however, remained central to politics, just in a different and less destructive way. Emperors had to acquire popularity with them through pay or personal command. One emperor, Septimus Severus, defined the central rule of Imperial politics as "enrich the soldiers and ignore the rest." Fortunately, soldiers remained loyal to their paymaster. For 230 of the 240 years following Augustus's rise to power, there were no military rebellions, though the remaining ten years were dominated by civil war. Soldiers rarely favored civil strife because this threatened the stability of their pay, though when it happened they sold their services to the highest bidder.

Imperial soldiers lived well. They saved 30 percent of their pay, owned slaves, and received first-rate medical care. On average, they lived five years longer than civilians. All forts had effective sanitation and fresh water, while large ones had a hospital. Military doctors had effective forceps, scalpels, surgical saws, and medicinal herbs. Doctors used opium to kill pain and conducted sophisticated and successful procedures like amputation and removing arrows from chest cavities. Through ligatures, tourniquets, and surgical clamps, doctors handled hemorrhages and minimized infection, gangrene, and blood loss from cuts to major arteries. Not until the days of penicillin did any soldiers have better medical care than the Romans. Their diet included wine, bacon, cheese, vegetables, fruit, wheat, fowl, fish, beef, mutton, and pork, not to mention snail, fox, and beaver. Rations could be gargantuan— three pounds of bread, two pounds of meat, and two pints of wine per man each day. There is one recorded instance of Roman armies suffering from scurvy, but there is no record of soldiers complaining about their food.

The army defended the empire and also helped to run it. Soldiers served as policemen, judges, and tax collectors and used these opportunities to suit themselves. They robbed and assaulted civilians and once fought the population of Rome for three days and burned down the city. Generals moved their men from one town to another simply to make local people pay to have them transferred. Not surprisingly, when asked by soldiers how to live well, Jesus Christ replied—"No bullying; no blackmail; make do with your pay!" The army also became territorial. Legions, recruited from and marrying into local populations, increasingly disliked transfers, hampering the strategic redeployment of Roman forces. Their discipline also became erratic. Some legionnaires were drunk on duty, did not carry their weapons, and treated the army as a part-time career. Officers left units undermanned so to pocket the pay of the ghost soldiers. These factors dulled the army's edge, but centuries were required to wreck the weapon forged by Augustus.

The Imperial military system was unique in antiquity. Legions, six thousand men strong, were divided into ten cohorts, each with an officer, six centurions, and six hundred men. This command system could form more sophisticated formations and could better survive close combat than any other classical one. Trumpets and flags controlled units during combat. All legionnaires became *hastati*, relying on javelins and swords. Their seven-foot javelins, with an effective range of thirty yards, were useful whether they struck flesh or shield. On impact the heads bent, disabling any shield they penetrated and pinning overlapping ones together. This forced enemy soldiers to drop their shields precisely as Roman swords flashed toward them. The two-foot-long double-edged sword was used primarily for a killing thrust but also to chop off limbs. Legionnaires learned the sword techniques of gladiators. They carried effective but light helmets and armor. Strong cylindrical shields, made of wood and edged with metal, two and one-half feet wide and four feet long, covered the body.

Their tactics rested on a high synthesis of fire and shock. Within a twenty second period each legionnaire threw two javelins, disorganizing the enemy's ranks, and charged into them before they recovered. In the process Roman command sometimes collapsed. Usually, however, Romans maintained order while the enemy fell apart. At close quarters, no ancient soldiers could match the Romans, especially not their most usual foe. The undisciplined infantry of northern Europe stood in clumsy mass formations. Their front rank could never be relieved, and their members fought until they won or died, while men in the rear could not reach the foe. They carried little armor (sometimes they fought naked) and used long slashing swords and pikes—two-handed weapons. The more space to fight, the deadlier their blows, the closer the combat, the more exposed to a killing thrust against the armpit, a standard drill for legionnaires. The Roman general Germanicus told his soldiers, "You must strike repeatedly, and aim your points at their faces. The Germans wear no breastplates or helmets. Even their shields are not reinforced with iron or leather, but are merely plaited wickerwork or flimsy painted boards. Spears, of a sort, are limited to their front rank. The rest only have clubs burnt at the end, or with short metal points. Physically, they look formidable and are good for a short rush. But they cannot stand being hurt. They quit and run unashamedly, regardless of their commanders. In victory they respect no law, human or divine; in defeat they panic."

Roman commanders read military manuals that analyzed Hellenistic, Carthaginian, and Roman stratagems, tactics, and means of using surprise, mass, and maneuver. They applied these with finesse and combined legionnaires with auxiliaries according to specific needs. The standard deployment involved two or three lines of cohorts, using "wedge" tactics—pushing units forward into the enemy line, pressing it close together, and striking adversaries from flank and front. Cavalry usually just covered the flanks, but sometimes it played a Hellenistic role in battle. Similarly, to break the charge of heavy horsemen, one Roman commander formed his men in a crescent formation with the horns toward the enemy. A line of auxiliary pikemen backed by bowmen stood before his legions, while *carroballistai* on the horns raked the front from both sides. Imperial Rome used *ballistai* for everything Hellenistic armies had done and more. Every minute each *carroballistai* fired three bolts that penetrated shields three hundred yards away. They were moved ready for action on carts and used as artillery. Roman armies often anchored their front with *carroballistai* given a long and clear field of fire, to make enemy formations charge, take cover, or die. Not until Napoleon would European armies possess greater fire support than the Roman legions.

The Imperial army was impressive but not irresistible. A combination of terrain and the enemy restrained conquests beyond the Rhine and Danube Rivers, in the Sahara, Arabia, Scotland, and Sudan. In the deserts and mountains of the Middle East, the Parthian military system matched the Roman one in quality. During 53 B.C., at the Battle of Carrhae, for example, armored Parthian lancers forced forty-five thousand Romans to keep tight formation. Horse archers, supplied with arrows carried on camels, fired from all sides into a packed target. If Romans stood, they died, as they did if they charged, lured into ambushes by a faster enemy which specialized in shooting backward at a pursuing foe. Over the next seven centuries, Rome lost as often as not in battle against Parthians and their Sassinid Persian successors. Only with large cavalry forces could Romans defeat these enemies, and, even then, faced with scorched earth tactics and a prolonged war of attrition, sooner or later Rome always abandoned its conquests.

As expansion became impossible, Rome turned to one of the most sophisticated defensive systems ever known. Hundreds of scattered oasis strongholds guarded the Saharan and Arabian frontiers. Powerful forts watched the Parthian border. Hadrian's Wall ran seventy-three miles from one seacoast to another on the Scottish frontier. Strong forts, along a wall, eight feet thick and twenty-one feet high, were spaced every few miles behind a ditch twenty-seven feet wide and nine feet deep, which overlooked the moors to the north. A similar, if less thick and complex, system, resting on a wooden palisade nine feet high and backed by fortified garrisons, covered the Rhine and the Danube frontiers. These fortified zones kept the enemy out of the empire. Only about 10 percent of their garrisons manned fortifications; the remainder served as mobile reserves. Such systems prevented small raids and forced attackers to use large numbers, which could be smashed before they reached the Roman frontier. Linked by flag and fire signals and roads, reserves could move quickly to any threatened area. Cavalry could intercept lesser raiding parties, and legions could trap great ones in open territory—Rome's preferred conditions for battle. Fifty thousand miles of paved and two hundred thousand miles of dirt roads let Rome concentrate most of its forces, field armies of 60,000 to 150,000 men, against any one enemy.

The Augustan system collapsed in the 200s A.D., as internal stability and external security both vanished in a vicious circle. Endemic civil wars weakened the empire while Roman diplomats lost their ability to divide their neighbors. Sassinid Persia and European "barbarians" became stronger and more aggressive and launched great and simultaneous attacks. Augustus's centralized army of heavy infantry could not meet these dangers. While any legion could move from one end of Roman Europe to the other during one campaigning season, none could defend both Europe and Asia at the same time. Rome no longer faced just one enemy at one time—danger was everywhere. Meanwhile, its military success declined. Two Roman field armies were annihilated in battle, and two emperors died with them. Persians ravaged Asia; "barbarians" devastated Europe.

Only a more costly and less efficient army could handle these dangers. By A.D. 320 Rome became increasingly militarized. It raised taxes, made every soldier's son a soldier, and adopted massive conscription. In order to defend every province at once, Rome divided the empire into two halves and the army into several local garrisons and two types of soldiers. *Limitanei*, static troops, defended the frontier against small raids and slowed major advances until the *comitatenses*, field forces, arrived. The army doubled in size, and relied on cavalry as much as legions. Because of corruption and the expense of additional horses, these six hundred thousand soldiers cost three times as much as the Augustan army, yet they never defended the frontiers as well as the latter. As expenses rose, income fell. Ravaged areas paid barely 10 percent of their previous taxes for decades thereafter. Rome increasingly paid its troops, especially the *limitanei*, in-kind. Their salaries declined; so did their loyalty and skill.

After 150 years of stress, the empire was so debilitated that for the first time it could not fully recover from the annihilation of one field army at the Battle of Adrianople in A.D. 378. Afterwards "barbarians" always remained in the empire, although sometimes serving Rome as allies, or *feoderati*. Other "barbarians" hammered the frontiers while Romans fought civil wars within. *Comitatense* casualties were staggering and their quality collapsed. Between A.D. 395 and 425 most *comitatenses* were recently promoted *limitanei* or newly recruited "barbarians." Rome, desperately short of manpower, conscripted slaves, "barbarian" prisoners of war and men who had deliberately amputated their own thumbs. After Adrianople, the Roman cavalry remained good, but the quality of its infantry collapsed. Much of it consisted of *feoderati*, using loose and undisciplined phalanxes. Although Romans still fought in close formation, they had lost the discipline and tactics to do so with effect—they no longer even used armor.

Rome fell because its army failed. In A.D. 360 Romans routinely whipped three times their number of barbarians. Thirty years later they were no better than "barbarians" and fewer in number. As Roman quality fell, so did its quantity. Until A.D. 378, Rome routinely maintained field forces of sixty-five thousand men or more. Over the next century, its armies varied between four and twenty-five thousand men, from a population of 60 million people, though the eastern empire very occasionally brought forty thousand to one hundred thousand soldiers into battle. Sixty-six percent of Rome's soldiers were *limitanei*. Most of the remainder garrisoned cities or inactive provinces. Rome's foes always threw their full force against a fragment of the empire's army and tiny enemies crushed the empire. Coalitions of fifty thousand soldiers inflicted disasters like the Battle of Adrianople, and tribes of twenty-five thousand seized crucial provinces.

Between A.D. 400 and 450, the western empire disintegrated. In particular, during just ten years, between A.D. 400 and 410, everything went wrong at once in Rome's military system. The *limitanei* were neither supported by the *comitatenses* nor paid by the state. They became a peasant militia, defending their farms but not the frontier. Border defenses and most of the army collapsed. Only seventy-five thousand *comitatenses* stood in the decisive theaters of Gaul and Italy, and, even there, armies and major garrisons rarely equaled five thousand soldiers. As many *feoderati* as Roman soldiers were in Italy. Between A.D. 405 and 407, the western empire withdrew garrisons from Gaul and Britain to prepare for civil war with the eastern empire. The remaining Roman forces in those provinces revolted and a coalition of "barbarians" crossed the Rhine, smashing the defenses of western Europe. Another coalition entered Italy and, because of civil strife, were joined by the *feoderati* there. Within five years Rome was sacked while Britain and much of the Balkans, Gaul, and Spain were gone. Great cities surrendered to enemies with primitive siege techniques. As "barbarians" occupied more territory, Roman resources collapsed. Men and money vanished at the same time, so did the Imperial Roman Army, and the Roman Empire was overthrown.

Suggested Reading

The foundation for the study of war and society during the classical period are surviving Greek and Roman historical works. Foremost among these in value are Herodotus, *The Histories*, trans. Aubrey de Selincourt and A. R. Burn; Thucydides, *The Peloponnesian War*, trans. Rex Warner; Zenophon, *The Persian Expedition*, trans. Rex Warner, and *Hellenica*, trans. Carleton L. Brownson; Arrian, *The Campaigns of Alexander*. trans. Aubrey de Selincourt; Polybius, *The Rise of the Roman Empire*; Livy, *The War with Hannibal*, trans. Aubrey de Selincourt, and *Rome and the Mediterranean*, trans. Henry Bettenson; Julius Caesar, *The Conquest of Gaul*, trans. S. A. Handford, and *The Civil War*, trans. Jane F. Mitchell; and Tacitus, *The Histories*, trans. Kenneth Wellesley.

Two useful surveys of classical war and society are Arthur Ferrill, *The Origins of War, From the Stone Age to Alexander the Great* (London, 1985), and, despite errors and exaggerations, Richard A. Gabriel and Karen S. Metz, *From Sumer to Rome, The Military Capabilities of Ancient Armies* (New York, 1991).

The fundamental studies of the relationships among war, the military, state, politics, and society in classical Greece are W. Kendrick Prittchard's magisterial four volume series *The Greek State at War* (Berkeley, 1971–85), augmented by some of the essays in Victor Davis Hansen, *Hoplites: The Classical Greek Battle Experience* (London, 1991). For the Roman period, see J. B. Campbell, *The Emperor and the Roman Army, 31 B.C.–A.D. 235* (Oxford, 1984); Roy W. Davies, *Service in the Roman Army* (Edinburgh, 1989); P. A. Holder, *The Roman Army in Britain* (London, 1982); Ramsay MacMullen, *Soldier and Civilian in the Later Roman Empire* (Cambridge, Mass., 1963); and Nathan Rosenstein, *Imperatores Victi, Military Defeat and Aristocratic Competition in the Middle and Late Republic* (Berkeley, 1990).

F. E. Adcock, *The Greek and Macedonian Art of War* (Berkeley, 1957), is a useful introduction to the topic. J. K. Anderson, *Military Theory and Practice in the Age of Zenophon* (Berkeley, 1970); Victor Davis Hansen, *The Western Way of War, Infantry Battle in Classical Greece* (New York, 1989); the essays in Victor Davis Hansen, *Hoplites: The Classical Greek Battle Experience* (London, 1991); and J. F. Lazenby, *The Spartan Army* (Warminster, 1985), offer the best scholarly accounts of Greek warfare. J. R. Ellis, *Philip II and Macedonian Imperialism* (London, 1968); A. B. Bosworth, *Conquest and Empire, The reign of Alexander the Great* (Cambridge, 1988); and N. G. L. Hammond, *The Macedonian State, Origins, Institutions and History* (Oxford, 1989), offer clear accounts of Macedon and its military system. J. F. C. Fuller, *The Generalship of Alexander the Great* (London, 1960), remains the best analysis of Alexander's campaigns. War in the Hellenistic period is not well served. The standard textbook on the topic, W. W. Tarn, *Hellenistic Military and Naval Developments* (Cambridge, 1930), is out of date and contains many errors. The best, if specialized, works on this general topic are Bezalel Bar-Kochva, *The Seleucid Army, Organisation and Tactics in the Great Campaigns* (Cambridge, 1976), and two works by Richard A. Billows: *Antigonos the One-Eyed and the Creation of the Hellenistic State* (Berkeley, 1990), and *Kings and Colonists: Aspects of Macedonian Imperialism* (Leiden, 1995). The best study of the Punic Wars is Brian Cavan and J. F. Lazenby, *Hannibal's War, A military history of the Second Punic War* (Warminster, 1978).

The standard accounts of the Roman army are Michael Grant, *The Army of the Caesars* (New York, 1974); Lawrence Keppie, *The Making of the Roman Army, From Republic to Empire* (London, 1984); and Graham Webster, *The Roman Imperial Army of the First and Second Centuries* A.D. (London, 1979). For Roman strategy and its military collapse, the best works are Edward N. Luttwak, *The Grand Strategy of the Roman Empire, From the First Century* A.D. *to the Third* (Baltimore, 1976); A. H. M. Jones, *The Later Roman Empire, 284–602: A Social, Economic and Administrative Survey,* 2 vols. (Oxford, 1964); and Arthur Ferrill, *The Fall of the Roman Empire, the Military Explanation* (London, 1986).

The best studies of ancient siege craft, fortifications, defensive systems, and their place in war and strategy are Edward Luttwak, *The Grand Strategy of the Roman Empire* (Baltimore, 1976); E. W. Marsden, *Greek and Roman Artillery, Historical Development* (Oxford, 1969); and Josiah Ober, *Fortress Attica, Defence of the Athenian Land Frontier, 404–322* B.C. (Leiden, 1985). While relatively little work has been done on ancient sea power, several excellent works are available: Lionel Casson, *The Ancient Mariners, Seafarers and Sea Fighters of the Mediterranean in Ancient Times* (New York, 1959), and *Ships and Seamanship in the Ancient World* (Princeton, 1971); Borimir Jordan, *The Athenian Navy in the Classical Period, A Study of Athenian Naval Administration and Military Organisation in the Fifth and Fourth Centuries* B.C. (Berkeley, 1972); J. H. Thiel, *A History of Roman Sea-Power Before the Second Punic War* (Amsterdam, 1954), and *Studies on the History of Roman Sea-Power in Republican Times* (Amsterdam, 1946); and, despite its eccentricities, H. T. Wallinga, *Ships and Sea-Power Before the Great Persian War, The Ancestry of the Ancient Trireme* (Leiden, 1993).

3. MIGRATIONS AND INVASIONS

Huns, Goths, Byzantines, Arabs, Vikings, and Magyars,

A.D. 300–1000

This chapter looks at the period of the disintegration of the Western Roman Empire and its successor, the Byzantine Empire. Following on from this are the creation of the Arab empire and further onslaughts on Europe by the Vikings and Magyars. Hence, barbarian styles and attitudes toward war opposed well-established Roman ideas, but it is interesting that both sides learned from each other and adapted.

The experience of war was undoubtedly brutal for those involved, yet there was a conscious effort by barbarians to organize logistically and to adopt new technology, especially siege warfare techniques. Byzantium developed a well-organized army and sensible strategies to defend its extensive territory. Meanwhile, Arab armies were small, but they used mobility and surprise effectively and benefited from a period of weakness among major powers in the area. The Vikings aroused horror from many of their victims and used this to extort tribute. Their method of warfare was unusual in using ships to reach the coast of their targets, then riding horses to move inland, and, finally, dismounting to fight. Finally, the Magyars showed a classic ability to adapt and produce a winning army, yet, like the Vikings, they too were able to be integrated into the societies they attacked. Overall, these migrations and invasions certainly hastened the decline of the Roman Empire and disrupted established societies, while producing fear and bloodshed. In military terms, a considerable emphasis on cavalry emerged, although infantry were always present and siege techniques were always needed.

Starting in the last quarter of the second century A.D., a bewildering variety of Germanic tribes were on the move, migrating because of internal upheavals, destabilized by Roman trading patterns, and seeking food, plunder, and slaves to trade through capture in warfare. By

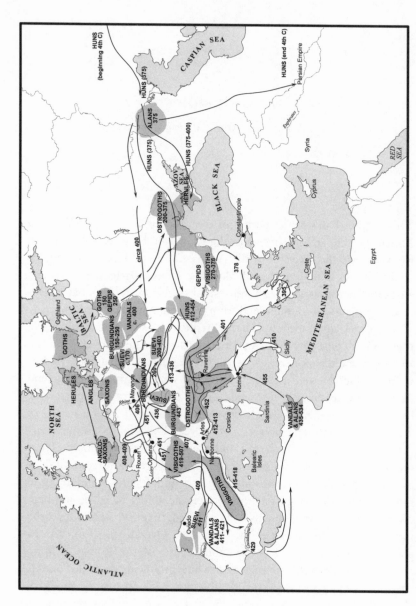

Map 3.1. Tribal Migration during the Later Roman Empire

the fifth and sixth centuries A.D., Goths, dividing into Ostrogoths and Visigoths, fought and moved into Italy, Greece, southern France, and Spain; Angles, Saxons, and Jutes invaded Britain; Vandals swept brutally through Germany and France and ended up controlling parts of Spain, the western Mediterranean seas, and grain-rich North Africa; Burgundians wound up in Burgundy; Lombards invaded northern Italy; and the Franks captured most of what was to become France. These groups sometimes made alliances, but they also warred against each other as well as against the remains of the Roman Empire, which in turn used the strategy of divide and rule against the barbarians. But perhaps most feared of all, the Asiatic Huns in the late fourth century A.D., subjugated the Ostrogoths and drove the Visigoths against the Roman frontier and then in the early fifth century turned toward western Europe and northern Italy.

The arrival of the Huns from central Asia gave both the Goths and the Romans a nasty shock—the Huns were described as prodigiously deformed and ugly, bearing little resemblance to humans. Moreover, their nomad style of horse-based warfare initially proved difficult to confront. According to the late-fourth-century writer Ammianus, the Huns

> divide suddenly in scattered bands [tribal units] and attack, rushing about in disorder [open order] here and there, dealing terrific slaughter; and because of their extraordinary rapidity of movement, they cannot be discerned when they break into a rampart or pillage an enemy's camp. And on this account you would not hesitate to call them the most terrible of all warriors, because they fight from a distance with missiles having a sharp bone, instead of their usual points [horsed archers] . . . then they gallop over the intervening spaces [i.e., close with the enemy] and fight hand to hand with swords regardless of their own lives; and . . . throw strips of cloth plaited into nooses [lassoes] over their opponents and so entangle them that they fetter their limbs and prevent them from the power of riding or walking.

In other words, the Huns were mounted archers who first disorganized their enemies with volleys of arrows delivered by rapidly moving but organized tribal units and then swiftly closed and finished off the battle on foot with their heavy iron swords. These swords likely were obtained by barter, but they also used indigenous weapons such as lassoes and, almost certainly, long lances to create a heavy cavalry. However, their key weapon was undoubtedly the powerful reflex composite bow, with the arrows tipped with bone. The bows were capable of an accurate range of 60 meters and an effective range of 175 meters. When this weapon was allied with the Huns' ability to use it accurately from extremely mobile and durable nomad horses, the result was a formidable fighting force. Tactically, they also used the ancient nomadic ruse of false flight and then renewed attack, usually through an ambush. In addition, since all Roman sources speak with horror of the Huns, it is evident that the Huns played on their fearsome physical appearance and ragged marmot-skin clothing to induce a psychological advantage in battle, since their actual numbers were quite small when raiding, often in the range of two hundred to twelve hundred men. Another advantage that the Huns possessed was their attraction for disaffected groups among both the Ostrogoths and the lower classes in the Western Roman Empire, who greeted their arrival in the fifth century with enthusiasm. Thus, many slaves, miners, and agricultural workers threw off their Roman servitude to join the Hun forces. Finally, the Huns' effectiveness was much improved when the independent tribal groups of raiding Huns started to form a confederacy around the 420s, and particularly after 435, when Attila became king of the Huns and was able to plan concerted campaigns.

Attila was described as having "a large head, a swarthy complexion, small, deep-seated eyes, a flat nose, a few hairs in the place of a beard, broad shoulders, and a short square body . . . and he had a custom of fiercely rolling his eyes, as if he wished to enjoy the terror which he inspired." However, apart from holding together the Hunnic confederation and revealing himself as a competent general, Attila also displayed considerable diplomatic skills. For example, he often allied himself with the Romans: he fought a war against the Burgundians in 436 on behalf of the Western Roman Empire, and he also received a large annual subsidy from the Eastern emperor. In fact, Attila and the general of the Western Roman Empire, Aetius, formed a friendly alliance, so much so that Attila sent Aetius his most exotic slave—a Moorish dwarf—as a gift. As another example, the Hun campaign in 441 in the Danube area was successful because Attila knew that the Romans were engaged elsewhere and would not intervene. Similarly, when Attila decided on a major campaign in 451 in Gaul, he took care by diplomacy to keep the powerful Vandals from intervening, while at the same time he allied himself with the Ostrogoths and with some Burgundians, Alans, and Franks. However, despite an initially successful campaign in Gaul, in which Metz, Strasbourg, Rheims, Cologne, Worms, and Trier fell to Attila, the Huns were defeated, or at least forced to retreat, by Roman forces led by Aetius at the battle of Chalons in 451.

Yet by this date Attila and the Huns were no longer fighting in their traditional way. After the Huns arrived in Europe, they no longer had the necessary grazing area for their horses, since each rider in the central Asian plains had formerly required around ten mounts. Thus, an army of ten thousand would have required grazing area for at least one hundred thousand horses, and the western European countryside could not have supported such a force. Therefore, although the Hun army in Europe would still have maintained an elite arm of mounted archers, there were now more infantry in the shape of dismounted archers and foot soldiers armed with captured or bartered weapons, such as swords and spears. In addition, Attila's Germanic and Ostrogothic allies were infantry. Yet at Chalons, after Attila's defeat by a combined army of Romans, Franks, Alans, and Visigoths, the chronicle relates that Attila retreated to his camp and threatened to cast himself into the flames of a funeral pyre made up of horse saddles in case he was attacked again and forced to surrender. If so, one can assume that the saddles indicated a still formidable body of horses in Attila's army. Nevertheless, the Huns were clearly no longer the terrifying nomad horse archers of the previous century. In another way as well the Huns were forced to fight differently, namely, in siege warfare. Clearly, they had no expertise in this area and were forced to rely on the siege warfare knowledge of Roman prisoners or deserters, or they called in tribes, who did know what to do, as occurred at the siege of Aquileia in 452. No doubt the Huns also took towns through deceit, bribery, and starvation and could build ramps up the walls of cities, and at the siege of Orleans in 451, they applied the "mighty hammering of battering rams," according to Gregory of Tours. But the Huns' main weapon, like the Assyrians', was probably the psychology of terror. Having utterly razed and destroyed some towns, like Aquileia in Italy, slaughtering all defenders and selling the remaining inhabitants as slaves, other towns simply opened their gates to avoid similar destruction. This may have been the case with Milan, Verona, Pavia, and Ticinum, which were left standing by Attila during his Italian campaign.

It will be recalled that Attila had retired to his camp after the defeat or forced retreat after Chalons, where he expected pursuit by Aetius. In fact this camp was composed of a laager of wagons formed in a circle and was a traditional barbarian defense that the Huns may have learned from the Goths and applied to the less mobile warfare of Europe. As it turned out,

Aetius permitted Attila and his remaining forces to escape after Chalons (perhaps he had no choice), and in 452 Attila turned his forces toward northern Italy and Rome. At first, he was very successful, and it seemed as though Rome was again fated to be destroyed. However, lack of provisions, sickness in his army, and an attack by the Eastern emperor across the Danube directed at the Huns' rear lines and home population forced Attila to withdraw. It may also be that Aetius deliberately abandoned northern Italy in order to save Rome, counting on famine, disease, and plunder to deflect the Huns. Rome survived, and the next year Attila took a new wife, named Ildico, but celebrated the occasion too heavily and on his wedding night suffered a nose bleed and either bled to death or drowned in his own blood as he lay in a drunken stupor. Effectively, the threat from the Huns was at an end, and the power of the Huns as a confederacy collapsed.

The Hunnic onslaught on the Western (and Eastern) Roman Empire was actually only one of many barbarian attacks, since Rome was besieged eight times and taken six times between 410 and 563. By the late fifth century the Roman Empire had essentially "fallen" to various barbarians (although Rome's army itself now contained a significant barbarian element), and Italy was largely ruled by the Goths. Originally, some Goths had been forced across the Roman Danube frontier by the Huns, while others were settled by Rome as federated allies and were enlisted in the Roman army in large numbers. The Goths had defeated the Roman emperor Valens at Adrianople in 378, where the Goth forces were largely infantry, although with a small number of very useful cavalry. Gothic infantry fought with shields, swords, lances, and occasionally wooden clubs. Only the Goth leaders had armor, and their tactics generally consisted of the simple mass advance of the horde, actually a deep phalanx, preceded by the barbarian *barritus*, or battle song, which started quietly and then swelled to a thunderous roar. Gradually, however, the Goths used captured or traded Roman weapons, began to employ infantry as archers, and around A.D. 400 started to increase their cavalry forces. In other words, their army began to resemble the Roman army, although their weak points were supply and logistics and an inability to mount successful sieges. The Goth cavalry carried heavy lances, or *contus*, as well as swords and shields and armor, though they did not use stirrups. Their cavalry tactics were to outflank, to use the false retreat, and then to apply the sudden ambush and attack. On foot, the Goths by the fifth and sixth centuries also used the two-handed *contus*, plus swords and shields, and wore leather battle tunics. There were also Gothic foot archers, who were limited in mobility and vulnerable to enemy cavalry. The Goths fought against each other (Visigoths against Ostrogoths) as well as against other barbarians and the Romans, but in 497 the Ostrogoth Theodoric the Great was recognized as king of Italy, and in 511 he also became king of the Visigoths. He attempted to imitate a kind of Roman state and rule, but with his death in 526, Gothic unity fell apart, the Lombards invaded northern Italy, and the continuing conflict against both the Eastern and Western Roman Empires was taken up by Ostrogoth military leaders such as Vitigis (536–40), Totila (541–52), and finally Teja in 552.

Goth Battle Module: The Siege of Rome (537–38) and the Battle of Busta Gallorum (552)

Opposing these last Gothic leaders was the great Eastern emperor Justinian (527–65), who in 533 launched his efficient general Belisarius first against the North African Vandal kingdom, which was rapidly conquered, and then against the Goths in Italy via Sicily. Belisarius initially took Naples by siege, and then Rome surrendered with little trouble, but in February 537 Belisarius was besieged in turn in Rome by the Ostrogoth military leader and king, Vitigis. The sixth-century historian of the war against the Goths, Procopius, was legal secretary to Belisarius and likely was present at Vitigis's siege of Rome. Procopius describes how initially Vitigis broke down the aqueducts to the city so as to cut off the water supply as much as possible and to prevent the aqueduct water from working the mills in Rome that ground the grain into flour. Belisarius got around this problem by placing the mills between boats on the Tiber River, thus using the force of the river to turn the mills. The Goths then floated dead Roman soldiers down the river to block up the mills, but Belisarius countered by throwing a chain across the river that prevented the bodies from reaching the mills. Meanwhile, water from the Tiber provided sufficient drinking water for the Roman defenders, while for those far from the river, enough wells were available. One other potential problem was the sewers, but since they discharged into the Tiber, it was not thought that the Goths could climb into Rome through them.

For his part, Vitigis set up seven well-defended camps around Rome, but he found that he could never make a complete cordon around the city due to the great distance involved. This, of course, enabled provisions to come into Rome, particularly during the night. For the attack on Rome itself, Vitigis constructed wooden towers as high as the walls of Rome and drawn by oxen, plus using many scaling ladders and four large rams operated by fifty men each. Then he ordered his men to prepare bundles of wood and reeds to throw into the moat and ditches around Rome so that the siege engines could be drawn across. In defense, Belisarius, who commanded only five thousand imperial defenders and the city militia and was heavily outnumbered, made up for his numerical inferiority with the fire power of stone and missile throwing catapults as well as a curious defensive weapon called a "wolf," which consisted of a massive wooden construction, similar to a large barn door, attached to which were several projecting "beaks." This machine was placed against an outside wall or gate, and when enemy soldiers approached, it was simply pushed over on top of them, thus dispatching whoever was caught underneath. Belisarius also overcame his lack of numbers by integrating Roman citizens as well as the local militia into defensive units—this also had the effect of maintaining morale in the city. Finally, to preserve provisions, Belisarius ordered all the "useless eaters," that is, the women and children and all domestics who were not helping the defense, as well as the male or female attendants of the soldiers, to leave for Naples.

On the eighteenth day of the siege, Vitigis tried for an all-out attack at several gates, towers, and weak spots around the walls. Clearly, Vitigis was not experienced at siege warfare, and he did not have enough siege towers so that at only one or two points could the towers approach the walls. For the rest of the attack, Vitigis could only use rams, mining, scaling ladders, the testudo of shields, and archers to keep the defenders away from the walls. Procopius describes the approach of the Goth towers toward the Salarian gate, where Belisarius himself was stationed: "Belisarius gave the signal for the whole army to put their bows into action, but those near himself he commanded to shoot only at the oxen [drawing the towers]. And all the oxen fell immediately, so the enemy could neither move the towers further nor in their perplexity do anything to meet the emergency while the fighting was in progress. In this way the forethought of Belisarius in not trying to check the enemy while still at a great distance came to be understood, as well as the reason why he had [earlier] laughed at the simplicity of the barbarians, who had been so thoughtless as to hope to bring oxen up to the enemy's wall."

Vitigis countered this setback by leaving a large force at the Salarian wall, with instructions not to waste men by attacking but to keep the defenders busy with missiles so as to prevent reinforcements from going elsewhere. According to Procopius this plan failed due to a strange incident: "A Goth of goodly stature and a capable warrior, wearing a corselet and having a helmet on his head [i.e., a tribal leader] . . . refused to remain in the ranks with his comrades, but stood by a tree and kept shooting many missiles at the parapet. But this man by some chance was hit by a missile from an engine . . . And passing through the corselet and the body of the man, the missile sank more than half its length into the tree, and pinning him to the spot where it entered the tree, it suspended him there a corpse. And when this was seen by the Goths they fell into great fear, and getting outside the range of missiles, they still remained in line, but no longer harassed those on the wall." Procopius perhaps "dramatized" this situation, since it is likely that the Goth force needed no dramatic incident to simply and sensibly retreat beyond missile range. However, the Gothic withdrawal did enable Belisarius to leave the Salarian gate and rapidly reinforce a weak area called the Vivarium, where the Romans had originally kept wild animals and where Vitigis was successfully undermining the wall. Belisarius solved the problem by keeping the Goths who had broken through enclosed in the limited space of the Vivarium, while massing the majority of his men for a surprise counterattack, which he achieved by suddenly opening the gate, dispersing the Goths and burning their siege engines. This counterattack was probably part of Belisarius's general instructions for defense, because the same tactic occurred at the Salarian gate and proved equally successful.

Vitigis's major assault was nearly successful, but he was never able to starve the defenders of Rome nor break down the walls of the city nor obtain entrance by bribery or deceit. Obviously, Vitigis was not sufficiently experienced in siege warfare and did not have sufficient siege engines (and probably engineers) to succeed, while Belisarius knew exactly what to do in defense. Thus, Vitigis turned next to diplomacy and a general armistice, which only gave Belisarius time to reinforce and reprovision. Vitigis tried one major battle outside the city gates, on the Plain of Nero, where he arrayed the Goths with a mass of infantry and archers in the middle and two massed cavalry squadrons on the wings. Although the Goths won the day, they could not prevent Belisarius's forces from escaping back into the city. Meanwhile, Roman cavalry reinforcements attacked Vitigis from the rear over the winter months and led into captivity the wives and children of his troops. When the Romans were close to his capital of Ravenna, Vitigis was forced to raise the siege of Rome in March 538. Procopius reported that the Goths had lost thirty thousand men in the siege of Rome, though the actual number is probably closer to three thousand.

A brutal campaign between the Goths and the Romans followed, which ravaged the countryside but was interrupted by an invasion of Italy by the Franks in 539. The Franks attacked both the Goths and the Romans, hoping for plunder and tribute while the Goths and the Romans were engaged with each other. The Franks' army consisted of an all-infantry force, carrying swords, shields, and throwing axes, and a small spear-carrying cavalry bodyguard around their leader Theudebert. Their tactics were simple: at a signal they first hurled their axes, aiming to break the shields of the enemy, and then closed as quickly as possible to finish off the battle with their swords. Neither Goths nor Romans could do much against the Franks, who reportedly threw Gothic men and women into the river after capturing Pavia and indulged in human sacrifice. However, the Franks were eventually forced out of Italy by the old enemy of armies—disease—in this case diarrhea and dysentery. Following this unpleasant episode, Vitigis found himself outmaneuvered by the Romans, since their strategy of depriving the Goths of their mobility by forcing them to defend strategically important sites proved successful. Eventually, Vitigis was forced to surrender both Ravenna and his own person, because of another age-old enemy of armies—hunger—though this was caused by the burning of the granaries in Ravenna at Roman instigation and by a naval blockade.

The next Goth military leader of note was Totila, who was elevated to the kingship of the Goths in 541 on the understanding that he would reconquer Italy. Totila made a promising beginning, attracting not only Goths from their estates but also other barbarians and many Roman soldiers. At the battle of Faenza in 542, Totila with five thousand men defeated a Roman army twice the size by the simple expedient of sending three hundred Gothic lancers behind the Romans before the battle began, thus disrupting the Roman army at a critical point. Following this victory, a battle of attrition raged across Italy for several years, mostly in Totila's favor. Rome was occupied by Totila in December 546, then abandoned, probably because he could not hold and provision it, then besieged and captured again by Totila through treachery in early 550. Totila reigned supreme in Italy, but he also ravaged Sicily and built a navy of three hundred ships with which he attacked the Greek mainland

and captured Sardinia and Corsica. However, the Roman fleet crushed the Goth navy in 551, and in Constantinople Justinian decided on "total war" and eventually appointed a particularly able man to reconquer Italy, Narses.

Narses was unusual in that he was a eunuch and even more unusual in that he was old as a military commander, in fact he was believed to be seventy-six years of age. However, he had had previous military and political experience at a high level, and, whereas Belisarius tended to follow a strategy of maneuver, Narses believed in direct military attack to settle matters with the Goths. Thus, in April 522 Narses marched overland with an army of some twenty-five thousand men from Constantinople to Italy. Narses fooled the Goths by marching along the marshes and estuaries of the coastline of northern Italy, rather than through the interior where the Goths had placed their defensive lines. Finally, in late June or early July 522, Narses met with Totila and his numerically inferior army at a battle site that has been identified as either Busta Gallorum or Taginae. Narses sent envoys to Totila to ask if he intended to surrender or, if he wished to fight, to name the day. Totila answered: "At the end of eight days let us match our strength." However, Narses knew his man and wisely took precautions, for the very next day Totila arrived within two bow shots' range, ready for battle.

Narses showed his ingenuity as a general both in his original formation and then in changing the final disposition of his troops at the last minute. In the center of his army, Narses dismounted his Lombard and other barbarian allies, allowing them to defend themselves with their lances. Possibly Narses did this because he suspected the loyalty of these allies, who may have harbored an admiration for Totila, and certainly it would make it harder for them to flee, but another reason was to offer these barbarian allies as an enticing target for the Goths. Next, Narses placed four thousand foot archers on either side of his barbarians, making a total of eight thousand archers in all. These archers were clearly a formidable force and obviously the key to the whole battle, so their positioning would be critical. On either side of the archers, Narses placed his two wings of regular cavalry, but he also stationed two detached groups of cavalry: one of one thousand horse and one of five hundred horse, "at an angle" on the extreme left wing, behind a small hill that existed on the far left flank of the imperial forces, which Narses had captured. Narses's instructions were that the body of five hundred horse was to be the mobile reserve, rushing to the rescue if the line faltered at any point, while the group of one thousand horse was to get behind the Goth army as it attacked and thus disrupt their offensive. The overall positioning of Narses's forces was made possible by his much larger numbers, and this also enabled the location of the extra fifteen hundred cavalry on the extreme left wing. Narses then placed himself in front of his regular left wing cavalry and awaited developments. The overall disposition suggests that Narses expected to use the archers to halt any Gothic charge and then to apply a left wing outflanking movement to win the battle.

Totila meanwhile was obviously in a quandary, partly because he was outnumbered and outflanked, partly because he had to somehow offset the power of Narses's archers and left wing cavalry, and partly because he was still awaiting the arrival of his subordinate general Teja with two thousand more Gothic cavalry. He therefore decided to play for time, but his initial dispositions, according to Procopius, were the same as Narses's, meaning that Totila must have put his infantry in the center and his smaller cavalry force on his wings. At first neither army advanced but waited for the other to attack, and there was no movement. Then Totila learned that Teja's two thousand Goth horsemen were rapidly approaching, so to give them time, he gave an exhibition of the *djerid*, the lance-ride of the horse nomads. Procopius describes Totila's unusual demonstration: "For he wheeled his horse round in a circle and then turned him again to the other side and so made him run round and round. And as he rode he hurled his javelin into the air and caught it again as it quivered above him, then passed it rapidly from hand to hand, shifting it with consummate skill, and he gloried in his practice in such matters, falling back on his shoulders, spreading his legs and leaning from side to side, like one who has been instructed with precision in the art of dancing from childhood. By these tactics he wore away the whole early part of the day." It is unlikely that Totila could have used up so much time on his *djerida*, but he did also send delegates to Narses to parlay, once again stalling for time.

The two thousand Gothic horsemen arrived at the stockade or defended circle of wagons in the Gothic rear, and Totila delayed once again by ordering his army to break formation and take their morning meal. This was partly to give the new cavalry arrivals time to rest and get into position, partly to feed his men, partly to give himself time to consider battle plans, and partly to try and surprise Narses with a sudden attack because he expected Narses to similarly stand down his men for a meal. But Narses again was prepared and had ordered his men to feed while standing in the ranks. Moreover, an important change now occurred in the dispositions of both armies, as Procopius relates: "for the Roman wings, in each of which four thousand unmounted horsemen [i.e., Narses's dismounted archers] had taken their stand, were moved forward at Narses's command so as to form a crescent." Why had Narses done this? Perhaps because he always intended to use this strategy or perhaps because he was reacting to the arrival of the two thousand extra horsemen, which made it possible for Totila to use the traditional cavalry charge as the centerpiece of his attack. Totila hoped to offset the superiority of Narses's archers in the only way he knew how; namely, by first routing the easiest and weakest target, the enemy barbarian center, with an overwhelming cavalry charge, he would then in the confusion turn his cavalry and infantry against Narses's two wings of archers and cavalry. So Totila massed his cavalry in front and his infantry in the rear, with instructions to the cavalry to fall back on the infantry if the cavalry charge failed and then both were to move forward together in a final assault. For his part, as previously mentioned, Narses had altered his own battle strategy from a left wing encirclement to an envelopment on both wings, using his dismounted archers to break the enemy cavalry charge and then rolling up the infantry.

Narses's last-minute dispositions sound like Hannibal's ideas at Cannae, but in fact he probably had a very good idea of how the Goths were likely to fight if sufficient cavalry was available to them, because Procopius relates that the imperial forces were aware of Gothic tactics. In an earlier speech by Belisarius in Procopius's *History of the Wars of Justinian*, he makes the point that the two sides fought in different ways: "Practically all the Romans and their allies, the Huns, are good mounted bowmen, but not a man among the Goths has had practice in this branch, for their horsemen are accustomed to use only spears and swords, while their bowmen enter battle on foot and under cover of the heavy-armed men. So the horsemen, unless the engagement is at close quarters, have no means of defending themselves against opponents who use the bow, and therefore can easily be reached by the arrows and destroyed; and as for the foot-soldiers, they can never be strong enough to make sallies against men on horseback."

Hence, Totila's final battle formation was in the Goth military tradition, with the cavalry in front and the bowmen and infantry drawn up in the rear. Thus, Totila failed to rise above the normal Goth method of attacking and gambled that a devastating heavy cavalry charge would turn the tables in his favor. However, when the battle commenced, the first Gothic cavalry charge was turned back. Procopius suggests that Totila's cavalry was surprised by the four thousand bowmen on each side, meaning that Narses's archers were probably still moving into their crescent position on either side of the battlefield as the battle opened. In any case, Procopius notes that after suffering heavy losses from the archers, the Gothic horsemen managed to close with the enemy, presumably after further charges, but the fight was inconclusive. As nightfall approached, Narses's army began to push the Gothic cavalry back, and then panic set in, for Totila's infantry phalanx in reserve neither provided lanes for the cavalry to pass through and regroup, nor stood firm, while the cavalry itself streamed back in great disorder and crashed into their own infantry. Both the Gothic cavalry and infantry then fled in disorder, and some six thousand of Totila's army perished, including many Roman soldiers who had earlier gone over to the Goths. Narses's army also took a large numbers of Goth prisoners, but these they later killed as well.

The Goth army was crushed, and Totila himself was slain, either at the very beginning of the battle or later as he fled the battlefield at night. Judging by the numbers given, Narses's army may have been twice as large as Totila's, and so the outcome was always likely to be a victory for Narses, in which case Totila's mistake had been to engage in a fixed battle at all.

Totila's death and defeat at Busta Gallorum was really the beginning of the end for the Gothic nation. Totila's commander Teja escaped after Busta Gallorum and fought on, but he was finally defeated at the battle of "Milk Mountain" in October 552. This ultimate defeat occurred partly because hunger forced the Goths out from well-defended positions, partly because the commander of the Gothic naval fleet treacherously surrendered, thus cutting off supplies to the Goths, and partly because Narses's forces again outnumbered the Gothic army two to one. With Teja's death during the fight and the crushing loss at "Milk Mountain," the Goth nation collapsed. The last Goths in Italy capitulated in 555, while the Visigoths, who had earlier invaded Spain in 415, briefly rejuvenated their kingdom there before being finally defeated by the Arab invasion of 711.

The army from the Eastern Roman Empire that had defeated the Goths was an extremely proficient one. It was distinguished by the variety of weapons it could bring to bear upon the enemy, by capable generals such as Belisarius and Narses, and, eventually, by the support of a sound administrative and economic structure. The centerpiece of the Byzantine (as the Eastern Roman Empire came to be known) army came to be the mobile horse archer, clad in mail, who could use either shock tactics or shower the enemy with arrows. These mounted archers, or *cataphracts* as they were called, have received considerable attention, but it is important to note that they were supported by light and heavy infantry, in a ratio of four to one. In other words, for every cavalryman, there were four infantrymen, which is what might be expected given the cost of maintaining and training mounted archers. There were also heavy lancer cavalry, but still, overall, the four to one ratio of infantry to cavalry was maintained over several centuries in the main Byzantine army.

The structure of the Byzantine army as it developed by the seventh and eighth centuries was twofold. In Asia Minor, Thrace, Greece, and southern Italy, there were armies called *themes*. By around A.D. 650, *themes* became administrative divisions as well as armies, and the soldiers who made up these armies held military lands instead of receiving a military stipend. The *themes* varied in military size, from around two thousand to eighteen thousand men, and by the mid-ninth century, the *theme* armies amounted to ninety-six thousand men in total. A *theme* was led by a commander called a *strategus*, under whom served a *turmarch*, if the *theme* was large enough, commanding four thousand men. Under him again, in decimal fashion, was the next rank, a *drungary*, who commanded one thousand men. Still lower, there existed units of one hundred, fifty, and ten men, each with their own commanders. A useful variation that emerged in the ninth century was the *bandum*, a district garrisoned by two hundred men. This soon became the basic administrative division of the Byzantine Empire.

Complementing the *themes* were the *tagmata*, a series of divisions stationed either in or near Constantinople. They carried names such as the Schools, the Excubitors, the Watch, the Numera, and the Walls, and in the mid-ninth century, together with a mule corps named the Optimates, the *tagmata* amounted to some twenty-four thousand men. Originally the *themes* were thought of as a defensive force to guard the boundaries of the empire, while the *tagmata* were conceived as a mobile force, including a higher percentage of cavalry that could conduct offensive operations or reinforce the *themes* as required. In practice, both types of army acted as both a mobile force and a defense force, though the *tagmata* were always more mobile. The two armies also included surveyors, quartermasters, and scouts and one surgeon for every twenty or twenty-five men, which shows an unusually high regard for the health of the men. Rounding out the land army was a sophisticated system of providing horses and mules from ranches in Asia Minor, although the cavalrymen of the *themes* provided their own horses.

A striking feature of the Byzantine armies, then, was their strong administrative control and clear structure. Reflecting the sophisticated nature of Byzantine warfare were the production of a number of military manuals. Some of these have survived and give detailed instructions to meet all possibilities. For example, a mid-sixth-century manual counsels how infantry can fight cavalry: "In employing an infantry phalanx against cavalry we should draw them up in the following manner. The men stationed in the first and second ranks should keep up continuous fire with the bow, aiming at the feet of the enemy's horses. All the rest of the men should shoot at a higher angle so that when their arrows drop down from above, they will cause all the more injury, since the horsemen cannot use their shields to protect both themselves and their horses." Eventually, after the enemy cavalry have been slowed down, the phalanx should pick up their spears and advance against them. Other advice for archers is that they should never aim straight at the enemy infantry, because they are covered by their shields, but should aim off to the side, although horses feet should always be aimed at straight ahead. No doubt, Narses's archers at Busta Gallorum used these tactics.

The manuals are full of measures to deceive the enemy. Thus, the same mid-sixth-century manual gave one ingenious method for fording a river in the face of the enemy: "By night the troops moved behind a hill so that they were not seen at daybreak. A detachment of the army was sent out. They carried a large amount of horse manure, and their orders were to ride a good distance up the river and dump the manure into the river. When the men who guarded the ford saw this carried down by the current, they were convinced that the army had crossed the river further up, and so they abandoned their position at the river. The troops hidden behind the hill then forded the river and went after the enemy." Later manuals reflected the needs of the time—for example, a tenth-century manual on skirmishing related to the continuous Arab raids of that century. This manual gave commonsense instructions about finding and destroying raiding parties and about the methods of setting up an ambush. One elaborate section explains how to follow an Arab raiding party. There should be three teams following the Arabs—the first close enough to hear "the murmuring of men and the neighing of the horses." Then the second team keeps the first team just in sight and similarly with the third team. Then behind the third team are three units of four men each, once again the first unit just keeps the third team in sight, and so on. Finally, the last team has two extra men attached, who act as messengers passing along the information gained by the first team.

In addition to the flexible response to different conditions of battle and irregular warfare reflected in the manuals and the well-organized and trained *themes* and *tagmata*, the Byzantines also defended their empire with a series of forts. These were arranged in a defense-in-depth system along the lengthy frontiers and were originally established by Justinian. According to Procopius, "Justinian bordered the river [Danube] with numerous fortresses and set up guard-posts along the banks to prevent the barbarians from crossing. But when these structures were completed he reflected that should the enemy succeed in penetrating this barrier they would find themselves among defenseless inhabitants. . . . He was not content, therefore, to ensure a general measure of safety by means of these river forts alone, but constructed great numbers of other defense-works all over the flat country, until every manor was either transformed into a fortress or was protected by a nearby fortified position." This system eventually covered both the Balkan and western frontier areas and the mountain passes of the Taurus and Antitaurus ranges of the eastern Arab frontier, and it was extremely effective in preventing conquest of outlying areas. When Arabs, Slavs, or Bulgars appeared, the threatened civilians and *theme* units simply retreated to the forts, where either active or passive defense tactics could be used. Since the Arabs generally did not have time for siege warfare and since the Bulgars and Slavs did not know siege warfare, it was simple to wait out the raid or expedition and then rebuild and restock the land. Even when forts were taken in an actual invasion, the flexible defense-in-depth system generally prevented serious defeats and conquests of territory, and although every year Bulgars and Arabs raided, the Byzantines simply reoccupied the land, rebuilt the forts, and replaced the men in an efficient manner. (Each man lost was supposed to be reported to Constantinople and immediately replaced.) On the other hand, the *themes* could not actually keep raiders out of Byzantine territory and could not easily defeat the invaders, and time after time, defenders were surprised by raids and attacks. Yet the system worked like an elastic band, expanding and contracting as required to meet different situations. Thus, as an inexpensive and adaptable defensive system, usually against much larger armies, it was excellent. Additionally, the system was reinforced with the normal Byzantine tactic of trying to corrupt and to foment dissension among attacking armies.

The Byzantine army, however, was not always on the defensive. Although the vast extent of the empire, the rugged mountains and the desert nature of the frontiers, the aggressive style of its opponents, and the desire for economy all kept Byzantium in a defensive mentality, there were also several moments of offensive warfare. The wars of Justinian are one case, but to take another example, in 811 after saving sufficient money, the emperor Nicephorus decided to deal the Bulgars a crushing defeat and remove their menace altogether. Gathering together the mobile elements of the *tagmata*, several *themes*, and civilian volunteers, an army of seventy-one thousand set forth for the Bulgar capital, Pliska. By various feints, Nicephorus deceived the Bulgar khan, Krum, and was able to burn Krum's wooden palace and eliminate the entire garrison of twelve thousand men. A relieving force of fifteen thousand Bulgars was also destroyed. But just as Byzantine's *themes* often ambushed Bulgar invaders, so Krum repaid the favor and blocked Nicephorus's army in a valley with the aid of high wooden barriers and deep ditches at either end. The *tagmata*, being cavalry, tried to escape but were drowned or crushed to death in the marsh and the river. Only when their bodies and horses provided a causeway, could some escape. Similarly, only when the barriers and ditches at either end of the valley were covered with the dead and disabled, could the remainder of the *themes* escape. Nicephorus himself was killed early in the battle, and Krum cut his head off, stripped away the flesh, lined the skull with silver, and happily toasted his achievements with this unusual cup.

In this particular case, the offensive failed, but as so often happened in Byzantium's wars with its frontier neighbors, action was met by counteraction and an offensive was followed by a counteroffensive. So in 813 Krum launched a major invasion of Byzantium. Adrianople was besieged and fell, and its forty thousand inhabitants were transferred as a colony to Bulgar territory. Now Constantinople itself was besieged, and, in April 814, Krum organized a massive siege train, using Byzantine engineers who had deserted to give him the skills he lacked. The siege train included rock, fire, and arrow throwers, catapults that threw stone balls and spiked missiles called "briers," battering rams and penthouses to protect the soldiers, siege ladders, and lesser equipment. All of the siege material was carried in five thousand wagons covered with iron plate to protect them from fire and drawn by ten thousand oxen. Possibly Krum intended to build wooden towers as well when he arrived before the walls, but in any case he planned to apply this strength against the one area of the land defenses of Constantinople that did not have double walls, namely, the Blachernae section. It is noticeable that Krum did not have the ability to use ships in the siege, and thus he could not completely surround and starve the city.

Luckily for Constantinople, Krum suffered a cerebral hemorrhage shortly before the attack started—blood flowed from his ears, nose, and mouth, and he died. The siege did not take place, and the city survived, although it is quite possible, given their success against Adrianople, that the Bulgars might have taken Constantinople more than five hundred years before it was actually lost forever. However, the mention of Krum's maritime deficiency reveals also one of Byzantium's initial strengths—its navy. In the sixth, seventh, and early eighth centuries, the Byzantine navy was powerful and even saved Constantinople in 717. In that year, the Arabs launched some 150,000 soldiers and 7,500 ships against the city and threatened to starve the inhabitants through a complete blockade. But the Byzantine emperor, Leo III, managed to burn the Arab supply ships, and the siege was lifted in 718. However, by the ninth century, Arab pirates, based in Crete, were ravaging the empire, while the Byzantines showed a surprising lack of interest in sea power. In the tenth century, Byzantium again built up its fleet, and, until the early twelfth century, the empire was again a strong naval power. Byzantium then began to rely more and more on Italian ships, particularly Venetian, to guard its western shores, though Venice and Byzantium were also rivals.

The capture of Constantinople by the misdirected Fourth Crusade between 1203 and 1204 underlined the weakness of the empire's navy, for at that time there were only twenty worm-eaten ships rotting in the harbor to oppose the crusaders. In this particular siege, the Byzantines were only able to reply to the crusaders' attack by finding enough merchant vessels to launch one fire-ship raid of seventeen ships filled with logs, shavings, pitch, and tow, but the crusaders were able to approach the fire ships with long boats and galleys and tow them out to sea with the aid of grappling irons. Yet the absence of a proper Byzantine navy was critical. The crusaders were able to take Constantinople by the method of lashing pairs of their tallest ships together and then raising, by block and tackle, temporary bridges made of ladders and slung between the masts of the two ships so that soldiers could run over these bridges onto the towers protecting the city. Unfortunately, the muddy shore prevented the crusaders' ships from getting close enough to use their ladder bridges. Then a favorable wind drove some of the tallest ships right onto the shore. One of the crusaders present, de Villehardouin, described the critical attack on April 12, 1204, and how two of the lashed ships managed to straddle one tower: "The assault had been going on for a considerable time when our Lord raised for us a wind called Boreas, which drove the ships still further on to the shore. Two of the ships which were bound together—the one called the *Pilgrim* and the other the *Paradise*—approached so close to a tower, one of them on one side and one on the other, as God and the wind drove them onwards, that the ladder of the *Pilgrim* made contact with it. Immediately a Venetian, in company with a French knight named Andre Durboise, forced their way in. Other men began to follow them, and in the end the defenders were routed and driven out." Another eyewitness, Robert of Clari, recounted how Andre Durboise "took hold of the sides of the window [of the tower] with hands and feet and pulled himself inside on his knees. As he entered they [the English, Danish and Greek defenders] rushed on him with axes and swords and struck him fiercely, but, because of his armor, by God's mercy they did not wound him." The tower was taken, but when the tide went out, the *Pilgrim*, which had been fastened to the tower, threatened to pull the whole tower down, and so the ship was cut free. Another tower was similarly taken, but it was the capture of a postern gate by a group of sixty sergeants and ten knights, who, storming out of a ship, really captured the city.

Byzantine's maritime problems in 1204 highlighted the fact that Constantinople was essentially a land-based power, and for most of its existence, Byzantium saw its navy as secondary in importance. Arabs in Sicily and Crete were annoying but not a vital threat to Byzantium as a whole. Thus, Byzantium's navy was usually quite small but at times grew rapidly when stronger threats were perceived. For example, there were 180 ships in the tenth century when the empire was opposed by determined Russian attacks and by Arab pirates. Byzantium's ships were primarily located in two or three maritime *themes*, particularly the southernmost Cibyrrhaeots theme, and there was also a central drungary of the fleet, whose ships transported *tagmata* and *themes* on expeditions. The chief Byzantine type of ship until the tenth century was the *dromond*, a *bireme* (two banks of rowers) with a wooden castle and a complement of three hundred men, of whom seventy were soldiers, and there were also smaller ships, manned by 130 to 160 men, often Russians. The overall lack of interest in the navy was curious, given the vulnerability of Constantinople itself to sea attack, as in 1204. Yet at some crucial moments, sea power proved decisive, for example, when the Arabs launched massive attacks in 678 and between 717 and 718 but were turned back to a large extent by a Byzantine secret weapon, usually called "Greek fire."

"Greek fire" was a petroleum based substance, reportedly brought to Constantinople in 678 by a Greek engineer named Callinicus and capable of being sprayed onto enemy ships so that they burned fiercely. A contemporary report in 678 said that the Arab ships that attacked that year were "engulfed in flames" and utterly destroyed. The Byzantines themselves called the secret substance "marine fire," "liquid fire," "prepared fire," or "artificial fire," and four characteristics separated it from the numerous incendiary devices of the period: it burned in water, it was liquid, it was propelled or sprayed through tubes or siphons, and some said that it produced a loud boom and was accompanied by smoke as it was sprayed from the tube or siphon. Probably as important as the chemical composition of the substance itself was the heating and propulsion device that made the system work. The substance was heated and pressurized in closed containers below decks, it was then passed through a pipe with a valve that released the jet of liquid. As it left the nozzle a torch ignited the substance, while the nozzle itself could be turned left or right or raised and lowered for elevation and distance. The substance burned and clung to wood, sails, oars, clothing—anything combustible—and could not be quenched by water. Unfortunately for the Byzantines, the secret of the substance and its propulsion system was so rigorously kept by the family descendants of Callinicus, and by a system of compartmentalizing knowledge of the weapon, that the secret was lost. Opinions vary as to when "Greek fire" was last used, but it may have been as early as the last great Arab attack between 717 and 718. After this, the Byzantines often spoke of using the secret weapon, but when they were on the offensive, such as the two expeditions to recover Crete in 828 from the Arabs, "Greek fire" was not employed, and in further defensive engagements, such as the Russian attacks of the tenth century, the evidence is vague.

The loss of this maritime secret weapon is symbolic of the greater loss of the Byzantine Empire. The arrival of the Seljuk Turks in Asia Minor signaled the erosion of the eastern portion of the empire so that the decisive defeat of the Byzantines at the battle of Manzikert in 1071 by the Turks was simply the culmination of fifty years of advancing Turkish power. Ironically, it was the light horse archers of the Turks at Manzikert that scattered, ambushed, and picked off the heavier Byzantine cavalry and won the day for the Turks—ironic because horsed archers had once been Byzantium's strength. By the end of the twelfth century, the empire in Asia Minor was only a narrow strip along the Black Sea and Anatolia. Then the capture of Constantinople in 1204 by the errant Fourth Crusade ultimately deprived Byzantium of much of the Balkans and Greece. Lastly, the emergence of the powerful Ottoman Turks in the fourteenth century completed the physical destruction of Byzantium, and though Turkish attacks on Constantinople in 1397 and 1422 were repulsed, the final successful Turkish assault on the capital took place in 1453. Yet the end of Constantinople was really an epilogue to a century of imperial decay in which financial decline and loss of territory had diminished the army so that the emperors turned to mercenaries of all kinds, including Turks. However, these soldiers were frequently undisciplined and of dubious loyalty. The army that had once been the hammer of the Goths was at the end a much smaller and dispirited force, indeed only eight thousand men were available in 1453 to defend Constantinople against an overwhelming army of one hundred sixty thousand Ottoman Turks. The basic defensive strategy of the Byzantine Empire, which had worked so well for almost nine hundred years, could not cope with internal disintegration and the power of the rival Turkish empires.

If the Seljuk and Ottoman Turks had dealt the final fatal blows against Byzantium, the dangerous enemies of earlier years had been the Persians and the Arabs. The Persian threat had been rolled back by a campaign in the early seventh century and was completed by a Byzantine victory at Nineveh in 626. Thereafter, Persia remained a rival for control of trade routes to the Far East, but it was not a serious threat. The Arab explosion in the seventh century was another matter. Muhammad, the founder of Islam, was born in Mecca around 570, and in 610, after experiencing a vision of the archangel Gabriel, he began to proclaim his monotheistic beliefs against the common polytheism of the area. Yet Muhammad did not intend to innovate, rather he announced that his doctrines went back to the original true religion of Abraham, from which Christians and Jews had since deviated, and he always saw the "people of the book" (Jews and Christians) as separate from other non-Muslims.

However, he faced considerable hostility in Mecca, perhaps because the leading Quarishi clan feared that Muhammad would deprive Mecca of its important Kaaba pilgrimage shrine. Thus, Muhammad was forced to depart with his small band of converts to the nearby town of Yathrib, which was a rival to Mecca. Yathrib was renamed Medina (city of the prophet), and it was not long before Muhammad was able to impress his personality on the town. Although Muhammad slowly gained converts, the new Muslims from Mecca (known as the Emigrants) were poverty stricken and relied on the converts in Medina (known as the Helpers) for assistance. Soon Muhammad announced that Gabriel had indicated the need to attack unbelievers, of whom the closest were of course in Mecca. A useful byproduct of this assault on Mecca and revenge on the Quraish was that a successful attack would relieve the poverty of the Emigrants from Mecca. Moreover, Mecca was an important staging post for the profitable caravan trade between the Yemen and Syria, and caravans were vulnerable to raiding. Thus, the first military endeavor of Muhammad and his followers was an attempt to capture, in January 624, a one-thousand-camel caravan as it approached Mecca.

Muhammad's force consisted of only 300 men, with a mere 70 camels and 2 horses, while the Quraish, who had learned of the raid, issued forth from Mecca with 750 camel riders and 100 horsemen in chain mail. Eventually, the two sides met at the wells of Bedr. Despite the disparity in numbers, the Muslims had every reason to fight, especially the Emigrants, who owned nothing except their swords, while the new religion promised instant paradise for those who were killed in battle for the Muslim cause. It is related that in this fight a young man overheard Muhammad call out: "All who die today will go to paradise." Throwing away the dates he was eating, the young man drew his sword and rushed into the fray to his death, crying: "What! is it only necessary to be killed by those people in order to enter paradise!" On the other hand, the Quraish felt no such fervor, and they were reluctant to shed the blood of fellow tribesmen or lose their own lives for little reason. However, the war party among the Quraish persuaded the others to fight, and, in Arab tradition, the battle commenced with single combats. In this case, three Quraishi chiefs stepped forward to challenge the Muslims, and Muhammad allegedly turned to his own clan, calling out "O Ben Hashim. Stand up and fight." Whereupon, Muhammad's uncle and two cousins stepped forward to meet the challenge. The first two Muslims slew their opponents with sword play, while the last combat resulted in the death of both the Quraishi and the Muslims. Then battle commenced, while Muhammad prayed fervently behind the lines, for if his cause was defeated and he himself killed, the Muslim religion would certainly disappear. Although early Muslim battles are often depicted as wild melees, Muhammad's force actually sent out archers to the wings to protect the flanks, and, since there was no cavalry, the main infantry force in the middle consisted of swordsmen and spear and javelin men. Chain mail armor was worn only by the wealthy few. No doubt the spear or javelin men commenced proceedings for the Muslims, followed by the swordsmen in a charge. The Quraish on the other hand dismounted from their camels to act as archers and infantry, and their horsemen advanced in front of the infantry, preceded by a shower of arrows.

The battle was undoubtedly of short duration, given the few reported casualties, but at one point Muhammad picked up a handful of gravel and hurled it at the Quraish, shouting: "Confusion on their faces." This apparently renewed the spirit of the Muslims, and their high morale soon prevailed. The Quraish evidently already had an eye on their line of retreat and rushed from the battlefield to nearby Mecca, leaving behind forty-nine dead and a similar number of prisoners. Muhammad's success drew in other tribes, including desert Bedouin, and, in 630, after several desert battles similar to that of Bedr, including some defeats and some victories, the Muslims were able to raise an army of ten thousand men and enter Mecca unopposed. The achievement brought in yet more support, although soon after, in 632, Muhammad died. Muhammad's only two sons had died in infancy, and, after some trouble, he was succeeded by his father-in-law, Abu-Bakr, who was named Caliph, or Successor. Abu-Bakr died shortly thereafter, but the new Caliph, Umar, carried out the policies of Muhammad as had Abu-Bakr, namely, to expand. Expansion was not conducted to convert unbelievers, since the Muslims initially wished to remain a separate racial entity as rulers and tax gatherers; nor was it the result of Arab tribal migrations, which occurred later; nor was it the result of religious enthusiasm, although this made the expansion possible. Rather, the primary motive seems to have been the desire to attain more fertile territory and to obtain plunder, which was what paid the Muslim armies. At the same time, Persia and Byzantium were involved in wars with each other, and both had reached a low ebb of military ability. Moreover, particularly in the Byzantine lands of Egypt and Syria, religious persecution by Constantinople made the inhabitants prefer the Muslims, who did not force conversion and who, especially for Jews and Christians (people of the book), demanded fewer taxes. So the time was right for expansion, religion provided the motive, and wealth was there for the taking.

The Arab Muslims in the early to mid-seventh century thus surged across Syria and Iraq, defeating Byzantine armies in 636 and 637 and occupying Antioch, Damascus, and Jerusalem. By 651 Persia was conquered. As far as Byzantium was concerned, the Arabs took the Byzantine province of Egypt by 646 and then North Africa. By the late seventh century, the Arabs had moved beyond the Persian Empire into central Asia and secured much of that territory, including Samarkand. Then in 711, using the recently conquered Berbers, the Arabs (or Berbers) occupied Spain, but their attempts to take Constantinople itself between 717 and 718 were thwarted by the triple walls of the city, by Byzantine allies, and, as we have seen, by "Greek fire" and the Byzantine navy. Although the Arabs/Berbers used Spain as a base from which to send out tentacles into western Europe, these forays were at the limits of their logistical and military ability and they were turned back, especially by Charles Martel at the battle of Poitiers around the year 732. In this battle, the Franks, wearing wolfskins and with their long matted hair hanging down to their shoulders, fought on foot and formed a huge unbreakable square. The Arab/Berber light cavalry could do nothing against the square and were forced to admit defeat and retreat at night. The Arab/Berber forces later seized Avignon and Lyons and held on to Narbonne until 759, meaning that Poitiers is not strictly a turning point. But it did indicate that the Muslim threat to Europe was likely to fail. The "Song of Roland," an eleventh-century poem supposedly celebrating the rousing defense in 778 of Charlemagne's army against the Spanish Muslims by the commander of the rearguard, Roland, showed the confidence of the West when facing the Muslims. Meanwhile, following the establishment of the *themes* and upgrading of its army, Byzantium prevented the Arabs from penetrating Asia Minor in any decisive way. Indeed the Byzantine emperor regarded the *theme* of Anatolia, facing the Arab threat, as the most important *theme* of all, and consequently chose its strategus extremely carefully. Thus, the Arabs were never able to bribe or subvert the strategus of Anatolia, which would have opened the way to Constantinople.

Nevertheless, within about one hundred years of Muhammad's death, the Arabs had created an empire through conquest that rivaled those of Persia and Rome. How did this occur? Not, it seems, by technology, for the Arabs did not create new weapons, and their technology was actually inferior to that of Byzantium and Persia. However, as previously mentioned, the Arabs did start to expand at a time when the Persian and Byzantine Empires were in disarray. Equally important, the Arabs managed to organize an expansionist movement out of a previously fragmented tribal society, partly through an aggressive and demanding religion and partly through the economic and political rewards that successful expansion brought. The previous feuding of Arab tribes was channeled into a communal obligation to perform jihad, or holy war, not to convert unbelievers but to achieve the universal domination of Islam. All of this obviously created a series of armies that had considerable incentives to succeed. The Muslim political elite also saw expansion as a way of retaining their position at the head of Arab society and as a method of securing trade routes through the Arab world, the old Persian Empire, and North Africa. In this case, economic success fed upon itself and fuelled further advances.

In a purely military sense, the Arab armies initially fought with their own particular style. Their armies campaigned on the edges of the desert and relied on their mobility in long marches across and around the boundaries of the desert, giving the Arabs the advantage of surprise as well as the ability to fade into the desert if things went wrong. Additionally, the desert was always useful as a raiding base. Arab armies were initially quite small, as might be imagined given the problem of logistics in covering long distances across difficult and waterless terrain. Thus, the Arab armies that conquered Syria and Iraq were no larger than five thousand to twelve thousand men, and sometimes even smaller. On the other hand, the size of the Arab army at specific battles, such as Yarmuk in Syria in 636 was over twenty thousand men. Some women and children accompanied these armies, to tend the flocks that provided milk and meat for the men, to look after the wounded, and even to participate in the battle. Hence, after the battle of Qadisiya (637) against the Persians, which reportedly lasted for three days, the Arab women and children went over the battlefield, helping the Arab wounded but dispatching the Persian wounded with wooden clubs. Tribes were the building blocks for the original armies, and, since there were at first no standing armies, armies were brought into being for specific campaigns by calling on volunteers from specific tribes, by requiring tax agents to raise a certain number of men, or by enlisting conquered tribes. Later on, other defeated groups such as the Berbers were integrated into Arab armies, but eventually by the ninth century lack of manpower led to the use of Turks and other nationalities such as mamluk slave soldiers. Sieges were often avoided, partly because the Arabs were not experts in siege warfare, although they were quite capable of undertaking sieges, but mainly because sieges slowed down Arab mobility. Therefore, sieges were embarked upon only where there were few alternatives—for example, the six month siege of Damascus in 635, when either deceit or surprise enabled the Arabs under Khalid to eventually take the city. There were also numerous sieges during the Arab/Berber occupation of Spain. Constantinople itself came under prolonged Arab siege between 674 and 678 and again from 717 to 718, because the Arabs believed that only the capture of the capital would end the Byzantine Empire.

The actual style of Arab warfare changed as it adapted to Persian and Byzantine methods. Originally, Arab armies were simply tribal groups fighting together, using spears, bows, and swords. Each tribe would have its own flag or standard which rallied the men, who fought as infantry because very few horses were available. Cavalry was not a factor, therefore, and the more widely available camels were used almost entirely as transports to the battlefield, whereupon the rider would dismount and fight on foot. After the obligatory single combats, tactics consisted mainly of the charge, although false retreats, ambushes, and infiltration around the flanks were also used. As more horses were captured and as the more sophisticated Byzantine and Persian forces were encountered, the Arabs adopted a more structured style of warfare. Thus, Arab armies rode on camels to the battlefield, horses were led alongside the camels, and soldiers transferred to the horses before the battle to form a cavalry. At Qadisiya, the Arab army possessed a cavalry force of about six hundred men, and they opened the battle with a series of charges. However, the bulk of the Arab armies were infantry, recruited mainly from the towns, and by 635 they were arranged not by tribes but by infantry formations. Thus, there were right and left flank units, a central brigade (the "heart"), a vanguard, a rear guard, and separate cavalry and archery units. Armies were broken down into units of ten, the infantry was frequently drawn up in deep ranks of eight or more, and a clear chain of command existed. Above all, the chief component of Arab armies was the infantry, not the cavalry, and success came through mobility, religious enthusiasm, high morale, and a certain Arab desert hardiness.

Curiously, many of the Arab battles seemed to take place over a number of days. So at the decisive battle of Yarmuk in 636, the conflict was reportedly spread out over a month and a half, while at Qadisiya in 637, there took place a four day conflict. Qadisiya was fought beside the Euphrates, when the Persian army under its commander Rustem was forced by his emperor to cross the river and engage the Arabs, thus losing the advantage of position to the Muslims. The Persian attack was led by several elephants, which scared away the Arab cavalry and bid fair to win the battle by themselves. However, the Arabs fired arrows at the soldiers on board the elephants, while others scrambled underneath the great beasts and cut the girths of the howdahs, thus throwing the Persians to the ground. But at the end of the first day, neither side had the advantage. After clearing away the wounded and dead on the morning of the second day, both sides set to fighting again, though the elephants failed to reappear. Some Arabs rode camels disguised with hoods and draperies, to frighten the Persian cavalry, while at the same time the advanced (cavalry) guard of Arab reinforcements arrived. Once again neither side prevailed, and once again the morning of the next day was spent clearing away casualties. The elephants made another appearance but were dispatched with lances, though not before an enraged elephant picked up with its trunk the leader of the Arab group attacking the animals, Qaqaa, and killed him by dashing him to the ground. The main body of Arab reinforcements arrived, but at the end of the third day, there was still a stalemate. Then an unexpected Arab night attack dismayed the Persians by its fury, and finally on the fourth day, the Arabs managed to penetrate the center of the Persian line and put the whole Persian army to flight. The details of this conflict show that the Arabs actually fought a battle of attrition, preserving their troops as much as possible and, with the aid of reinforcements, were able to launch the last decisive attack. Other Arab battles reveal similar features, and so the concept of attrition was evidently an Arab strategy.

The Arab conquests were remarkable in their speed and extent. Yet internal political and military conflicts divided the Arab world, for example, Shi'a versus Sunni. The Arab dynasties of the Ummayyads (c. 661–750) and the Abbasids (750–945) were followed by decentralization of the Arab empire and the growth of the power of the Muslim Seljuk and Ottoman Turks, who took over leadership of the Muslim world. Nevertheless, the Arab Muslim empire was unusual in that it began in the mind of a single individual—Muhammad. In contrast, another nearly contemporary series of rapid conquests and settlements in the Western world by the Vikings rivaled the Arabs in speed and surprise, but their conquests stemmed from several factors and not from one individual.

The Vikings were one of the few groups that raided and settled as conquerors from the sea. Starting in the late eighth century, Scandinavians known as Northmen spread as traders, pirates, and fighters to England and Ireland; to the Frankish lands of western Europe (especially Normandy); to the Mediterranean lands of the Muslims and Byzantines (around the year 1000, Vikings actually formed the Varangian Life Guard for the Byzantine emperors); to the southern lands of the Slavs; and westward across the Atlantic as farmers and settlers to Iceland, Greenland, and briefly to North America. What caused this explosion of activity? Certain factors explain the Viking expansion: population growth pressing on limited farming areas, climate change that restricted land for farming, internal dynastic conflicts, knowledge of wealthy foreign lands and routes from Scandinavian traders, the simple desire for loot, plunder, and land, the transference of Scandinavian piracy from the Baltic to western Europe; the development of an efficient ship with sails, and the evolution of seagoing navigational skills. Referring to these last two factors, the Vikings had developed sails at least by the eighth century to supplement their rowers, for without sails long voyages were impossible. This critical development probably came from contact with Western traders.

There were many sizes of Viking ship, but the ninth-century boat excavated at Gokstad was typical of the larger sea raiding ships. It was 23.33 meters long and 5.25 meters amidships and clinker-built entirely of oak. There were sixteen oar holes on each side, and spaces for thirty-two shields on each side, thus the crew numbered at least sixty-four. The ship was steered by a lengthy rudder, placed near the stern on the steer-board (starboard) quarter. Each end of the boat featured a prow; there was a deep enough keel to allow efficient sailing, a mast that could be stepped or laid down, and a nearly square sail made of rough wool. Finally, the boat drew very little draft, so it could easily be beached. With regard to navigation, the Vikings did not know longitude but relied on latitude only, taking bearings from the sun and the polar star. They therefore sailed along a particular latitude until gaining their objective and then turned north or south as required. Without question, the Vikings also built up experience of the seas they sailed and passed this knowledge on to succeeding voyagers, as obviously occurred after the first landfall on the North American coast around the year 1000.

Fig. 3.1. The Gokstad ship, a classic Viking seagoing warship, which also may have been used as a merchant ship. Note the clinker-built style of construction. (c) University Museum of Cultural Heritage—University of Oslo, Norway. Photo: Eirik Irgens Johnsen.

The first Vikings (Danes and Norwegians), raided for plunder in the 780s on the coasts of Britain, and these were followed by Danish attacks on the Frankish kingdom of Charlemagne at the beginning of the ninth century. Then came mixed trading-raiding incursions by primarily Swedish Vikings in the early ninth century into what was to become Russia. Thus, as early as 860 a fleet of two hundred Viking ships from Swedish Kiev besieged Constantinople, and although they could not take the city, the Vikings laid waste to surrounding monasteries and the suburbs of the capital. In what was a familiar reaction by churchmen to the Vikings, the patriarch Photius bewailed the ferocity of the raiders, finding it difficult to fully express his horror:

> Woe is me that I see a fierce and savage tribe fearlessly poured round the city, ravaging the suburbs, destroying everything, ruining everything—fields, houses, herds, beasts of burden, women, old men, youths—thrusting their swords through everything, taking pity on nothing, sparing nothing. The destruction is universal. Like a locust in a cornfield, like mildew in a vineyard, or rather like a whirlwind or a typhoon or a torrent or I know not what to say,

it fell upon our land and has annihilated whole generations of inhabitants. I consider them happy who have fallen prey at the hands of the murderous barbarians because, having died, they are unaware of the disaster that has befallen us.

The initial raids of the Vikings on England and Scotland were often aimed at monasteries because they contained wealth and were poorly defended, and, being pagans, the Vikings saw nothing wrong in attacking such targets. In 793, for example, the Norwegian Vikings attacked the monastery at Lindisfarne, killing priests and nuns, desecrating the holy relics, taking away treasures, and even enslaving a few of the monks. The churchman Simeon of Durham later wrote that the raiders of 793 "laid everything waste with grievous plundering, trampled the holy places with polluted steps, dug up the altars, seized all the treasures, killed some of the brothers, some taken away in fetters, many driven out naked and loaded with insults, and some they drowned in the sea." The raids on what came to be France and Germany were on a larger scale, starting in 834, and by the mid-ninth century, the Vikings were confident enough to winter over. The Vikings soon aimed at towns and cities on rivers or on the coast, such as Hamburg, Antwerp, Nantes, Chartres, Orleans, Bordeaux, Toulouse, and Paris. Despite their seagoing nature, the Vikings proved capable of undertaking siege warfare, besieging Paris between 885 and 886, where they used battering rams, stone hurlers, and volleys of arrows. The Vikings also were able to go far inland, riding on horses to reach their objectives and then dismounting to fight on foot. Finally, by about the year 900 the Vikings began to settle in France, especially in Normandy. There was a similar pattern in the British Isles, first raids from the 790s onward, then, particularly by the Danes, extended inland campaigns between 865 and 954, and again from 980 to 1035, and finally settlement and integration.

How did the Vikings fight? In their earlier raids, a simple hit and run strategy was employed. Larger raids inland required the use of a base camp, often located on an island at the mouth of a river, such as the island of Northey on the Blackwater River of the east coast of England, which was used as a base during the inland raid of August 991. The camp was normally fortified with a ditch and rampart and a few guards, and then the Vikings moved inland toward their target, either by river, or if a river was not available, by riding horses which might have been brought with them or stolen from local communities. On reaching their target, the

Vikings dismounted to loot and plunder or if necessary to fight. These raids took place in the summer, and the Vikings then sailed home before the winter. But as Viking confidence grew, it was possible to winter over in their fortified camps. When the Danish Vikings conducted their major campaigns in England between 866 and 886 and between 892 and 896, they did so not by river but by horse, setting up bases and then using the still existing Roman roads to cross the entire country on horseback. Because defenses were geared to river and sea, the use of the Roman roads made a critical difference to the Viking success in grabbing large areas of land.

However, larger raids or attempts to actually take territory required different battle tactics. For example, in a pitched battle, the conflict opened with a hail of arrows, then spears were hurled, and finally the Vikings closed to fight with swords and long battle axes called *skeggox* or "beard" axes. They wore mailed coats and leather or iron helmets (without horns) and carried long triangular wooden shields. As the Vikings came hand to hand with the enemy, the chief tactic was to form the ranks together in a "battle hedge" or shield wall, with overlapping shields, and then attempt to break open the normally similar closed ranks of their opponents by the use of spears, swords, and axes. Once the enemy ranks were broken up, it was usually then a simple matter to deal with the isolated groups that remained. Sometimes, the front ranks of the Vikings consisted of "berserkers," a group of frenzied warriors, who were "bare sark," that is, shirtless, meaning without armor. A saga describes the berserkers of Odin, who "refused to wear mail-coats and fought like mad dogs or wolves, biting their shield-rims; they had the strength of bears or bulls. They cut down the enemy, while neither fire nor iron could make an impression on them."

The Vikings liked to spread an image of terror in their warfare, because it was then easier to demand tribute of the threatened towns or areas rather than have to fight. Thus, the English paid thousands of pounds of Danegeld silver to protect themselves from 992 until 1012, when the tribute simply became part of the tax structure. Equally, in what came to be France, between 845 and 926, the Franks paid many thousands of pounds of silver in what was really protection money and raised this money by a kingdomwide tax system. Alternately, if fighting did take place, then psychologically the defenders were already in fear of their lives from the terror of the Vikings. Tales of Viking violence grew, such as the "blood-eagle sacrifice," in which the victim's rib cage was torn open, and the lungs pulled out to form the shape of an eagle. Accounts of this practice are suspect, but they helped create an image of ruthlessness that assisted the Vikings, especially because Viking armies were really quite small, often two thousand men or less.

How did the Franks and the English defend themselves against these violent raiders? One obvious choice was the payment of tribute. Towns also rebuilt their walls, and methods of raising local infantry levies were instituted. Another tactic was to build fortified bridges or upriver forts to prevent Viking raids from reaching their targets. Forts could also be built at vulnerable places on the coastline. Yet another response by King Alfred of Wessex in England was to build a fleet and to meet the Vikings at sea. Alfred believed that bigger was better and built ships with sixty oars or more and with wider decks. But the ships proved difficult to navigate and were defeated. Inland, Alfred mounted several attacks on the Danes and launched a low-level guerrilla campaign, but without decisive success, and he was frequently compelled to pay tribute. Ultimately, in eastern and northern England an Anglo-Scandinavian society was created through two waves of settlement, first by warrior-settlers, and then by straightforward settlers. These Vikings sought land to farm, although recent excavations at York (Viking Jorvik) suggest the Vikings also devoted considerable energy to trading, leather working, wood working, and jewelry making.

Not only did the Vikings create new societies through conquest and settlement in what were to become Russia, France, and Britain (particularly England, Ireland, including the founding of Dublin, and the Scottish islands), but they also used their navigational skills to cross the Atlantic and founded settlements in Iceland and Greenland and briefly at L'Anse aux Meadows in Newfoundland. Thus, the Vikings preceded Columbus to North America by nearly five hundred years. Although the Vikings' greatest conquests had been in Europe and among the Slavs, their impact was soon absorbed, and their quite rapid integration with local populations created new societies. This role was similar to the Germanic barbarians who, although defeated by Byzantium in the east, established a number of new societies in western Europe. However the Muslims could not easily be integrated into Europe, since they wished to conquer, while their faith, though tolerant to others, was incompatible with the growth of Christianity and with different political and cultural institutions in the west. Therefore, over some seven hundred years from A.D. 300 to 1000 a new pattern of states had been established in the western world, largely by warfare, to replace the old Roman Empire.

The traditional Roman art of war by infantry legions also had been replaced by a more cavalry-oriented style of warfare, which the later Romans themselves had already begun to adopt. The Huns, some of the Germanic barbarians such as the Goths, the Arabs, and to some extent the Byzantines had all demonstrated the value of light cavalry and cavalry archers. Yet it is important to notice that infantry never lost its value and in fact remained a critical part of almost all armies. The Vikings were unusual in being seaborne warriors, but they also fought on foot. However, the last threat to Europe before an organized feudalism emerged, with its heavy cavalry, was the eruption of yet another nomad group from north of the Black Sea, the Magyars.

The Magyars fought as a horse-borne army of archers, though they also carried slightly curved swords, short spears, and axes for close order combat. The Magyars wore light armor of mail shirt, leather helmet, and even used their hair as armor, braiding it into two ponytails on each side of the neck to protect the main arteries. Important was their use of stirrups, stemming either from the Turks or from the Avars, who introduced this innovation to the west in the late sixth century. Stirrups enabled quicker stops, starts, and turns and the ability to maneuver in formation. Thus, the Magyars fought in a loose line of several brigades, with gaps between the units to enable the brigades to make turns, to retreat if necessary, and to simulate false attacks and retreats. The Magyar style of fighting was based on cavalry archers firing volleys of arrows and then circling the enemy to attack from several directions. Then the reserves pursued the enemy as long as necessary for complete destruction. Similar to the Huns in the past and the Mongols in the future, the Magyars were able to travel large distances, in their case by each soldier trailing three or four horses as remounts and by carrying supplies on pack horses. Finally, discipline was fierce and cruel.

From about the year 900, the Magyars raided widely in the Rhine, Moselle, Loire, and Rhone Valleys; in northern Italy; in the Balkans; and as far as Constantinople in 942. Then in 955 the Magyars launched a strong invasion of the lands of Otto I (936–73), ruler of the east Frankish kingdom. The Magyar army numbered some thirty-five to forty thousand light cavalry, under the command of "Bloody Bulcsu," so-called because of his tough discipline. The army of Otto I was smaller, perhaps twenty to twenty-five thousand, of more heavily armored cavalry, and it met the Magyars just south of Augsburg. Bulcsu attempted to besiege Augsburg, but, like most nomad armies, the Magyars were not proficient at siege warfare, and they were forced to lift the siege. This led to a decline in Magyar morale and also released Augsburg's garrison to join Otto I's army. Bulcsu devised a reasonable battle plan in which a smaller force crossed the Lech River to the south and attacked Otto I from the rear, while the main group made a wide circle to the north, crossed by a ford, and attacked Otto I from the front. This maneuver is similar to the successful future Mongol strategy at the battle of Mohi Heath in 1241 against the Hungarian descendants of the Magyars. However, in 955, Bulcsu's strategy failed to work because the rear attack was defeated and dispersed by Otto I before the frontal attack could take place. When the main attack went in, Bulcsu's light cavalry archers made no impression against the deep phalanxes of Otto I's heavy cavalry, partly because the steady rain lessened the effectiveness of the Magyar archers. Bulcsu then had recourse to the usual nomadic false retreat, but when this did not work either, Bulcsu simply launched his light cavalry in hand-to-hand action against the heavily armored knights of Otto I in their phalanx formations. Not surprisingly this led to the massacre of the Magyars, either on the field of battle or when they were later pushed into the Lech River.

Thus, in 955 the Magyar offensives were halted, and some decades later the Magyars accepted Christianity, settled down as agriculturalists, and became the kingdom of Hungary under Stephen I. Symbolically, the Magyars had been defeated by heavy cavalry, for the European medieval age of the knight on horseback was already under way.

Suggested Reading

A rather simple—aimed at the younger reader—but complete overview of the complex area covered by this chapter is Trevor Cairns, *Barbarians, Christians and Muslims* (Minneapolis, 1975). Another useful introduction is Lucien Musset, *The Germanic Invasions: The Making of Europe*, A.D. 400–600 (University Park PA, 1965, 1975). For the slightly later period, a good background study is Geoffrey Barraclough, *The Crucible of Europe, the Ninth and Tenth Centuries in European History* (London, 1976).

There is no single good modern book on barbarian warfare, so information has to be ferreted out of many sources. The traditional reference, originally published in 1921 and therefore now outdated but intelligently written, is Hans Delbrück, *The Barbarian Invasions: History of the Art of War, Volume II*, trans.

Walter Renfroe Jr. (Lincoln NE 1980, 1990). An overview of varied quality is Gerald Simons, *Barbarian Europe* (New York, 1968). For the late Roman period Arther Ferrill, *The Fall of the Roman Empire: the Military Explanation* (New York, 1986), is a good military introduction to some barbarian groups and their styles of warfare. Less useful is Justine Randers-Pehrson, *Barbarians and Romans: the Birth Struggle of Europe*, A.D. 400–700 (Norman OK, 1983). The complicated relationship between Roman and barbarian is also explored in Patrick Geary, *Before France and Germany: the Creation and Transformation of the Merovingian World* (New York, 1988). More focused is Bernard Bachrach, *Merovingian Military Organization, 481–751* (Minneapolis, 1972). An overview of the important barbarian group, with some military matters included, is Edward James, *The Franks* (Oxford, 1988). An introduction to Charlemagne is E. M. Almedingen, *Charlemagne, A Study* (London, 1968).

For the Huns, see chapter 5 in J. Otto Maenchen-Helfen, *The World of the Huns*, ed. Max Knight (Berkeley, 1973), and also E. A. Thompson, *A History of Attila and the Huns* (London, 1948). For the complicated history of the Goths, the best introduction, though only partially concerned with warfare, is Herwig Wolfram, *History of the Goths* (Berkeley, 1979). Chapter 8 in Thomas Burns, *A History of the Ostro-Goths* (Bloomington IN, 1984), specifically deals with the Ostrogoth military system. Extremely valuable primary sources are the works of two sixth-century observers of the Goths, namely, Jordanes, *The Gothic History*, and Procopius, *History of the Wars*.

Turning to Byzantium, there is Warren Treadgold, *The Byzantine Army* (Stanford, 1995). For the later Byzantine army, stressing the army as an institution and its role in policy, is Mark Bartusis, *The Late Byzantine Army: Arms and Society, 1204–1453* (Philadelphia, 1992). Of considerable value is Stephen Williams and Gerard Friell, *The Rome That Did Not Fall* (London, 1999), dealing with the fifth century and including much barbarian material; J. A. S. Evans, *The Age of Justinian* (London, 1996), which tends to downplay Belisarius' abilities; and Walter Kaegi, *Byzantium and the early Islamic conquests* (Cambridge, 1992), which has a useful chapter on the battle of Yarmuk. Other titles include L. H. Fauber, *Narses, Hammer of the Goths* (New York, 1990); Walter Kaegi, *Byzantine Military Unrest, 471–843: An Interpretation* (Amsterdam, 1981); Walter Kaegi, *Army, Society and Religion in Byzantium* (London, 1982); Warren Treadgold, *The Byzantine Revival, 780–842* (Stanford, 1988); George Huxley, *Why Did the Byzantine Empire Not Fall to the Arabs?* (Athens, 1986); and Blondal, *The Varangians of Byzantium* (Cambridge, 1978). Contemporary sources include Procopius, *The History of the Wars* (Cambridge, 1916); de Villehardouin, *The Conquest of Constantinople* in Joinville and Villehardouin, *Chronicles of the Crusades* (New York, 1963, 1986); and George T. Dennis, *Three Byzantine Military Treatises* (Washington DC, 1985).

There is an extended literature on the Arabs, although it is difficult to find a single modern source specifically concerned with Arab styles of warfare. The closest is Lt. Gen. Sir John Glubb, *The Great Arab Conquests* (London, 1963). Valuable articles are in V. J. Parry and M. E. Yapp, *War, Technology and Society in the Middle East* (London, 1975), which also contains articles on Byzantine warfare. Less useful than the title indicates is Fred Donner, *The Early Islamic Conquests* (Princeton, 1981). Tightly written and partially concerned with military affairs is Patricia Crone, *Slaves on Horseback: The Evolution of the Islamic Polity* (Cambridge, 1980). Disappointing because of its mainly political focus is Roger Collins, *The Arab Conquest of Spain, 710–797* (Oxford, 1989). Some sidelights occur in Ronald Finucane, *Soldiers of the Faith: Crusaders and Moslems at War* (London, 1983). The Arab conquest is put into context in Philip Hitti, *The Arabs: A Short History*, 2nd rev. ed. (Chicago, 1970).

There is a vast literature on the Vikings, and much of it contains good chapters on the nature of their conquests. It is only necessary to mention three titles, Johannes Brondsted, *The Vikings*, trans. Kalle Skov (New York, 1965); P. H. Sawyer, *Kings and Vikings* (London, 1982); and F. Donald Logan, *The Vikings in History*, rev. ed. (London, 1992). A contemporary account of a raid on England in 991 is the poem *The Battle of Maldon*, while several of the Viking Sagas have been translated into English, as has the Russian Primary Chronicle.

Finally, a brief but specific look at Magyar warfare is Anthony Komjathy, *A Thousand Years of the Hungarian Art of War* (Toronto, 1982).

4. EUROPEAN CHIVALRY AND THE RISE OF ISLAM

The period from the Roman Imperium to the High Middle Ages is generally depicted as the "dark ages," that is, one in which little advancement of knowledge and practice took place. This is somewhat misleading in the area of military history because there were basic realignments in social, economic, and military relations as well as major refinements in existing tactics and weaponry.

Beginning with Charles (the Hammer) Martel in the eighth century, the Franks—a group of Germanic tribes first mentioned in the fourth century in the lands between the Maas (Meuse) and Scheldt Rivers and that thereafter occupied most of central and western Europe—developed the feudal system largely as a military order. The king granted distinguished soldiers sufficient land from the royal estates to permit these noble knights (*comitatus*) to purchase mounts, armor, lances, swords, and shields and to undergo basic military training, honed in grand tournaments. The knights, for their part, swore an oath of loyalty to serve the king as vassal and warrior—usually for forty days out of the year. Fortified castles and mounted knights became the dominant feature of feudalism. The poorer freemen became serfs and rarely rendered military service.

The feudal system did not develop concepts such as unity of command, tactics, and training because of the very nature of its part-time and disparate service. What cohesion it achieved came about from its devotion to Christianity, for the Frankish knights developed a code of honor closely bound to Christian values such as truthfulness, mercy, and loyalty, a code that would become known as chivalry.

Religious fervor and military protection also highlighted developments in the Arab world. The rise of numerous largely independent Muslim religious principalities generated a centrifugal force that collided with Christian Europe during the First Crusade (A.D. 1095–99). Frankish knights in mail body armor encountered mobile Muslim light horse archers. Straight and long Frankish swords crossed finely honed, curved-blade Muslim scimitars. Missile-hurling machines (mangonel, or trebuchet) were matched against Muslim fortifications. And by the end of the First Crusade, both East and West had adopted combined-arms tactics, coordinating the movements of cavalry and infantry in battle.

Naval warfare, on the other hand, changed little. Long, low galleys rowed by slaves remained common, and the object of war at sea remained ramming or boarding the opposing vessel. Yet during the First Crusade, sea power showed its crucial role for logistical support. The maritime states of Italy—in particular Venice, Genoa, and Pisa—ferried crusaders to the Holy Land and thereafter provided them with resupply. In the process, they enhanced interaction between the Muslim and Christian worlds.

Knights and Saracens are the stuff of fairy tales and Hollywood movies. Myths and shibboleths abound. Over the centuries, stereotypes have hardened into accepted fact. The task for the historian, then, is to try to sort out myth from legend, reality from illusion, in order to arrive at a rational and balanced view of warfare during this period. The central problem is one of hard, documentary evidence. There exist no non-Muslim sources on the prophet Muhammad. The sacred revelations made to Muhammad by Allah through the angel Gabriel, the writings of the Qur'an, were written after the Prophet's death and are in no chronological order. For the West, many of the sources are in the form of chronicles either by participants in the Crusades or by religious scholars, most of whom exaggerated accounts through "pictorial" or "illustrative" figures of combatants and casualties.

A second major problem is that of statistics. With regard to Islam, for example, the Damascene chronicler Ibn-al-Qalanisi documented the arrival of crusader armies "with forces so numerous that their numbers cannot be reckoned." Estimates of combatants for the First Crusade alone range from 360,000 Muslims to 600,000 crusaders. Specifically, Fulcher of Chartres and Albert of Aix insisted that 600,000 warriors went on the First Crusade; Ekkehard of Aura stands on 300,000; Raymund of Agiles speaks of at least 100,000. Anna Comnena recorded that Godfrey of Bouillon alone brought 10,000 horse and 70,000 foot to liberate the Holy Grave. And with regard to the celebrated Templars, Bernard of Clairvaux in 1125 assured the Christian world of their ferocity in com-

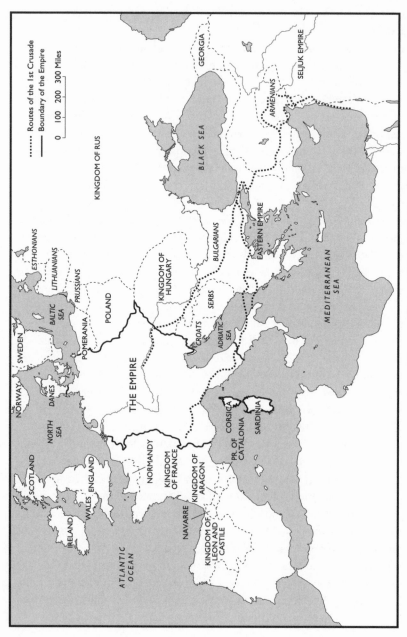

Map. 4.1. Clash of Cultures: The First Crusade

bat: "Often 1,000 men are put to flight by one of them, and 10,000 by two." These figures, widely celebrated in the chansons de geste, will be adjusted more realistically later.

Finally, we encounter the problem of semantics. Apart from the imprecise meaning of terms such as "strategy," "operations," and "tactics" during this period, neither side used the language that we have adopted. The Muslims, for example, did not use the term "crusaders," and their chroniclers spoke only of "Franks" and "infidels." The Christians, for their part, generally recorded encounters with "infidels" and "paynims," at best with Saracens and Moors or Turks and Tatars.

Warfare had not changed dramatically since the days of Rome. Armies of eight to ten thousand men were considered large. Battle fronts remained stable at about six to seven kilometers wide from the time of Rome to Napoleon Bonaparte. Opposing armies generally continued to form up a thousand meters apart and basically to leap, grunt, and hack at each other. Soldiers served for a plethora of reasons—with drink, physical coercion, religion, and enrichment being the prime motives. Indeed, there really existed no way for a man of the times to make a quick fortune except on the battlefield. Prisoners and their equipment thus constituted a shortcut to wealth; special bounty hunters tackled fugitives from battle.

The commonplace character of violence in the medieval world combined with the traditional carnage of battle to produce grisly encounters. After a major battle, local villagers looted the corpses and carved up the horses and pack animals. Those too poor to ransom or too badly hurt to take as captives were killed. The two dozen "surgeons" who normally accompanied an army set and splinted broken arms and legs but could do little else. Depressed fractures of the skulls were lethal as the secret of trepanning had not been unlocked. Wounds from lances and arrows that had pierced the intestines were fatal as peritonitis was inevitable. Penetrations of the chest cavities routinely resulted in sepsis. Broken backs caused by falls from mounts likewise almost always resulted in death. Countless combatants were left on the field of battle and either bled to death or fell victim to shock and exposure. It was almost an act of mercy for the victorious side to return to the battlefield the next day to dispatch those whom they found to be still alive.

Medieval armies were at once small and expensive. The former meant that it was difficult to wage offensive war over time; the latter dictated war by maneuver and the need to avoid bloody battle in order to minimize losses. War aims thus tended to be limited and campaigns often were little more than plundering expeditions. While Charlemagne and Louis the Pious had developed the strategy of multiple concentric attacks, there existed no great theoretical treatise on strategy. Communications likewise had changed little. Smoke signals by day and lights or beacons by night along coasts or on prominent sites augmented the ancient horseback messenger. Church bells were rung to signal hostile attack. Carrier pigeons were introduced after Godfrey of Bouillon learned of this Muslim practice during the First Crusade.

To be sure, there had been some modest technological advances. Stirrups arrived from China in the eighth century and the nailed horseshoe became common around A.D. 900. The Franks developed diamond-shaped shields to protect thighs and legs. Coats of mail, with ring joined to ring, covered warriors in the tenth century, and their mounts were likewise caparisoned by about 1150. Mail shirts, breeches, and hoods as well as metal pot helmets rounded out the knights' defensive armor. Swords became heavier and longer, used mainly for cutting rather than thrusting.

Mobile siege towers and beam-sling artillery firing stones enhanced siege warfare. The Franks first encountered and quickly adopted from the Near East petroleum-based "Greek fire," hurled either by mangonels or later fired out of bronze tubes. But the principal weapon of siege warfare remained starvation. The problem of land logistics was eased with the appearance of the horse-collar and breast-strap harness by 800 and of the whippletree for supply wagons by the mid-eleventh century. At sea, skeleton-first ship construction reduced cost and increased available tonnage.

A true "revolution in military affairs," however, came in the field of social, economic, and military relationships. As the nineteenth-century German historian Leopold von Ranke stated, Latin Christendom consisted of two major institutions: the Church, a spiritual universal state whose parts were formed by the individual kingdoms that were more or less firmly established units unto themselves, and the feudal state with its various layers of authority and power. Feudalism was essentially military, a social organization designed to produce and support cavalry. In a basically agrarian barter society, land endowment constituted wealth, which was required for mounted warriors. Thus, it was Charles Martel's vast and ruthless annexations of Church lands that allowed the mayor of the palace and his loyal retainers not merely to strengthen their forces but to shift the focus from foot to horse. Over time, the Franks fused vassalage, the ancient custom of swearing allegiance to a leader, with benefice, the granting of an estate, to produce feudalism. Loyalty to one's liege and prowess in battle became the twin features of the new sociomilitary system. Conversely, failure to fulfill one's military obligation entailed forfeiture of the land endowment. The crisis that generated feudalism was the Saracenic invasion and the need to pursue Islam's forces after their advance had been halted by infantry at Poitiers in 732.

Military strategy—the art and science of deploying armed forces to attain political objectives by the application of force—did not exist in the Middle Ages in the modern sense of the term. Armies were small in numbers, had little discipline, and usually served only for limited periods. The great vassals constantly challenged the authority of the crown, while the latter could undertake extensive campaigns only with the unanimous agreement of the former. Moreover, campaigns were conceived of in terms of individual battles and victory was something to be exploited for plunder rather than pursuit. In most cases "strategy" translated into a single campaign or even a single battle and depended upon the personal skill and dedication of the commander.

Given that feudal armies were too small and too weak to exploit victories in the open field, it is not surprising that the strength of the defensive in fortified places remained decisive. Sieges tended to last a long time and to accomplish their purpose only at great expense and with great difficulty. Nor does there seem to have been a recognition of the fact that siege armies were highly vulnerable to relief counterattacks. By and large, battle remained little more than a series of small combat actions.

Operations—the actual deployment of combat forces—received more attention than did strategy. Knight and horse became the outward symbols of the Franks' military system. The "age of chivalry," as the term suggests, was dominated by the horse. A contemporary adage stated that "One hundred horses are worth as much as 1,000 men on foot." The horse accorded its owner first social and then legal superiority, for horses were costly and only the wealthy could afford either the requisite mounts (at least three per knight) or the large quantities of grain that they consumed. Additionally, horses had the unfortunate habit of getting killed in battle. In short, only those recently enriched by the seizure of Church lands and the benefice of royal estates could afford to fight on horseback, and from this derived the social and legal superiority of the mounted warrior. By about 1000, the term *"miles"* changed meaning from the generic "warrior" to the specific "knight." The Frankish warrior progressed from vassal to knight and finally to noble: knighthood became synonymous with nobility. The *miles* formed a hereditary class, almost a caste unto itself, and a wide gulf soon divided the mounted warrior aristocracy from the mass of peasant foot.

The medieval saying that people existed to work, knights to fight, and priests to pray accurately reflected the emerging sociomilitary system. The costs not only of purchasing, maintaining, and replacing mounts but also of acquiring armor and weapons, of hiring servants and squires, footmen and bowmen all limited knighthood to the wealthy elite. The Hohenstaufen emperor Frederick II confirmed the dominance of this class when he stated that "the fame of his empire and his own power rested in the body of knights."

The complete knight was a costly creature. With at least three mounts (later protected by chain mail), a knee-length mail shirt (hauberk), mail coif, metal-plate armor, helmet, lance, sword, silk pennon, tent, beasts of burden to haul and to carry kitchen, kettles, victuals, and wines— this medieval "battleship" cost the equivalent of fifteen mares or twenty oxen, equal to the plow teams of ten peasant families. Put differently, it required the revenues of at least 300 to 450 acres of fertile land to launch and sustain a knightly career. Even infantry became a costly endeavor. A standard arsenal of pike, mace, axe, halberd, and short mail shirt around 1300 could cost half a year's wages. The *Domesday Book* reveals that iron production in England trebled between 1066 and 1086, with similar metallurgical expansion assumed for the Continent, making armor protection for rider and mount feasible.

Aside from birth, entry into the knighthood was purchased through rigorous training. In fact, formal training welded together this self-conscious cosmopolitan military elite. Conducted either at the court of a prince or supervised by another knight, training was both mental and physical. Wolfram von Eschenbach has left a clear picture of what was expected of an aspiring knight: "manipulating the shield, fighting with the sword, firing at the target, broad jumping, and gripping the lance well, and sitting straight in the saddle." The joust, or tournament, was designed to test the aspirant's skills and mettle. Despite a prohibition against using sharp weapons in tournaments at the Council of Reims (1131), knights in France developed highly realistic combat simulation by abandoning blunt in favor of sharp weapons for jousts. The sword became the symbol of class and honor. Wirnt von Gravenberg gave testimony to the link between the two in his treatise *Wigalois* (1204–1210): "May God strike down those who even give a sword to him who cannot measure up to the knightly life, who from his origins is not born to it."

Troubadours and Minnesänger in the *Chanson de Roland* and the *Nibelungenlied* have handed down a romantic, lyrical glorification of knighthood and chivalry. The literary image of the knight errant, the romantic appeal of knighthood in flower, the formation of chivalric orders, the flattering portraits of the courtly life of the nobility, and the heroic descriptions of tournaments have dominated our perception of the age of chivalry. Such images, however, need to be balanced by the existence of a horde of robber barons whose function was closer to that of the brigand than to that of the valiant protector of honor and fair maidens. Images also need to be tempered by realization of the human fear that even the bravest chevaliers must have held of wounds, mutilation, and death.

The medieval knight was much more heavily armed and protected than the cavalry of antiquity. Decision in battle depended solely on the knight, and the new *miles* was unique insofar as no other combat branch could stand up against him. The widely held notion that only at Courtrai in 1302 was Flemish infantry able to score foot's first victory in battle since the days of Rome probably is too extreme. Nevertheless, modern scholarship maintains that decision in battle was brought about mainly by the personal skill and bravery of individual knights—and not, as in the case of a Roman legion, by steadfastly maintaining a position, executing a clever maneuver, or uniting disciplined and trained tactical units as shock troops. Uniformity and excellence of weapons, of course, were also decisive in combat—the lance that did not splinter, the sword and arrow that pierced iron, the armor that was impenetrable.

While little in the way of theory has survived on how knights were actually deployed in battle, it is generally accepted that they were not used for maneuver warfare or enfilading actions. Terrain played no great role as knights could operate effectively only on a plain. There were no knightly drills for riding in close formation, deploying on the field of battle, or performing wheeling movements. Once engaged in combat, command and control were limited to rallying to one's banner. Commands, signals, and bugles were ineffective in the resulting din of the melee, which knew neither fronts nor flanks. The characteristics of the knight, then, determined the nature of battle.

Tactics—the art of conducting battles, engagements, and attacks in order to accomplish tactical objectives in a given combat area—received the most attention from medieval warriors. As a rule, knights formed up in closely serried ranks: a rectangular formation of fifty to sixty knights in front, two or three rows in depth. The chief tactical aim was the breakthrough. The initial charge of heavy units in serried formation was designed to breach the enemy front, whereupon the knights would penetrate other enemy units. At times, the battle would be decided by the initial assault, with one side signaling defeat by fleeing to the safety of a castle. At other times, when the first ride through the enemy's line failed to settle the issue, the knights would turn and ride through the hostile line again (*kêre*) and again.

Available sources indicate that after the initial charge the battle deteriorated into individual fights between knights. There existed no common sense of discipline, for in feudal Europe the very spirit of the hereditary warrior class militated against this. The personal honor and prestige of the individual knight was paramount. And knights attacked knights because their action alone was decisive in battle. Hence, they usually ignored the unmounted rabble for it was not worth the trouble of pursuit. No evidence exists to shed light on the degree of cooperation between fully armored knights and lightly armed horsemen. We do not even know for certain whether the latter were ever used as scouts or as light cavalry. Most scholars agree that light horse was usually massed with infantry.

In knightly combat, the critical blow was delivered by the combined momentum of horse and rider. By 732 the Carolingian court had developed the tactical charge of knight on horseback, shield in one arm, spear tucked firmly under the other. At the moment of impact, the knight in his high saddle leaned forward over the horse's neck with feet firm in the heavy stirrups. Once forced out of the saddle, the knight was awkward and immobile. Remounting was a daunting task. Indeed, even getting back on one's feet was a major challenge for a man encumbered by chain mail or plate armor. Pursuit of the adversary on foot likewise was virtually impossible.

Above all, medieval cavalry should not be confused with its highly mobile and disciplined successor, be it on the early modern European battlefields or on the North American plains. Knightly combat was laborious and slow. Two or three large hunter-type horses (such as Percherons, for example) were required to transport the knight (150 pounds), his armor (60 pounds), and his saddle and trappings (40 pounds) to battle. Once astride his best mount, a knight's charge of five hundred yards per minute was extraordinary; best speed on horseback has been estimated at around twelve to fifteen miles per hour. It remains a matter of conjecture as to how many knights and horses, exhausted by both approach and charge, were able to perform the *kêre*.

Archers were the bane of knights. At once tough professionals and yet outside the chivalric system, bowmen were a threat especially to the knight's mount. Conversely, there was no honor to be gained in fighting them. Archers were armed with the composite reflex bow made of wood, sinew, and horn glued together as well as with a sheaf of about two dozen chisel-headed arrows. A good bowman could loose a shaft every ten seconds, and the effective range was about two hundred to three hundred yards. The clouds of arrows shot at an approaching adversary by bowmen either in front or to the side of the knightly host usually wreaked havoc among hostile horses. Many a chronicler recorded the cries of animals in pain. The vaunted crossbow, a hand ballista that could fire metal bolts farther, faster, and more accurately than the composite reflex bow, was especially effective against knights as it could penetrate mail and even plate armor. Not surprisingly, its use was outlawed by the Lateran Council in 1139—but only against Christian warriors. It remained an ideal and just weapon against Saracens.

The Franks initially encountered massed mounted archers during the First Crusade. This frightful combat arm with its great mobility was so effective that the crusader armies quickly incorporated Turkish mounted archers into their own ranks. On the whole, however, Latin Christendom did not hold the bow in high esteem. It was considered a weapon of the devious Orient (Persians and Parthians) and it belonged to the socially inferior class of footmen. Hence, it was not unusual for knights to mutilate or execute captured bowmen as a sign of disdain—and fear. As well, bowmen had no ransom value.

Infantry was universally viewed as constituting the bottom rung of the social and military ladder. Even with protective harness and piercing as well as cutting weapons, foot was seen but as an auxiliary of the mounted warrior. As far as is known, it developed no offensive tactics, perfected no maneuver capability, received no training for use in closed movements, and was accorded no strong tactical system of discipline. The only theoretical tract for foot remained Vegetius's *Epitoma rei militaris*, yet this fourth-century manual required troops with skill and dis-

cipline, capable of marching in tight formations and executing sophisticated wheeling movements. European armies, consisting of feudal host,
popular levy, mercenaries, and pilgrims, boasted no such formations. Infantry was armed with pike, spear, mace, and axe. By adding an axehead
near the point of the pike in the halberd, infantry could both thrust and
cut. Leather or quilted linen—later, a short chain mail shirt—served as
body protection. Perhaps an iron cap and a shield completed the arsenal.
In battle, infantry either screened the approach of knights or became involved from the rear in the wake of the knights' assault. At its best, foot
provided refuge and cover for knights in distress.

The work of infantry was akin to butchery. Its ability to inflict damage ("killing zone") was restricted to a small circle around the body,
where arm's reach permitted footmen to club, slash, or stab. A spear
thrust through the visor or armor joints, an axe stroke delivered behind
the knee, a slash with a two-handed mace or pike at the legs, belly, or
head of a knight's mount—these were the tool and trade of foot in close
combat. Charles of Anjou graphically attested to infantry's role when,
before the Battle of Benevento (1266), he admonished his footmen to
"hit the horses rather than the men" in order "more freely" to "catch
the riders of the horses and kill them, thus lying on the ground and
slow by the weight of their armor." Additionally, the brother of King
Louis IX encouraged his knights to retain foot soldiers to "destroy the
horses of the enemy as well as kill those who will be shaken off by their
horses."

Given the frightful slaughter of infantry during the First World War
and the return to battlefield mobility late in the war with the appearance of the "tank," it is perhaps not surprising that modern scholars
have tended to be unsympathetic to the value of foot soldiers and to
glorify the knight as the medieval version of the "tank." But one may
well question whether knights were central to and dominant in combat.
Indeed, how effective were knights against well-sited and protected castles? Or against archery and other missile weaponry? Or against long
sharpened stakes or spikes stuck in the ground at an angle suitable for
impaling a horse? Or even against foot armed with halberds and pikes?
Were horses, in fact, so stupid as to impale themselves on such obstacles, or did they not instead follow their natural instincts either to take
an evasive course around the obstacle or simply to bolt? The upended
horses in the Bayeux Tapestry (around 1092) might well prompt us to
rethink the efficacy of foot against mounted shock combat.

SIMVL: ANGLI ET FRANCI: INPRELIO :·:

Fig. 4.1. "Mounted Shock Combat Meets Foot." Bayeux Tapestry, c. 1092, *Vetusta Monumenta*. Society of Antiquaries of London.

Perhaps it might be more profitable to see medieval warfare as a function of mixed combat, of what today we call combined-arms formations—knights used in conjunction with archery and infantry. It is conceivable that the supporting arms were more closely grouped around the principal arm, knights, than medieval chroniclers allowed. The highly romanticized literature of the age of chivalry undoubtedly singled out the knight for distinction more for social and legal than for military reasons. But perhaps mixed formations of heavily armed knights, lightly armed horsemen, mounted archers, longbowmen and crossbowmen on foot, and infantry with close-combat weapons were the norm rather than the exception in the Frankish way of war by A.D. 1000. Richard the Lionhearted in the Levant made use of combined infantry and cavalry arms and of missiles and shock action. Still, it remains an open question how much the armies of the Christian West learned in their encounters with the forces of Islam.

Islam (meaning "submission") was a political-military organization based upon the power of religion. All devout Muslims (followers of the Prophet) saw themselves as bearers of God's truth with a sacred duty to bring it to the rest of mankind, mired in barbarism and unbelief. The Qur'an was explicit on the symbiosis between belief and war: "The best theology is to help God with the sword." Islam's military might rested upon a tenuous triad. The military arm was centered on the warlike nomadic Bedouins of the desert, on what Muhammad called the "hoofs" of the Community's horses and "the points of its lances." A common culture and language bound these warriors to the economic backbone of Islam, the city-dwelling, sedentary merchant citizenry. Finally, the Prophet himself represented the political and religious unity of the movement. Beyond that the religious teachings of fate (kismet) and Paradise ("Swords are the keys of Paradise") combined with the military discipline assured by the authority of Allah to make possible the conquests of Egypt and Palestine, Syria and Iraq, North Africa and Iberia, and advances as far as Tibet and the Loire River. The new religious state was centered at Medina after the hyra of 622.

Islam was more a militant religion than a modern state. To be sure, at first the Prophet and later his successor, the caliph, was entitled Commander of the Faithful. Muhammad was at once the spiritual head, the temporal ruler, the interpreter of the will of God, and the military leader. But there existed no written constitution in the modern sense and there could be no certain principle of succession to the caliphate. Theocracy, by its very nature, is not hereditary. In addition, the dispersal of tribes along the expanse of the Fertile Crescent as well as the primitive nature of desert communications militated against the development of a modern centralized state. Bitter and often violent civil wars usually determined the succession.

Whereas Muhammad was an impostor to Christians, Christ was but a precursor to Muslims. The latter depicted the Christian states, collectively, as the House of War and Europe, particularly, as the seat of barbarism. In 1068 Said-ibn-Ahmad, qadi of Toledo, described the temperament of north Europeans (the "seventh climate") as "frigid, their humors raw, their bellies gross, their color pale, their hair long and lank." The Qur'an admonished the faithful to "fight the polytheists completely, as they fight you completely." Before the Crusades, the Christian and Muslim worlds had studiously ignored one other; a medieval iron curtain separated the two theocracies, allowing little intercourse in diplomacy, travel, or trade. What few contacts Islam had were largely with the Greek Christian empire of Byzantium. Cultural influences from Ethiopia and from Judaism further helped shape the Muslim state.

In the military sphere, however, the Prophet's axiom that "whoever imitates a people becomes one of them" was routinely set aside. It was accepted practice to fight the infidel with his own weapons and devices. Thus, Islam borrowed heavily from the general military systems of the old Zoroastrian Persians and Christian Byzantines and adopted specific technical innovations such as "Greek fire" from the Byzantines and gunpowder from Christendom. But there existed no great Muslim theorist of war and there is no evidence that Muslim strategy was influenced by any specific Byzantine or Sassanian Persian treatise on warfare. Nor is there any evidence that the Muslims ever read existing Byzantine, Persian, or Greco-Roman treatises on war. Most likely, Byzantine and Persian influences came to Islam through adaptation by direct observation or by verbal reports about those societies' military establishments and practices. It is questionable whether there even existed a formal term for strategy during the early Muslim conquests.

Given the diversity of Muslim influences, it is difficult to talk of a specific attitude to war, much less of a distinct strategic culture. Apocalyptic visions of calamitous warfare dominated Islam. Its warriors considered a state of war as the norm, raiding (*ghazw*) as the customary form of warfare. Above all, they accepted a communal (though not individual) obligation to perform jihad, armed struggle against non-Muslims. Their political aim was universal domination by Islam, not the total conversion of unbelievers. Above all, Islam was not simply a new military system because its military dimension was first and foremost the byproduct of the Prophet Muhammad's apocalyptic religious message as laid down in the Qur'an.

Muslim armies at first came as volunteers from the tribes of the Arabian Peninsula. Later, tax agents operated among the tribes to raise contingents. Islam's greatest leaders grouped separate tribes such as the Banu Shayban, Banu 'Ijil, Banu Hanifa, and Banu Yashkur into larger tribal units such as the Bakr b. Wa'il. Only during the later stages of the second jihad in the eleventh and twelfth centuries did Islam turn first to mercenaries such as the Seljuk Turks and finally to a military-slave institution (*mamluk*) in order to overcome the pressing need for soldiers. Tribal kinsmen, however, formed the military aristocracy of Islam. Only leaders whose allegiance to Islam was unimpeachable received upper-level commands. The early followers of Muhammad, the Meccan Immigrants (*muhajirun*) and the Medinese Helpers (*ansar*), constituted the highest rungs of this warrior aristocracy.

The operational art of war in Islam can be gleaned roughly from extant sources. The Muslims sought short, violent battles that featured knights and mounted archers. Muslim mounted archery, quicker and more flexible than its Occidental counterpart, was based on the speed and agility of Arabian mounts as well as on lighter weapons such as bow, shield, lance, sword, and club. This mobility, in turn, allowed Muslim forces to stay at a distance from Christian knights and to choose the moment and place to close. Arabs used the bow from the saddle without halting or dismounting. Their high rate of fire, generally aimed at knights' horses, often destroyed the westerner's cohesion in battle.

Additionally, Muslim armies repeatedly used the stratagem of the feigned retreat to draw weary knights either from their horses or into prepared ambushes. Islam's warriors perfected the art of attacking enemies on the march and forcing them to fight under improvised conditions, without being able to marshal their forces for battle. Moreover, they appreciated such basic principles as avoiding encirclement, striking the main body of the enemy, and maintaining a reserve as relief force. Numerical superiority, flanking assaults, and use of terrain were also part and parcel of the Islamic art of war around 1100. Generally speaking, Saracenic warfare as experienced by the crusaders—which will be taken up later in the case study—probably differed little from that conducted by Rome's Parthian enemies at Carrhae in 53 B.C.

To gain a more accurate picture of the nature of the Muslim military establishment, it might be profitable to turn to one of the few surviving primary documents, the Chronicle of Tabarî from the year A.D. 923. Survival of this document is critical since virtually all scholars of Islamic warfare agree that few sources exist on the organization of Muslim armies and that practically nothing has survived on the strategical or tactical practices of the Arabs. Moreover, there exist no records or memoranda of major councils, no original dispatches between Medina and front commanders, no letters between military leaders, and, perhaps most importantly, no record of how the caliph and his advisors at Mecca implemented strategies and operations.

The military administration of the Omayyad Caliphate was adopted basically from the Persians, and its initial function was to distribute booty. In time, it evolved into a payroll office at Medina, maintaining rolls of eligible warriors who received an annual stipend (*ata*) paid in the first month of the Islamic calendar, special bonuses, and booty shares. Muhammad, who had centralized the system of taxation and justice, had decreed: if you capture a warrior, he is yours; if you kill him, his possessions are yours. Supplies and treasures seized especially in cities were divided as follows: the head of the raiding force generally received one-fifth; slaves (white Turkish and black African) as well as precious metals (often melted down on the spot for ease of transport) went to the leader and to Islam; weapons, coins, cattle, sheep, camels, and donkeys of the defeated became booty for the victorious warriors. Finally, land grants from conquered territories to Muslim warriors also fell under the purview of the army administration. The military also administered the taxes levied upon conquered unbelievers—a head tax (*jizya*) and a land tax (*kharaj*) in lieu of military service owed Islam in exchange for personal safety and use of property. The head tax reportedly was the primary source of income. Levies of two hundred thousand dinars were not uncommon for conquered territories, and members of the highest levels of the military aristocracy could expect as much as five hundred dinars per month from this.

Logistics comprised a third major aspect of military administration. While especially the Bedouin tribes mainly lived off the conquered land, merchants were engaged to lay in stores for major campaigns. Sheep were taken along for meat while flour, bread, and pastry were dietary

staples. Advanced supply stations also served as the bases for future conquests. Camels carried twenty bags of water each as well as a vial of date
wine, while donkeys hauled other requisite supplies. Fodder for the animals was foraged in conquered territories and standard army rations
(*rizq*) consisted of bread, oil, and vinegar.

Medina established a basic system of military administration that included such modern components as a department of the army, pay-
master-general, and quartermaster-general. Regular reviews were introduced to inspect, pay, and promote (or demote) troops, which were rated
as excellent, moderate, and inferior. Jousts, in which riders sought to run
lances through metal rings mounted on wooden poles, were common.
And at the Cairo Citadel, the Mamluk Faris instituted the equivalent of
a modern military school with emphasis on archery, equitation, fencing,
and lance games.

The Chronicle of Tabarî suggests that Muslim forces—generally between six thousand and twelve thousand men during the major battles
of Yarmuk (636) and Qadisiyyah (637)—were commanded by a leader
(*amir*). The latter, though subordinate to Medina, enjoyed great latitude
to decide terms of peace and to appoint the commanders of various tactical formations within his army. He was assisted by special aides (staff)
without command function. There existed no midranks; the basic units
of "tens" were the next command level. The *amir*'s army usually consisted of an advanced guard, two wing formations, a center of about three
thousand warriors, and a rear guard. Standing armies, modern formations such as regiments and battalions, and routine drills and regulations
as well as rigid discipline were unknown. Raiding forces customarily
were demobilized after each campaign, but garrisons were maintained
on a permanent basis along Islam's extended frontier. Flags, usually in
tribal colors, were used to signal troop movements. Morale was maintained by premiums paid for enemy heads and by the promise of Paradise
for those who fell fighting the unbelievers. But on occasion, Muslim warriors deserted or changed sides for higher pay.

The Muslims enjoyed no technological advantages. Indeed, it could
be argued that both the Persians and Byzantines were superior in terms
of technology, metallurgy, armor, and ballistics. Moreover, the Franks,
called "iron people" by the Turks, enjoyed heavier armor protection.
Sources generally speak of crusaders as being "armed" or "heavily
armed," of Muslims as being "naked" or "disarmed." Unfortunately, it
is not known whether any of the state arms factories of the later Roman

Empire still operated at the time of the Muslim conquests. Caravan trade and tribute exacted from conquests financed the expansion of Islam, and hence vast destruction of conquered lands did not become a conscious part of their strategy. Not surprisingly, in a centuries-old camel culture, Muslim warriors proceeded to battle in groups of two per camel. Dromedaries, which had already been used by Alexander the Great, could cover up to fifty miles per day for a week and go for as much as a month without water. Customarily, a Muslim army advanced at a top speed of twenty miles per day. Mobility, surprise, and swift evasion were the hallmarks of Bedouin warfare.

Once at the scene of battle, the warrior changed to his battle horse. (Indeed, horses were in short supply especially during the early conquests.) His saddle customarily was one of leather-covered wood with metal stirrups, and the front part of his mount's hooves often were cut to produce greater speed. Chroniclers claim that the warrior often injured his horse in order to get it riled for combat, but one may question whether an injured horse became mean or simply frightened.

Geography favored the Muslims. Not only did they enjoy interior lines of communications and logistics, which enabled them to shift troops between Persian and Byzantine fronts, but the desert terrain made it almost impossible for their opponents to strike at the center of the Arabian Peninsula. Intelligence was gathered not only from merchants and travelers but also from friendly dissident circles such as Arab populations, and from malcontent religious sects such as Christians, Jews, and Samaritans ("People of the Book"). Muslim maps, if any, were generally inferior to those of their Byzantine opponents. Carrier pigeons and horse-mounted couriers were the primary means of communication. Eunuchs were reserved for highly confidential missions.

Cavalry units usually consisted of three-thousand- to four-thousand-man formations, which, in turn, were subdivided into units of one hundred to six hundred warriors. Heavily armored cavalry (*mugaffafa*) was used sparingly, usually for pursuit, and the weapon of choice was the supple yet sturdy curve-bladed scimitar (deployed either from horseback or dismounted). Armor (*dir*) was expensive and hence reserved for rich warriors. Body armor was heavy and usually discarded during retreat, while plate armor was rare due to cost, weight, and heat. Two coats of chain mail, separated by a cloth gown, became standard for the heavy cavalry, whose horses later were also protected by chain mail. Since body armor did not extend below the ankles, mutilated feet were common.

Shields were made of leather, curved and round; helmets were either of leather, leather covered with iron, or metal. Much more common were marksmen equipped with bows and arrows on light, fast horses.

Infantry, which was rarely used in the Omayyad Caliphate without cavalry, was armed with lances, bows, and swords. Lances were either long bamboo shafts with iron tips or shorter all-metal spears. Indian steel was highly revered. Iron-covered wooden clubs, mace, javelins, slings, naked axes, and daggers completed the weaponry. As a last resort, foot hurled either burning bamboo bundles or stones at pursuers. Showing their determination to fight to the death, infantry at times intentionally broke their wooden or metal scabbards at the height of battle. By and large, infantry bore the brunt of the fighting. The bow (*kaus*) was the most feared weapon in the Saracen arsenal, and archers, often organized as distinct units, had an effective range of about one hundred yards. The prowess of Muslim bowmen at close range was legendary: chroniclers frequently noted victims stuck with arrows like porcupines. Archers carried between thirty and fifty arrows made of wood or bamboo, with metal tips (often dipped in poison). The primary task of archers was to shield their cohorts from Byzantine and Sassanian heavy cavalry.

In the area of siege warfare, Muslims again enjoyed no advantage over their adversaries. Indeed, it has been suggested that they paid less attention to engineering than did the Franks. To be sure, Islamic armies already at the time of the Prophet relied for defense upon city fortresses (*hisn*) and walled castles (*kasr*) as well as mountaintop fortresses (*kal'a*). Muhammad likewise initiated the use of ditches covered with reeds and sand as deception, both in the open terrain as traps and around cloth-tent encampments as protection from surprise attack. Rudimentary catapults had been adapted from Persian prototypes. Their Greek name, *maganik* ("hurls stones"), effectively described their function.

Medical units in the modern sense were unknown. The wounded were carried back to camp to be treated by the women with cotton bandages, while the dead were buried on the field of battle. What passed for medics not only labored to remove arrows from the wounded, but also served the *amir* to cut out the tongues and gouge the eyes of the condemned. Prisoners were disposed of immediately: warriors were routinely put to death; children were drowned; and noncombatants were sold into slavery. To be sure, every *amir* developed his personal style. At Tabri, for example, a victorious Muslim leader put to death between six and forty thousand enemy warriors. As a nearby stream ran red with

Fig. 4.2. "Archers in Action." Bayeux Tapestry, c. 1092, *Vestuta Monumenta*. Society of Antiquaries of London.

blood, the *amir* not only painted with it but mixed it with flour for his bread. A general rule of thumb in the Omayyad Caliphate stated that one-third of all military prisoners were to be crucified, one-third to have their hands cut off, and the remainder to lose both hands and feet. Hostages held during negotiations were put to death if trickery was tried or war resumed.

On occasion, between seven hundred and one thousand women would accompany a Muslim army to battle. Their tasks were to tend the flocks that supplied meat and milk to the warriors, to treat the wounded, and, as a signal of utmost disgrace, to scold and even stone Islamic warriors who had left the scene of battle. It was not unknown for Arab women to render the coup de grâce to wounded hostile warriors.

Formal declarations of war were not known. The Chronicle of Tabarî documents an interesting encounter between hostile armies in the Islamic year 85 (A.D. 707). The leader of a Turkish force sent a courier bearing poison (war to the bitter end), arrows (normal combat), and musk (peace). His Muslim counterpart in disdain burned the poison, broke the arrows, and poured the musk on the ground—whereupon the Turks lost their desire to attack.

Finally, the chronicle gives a description of battle around the year A.D. 923. An Omayyadan army advanced in the field in columns of about two thousand yards long and by ships on the Euphrates, Tigris, and Oxus Rivers. On land, the march order (*ta'biza*) combined foot and horse in vanguard, center, wings, and rear guard. The center consisted mainly of infantry as well as of general headquarters. The *amir* was carried to battle in a chair. About forty to eighty scouts undertook reconnaissance as well as courier duties. The battle order (*saff*) saw the army deploy in rows (often seven in number) and spread out—precisely in the manner that the devout were ordered to assemble in the mosque by Umar I. The Prophet had decreed that his armies were to be more than wandering, disorganized tribal hordes: "God loves those who fight for him in a battle order as if they were parts of a firmly assembled building."

Nonetheless, there rarely was a detailed plan of battle. Instructions were verbal and vague: "I will attack their right wing; thereafter, my right wing will engage their left wing; the center will await my orders." Battles of encirclement were rare, and victory generally fell to the side that remained on the field of battle. A beaten foe was pursued vigorously—or at least until his main camp was found and plundered. Muslim leaders knew how to strengthen either wing of their army for the decisive assault and how to use a hill or ridge to protect one flank in order to reinforce the other.

Cavalry adopted a breakthrough strategy. Muslim horse almost always attempted a frontal assault in the hope that sheer mass (and noise) would decisively breach the enemy line. Once this had been accomplished, the battle often degenerated into a melee wherein individual warriors challenged each other one-on-one for glory. A favorite tactic developed over millennia of Bedouin warfare was to strike the opponent at the seams of his formation with small cavalry squads, then quickly withdraw, only to repeat the process again and again until the enemy ranks had been broken. Human wave tactics were eschewed as they would only lead to a severe drain on morale.

Infantry in battle first used their bows (especially against enemy horses to force their riders to dismount), then hurled their spears, next charged with lances, and finally closed with swords and clubs. On occasion, deception was practiced: the first row of infantry put saddle blankets on lances stuck in the ground in order to obscure the adversary's vision. When deployed in defense, infantry planted their lances in the ground and kneeling archers aimed at the oncoming mounts. During close combat, foot soldiers sought to stab enemy horses in the nostrils, and finally stood back-to-back with drawn swords in order to offer two fronts.

Siege warfare was an arduous undertaking, often lasting six months to a year before a city fell. The siege of Aleppo, in fact, lasted six years. Hostile citadels were flooded to prevent supply and reinforcement. Their fresh water supply from nearby streams was cut off, and their wooden walls were set on fire. Sappers dug ditches to advance assault troops to their walls. The enemy's protective ditches were filled with dirt hauled up by donkeys at night. And as many as eighty catapults hurled stones against the citadels' walls and gates. Two hundred years later, special mangonels flung naphtha: a volatile mix of 10 pounds tar, 3 pounds resin, 1.5 pounds each sandarac and lac, 3 pounds high quality sulphur, 5 pounds melted dolphin fat, and 5 pounds liquefied and clarified fat from goats' kidneys. In most cases, however, a skillful combination of diplomatic negotiation, psychological pressures, fear of starvation, and the conviction of inevitability rather than military siege brought about the surrender of fortified places.

Several general conclusions can be drawn about the nature of Muslim warfare. At both the strategic and tactical levels, the Islamic military proved surprisingly capable as well as flexible. It knew how to choose critical pressure points and to concentrate force against them. It adopted economic blockade, leading to famine and strangulation of trade, as a standard weapon. It sought decisive battles and exploited ruthlessly all victories and breakthroughs. It combined high-intensity bursts of violent military activity with protracted and patient negotiations to attain political goals. Islam did not ignore ambush in strategy. "Warfare is deception," the Prophet had stated. Flexibility was manifested in Islam's willingness to negotiate, to mediate, even to compromise for the moment. Islam did not always insist on total victory. Nor was there a dogmatic policy to hold everything forever. And finally, the caliph and his advisors were flexible in their means: threats, negotiations, duplicity, craft, patience, and violence were all part of Medina's arsenal.

Since Muslim armies did not owe their spectacular conquests to technical, organizational, or tactical advantages, it remains to identify potential keys to victory. To be sure, Islam benefited greatly from the weakness of its opponents—the exhaustion of the Byzantine and Sassanian Empires due to prolonged wars—and the natural calamities that befell them, especially vast floods in Iraq. But the key to Muslim conquest lay in a new attitude toward war. The old notion of fighting for one's community gave way to *umma*: to fight (and die) for a unique, separate, and unified Islamic community. In other words, the psychological dynamism of a new universal prophetic religion integrated Arabia's fragmented tribal societies in order to achieve well-defined political and military goals. While hunger and avarice may well have played their parts in the expansion of Islam, the religious state centered at Medina welded the often quarreling tribes of the Arabian Peninsula into an effective fighting force. In the process, Islam opened political horizons that lay beyond the individual tribe. The secret, then, lay in the remarkable degree to which "a new Islamic state with an expansionist policy could harness for its purposes the rugged warriors of Arabia."

The actual conquests, for the most part, were probably driven by a complex nexus: the ideological message of Islam; the need to secure trans-Arabian trade and to recover trade routes that had shifted farther north; the lure of booty in terms both of treasure and of slaves and of new taxes to levy and lands to divide; and the leaders' needs to preserve their dominance in the new hierarchy. Islam's expansion was halted in the eleventh century primarily by a classic policy of overreach. The Kingdom of Georgia repulsed Muslim invaders. Sardinia and Sicily were re-

taken by Christendom. The Reconquista on the Iberian Peninsula secured Toledo and Coimbra. And the crusaders seized the coastal plains
of Palestine and Syria.

Case Study: The First Crusade

Armed Christendom and Islam clashed dramatically during the First
Crusade, publicly launched by Pope Urban II at the Council of Cler-
mont in 1095 as a holy war to free Jerusalem from the infidels. From
the start, the First Crusade consisted of both a domestic "truce of God"
and a fervent call to arms. "God wills it" (*Deus vult*). Its deeper motives
were many: the ambitions of adventurer princes; the desire of younger
sons restricted by primogeniture in the West to gain a principality in the
East (Bohemond of Taranto, Prince of Antioch, is a prime example); the
interests of Italian city-states for trade and emporia in the Levant; and
the need to escape famine (Lorraine) and pestilence (Bohemia) at home.
For the first time since the decline of the Roman Imperium in the West,
Europe was sufficiently powerful to attack the Muslim East.

The Crusades in many ways are emblematic of medieval Western
warfare. They form a unity in terms of military history and offer a cogent
case study of similar elements struggling over time almost continuously.
And yet, their chronological sweep almost defies analysis in a case study.
Thus, for this case study, the Crusades are divided in terms of time by
being restricted to the First Crusade. This period allows the historian to
compare and contrast warfare in the age of chivalry with that during the
rise of Islam.

The First Crusade should not be confused with a modern-day grand
strategic operation such as Overlord, the Allied invasion of France in
1944. The crusaders drafted no single coordinated strategy, appointed
no supreme commander, devised no complex tactical plans or formations, and after initial conquest promulgated no further coordinated effort at expansion. At times, the irrational dominated, as witnessed by the
emphasis upon the notions of purgatory and indulgences, the combination of apocalyptic frenzy and stark brutality, the miraculous discovery
by Peter Bartholomew of the lance which had pierced Jesus' side and
that allowed Bohemond to turn the tide of battle against Kerbogha, the
Atabeg of Mosul, after the fall of Antioch, and finally the appearance of
psychotic elements in the children's crusade and the pilgrimages of Peter the Hermit and Walter the Penniless. Put differently, the crusaders'
oath to liberate the Holy Grave did not translate into the permanent

occupation of Palestine to defend it. Nor did it translate into practical goals; its force was constantly consumed fruitlessly.

Of course, the moral power of religion was ever present. Crusaders accepted fasting, said prayers, underwent confession, and celebrated mass before as well as after battle. Like Muslims, they equated death through combat with eternal bliss in Paradise. Oaths of brotherhood were sworn and the Cross as well as the Holy Lance served as emblems of their undertaking. The intervention of the Virgin Mary in battle was not uncommon in chronicles. Religious orders such as the Templars and the Knights of St. John again underscored the religious motive, as did the customary war cries *Diex aie*, *Saint Sépulchre*, *Christus vincit*, *Christus regnat*, and *Christus imperat*.

Total Christian forces for the First Crusade probably amounted to 12,000 warriors, of whom 1,200 to 1,300 were knights. Muslim armies are estimated at equal strength. At the siege of Antioch in 1097, for example, about 700 knights and 2,000 foot defeated a Muslim army of 3,000. Two years later at Ascalon, 1,200 horse and 9,000 foot constituted probably the largest crusader force put in the field. A typical engagement might encompass 500 to 1,000 knights per side. Contemporary exaggerations, such as Orderic Vitalis's claim that at Antioch (1098) 113,000 men crossed a single bridge in one day, need to be laid to rest. A force of this magnitude would have comprised a column twenty-eight miles long.

While the sources with regard to this violent interaction between East and West are spotty at best, several observations nevertheless are possible. Soldiers of fortune and weapons traders served both sides. The Arabs purchased high-quality Frankish swords and white slaves from the West; the crusaders engaged Muslim, Jewish, and Byzantine physicians from the East. Both sides learned the art of the sapper and miner, the use of siege instruments and liquid fires. The knightly concept of chivalry was paralleled by the Islamic notion of *farsia*. Perhaps the crusaders benefited from two Byzantine tracts they encountered: Maurice's *Strategikon* (580) and Leo the Wise's *Tactica* (886–912). But both tracts were designed for a well-drilled and professional army. In feudal Europe, however, armies tended to be temporary and amateur.

It would be absurd to suggest that either side enjoyed a technological or doctrinal edge. Technological change, in fact, was minimal during this period and no battle was won due to the clear-cut effect of a superior weapon. At best, both sides endlessly altered old weapons or combinations of the same, with the result that tactics likewise differed little over time. One can speak of "superiority" only in terms of the superiority of the man on horseback over the soldier on foot.

The problem of supply devolved upon the Italian city-states, and it would not be amiss to state that western sea power was decisive for the success of the First Crusade. The Genoans sent a fleet to assist in the siege of Antioch, and the Pisans by 1099 had joined in the Levant trade. But the principal middlemen between Latin Christendom and the Levant were the Venetians. In 1100 they resupplied the crusaders at Haifa with a fleet of one hundred ships, thus launching what would become their overseas empire. Four years later, the Venetian Arsenal became the prototype of a modern supply center, featuring specialization for craftsmen, standardization of replaceable ship parts, and stockpiling of spare parts. These innovations gave Venice the edge at sea.

The financial costs of the Crusade were met by a combination of church tithes, alms, the sale of horses and weapons of deceased princes and prelates, special legacies and gifts for the liberation of the Holy Land, private princely funds, and money secured from those who opted to buy out of the pilgrimage. But funds often were insufficient to meet the needs of the crusaders. Contemporary chroniclers noted that famine, followed by severe colds, swollen feet, and rotting teeth, plagued the Franks throughout the First Crusade. Other diseases and plagues undoubtedly beset the host of knights in the Levant.

Loot and plunder were routine. At Dorylaeum in 1097 the crusaders prayed: "Be of one mind in your belief in Christ and in the victory of the Holy Cross, because you will all become rich today, if God wills." The desire and need to loot often detracted from the main thrust of a campaign. Armies slowed down to plunder towns and fertile fields. Booty had first to be gathered, then usually melted down, and finally hauled to safety. Above all, the high costs of mount, armor, and weapons had to be met. Loot and prisoners taken for ransom were a convenient way to make ends meet—despite stern punishments for plundering (loss of ears and nose) established by the leaders of the First Crusade.

In terms of what may loosely be defined as "operations," both sides practiced limited warfare. Each tried with economy of effort to attain the immediate objective of a single campaign; complete overthrow of the adversary was not a war aim. Despite reckless fury in combat, the Muslim chronicler Usamah noted: "Of all men, the Franks are the most cautious in warfare." The reasons for this were manifold. Encamped at the fringe of Muslim Asia, the crusaders could hope to seize but a few coastal bastions. The conquest of Arabia was beyond their wildest ambitions. Victory often proved an illusion. Muslim armies usually disbanded after each campaign and before winter, only to reappear in force the following spring. The acquisition of castles and walled towns, then, constituted the highest prize of warfare. Most importantly, the Franks were keenly aware that the consequences of defeat were immense: loss of bases, castles, and horses.

The crusaders customarily subdivided their army into a number of smaller units and then concentrated them on the field of battle in a prearranged order. They understood that it was critical to maintain solidity and cohesion of marching order. At Antioch in 1098, for example, the crusaders marshaled their forces in four divisions, each consisting of two squadrons, changing from column to line as they approached the enemy. The following year at Ascalon, however, the Franks approached the Muslim enemy in nine squadrons (acies) organized into three ranks of three squadrons each as vanguard, middle, and rearguard. This square formation allowed them to repel a hostile surprise attack equally on all sides. But at Ascalon the Franks assumed the offensive. They attacked the Fatimids of Egypt in a carefully devised order: bowmen and foot preceded knights and harassed the enemy sufficiently to allow several decisive charges by six separate squadrons of knights. Mixed combat (horse and foot) came about by accident rather than design as the high casualty rate among horses in the desert terrain forced many knights to deploy as foot soldiers. In short, there existed no standard operational order.

Tactically, the role of infantry in the First Crusade remains in dispute. Foot is mentioned in the documents only when put to rout and massacred. Yet, at Dorylaeum (1097) it deployed a thick forest of lances to rally its own retreating knights, but the next year at Antioch, it bolted at the mere sight of runaway horses. Infantry's role on the battlefield included dispatching dismounted Muslim knights, assisting its own knights back into the saddle, carrying the wounded to the rear, and killing scattered Saracen mounts. Undoubtedly, foot fought as well as could be expected since defeat or surrender meant captivity and slavery. By contrast, the unskilled rabble that followed Peter the Hermit and Walter the Penniless on the First Crusade was slaughtered with reckless abandon by mounted Muslim marksmen.

Psychological warfare became a regular feature of the First Crusade. At Dorylaeum the Franks recalled the fierce battle cries and the "barbarous sound" of their adversaries. At Antioch they slew several hundred

Muslims and paraded their severed heads on pikes as trophies. Again, at Nicaea, the crusaders cut off the heads of their foes, fixed them on pikes, and paraded them publicly in order to weaken Muslim morale. At other times they hurled the heads of their fallen foes off castle walls as a sign of disdain. Islam, for its part, replied not only with similar atrocities but above all with utter contempt for the Christians. The chronicler Ibn Jubayr noted with regard to Acre, the chief port of the crusaders: "But it is a land of unbelief and impiety, swarming with pigs and crosses, full of filth and ordure, all of it filled with uncleanliness and excrement." Crusader princes in former Muslim lands were accorded the special term *mutamallik*: one who pretends to be a king. Bedouins, especially, held the crusaders in contempt. Perhaps because they lacked the elaborate protective armor of their opponents, they questioned their valor: "The Franks wear armor because they fear death!"

The capture of Jerusalem in 1099 is a classic study of defense and siege warfare—as well as of brutality. The city was defended by a force of Fatimid Muslims numerically superior to the crusaders, thus denying the Occidentals the option of blockading the city and thereby starving it into submission. Their leader, Godfrey of Bouillon, decided to attack Jerusalem's powerful fortifications. The crusaders deployed mangonels to hurl liquid fire against the hay and cotton protection that the Muslims had placed around the city's towers. Scaling ladders, small wooden castles with catapults on wheels, a battering ram, and a traditional siege tower were deployed against the walled enclave. The Muslims, in turn, bombarded the approaching towers with stones and liquid fire. There was a lack of water and the Franks suffered fearfully from the heat of a desert sirocco. Finally, Godfrey led his force over a wooden drawbridge from the siege tower to the city's walls. Others scaled the wall with ladders. Jerusalem fell between July 13 and 14, 1099. The conquest gave occasion to a great massacre of Muslim men, women, and children. The Dome of the Rock and the Mosque of al-Aqsa were desecrated. The Jews, who were said to have assisted the Muslims, were burned in their chief synagogue. Thereupon, the Soldiers of God marched in their blood-soaked tunics to celebrate their deeds at the Church of the Holy Sepulchre.

It might be profitable to close with a contemporary account of the crusader way of war by Anna Comnena, daughter of the Byzantine emperor Alexius I. After the capture of Antioch in 1098, she noted of the Franks, whom she called Celts: "They have no military discipline nor

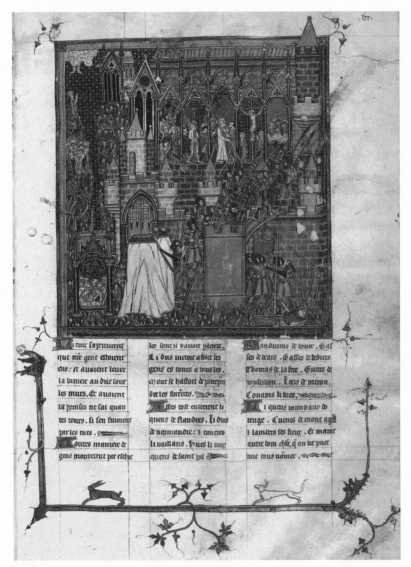

Fig. 4.3. "Christian Warfare: The Sack of Jerusalem, 1099." Bibliothèque nationale de France, Paris.

strategic skills but as soon as they have to fight and do battle, a raging fury seizes their hearts and they become irresistible, common soldiers and leaders alike. They hurl themselves with invincible impetus into the midst of the enemy ranks as soon as the latter give a little ground." The

Emir Ousama-ibn-Munquidh concurred fully: "Anyone who knows any-thing about the Franks looks on them as beasts, outdoing all others in courage and warlike spirit, just as animals are our superiors when its comes to strength and aggression." But such warlike spirit and aggres-sion were not limited to either Latin Christendom or the Levant.

In conclusion, the case study of the First Crusade while in some re-spects a "black swan," nevertheless offers insight into at least four of the five subthemes of this book: the idea of war, the impact of technological innovation on warfare, the nature of armies, and the experience of the soldier.

Suggested Reading

Books on medieval warfare are legion. A brief overview can be gleaned from Lynn White Jr., *Medieval Technology and Social Change* (London, 1962). The me-dieval military system in general can be found in William H. McNeill, *The Pur-suit of Power: Technology, Armed Force, and Society since A.D. 1000* (Chicago, 1982); Sir Charles Oman, *A History of the Art of War in the Middle Ages,* 2 vols. (New York, 1924); and Philippe Contamine, *War in the Middle Ages* (London, 1984). Jean Froissart, *Chronicles* (New York, 1968), offers a highly readable account of medieval warfare, as does John Keegan, *The Face of Battle: A Study of Agincourt, Waterloo and the Somme* (New York, 1976). Martin van Creveld, *Technology and War: From 2000 B.C. to the Present* (New York, 1989), is a basic nuts-and-bolts tabulation of the weapons of war as they evolved over the last three millennia. The two major sources for this section were J. F. Verbruggen, *The Art of War-fare in Western Europe During the Middle Ages: From the Eighth Century to 1340* (Amsterdam, 1977), and Hans Delbrück, *History of the Art of War: Within the Framework of Political History,* vol. 3, *The Middle Ages* (Westport CT, 1982). The latter is especially useful for its cogent analysis of knighthood as a social caste.

With regard to Islamic warfare, the best work in this field, unfortunately, remains in German: Nicolaus Fries, *Das Heerwesen der Araber zur Zeit der Omai-jaden nach Tabarî* (Tübingen, 1921). This slender but brilliant volume deserves translation for it details the military system of the Omayyaden Caliphate in 923 in a lucid and rational manner. Its closest rival in the English language is G. H. A. Juynboll, trans., *The History of Al Tabari,* 13, *The Conquest of Iraq, Southwest Persia, and Egypt* (Albany, 1998); see also Fred McGraw Donner, *The Early Is-lamic Conquests* (Princeton, 1981). Hans Delbrück's *History of the Art of War,* vol. 3, *The Middle Ages,* is disappointing on the Arabs in light of the author's masterly treatment of warfare in the age of chivalry in the same volume. V. J. Parry and M. E. Yapp, *War, Technology, and Society in the Middle East* (London, 1975), offers some nice comparative views of Franks and Saracens.

General background material on Islam is available in G. E. von Grunebaum, *Classical Islam: A History 600–1258* (London, 1970); *The Cambridge Medieval History*, vol. 2, *The Rise of the Saracens and the Foundation of the Western Empire* (New York, 1913); Bernard Lewis, ed., *Islam from the Prophet Muhammed to the Capture of Constantinople*, vol. 1, *Politics and War* (New York, 1974); and Oman, *Art of War in the Middle Ages*, vol. 1. A brief summary of the genesis of Muslim warfare can be gleaned from John W. Jandora, "Developments in Islamic Warfare: The Early Conquests," *Studia Islamica*, vol. 64 (1986): 101–13. The technical side of Islamic warfare has been examined by David C. Nicolle, "The Military Technology of Classical Islam," unpubl. Ph.D. diss., University of Edinburgh, 1982. Finally, a new analysis of the Islamic military system has been offered by Daniel Pipes, *Slave Soldiers and Islam: The Genesis of a Military System* (New Haven CT, 1981).

The interaction of Christendom and Islam has been studied by Bernard Lewis in *The Muslim Discovery of Europe* (New York, 1982), while the Byzantine reaction to Islam has been superbly analyzed by Walter E. Kaegi Jr. in his pioneering study *Byzantine Military Unrest 471–843: An Interpretation* (Amsterdam, 1981), as well as in a series of edited essays, *Army, Society and Religion in Byzantium* (London, 1982). Another useful study is Mark C. Bartusis, *The Late Byzantine Army: Arms and Society, 1204–1453* (Philadelphia, 1992).

The classic history of the First Crusade remains Steven Runciman, *A History of the Crusades*, vol. 1, *The First Crusade and the Foundation of the Kingdom of Jerusalem* (Cambridge, 1951). Also still useful is *The Cambridge Medieval History*, vol. 5, *Contest of Empire and the Papacy* (New York, 1926). William H. McNeill, *Venice: The Hinge of Europe 1081–1797* (Chicago, 1974), sketches in the role of the Italian maritime states in providing the logistical support for the Crusade. Jean de Joinville and Geoffrey de Villehardouin, *Chronicles of the Crusades* (New York, 1982), offers a richly descriptive account of an albeit later Crusade. The military aspects of the First Crusade are provided by R. C. Smail, *Crusading Warfare (1097–1193)* (Cambridge, 1956); and Verbruggen, *Warfare in Western Europe During the Middle Ages*. Lewis, *The Muslim Discovery of Europe*, again offers insights into the interaction between East and West during the First Crusade. The Byzantine view is readily available in Anna Comnena, *Alexiad*, trans. E. A. S. Dawes (London, 1928).

5. EASTERN STYLES OF WARFARE
The Mongols, India, China, and Japan

War took place primarily within the context of state formation and modernization for the societies involved in Eastern warfare. Hence every aspect of society tended to be involved in this process, while the experience of individuals and soldiers was frequently brutal as armies used strict discipline and terror tactics to gain their ends. There was also an attempt to formalize rules of warfare, made more difficult in this period by the fact that armies were forced to grapple with and adapt to the development of gunpowder weapons. Culturally, this proved to be a serious problem for all the societies involved. Indeed, Japan actually gave up the gun and reverted to a pregunpowder stage of warfare, while China delayed its adaptation to these weapons. On the other hand, some Moghul emperors adapted rather well to gunpowder warfare. Hence, technical change was of crucial importance in this period.

While land warfare in medieval western Europe was built around knights on horseback, together with foot archers and siege techniques as required, Eastern styles of warfare at the same time showed striking differences. The most obvious difference was the presence of light cavalry armed with the composite bow, which dominated central Asia for centuries. And the most successful of these Eastern approaches to warfare was practiced by the Mongols, who created the largest continuous land-based empire in history. Their expansion also involved invasions of other major Eastern powers, some of whose styles of fighting will also be considered in this chapter, namely, India, China, and Japan.

The Mongols
Mongol power was first established by Temuchin, the future Chingiz Khan (c. 1167–1227). After a very difficult childhood, Temuchin managed to unite the tribes of Mongolia by 1206, at which time he was

acclaimed Chingiz Khan, or emperor of the Mongols, at a *quriltai*, or gathering of Mongol princes. Chingiz then embarked on a series of expansionary wars, partly because of the need to employ his newly organized army; partly for preemptive reasons, to secure his borders (particularly against the Chin government of northern China); partly for trade reasons; partly simply to obtain plunder; and partly because of a sense of religious destiny, namely, that the Mongols would "conquer every country in the world." Chingiz is reported to have said that his supreme joy was "to chase and defeat his enemy, seize his total possessions, leave his married women weeping and wailing, ride his gelding, use the bodies of his women as a nightshirt and support, gazing upon and kissing their rosy breasts, sucking their lips which are as sweet as the berries of their breasts." At his death in 1227, Chingiz controlled an area from the Caspian Sea across to the Pacific Ocean, including northern China. However, it does not seem that Chingiz intended to create an empire, and so, strangely enough, his conquests can be seen as creating an accidental empire. Ultimately, at its greatest extent around 1280, the Mongol empire stretched from Hungary to Korea and included most of Asia, apart from India and some stubborn areas in southeast Asia.

What was the secret of Mongol success in war? It was not technical superiority; in fact, the Mongol weapons of compound bow, sword, axe, and lance were similar to others of the time, and indeed initially the Mongols were actually deficient in siege weapons and techniques. Nevertheless, Mongol soldiers were strictly disciplined and fought with great tenacity, while their tactical skills as light cavalry were exceptional. Their commanders were appointed according to merit and showed a high level of tactical and strategic ability. In addition, the logistical and organizational aspects of Mongol campaigns were carefully worked out. Finally, the impact of the enormous size of Mongol armies was important. Despite the small Mongol population base of only around seven hundred thousand, which was obviously insufficient for major campaigns against areas the size of China, the Mongols compensated by mobilizing a high percentage of the available males over the age of twenty and under the age of sixty. Then, by incorporating the soldiers of defeated populations into their armies, and later, under the khan Ogodei (1229–41), by enforcing a kind of *levée en masse* of conquered populations serving as infantry auxiliaries, the Mongols were able to put into the field armies of two to three hundred thousand men. Mongol army size did vary considerably according to need and local populations, and in many cases,

Fig. 5.1. Chingiz Khan, founder of the Mongol Empire. National Palace Museum, Taipei, Taiwan, Republic of China.

the large numbers often quoted by contemporaries included reservists as well as active soldiers. Nevertheless, large Mongol armies, formed of nomadic Mongol cavalry, infantry auxiliaries from captured sedentary areas, and conscripted Muslim or Chinese siege crews, did frequently have an impact through sheer mass.

These large numbers were controlled by structuring both the Mongol army and the auxiliaries in a decimalized system, a method that was not new since nomads of the steppes had used decimalized forces for centuries. Chingiz Khan applied this idea to his army between 1203 and 1206, with ten men designated as an *arban*, one hundred as a *jagun*, one thousand as a *minghan*, and ten thousand as a *tumen*. An army usually consisted of three or more *tumen*, and in a major campaign often three armies—of the west, center, and east—operated separately, coming together at crucial junctures. However, just because an army operated with three *tumen*, it did not mean that that the army consisted of thirty thousand men because *tumen* were never at full strength and often considerably under strength, especially among the auxiliary forces. Thus, three *tumen* might actually only consist of fifteen thousand men. Whatever the actual number, one of the main reasons behind this decimalized system, besides military efficiency, was Chingiz's effort to overcome tribal loyalty by creating stronger ties to military units, especially at the *minghan* level. In the same way, Chingiz created an imperial guard, called the *keshig*, which numbered ten thousand men by 1206 and which also cut across tribal lines. It was a great honor to belong to the *keshig*, which provided military commanders and administrators for the growing empire and which formed a group with specific loyalty to Chingiz himself. In general, Chingiz was innovative by removing loyalty from the tribal structure and focusing that loyalty on himself.

Mongol armies were all-cavalry armies until the invasion of China, when siege specialists and auxiliary infantry were added. Originally, under Chingiz Khan, the army consisted of light and heavy cavalry. The light cavalry dressed in blue or brown leather tunics called *kalats* and possibly had a cuirass of lacquered leather strips. On their heads they wore cone-shaped hats of fur and leather, with each tribe sporting a different design or color. The heavy cavalry switched to iron helmets on active service and wore a coat of mail with oxhide or iron strips covered in leather. Additionally, all Mongol soldiers wore a long undershirt made of silk, which prevented arrows from penetrating too deeply as well as permitting the soldier to withdraw the arrow from the wound by carefully drawing out the silk and untwisting it along the same path the arrow had originally taken.

Both light and heavy cavalry carried their most important arm—the compound bow, made of layers of bone and sinew and with a range of 350 yards. The Mongol soldier also used the thumb lock, a device whereby the string was drawn back by a stone ring worn on the right thumb, which released the string more quickly and powerfully than simply with the fingers. Each Mongol carried two bows hung on the left side, one for short range and one for long range. A variety of arrows were used, light arrows for long range and heavy arrows for short range, whistling arrows for signaling, incendiary arrows for creating fires, and three-foot armor-piercing arrows with tips hardened by plunging them into salt water after heating. Other weapons carried included a lasso, a dagger strapped to the inside of the left forearm, and a wooden shield. The light cavalry also carried a small sword and javelins, while the heavy cavalry used a long curved sword, an axe, and a twelve-foot lance with a hook near the tip for unhorsing opponents. Finally, the Mongols looked after their cavalry horses very well, and each soldier usually campaigned with a string of five remounts following behind as well as a herd of remounts following each *tumen*. Mongol soldiers preferred to ride mares, for their milk, and, if necessary, the rider could also cut the haunch of his horse and drink the blood.

Mongols rode even before they could walk and learned to live on their horses for days on end, subsisting on dried meat, millet, yogurt, and koumiss (fermented mare's milk). Originally Mongol soldiers were not paid but lived on plunder, which was divided up according to strict rules. In fact, the soldiers contributed a tax-in-kind to their commanders, called the *qubchur*, for the maintenance of poor and disabled soldiers. Later on, when the empire ceased to expand and plunder was no longer available, Mongol khans such as Khubilai (1260–94) in China resorted to the time-honored system of granting agricultural land to military households and exempting them from half of the annual tax required of civilians. These military households also had to provide their own military supplies, and this, together with their half tax and military duties, proved a serious burden. Mongol armies were strictly disciplined, with flogging for minor offences and beheading for major offences. For example, according to a Western observer: "When they are in battle, if one or two or three or even more of a group of ten run away, all are put to death, and if the whole group of ten flees, the rest of a group of a hundred are all put to death if they do not flee, too. In a word, unless they retreat in a body, all who take flight are put to death. Likewise, if one or two or more go forward boldly to the fight, then the rest of the ten, if they do not follow, are put to death. And if one or more of the ten are captured, their companions are put to death if they do not rescue them."

Another Western observer noted the quiet discipline and confidence with which the Mongols around the 1270s struck camp:

And if the chieftain wishes to move camp, when midnight is passed, he orders the drum to be struck and the man who is allotted this task grasps two wooden maces in his two hands . . . and strikes as hard as his strength and breath allow him to do. . . . Immediately, great and small prepare their horses and put their equipment on them. After a good interval, the drum is beaten for the second time, then they strike their tents and load up all their possessions, and the divisions assemble, and those who advance on the outside go in the vanguard and after them the others in order right up to the chief who comes last or in the middle. . . . Then the drum is struck for the third time and the vanguard moves off and all the others follow, in very good and regular order. Nor would you ever hear any outcry or uproar except for the horses' hooves, for no one dares to exclaim or shout when the camp moves nor can any man ride in front of another except according to the order prescribed for the divisions. When the camp is led off in this way, a set of people allotted to the task, search through the whole area occupied by the army to collect up the things that have been forgotten. . . . Those who have lost something ask these search parties about it and bring witness and guarantor. Thus they recover by pledged word all the things they have forgotten and lost.

Helping to create the discipline and order of the Mongol army was the ritual of the great hunt, which trained the army in the strategy and the tactics of encirclement. At the beginning of each winter, when the Mongols were not on campaign, the great hunt was organized: a starting line eighty miles long was marked with flags set up to mark the collecting point for each *tumen*, and, hundreds of miles away, a finish line was established. Lasting for three months, the army drove forward, keeping the animals in front of them, and then sent two wings out in order to encircle the animals. Gradually, the circle tightened, with penalties for any soldier that allowed an animal to escape. On the final day, the khan fired the first arrow, and all the animals except for the scrawny ones and those that were permitted to live were then killed for food over the winter. The great hunt provided training in coordinating the actions of three armies over hundreds of miles—in communicating by flags, by burning torches at night, and by couriers—and in methods of encirclement. Other strategies employed by the Mongols included the use of surprise, via large-scale ambush or the unexpected appearance of swift armies; the Napoleonic style convergence of armies after hundreds of miles of maneuver; the well-known nomad and Turkish tradition of the false retreat; and the psychology of terror, by which the extensive massacre of citizens after the capture of certain cities presumably persuaded other cities to capitulate without offering resistance.

In regard to terror, an infamous example is Baghdad, where the Abbasid caliph initially refused to surrender in 1258. When the city was taken and sacked by the Mongols, two hundred thousand or more citizens were massacred, in particular Muslims by the Christian auxiliaries of the Mongol army. The caliph and his sons were reportedly rolled into carpets and trampled to death by horses, following Mongol tradition that royal blood should not be spilled. This particular terror strategy seems to have worked, for following the example of Baghdad, many Muslim princes of the Middle East came in to the Mongol commander's camp to offer submission and several towns, such as Damascus, accepted Mongol terms.

In battle, the Mongol army advanced with a vanguard of light cavalry, with wings of light cavalry on the flanks, and these engaged the enemy first. Behind the vanguard were two ranks of heavy cavalry and, behind them, three ranks of light cavalry. After the vanguard pinned the enemy, the main body of light cavalry rode through the ranks of heavy cavalry and approached the enemy but did not charge. Instead, they rode across the front, discharging arrows in an attempt to break up the enemy front. If this was accomplished, the light cavalry moved to the flanks and the huge camel-borne kettle drum known as the *naccara* was beaten to sound the attack of the heavy cavalry, which then charged home and routed the enemy. If this frontal attack failed, another tactic, known as the *tulughama*, or flanking maneuver, was employed, by which the light cavalry attacked one of the flanks of the enemy followed by the heavy cavalry that galloped around to charge the same enemy flank. Another favorite battle tactic was the use of the *mangudai*, or false retreat light cavalry group. In front of the army the *mangudai* charged the enemy and then fell back in apparent confusion. Sometimes, the *mangudai* was an entire *tumen*, or even an army, as at Savo in 1241. In any case, the idea was that as the enemy pursued the retreating Mongols, an ambush of waiting archers greeted the pursuers, followed by a heavy cavalry charge. Smoke bombs were also used to confuse the enemy and to shield the ambush. Although Mongol opponents knew of the common false retreat trick, it is surprising how often this tactic worked.

In one area the Mongols were deficient: siege techniques. On the plains of central Asia there was no need for siege weapons, but the cities of northern China presented a serious problem when Chingiz invaded in 1211. Quickly recognizing the problem, Chingiz conscripted Chinese craftsmen and engineers, who showed the Mongols how to operate the light Chinese-type catapult, which required forty men to pull back the ropes connected to the wooden arm under tension, while the heavy catapult required one hundred men. These catapults had limited ranges of 100 to 150 yards, and their missiles were small, ranging from two to twenty-five pounds. However, after the fall of Samarkand in 1220, Persian and Middle Eastern catapults were copied, meaning that the catapult operated via a counterweight, like the Western trebuchet, and longer distances and heavier stones could be used. Chingiz also used other traditional means of besieging cities, such as bribery and deception, cutting off supplies by surrounding the walls, mining, and assault through escalade. In addition, the Mongols forced prisoners either to advance in front of them as a human shield as they stormed the walls or to do dangerous siege work such as filling in moats and ditches or building approaches to the walls. These methods worked well enough, and northern China was conquered by 1234. Later, under the khan Mongke in 1252, all Chinese metal workers, carpenters, and gunpowder makers were registered as catapult operators, and these formed the basis of the one thousand catapult crews who accompanied the Mongol armies to Persia in 1253.

Even so, when Khubilai Khan decided to defeat the Sung of southern China, he experienced great difficulty with the siege of Hsiang-yang, which lasted from 1268 until 1273. This city was located on the Han River and was the major obstacle en route to the Yangtze River basin. Hsiang-yang was defended by a castle, a strong wall, and a deep moat on the landward side and was also protected by another town on the opposite bank of the Han River. Naturally, the Han River supplied water as well as a route for resupply from the south for Hsiang-yang. The Mongols attempted to starve the city and were forced to build five hundred ships to prevent supplies coming up river. But the defenders of Hsiang-yang had ample supplies of food, and the siege engines being used were obviously insufficient.

In 1271, Khubilai appealed to his nephew the Il-Khan of Persia for help, and two Muslim siege experts, Isma'il and Ala al-Din, arrived in late 1271. These engineers built two large siege engines on the spot, a catapult and a mangonel. These trebuchet-type machines soon reduced the town across from Hsiang-yang, and in early 1273 the two Muslims set up another large engine at the southeast corner of the city itself: "The missile weighed 150 catties [pounds]. When the machinery went off the noise shook heaven and earth; everything that [the missile] hit was broken and destroyed." With this, the walls of Hsiang-yang crumbled and the defenders surrendered.

The Mongols then carried on a similar catapult-style conquest of the Sung towns and fortifications of southern China, under their excellent general Bayan. Most towns capitulated, but those that did not were destroyed by the catapults and flame throwers (naphtha hurled by the trebuchet-style machines) designed by the two Muslim engineers. This siege campaign was successfully concluded by 1276, when the Sung Empress Dowager surrendered the royal seal to Bayan. But what is notable is that even with fifty years of experience neither the Mongols nor their Chinese allies were able to build siege engines good enough for the job. Instead, they relied on imported Middle Eastern experts, who alone brought the five-year siege of Hsiang-yang to an end and provided the siege expertise for the defeat of the rest of Sung China.

The Mongols were extraordinarily adaptable, for example, in the warfare of south China. There, despite heat, lack of fodder for the horses, tropical diseases, and the forests and waterways of the south, the Mongols succeeded, including the building of a viable navy with the help of their expert Chinese and Korean subjects. The Mongols excelled, however, in the large-scale maneuvers and cavalry battles of the open plains.

Battle Scene: Mohi Heath, 1241

A particularly impressive campaign was the Mongol invasion of Poland and Hungary. Under the rule of the khan Ogedei, the great general Subedei planned the Mongol drive westward. In 1237 Subedei invaded Russia, and, by the end of 1240, Kiev and many other Russian cities and principalities had fallen. Subedei then planned a winter campaign for eastern Europe because the Mongols were used to winter conditions and because the frozen rivers were easier to cross. No maps were available, but spies and deserters brought in information about roads, towns, military forces, and sources of food. So early in 1241 Subedei divided his army into four forces, one to go north into Poland to draw off and disperse any threat from the right flank of his main army of three groups. At Liegnitz, on April 9, 1241, Prince Henry of Silesia and his motley army of twenty thousand met the northern force of Mongols, probably of similar or smaller size, and was taken in by the usual Mongol false retreat tactic. Henry and his cavalry foolishly pursued the Mongol *mangudai* and were met by a storm of arrows followed by the Mongol heavy cavalry charge. Behind Henry and his cavalry, the Mongols set off smoke bombs to screen the action from Henry's infantry and disposed of Henry's cavalry. The Mongols then rode through the smoke and shot down the helpless infantry. Prince Henry fled with a small bodyguard, but these were cut down by the Mongol pursuit. Finally, when Henry's horse collapsed, he tried to run in his armor, but he was swiftly ridden down and beheaded. His head was then paraded around the walls of Liegnitz on a lance, but the city held out. Nevertheless, the diversion of attention from the main invasion to the south was achieved.

After the battle at Liegnitz, the Mongols recorded the number of enemy dead by cutting off the right ears of the dead—nine large sacks of ears were thus sent to Batu, khan of the Golden Horde in Russia and nominal commander of the invasion. The northern Mongol force then drew another Western army led by Wenceslas of Bohemia after them, and, finding it too large to fight, they simply broke up into small groups and rode around Wenceslas into Hungary. Meanwhile, to the south, the three Mongol armies of around fifteen thousand cavalry each, moved swiftly, far apart from each other, with the vanguard traveling 180 miles in three days. With excellent communication the three armies met on the Danube near the Hungarian capital of Gran. Subedei decided it would be unwise to cross the Danube under the eyes of the large army of some one hundred thousand that King Bela of Hungary had collected. So, Subedei started a large-scale false retreat—for six days, until the three armies had crossed the Savo (or Sajo) River by the only bridge, constructed of stone—and then continued for ten miles into Mohi heath.

Subedei's plan was to take half the army and recross the Savo River by a quickly constructed wooden bridge to the north and then come in behind Bela's army while at the same time Batu attacked and pinned the Hungarian army across the original stone bridge. At dawn on April 10, 1241, Batu attacked with catapults and flame throwers and perhaps gunpowder bombs, and behind this his cavalry fought for two hours to keep the enemy pinned. At last, Subedei appeared, late because the bridge had taken longer to build then expected, and surrounded the Hungarian army from the rear. But King Bela retained his composure; his army formed into columns and retreated to their fortified camp. Batu had taken heavy casualties and considered retreat, perhaps another false retreat, but Subedei insisted on attacking the camp. The Mongols surrounded the camp and broke down the defenses by catapult, leaving an escape route for the Hungarian army. As the Mongols attacked, many of Bela's knights formed into a wedge and charged. They were met by the usual hail of arrows and then defeated by the Mongol heavy cavalry. The retreat was on, and, as the Hungarian army fled down the escape route, the Mongol light cavalry rode beside the unfortunate fugitives, shooting them down. Soon the road back to the city of Pest was littered with Hungarian dead so that "their bodies were strewn everywhere like stones in a quarry." Some sixty to seventy thousand of King Bela's army were killed, and the road to western Europe was open to the Mongols.

The Mongols actually reached Neustadt near Vienna and summered on the Hungarian plain, where forage for their horses was available. However, in December 1241, the great khan Ogedei died in Mongolia, and Batu and Subedei withdrew their armies from Hungary to Russia. Whether this withdrawal was primarily because of the death of the khan or because the Hungarian plain could not permanently provide sufficient pasturage for the Mongol horses is not clear.

Nevertheless, although the Mongols continued to intervene in Hungary in the 1280s and 1290s, they never again threatened western Europe. Indeed, after about 1260, following the death of the great khan Mongke in 1259, the Mongol empire split into four parts: the Chaghadai khanate in central Asia, the Yuan dynasty in China founded by Khubilai, the Il-Khans of Persia, and the Golden Horde in Russia. The focus had already shifted south and east—to the Middle East and China under Mongke; to China, Korea and the abortive invasions of Japan, Java and southeast Asia under the great khan Khubilai; and once more to the Middle East and northern India by the Turkish-speaking Muslim, Timur the Lame, or Tamerlane (1320s and 1330s–1405). Ultimately, Mongol rule collapsed first in China and Persia but lasted longer in the more nomadic territories of Russia and central Asia.

Tamerlane's conquest of Delhi and northern India was in the nature of a massive plundering expedition. With the same kind of Mongol army as that of the previous khans, Tamerlane successfully besieged various cities in northern India before arriving near Delhi in December 1398. Here, between Panipat and Delhi, the decisive battle was fought, with the Indian forces of Sultan Mahmud Shah relying on 10,000 cavalry and 40,000 infantry, plus 125 war elephants. Tamerlane's army was reported to consist of 90,000 cavalry but was likely much smaller since Tamerlane took considerable defensive precautions to reassure his men. However, the Mongol advance guard slipped in behind the Indian advance guard and caused considerable confusion, while the two light cavalry wings in a double *tulughma* attacked both flanks and caused the left and right Indian wings to break and flee. Then the center of the Indian line, led by the war elephants, drove forward. But the Mongol cavalry archers were told to aim for the mahouts of the elephants and then wound the beasts, while at the same time Tamerlane reinforced his center with the *keshig*, or royal guard. This was sufficient, and "soon one saw the ground strewn with elephants' trunks mingled with the bodies and heads of the [Indian] dead." The Sultan fled, and the next day Tamerlane entered Delhi. At first he restrained his troops, but the inhabitants resisted the Mongol style of plundering, which led to indiscriminate slaughter. Soon vast piles of severed heads arose at the four corners of the city, although in Mongol tradition qualified craftsmen were spared and sent to Samarkand (Tamerlane's capital) to beautify that city. Then Tamerlane departed without leaving any administrative or imperial structure behind him.

India

India was not done with the Mongols, for in 1519 a Transoxanian prince named Babur (1483–1530), a descendant of both Tamerlane and Chingiz Khan, first invaded northern India. Chased out of his homeland around Ferghana by the Turkish Uzbegs, Babur finally succeeded in capturing Delhi and Agra in 1526 and thus founded the Moghul dynasty in India, "Moghul" being a corruption of the word "Mongol." Babur was a cultured individual, besides being an outstanding general. He spoke and wrote both Turkish and Persian and composed much fine poetry as well as music. He loved nature and planned and planted many gardens with fountains and running water. Although a Sunni Muslim, Babur enjoyed parties, drank much wine and arrack, consumed on the four drinking days of the week, and on the non-drinking days, he ate cakes spiced with marijuana. Babur loved his family and children; for example, he religiously visited his aunts every Friday, whatever the weather. Babur was, therefore, an unusual and humane man but, in the spirit of the times, could be ruthless. Thus, when an attempt to poison him occurred in 1527, Babur related his punishment of the guilty: "That taster I had cut in pieces, that cook skinned alive; one of those women I had thrown under an elephant, the other shot with a matchlock. The old woman [the instigator] I had kept under guard; she will meet her doom." In fact, she drowned herself.

With his varied background and cultivated mind, it seemed likely that Babur would bring a masterful touch to the battlefield, and he did. Babur's first main opponent was Ibrahim Lodi, the sultan of Delhi, whose Afghan troops he met on the battlefield of Panipat in 1526. Babur possessed some twelve thousand cavalry, matchlockmen, and artillery, while Lodi put into the field perhaps twice that number of cavalry, plus a large number of elephants. Babur's main strength was in the firepower of cannon and matchlocks, which were new to India. Here Babur was assisted by an Ottoman gunner, Ustad Ali-quli, who had experienced the Ottoman system of chaining together the cannon or carts behind which the cannon fired and behind which the matchlockmen were also protected as they fired and reloaded. In Babur's memoirs, he states that he collected seven hundred carts and that they were joined together "in Ottoman fashion, but using ropes of raw hide instead of chains, and that between every two carts five or six mantelets should be fixed, behind which the matchlockmen were to stand to fire. To allow of collecting all appliances, we delayed 5 or 6 days in that camp." This system seems to have been a useful defensive-offensive method of warfare, and it is notable that in the very same year as Panipat, the Ottomans used an exactly similar system to defeat the Hungarians at the important battle of Mohacs. Babur continued his careful preparations, no doubt to offset the numerical superiority of Ibrahim Lodi: "On our right was the town of Panipat with its suburbs; in front of us were the carts and mantelets we had prepared; on our left and elsewhere were ditch and branch. At distances of an arrow's flight sally-places were left for from 100 to 200 horsemen." In other words, Babur had secured both flanks as well as the center but left room for counterattacks through the center as well as on the flanks. Babur then structured his cavalry forces in the traditional Mongol way—a vanguard (or advance), a center, a left and right center, a left and right wing, two *tulughama* (turning parties of mounted archers) on the two wings to converge on the enemy rear, and a left, center, and right reserve.

The two sides waited for seven days, each hoping to entice the other to attack, meaning that Babur did want to fight a defensive-offensive style battle. Eventually Babur sent off a night attack with some four thousand cavalry that failed to disrupt Lodi's camp but convinced Lodi to launch an attack on April 21. His plan was to cut off Babur from Panipat and then wheel around the guns in the center to take Babur's army in the flank. However, he was not able to do this since Babur sent his reserves to protect that flank while the artillery and matchlockmen were effective in the center. Babur's plan was to send the *tulughama* to the rear of the enemy and for the left and right wing cavalry to attack the flanks. Eventually, Babur's cavalry hemmed in the Afghans so that they "could neither move forward against us nor force a way for flight." Neither did Lodi's elephants do much damage as the mahouts were shot off the beasts by gun and arrow. By noon the Afghans were defeated and had lost about fifteen thousand men.

In Babur's own words, Lodi "was an inexperienced man, careless in his movements, who marched without order, halted or retired without method and engaged without foresight." Reflected in these words is the fact that Babur was a careful general, demonstrating the care, method, and preparation that is the mark of all successful and outstanding military leaders. In addition, Babur's artillery and matchlockmen provided a useful addition to his army, although they were not decisive. Finally, Babur's cautious defensive-offensive formation permitted the best use of his cavalry and firepower. Babur's battle strategy was so successful that when he faced the Rajputs and the remains of the Afghans at the battlefield of Kanwa the next year, 1527, Babur adopted the very same strategy. The Rajputs were led by Rana Sanga, a veteran of many fights who had lost an eye and an arm and had suffered some eighty wounds in his life. Additionally, Sanga outnumbered Babur by two to one or more, plus the usual contingent of elephants. Babur proved even more cautious, digging ditches around his army, setting up the chained carts for the artillery, positioning more reserves than before, and inventing a new wheeled tripod device for his matchlockmen such that it protected the firers but was mobile, giving the matchlockmen the opportunity to advance or retreat.

It is interesting that Babur also used considerable psychology on his troops before this battle, giving a stirring speech to his army, remitting the tax (*tamgha*) on all Muslims, and then personally giving up wine: "And I made public the resolution to abstain from wine . . . The victorious servants . . . dashed upon the earth of contempt and destruction the flagons and the cups, and the other utensils in gold and silver . . . They dashed them in pieces, as, God willing! soon will be dashed the gods of the idolators [the Rajputs], —and they distributed the fragments among the poor and needy." No doubt all this helped the wavering troops, whose morale in the face of the numerous and tough Rajputs was probably low.

As at Panipat, the enemy tried various attacks on the left and right flanks of Babur's army, not being able to attack the center with its interlocking carts, artillery, and matchlocks. Babur skillfully sent reserves as required to his flanks, while it appears that the artillery and matchlockmen had a greater impact on this battle than at Panipat. Thus, when the Rajput cavalry charges had been blunted, Babur ordered the *tulughama* to envelop, while the household cavalry issued out from behind the left and right of the carts of the center. Surprisingly, the carts and the artillery, and the matchlockmen with their tripods, were also ordered to advance: "The matchlockmen of the royal center, in obedience to orders, going from behind the carts into the midst of the battle . . ." and "Just at this time came an order from his Majesty . . . that the carts of the center [the artillery] should be advanced." The Rajput army also suffered some defections during the battle, but in any case they had no answer to the advancing artillery and matchlocks and were surrounded by the usual *tulughama* and cavalry wings. Soon the survivors fled toward the nearby hills, and the victory was so complete that the Rajputs never threatened Babur again.

Babur was also unusual in his attention to technology and encouraged Ustad Ali-quli to create a foundry in order to build mortars for use against enemy forts. One such attempt was reported: "Round the mortar-mould he [Ustad] had had eight furnaces made in which were the molten materials. From below each furnace a channel went direct to the mould. When he opened the furnace-holes on our [Babur's] arrival, the molten metal poured like water through all these channels into the mould. After awhile and before the mould was full, the flow stopped from one furnace after another. Ustad Ali-quli must have made some miscalculation either as to the furnaces or the materials. In his great distress, he was for throwing himself into the mould of molten metal, but we [Babur] comforted him, put a robe of honor on him, and so brought him out of his shame." As it turned out, after the mould cooled, the main chamber was found to be without defect, while "to cast the powder-chamber is easy," said Ustad.

Babur was thus a general who understood all aspects of warfare and appreciated the problems of individuals. The result was that Babur conquered all of northern India. Not so capable was his son, Humayan, who lost two battles to the Afghan Sher Shah, due primarily to Humayan's incompetence. However, Humayan was succeeded by perhaps the greatest Moghul emperor of all, Akbar (1556–1605).

Akbar was an exceptional monarch because of his military abilities and successes, his great tolerance of other religions and ideas, including Hinduism, his love of learning and of the arts (despite being illiterate), of his enquiring and visionary mind, which resulted in his creation of a new emperor-centered religion of the sun, and because he was a capable administrator, who organized the structure and economy of the Moghul empire in an efficient manner. Akbar considerably widened the Moghul empire by expanding it to the coastline of Baluchistan, Sind, Cutch, and Kathiawar in the west, to central India in the south, and to Bengal and Orissa in the east. Akbar also understood the strategic value of fortresses, and he constructed four large forts, guarded by artillery, at Allahabad, Lahore, Ajmer, and Agra, that were virtually impregnable. These formed a large square in the center of the Moghul empire and anchored the defense of the empire. Akbar then made sure to destroy those forts that offered a challenge to Moghul supremacy, and the successful sieges of Chitor and Ranthambor signaled to all that none could defy the emperor. In the many campaigns to suppress rebellions or extend the empire, it is noticeable that Akbar often left the conduct of these campaigns to trusted commanders and did not accompany them himself. However, Akbar did move about his empire with his army and did lead the attack on the two major fortresses mentioned above.

The Moghul army on the march attracted the attention of many observers. Just as in the Ottoman Empire of Suleiman, the huge army as it crossed the territories of Akbar emphasized the power and authority of the emperor. Some one hundred thousand soldiers and camp followers accompanied Akbar as he campaigned, including fifty thousand cavalry, five hundred war elephants, twelve thousand matchlockmen of the standing army, and some thirty-five thousand infantry. Later on, as Akbar's empire increased, these numbers would have been even larger. The mobile artillery at one time consisted of only twenty-eight field guns, but larger siege guns were either produced at the siege site or were drawn on platforms by oxen and elephants. In regard to logistics, Akbar used agents to scour the countryside for food, and local merchants and traders were encouraged to come to the bazaars in the encampment with supplies to trade. As in Alexander the Great's time, emissaries were also sent ahead to local chiefs and princes along the way with requests for submission and orders to gather food supplies for the army or suffer reprisals. Surprisingly, given the size of the royal encampment and army, the logistics system worked. Equally, given the possibility of confusion due to the size of the army, the encampment on the march was so organized that each camp was set up in a similar fashion. For example, "The guards for Thursday, Friday and Saturday encamp in the center; those for Sunday and Monday, on the right; and those for Tuesday and Wednesday, on the left." Moreover, three hundred scouts were sent out to a distance of eighteen miles at all points of the compass to keep watch and to check the route, while sappers and miners were sent ahead to level roads and build bridges.

Discipline was strict but fair in Akbar's army, as one incident shows: a scout had been sent ahead to see if a river crossing was feasible but had relied on village accounts rather than seeing for himself. So,

> the King ordered him to be seized, dragged to the place which he had told him to go to, bound prostrate on an inflated bag of ox-hide, and launched upon the river. When the report of this was spread through the camp, almost the whole army flocked to the river-side to see this strange sight. The officer was being carried hither and thither in the middle of the river at the mercy of the current. He was weeping, imploring pardon with miserable cries, and trying to move the King to mercy. As he was carried past the royal pavilion, the King gave orders for him to be rescued from the river, entered in the inventories as royal property, exposed for sale in all the bazaars, and finally auctioned as a slave.

In regard to administration, Akbar perfected the *mansab* system, adapted from the Mongol decimal system, in which all officers in the imperial system were awarded a personal *zat*, or rank. This rank defined a person's status, pay, privileges, and titles and was strictly at the discretion of the emperor. Later, in the 1590s, another decimal rank came into use, the *sowar*, or trooper ranking, by which each *mansabdar* was required to produce a certain number of heavy cavalrymen according to their ranking. *Mansabdars* were required to recruit, pay, train, and maintain this cavalry with up to as many as five thousand horse and were in turn paid by the emperor. This system shifted the problem of maintaining a large standing army to those individuals in imperial service and yet centralized authority with the emperor. Eighty-five percent of Akbar's budget was devoted to *mansabdar* salaries and only 9.5 percent to the royal or central military establishment. Meanwhile, Akbar's imperial household, with all its size and pomp, only took up 5 percent of the budget. Moreover, because of the constantly expanding empire, income exceeded expenditure by around 4.5 percent.

Akbar also organized, ordered, and structured his empire to an extraordinary degree. Every aspect of his empire was reduced to ranks and categories. For example, Akbar gave minute instructions with regard to the amount of food to be fed to the animals of the court (war elephants, cavalry horses, transport camels, etc.) and then introduced regulations for measuring the fatness and leanness of each animal, plus rules for fining the attendants who allowed each animal to deviate from the norm: "His Majesty first determined the quantity of daily food for each domestic animal, and secondly determined the results, which different quanta of food produce in the strength of the animal." An investigator then reported on each animal, and "His Majesty then inspects the animals himself, and decreases or increases the degrees of their fatness and leanness as reported, fixing at the same time the fine for leanness. . . . The leanness of an elephant has been divided into thirteen classes."

Akbar paid particular attention to his war elephants for their symbolism and value in battle, and his contemporary biographer, Abu Fazl, states: "Experienced men of Hindustan put the value of a good elephant equal to five hundred horses; and they believe that, when guided by a few bold men armed with matchlocks, such an elephant alone is worth double that number." Nevertheless, in battle the elephants were placed in the rear behind the infantry and matchlockmen, who were themselves behind the three divisions of cavalry in the front of the army. This location of the elephants was to ensure that they did not panic and run amok. Behind the elephants were the substantial reserves of the army, who were often the key element of the battle, either in ambush or as the impetus of the final surge to victory. On the other hand, Akbar frequently used the elephant charge as a battle-winning tactic, for example, in 1567 against the rebel Bahadur.

The matchlockmen were also significant, for Akbar paid great attention to muskets and cannon. Akbar established a musket foundry and inspected himself the muskets that were produced. The fact that his standing army contained twelve thousand matchlockmen, although their numbers were only one-quarter the size of the traditional cavalry, indicates their rise in importance. There is also a significant suggestion in Abu Fazl's biography that Akbar's gunsmiths actually invented a flintlock: "guns are now made in such a manner that they can be fired off, without a match, with a slight movement of the cock." Cannon also were made in Akbar's foundries or were purchased from Westerners. They were distributed around the kingdom to protect Akbar's forts, while separate cannon and mortars were made for siege work. Although Akbar's forces engaged in numerous battles of imperial expansion or against rebels, a greater effort was probably expended against enemy forts, for these really controlled areas of country, and their reduction was essential to winning a particular campaign.

One such campaign entailed the conquest of the state of Mewar in Rajputana, whose reduction would mean the eventual conquest of all of Rajputana. The capital of Mewar was Chitor, and in October 1567, Akbar arrived to capture the fort at Chitor. But the ruler of Mewar adopted scorched earth tactics and then departed for the hills, leaving eight thousand Rajput warriors and forty thousand peasants to defend the fort. The fort itself was a large structure, on top of a high hill and well-supplied with water and provisions. Akbar did not have a large siege train, and, with the aid of his surveyors, Akbar initially surrounded the fort with defensive lines, which took a month. Then several assaults were launched, but these could not overcome the fire of the defenders. Akbar then decided to capture the fort in a methodical manner. Thus, mines were dug toward the key points of the walls, and a *sabat* was started toward one part of the walls. *Sabats* were a unique feature of siege warfare in India, in which a covered passage was constructed above the ground in zigzag fashion toward the walls. Through this covered passage, soldiers could pass protected from arrows and missiles. At Chitor, the particular *sabat* was so "extensive that ten horsemen abreast could ride along it, and it was so high that an elephant rider with his spear in his hand could pass under it." Meanwhile two mines were set off, but one mine was delayed in its firing, which destroyed the storming party of some five hundred Moghuls. Akbar also caused a large mortar to be cast at the site, since it would take too long to bring mortars from the central artillery park. The chronicler notes that when the garrison of the fort became aware of this mortar, "the smoke of astonishment suffused their obfuscated brains." Akbar himself then went to the *sabat* to encourage his soldiers and seizing his favorite gun, "Sangram," fired at an aperture where a marksman was doing damage to the *sabat* workers. Akbar had shot and killed Ismail, the chief of the musketeers at the fort. Similarly, as the chronicler adds, "H. M. [Akbar] killed many of the noted members of the garrison and sent them to the sleep of annihilation." Finally, the *sabat* reached the wall, a concerted attack with mines was made at several points, Akbar also reportedly shot the leader of the garrison, and soon the *johar* fires were burning inside the fort, indicating that the Rajputs' principal women were going to their death on funeral pyres, while the men prepared to fight to the death. At dawn on February 23, 1568, Akbar entered the fort with three hundred elephants, and after fierce fighting, some thirty thousand defenders were slain.

Chitor had fallen, and soon after another hitherto impregnable fort, Ranthambor, was taken by Akbar in 1569. These forts controlled trade routes west to the Arabian Sea and illustrate the significance of forts in India in the Moghul period. Similarly, the capitulation of Burhanpur and the extensive sieges of Ahmadnagar and Asirgarh in 1600 in the Deccan were undertaken because they effectively controlled key routes to the Deccan and were too dangerous to leave untaken in the rear of Akbar's invading army. Akbar never did manage to conquer the Deccan, which was left to his great grandson, Aurangzeb. By his death, Akbar had created a highly effective army built around the traditional light cavalry, but he increased the numbers of infantry, and he appreciated firepower. Thus, his artillery park and musketeers were important parts of the army, and his armories were capable of casting muskets, mortars, and both light and heavy cannon. Many of these were successfully used in the all-important sieges of the period. On the other hand, Akbar remained committed to the traditional large-scale use of elephants in warfare, although these were effective only against lightly armed opponents.

Akbar was followed by Jahangir (1605–27), who succeeded in spending most of the funds amassed by Akbar. Then came Shah Jahan (1627–58), who considerably extended the Moghul empire, restored its finances, and constructed palaces, forts, and gardens in the grand Moghul manner, including the Taj Mahal. Shah Jahan's son Aurangzeb (1658–1707) became involved in a bloody war of succession, particularly with his brother Dara. The French medical doctor Francois Bernier, present at a battle between the two brothers near the River Jumna in 1658, provides a valuable description of the preparations for the conflict: Dara "placed the whole of his cannon in front, linked together by chains of iron, in order that no space might be left for the entrance of the enemy's cavalry. Immediately in the rear of the cannon, he ranged a line of light camels, on the forepart of whose bodies small pieces of ordnance, somewhat resembling swivels in our vessels, were fixed. . . . Behind these camels was posted the most considerable part of the musketeers. The rest of the army consisted principally of cavalry, armed either with sabres, and those kind of half-pikes [lances] . . . or with sabres and bows and arrows, which latter weapon is generally used by the Moghuls." Dara's army was formed into three divisions, and Aurangzeb set up his forces in the same manner except that he concealed light artillery on the wings. The battle went Dara's way until he dismounted from his elephant, either from fear or persuasion, which disheartened his followers, and this gave the victory to Aurangzeb.

What is notable about these formations is that the same defensive-offensive chaining together at the forefront of the army was still taking place as occurred in the time of Babur, except that chained carts had been replaced by the recently developed artillery. Meanwhile, apart from the artillery on the wings, much the same emphasis was placed on cavalry as in Babur's campaigns. During his long rule, Aurangzeb went on to improve his artillery, dividing it into heavy and light pieces and initially paying foreigners to serve the arm. For example, on campaign after the royal camp came the light artillery, including some three hundred small swivel pieces on camels, firing a ball of between ten and twelve centimeters and about sixty small field pieces made of brass. The latter, according to Bernier, were "mounted on a well-made and handsomely painted carriage, containing two ammunition chests, one behind and another in front, and ornamented with a variety of small red streamers. The carriage, with the driver, was drawn by two fine horses and attended by a third horse, led by an assistant driver as a relay." Bringing up the rear came about seventy heavy cannon, mostly brass, drawn by oxen and elephants and not always capable of following the royal progress in the mountains or across rivers. However, it seems that Aurangzeb paid little attention to his musketeers, for Bernier notes that they received the lowest pay and cut a "sorry figure at the best of times . . . when squatting on the ground, and resting their muskets on a kind of wooden fork which hangs to them. Even then, they are terribly afraid of burning their eyes or their long beards, and above all lest some Djinn, or evil spirit, should cause the bursting of their musket." Bernier went on to note that Aurangzeb employed a large number of cavalry, perhaps two hundred thousand in the whole empire, but that the infantry were few and in the royal army numbered only some fifteen thousand, mostly musketeers and artillerymen.

Thus, it seems that Aurangzeb preferred a rather traditional army, except for a certain amount of emphasis on his artillery. However, on achieving the throne, Aurangzeb proved to be an austere and puritanical Muslim who continued to expand the empire but also spent twenty-five years engaged in a difficult war against an increasingly powerful force in the south—the Marathas.

The Marathas were a Hindu warrior society that unified under the direction of a talented leader, Shivaji (1627–80). Shivaji introduced a patriotic tone to his cause, calling for a Hindu empire, a Maratha kingdom, and a land of virtue and honor. He undercut feudalism, pulled down the castles of local tyrants, did away with hereditary appointments, and rejected the jahgir system of payment by land grants. Instead Shivaji created a standing army and navy that were well disciplined and paid. With regard to discipline, for example, Shivaji ordered that women, Brahmans, and cows were not to be touched, and female slaves and dancing women were forbidden to enter army camps. As one European visitor noted in 1671, Shivaji "was extraordinarily careful that no woman should be in his army; and if he happened to find one, he immediately turned her out, first cutting her hair and ears." Then in regard to pay, Shivaji obtained his funds by forcing a *chauth*, or tax, on conquered and neighboring lands, which was then used to pay his forces.

Shivaji understood the limitations of his forces, so in his land warfare against the local sultans of Bijapur and then against the Moghuls he relied mainly on swift raids by light cavalry and infantry. Due to cost and because of the hilly terrain, Shivaji's army consisted of more infantry than cavalry, and perhaps for the same reasons, his army was deficient in artillery. But the high morale of his forces and their mobility made them equal to the heavy cavalry and the efficient artillery of the Moghuls. Defensively, to maintain security in his empire, Shivaji understood the strategic value of forts to guard passes, valleys, and hilltops, and he either built or obtained by force or bribery a network of 240 forts throughout his domains by 1671. These forts were to prove a sore trial to Aurangzeb when he sent armies south to defeat Shivaji.

Shivaji delighted in daring raids. For example, he led four hundred men into the Moghul-controlled town of Puna in 1663, where they entered the Moghul governor's palace at night. Shivaji himself entered the governor's bed chamber and narrowly missed killing him in the dark, although he did cut off the governor's thumb and three fingers. At other times, Shivaji led raids on Moghul towns such as the port of Surat, where in 1664 he spent six days plundering the town of goods and treasure. Later, in 1670, he repeated his raid on Surat, this time as a major assault and made off with another rich haul. But when Aurangzeb decided to launch a large-scale offensive against Shivaji, the Maratha chief could not meet the superior Moghul army in battle nor prevent the successful siege of one of his major forts, Purandar. Shivaji was forced to surrender this fort after sapping, mining, and the use of siege artillery under the Italian Manucci made its fall inevitable. Thus, Shivaji was forced to make peace with the Moghuls, giving up twenty-three forts and eventually going to the Moghul capital, then at Agra, as a virtual prisoner.

However, Shivaji engineered a daring escape in disguise and returned to Maratha territory. Here, he consolidated his power and made an uneasy peace with the Moghuls. But this agreement did not prevent his troops from recapturing the Moghul-held Lion fort through the unusual expedient of having a large iguana scale the sheer walls with a rope tied to it. Then in 1674, after four years of successful raiding and financial rewards from the *chauth*, Shivaji crowned himself as a Hindu monarch and thus asserted his independence from the Muslim Moghuls. Shivaji then embarked on further campaigns to conquer the Carnatic coast and Mysore but fell ill and died in 1680.

Shivaji succeeded by building a strong financial base through constant raiding, expansion, and taxation; by creating a spirit of nationalism and discipline among the Marathas; by focusing on adaptable light infantry armed with muskets, swords, and bows, apparently a more significant arm than his cavalry; by avoiding large-scale battles with the Moghuls; by creating a navy; and by organizing a defense-in-depth system of fortresses. However, he was deficient in artillery and could never overcome this obstacle, despite attempts to acquire cannon from Surat and Golconda.

Indeed this was a problem for both Shivaji and Aurangzeb, who generally relied on foreigners for their artillery expertise, although the Moghuls did cast their own cannon. At the same time, the Moghuls innovated with their use of mobile camel-borne swivel guns. Both Moghuls and Marathas adapted reasonably well to the matchlock musket and learned to make their own matches, but they were slow to convert to the flintlock. However, conversion to the flintlock was also backward in parts of Europe. In the manufacture of gunpowder, the early use of Indian gunpowder, probably in the thirteenth century for pyrotechnics and later for siege mining, enabled Moghuls and Marathas to make their own powder, although it was not well corned and did not retain its potency in storage. Overall, in regard to gunpowder weapons, it seems that both Moghuls and Marathas were content to take the sensible course of borrowing the technology and expertise whenever needed while building their own cannon as far as possible. Musketeers, however, were not well regarded, probably because of the unreliable technology of the muskets themselves. Moreover, if traditional armies and weapons worked well and if opponents did not force alterations by innovation, why change?

By the early eighteenth century as the Moghul empire fell prey to internal feuds, it is clear that there was confusion over the role of gunpowder weapons. While equal numbers of infantry and cavalry took the field, the infantry were divided into footsoldiers, bowmen, and matchlockmen, and on one occasion in 1722 the rebellious Raja of Ajmer produced a force of twelve thousand men mounted on camels, each camel carrying one matchlockman and one archer. Earlier, in 1720, the emperor Muhammad Shah, mounted on an elephant, conducted a large-scale battle against rebellious nobles, where the idea of warfare was to advance the artillery first, behind which the foot soldiers initially sheltered. If the contemporary Hindu chronicler Das Lakhnawi is to be believed, even this was problematic, since the Imperial army commander was forced "to give gifts to gunners, matchlockmen and musketeers, and rewarded them for each volley they fired. As the artillery advanced immediately the troops occupied the ground in its rear. The artillery men, being encouraged by the gifts and presents and the generosity of Haidar Quli Khan [the commander of the royal artillery], fired one of the guns at the time and (simultaneously) loaded the other."

The obvious shortage of artillery may be due to a lack of mobile artillery or to the sheer difficulty of moving the huge cannon of the time. Again, Das Lakhnawi remarks of a particular siege in 1719 where the artillery train was so enormous that one cannon, nicknamed the Lord Champion, firing balls of eighty pounds weight, required "four big elephants, [and] fourteen hundred draught oxen." Another cannon, named Fort Opener, delivering balls of one hundred pounds weight, needed four elephants and seventeen thousand oxen to draw it along. Since it had rained heavily, these and other cannon took twelve days to cover a distance of one *kuroh*, part of the problem being that houses and shops in the town of Akbarabad had to be pulled down to make way for the passage of the cannon. Generally, it seems that in the 1720s the integration of muskets into the Moghul army was about fifty years behind similar developments in Europe, while the reduction in size and weight of siege cannon was about a century behind.

Nevertheless, later in the eighteenth century, the Maratha, Mysore, and Moghul successor states were forced to make considerable efforts to overcome their gunpowder deficiencies to deal with the British. Only in hindsight, after the large-scale arrival of Europeans, does it appear that the earlier Moghuls and Marathas should have done more in adapting to gunpowder weapons. The exception is siege artillery, which proved its value at an early stage, although development afterwards lagged, as indicated above. And, as in other areas of his life, Akbar was unusual among the Moghuls in his positive attitude to gunpowder weapons.

However, the Moghul empire began to crumble in the late seventeenth and early eighteenth centuries, partly due to Aurangzeb's lengthy and costly wars in the Deccan against Shivaji's successors, partly due to internal rebellions and conflicts, especially four destructive wars of succession, and partly because of clever Maratha tactics. These tactics consisted of Maratha light cavalry attacks and raids against the forts and garrisons of Moghul power in the 1730s. The Marathas controlled the countryside, while the Moghuls could not move out of their forts and garrisons. Through this the Marathas slowly built up their strength until they could meet the Moghuls in battle, for example, at Bhopal in 1738.

The Maratha empire continued to prosper after Shivaji's death and eventually engaged in three wars against the British in the late eighteenth and early nineteenth centuries. While initially successful, the large Maratha armies, with cavalry predominating, found they could not ultimately defeat the better-disciplined British forces, and finally in 1819 the Maratha princes were subjugated and their lands annexed.

China

Meanwhile, another huge power to the east, China, although initially conquered by the Mongols, threw off Mongol rule in the 1350s and 1360s. The chief leader of this revolt was Chu Yuan-chang, a former monk who entered Peking in 1368 and founded the Ming dynasty. Known as the Hung-wu emperor, he exacted strict discipline in his army. Hung-wu in his earlier days used to say: "When I was still a Mr. Nobody in the army, I was disgusted to notice how among the leaders there was such lack of discipline. Later on I was promoted to the command of an army in which all the soldiers were newly enlisted. One day when I was leading them out to fight, two of the men disobeyed me. I immediately ordered them to be executed. From then on, all submitted to my commands with trembling and no one dared violate my orders. Nothing is impossible to a man of strong will." Later in his reign, in 1389, Hung-wu ordered that officers who allowed their sons to spend time singing songs instead of learning to ride horses and use the bow were to have their tongues cut out. Those who played chess or football were to lose arms or feet. This kind of discipline apparently produced useful soldiers and many good generals from among the officer class.

Besides discipline, Hung-wu instituted the *wei-so* army system, with the purpose of producing a powerful army that did not link the army to ambitious commanders. Thus, each prefecture contained a military district called a *so* responsible for providing 1,128 soldiers, while a military district covering two prefectures was called *wei* and produced 5,600 soldiers. Eventually, this system produced around 1 million soldiers. The military staff (Wu-chun tu-tu fu) were responsible for keeping the military registers of the country, while the central Board of War mobilized the relevant districts and set strategy. The idea was that troops were mobilized according to need from across the empire, and commanders were chosen from the military staff. When the campaign was over, the commanders lost their commands, while the troops returned to their *wei-so* districts. Hence, no commander could build up loyalty within a particular army and pose a danger to the state.

In order to pay for this system, soldiers were given land in order to be self-sufficient. Thus, soldiers generally supplied their own equipment, and sons were obliged to follow army service in hereditary style. At any one time, only 20 to 30 percent of the soldiers were actually on duty, the rest farmed and produced enough grain to pay for the whole *wei-so* system, including the officers. Hung-wu boasted that "I keep a million soldiers without causing my people to spend one penny!"

Unfortunately, later Ming rulers were not so capable; emperors became absolutist and isolated from reality; corruption crept into the system so that far fewer soldiers and horses were actually available than the military register indicated; and during and after the reign of the emperor Yung-lo, self-interested eunuchs gained too much power. As a result, there occurred such disasters as the T'u-mu incident of 1449. In this case, the problem started with the young and foolish emperor Cheng-t'ung, who was dominated by the eunuch Wang-Chen, who in turn basically ruled China. The 1449 T'u-mu incident occurred at this time because the perennial problem of the Mongol frontier reasserted itself, due to the activities of the ambitious Mongol khan Esen. Despite a considerable effort to rebuild the Great Wall during the last decades of the fourteenth century, the northern frontier remained unstable. This was due to a number of factors: the incompatibility of Mongol nomad and Chinese sedentary agricultural societies; the inability and disinterest of Chinese emperors in regulating frontier trade so that the nomads were frequently cheated; the naturally chaotic nature of the frontier, so, for example, some Chinese generals initiated attacks against the nomads simply in order to obtain greater reputations and rewards for themselves; and perhaps the imperative needs of the nomads for particular Chinese supplies such as iron and grain, which forced the Mongols to raid at certain times.

However, in 1449 Wang Chen proposed that the Mongols be taught a lesson for their recent raids, following on from Mongol dissatisfaction, even humiliation, over Wang Chen's trading practices with them. Wang Chen advised that the emperor accompany the large-scale campaign that he proposed to lead against the Mongols. The Ming army comprised around half a million men, but morale was poor, Wang Chen was exceedingly unpopular, and the route northward beyond the Inner Great Wall experienced almost continuous rain. Eventually, Wang Chen was forced to turn back before the emperor's army reached the Outer Great Wall and before the Mongols had been punished.

The Mongols, however, had other ideas, and in a classic Mongol ambush and encirclement, they surrounded the Ming army near T'u-mu and cut it off from water supplies. In confusion, the huge Ming army collapsed under a rain of Mongol arrows, Wang Chen was killed, or perhaps murdered by Chinese officers on the field of battle, and the emperor simply sat down on the ground to await his fate. Esen was surprised to find he had captured an emperor but did not know how to exploit the situation. Esen wasted time negotiating for a month, and when he arrived before the walls of Peking, he discovered a new emperor had been chosen and defensive measures undertaken. Thus, the Mongols proved incapable of besieging the city. Esen was obliged to retreat, and eventually he simply released the discredited emperor.

The Ming learned some lessons from T'u-mu but not necessarily the correct ones. The Mongols and the northern frontier became the obsession of the Ming, who focused on military solutions rather than diplomatic or commercial possibilities, while the real threats of the early seventeenth century, internal rebellion and the nomad Manchus, were given less attention. At the same time, the Ming decided to abandon the defense-in-depth concept of northern defense, where forward garrisons beyond the Outer Great Wall provided a flexible response system and established instead a simpler linear defense based on the Great Wall.

Other signs of strain included the decline in the numbers of soldiers actually available to defend the empire. For example, the twelve divisions in Peking, originally 107,000 strong, by 1528 numbered only 54,400, and the original 150,200 horses had fallen to 19,300 by the same date. Yet the Ming empire showed great resilience dealing with Japanese pirates along the coasts in the 1530s and another Mongol assault on Peking in 1550.

A symbol of this Ming tenacity is the generalship of Ch'i Chi-Kuang from the 1550s to the 1580s. Originally posted to the coastal region of Chekiang to deal with Japanese pirates, Ch'i Chi-Kuang recruited sturdy peasant soldiers from inland areas, maintained strict discipline by cutting off the ears of disobedient soldiers or by threatening the death penalty for squads that retreated or failed in their duty, and instituted small infantry teams of soldiers. These teams of twelve men were called "the mandarin duck formation" because the team structure resembled the outline of a duck, but the teams were vital to overcoming the superior close-order fighting skills of the Japanese pirates.

The team was formed of four pikemen, carrying pikes of twelve feet in length. Four soldiers moved ahead of the pikemen, two carrying shields and swords to protect the pikemen, plus another two soldiers carrying long bamboo trees with foliage to obstruct and confuse the enemy. Behind the pikemen were two soldiers carrying weapons that discharged fire arrows. The team was completed by a corporal as leader and a cook-porter. Ch'i Chi-Kuang did not favor firearms because they were unreliable at this date and probably because the pirates could be defeated without them. Ch'i Chi-Kuang's chief battle tactic was to aggressively attack the enemy and, after sustaining initial losses, to keep attacking, at which point the pirates normally lost cohesion and fled.

Ch'i Chi-Kuang eventually built up an army of ten thousand men and, by the mid 1560s, defeated the pirates. He was then transferred in 1567 to the region of Chichou, a garrison city north of Peking. Here, Ch'i Chi-Kuang developed some further intriguing tactics to deal with the cavalry charges and arrow volleys of the Mongols. Central to his idea was the "battle wagon," a large two-wheeled cart, drawn by mules, with wooden screens instead of the normal sides of the cart. In combat, the carts lined up side by side to form a wall, but the end screens acted as swing doors, enabling soldiers to exit and return. Meanwhile each cart carried two pieces of light artillery, called *fo-lang-chi*, meaning "of foreign origin." These artillery pieces resembled European culverins and were three to seven feet long, cast in bronze or iron, with a caliber of two inches or less. The gunpowder was breech loaded in a flask-shaped container, although the lead bullet was muzzle loaded. Matchlock muskets were also used, and both muskets and the artillery were fired from the carts through holes in the screens.

Supporting each battle wagon were twenty men, ten of whom stayed with the cart at all times, maneuvering it and serving the artillery. The other ten formed an offensive team near the wagon, similar in function to the original "mandrake duck formation." Four of the team carried muskets, while the others carried lances or swords to deal with the Mongol horse and rider. The familiar bamboo tree was also carried to project forward and to disorient the enemy. This offensive team was not allowed to move more than twenty-five feet from the wagon; indeed the wagon had to follow should the team advance.

Infantry counterattack was also seen as crucial, with waves of infantry emerging from underneath or between the wagons when the Mongols were thought to be in confusion. Cavalry were used to screen the battle wagons as they formed a square or circle at the beginning of the action and then retreated inside the wagon laager when the Mongols attacked. Occasionally, heavier artillery pieces, including one weighing thirteen hundred pounds and known as "the great general cannon," were carried, this time on four-wheeled carts. The larger cannon fired antipersonnel stones and small iron balls at point blank range. Other weapons carried included a light mortar and fire lances.

According to Ch'i Chi-Kuang, an ideal brigade consisted of 3,000 cavalry, 4,000 infantry, 128 heavy battle wagons, and 216 light wagons. However, it does not seem that this brigade scheme met with much approval, because the empire was focused on defense rather than attack. Ch'i Chi-Kuang was told: "Our main concern is defense. It is already a great achievement if the nomads are contained. As long as you are keeping Chichou peaceful your mission has been accomplished." Unfortunately for the empire, even this was not possible when in the early seventeenth century internal problems and nomad attacks produced grave problems for the Ming.

Then in the 1640s internal rebellions of discontented soldiers and starving peasants led to a successful revolt by Li Tzu-ch'eng, who actually entered Peking in 1644. On the same day, the emperor hanged himself so as not to fall into the hands of the rebels. An imperial army to the north under Wu San-kuei blocked the frontier against the Manchus, who were nomads of the forests of southern and eastern Manchuria. Hearing of the fall of Peking, Wu San-kuei enlisted the Manchus as allies, routed Li Tzu-ch'eng, and entered Peking in turn. However, when he sought to dismiss the Manchus, the nomads refused to leave the capital and declared that the Ming dynasty had forfeited the Mandate of Heaven. The Manchus in 1644 now ruled north China, but in the south Ming princes and warlords maintained their independence. Hence, the Manchu armies turned south and, using the traditional Mongol-style three-pronged offensives, conquered the remainder of China in the 1640s and 1650s.

Partly because of geographical problems, partly because of sieges that the Manchus found difficult to conduct (similar to the Mongols' experience earlier), and partly because the Ming were assisted by the Jesuits and Portuguese with firearms and artillery, this was not an easy conquest. Thus, the Manchus were forced to occasionally change from their normal Mongol-style warfare of cavalrymen using the compound bow to a more gunpowder-oriented style. So the Manchus, like the Mongols before them, began to learn gunpowder technology from their enemies. As early as 1631 the Manchus used Ming defectors and examples of captured cannon to cast their own cannon, and by 1635 they were also using muskets. However, a series of informative pictures from the slightly earlier period of the 1630s in the *Thai Tsu Shih Lu Thu* shows that, even so, the speed and tactics of traditional Manchu cavalry archers and infantry bowmen could still overcome the firepower of Ming cannon and muskets so that the Manchus preferred to use their cavalry wherever possible. Other factors that helped the Manchus were their high morale, while the Ming princes and warlords fought against each other and the local peasants often feared the armies of the Ming supporters more than the Manchu forces, independent bandits often created chaos, and the Ming armies suffered from poor morale and disorganization. Finally, like the earlier Mongols, the Manchus were capable of using terror tactics to induce armies and towns to surrender.

One such example of the latter tactic is the Manchu siege of the city of Yang-chou in 1645. When the defenders of Yang-chou refused to surrender, the Manchu forces used cannon to breach the walls and then instituted a massacre, as one survivor recalled:

> The women wore long chains around their necks, like clumsy strings of beads, and they stumbled at every step so that they were covered with mud. Here

and there on the ground lay small babies who were either trodden under the hooves of horses or the feet of men. The ground was stained with blood and covered with mutilated and dismembered bodies, and the sound of crying was heard everywhere in the open fields. Every gutter and pond was filled with corpses lying upon one another, and the blood turned the water to a deep greenish-red.

Where the sword hilts clattered and fell, waves of bitter cries arose and hundreds begged for their lives. Whenever soldiers appeared, all the southerners, no matter how great their number, squatted down and dropped their heads. None dared to flee, but each stretched out his neck, expecting the stroke of the sword.

Suddenly I saw a very handsome man of less than thirty wearing a Manchu-style hat, a red coat, a pair of black shoes, and carrying a two-edged sword hanging by his side, accompanied by a follower, also very gallant and brave in appearance, wearing a yellow jacket . . . The man in the red coat looked into my eyes and said, . . . "Tomorrow His Highness the Prince [the Manchu military commander] will order the swords to be sheathed and all of you will be spared."

Other sieges, however, were more difficult. For example, the siege of Nan-ch'ang, which lasted for six months in 1648 and 1649, only came to an end when some soldiers betrayed the city and Manchu forces scaled the walls. Evidently, cannon alone were insufficient to take this city. The same thing happened in 1650, when the Manchu forces were obliged to besiege Kuang-chou in the heat and malaria of southern Kuang-Tung province. Despite the heavy use of cannon, this siege lasted eight and a half months, and even then the city defense only collapsed when the Ming commander of a section of the outer wall defected and opened the inner city walls to Manchu soldiers and cannon bombardment. These sieges show that Manchu cannon and siege techniques were not really up to the task and that Ming cities with good defenses could only be taken by deception. Nevertheless, through good discipline, tactics, and strategy, together with corresponding confusion and rivalry among the Ming defenders, the Manchus completed their conquest of south China by 1662.

Thereafter, the Manchu dynasty proved very durable indeed and lasted until 1912. Among the great Manchu emperors, K'ang-hsi (1662–1722) stands out as a forceful ruler who defeated internal revolts and engaged in successful campaigns in Outer Manchuria and Tibet, including a 1685 victory over the Russians at the fort of Albazin. This victory was accomplished through an expeditionary force of fifteen thousand, using 150 cannon and 50 mortars provided by the Jesuits. Indeed, K'ang-hsi benefited considerably from the cannon-founding expertise of the Jesuit father Ferdinand Verbiest in 1675, as a contemporary Jesuit account recalls: "After the Emperor had tried many several ways to no purpose, he saw plainly that it was impossible to force them [the rebel troops] from the places where they had entrenched without using his great Artillery: but the Cannon which he had were Iron, and so heavy that they dared not carry them over such steep Rocks, as they must do to come to him [the rebel leader]. He thought Father Verbiest might be assistant to him in this matter; he commanded the Father therefore to give directions for casting some Cannon after the European manner."

Father Verbiest declined, citing religious convictions. The emperor ordered obedience to his request on pain of Verbiest losing his life and the Jesuits being rooted out of China. Verbiest reconsidered and cast the cannon admirably: "All the Pieces of Cannon were made very light and small, but strengthened with a stock of Wood from the mouth to the breech, and girt with several bands of Iron. . . . This new Artillery did every way answer what they proposed from it. The Enemy were obliged to leave their Entrenchments in disorder, and soon after to Capitulate."

Verbiest cast some 340 of these light cannon in the first year, blessing them liturgically and giving each the name of a saint, which was then inscribed on the cannon. It appears, however, that Verbiest did not actually introduce Western techniques of casting cannon but simply improved on long-established Chinese traditions of producing lightweight cast-iron weapons, in which field they were in advance of Europe. In fact, cast-iron cannon had been made in China from 1356, while Europe could not safely make cast-iron cannon until the second half of the sixteenth century. Similarly, the Chinese were making cast-iron mortars and large bombards in the 1370s. However, Chinese bureaucracy regarded gun founding as a secret art, and this may have restricted the development of Chinese methods of casting cannon. By the early sixteenth century, Portuguese breech-loading cannon arrived in China, and, over the course of the sixteenth century, European artillery came to be imitated in China. Although Western visitors in the late 1500s continued to be impressed by Chinese artillery, by 1600 the lead over the West in cannon technology was evaporating, and in the early to mid-seventeenth century, Chinese emperors were relying on the highly educated Jesuits and on Portuguese detachments of artillerymen to produce and operate artillery.

All of this occurred despite a long Chinese lead in gunpowder production, since "fire arrows" and "fire cannon" were already in use in the twelfth century. Similarly, Chinese rockets appeared by 1340, and "rocket arrows" were especially significant between 1550 and 1580. Exploding bombs containing caltrops and "ground rats" of gunpowder that ran across the floor were also in use by the first half of the fourteenth century, with vividly descriptive names such as the "bandit-burning vision-confusing magic fireball." But Chinese gunpowder was low in nitrates and therefore lacked punch, and for this reason it did not develop in artillery use ahead of other countries.

It seems also that while the first Chinese handgun appeared in 1288 and various devices were used intermittently for the next two hundred years, nevertheless, the first muskets arrived from Turkey around 1530 and were followed by Japanese and Portuguese models. The Chinese then developed double-barreled muskets and even muskets with three to five rotating barrels. These were all matchlock muskets, and what is most striking is that there did not then occur a flintlock period, as in Europe around 1700. Instead, China went directly from the matchlock musket to the percussion cap and cartridge rifle of the mid to later nineteenth century. Indeed, the first modernization of Chinese arms since the seventeenth century only took place in 1864, when Li Hung-Chang equipped his army with fifteen thousand foreign-made rifles. Once again, an early lead in technical military development in China already had begun to slow down around the fifteenth century, and by the time of the Opium War (1840–42), China was vulnerable to the military technology of the West.

A similar situation occurred with naval developments. The famous voyages of Cheng Ho between 1405 and 1431 as far as the Indian Ocean, the Persian Gulf, Aden, and the east coast of Africa were ahead of European capabilities at the time. Some of Cheng Ho's oceangoing junks measured 517 feet in length by 212 feet in width, were built with four decks, and contained watertight compartments. The compass, originally used in China to locate proper burial places for the dead, was readily adapted to long-range voyages. Additionally, these junks carried naval cannon for defense and offense. But the voyages were discontinued suddenly, the immediate reasons being cost and the fact that the northern frontier now demanded all the attention of the state.

However, deeper cultural reasons were more significant. First, the Chinese were unusually self-centered in a cultural sense and felt no need or motivation to explore or discover other lands. Second, there existed a traditional anticommercialism in China, which looked down on merchants as exploitative and parasitic and saw no virtue in merchants or explorers going overseas to ply a trade. Third, Chinese scholars and bureaucrats believed that China was self-sufficient economically and needed nothing from foreign lands. Hence by 1500, Europe had once again overtaken China, this time in maritime affairs.

Thus, the fundamental reason why Chinese technical military evolution fell behind the West seems to be cultural. Chinese tradition consistently elevated *wen* (literate culture) over *wu* (military force). Unity, hierarchy, peaceful order, scholarship, bureaucratic control, self-discipline: all were extolled above warfare and the military as ideals. Confucian teaching stressed the classical ideal of the individual who attained his ends without violence. Moral authority rather than physical force was revered. In order to preserve the social order, the first level of control was through education, in which each person understood how to act and live peacefully in a social hierarchy. The second level of control was a social system of rewards and punishments. Only as a last resort would the state revert to the third level of control—military persuasion. But for the emperor to actually use violence to preserve order was an admission of failure, he was incapable of properly pursuing the art of government so that *wen* operated rather than *wu*. In this atmosphere, military technology was seen as a low priority and indeed could often be left to degraded foreigners. In the last resort, uniformity, common ideals, stability, and the status quo were more important than technical development.

Japan

Strangely enough, a different scenario with similar results was the case of Japan. Japan was a country even more isolated than China, and developments in the art of war took place through internal processes until the arrival of firearms via the Portuguese in the 1540s. In fact, the military history of Japan through the arrival of gunpowder seems to have evolved through four internal stages. Initially, warfare in the eleventh and twelfth centuries featured mounted warriors—the samurai—carrying swords and lengthy compound bows. The samurai were originally the retainers of wealthy landlords and simply served the landowners in a feudal-style relationship. The word *samurai* comes from the verb *samurau* or *saburau*, meaning "to serve," which generally meant military service. As with the knights of the feudal west, the samurai developed a number of formal rules of warfare, such as individual combat, formalities before the battle, and rules of conduct set down later as *bushi-do*, the way of the warrior.

One example of early samurai formality was the tendency for well-known samurai to introduce themselves to the enemy before a battle, often as a challenge to individual combat. Thus, at the battle of Ichi-no-tani in 1184, Kajiwara Kagetoke introduced himself to the enemy (incorrectly as it happened), by shouting out: "Ho! I am Kajiwara Heizo Kagetoki, descended in the fifth generation from Gongoro Kagemasa of Kamakura, renowned warrior of the East country and match for any thousand men! At the age of sixteen I rode in the van of Hachiman-taro Yoshiie at the siege of Sembuku Kanezawa in Dewa and, receiving an arrow in my left eye through the helmet, I plucked it forth and with it shot down the marksman who sent it, thereby gaining honors and leaving a name to posterity!"

Another less attractive feature of samurai warfare was the tradition of cutting off the heads of the enemy, whether they were wounded or dead. This was done in order for the victorious general to view the heads afterward to make some kind of count of the defeated and for the simple honor of demonstrating one's prowess in warfare by carrying off the head of one's opponent as a trophy. An example of the ritualistic quality of this tradition occurred in 1562 at a battle wherein a general named Ota Sukemasa got into individual combat with a samurai called Shimizu. Because he was already wounded, Ota was thrown to the ground, but Shimizu tried in vain to cut off Ota's head. At this turn of events, Ota, his eyes flashing with anger, cried out: "Are you flurried, sir? My neck is protected by a Nodowa [an iron neck piece]. Remove this, and take off my head." Shimizu bowed and replied: "How kind of you to tell me! You die a noble death. You have my admiration!" But just as Shimizu was removing the Nodowa, two of Ota's retainers ran up and threw Shimizu to the ground, where in a reversal of affairs, Ota then decapitated Shimizu.

One other aspect of samurai warfare has attracted attention: the tradition of *hara-kiri*, or suicide, as an honorable way to end one's life. Suicide was often undertaken when a battle was lost or when no other possibility of continuing the fight was possible. The tradition appears to start with the giant samurai Tametomo in the mid-twelfth century, but the most celebrated case concerns Minamoto Yorimasa, the leader of the Minamoto clan who fought against the Taira clan during the Gempei war (1180–85). At the battle of Uji in 1180, the Minamoto were defeated, and Yorimasa, wounded in the arm, rested in the Phoenix Hall of the nearby Byodo-in country villa. While his sons held the gate against the Taira, Yorimasa, aged seventy-four, wrote a farewell poem on his war fan:

Like a fossil tree from which we gather no flowers
Sad has been my life, fated no fruit to produce.

Yorimasa then cut open his stomach and soon died. A retainer cut off his head, fastened stones to it, and sank it in the river where no Taira could find it. Yorimasa's eldest son then followed suit. This tradition of honorable suicide continues throughout Japanese history, although in later times it was sufficient to make an initial stomach cut and then a retainer would take off one's head.

The initial stage of Japanese warfare not only included the elite samurai cavalry but there were also unmounted soldiers who were farmers recruited for a particular campaign. These farmers normally tilled the samurai's rice fields and were poorly equipped, generally with spears or pikes. There must have been large-scale recruitment at times, for armies during the Gempei war sometimes numbered in the tens of thousands. Another weapon for dismounted warfare, generally favored by the fighting monks of the time, was the *naginata*, a heavy glaive, with a blade four feet long.

The strategy and tactics of the early period featured mobility, with the samurai cavalry moving swiftly in flanking movements, ambushes, pursuits, and unexpected appearances. This mobility was combined with a gradual replacement of the continued formality of warfare in which individual combat or combat in carefully numbered groups or in small melees shaped the battlefield.

At the critical battle of Kurikara in 1183, during the Gempei war, the Minamoto forces sent picked groups around to the rear of the Taira army. Then, to gain time, the Minamoto indulged in formal archery duels with the Taira, followed by combat between thirty, fifty, and one hundred selected samurai. While this was happening, the Minamoto prepared a herd of oxen with pine torches bound to their horns, which were then lighted as dark fell. The Minamoto then attacked from front and rear, assisted by the oxen so that the Taira fled down a narrow valley, as the Minamoto anticipated. Here they were slaughtered, although probably not in the numbers cited in a contemporary chronicle: "Thus did some seventy thousand horsemen of the Taira perish, buried in this one deep valley; the mountain streams ran with their blood and the mound of the corpses was like a small hill; and in this valley, it is said, there can be seen the marks of arrows and swords even to this day."

Formal styles of warfare, especially individual combat, received a further blow from the Mongol invasions of 1274 and 1281. The Mongols taught the samurai a lesson in integrated tactics in their 1274 invasion, although the Mongols did not have the strength to take over Japan. The second, much larger invasion force landed at the same place as before, Hakata Bay, but this time the Japanese erected a long wall behind which they defended desperately. The Mongols suffered considerable losses and were forced to re-embark. Moving along the coast to meet up with another Mongol fleet, both fleets were overtaken by a typhoon off Takashima. This kamikaze, or divine wind, on August 15, 1281, probably sank most of the Mongol fleet and thus saved Japan. Still, these invasions helped prepare for a new, second period of war in Japan, which emerged in the fourteenth and fifteenth centuries. Here, warfare left the formality of the past still further behind and also turned away from long-range cavalry campaigns. Instead, conflict tended to occur between neighboring princes, where larger armies on foot were capable of offensive and defensive operations, because they generally did not have to move large distances. In addition, siege warfare became increasingly important, which again put a premium on dismounted actions.

In the lengthy fourteenth-century war between the Courts, loyalty all but disappeared so that samurai values also largely declined. Finally, in the first half of the fifteenth century, the Japanese peasant farmers staged a series of peasant revolts, using the system of mutual defense leagues called *ikki*. Warrior monks also successfully revolted against the samurai in the later fifteenth century. In addition, peasant soldiers, the *ashigaru*, discovered that joining a local army was more profitable than farming, and they too contributed to the trend known as *gekokujo*—the low oppress the high.

Given all these developments, the fourteenth and fifteenth centuries saw a much greater emphasis on foot combat so that samurai dismounted and fought with a short-bladed *naginata* and a long sword, called a *no-dachi*, with a four-foot blade. Foot soldiers relied on the bow and the spear. These weapons were useful in the Onin War, which commenced in 1467, between two major clans in Kyoto, the Yamana and the Hosokawa. The war was unusual in that it was fought mainly in the city of Kyoto, and it evolved into a battlefield reminiscent of World War I in that there was a neutral zone with a trench twenty feet wide and ten feet deep separating the contestants. The two clans fought behind barricades and made surprise attacks or attempted to burn out their opponents. Each side recruited some eighty thousand soldiers, and the war dragged on for ten years. Even here, aspects of formality continued so that after a particularly fierce day's fighting, a small but desperate band of defenders holding the Goryo shrine area, under one Masanaga, sent a message for help to his ally: "We are exhausted from the day's battle. . . . Would you please send me a cask of sake? I will present it to Masanaga and will attend to his final banquet. Then we will cut our bellies together. One more thing. A number of our arrow bearers got lost . . . and never reached camp. Could you supply us with some arms?" However, the messenger only returned with a single arrow, meaning that the fight should continue. So Masanaga and his remaining men gathered their dead together, set fire to them and the Goryo shrine, and escaped through the undergrowth.

Ultimately, the leaders of the two clans died, and the Onin War wound down. But a new period of warfare ensued, the age of the country at war, from 1490 to 1600, when central authority was absent and major families fought for control of large areas of Japan and ultimately for control of Japan itself. During this third period of warfare, three features of war become prominent: the importance of castles, the introduction of firearms, and the increased size of armies. This may be seen as a military revolution similar to that going on in the West.

During the second half of the sixteenth century, castle building accelerated, partly as a response to the introduction of cannon and firearms, partly due to the economic consolidation of local feudal lords (*daimyo*), and partly due to the *daimyo's* desire to use the castle as a symbol of wealth and power. The most famous example is the Azuchi castle, built by the leading warlord of the time, Oda Nobunaga. He began work on the castle in 1576 and developed a huge structure, with four concentric baileys, that was a mansion as well as a defensive castle. Similarly, castle towns developed, for example, Hachigata castle, as described in the late sixteenth century: "The main castle fronted on a river bank, the other sides being protected by moats and embankments. Around the castle were the dwellings of samurai, merchants, and craftsmen (especially those engaged in arms production), and peasants. The inner sector of the town was filled with inns, markets and shops, while on the edges of the town were temples and shrines."

Finally, it is clear that castles and fortifications became offensive weapons in warfare as a way of penetrating and holding an area. Similarly, castles provided an interlocking system of defense for an area, and all major lines of communication were guarded by castles. Hence, castles and sieges became all-important in Japanese strategy. As in other lands, sieges of these castles used the same wide variety of techniques such as bribery, flooding, mining, starvation, scaling ladders, palisades, "tortoise shell" wagons, and direct assault, although cannon were used sparingly.

Hand-held firearms, however, revolutionized warfare in Japan due to the adaptability of such men as the celebrated warlord Oda Nobunaga. The first and most celebrated battle in which matchlock muskets proved decisive was the battle of Nagashino in 1575.

Here Nobunaga offset the cavalry of his opponent, Takeda Katsuyori, by fielding ten thousand musketmen. Nobunaga picked his three thousand best marksmen and lined them up in three ranks of one thousand each, with instructions for each rank to fire volleys alternately, because of the slowness of reloading the matchlocks. They were also to fire only when the enemy was close, because of the inaccuracy of the muskets. Finally, a palisade was constructed in front to protect the musketmen and to prevent the cavalry leaping over them. Gaps were left every fifty yards or so in the palisade, to permit counterattacks. The palisade and the musketmen were placed in the center of the line, and a "bait" of two groups of samurai were placed in front of the palisade to draw Takeda's cavalry onward. The battle went exactly as Nobunaga planned, and Takeda's cavalry fell in heaps under the measured volleys of the musketmen, although there was also a good deal of hand-to-hand fighting in traditional style. Nagashino revolutionized warfare in Japan, although muskets continued to be reserved for lower-class soldiers, while the samurai still preferred sword, bow, and spear.

Then, to complete the military revolution, by the late sixteenth century, armies became much larger, reflecting the consolidation of power by the leading warlords such as Nobunaga, Hideyoshi, and Iesayu. Hideyoshi, who eventually unified Japan under one central government, was able to put armies of 250,000 men and more into the field by ordering his daimyo to conscript set numbers of peasants and townsmen as pikemen and by having the power and finances to organize large scale

Fig. 5.2. *The Battle of Nagashino*, 1575. Tokugawa Art Museum, Nagoya, Japan.

logistics. For example, Hideyoshi's 1589 Hojo campaign required two hundred thousand *koku* of rice (one *koku* equals five bushels), carried by ship to the campaign area, plus the provision of ten thousand gold coins to purchase rice along the campaign trail. Additionally, thousands of pack horses were hired to carry the rice inland from the sea ports. Similar to Europe, it appears that the largest armies won the battles.

The unification of Japan was completed in 1590 by Hideyoshi (1536–98), due partly to clever generalship, partly to his keen diplomatic skills, and partly to his command of vast armies and resources. But Hideyoshi did not rest there, because he had already turned his attention to no less a project than the conquest of China via Korea. The reasons for this campaign are obscure, perhaps to use Hideyoshi's army (which was unemployed) at home, perhaps to expand the land bank for use as rewards to samurai and daimyo, or perhaps because of the economic need to obtain direct trading relationships with China and Korea. Most likely it was simply Hideyoshi's ambition to create an empire. As he told the Korean envoys in 1590, explaining why he wished to obtain free passage through

Korea to China: "Taking wings like a dragon, I have subdued the East, chastised the West, punished the South, and smitten the North. Speedy and great success has attended my career, which has been like the rising sun illuminating the whole earth. . . . I will assemble a mighty host, and invading the country of the Great Ming, I will fill with the hoar frost from my sword the whole sky over the four hundred provinces. Should I carry out this purpose, I hope that Korea will be my vanguard."

Unfortunately for Hideyoshi, Korea had no intention of becoming a vanguard and certainly did not want to allow Japanese forces to simply march through Korea. Instead, Korea prepared for war while Hideyoshi did the same. In 1591 he set up a base at Nagoya, on the northwest coast of Japan. The plan was for seven divisions, totaling 140,000 men, to invade and occupy Korea, then three more divisions, totaling another 52,000 men, were to land and join up with their comrades for the actual invasion of China. Another 100,000 men formed the garrison at Nagoya. All of these men were supplied and paid for by the northern daimyo, while the daimyo whose lands bordered the sea supplied the junks to ferry this army across. More junks following behind carried vast supplies of rice and beans as well as horses for the cavalry.

Fortunately for the Japanese, no Korean ships contested the invasion, and, once landed at Pusan, the Japanese divisions rapidly advanced on Seoul, the capital of Korea. The Korean defenders were poorly led peasants, and their weapons consisted of short swords, bows, and flails but no firearms. Although the Koreans did possess small battlefield cannon, borrowed from the Chinese, these were outshot fairly easily by the Japanese matchlocks. In fact, perhaps one-quarter of the Japanese forces were musketmen, plus some infantry pikemen, while the rest were samurai, carrying their usual two swords and either a bow or *naginata*. Within three weeks, Seoul fell, and the Japanese divisions fanned out across Korea. Kato Kiyomasa's Second Division actually reached Manchuria and the Tumen River, while Konishi Yukinaga's First Division captured Pyong-yang. However, as autumn arrived three factors turned the invasion against the Japanese. First, Korean guerilla warfare wore down the Japanese samurai in their forts and towns and prevented them foraging for food. Second, the famous Korean admiral Yi Sun Sin, with his "turtle" boats made of iron, plus cannon, made short work of the Japanese junks in various engagements. And third, the Chinese intervened, and a large Chinese army forced the evacuation of Pyong-yang in early 1593. The Japanese divisions withdrew to Seoul, and, despite a crushing Japanese victory in front of Seoul, when the samurai used superior weapons and tactics to leave ten thousand Chinese dead on the battlefield, Seoul was abandoned by the Japanese in May 1593. Lack of supplies and low morale led to a retreat to the coast, where fortified camps were set up, but most of the army returned to Japan. Peace negotiations did not please Hideyoshi, whose conduct became less and less rational. He ordered a second invasion in 1597, which like the first achieved considerable successes on land but could not solve the problem of the Korean navy nor of logistics. Hideyoshi's death in 1598 then led to a second Japanese evacuation and the end of Hideyoshi's dream of an empire.

One frequently quoted letter from the second invasion comes from Asano Yukinaga, who wrote to his father in Japan in 1598 after surviving a bitter siege by Chinese and Koreans in Uru-san: "When troops come [to Korea] from the province of Kai, have then bring as many guns as possible, for no other equipment is needed. Give strict orders that all men, even the samurai, carry guns." Despite these progressive sentiments, the fourth stage of Japanese warfare emerged when, starting with Hideyoshi and carrying on through the rule of Tokugawa Ieyasu (1542–1616), who was proclaimed shogun in 1603, firearms were forcibly withdrawn from general use. In fact, in a series of stages, Japan was disarmed in order to create a strong central government without fear of rebellions and at the same time preserving a sharper distinction between samurai and farmer. Hideyoshi originally issued the order for the "sword hunt" in August 1588 with the overt intention of building a vast Great Buddha but actually intending to disarm the country: "The people of the various provinces are strictly forbidden to have in their possession any swords, short swords, bows, spears, firearms or other types of arms. The possession of unnecessary implements [of war] makes difficult the collection of taxes and dues and tends to foment uprisings. . . . Swords and short swords thus collected will not be wasted. They shall be used as nails and bolts in the construction of the Great Image of Buddha."

By 1607, under Ieyasu, firearms could only be made under license from the central government, and over the next century the making of firearms was more and more restricted. In fact the Shimbara Christian rebellion of 1637 was the last time that firearms were seriously used in Japan for two centuries. And just as in China, Japan never went through the flintlock revolution, at least until the nineteenth century. Only with the arrival of Commodore Perry in 1853 did the Japanese again begin to seriously promote the manufacture of firearms. Why did Japan turn back the clock on their firearms, when in the late sixteenth century they were actually ahead of the West in their firearm tactics and volley firing?

Besides the idea of disarming the country in order to achieve a strong central government, which must be the most significant reason, five other mainly cultural explanations have been advanced for giving up the gun. First, the samurai did not want them, and especially they did not want the lower-class farmers to possess firearms. Second, Japan was secure geographically and did not need firearms to protect the country. Third, the sword had an aesthetic and symbolic appeal in Japan so that the idea of replacing swords by firearms was unacceptable. Fourth, there was a reaction in Japan in the seventeenth century against foreign influences, and firearms were seen as foreign. Fifth, firearms were seen as ugly and only to be used by the lower classes. Firearms also involved ugly movements of the body, compared with the graceful movements of the sword and spear. Probably as much for political and cultural reasons, then, Japan, like China, went into a self-imposed reaction against firearm weapons and thus became vulnerable later on to Western power.

In conclusion, it seems that Eastern styles of warfare depended heavily on inherited traditions. This was particularly the case with the general emphasis on light cavalry. Once these armies proved successful, there was little need to change. Strict social and military discipline, strong military leadership, and economic consolidation then paved the way for further military success in all these empires. But where it was imperative to adapt, this was done, as with the Mongols and siege techniques, the Moghuls and firearms, Chinese defensive measures against the nomads, and Japanese adaptation to castle building and muskets. But then cultural traditions resurfaced again and tended to limit further innovation, especially as these Eastern powers were isolated geographically. Ultimately, the lack of external challenges induced a certain status quo mentality, especially in regard to gunpowder weapons. This only changed when the arrival of the imperialistic Western powers in the nineteenth and twentieth centuries forced further innovation and adaptation. (The exception was the Mongol empire, which did not survive to the modern period, having disintegrated earlier for internal reasons.) Yet while each of these empires was at its height, their styles of warfare were extremely effective and generally tended to be ahead of contemporary Western developments.

Suggested Reading

The Mongols

The standard text for the Mongol style of warfare is still J. J. Saunders, *The History of the Mongol Conquests* (London, 1971). An older classic, originally published in French in 1939 and translated by Naomi Walford, is Rene Grousset, *The Empire of the Steppes: A History of Central Asia* (New Brunswick NJ, 1970). Although outdated, Grousset's book contains many details absent in other works. A recent useful overview, with stimulating interpretations and an up-to-date bibliography, is David Morgan, *The Mongols* (Oxford, 1986). A book that concentrates on the Mongols in the West and contains a concise chapter on Mongol warfare is James Chambers, *The Devil's Horsemen: The Mongol Invasion of Europe* (London, 1979). Texts concerning particular Mongol khans include, for Chingiz Khan, the much debated contemporary account, perhaps written in the 1220s, *The Secret History of the Mongols*, trans. F. W. Cleaves (Cambridge MA, 1982). On Chingiz Khan, see Paul Ratchnevsky, *Genghis Khan: His Life and Legacy* (Oxford, 1991). On the khan Mongke and also containing useful material on Mongol politics and recruiting practices is Thomas T. Allsen, *Mongol Imperialism: The Policies of The Grand Qan Mongke in China, Russia, and the Islamic Lands* (Berkeley, 1987). A recent book that stresses Khubilia's administration as well as his life is Morris Rossabi, *Khubilai Khan: His Life and Times* (Berkeley, 1988). Finally, for Tamerlane, Beatrice Forbes Manz has produced a book that avoids much mention of warfare, *The Rise and Rule of Tamerlane* (Cambridge, 1989).

The Moghuls

The best background volume, containing an excellent bibliography, is John F. Richards, *The New Cambridge History of India, The Mughal Empire* (Cambridge, 1992). There are a number of rather outdated military histories of India that cover the breadth of Indian military history and, of course, Moghul activities: for example, Major Gautam Sharma, *Indian Army Through the Ages* (Bombay, 1966), and Lt. Col. H. C. Kar, *Military History of India* (Calcutta, 1980). For the Moghuls specifically, there is the classic but outdated William Irvine, *The Army of the Indian Moghuls* (London, 1903). A corrective to Irvine on the relative numbers of cavalry and infantry comes in Dirk Kolff, *Naukar, Rajput and Sepoy* (Cambridge, 1990). Also useful but disjointed, like Irvine, is Raj Kumar Phul, *Armies of the Great Mughals (1526–1707)* (New Delhi, 1987). For Akbar, a sympathetic short introduction is S. M. Burke, *Akbar, the Greatest Mogul* (New Delhi, 1989). Fortunately, for many of the Moghul emperors, lively and revealing contemporary accounts and memoirs were prepared, such as *Zahiruddin Muhammad Babur Padshah Ghazi*, trans. Annette Beveridge, and *The Baburnama in English* (Memoirs of Babur) (London, 1969). Akbar is represented by Abu Fazl, *The Akbarnama*, 3 vols., trans. H. Beveridge (rpt. New Delhi, 1973), and by Abu Fazl, *The A'in-i Akbari*, 3rd ed., trans. H. Blochmann, rev. Lt. Col. Phillott (New Delhi, 1977, 1978). An excellent snapshot of Aurangzeb's reign is found in the letters and memoirs of the French doctor Francois Bernier, for example, his *Travels in the Mogul Empire*, A.D. *1656–1668*, rev. ed., by Archibald Constable (1891), 3rd ed. (New Delhi, 1972). A good look at the reasons for the decline of the later Moghul emperors in the early eighteenth century is contained in the contemporary chronicle of Das Lakhnawi, *Shahnama Munawwar Kalam*, trans. and ed. Syed Hasan Askari (Patna, 1980). A book that has chapters on the transition to the Marathas is Stewart Gordon, ed., *Marathas, Marauders, and State Formation in Eighteenth-Century India* (Delhi, 1994). On the Marathas, there exists a well-researched book by Surendra Nath Sen: *The Military System of the Marathas*, 2nd ed. (Calcutta, 1958). The Maratha military leader Shivaji is covered by Jadunath Sarkar, *Shivaji and His Times*, 6th ed. (Calcutta, 1961). Finally, Ahsan Jan Qaisar discusses the vexed question of technology transfer in his *The Indian Response to European Technology and Culture* (A.D. *1498–1707*) (Delhi, 1982).

China

China is not well served by military historians, apart from Frank A. Kierman and John K. Fairbank, eds., *Chinese Ways in Warfare* (Cambridge MA, 1974), and now Hans van de Ven, ed., *Warfare in Chinese History* (Leiden, 2001). On gunpowder technology, a remarkable achievement is Joseph Needham's *Science and Civilisation in China*, vol. 5, *Chemistry and Chemical Technology*, part 7, *Military Technology: The Gunpowder Epic* (Cambridge, 1986). An overview with some military history, though now rather outdated, is Rene Grousset, *The Rise and Splendour of the Chinese Empire* (Berkeley, 1968). A more recent overview, again with military references, is Dun J. Li, *The Ageless Chinese*, 3rd ed. (New York, 1978). Concerning the northern frontier, there exists Sechin Jagchid and Van Jay Symons, *Peace, War, and Trade Along the Great Wall: Nomadic-Chinese Interaction through Two Millenia* (Bloomington IN, 1989). Providing a snapshot of one year, with a fine chapter on Ch'i Chi-kuang is Ray Huang, *1587, A Year Of No Significance: The Ming Dynasty in Decline* (New Haven, 1981). Albert Chan has produced a useful book on the Ming, with military history sections: *The Glory and Fall of the Ming Dynasty* (Norman OK, 1982). A work with a political emphasis is Lynn Struve, *The Southern Ming, 1644–1662* (New Haven, 1984). Robert Oxnam provides a view of the Manchus in his *Ruling From Horseback: Manchu Politics in the Oboi Regency, 1661–1669* (Chicago, 1975). More information on the Manchu emperor K'ang-Hsi can be found in Jonathan Spence, *Emperor of China: Self-Portrait of K'ang-Hsi* (New York, 1975). On warfare in the later Manchu period, Peter Ward Fay, *The Opium War, 1840–1842* (New York, 1976), gives a sense of Chinese-Western mutual incomprehension.

Japan

The most accessible works on Japanese military history are those by S. R. Turnbull, although they tend to reflect the attitudes of the time by focusing on personalities and geographical military moves rather than on underlying trends in
warfare. Turnbull's most useful titles are *The Samurai, a Military History* (London, 1977); *The Book of the Samurai: The Warrior Class of Japan* (New York, 1982);
and *Battles of the Samurai* (London, 1987). The institutional background in the
period before the move to central government and unification is provided in
Paul Varley, *The Onin War (1467–1477)* (New York, 1967). A clear biography
of the man who unified Japan but failed in his strange effort to conquer China is
Mary Berry, *Hideyoshi* (Cambridge MA, 1982). For the sixteenth century, see relevant chapters in George Elison and Bardwell Smith, eds., *Warlords, Artists, and
Commoners: Japan in the Sixteenth Century* (Honolulu, 1981). The unusual story
of Japan's effort to outlaw firearms is told in the well-illustrated book by Noel
Perrin, *Giving Up the Gun: Japan's Reversion to the Sword, 1543–1879* (Boston,
1979). A brief overview of Japan's history, with short authoritative sections on
the military is Conrad Totman, *Japan before Perry: A Short History* (Berkeley,
1981). More specifically, this period is covered by George Sansom, *A History of
Japan, 1334–1615* (Stanford, 1961). A comparison of Japanese and European castle building and adaptation to firearms is found in Geoffrey Parker, *The Military
Revolution: Military Innovation and the Rise of the West, 1500–1800* (Cambridge,
1988).

6. THE AGE OF GUNPOWDER AND SAIL

Gentleman: I hear many say, "What need so much ado and great charge in caliver, musket, pike, and corselet? Our ancestors won many battles with bows, black bills, and jacks." But what you think of that? Captain: Sir, then was then, and now is now. The wars are much altered since the fiery weapons first came up. – Robert Barret, 1598

Blessed were the times which lacked the dreadful fury of those diabolical engines, the artillery, whose inventor I firmly believe is now receiving the reward for his devilish invention in hell; an invention which allows a base and cowardly hand to take the life of a brave knight, in such a way that, without his knowing how or why, when his valiant heart is fullest of furious courage, there comes some random shot—discharged perhaps by a man who fled in terror from the flash the accursed machine made in firing—and puts an end in a moment to the consciousness of one who deserved to enjoy life for many an age. – Miguel Cervantes, 1604

Looking backward, many sixteenth- and seventeenth-century writers expressed reservations about the changes in warfare wrought by gunpowder weapons that had altered their world and forever closed what in fanciful retrospect appeared to have been a more ideal age. Nevertheless, knowledgeable Europeans also expressed great pride in having broken out of the geographical constraints of their eastern Atlantic and Mediterranean world and at least held off the infidel Turks following the disastrous loss of Constantinople in 1453.

Quite without fully understanding the extent of their achievements, Europeans had developed weapons and technology that before long allowed them to dominate, or at least to influence, all other civilizations around the globe. However, those same primitive engines—firearms—that helped to make possible worldwide military superiority also contained the seeds of internal self-destruction. In internecine warfare committed in the name of religion and of naked competitions for economic and political dominance, armies and navies equipped with gunpowder artillery, arquebuses, muskets, oceangoing vessels, and sophisticated fortifications blasted continental competitors and opponents. With old certainties challenged in many different areas of human endeavor, perhaps for the first time at a world level the intrusion of technology in the field of military sciences compelled all nations, monarchs, city-states, religious leaders, and soldiers to accept the concepts of quite rapid change or progress. Already by the end of the sixteenth century, the most successful nations were those that by one means or another adapted to military developments that in some respects provoked events some historians describe as military revolutions.

The enormous cost of the new technologies and of the resources needed to mobilize military and civilian forces, to secure greater quantities of metal, and to manufacture firearms and gunpowder stimulated competitions that could be joined only by the most wealthy and powerful and by those blessed by proximity to natural resources and good strategic location. Many smaller jurisdictions gave way to larger ones and a few super states coalesced territories into empires and then mobilized against one another in what would become the first global struggles for domination. Portugal, Spain, France, England, Holland, Sweden, the Holy Roman Empire, and other states competed with new military hardware and organizations based on gunpowder weapons. For a variety of reasons, some nations could not maintain the momentum essential to exert power and either dropped into secondary status or were replaced by states that possessed the resolve, the resources, and often the religious zeal to build fleets, recruit armies, develop industries, and obtain new weapons of war.

The great multi-decked galleons, heavy artillery siege trains, the musket- and pike-equipped infantry forces, and the nearly impregnable fortifications of the sixteenth century could not have been foreseen by those who first experimented with gunpowder and evolved primitive firearms. Indeed, many sixteenth- and seventeenth-century writers on military subjects looked back with open awe upon the near revolutionary changes that even with the most acute hindsight were difficult to explain. Twentieth-century military historians such as Michael Roberts, Geoffrey Parker, Jeremy Black, John Lynn, David Eltis, and others have identified specific periods in which "military revolution" dramatically altered the face of war.

Despite recent research, the discovery, early distribution, and adoption of gunpowder and of gun technology still remain shrouded in mystery. Most historians, including those of sixteenth-century Europe, acknowledged that gunpowder was most probably a Chinese or Mongolian invention. The Chinese manufactured fireworks, developed rocket propulsion for use in warfare, and experimented with devices designed to harness explosive power. Carried westward across Asia to India and then to Arab civilizations, gunpowder and its attendant technologies reached the Mediterranean world around the thirteenth century. The Arabs described saltpeter as "snow from China," which further underscored its Asian provenance.

Diffused by the Byzantines, Venetians, and others who recognized the curiosity and likely the potential of gunpowder, the substance showed up in different parts of Europe and about the Mediterranean littoral. Explosive gunpowder requires a mixing ratio of approximately six to seven parts saltpeter, one part sulfur, and one part charcoal. The first known formula, written in cryptic language by Roger Bacon in England, can be traced to the mid-thirteenth century, indicating likely diffusion of information from Arabic sources in Spain and elsewhere.

Early gunners called saltpeter "the soul," charcoal "the body," and sulfur "the life" of powder. During combustion, the explosive ignition of gunpowder releases gases that expand to require over a thousand times the space of the original mixed product. The diverse potential applications for this energy did not fail to escape fertile minds, and we can assume that in addition to passing on existing technical information, early scientists made multiple separate discoveries, sometimes without direct intercommunications, that harnessed the explosive force needed to propel rockets and to fire projectiles.

By as early as 1400, the ideal ratio of seventy-five to twelve to thirteen for the components of gunpowder was well known among the fraternity of gunners as were methods to mix the powder properly. They developed engraining, or "corning," to make stable granules that permitted a better flow of oxygen thus enhancing the explosive characteristics. Corning also prevented the heavy saltpeter from sinking to the bottom and carbon rising to the surface within flasks or containers. By the beginning of the sixteenth century, quite efficient technologies and powder mills increased output, reduced prices significantly, and produced specialized types of gunpowder for different artillery pieces and handguns.

For early historians, the complexity and even mystery that accompanied the appearance of firearms caused them to seek a single inventor upon whom to bestow the glory or ignominy of having discovered powerful weapons often considered abhorrent to peaceful humanity. It was convenient to blame the Chinese, who were distant, foreign, and pagan, or the infidel Moors of Spain and North Africa, who could be linked to Islamic Turkish threats against Christendom. Many later writers—especially the northern European Protestants, who published a great deal and whose writings still influence thinking about military history—fixed upon the figure of Berthold Swartz, an obscure German Franciscan friar and alchemist. According to one version of the story, in 1300 Swartz heated a covered vessel containing sulfur and niter and in the process touched off a violent explosion that blasted the lid into the ceiling of his room. Intrigued by this spectacular result, Swartz pursued his experiments and "found out Gunpowder, the Mother of all Fire-Engines and Works." He was said to have invented a primitive pipe gun that he sold later to the Venetians, who employed it in their wars against the Genoese.

Compelling though the Swartz story may be, as is so often the case in history simplicity obscures a most complex period of experimentation, failures, and successes that eventually led to the invention of new weapons. Many writers such as Miguel Cervantes and William Shakespeare absolutely deplored the introduction of firearms, which they blamed for multiplying the atrocities of warfare and for allowing cowardly weaklings of base origins—even lowly foot soldiers—to slaughter mounted knights who were the trained elite of European chivalry. Moreover, the Catholic monk Swartz fit another stereotype for writers who assigned the origins of guns to devilish agency. For example, some Protestant enemies of Catholicism illustrated tracts referring to gunpowder with gruesome woodcuts showing demonic interventions directing Swartz in experimentation. If Satan himself could be shown to play a maleficent role in Swartz's technical breakthroughs, then all Catholics might be blackened for embracing and advancing truly evil inventions.

For a long time neither scientists nor soldiers could explain the principles governing the almost instantaneous passage of a bullet from the muzzle of a gun barrel to strike a distant object with such brutally destructive force. One early gunner who managed to hit his target with three successive shots was believed to be in league with the devil and condemned to undertake a pilgrimage to atone for his manipulation of magic. In an age when Europeans identified, persecuted, and killed witches thought to be at work in their midst and sanctioned holy inquisitions to protect Christianity, it is scarcely surprising that they perceived gunpowder weapons with fear as well as admiration.

Many leaders, including Martin Luther, insisted that cannon and arquebuses were the production of the devil and hell itself. Little wonder then that fifteenth- and even sixteenth-century soldiers often expressed deep personal ambivalence about their firearms. In Italy some commanders stuffed captured cannoneers into the barrels of their own great guns and blasted them out. In the late fifteenth century, Paolo Vitelli sentenced captured arquebusiers to the horrendous penalty of having their hands chopped off and both eyes pierced. Frequently, those who employed firearms chose to proclaim their victories in more traditional terms of impetuous charges, hand-to-hand combat, effective swordplay, and the concentrated power of disciplined pikemen. The work of cannon and arquebuses—especially against pagan forces discombobulated by thunderous reports, flashes, and unprecedented horrible wounds—often remained underreported in the chronicles of overseas conquest.

With time, of course, this reticence to credit gunpowder technology dissolved. By 1670 Sir James Turner, a veteran soldier of the Continental wars simply dismissed the tiresome gunpowder debates: "I will not at all amuse myself here with the needless disputes of some, whether this invention be destructive to mankind or not, since we read of many more men kill'd in Battles and Sieges before the noise of it was heard, than have been since. I shall only say that never anything was invented before it that offer'd so great violence to Nature, and yet is a ready servant and agent of Nature, it being able to make the heaviest bodies, stones, houses, and walls ascend in an instant, and waters suddenly to leave their habitations in the bowels of the earth, and appear on the surface of it; and all this perhaps, to avoid something which nature doth more abhor."

The earliest documented reports of guns appearing in European inventories can be traced to the first decades of the fourteenth century. Although the translation of terms in different languages can provoke great confusion and apparent references to explosions might also refer for example to Greek fire projected by catapults or pumps, there is pictorial evidence from a 1327 manuscript at Oxford University that illustrates an armored soldier preparing to discharge a primitive "thunder jar" (*pot de fer* in French and *vasi* and *scioppi* in Italian) loaded with a protruding bolt or quarrel.

Obviously, weapons such as these had been deployed and used prior to this date. Designed for use in sieges and against barricaded gates, the device was fired by a lighted match or heated wire at a touchhole situated at the top of the barrel behind the loaded charge. There are manuscript references to stone firing guns (*pedreros*) used by Spanish Christians and Islamic forces in the wars of Granada and in clashes along the coasts of North Africa. Other documents from Florence, Ghent, and elsewhere list inventories of small cannon and both iron and stone shot. With a developed grasp of this sort of technology and the use of firearms during sieges, Europeans and other peoples could move ahead to consider better methods of founding metal guns, transporting heavy pieces, furnishing munitions, dealing with recoil, and numerous other associated technical problems.

By about 1325 early cannon appeared throughout Europe. Although it is difficult to trace the process of proliferation and the battlefield successes or failures of the new weaponry, English forces used cannon in the siege of Calais (1346–47) and likely at the Battle of Crécy (1346) in the early stages of the Hundred Years' War (1337–1453). Islamic Iberians employed guns during the siege of Algeciras (1342–44), but since they were on the defensive side the clumsy weapons were most likely not particularly effective. On the offensive, the Christian Castilians benefited much more from their use of firearms, using artillery pieces as siege weapons against Moorish castles and other fortifications. Indeed, while both sides in the Iberian wars understood and used gunpowder weaponry, the Castilians and Aragonese exploited the technology offensively, learned how to deploy their guns, to protect gunners in sieges, and to plan the logistical systems needed to supply their pieces with gunpowder and cannonballs. Cannon also appeared during sieges of Cairo and Damascus in the 1360s and 1370s. Between 1389 and 1390, an observer at Damascus reported during a siege, "People never slept a wink because the cannon bellowed night and day to such an extent that the country was shaken as if by an earthquake."

Although the introduction of firearms into warfare followed an uneven course, it is important to note that technical advances took root first in those regions where for one reason or another war was an endemic factor in relationships between distinct peoples. Much like the great tec-

Fig. 6.1. *Assault on the Strong Town of Afrique,* The Siege of Tripoli. From Froissart's *Chronicle,* the British Library, London. Courtesy of Compagnie Royale D'Artillerie, La Prairie, Quebec.

tonic plates of the world's continents that collide to produce cataclysmic eruptions along the fracture lines, so too the frontiers between vastly different cultures, opposing religions, and aggressive competitors for resources created a number of flash points for chronic warfare. Within these frontier zones, no participant society safely could forswear military preparedness, forgo the use of potent new weapons, or delay the adoption of better tactical and logistical organizations for their armed resources.

While the frontier zones of chronic warfare altered through time, for the early epoch of gunpowder weapons we can identify conflicts such as the Hundred Years' War between France and England that occurred spasmodically during the span when guns ceased to be mere adjuncts of siege warfare. By the early decades of the fifteenth century, great bombards had become effective destroyers of defensive fortifications. Another example with later ramifications for world military history was the Christian-Islamic frontier involving Portugal, Castile, Aragon, Morocco, Italy, and northern Mediterranean Christian countries against Iberian Granada, the North African states, the Ottoman Turks, and other Islamic nations.

By the end of the fifteenth century, Castile and Aragon concluded the military campaigns of the Iberian *Reconquista*, centuries of crusading warfare directed against gradually eroding Islamic power centered in Granada. From these campaigns emerged Spanish soldiers such as Gonzalo de Córdoba who produced the first great gunpowder armies and fleets with ideas and aspirations directed toward conquest and even global domination. With their arquebuses, cannon, and disciplined military organizations, small numbers of Castilian soldiers led by Hernando Cortés, Francisco Pizarro, and other conquistadores toppled the great Aztec, Inca, Maya, and other indigenous civilizations of the New World. With ships and guns, the Portuguese circumnavigated Africa to dominate populous civilizations of the Indian Ocean, pressing on to China and Japan. In the eastern Mediterranean, the rise of the Ottoman Turks coincided with the practical application of gunpowder technology. Their powerful forces crushed Constantinople in 1453, extended through the Balkan lands eventually to threaten Habsburg, Vienna, and moved westward by sea and land to occupy North Africa, endanger Italy, and challenge emerging Spanish military power. Although gunpowder migrated originally from the east, the Ottomans and the Europeans returned its powerfully mutated technologies back from the west to dominate the Indian Ocean littoral and to open the sea routes to China and Japan.

In France, Flanders, and the German states, metallurgy, gun-founding, and good practical ideas produced better weapons and specialists. However, many of the real lessons of how to apply offensive and defensive elements of the new technologies emerged in Italy, which in the fifteenth and sixteenth centuries was a chronic battleground that contained dynamic mutually hostile states and attracted outsiders anxious to grab rich territories. The French, the Spanish, and even the Ottomans coveted the wealth of Italy and harbored an even broader vision of Mediterranean domination.

In the early sixteenth century, Italy became a kind of laboratory for rapid battlefield military experimentation involving firearms and for the development of remarkable defensive fortifications designed to resist heavy siege guns. In Italy, we can identify a quickened pace of changes that in many respects set the scene for much broader sixteenth-century wars that divided Europe and spilled over into the Atlantic Ocean world and then round the globe.

From the beginning, gunpowder weapons divided into two basic classes—handguns and artillery. Heavier firearms supported sieges to collapse gates, fortifications, and castle walls. At first, lighter guns served principally to defend parapets and walls against attackers. Early hand-guns were simple metal or even wooden tubes closed at one end with a drilled touchhole at which a lighted linstock, or hot wire, ignited the powder charge that propelled a projectile or projectiles. For use during the chaotic and mobile conditions of battlefield combat, such weapons were close to useless since they had to be secured to absorb recoil and required two or three gunners to serve them. Nevertheless, by the 1350s many city and town garrisons possessed inventories of handguns, or *scioppi*, that by now were metal tubes attached to long staffs designed to rest upon the ground. The use of a wooden stock, or "tiller," attached to the barrel had not evolved and the method of firing from the shoulder remained for future innovators.

Early gunners cast firearms in bronze (copper and tin), brass (copper and zinc), copper, and iron, and they experimented with wood barrels strapped by metal bands. Bronze was more expensive than iron and re-quired access to copper, which was quite common (from Hungary, Ty-rol, Saxony, Bohemia, and Spain), and tin, a more expensive metal mined in few locations (England, Spain, and Germany). Good fortune awarded strategic ore deposits to some nations, while others had to depend on commerce or conquest to obtain adequate supplies. Wars or other dis-ruptions often limited the availability of metal and interfered with the manufacture of weapons. Wooden guns, while cheap to make, wore out quickly, sometimes exploded, and were wildly inaccurate. While they dropped out of use among major powers, they would appear time and again almost up to the present around the world in revolts and uprisings where metal was expensive or simply unavailable.

Almost from its introduction, gunpowder increased pressures for re-sources, impetus for commerce, and hastened technological innovations designed to seek efficient applications. The art of bell founding was an excellent background to highly skilled craftsmen who now turned their energies to founding bronze cannon. Other specialists manufac-tured gunpowder, constructed carriages suitable to move the cumber-some and heavy pieces, and mastered the specialized skills required to make artillery effective in defensive and offensive applications. Iron guns were heavier and more liable to explode or fracture than those made of bronze, but they were also much cheaper. Iron casting left flaws and air holes—especially where the ores contained sulfur. To avoid these dangers, gun makers used wrought iron rods or bars that they built up about a wooden mandrel (core) and beat them while red hot to remove impurities and to weld them into a solid tube. Heavy iron hoops were clamped and then shrunk onto the tube in the form of barrel hoops for additional strength. Nevertheless, accidental explosions and burns from the "breath" of bombards and other guns were quite common. Gunners exercised care to avoid blasphemy, to eschew immorality, and to make certain that they kept their spiritual lives perfectly in order. In 1460, for example, James II of Scotland died instantly at the siege of Roxburgh Castle during an inspection when a hooped bombard of Flemish manufacture burst and one of its quoins (wedge-shaped blocks) crushed his chest. As might be expected, given the nature of their craft, gunners exploited secrecy guarding formulas and protecting specialized technology. Forming tightly knit brotherhoods they contracted their services to the highest bidders.

Despite the element of mystery surrounding the work of gunners, inventive minds of the fourteenth century produced many advances to make gunpowder weapons more efficient and fearsome. The idea of breech-loading developed in this formative period and heavy guns often had separate breech-blocks or chambers. Some guns became so large that they were cast in two or three sections for transport. Screwed together and braced for firing, such pieces were suitable only in sieges where there was adequate time for reassembly and stationary targets that could be battered from fixed positions. Breech-loading was especially useful for shipboard applications where space was at a premium and light swivel guns came into use to defend decks against possible enemy boarders. Generally speaking, however, like many other good ideas breech-loading of heavy and light guns had to be discarded for technological reasons. Until nineteenth-century advances in the science of metallurgy, gunners could not effectively seal the breech during firing to prevent the escape of gasses.

Technological limitations also deterred those who designed and sometimes attempted to build experimental mass fire and repeating firearms. Heavy carts or carriages equipped with multiple barreled guns designed to be fired simultaneously foreshadowed nineteenth-century inventions but could not be made to operate efficiently or safely in the fourteenth or fifteenth centuries. Jamming, leakage of gasses, explosions, and other technical and safety problems convinced gun founders that muzzle-loading was the most efficient method to follow. Gradually, different classes of heavy guns emerged: artillery pieces designed to fire on flat trajectories and wide-mouthed mortars and howitzers that fired on higher trajectories to lob projectiles and bombs over walls and into fortifications. At the same time, experiments continued with lighter handguns useful for many defensive and offensive applications.

As in so many different areas of human endeavor, gunners concluded that if a big gun was effective to obliterate defenses or to batter psychologically an opposition force, then even larger guns would do a better job. Beginning in the 1370s, gun founders began to produce truly enormous bombards with tube or barrel diameter of up to half a yard that fired sculpted stone balls weighing as much as five hundred to fifteen hundred pounds. Cast-iron shot—cheaper and with more penetrating power than stone—appeared in Italy during the fourteenth century, and the French adopted it to reduce English castles during the latter stages of the Hundred Years' War. By the fifteenth century, gigantic bombards appeared throughout Europe and around the Mediterranean littoral. Some of these great guns still exist such as "Mons Meg," an iron bombard of the mid-fifteenth century displayed at Edinburgh castle, and "Mad Margaret," which is five meters in length, has a diameter of 0.64 meters, and weighs 16,400 kilograms, at Ghent, Belgium. These great bombards as Sir James Turner noted, "take frequently their denominations from the Inventors, or from beasts and Birds, whom for their swiftness, rapacity, and cruelty, they seem to represent." In the 1450s, French siege guns each unique in caliber prior to standardization so that they required special individual ammunition, bore names such as Enea, Silva, Vittoria, and La Plus du Monde. Henry VII (1509–47) of England purchased 140 bronze guns from the Flemish gun founder Hans Poppenruyter including "the twelve Apostles."

The tendency toward the gigantesque in bombard making became even more evident in the 1453 Ottoman siege and conquest of Byzantine Constantinople, which took place at about the same time that the French employed heavy guns to overthrow English castles at the end of the Hundred Years' War. Sultan Mehmed II employed a Hungarian gun founder from Adrianople named Urban who according to some sources abandoned his employment with the Byzantines following a dispute over wages. Anxious to capture Constantinople, the sultan demanded guns large enough to fire stone balls that would bring down extremely thick walls. One bombard cast by Urban was said to be almost nine meters (twenty-seven feet) in length with walls eight inches thick and a bore of thirty inches. It fired stone balls that weighed twelve hundred pounds.

Anticipating a test firing at Adrianople, some observers expressed anxieties that the shock of the explosive blast would "leave some speechless or cause pregnant women to abort." While these dire warnings proved groundless, the event was memorable enough as "the stone when discharged, was propelled from the cannon with a piercing air-rending sound, and the air was filled with smoke and haze." The enormous ball traveled almost a mile and slammed into the earth carving a crater six feet deep.

It was one thing simply to test fire the bombard that the gunners placed on a cumbersome sledge that used the ground to absorb recoil and quite another to transport it overland to Constantinople with its attendant equipment and crew, heavy ammunition, and enormous appetite to consume gunpowder. To commence the siege, the Ottomans faced difficulties that confronted all those of the period who conceived large-scale military operations. Where transport by sea was unavailable, armies faced the daunting task of upgrading or constructing roads and bridges that throughout the continent were either in poor shape or nonexistent. Nevertheless, during March and April 1453, crews of Christian prisoners smoothed the surface of the road from Adrianople to Constantinople, and a team of fifty carpenters constructed and reinforced bridges. Contemporary sources indicate that for the great bombard alone, thirty wagons had to be linked together and hauled by sixty oxen. A crew of four hundred laborers supported the gun during its passage. On Monday, April 2, 1453, the first Turkish detachments came into sight of the city and within a few days a force of eighty to one hundred thousand troops established a siege.

Case Study: The Siege of Constantinople

Although vastly outnumbered and outgunned, the defenders of Constantinople answered their Turkish besiegers with arrows, crossbow quarrels, and bullets from light guns situated on the parapets. Some of these loaded with five or six lead balls struck victims with such force that the projectiles passed through the shield and body of the first Turkish soldier, through a second man, and sometimes even penetrated a third. In the meantime, the besiegers dug trenches, established their encampments, cut off the harbor, and laboriously set up their great bombards and smaller siege guns. A Venetian ship attempting to run the marine blockade was struck and shattered by one enormous stone bombard ball. The captain and thirty survivors made it to shore where they fell into the hands of the Turks. Mehmed ordered all of them beheaded except the captain who suffered a horrible, slow death impaled upon a stake through the anus.

When the first great bombard blasts struck the city walls, the shocked Constantinopolitans were said to cry out in shock, "Lord, have mercy." Fortunately for the defenders, the largest guns were so cumbersome to operate that they fired only six or seven rounds per day. To prevent shattering or fractures after two or three shots, the gunners covered the hot barrels with heavy wool felt soaked in oil. Although one great bombard cracked after a few shots and could not be repaired, the bombardment soon wreaked havoc on the high stone works.

At first, the defenders rushed to repair broken and crumbled walls and towers with barrels filled with stones or they suspended padded hides and mattresses of wool to absorb the crushing blows. At the same time, they listened below ground for the ominous sounds of Turkish miners. Before long, however, supplies of gunpowder within Constantinople ran short so that by mid-May the city faced a day-and-night barrage of over two hundred stone balls that obliterated sections of wall. Where possible, the defenders repaired the breaches with hastily erected earthworks.

After some experiments, Mehmed's commanders learned that they obtained the best results when they aimed heavy and medium bombards in batteries directing fire in triangular patterns against specific sections of walls, towers, and gateways. The constant din of bombards and crash of stone projectiles that pulverized the walls sent stone splinters flying through the city to wound the unwary and to inspire fear in everyone. Gradually the morale of the Byzantines fell as they could no longer repair the damage. Women were said to faint from the shock caused by the noise and concussion. If this cacophony of heavy bombard explosions was not sufficient, the Turks attacked the breaches—using conscripted Christian soldiers first—bellowing their war cries, rattling their castanets, and pounding tambourines. They excavated several underground tunnels that the defenders discovered and burned out after ferocious hand-to-hand skirmishes within the constricted passages. The defenders captured two Turkish commanders, whom they beheaded summarily and then catapulted their dismembered bodies over the walls into the midst of their erstwhile comrades. Beginning on May 29, massed wave attacks again of conscripted Christians were sent by Mehmed on suicidal missions up siege ladders directly into the faces of the desperate defenders. These attackers possessed no alternative but to advance since

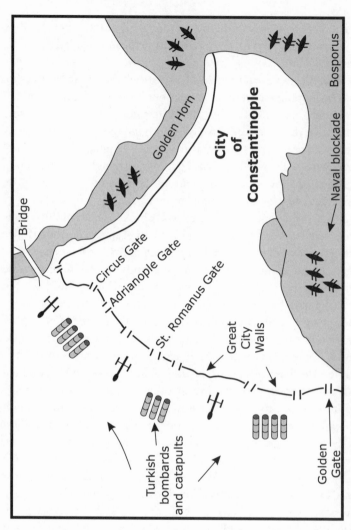

Map. 6.1. The Siege of Constantinople, 1453

retreat meant instant slaughter by Turkish forces behind them. Gradually, the withering fire and wave attacks exhausted the defenders. In the
third assault, veteran Janissaries rushed through the acrid smoke of the
cannon fire, clambered over the breaches and flooded into the city.

Despite technical difficulties with gun carriages and platforms, the
Turks combined the effectiveness of bombard firepower with other
more traditional siege methods such as mining, escalade, and the use
of towers. Without doubt, the great bombards situated behind earthen
breastworks provided the offensive edge needed to knock down the
concentric rings of walls and towers that for centuries had made Constantinople almost invincible. Through the fifty-five day siege, the heavy
Turkish guns fired at least 100 to 120 times daily consuming over one
hundred pounds of gunpowder. Smaller more mobile guns fired shot
that irritated the Byzantines who quickly ran through their own supplies
of gunpowder and munitions that could not be replaced. Nevertheless,
many Turks died and suffered wounds from defensive gunfire directed
against massed attackers and at their entrenchments. With the final collapse, Turkish forces rushed into the city to massacre, rape, enslave, and
to pillage the remnants of Christendom's now defunct eastern bastion.

The traumatic shock of the fall of Constantinople and the Byzantine
collapse opened the way to Turkish expansionism northward through
the Balkans, westward into Christian territories of the Mediterranean,
and east and south against other Islamic competitors. In Mamluk Egypt,
cannon had been well known and used in sieges since the mid-fourteenth
century even before the Ottoman Turks adopted firearms. Notwithstanding their foreknowledge, the Mamluk army rejected handguns
which by the fifteenth century had begun to be more than just a novelty.
A thoroughly military society based on martial codes of chivalry that
recognized the horseman armed with sword, lance, and bow as soldier
and noble, there was no place for infantrymen bearing handguns.

While large guns might be employed in siege warfare, Mamluk warriors clung to their horses and older ideas. They assigned the new infantry weapons to lower class men and slaves who could not be permitted
to develop sufficient offensive strength or experience to take on horsemen. When the Ottomans arrived and the Portuguese sailed into the
Red Sea from the Indian Ocean, the Mamluks were unable to defend
themselves. Massed Janissary infantry and Turkish artillery cut them
down and Portuguese gunners did the same.

Having employed bombards and handguns in Morocco as in a siege of Ceuta during 1456 where they faced Moroccan forces that possessed thirty bombards, the Portuguese gradually achieved operational dominance and tactical superiority. When Vasco da Gama sailed north into the Red Sea after having opened the Cape of Good Hope route, the Portuguese already possessed effective firepower sufficient to overwhelm Islamic opposition. Artillery bombardments from ships supported destructive assaults by soldiers armed with handguns as well as traditional hand weapons. A very few Portuguese interlopers tilted the balance of power against the Mamluks and other peoples from the Red Sea to the Persian Gulf, India, and eastward to the Straits of Malacca. In the process, they began the transformation of south and southeast Asian warfare.

Although changes involving gunpowder weapons occurred over many decades, the culminating impact on warfare was quite spectacular—especially so if one side lacked the technology or inadvertently fell behind. In addition to the heavy bombards used by the Turks at Constantinople or the French in the last years of the Hundred Years' War, light guns frequently served in defensive roles and occasionally even on battlefields. Primitive handguns (*bombardellos*) appeared as early as the fourteenth century, but these were fired from poles set against the ground, from the center of the breastplate, sometimes from the shoulder, or held away from the body altogether. With a slow match or hot wire in one hand, the gunner encountered difficulties achieving accuracy and handling recoil—particularly since the match at the touchhole on top of the barrel obscured attempts to aim at a target. With two men assigned to a gun they could use a forked rest to stabilize the heavy weapon. Despite many obvious disadvantages, however, when compared with bows and crossbows soldiers soon recognized that bullets flew over long distances and sometimes hit targets with great penetrating power. For doubters, some early handgun designs included built-in war clubs or battle-axes that could be used in case of misfire. Descriptions of handguns appeared in Italian sources during a 1431 siege of Lucca by a Florentine army and in Bohemia during the 1420s where Hussite forces used them to defend wagon forts during their struggles against Catholic domination.

The exact steps that moved handguns from mainly defensive roles into offensive actions is difficult to date, but by the 1430s some armies had organized specialists in the uses of these weapons. During the 1440s,

Milanese handgunners caused havoc and notable casualties among Venetian forces. In 1448 at the Battle of Caravaggio, smoke from gunfire obscured the field—a phenomenon that soon became an integral aspect of battle. The execution of handgunners by Italian *condottieri* commanders underscored that these weapons had become effective. Notwithstanding criticisms from writers about the unchivalric element of shooting down knights, by the mid-fifteenth century, handgun formations were present in all Italian standing armies—gradually pushing crossbows into subsidiary uses.

Although the Italians and the Germans played major roles improving handguns, the Castilians and Aragonese of Iberia during the final stages of the wars of the Reconquista against Islamic Granada also embraced light firearms. In this frontier zone of endemic conflict, Castilian forces absorbed and improved upon new ideas and created better military organizations to harness the firepower potential of massed handguns. Even prior to the unification of Iberian power, Spanish forces played active roles in the wars of Italy. In 1438 during the siege of Capuana at Naples, Don Pedro the brother of the King of Castile suffered instant decapitation when he stepped into the trajectory of a cannonball. The Spaniards were either the first or among the first to adopt shoulder firing that permitted men to absorb recoil effectively—especially when compared with firing from the breastbone—an advance that allowed the development of more powerful small arms.

By the mid-fifteenth century, cumbersome handguns consisting of a closed tube with a touchhole and a wooden stock gave way to much improved models that employed mechanical methods to discharge the weapon. Instead of requiring the gunner or his assistant to insert a burning match or a hot wire into the touchhole, innovators developed devices called "serpentines" or "cocks" that held a lighted match-cord. When triggered, the arm of the cock pivoted the burning material bringing it into contact with fine gunpowder in a flash pan that in turn fired the primary charge driving the bullet out of the barrel.

On the negative side, this method of firing handguns was cumbersome, impossible to conceal at night due to the glow of the matches, and almost useless in inclement weather that extinguished matches and either dampened or scattered the flash powder. Nevertheless, the matchlock arquebus was a relatively simple, rugged, and comparatively safe weapon for soldiers who showed little respect for their weapons. Remarkably, the matchlock arquebus and the heavier musket were to

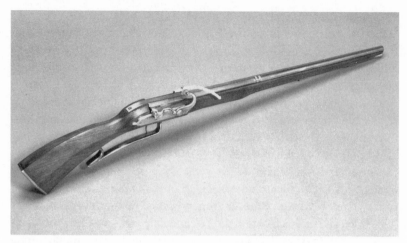

Fig. 6.2. Matchlock musket. Courtesy of Compagnie Royale D'Artillerie, La Prairie, Quebec.

remain in general service until the late seventeenth century and the development of the flintlock.

Despite the claims of military thinkers who continued to sing the praises of bows and crossbows, the arquebus and musket inevitably drove the older weapons into retirement from the battlefield. Notwithstanding the many shortcomings of guns, soldiers preferred firearms over bows and recognized the prestige and potential of the new weapons. If an ideal bowman could shoot four or five times faster, other soldiers insisted that well-trained arquebusiers could inflict even greater damage. And after a few months of hardships and privations on active combat duty, while many archers lost their physical strength arquebusiers no matter if they suffered were still able to fire balls that penetrated enemy armor. Other observers pointed out that powder and bullets could be supplied much more easily than well-crafted arrows suitable for military uses. Commenting from his own experience in sixteenth-century warfare, Sir Roger Williams noted:

> Touching bow-men, I perswade my selfe 500 musketeers are more seruiceable than 1,500 bow men; from that rate to the greater numbers in all manner of seruices by reasons are thus: among 5,000 bowmen, you shall not finde 1,000 good Archers, I meane to shoot strong shootes; let them be in the field 3 or 4 months, hardlie find of 5,000 scarce 500 able to make any strong shootes.

Moreover, as a rule bowmen feared soldiers equipped with firearms and often expressed terror if they had to expose themselves to gunfire in attacks against fortified positions. After the mid-fifteenth century, hand-gun companies became an increasingly important part of many standing armies. By the 1470s, about twenty percent of Milanese infantrymen carried guns that were more effective weapons than some historians have believed. While crossbows did not disappear entirely, their numbers declined progressively as the matchlock arquebus replaced older less efficient handguns.

As in the previously discussed case of the Ottomans against the Byzantines, it is instructive to follow the introduction of handguns in a frontier zone of chronic warfare—this time of the Castilians who played such an important and dominant role in European warfare of the sixteenth century and extended their military power to the Americas. First in the wars against the Moors and later in Italy, they introduced tactical innovations that would make the arquebus and the musket extremely potent in both offensive and defensive applications. By the second half of the fifteenth century, the Castilians with shoulder firing developed heavier small arms needed to pierce armor. Guided by the effective leadership of Isabel of Castile and Fernando of Aragon who launched the final chapter of the *Reconquista*, the Iberian Christians eliminated Islamic Granada.

In frontier warfare between Christianity and Islam, the Spaniards developed gunpowder weapons and tactics that played crucial roles in the rise of armies that dominated sixteenth-century warfare. While both Islamic and Christian Iberians were experts in the use of guns of all types, Granada found itself pressed into static defensive warfare cut off from reinforcements and from Ottoman or other Islamic assistance. In the meantime Queen Isabel scoured Europe to hire gunners, gun founders, and to assemble munitions, eventually organizing a large hired artillery force suitable to undertake prolonged sieges and campaigns. The Granadans like the Mamluks of Egypt and many other cultures retained a strong affection for cavalry and were somewhat slower than the Christians to recognize the potential blend of handguns and foot soldiers. In ten years of warfare culminating in the 1492 surrender of Granada, the Castilians experimented with heavy siege guns needed to reduce Islamic citadels and recruited a large infantry army of about sixty thousand troops armed in part with handguns as well as other hand weapons. Although the Castilians loved horses and cavalry as much as their Moorish enemies, they recognized that guns and infantry provided the keys to overpowering Granada.

During the 1480s, Isabel and Fernando imported engineers, gunsmiths, smelters, and blacksmiths from Italy, Germany, and Flanders to accomplish their project of conquest. They purchased heavy bronze guns from France and Germany called *lombardas* with twelve-foot-long barrels that fired iron or stone balls weighing up to 165 pounds. Some great guns arrived as gifts with supplies of gunpowder from Christian leaders who wished to demonstrate their solidarity in the final crusade against Iberian Islam. In total, Isabel assembled two thousand large and small artillery pieces, and also recruited six thousand sappers and engineers to construct roads and bridges and to prepare sieges against the well-defended walls of Muslim towns. To coordinate her artillery, Isabel hired a brilliant military engineer, Francisco Ramírez de Madrid, known as *El Artillero*.

Commencing with the fall of Ronda in 1485 and Málaga in 1487, the Granadans experienced the horror of witnessing their walls, bastions, gates, and other defenses reduced to rubble with many noncombatants killed by gunfire even if they attempted flight. According to contemporary accounts, the overpowering din of bombardment utterly destroyed Islamic morale and drove many close to insanity. Concentrating their artillery and using systematic interlocking fire, the Castilians learned to deploy a combination of heavy, medium, and light guns to the best advantage. Annual assaults gradually left the city of Granada isolated, panic-stricken, starving, and clogged with refugees dispossessed from other towns that had been pounded into surrender.

By 1491 Isabel and Fernando were able to assemble a besieging army of up to eighty thousand troops before Granada. Unlike Constantinople that had fallen spectacularly to artillery fire from bombards and bloody assaults at breaches, the Castilians employed an older style of siege over eight months that literally garroted the city in a deadly artillery cordon. On January 2, 1492, Isabel and Fernando entered Granada, inspected the artillery of the defeated Islamic troops, and ordered them to lay down their firearms. For some decades until defensive engineers in Italy altered the science of fortification construction to compensate for gunpowder artillery and infantry armed with handguns, offensive forces appeared to possess distinct advantages. Moreover, the combination of gunpowder weapons now heralded an era in which European military technology utterly overwhelmed the defensive and offensive capabilities of other military cultures round the globe.

The Castilian-Aragonese campaigns against Granada provided a quite remarkable testing ground for gunpowder warfare. The rugged geography and well-fortified towns of Islamic Granada forced the Christian Spaniards to develop better infantry to assault prepared positions. In these mountainous regions, heavy artillery and light handguns became essential components. Like the Hussites in Bohemia, the Castilians mounted guns on carts protected by large shields (mantlets). Especially in summer, infantrymen used light armor over leather clothing—wearing a simple basin helmet, polished knee pieces, and red calf-high boots made in the Moorish style. To maintain essential agility, arquebusiers often discarded chain mail shirts and wore layered leather that was almost as effective in resisting glancing blows. To increase speed and allow for the possibility of surprise, Spanish forces carried limited baggage, lived off the land, and attempted to forbid female camp followers.

With Granada conquered, Christopher Columbus dispatched, the Canary Islands occupied, and amphibious raids launched into Islamic North Africa, one might have expected to see Spanish military efforts concentrated in these directions. However, in 1495, following another Iberian interest, Gonzalo Fernández de Córdoba (the Great Captain), who had been born in 1453, the year Constantinople fell, and spoke perfect Arabic, received orders from King Fernando to lead a Spanish expeditionary force to intervene in Sicily and Naples. Trained in the hit-and-run raiding tactics learned in the Granadan War, Córdoba's infantry employed a higher proportion of arquebuses than other armies and protected these troops with soldiers armed with pikes, lances, and swords. During the early campaigns in Naples, the Spaniards deployed arquebuses offensively on the battlefield, in ambushes and in defense of fortified earthworks, ditches, and walled castles. Under Córdoba and other commanders, the successes of the arquebusiers illustrated that handguns had become much more potent. It is interesting that even as a great hero and army commander, Córdoba also had to keep detailed financial records of his military expenditures and to suffer the fiscal restraints of civilian bureaucrats who served their budget-conscious king.

For this period, Italy became a testing ground for weapons, tactics, and different military offensive and defensive combinations. In 1494, Charles VIII of France invaded Italy with an army of eighteen thousand men and an artillery train of over one hundred heavy, horse-drawn guns that made short work of existing medieval fortifications and carried the invaders as far south as Naples. By this point toward the end of the fifteenth century, effective though cumbersome gun carriages had been developed and muzzle-loading bronze or iron guns weighed much less than the earlier bombards. Even so, heavy cannon mounted on wheeled carriages weighed over eight thousand pounds. For better mobility, lighter guns on two-wheeled carriages began to play larger roles that extended to the battlefield. The addition of trunnions—projections from the gun barrels that fitted into sockets on the carriages—allowed gunners to aim more accurately and to raise and depress the muzzles of their guns. With the proliferation of artillery, the cost of gunpowder and cast-iron balls declined significantly. With these developments, French artillery gained a reputation for excellence—mostly in sieges but also on the battlefield. Skillful gunners supported by an effective siege train and much better logistics gave the French a potential battle-winning advantage.

Behind the scene, Niccolo Machiavelli and other writers grappled with the changes in warfare, considered the possibilities of wedding gunpowder weapons with ancient formations such as the legion and phalanx, and argued in favor of conscripted armies of citizens rather than of paid foreign mercenaries such as the *condottieri*. Renaissance scientists such as Leonardo da Vinci and Michelangelo planned fortifications to resist gun fire, designed mortars, and even considered mass fire weapons such as submarines and aircraft that were to remain outside the practical reach of military builders until the nineteenth and twentieth centuries.

By the beginning of the sixteenth century, artillery pieces of different calibers and weights were developed according to the special needs of field forces, sieges, and naval applications. Artillery trains and arsenals included heavy, medium, and light guns with names such as full cannon, culverin, demiculverin, *perrier, saker*, falconet, *moschetto*, and many others. For mobile siege warfare, the forty-five-hundred-pound half-cannon fired a twenty- to thirty-pound iron shot, the culverin a twenty-five-pound shot, a half culverin a twelve-pound shot, and the *perrier*, or *pedrero*, stone balls that were effective against ships and tightly packed squares of soldiers.

At the Battle of Novara in 1513, for example, French artillery fire slaughtered seven hundred Swiss infantrymen deployed in a densely packed square formation. With these developments, logistics assumed ever greater importance. A train of heavy guns, powder, cannonballs, instruments, and other equipment needed an enormous number of horses, mules, and oxen. One demi-cannon with carriage weighed at least six thousand pounds and required approximately twenty pounds of powder to fire a thirty-pound iron ball. With increasing rates of fire, sixteenth-century armies had to assign at least forty horses to move a gun and ammunition. This was prior to considering the additional baggage wagons that conveyed other equipment, tents, spare parts, provisions, clothing, and the multitude of men and women who served an army on the move.

In Italy, Spanish forces fresh from their victories against Granada encountered the French. In a series of epochal battles such as Cerignola (1503), Ravenna (1512), Bicocca (1522), and Pavia (1525) involving gunpowder weapons, tactics, and logistics, they also experimented with linear formations and different combinations of troops that would allow the matchlock arquebus and a little later the heavier musket to maximize flexible firepower on the battlefield. During the Italian wars of the early sixteenth century, the Spaniards evolved the *tercio*, a tactical formation of 1,000 to 3,000 men that now gave infantry the offensive and defensive firepower to achieve decisive predominance on the battlefield. Named after the jurisdictions where they were raised such as Málaga, Sicilia, Lombardía, and Sardinia, some *tercios* were to endure for almost two hundred years. Organized around twelve companies of 250 men each, the *tercio* drew upon the traditions, organization, and inspiration of the Roman legion and of the Swiss infantry.

In the process, the Spaniards set the scene for the evolution of the modern regiment. A *maestro de campo* (colonel) commanded with a *sargento mayor* (major), an adjutant, and other staff officers. Each company had a captain, an ensign, a sergeant, and ten corporals. As the century progressed, the Spanish infantry increased its firepower with companies of musketeers, arquebusiers, and pikemen. The pikes served to protect the gunners against cavalry attacks and from opposition infantry during the cumbersome reloading process. In defensive situations, the *tercio* formed an almost impenetrable square protected by pikes that could adopt a linear form to charge. While the *tercio* was a quite flexible independent force, its subordinate companies including all infantry arms could be detached for a variety of different specialized duties in patrols, garrisons, or to support other formations.

Gradually, the Spaniards increased the ratio of arquebusiers to pikemen. Innovative commanders such as Gonzalo de Córdoba, Pedro Navarro, and the Marqués de Pescara developed field fortifications utilizing parapets and entrenchments, gunpowder mining techniques to attack fortifications, and more flexible as well as effective light infantry formations. In the same years, the French deployed their excellent artillery more often to support forces on the battlefield as well as to batter fortifications. At the Battle of Ravenna (1512) for example, the French used effective enfilading fire to harass Spanish entrenchments, eventually compelling the vexed troops to undertake an ill-conceived charge. One iron cannonball mowed down thirty-three soldiers. Even in defeat, however, the Spanish arquebusiers, pikemen, and swordsmen fought courageously and retreated in disciplined order. At the Battle of Pavia (1525), Spanish and German arquebusiers supported by pikemen under the Marqués de Pescara not only held off the French artillery and cavalry with their firepower but were sufficiently mobile to surround the French and to capture King Francis I, who remained a prisoner of war for a year.

In the New World, the Spanish *conquistadores* exploited a combination of European military technology, tactical formations, firepower, psychological factors, and outright treachery to overthrow the great and populous empires of the Aztecs, the Incas, and other civilizations. Because the natives of the New World lacked biological resistance to influenza, measles, smallpox, and many other common ailments, disease epidemics were the allies of the Spaniards and other European invaders. To conquer Mexico, in 1519 Hernando Cortés organized a small army of only six to nine hundred men most of whom in the first instance brought their own armor, weapons, war dogs, and horses. As was customary, Cortés's followers elected him *adelantado* (military and political governor) and swore to follow his command. According to their individual investments of funds, arms, horses, and retainers in the expedition, each soldier hoped to receive a share of booty, land, and, later, access to the native labor force. Discovering that recently conquered subject peoples close to the Gulf of Mexico coast were restive under the heavy-handed rule of the Aztecs, Cortés made masterful use of the principle of divide and conquer. Accompanied by armies of native warriors, porters, and auxiliaries, Córtes built a coalition of disaffected native states. Where necessary, the Spaniards fought battles using their firearms, horses, and steel weapons.

In what was a truly audacious project, Cortés marched inland to visit the Aztec emperor Montezuma in Tenochtitlán (today's Mexico City). Leaving a small garrison at Veracruz, the actual Spanish forces numbered just over three hundred soldiers. Even with the chronicles by soldiers such as Bernal Díaz and some other observers, letters by Cortés, and some partial native observations recorded after the conquest, the ensuing battles, alliances, psychological tricks, and tactics used by the Spaniards make the conquest appear more like fiction than fact. In some respects, the conquests in the Americas continued many aspects of crusading warfare during the *Reconquista* in Iberia. Nevertheless, even with the presence of significant numbers of native allies, it is difficult to explain how a warlike, wealthy, and populous empire fell to so few. As might be expected, the role of gunpowder weaponry and field tactics played significant roles in the overthrow of the greatest New World native civilizations.

Although historians continue to debate the impact of gunpowder technology as opposed to other factors, Cortés's campaign employed native porters to transport a small number of light bronze cannon and heavier iron naval guns. Only a few of the Spaniards carried arquebuses and crossbows. Most of the invaders made effective use of their sharp-edged steel swords and defensive armor against natives who wore light quilted cotton armor and used war clubs imbedded with sharp obsidian chips. Aztec warriors who sought to capture prisoners for sacrifice rather than to kill them on the battlefield were no match for arquebusiers and swordsmen. Attacking in mass formations, they were perfect targets for slaughter. Even with a limited number of horses, the Spanish employed shock to break through and crush native infantry. Historians who downplay the impact of cannon and handguns do agree that at first firearms produced powerful psychological advantages. However, they argue that native familiarity with the weapons quickly produced defensive responses. Some sources refer to Aztec soldiers throwing themselves on the ground when they saw that a cannon was about to be fired and attacking in zigzag form to evade gunfire.

In spite of these views, even a few cannon and handguns acted as a catalyst to hasten the collapse of native resistance. Bernal Díaz recalled in his memoirs, "The steadfastness of our artillery, musketeers, and bowmen did much to save us, and we inflicted great casualties on them." Regarding the battles, he concluded, "One thing alone saved our lives: the enemy were so massed and so numerous that every shot wrought havoc among them." In the final siege of the Aztec capital that was surrounded by lakes and joined to the land by causeways, the Spaniards built small brigantines and mounted bronze and iron bow guns to bombard native canoe fleets, the causeways, and then to besiege and smash the city. Cut off and abandoned by former allies and now the victims of epidemics of *viruelas* (smallpox) or other European diseases, in August 1521 the last native emperor, Cuauhtémoc, opened negotiations for a surrender and then was captured while attempting to flee the city later that month. In many respects, Cortés inherited a city of the dead.

The treachery of Cortés in capturing Montezuma was to be replayed by Francisco Pizarro and his band of *conquistadores* against the Incan Empire of Peru. Again, divide and conquer techniques and the arrival of European and African microbes played important roles in conquest. The Spaniards achieved great success against sedentary agricultural civilizations ruled by powerful leaders and centralized systems. In many respects, the conquest was one of a few Spaniards with their gunpowder weaponry supported by native insurgent forces against the Aztecs or Inca factions that lacked this morale boosting support. Elsewhere in the Americas, seminomadic and nomadic peoples defended themselves more effectively against European arms and gunpowder technology. Cannon were useless if there were no opportunities for sieges, and handguns of the sixteenth century posed only limited threats. Shortages of gunpowder and of lead for balls often made traditional weapons more suitable for hit-and-run guerrilla-style combat and skirmishing. When the natives adopted horses, they rather than the Spaniards dominated many great frontier zones.

Remarkably, the military system evolved by the Spaniards during the *Reconquista* and improved in the training ground of the early-sixteenth-century wars of Italy, also opened the way to long-term military domination of Europe and the Americas. As Holy Roman Emperor Charles V drew upon enormous resources. His son, Philip II, though not a field soldier, taxed his empire and borrowed for grand military purposes until he literally bankrupted his possessions. The infantry *tercios* recruited multinational forces of Spaniards, Italians, Portuguese, Walloons, Burgundians, Germans, and attracted Catholic volunteers from Ireland, Scotland, and England as well as other countries. Effectively trained, well organized, led by excellent commanders, and conditioned over time to anticipate victory, even with mutinies during the wars of the Netherlands, the Spanish army retained its dominance until well into the seventeenth century. Adopting Swiss organization and some elements of the ancient legion, these multinational forces employed heavy rectangular and square tactical formations that offered excellent defensive cover as mobile bastions and possessed much greater mobility for rapid offensive action than some modern historians have argued.

Based on pikemen selected for their size and physical stamina and arquebusiers, these well-trained infantrymen formed flexible units capable of explosive attacks, offensive firepower, and intimidating defense behind a hedge of eighteen-foot-long pikes that overawed opposition infantry and cavalry. As the century progressed, the Spaniards increased the ratio of arquebusiers and then musketeers to pikemen until their numbers were roughly equal. However, writers of the period stressed the perils for any infantry force to deploy too many firearms for the number of pikemen or to permit the quality and training of pikers to deteriorate.

Fired from the shoulder using a forked rest in the "Spanish manner" to absorb recoil rather than from the breast in the "French manner," the musket was simply a large arquebus with a bore of twenty millimeters that fired a heavy single ball or five or six lighter ones over a lethal range of about four hundred meters. Compared to other weapons, the musket had the advantage of great flexibility for use on the battlefield, to defend trenches, to assault fortifications, and to fire bullets that could bring down even the most heavily armored cavalryman. In battle, musketeers formed deep lines of four or more ranks that fired and then countermarched to the rear to reload so that the unit could maintain a steady volley. Sir Roger Williams estimated that five hundred musketeers were worth one thousand troops armed with arquebuses or *calivers*. All European armies followed the Spanish example and adopted muskets over other firearms. Indeed, most soldiers demonstrated a strong preference for firearms over other weapons and recognized the prestige of the infantry musketeer.

Quite aware of the uncertainties involved in the use of arquebuses and muskets, veteran Spanish forces withheld their full volleys until enemy infantry or cavalry units were within twenty to fifty paces. As the enemy approached, a few Spanish soldiers opened a harassing fire at long range designed to "attract and to deceive fools" or to provoke a premature volley that would permit the men of the *tercios* to close rapidly to within twelve to fifteen paces of their opposition before they unleashed their own deadly volley. Wet weather made matchlock weapons almost useless and in the heat of battle faulty loading reduced the effectiveness of all but the best trained infantrymen. Often, soldiers fired seven or eight precip-

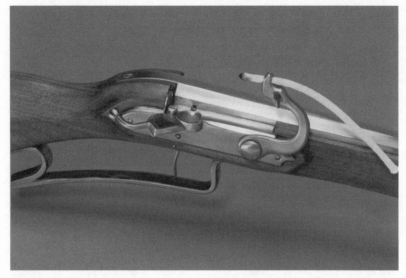

Fig. 6.3. Firing mechanism of a matchlock musket. Courtesy of Compagnie Royale D'Artillerie, La Prairie, Quebec.

itate rounds—heating up the barrels of their arquebuses or muskets so that their firearms functioned poorly and were more likely to misfire or even explode. If the matches were damp or poorly twisted, the weapons would not discharge. If the gunpowder carried by the infantryman was not well corned, bullets simply did not carry over much distance and fell short without damage to the opposition force. Some nervous men lowered the muzzles of their weapons so that the lead bullets rolled out harmlessly upon the ground. Commonly, in the heat and duress of battlefield conditions, anxious soldiers overcharged their muskets and were knocked flat by the recoil.

While infantrymen of the period did not dress in uniform clothing, they wore topcoats, breeches, jackets, shirts, underwear, wool stockings, and leather shoes. Before midcentury most protected themselves with armor including an iron helmet or morion, a heavy breastplate, and thigh pieces. The defensive pikemen wore mail shirts and hose, padded headpieces and iron codpieces, and padded gauntlets, and they used swords and daggers for personal defense. In addition to their heavy firearms, the arquebusiers and musketeers carried powder flasks, bandoleers of powder charges, touch boxes, scouring sticks, purses for bullets, priming irons for cleaning the touch holes, their own molds to cast bullets, steel and flint to strike fire, and dry, well-made matches. As the century progressed and as battles gave way to sieges and smaller skirmishes, many soldiers discarded the morion and cuirass, preferring flexibility over protection. Indeed, Spanish soldiers were given considerable latitude to dress themselves in the brightest colors and flamboyant fashions under the belief of commanders that individuality enhanced ferocity and warlike characteristics. As might be expected, soldiers who served for any length of time under combat conditions soon appeared to be little better attired than a band of ragged beggars.

Against cavalry, the infantry combination of pikes and muskets proved highly effective. Musket balls maimed and killed horses, penetrated the best armor, and often removed the advantage of shock traditionally enjoyed by mounted troops. While on occasion cavalry troops used velocity and shock to wreak havoc among unprepared pikemen mixed with musketeers, the discipline and training of Spanish forces made this a rare occurrence. On the positive side for cavalry, the invention of the wheel lock carbine and pistol early in the century opened the way for new tactical formations and increased the flexibility of mounted troops.

The wheel lock trigger mechanism operated on a coiled spring wound by a key much like an old fashioned wind-up toy. A pull of the trigger released a rapidly turning iron wheel that when pressed against a flint showered sparks into a pan that ignited its fine gunpowder and set off the main charge within the barrel and dispatched the bullet. Despite the high cost and relative fragility of the wheel lock pistol or carbine compared with matchlock muskets, this system had obvious advantages for cavalry use. The wheel lock did not require a lighted match and mounted soldiers needed to fire with only one hand—often carrying a reserve of two or three additional pistols in holsters. Some mounted troops abandoned the lance and developed a new tactical system called the caracole in which during charges the front rank of a cavalry formation fired, wheeled their horses, and rode to the rear to reload.

Although there are many theories about the offensive and defensive implications of the new elements of warfare and the rise of much larger armies, it is important to recall that monarchs such as Emperor Charles V and King Francis I of France possessed greater financial resources, larger populations, and more sophisticated bureaucracies required to recruit, train, deploy, and to supply their forces. Moreover, beyond their struggles to dominate the European and Mediterranean worlds, the ma-

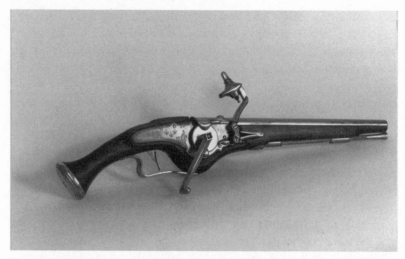

Fig. 6.4. Cavalry wheel-lock pistol. View of the mechanism and the gun. Courtesy of Compagnie Royale D'Artillerie, La Prairie, Quebec.

jor powers now reached outward to the Atlantic world and beyond to other continents, oceans, and seas. Global ambitions to dominate sea routes as well as islands and continents were supported by superior military and naval technology, by political and economic rivalries, and by deeply held beliefs that Christianity must prevail against Islam or other religions. In the process, the reputation of Spanish soldiers for their sanguinary brutalities remains alive even today. Catholic armies rampaged through the Protestant Netherlands and in the Americas, bands of Spanish *conquistadores* sometimes committed acts of untrammeled cruelty against the indigenous peoples. Part of this evil reputation resulted from effective Protestant wartime propaganda employing the newly invented printing press, but general cruelties and horrendous atrocities were common to all sixteenth-century armies and soldiers.

Military historians often have stressed these most negative themes and have neglected to note the importance of Spanish military organization that would influence Maurice of Nassau, Gustavus Adolphus, and other later military innovators. Because of the level of discipline, system of promotions, and effective organization, the Spanish army inculcated loyalty and professional pride unknown elsewhere during the period. In the Netherlands, commanders such as the dukes of Alba and Parma promoted officers of proven battlefield talent rather than selecting candidates based upon their noble birth alone. Parma achieved widespread contemporary recognition as the best general of his epoch. Following enlistment and the oath of allegiance to uphold the articles of war that defined discipline and duties, Spanish soldiers received excellent training and careful supervision from their captains and noncommissioned officers who taught them to play effective roles within their companies. They practiced how to handle muskets and other weapons, learned tactical maneuvers by constant repetition, and became fully accustomed to the disciplined evolutions used during combat. Because Spanish units tended to stay together for long periods, the soldiers developed high morale, discipline, and level of training. Although mutinies became a problem later in the century among unpaid battle weary forces stationed in the Netherlands, rigorous discipline and harsh punishments under military justice made soldiers think carefully before they contemplated resistance to their officers.

With lengthy sieges much more frequent than conventional battles through much of the sixteenth century, the Spanish army led in the development of techniques required to assault fortifications. First, the besiegers fortified their own encampments and approached the enemy walls with carefully constructed trenches starting outside the effective range of defensive artillery fire. With the establishment of a strong fortified position, the attackers deployed up to half of their forces to interdict commerce, raid, secure food supplies, and to construct roads, bridges, and other works needed to site their heavy siege artillery. Guided by the published treatises of experts such as Bernardino de Mendoza, Spanish pioneers were methodical in their construction of intricate networks of well-designed zigzag and winding trenches protected by temporary bulwarks, towers, and built up flanks. Often the deep trenches that approached the enemy walls and fortifications were of a breadth to permit two or three soldiers to move comfortably through the system abreast and in case of counterattacks to allow for movement and possible hasty withdrawals of the most advanced artillery positions. They constructed protective works for their artillery pieces that battered enemy fortifications from ranges outside of effective defensive musket fire, and they dug deep bunkers to protect assault troops assigned to attack enemy breaches.

Once defensive flanking fire had been eliminated, Spanish units competed—often throwing dice—for the dubious honor of leading the first charge. Supported by arquebus and musket fire, they attacked with pikes and muskets—attempting to drive the defenders back and to consolidate their advance with gabions, sandbags, and wheeled portable wooden screens designed to deflect shot. They drew up their own artillery pieces to expand the breach and to bolster an advance into the city or fortress. If the enemy capitulated or collapsed without terms, the victorious Spanish soldiers often sacked, plundered, and looted everything of value and sometimes committed brutal acts common in all armies during an epoch that condoned cruelties. In 1553 at the bloody conclusion of the siege of the Château of Hesdin for example, French captives were tied together by their genitalia with arquebus fuse cords and tortured by violent yanks at the tethers so that they would reveal which soldiers were of families wealthy enough to make them worth holding for ransom. Having gained information, the captors slit the throats of all French prisoners determined to be too poor to provide sufficient profit.

To counteract the offensive firepower of armies equipped with cannon, culverins, demi-culverins, and the lighter *sakers* and falconettes as well as arquebuses and muskets, even by the beginning of the sixteenth century Italian engineers had begun to design expensive new types of defensive fortifications that were quite unlike earlier medieval square or round towers and curtain walls. Engineers such as Antonio da Sangallo the Younger developed angle bastions constructed of earth faced with stone that to eliminate enemy flanking fire were built to project outward from curtain walls much like arrowheads. This system, called the *trace italienne*, or bastioned trace, soon spread throughout Europe and then the world in port facilities designed to protect overseas colonies. Where older medieval walls and towers remained, military architects added modern star-shaped bastions, interlocking fields of fire, moats, ravelins, and other sophisticated defensive elements.

Whether as some historians argue this system that permitted defensive forces to employ heavy guns against attackers also contributed to a military revolution and much larger armies is a debatable question. Until the end of the century, heavy guns—offensive and defensive—remained inaccurate, inefficient, and cumbersome. Even with the addition of crude sights in the 1570s and the use of quadrants to determine elevation, uncontrolled recoil, changeable weather, fractures, the condition of gun carriages, and the quality of gunpowder and shot made the artillery commander's work an art as well as a science. Muzzle-loading guns fired slowly and had to be sponged out carefully between rounds to remove partially burned powder that otherwise might lead to disastrous explosions. Even with the development of cloth or paper cartridges around midcentury, the maintenance of an effective rate of fire delivered accurately was the exception rather than the rule for most battles and sieges.

The development of the bastioned trace did enhance the strength of defensive forces and made lengthy sieges rather than open field battles a common element of sixteenth-century warfare. Major cities of Flanders, the Netherlands, Germany, and North Africa suffered a succession of prolonged sieges. In France where religious civil war raged between Catholic and Protestant Huguenot forces, Paris faced sieges in 1589, 1591, and 1594. As a result, advances in engineering and in the adoption of new types of fortifications spread rapidly from one theater of war to another.

Based upon more and more complex geometric planning, the new designs of the *trace italienne* resisted the battering impact of cannon fire and of mining. Low lying brick-faced earthen ramparts absorbed shot and even exploding mines without collapse or crumbling. The interlocking fields of fire from bastions deterred attempts at escalade, protected defenders from the fire of attackers, and eliminated blind spots that might be used to approach the curtain walls. The defenders of these fortifications often held the advantage of being able to fire on attackers with their own artillery without exposing themselves to the besiegers. Carefully engineered bastions or firing platforms projecting outward into the moat or ditch protected the curtain walls and removed any possibility of flanking attacks. By the end of the century, these designs had become progressively more complex with the addition of ravelins, *horneworks*, and *demilunes* to create self-contained yet interconnected fortresses to support the general defensive system of the entire structure.

The construction of great earth fortifications at Antwerp, Maastricht, Ostend, and at other strategic locations in the Netherlands and in other places where wet ditches supplemented older and new defensive works, made offensive warfare much more expensive. Naturally, besieging and assaulting forces required more troops and significant attention to finance and logistical support. Whether or not the newer fortifications required larger garrisons, cities and governments had to have sufficient economic vitality to maintain defensive troops, to undertake expensive maintenance and expansion programs and to provide the heavy artillery pieces and munitions needed to sustain a possible siege. Even today, a walk around the massive walls and fortifications of Italian cities such as Lucca or Siena cannot fail to impress modern observers. Of course, the complexity and immensity of these defensive works underscores the fact that at least for some time these vibrant economies possessed the tax base or the credit needed to fund the enormous costs.

Even if the offensive forces and defensive garrisons were not sufficiently different to evoke the term "revolution" connected with warfare, clearly, both at home and abroad during the sixteenth century, many European powers possessed surplus funds to undertake continuous military expenditures. Following the Treaty of Cateau-Cambrésis in 1559, for example, the Continent faced chronic warfare for two entire generations. The Turks continued their assaults by land and sea, Protestant states resisted Catholic dominance, and France fought a series of debilitating civil wars that reduced its influence as a major military power. As a result, the costs of war continued to escalate, armies and navies became more permanent and professional, and monarchs sought to exercise greater centralized authority.

Even for the greatest states, the structural and financial demands of offensive and defensive warfare in terms of fortifications, weapons, equipment, transport, and ongoing expenditures to pay and maintain forces presented immense—even insoluble—problems. Adding the costs of fleets to defend coasts and to carry warfare overseas, nations needed to devise new ways to raise funding and to tax their subjects. Notwithstanding the best efforts of the Habsburg kings Charles V and Philip II, they lacked the bureaucracies and the will to extract funding among diverse populations that often resisted the burdens occasioned by defense and the spiraling costs of warfare. Indeed, the logistical demands of global military power were well beyond the fiscal capabilities of any sixteenth-century state. For Spain, the acquisition and distribution of pay and fresh rations for troops stationed in coastal watchtowers, aboard fleet vessels, garrisoned throughout the Mediterranean and in the Low Countries, devoured domestic revenues and compelled significant borrowing. Italian and Spanish soldiers stationed at Algiers, Oran, Tunis, Tripoli, Melilla, Mers el-Kebir, Bougie, and other distant North African presidios often ate contaminated rations, suffered through famines, felt totally abandoned amidst hostile Islamic cultures, and passed their lives in misery awaiting pay, supplies, and reinforcements that came only intermittently if at all.

Despite the windfall treasure of the Americas and increased revenues raised in Europe, Spain's military commitments vastly exceeded income. Huge loans made bankers the unhappy partners of the Habsburgs as they saw no alternatives to lending new funds in the vain hope of eventual repayment. Charles V spent lavishly to raise armies that totaled more than 150,000 men. Philip II expanded his land and sea forces even further to deal with Turkish expansion in the Mediterranean and Balkans, the Dutch Rebellion (an average of 65,000 troops in Spanish pay over an eighty-year period), and the assaults directed against England and Ireland.

In 1557, the Spanish crown declared bankruptcy for the first time, later defaulting on several other occasions before the century ended. Each crisis caused by ballooning military expenditures also provoked mutinies among distant unpaid army garrisons. When this occurred, major bankers in Italy, Germany, and elsewhere faced the prospect of ruin. In the Netherlands, long unpaid and desperate Spanish troops mutinied on at least forty occasions to loot cities and to commit brutalities against civilian populations. Angry troops, drawn out sieges that endured for months and left soldiers soft and in poor physical shape, and sharp religious divisions between Roman Catholicism and Protestantism made warfare even more brutal and inhumane than was common in this period. For example, the sack of Antwerp by Spanish and allied troops following a surprise attack upon a breach permanently damaged the reputation of Spain's soldiers. Described by Protestant writers as the Spanish Fury, this cruel wartime atrocity cost as many as eight thousand Dutch lives and contributed to the burgeoning negative propaganda campaign against Spain known as the Black Legend.

Although the Spaniards with all of their world military commitments suffered most severely from having to support expeditionary campaigns as well as standing armies and navies, France also declared bankruptcy in the 1550s and again in 1588. In England, Queen Elizabeth's advisors feared that the costs of equipping and training a force of twenty thousand troops to defend against a possible Spanish Armada invasion would overwhelm the nation's finances. In fact, relatively limited English military intervention in the Netherlands rose from a cost of £23,000 in 1588 to £175,000 in 1597. In Ireland during the last decades of the century, the costs of the English occupation army reached almost £2,000,000.

Despite rapidly growing expenditures, individual soldiers of the gunpowder age cannot be said to have lived more comfortable lives. Machiavelli's ideal published in his *Art of War* in 1521 that wars should be waged by citizen armies and not by foreign professionals fell upon deaf ears. German, Flemish, Spanish, Italian, and other troops recruited, trained, and paid by Charles V and Philip II served for decades away from their homelands in the Netherlands, Austria, Germany, in Mediterranean island garrisons such as Malta, and in the North African presidios of Algiers, Oran, and Tunis where Khereddin Barbarrosa and other Islamic chiefs became chronic threats as allies of the Ottomans. Many soldiers who managed to survive harsh conditions, injuries, and disease settled permanently near their overseas garrisons and never returned to their native lands. For Spain, Italy, and parts of Germany, for example, the chronic drain of young males into permanent military service produced a negative influence upon industry and agriculture. Most soldiers suffered in poverty, borrowed money against their pay, dealt with rapacious captains and paymasters, and sustained themselves with dreams of windfall plunder that might result from a successful siege or the capture of a wealthy prisoner. Soldiers stationed in North Africa suffered chronic shortages of food and were hungry almost all of the time. Most ate bad food and consumed contaminated water that gave them food poisoning, dysentery, typhoid, and other diseases. They lived in wretched conditions and more often than not dressed in clothing that was little more than a collection of rags. Many went barefoot and even during active campaign duty they lacked adequate clothing and footwear. One can only imagine the horror of Spanish soldiers in North Africa in 1569 who received a shipment of two thousand pairs of shoes, but only in sizes suitable for little girls.

In addition to these hardships, a variety of diseases such as measles, typhus, smallpox, influenza, cholera, and malaria spread in crowded garrisons where the troops suffered from unhygienic conditions. Commencing with Charles VIII's invasion of Italy during the 1490s, soldiers and civilians reported a new disease that produced pustules, running sores, and the "pestiferous buboes," known later as the *morbus gallicus*, French Pox, *Mal de Nápoles*, or syphilis. Originating in the New World and most likely carried by Spanish troops into Italy, syphilis became a permanent companion of military forces and a destroyer of lives. Hardened by diseases, difficult conditions, and everyday brutalities, notwithstanding that fact that many of the sixteenth-century wars were fought over religious principles, veteran soldiers of different armies were well known for their blasphemous expressions and sometimes even for their denial of God.

In many instances, women and children accompanied their men as wives or companions serving in many roles in support of military forces. Women foraged for food and fuel, cooked, sewed and laundered clothing, cared for wounded and convalescent soldiers, constructed camps and fortifications, and fulfilled numerous other essential services. Accompanying armies on the move, the so-called camp followers (*forces courtisanes*) often more than doubled the total numbers of fighting men. While officers and other observers often condemned these women as lowly soldiers' whores, such a definition disguised essential roles well beyond casual sexual relationships. Many commanders recognized that married soldiers stood up better to the rigors of duty at sieges than bachelors who had to provide and care for themselves. Indeed, with pay often in arrears for months or years, soldiers' women and children worked, stole, begged, or prostituted themselves to earn extra income. The Germans appointed a special officer, the *Hurenweibel* ("sergeant of whores"), to organize women noncombatants. The duke of Alba who had to move forces northward from Italy to the Netherlands, appointed officers to organize the many women who accompanied his army.

While women served armies in large numbers, they were not present on the battlefields except in the aftermath of combat, when they helped to rescue wounded soldiers, scavenged, and often plundered the enemy dead. During sieges where they were trapped in fortifications and towns with the rest of the populace, women often joined their men in desperate defense of breaches against enemy attackers who threatened rape, pillage, and barbarous atrocities if they succeeded. With blind intolerance between Protestants and Catholics and passionate hatred between Christians and Islamic opponents, women could not afford to confine themselves to noncombatant roles. At Maastricht in 1579 as at other Dutch towns besieged and threatened by Spanish troops, women fought alongside their men, threw pots of boiling water, and cast blazing hoops soaked in pitch in the faces of attacking soldiers. When the town collapsed, a bloody general massacre ensued as invading soldiers took revenge upon the now defenseless women and children as well as the men.

In addition to the dangers of diseases such as typhus, dysentery, scurvy, bubonic plague, diphtheria, smallpox, malaria, tuberculosis, and venereal complaints that accompanied sieges and campaigns—not to mention inadequate sanitation or the absence of basic hygiene—soldiers almost invariably died from infections resulting from gunshot wounds, pike thrusts, burns, or other injuries. At the siege of Metz in 1552 where the duke of Alba commanded roughly 120,000 troops, his military surgeons were so incompetent that the death rates convinced the troops that there was some secret conspiracy to poison all of the wounded.

While there was no plot, the impact of large low-velocity lead and iron bullets and balls fired by muskets and artillery pieces produced ragged wounds that were most difficult to repair. Invariably, projectiles drove fragments of armor, clothing, and shattered bone deep into the soft tissues of victims.

Most surgeons of the period believed that gunpowder was a poisonous substance that infected wounds. If simple amputation of a damaged limb above the injury was not possible, surgeons dilated wounds, probed with their fingers and unsterile instruments, and then either injected boiling oil or cauterized injured tissue with heated irons. Sometimes the oil included ten or more additional ingredients such as white wine, olive oil, *hypericum, cardius benedictus*, valerian, sage, Venice turpentine, *olibanum*, myrrh, butter, barrow's grease, and *sanguis draconis*. Following this treatment, surgeons applied ointments such as precipitate of mercury and covered wounds with plasters and messy dressings containing quite vile ingredients such as ground frogs, worms, and vipers. The intention was to produce suppuration or the "laudable pus" thought to have been recommended by Hippocrates and Galen. Almost invariably, however, such treatments produced sepsis, gangrene, and other infections that killed patients within a short time or produced long-term disabled veterans who lived miserable lives wracked with pain.

With the proliferation of firearms and increase in the size and use of armed forces, surgeons did learn from practical experience about how to improve their techniques. In 1559, Henry II of France suffered a head wound during a sporting joust when his opponent's lance entered his visor and pierced his forehead. The army surgeon Andreas Vesalius (1514–64)—now known as the father of modern anatomy—experimented to learn the nature of the king's injuries by duplicating the angle of the thrust upon the heads of four decapitated criminals. Vesalius determined correctly that the French king had suffered what would be a fatal wound from splinters that pierced his brain.

Similarly, Ambroise Paré (1510–90), a self-educated French barber surgeon, through his observations and experiments during a long career as an army surgeon, invented surgical instruments, wrote about treating gunshot wounds, and even developed artificial limbs. On one occasion while following the accepted treatment of cauterizing bullet wounds by injecting scalding oil and treacle, Paré ran out of oil and had to leave some patients untreated overnight. The next morning he discovered that these wounded soldiers suffered less inflammation, infection, and pain than those who had received the hot oil treatment. Accustomed to treating many soldiers who suffered deep facial burns caused by gunpowder flashes, Paré learned from knowledgeable country women that binding up such injuries after the application of heavy balms and oils was much less successful than leaving the wounds open and dressing them with crushed onions and salt. For amputations, Paré reintroduced the old Roman practice of ligature of blood vessels in amputations, rather than cauterizing with hot irons. As a result, Paré's patients suffered much less bleeding, shock, and tissue damage. Through direct observations, Paré abandoned older approaches and wrote practical handbooks to assist other surgeons.

Unfortunately, wounded soldiers did not always encounter medical practitioners of Paré's high ability. Although some armies organized permanent medical facilities and temporary field hospitals, these were seldom adequate. Armies on active duty appointed medical personnel, assembled supplies of medicines and hospital tents, and appointed medical attendants. Nevertheless, most forces lacked the organization to dispatch rescue teams onto battlefields immediately following combat or to organize the effective withdrawal of wounded soldiers from advanced siege lines. As a result, army surgeons contended with putrefied wounds often filled with maggots and gangrene that made amputations and removal of corrupted flesh absolutely essential. Some surgeons treated wounds with "arsenic and rusty Bacon" and used a jumble of resins, oils, wine, syrups, and extracts, and even mothers' milk and strong beer. They drained wounds by inserting lead and silver pipes and kept them open to allow the expurgation of "superfluous humors." Without adequate medical personnel, almost all battlefields such as that of San Quentin in August 1557 were left literally covered with dead and dying men and horses. Beyond the horrendous stench of putrefying flesh that emanated from the cadavers of men and horses in the summer heat, observers described clouds of buzzing blue and green flies that rose up in clouds that almost obliterated the sun when disturbed.

For every good army surgeon available, there were hundreds of charlatans, cranks, and impostors whose false cures did much more damage than good. Other dubious assistants such as corrupt priests who wished to obtain legacies from drawing up soldiers' wills and medical quacks followed armies to prey off the misfortunes of injured and sick soldiers. Some impostors prescribed absolutely ridiculous and dangerous concoctions, prayed reverentially over the wounded, placed signs of the cross

upon their injuries, and even promised to transfer to themselves the op-
pressive pain and suffering of their wounded patients. Inevitably, the
deaths of sick and injured soldiers from neglect and infections forced
many charlatans to flee precipitously if they were to avoid being hanged,
garroted, or shot for their evil interventions.

At sea, gunpowder weapons, new designs, and changed tactics paralleled innovations in land warfare. Although exact dating is difficult,
guns appeared aboard the cumbersome round ships used in the Atlantic
by as early as the mid-fourteenth century. With a length to beam ratio of about two to one and the use of towering fore- and stern castles designed to gain the advantage of height over potential foes, soldiers aboard these ships experimented with light guns in place of other
weapons and archers.

Prior to the sixteenth century, warships were almost always converted
merchant vessels that with garrisons of soldiers and guns placed on the
main deck and in the castles became floating fortresses. These vessels
were often poor sailors incapable of handling heavy weather and prone
to capsizing and other accidents. In their techniques of fighting, commanders first ordered an exchange of gunfire and then proceeded to
grapple and board enemy vessels for hand-to-hand combat. Seagoing
battles were made similar to attacks against fortresses on land. Often,
defenders retreated to the castles or below decks, defending themselves
until driven out by fire, force of arms, or negotiated surrender.

In the Mediterranean, the ancient naval workhorse the oared galley inspired the development of galleasses, contributed elements to the
sixteenth-century ocean-going galleons, and finally to the ships of the
line of the seventeenth century. Although boarding and hand-to-hand
combat characterized Mediterranean naval warfare, heavy guns placed at
the bow and stern of galleys enhanced the military potency of these vessels. Directing the galley toward its target—much like a modern fighter
aircraft—the objective was to use flank attack to strike at the exposed
banks of oars and the galley slaves and finally to ram and lodge the projecting bow spur into the enemy vessel.

Sixteenth-century warfare in the Mediterranean Sea directly paralleled the great land struggles between Hapsburg power centered in
Spain, Italy, and Austria against the Ottoman Turks. Following the
fall of Constantinople in 1453, the Turks attacked Venetian fleets and
moved to conquer island bases that would open the sea lanes to the
west. In 1480, an Ottoman force commanded by Gedik Ahment Pasha

attacked southern Italy and captured Otranto—alarming all Christian powers. Although these raids stopped for a time, in 1488 an Ottoman force attacked Malta and opened an expansive phase that was to carry Turkish power across North Africa. Moving against the Balkans, Sultan Suleiman captured Belgrade (1521), Rhodes (1522–23), and his forces attacked Hungary (1526) and besieged Vienna (1529).

Employing gunpowder weapons, modern fortifications, and galley fleets rowed by thousands of Christian captives, by the 1530s corsair fleets commanded by Khereddin Barbarossa carried seagoing guerrilla warfare against Spain and other Christian powers. In 1529, Spanish forces at Algiers suffered defeat in their forts that were pounded by effective Islamic artillery fire. Responding with a Christian alliance called the Holy League, Charles V had to divert forces and attention away from Germany and the wars against the Protestants to defend the Mediterranean against Islamic expansion. In 1541 for example, the emperor, accompanied by many illustrious soldiers including Hernando Cortés, the conqueror of Mexico, commanded sixty-five galleys and 450 supply vessels with twelve thousand sailors and twenty-four thousand soldiers in an attack to regain control of Algiers. Although Barbarossa had only six thousand troops, heavy rains and violent storms soaked Spanish gunpowder. Many ships were wrecked on the Algerian coast and the invasion failed utterly.

The indented Spanish and Italian coasts were a paradise for corsair raiders and effective defense required extensive garrisons and constant vigilance. By the 1560s military engineers such as Gian Baptista Antonelli planned extensive port fortifications and systems of coastal defense towers equipped with artillery. In the New World, attacks by English, French, Dutch, and others led Antonelli and fellow engineers to plan massive port fortifications at strategic locations such as Havana, Veracruz, Campeche, Cartagena, Panama, Santo Domingo, and Puerto Rico. As might be expected, effective defensive systems based upon complex fortifications and artillery were seldom completed, extremely expensive to maintain, and difficult to garrison. Without an imminent threat of attack, most defense systems cost so much that they crumbled rapidly, garrisons lost combat effectiveness and gun carriages rotted in tropical heat. In some instances, Spanish soldiers stationed in North African presidios suffered so much from isolation and lack of supplies that either they deserted or allowed themselves to be captured. In the New World, corruption, diseases, and loss of morale among defensive forces permitted small numbers of raiders to overwhelm defended port towns and cities.

In 1565 a large Turkish force besieged the Island of Malta defended by the Knights of St. John. For a month, Turkish forces attacked the fortress of St. Elmo with heavy artillery fire and dug trenches that permitted them to advance close to the walls where they opened several breaches. After many furious assaults, St. Elmo fell and the victors executed all of the survivors, incised their bodies with crosses, and threw them into the harbor. Having lost up to eight thousand troops in the first siege, the Turks now turned their heavy batteries against the castles of St. Michael and St. Angelo. The bombardment smashed the older fortifications, but the modern bastions, artillery, and arquebusiers backed by pikemen repulsed each attack against open breaches. After months of debilitating assaults, the Turkish invaders suffered so many battle and disease casualties—as many as twenty-four thousand deaths—that they had no alternative other than to withdraw. Hastened by a Spanish fleet, they left behind twenty-four great artillery pieces, many smaller guns, and a litter of abandoned ships and equipment. Five years later, however, the Turks assembled an army of fifty thousand troops and 116 galleys that assaulted and occupied the island of Cyprus.

With Venice and its empire threatened by Turkish expansion, Philip II of Spain assembled a Mediterranean galley fleet commanded by his half-brother, Don Juan de Austria, who was only twenty-six years of age at the time. Alessandro Farnese of Parma, who, like Don Juan, was later to lead Spanish forces in the Netherlands and to be involved in the 1588 Armada scheme against England, served with the Christian fleet and commanded Italian troops aboard the galleys. On October 7, 1571, at Lepanto on the Gulf of Corinth, the two great galley fleets collided— the Christians with over 200 galleys, including six large heavy-gunned Venetian galleasses, against about 230 Turkish galleys. In terms of firepower, the Christians deployed some 1,815 cannon against only 750 in the Turkish galleys. Don Juan arranged his fleet in the form of a broad crescent—with right, center, and left wings—and backed this main force with a strong rearguard reserve squadron. To prevent desertions common in coalition forces involved in galley warfare, he mixed the ships of different allied nationalities.

As in many epochal naval clashes, in some respects the Battle of Lepanto caught both sides by surprise. With almost twenty to twenty-five thousand Spanish, Italian, and German troops aboard the Christian galleys, many of whom were arquebusiers, and sixteen thousand Turkish land troops, including six thousand Janissaries armed with arquebuses, the battle transformed seagoing warfare essentially into a series of bloody land-style skirmishes waged from deck to deck as the galleys grappled in mortal combat and soldiers swarmed from ship to ship to assault their enemies. The Christians wore heavy armor and possessed many more firearms than the unarmored Turks, many of whom still used bows and arrows. At the beginning of the battle, the six great Venetian galeasses advanced to lead the Christian crescent firing their heavy batteries and employing irresistible ramming power to splinter the much lighter Turkish galleys.

After several hours of bloody combat and fierce fights between individual galleys and squadrons of galleys, the Christians began to prevail and in the end annihilated the Turks. That the Christians out-gunned their enemies in both heavy artillery and arquebuses played a significant role in the outcome. In what was in some respects a most decisive sea battle, for eight thousand Christians killed, the Turks lost almost two hundred galleys, thirty thousand soldiers, and fifteen thousand galley slaves. Don Juan ordered the head of Ali Pasha, the Turkish admiral, raised on a pike aboard his galley *Real*, and the great battle standard from Mecca was sent with the spoils of victory to Philip II at the Escorial in Spain, where they may be seen today.

Turkish casualties included some of their best trained naval officers who were impossible to replace and many heavy guns. In the aftermath, large numbers of captured Turkish soldiers suffered summary execution. However, while many observers and later historians viewed Lepanto as a decisive watershed, the Turks managed to replace their losses and for decades maintained pressure upon the Christian powers. With chronic warfare on land and sea in North Africa and many well-trained Islamic arquebusiers exiled from Spain, who were desirous of revenge against their Christian oppressors, there would be little peace and many opportunities for both Christians and Moslems to end up as prisoners for ransom, galley slaves, and servants in the service of their enemies.

In 1578, King Sebastian of Portugal and two Islamic contenders for power in Morocco perished in the Battle of Alcázarquivir in which Spanish Moslem arquebusiers and effective Moroccan artillerists fought against Portuguese forces. Between ten and twenty thousand Portuguese and mercenary soldiers from as far away as England became prisoners and galley slaves. As a direct result, Philip II invaded Portugal, making

Fig. 6.5. *The Battle of Lepanto* (anonymous artist). National Maritime Museum, London. Courtesy of Compagnie Royale D'Artillerie, La Prairie, Quebec.

Spain a veritable global empire that spanned Africa, the Americas, the Indian Ocean, and the Pacific world.

The dramatic thrust of Europeans to achieve hegemony in the Atlantic Ocean and around the globe grew in large part from the technological advances and adaptations emerging from the Mediterranean area. Sixteenth-century ship designs improved sea worthiness, sail carrying capacity, and, above all, fighting power that advanced European ships from technical inferiority compared with Chinese vessels to a point that they gained absolute global dominance. In 1519 the expedition of Ferdinand Magellan with five ships set out from Seville, Spain, to circumnavigate the world, by way of the Strait of Magellan and across the Pacific Ocean, and to tap the fabled riches of Asia. Although few men survived to return to Spain, this epic voyage underscored Europe's preeminence in maritime technology and fueled the expansive dreams of nations that possessed new ship designs and gunpowder weapons. The ships were armed for possible military action and Magellan perished in the Philippine Islands as he led some of his men armed with guns in a local conflict used to underscore the military potency of Europeans.

Although the subject of naval development is complex, during the fifteenth century the Portuguese, Castilians, and Basques altered the square-rigged ships of western Europe and experimented with different hull designs and Arab-style triangular lateen sails used in the Mediterranean. One can trace two separate streams of marine development, one Atlantic based that produced the merchant hulk, *nao*, and *carrack* constructed to carry bulk cargoes and the agile caravel developed by the Portuguese and Spanish. With much longer Atlantic voyages of exploration and conquest, Portuguese builders added a third mizzenmast or later even four masts to their vessels so that they could combine square-rig and lateen-rig in what became the *caravela redonda*. These caravels allowed for a greater spread of canvas and for better qualities of sailing close-hauled to the wind.

Gradually, marine builders altered these vessel designs to improve oceanic cruising capabilities. They increased size and complexity to enable ships to carry heavy artillery and larger crew complements including specialist gunners and soldiers. In 1502, for example, Vasco da Gama's ships bombarded the Indian port city of Calicut into submission, and in 1508, a Portuguese squadron used artillery broadsides to overwhelm a fleet dispatched by the Mamluk Sultan of Egypt. By the 1530s and 1540s, a recognizable *nao*- or galleon-style of vessel suitable as warship and cargo carrier emerged in several different countries. Often, these sailing vessels were heavily armed, well equipped, and able to carry war materials, large crews, and sufficient provisions for lengthy voyages and distant combat. Unlike the galleys discussed previously, *naos* and galleons could remain at sea for protracted periods or undertake prolonged coastal blockades. And as land fortresses evolved to deal with the battering impact of heavy siege guns, the seagoing galleons followed a complex course of development.

Until this period, even a major power like Spain possessed no permanent Atlantic navy to match its Mediterranean galley forces, and ocean-going squadrons had to be hired or pressed into the service of nations. For wartime uses, shipyards converted merchant ships by adding heavier guns, altering the superstructure to strengthen and raise the castles, and by placing on board a detachment of marine troops.

By the 1550s—after years of maritime warfare against the French—the great Spanish admiral Alvaro de Bazán, marqués de Santa Cruz, pressed for the development of specialized galleons of over five hundred tons and equipped with heavy broadside armaments. These purpose-designed warships were to have finer lines than merchant *naos* converted temporarily for naval functions. These designs duplicated similar evolutionary changes in Elizabethan warships of types that would be employed against Spain during the 1588 Armada campaign.

By the beginning of the sixteenth century, many Atlantic vessels like those of the Mediterranean carried a variety of defensive firearms designed to ward off pirates and other potential boarders. Placed in the bows and poop, mounted on the main deck to fire over or through embrasures in the gunwales, and in the high fore- and aft-castles, the weight of cannon made ships dangerously top heavy. Moreover, uncontrolled recoil sometimes sent heavy guns crashing across the decks to wreak havoc with gunners and equipment.

The obvious solution of situating the heavy bronze or iron muzzle-loading guns lower down between decks and of piercing the ship's sides with gun ports demanded new thinking by mariners and ship builders who at first resisted any weakening of hulls. Nevertheless, by about 1500 French and English shipyards introduced hinged ports or scuttles that could be closed securely to prevent leakage during bad weather. With this innovation, heavy guns could be placed on one or more decks along the length of the vessel.

In England, King Henry VIII (1509–47) ordered bronze guns from the master gun builder Hans Poppenruyter of Malines, and directed the manufacture of cheaper cast-iron guns founded from Sussex ores that had high phosphorous content and almost no sulfur to cause flaws and cracks. With time, English gun manufacturers learned how to pour molten iron and to cool their castings slowly without quenching. Aboard ships, these guns were set on sledges and on four-wheeled carriages fitted with wedges and tackles to improve aiming and to control recoil. With these developments, ships equipped with heavy guns became floating fortresses capable of massed broadside fire that could severely damage other vessels and permit attacks against shore fortifications.

Although broadside firing would change naval tactics dramatically through the century, it would take some time for the new ship designs and best tactical uses to be fully understood. Henry VIII's one-thousand-ton ship *Henry Grace a Dieu*, the six-hundred-ton *Mary Rose*, and the *Great Harry* were heavily gunned, but at the same time they were unwieldy vessels. The *Great Harry* carried 184 guns, but only forty-three were of heavy caliber capable of really damaging other ships. The heaviest guns aboard were four great cannon, sixty-pounders that were over eight feet in length. The *Mary Rose*, also heavily gunned, capsized and sank off Portsmouth in 1545 with the loss of over four hundred men. As if to underscore the embarrassment as well as the need for changes, Henry VIII and a large crowd had assembled on shore to observe a good sea battle against marauding French warships. Much to general consternation, even prior to engaging the enemy, *Mary Rose* heeled over suddenly and sank—possibly because the lower gun ports situated near the waterline had been left open.

With voyages to the Americas, Africa, and the Indian Ocean, European ships had to fulfill a variety of defensive and offensive requirements—without even mentioning the capacity to handle dangerous new routes, storms, treacherous currents, and other little understood meteorological conditions such as hurricanes and typhoons. At first, Spanish ships traversed the Atlantic alone, but by as early as the 1520s returning vessels—often Basque multipurpose *naos*—laden with treasure and other products ran the gauntlet of heavily armed French and North African pirate squadrons that lurked in the sea lanes of the eastern Atlantic. Before long, pirates and privateers crossed the ocean to pursue their depredations in the Caribbean. In response, Charles V authorized a small fleet of warships to patrol the Atlantic paid for by a new tax called the *avería* levied on all merchandise and cargo shipped in both directions. The patrols covered a vast ocean area from the Canary Islands to the Azores and the Portuguese coast.

With the ongoing struggles between Charles V and Francis I, maritime defense became both enormously expensive and difficult to maintain without much larger fleets committed to regular patrols. By the 1530s the Spaniards adopted a defensive approach of arming merchant ships with heavy guns and organizing them into convoys protected by small squadrons of warships. Gradually, this system evolved so that by midcentury there were two annual fleets (*flotas*) outbound to the Americas, subdividing once they reached the Caribbean to service the markets of Cartagena, Panama (including trans-Isthmian Pacific destinations), Veracruz, and other fortified ports. The fleet reassembled at Havana, Cuba, passed through the dangerous Bahamas Channel where enemy raiders sometimes waited and returned to Europe.

Regulated by detailed naval ordinances, these fleets returned the American treasure that helped Charles V and Philip II fund their vast European military enterprises. As might be expected, the enemies of Spain soon sought to broaden their trans-Atlantic attacks. In 1556, a force of French raiders landed in Cuba and sacked the port of Havana. By the 1560s, English contrabandists and corsairs such as John Hawkins and Francis Drake set the scene for major future sea and land confrontations in American waters. In 1568, Hawkins with five ships—one commanded by Drake—eluded Spanish warships and occupied Veracruz on the Mexican coast only to be trapped in harbor by the much stronger incoming Spanish fleet. Following negotiations in which the English sought to seek some means to flee, the Spaniards attacked the illegal intruders and destroyed most of their ships. Drake managed to escape and like many other Elizabethan mariners swore to have his revenge against the nefarious Dons.

On the Spanish side, adequate defense of New World ports now demanded the construction of impregnable fortresses based upon the latest European designs and garrisoned by regular troops. In the struggle for domination of the seas, the opposing contenders moved inevitably toward more definitive confrontations. By 1585 Drake in command of a fleet of twenty warships entered the Caribbean with plans to capture Cartagena, to occupy the Isthmus of Panama, and to destroy the port of Havana. While Cartagena fell, disease and battle casualties prevented the English on this occasion from attempting a more permanent occupation of Spanish territories in the New World.

The epochal but scarcely definitive expedition of the 1588 Spanish Armada dispatched by Philip II against England could not have come as a great surprise to Elizabeth I or any other knowledgeable English observer. Defender of Roman Catholicism, his Netherlands possessions, and a vast overseas empire, for Philip II the events of 1588 were simply the culmination of decades of growing enmity and xenophobia. Both sides characterized the other as truly loathsome and devilish. Queen Elizabeth I had sent funds and troops to support Dutch Protestant rebels, and English interlopers attacked and plundered Spanish shipping and the New World possessions. In the waters off the Netherlands, Zeeland's powerful Sea Beggars defeated Spanish naval squadrons and captured ports such as Brill, Flushing, and Leyden. The Spanish plan to invade England matured from ideas first discussed in the 1570s that involved a marine assault against Britain utilizing the land forces of the duke of Alba based in the Netherlands. In 1583 following the Marqués de Santa Cruz's naval victory over the Portuguese at the Azores where he commanded a fleet of thirty-five major warships, Santa Cruz proposed the much larger and more complex project of an assault against England. Ongoing English contacts with Islamic Morocco, raids on Spanish shipping and ports, harassment of Roman Catholics, military assistance to Dutch rebels, and other hostile acts exacerbated relations and headed both nations toward open war.

Santa Cruz's plan of 1586 envisaged great maritime and land campaigns requiring almost 800 ships (150 front-line warships) and ninety-four thousand troops with full equipment and provisions for an expedition of eight months. While the projected fleet consisted mostly of troop and equipment transports including many oared vessels, such a congregation would have been the greatest military project of the sixteenth century. In fact, despite the power of Philip II to lease, requisition, seize, and otherwise to press ship owners of different jurisdictions and nations, Spain lacked the wealth or the organizational capacity for such a grand design. In 1586, the duke of Parma presented a different plan for an invasion of England offering an army of thirty thousand troops from Flanders that was to be transported across the English Channel in shallow-draft barges to land at the mouth of the Thames River to commence a rapid assault on London.

By 1587, Philip II launched the business of acquiring shipping, supplies, and assembling forces at Lisbon and Spanish ports. Drake raided Cádiz to disrupt preparations and destroy vessels, but the Spaniards also had to worry about the overall impact of weakening Mediterranean defenses and thus encouraging the infidel Turks and North Africans to take advantage of Spanish preoccupation with the English invasion project. For his part, Parma soon recognized that Anglo-Dutch naval preeminence presented a formidable obstacle to his strategic planning—particularly since his own forces lacked adequate deep-water ports suitable for launching the cross-Channel invasion. Before any invasion attempt, the fleet from Spain would have to gain local superiority off the Dutch coastline. Meanwhile, in Lisbon and other Spanish ports, shortages of provisions, epidemics, and lack of supplies weakened the crews and troop complements crowded aboard ships that awaited final sailing orders. Even before the sudden death of the Marqués de Santa Cruz, myriad logistical weaknesses underscored the fact that even the best organized enterprise to dispatch an invasion against such a distant target required resources that stretched the capacity of a sixteenth century bureaucracy and state.

Case Study: The Spanish Armada

With expenses rising rapidly and the fleet deteriorating even faster, by the beginning of 1588 the grand design had to be launched quickly or scrapped. Philip II appointed the Marqués of Medina Sidonia to command, recognizing his organizational skills in planning large military

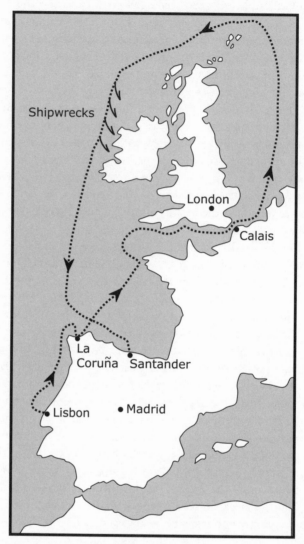

Map. 6.2. Track of the Spanish Armada, 1588

operations, his high social standing, and taking into account the negative consideration that he was not an experienced naval officer. This fact
led to criticism later of Philip's choice by many historians, but Medina
Sidonia could call upon numerous subordinate naval commanders for
tactical and strategic advice concerned with maritime questions. Philip
selected Medina Sidonia because he could organize shipments of water
casks, anchors, food, utensils, gunpowder, heavy guns, arquebuses, and
broaden the search for additional shipping.

Finally, at the end of May 1588, the Armada of some 125 Spanish,
Portuguese, German, Venetian, Levantine, and other foreign ships of
many different types set sail from Lisbon with a multinational force of
some twenty-seven to twenty-nine thousand men (8,000 seamen and up
to 21,000 troops). This motley collection of vessels carried an equally
unmatched assortment of 2,431 light and heavy guns of different calibers and origins that had been scrounged and purchased from every
possible source throughout Europe including all those merchant vessels
that happened to stop at Lisbon. Shortly after the fleet sailed, a violent
storm dispersed the ships even before they could gather for their final
assembly at La Coruña for the voyage to the English Channel. By July
1588 desertions and illnesses had begun to erode morale.

Although Armada strategy remains somewhat obscure, the main objective of the fleet was to convoy the duke of Parma's army from the
Netherlands to the Thames River for a joint land assault on London.
Heavy siege artillery shipped with the fleet was to make short work
of English fortifications and hastily thrown up earthworks that were
by no means as impregnable as the modern bastioned trace system
adopted on the continent. Against the invasion force composed mostly
of experienced veteran soldiers, the English militias had a significant
advantage in total numbers, knowledge of the country, and an established system of headland and hilltop beacons that could keep close
watch on Spanish movements. On the other hand, some experienced
English soldiers expressed deep reservations about the resolve and the
abilities of their green defensive forces. Sir Roger Williams who had
fought in the Netherlands declared, "But to speake troth, no Armie that
I ever saw, passes that of Duke de Parma for discipline and good order."
While the outcome of defensive actions against an invasion led by the
army of Parma and Medina Sidonia is a matter for pure speculation, the
English were inexperienced in late-sixteenth-century combat. Whatever
their capacities, they were most fortunate that their country avoided the

violence, atrocities, and other horrors that interminable warfare had brought to the Netherlands.

Under the overall command of the duke of Medina Sidonia, the division of the Spanish fleet into eight squadrons brought some order to the different ships types from galleons, *naos*, hulks, *pataches* and *zabras*, and the rowed galleasses and galleys. The officer appointed second-in-command, Juan Martínez de Recalde, captain-general of the Biscayan Squadron, was an experienced marine commander who could guide Medina Sidonia though he lacked experience as a fleet admiral. Aboard the ships, soldiers of the five *tercios* and assorted companies of troops served under their own officers. Packed onto overcrowded ships during the tempestuous weather of 1588, they suffered dreadful hardships well before they arrived in English waters. While the officers enjoyed slightly better quarters, the soldiers lived between decks where inadequate sanitation, lack of food preparation facilities, and limited sleeping accommodations caused constant problems. Some cooking took place well below decks on the bed of ballast materials where fouled bilge water mixed with rotten food, human excrement, and garbage. Constantly soaked by water that leaked through the decks, seasick, often weakened by dysentery, sometimes unable to maintain cook fires for many days, the Spanish invaders had to accomplish their mission quickly while there were still sufficient troops. Under such distressing conditions, many officers recognized that within a short period scurvy would appear to complete the devastation of all men aboard.

To meet the challenge, the English organized a fleet of 34 royal ships that belonged to Queen Elizabeth and 192 assorted privately owned vessels of different types, sizes, and capacities. Although many of these ships were small and not adapted for sea fighting, it is important to note that some of the royal ships were of new design with reduced fighting castles fore and aft and much lower superstructures. In a word, these vessels performed and maneuvered better in almost any winds than the larger, more cumbersome ships in the Spanish fleet. However, by streamlining the English gave up the advantage of height needed for close-in actions preceding boarding. On Spanish ships, the soldiers trained for boarding by firing light swivel guns and arquebuses, preparing to throw stones and darts, and to launch fireworks from poles called firepots just before grappling. For their part, the English adopted new tactics, which were to use their maneuverability and greater speed to fire cannon from a longer range. Recognizing that they could not match the Spaniards in a boarding melee, the English commanders Charles Howard, Francis Drake, John Hawkins, and Martin Frobisher rejected that approach entirely.

These English innovations set the scene for future maritime battles in which batteries of heavy guns exchanged broadsides designed to debilitate opposing crews and vessels. In 1588, however, the Spaniards depended much less on heavy artillery—deploying perhaps a third less weight in armaments than the English. Indeed, the motley collection of different sizes, types, and calibers of guns aboard the Spanish ships each requiring special ammunition underscored the fact that artillery was simply a secondary support prior to boarding and hand to hand combat. Armada officers opposed long-range artillery exchanges that merely wasted ammunition. Accuracy was poor and even heavy guns did little structural damage beyond 200 to 250 meters.

Instead, Spanish commanders loaded their diverse artillery pieces and prepared to fire a close range broadside that would provoke chaos just as boarders swarmed to the attack with concentrated fire of light arms. In this tactical approach the Spaniards did not anticipate reloading for prolonged artillery duels. They had not adopted the heavy four-wheeled gun carriages of the English that allowed for absorption of recoil, relatively rapid reloading, and better aiming. On some Spanish ships, larger guns using two-wheeled land carriages may even have had to be reloaded outboard with all of the attendant difficulties such operations would have entailed during combat.

As a result, Spanish officers reported that the English gunners fired three shots for their every one. If they attempted to fire the heavy forty- and sixty-pounders intended for land siege work in England, recoil would have been a major obstacle aboard ships and reloading in the confined spaces between decks would have taken at least an hour between shots. Confronted with English refusal to permit boarding, the Spaniards found themselves at distinct disadvantages. While neither side possessed the heavy fire power actually to sink opposition ships, artillery fire produced casualties and weakened the vessels for the voyage ahead.

Following a stormy and difficult voyage, on July 29 the Armada arrived off Plymouth and the next day assumed battle order with the galleasses in the vanguard, Medina Sidonia in the center to protect the troop and supply hulks, and Martínez de Recalde following with the rearguard. With news of this eventuality, Howard and Drake with fifty-four ships beat their way out of Plymouth and took the weather gage allowing them to pursue and to bear down upon the Armada. Skirmishing commenced

Fig. 6.6. *The Spanish Armada*, by H. C. Vroom. Private collection. Courtesy of Compagnie Royale D'Artillerie, La Prairie, Quebec.

between ships and squadrons that soon established that English tactics were to harass at distance, maneuver, and where possible to fire broadsides at close range. The Spanish adopted defensive cohesion as Medina Sidonia formed his fleet into the well-known great crescent formation. Although the Spaniards lost two vessels to the English following accidents and suffered some casualties, despite heavy exchanges of gunfire involving stragglers and the powerful galleasses, the Armada carried on without receiving significant damage. Nevertheless, the early skirmishing consumed powder and shot, illustrating England's advantage of proximity to port for resupply. Medina Sidonia dispatched letters to Parma requesting gunpowder, additional ships, and detailed intelligence about the readiness of his invasion forces to embark for England.

By August 6, the Spanish fleet had made its way up the English Channel to anchor in the dangerous road off Calais with the English fleet of 140 vessels positioned nearby just out of culverin range. Given the prevailing winds, the Spanish pilots warned that any further advance eastward might push the entire Armada into treacherous North Sea waters away from the planned rendezvous point with Parma's forces. Although success had eluded both sides up to this point, at a council of war the English captains conceived a plan to use the tides, currents, and winds to launch eight of their vessels converted hastily into fire ships for a night attack on the Spanish fleet. While the Spanish anticipated fire ships in such a closely packed anchorage, they also worried about new types of fireworks and vessels loaded with gunpowder to make them into floating bombs. Although Medina Sidonia stationed a screen of fast pinnaces to intercept any assault by unmanned fire ships, the English sent six to eight burning vessels with cannon double-shotted to fire when the flames heated them sufficiently as they drifted through the packed anchorage. Receiving signals about the impending danger, anxious captains slipped or cut their cables to move out to sea—and in the process saved their ships but lost precious anchors that they would need desperately during the epic voyage that lay before them. Only the galleass *San Lorenzo* was lost at Calais when it collided with another ship, broke its rudder, and ran aground on a sandbank close to shore.

At dawn's light on August 8, the English viewed a disorganized Spanish fleet and moved in quickly to take advantage of defensive lapses to press home their attacks. The Battle of Gravelines that followed was a confusing affair of many small engagements. Drake with *Revenge*, *Triumph*, and *Victory* maneuvered to take on Medina Sidonia's flagship *San Marcos* which with several other galleons moved to screen the dispersed fleet. Medina Sidonia's ship absorbed an estimated two hundred hits from heavy balls and the rigging suffered considerable damage from lighter arms. Despite the fact that many Spanish ships now lacked adequate supplies of cannonballs, they managed to reorganize their crescent formation. Before they completed their recovery, however, several vessels received such severe poundings from English gunfire that the crews suffered heavy casualties. Several ships drifted ashore on the Dutch coast and one or two may have foundered during stormy conditions that night. Other vessels received many hits at and below the waterline and damage to rigging that required rapid response by caulkers, carpenters, and riggers. Of even greater concern, the Spanish fleet was driven toward certain destruction in shallow shoal waters along the Dutch coast before a change of wind restored it to deeper water and propelled it northward with the English fleet in close pursuit.

For Medina Sidonia and his commanders, the first objective was to get back into position to coordinate operations with Parma. Unfortunately for their cause, however, they now recognized that the Spanish army of Flanders was unprepared to embark troops for an invasion of England. Indeed, Parma's forces had become bogged down against the

Dutch and the duke feared that by dividing his army to attack London, he would encourage a major Protestant outbreak in the Netherlands. Moreover, Parma had not taken into consideration fully Dutch offensive naval power or the slowness of his own forces to build and to assemble a fleet of boats suitable for the cross-channel invasion. After a few days during which Medina Sidonia tried twenty of his captains for cowardice and actually hanged one to strengthen the resolve of others, he determined that the Armada would have to circumnavigate the British Isles and return to La Coruña.

The voyage to the Shetland Islands and southward off the rugged Irish coastline exposed the crews to cold as well as to growing shortages of food and water. Already damaged by combat, some of the Armada ships foundered and many others attempted without adequate charts or anchors to put into Irish ports for water, repairs, and supplies. It was during the return voyage that the Spanish fleet suffered its real defeat to inclement weather as thousands perished at sea, on Scottish and Irish beaches, offshore in the raging surf of treacherous reefs, and at the hands of English soldiers ordered to execute all Spaniards who made it to shore. Few survived to tell of their hardships and of the horrible ordeals they suffered—sometimes being rescued two or three times as their ships foundered until they met their end on the rock bound coastline of Ireland. One who survived, Captain Francisco Cuellar, left a detailed journal of his harrowing escape across Ireland, into Scotland, and eventually back to Spain. Recently, marine archaeologists have studied some of these Armada wrecks to piece together information about Spanish ships, guns, equipment, and daily life aboard sixteenth-century warships.

Much like the Battle of Lepanto, the Armada defeat was by no means a watershed that marked a definitive diminution of Spanish power. Philip II overcame his grief about God's apparent unwillingness to support his grand Roman Catholic cause and rebuilt his fleets, assembled heavy weapons, and launched new expeditions. Although the English had illustrated new directions in marine combat, the Spaniards were not as backward as some historians have suggested. Indeed, it is totally simplistic to state that the failure of 1588 illustrated the inadequacies of Mediterranean warfare projected into the Atlantic. Instead, the Armada demonstrated the uncertainties of factors such as weather that in any military campaign can emerge to confound the best conceived plans of commanders and the difficulties of sixteenth-century logistics and communications. Nevertheless, Spain and its allies had lost at least eleven thousand trained seamen and soldiers as well as many ships that were expensive to replace. There were to be many raids back and forth during the 1590s and new "Protestant" storms to batter a succession of fleets sent by Philip against England and Ireland. Until the peace of 1604, the war switched to land campaigns in the Netherlands and France. In December 1592, Parma, one of the brilliant soldiers of his age, died in France worn out and wounded. By this point, other commanders had learned his techniques and improved the organization on the battlefield of musketeers and pikemen. Some like Count Maurice of Nassau of the Netherlands, sought to emulate Spanish discipline and organization and thus to achieve even greater firepower.

Although the size of the Spanish *tercio* had been reduced by a 1584 ordinance to fifteen companies of one hundred soldiers, Maurice observed that even closer study of the ancient Roman army might improve drill, discipline, and especially precision of soldiers in reloading their muskets. Maurice reduced company size to eighty soldiers dividing them equally between musketeers and pikemen. He organized musketeers into six to ten ranks so that they could fire efficiently by volley and maintain a constant hail of lead against opposition forces. Soldiers in the front rank fired and then wheeled to the rear to reload. With effective training, they preserved good order, maneuvered to take advantage of situations, and could still depend on their pikemen when enemy cavalry or infantry advanced to engage them. As a result of these reforms, the Dutch deployed their units to occupy a much wider battle front. This more flexible organization became evident in July 1600 at the Battle of Nieuport on the Flemish coast where sand dunes and other obstacles confused the situation. While both armies totaled about ten thousand infantry and fifteen hundred cavalry, the Dutch fired steady volleys that distressed the *tercios* and eventually caused them to lose effective order. When the Spaniards faltered and then retreated in complete chaos, the Dutch pursued to exterminate half of their total force. While some observers noted that the Spanish infantry had marched for many hours to get to the battle and the men were exhausted even before they fought, Maurice's reforms made Dutch forces able to challenge former Spanish invulnerability. With equal success at siege craft against Spanish-held towns and fortifications involving speed and concentration of artillery fire upon selected sections of the defenses, Maurice pushed the Spaniards from the northern Netherlands and set the scene for a general truce in 1609.

Suggested Reading

For general works on the topic of military revolutions that continue to fascinate historians, see Michael Roberts, *The Military Revolution, 1560–1660* (Belfast, 1956); Geoffrey Parker, *The Military Revolution: Military Innovation and the Rise of the West, 1500–1800* (Cambridge, 1988); Jeremy Black, *A Military Revolution? Military Change and European Society, 1550–1808* (Atlantic Highlands, 1991); Christopher M. Duffy, *The Military Revolution and the State, 1500–1800* (Exeter, 1980); David Eltis, *The Military Revolution in Sixteenth Century Europe* (London, 1995); John A. Lynn, ed., *Feeding Mars: Logistics in Western Warfare from the Middle Ages to the Present* (Boulder CO, 1993); John R. Hale, *War and Society in Renaissance Europe*; William H. McNeill, *The Pursuit of Power: Technology, Armed Force, and Society since A.D. 1000* (Chicago, 1982); and Clifford U. Rogers, ed., *The Military Revolution Debate: Transformation of Early Modern Europe* (Boulder CO, 1995).

Students interested in the evolution of arms, strategies, and tactics should examine Archer Jones, *The Art of War in the Western World* (Chicago, 1987); Philippe Contamine, *War in the Middle Ages*, trans. Michael Jones (Oxford, 1984); Carlo M. Cipolla, *Guns, Sails and Empire: Technological Innovations and the Early Phases of European Expansion, 1400–1700* (New York, 1965); Sir Charles Oman, *A History of the Art of War in the Middle Ages* II (New York, 1924), and *A History of the Art of War in the Sixteenth Century* (London, 1937); Christopher Duffy, *The Military Revolution and the State, 1500–1800* (Exeter, 1980); Andre Corvisier, *Armies and Societies in Europe, 1494–1789* (Bloomington IN, 1979); Clifford Rogers, "The Military Revolution of the Hundred Years' War," *The Journal of Military History* 51:2 (1993): 241–78; Michael Mallett, *Mercenaries and Their Masters: Warfare in Renaissance Italy* (London, 1974); John R. Hale and Michael Mallett, *The Military Organization of a Renaissance State: Venice c. 1400 to 1617* (Cambridge, 1984); John F. Guilmartin, *Gunpowder and Galleys: Changing Technology and Mediterranean Warfare in the Sixteenth Century* (London, 1974); and J. R. Hale and Michael Mallett, *The Military Organization of a Renaissance State: Venice, c. 1400 to 1617* (Cambridge, 1984).

For specific studies on the evolution of firearms and fortifications, see Hans Delbrück, *The Dawn of Modern Warfare*, volume 4 of his *History of the Art of War* (Lincoln NE, 1990). For more recent studies, see Simon Pepper and Nicholas Adams, *Firearms and Fortifications: Military Architecture and Siege Warfare in Sixteenth Century Siena* (Chicago, 1986); Michael Mallett, *Mercenaries and their Masters: Warfare in Renaissance Italy* (London, 1974); J. R. Hale, *Renaissance War Studies* (London, 1983); Christopher Duffy, *Siege Warfare: The Fortress in the Early Modern World, 1494–1660* (London, 1979); Bert S. Hall, *Weapons and Warfare in Renaissance Europe: Gunpowder, Technology and Tactics* (Baltimore, 1997); Brenda J. Buchanan, ed., *Gunpowder: The History of an International Technology*

(Bath, England, 1996); F. L. Taylor, *The Art of War in Italy, 1494–1529* (London, 1921); A. Al-Hassan and D. Hills, *Islamic Technology* (Cambridge, 1986); David Ayalon, *Gunpowder and Firearms in the Mamluk Kingdom: A Challenge to a Medieval Society* (London, 1978); Weston F. Cook, "Warfare and Firearms in Fifteenth Century Morocco, 1400–1492," *War and Society* 11:2 (1993): 25–40; John A. Lynn, "The *trace italienne* and the Growth of Armies: The French Case," *The Journal of Military History* 55:3 (1991): 297–330; and Mahinder S. Kingra, "The *trace italienne* and the Military Revolution during the Eighty Years' War, 1567–1648," *The Journal of Military History* 57:3 (1993): 431–46.

For the Ottoman conquest of Constantinople employing bombards, see Steven Runcinan, *The Fall of Constantinople, 1453* (New York, 1965), and Robert de Clari, *The Conquest of Constantinople* (New York, 1966). There are a number of published primary sources including Nicolo Barbaro, *Diary of the Siege of Constantinople* (New York, 1966); Doukas, *Decline and Fall of Byzantium to the Ottoman Turks*, trans. Harry J. Magoulian (Detroit, 1975); Makarios Melisserios, *Chronicle of the Siege: April 2–May 29, 1453*, trans. Mario Philippides (Amherst, 1980); J. R. Melville Jones, *The Siege of Constantinople: Seven Contemporary Accounts* (Amsterdam, 1972); and Gregorios Phrantzes, *A Contemporary Greek Source for the Siege of Constantinople* (Amsterdam, 1955).

On military medicine, see Richard A. Gabriel and Karen S. Metz, *A History of Military Medicine I* (New York, 1992); J. F. Malgaigne, *Surgery and Ambroise Paré*, trans. W. B. Hamby (Norman OK, 1965); Francis R. Packard, *Life and Times of Ambroise Paré, 1510–1590* (New York, 1921); W. J. Bishop, *The Early History of Surgery* (London, 1960); and Henry J. Webb, *Elizabethan Military Science: The Books and the Practice* (Madison WI, 1965).

For the military and naval history of metropolitan Spain and Spanish activities in the Mediterranean, see Fernand Braudel, *The Mediterranean and the Mediterranean World in the Age of Philip II*, 2 vols. (New York, 1966), and John H. Elliott, *Imperial Spain, 1469–1716* (New York, 1963). Although the military history of the *Reconquista* remains difficult to follow in English language works, see Weston F. Cook, "The Cannon Conquest of Nasrid Spain and the End of the Reconquista," *The Journal of Military History* 57:1 (1993): 43–70. Also see L. P. Harvey, *Islamic Spain, 1250–1500* (Chicago, 1990); J. Hillgarth, *The Spanish Kingdoms* 2 vols. (Oxford, 1978); Nancy Rubin, *Isabella of Castile: The First Renaissance Queen* (New York, 1990); and Paul Stewart, "The Soldier, the Bureaucrat, and Fiscal Records in the Army of Ferdinand and Isabella," *Hispanic American Historical Review* 49:2 (1969): 281–92. For Spanish activities in Italy, see Gerald de Gaury, *The Grand Captain: Gonzalo de Córdoba* (London, 1958). John F Guilmartin's *Gunpowder and Galleys* is the best account of Spanish-Turkish naval conflict and the Battle of Lepanto. For Spain's struggles against Islam in North Africa, see John B. Wolf, *The Barbary Coast: Algeria Under the*

Turks, 1500–1830 (New York, 1979); Andrew C. Hess, *The Forgotten Frontier: A History of the Sixteenth-Century Ibero-African Frontier* (Chicago, 1978); and Ellen G. Friedman, *Spanish Captives in North Africa in the Early Modern Age* (Madison WI, 1983).

For Spanish military activities involving the Spanish army in northern Europe, Geoffrey Parker's *The Army of Flanders and the Spanish Road, 1567–1659* remains a key work. Also see Parker's *The Dutch Revolt* (London, 1977). Earlier accounts by John L. Motley, *Rise of the Dutch Republic*, 3 vols. (London, 1856), and Pieter Geyl, *The Revolt of the Netherlands, 1555–1609* (London, 1932), contain a great deal of information but must be used with caution. William S. Maltby's *Alba: A Biography of Fernando Alvarez de Toledo, Third Duke of Alba, 1507–1582* (Berkeley, 1983), offers useful detail on his military career. Also see J. J. Silke, *Kinsale: The Spanish Intervention in Ireland at the End of the Elizabethan Wars* (Liverpool, 1970).

The Spanish conquest of the Americas has attracted a great number of historians, and there is a rich bibliography. For a general overview, see John H. Parry, *The Spanish Seaborne Empire* (New York, 1966), and *The Age of Reconnaissance* (London, 1963); and Tzvetan Todorov, *The Conquest of America*, trans. Richard Howard (New York, 1984). For the military implications and impact of gunpowder weapons, see Ross Hassig, *Mexico and the Spanish Conquest* (London, 1994); Richard C. Padden, *The Hummingbird and the Hawk: Conquest and Sovereignty in the Valley of Mexico, 1503–1541* (New York, 1970); C. Harvey Gardiner, *Naval Power in the Conquest of Mexico* (Austin, 1956); and James Lockhart, *The Men of Cajamarca: A Social and Biographical Study of the First Conquerors of Peru* (Austin, 1972). For a participant soldier's account, see Bernal Díaz, *The Conquest of New Spain* (London, 1963). For the native perspective, see Miguel Leon-Portilla, *The Broken Spears: The Aztec Account of the Conquest of Mexico* (Boston, 1962).

As might be expected following the 1988 celebration of the four hundredth anniversary of the 1588 Armada, there has been a significant outpouring of books and articles. Nevertheless, a good starting point is still Garrett Mattingly, *The Armada* (Boston, 1959). Perhaps the best book published in 1988 was Felipe Fernández Armesto's *The Spanish Armada: The Experience of War in 1588* (Oxford, 1988). For outstanding illustrations and an excellent bibliography, see M. J. Rodríguez-Salgado et al., *Armada, 1588–1988: An International Exhibition to Commemorate the Spanish Armada* (London, 1988). The significant results of archaeological expeditions off the Scottish and Irish coasts are described in Lawrence Flanagan, *Ireland's Armada Legacy* (Dublin, 1988). Also see Michael Lewis, *Armada Guns: A Comparative Study of English and Spanish Armaments* (New York, 1961); Peter Pierson, *Commander of the Armada: The Seventh Duke of Medina Sidonia* (New Haven, 1989); T. P. Kilfeather, *Ireland: Graveyard of the Spanish Armada* (Dublin, 1967); N. A. M. Rodger, *The Safeguard of the Sea:*

A Naval History of Britain, 660–1649 (London, 1997); Winston Graham, *The Spanish Armadas* (London, 1972); Peter Kirsch, *The Galleon: The Great Ships of the Armada Era* (London, 1990); Roger Whitling, *The Enterprise of England: the Spanish Armada* (New York, 1988); and Colin M. Martin and Geoffrey Parker, *Spanish Armada* (London, 1988).

7. NEW SIGNS OF TOTAL WAR

The Seventeenth Century

A hungry army observes no discipline.

These [men] of whom I speak, who know no Art or way of livelihood but by the trade of souldiery, are ordinarily called, *Souldiers of Fortune*; though most of them might rather be call'd the *Sons of Misfortune*. – Sir James Turner, 1671

Armistice (1609–21) in the interminable Eighty Years' War between Spain and the Netherlands was the result of physical and economic exhaustion on both sides rather than any real desire for a permanent peace. Soldiers and civilians inured to hunger, epidemic diseases, appalling conditions of trenches and fortresses, bloody massacres, and army mutinies savored the temporary respite from omnipresent hostilities connected with religious strife, ethnic rivalries, economic conflicts, and the expansive pretensions of their rulers. In the Netherlands the prosperous textile and manufacturing centers suffered, agriculture declined by as much as 90 percent in some districts, and many civilians fled from the southern provinces to cities such as Antwerp and Amsterdam.

During the years of the truce, Dutch ships attacked Spanish commerce and raided overseas territories from the Caribbean to South America and into the Pacific Ocean. Even prior to 1621, it was obvious that the heavily populated, religiously heterogeneous, and economically productive Netherlands would once again become a regional and international cockpit of war between Spain and the Dutch Republic. The monarchs and strategists of France, England, Denmark, Sweden, and the German states observed from the sidelines pondering military intervention and evaluating what advantages might fall their way. For many Europeans and people of distant lands around the globe under Spanish, Dutch, Portuguese, French, or English influence, seventeenth-century warfare became ubiquitous, interminable, and often inescapable.

Europe was torn by uprisings, rebellions, civil wars, territorial disputes, and internecine religious conflicts between Catholics and Protestants. Along the eastern European frontiers between Christianity and
Islam and in the Balkans, bloody combat and even genocide between
the Turks and Austrians shredded the fabric of civilization. The Thirty
Years' War (1618–48) laid waste some regions of Germany and central
Europe, leaving the land sterile and breeding stock consumed. Marauding armies looted the countryside, disrupted society, and halted normal economic activities until there was nothing left to steal. During the
1630s a Swedish chronicler reported "plundered cities, towns, and villages, victimized princes and nobles, slaughtered populations, ravaged
churches and houses of God, ministers stripped bare, women and vir-
gins violated without distinction of estate or age, cruelties that were
more than barbarous and devilish." Endemic warfare unleashed diseases
such as typhus fever, malaria, typhoid, bubonic plague, smallpox, scurvy,
dysentery, and many other infectious ailments that committed havoc
among a weakened population. Epidemics swept away civilians as well
as soldiers and extended the impact of war far beyond the actual combat zones. In some regions, successions of epidemics, crop losses, and
raids by nearly autonomous marauding armies and gangs of pillagers
triggered significant demographic disasters. Even though the population
losses were not as extreme as earlier observers and historians insisted, the
population loss was probably as high as 30 to 40 percent in some regions.

In England the Puritan rebellion and civil war (1642–48) led to the
execution of King Charles I, the declaration of a republic named the
Commonwealth under Oliver Cromwell, and the brutal suppression of
Scotland and Ireland as independent countries. The slaughter of English
Protestant settlers in Ulster by the Catholic Irish called the "great massacre" opened wounds that demanded revenge. In 1649 Cromwell led his
well-equipped veteran army into Ireland against an undisciplined coalition of Irish Royalists. At the siege of Drogheda in Leinster, Cromwell
refused mercy after the Catholic garrison at first refused to surrender.
The frenzied English soldiers put every man to the sword. Turning
south to besiege Wexford and Munster, the English again butchered the
garrison and thousands of Catholic civilians including priests, women,
and children. Cromwell defended his brutality as "a righteous judgment
of God upon these barbarous wretches who have imbued their hands
in so much innocent blood" and as a means to "prevent the effusion of
blood for the future." Epidemic diseases, starvation, and arbitrary con-

fiscation of lands left a bitter heritage among succeeding generations of dispossessed Irish Catholics. Even in regions that escaped direct violence and military occupation, army recruiters, soldiers, and tax collectors who grabbed scarce resources to support martial activities were viewed with hatred by the civilian population.

Although Spain's great military power waned in the seventeenth century, the decline was not as fast or as precipitous as some modern historians have suggested. Most research on military topics during this period has centered on the technical advances and reformed tactical systems evolved by reformers such as Maurice of Nassau in Holland and Gustavus Adolphus in Sweden. Researchers beginning with Michael Roberts identified and studied "military revolutions" in early modern Europe. They centered their research on the northern Protestant nations, the Swedish armed interventions in Germany, and the rise of France to military preeminence during the age of Louis XIV.

For some English-speaking historians, the civil war in England took on centrality and importance for broader military trends quite beyond its actual regional impact. Roberts identified the significance of linear formations developed by Maurice and Gustavus Adolphus from Ancient military histories and applied to modern infantry and cavalry. Extracting the highest levels of operational efficiency from soldiers who carried the matchlock musket, these reformers organized smaller units, thinned out the heavy infantry formations, and disciplined their soldiers with regular training and repetitive drills.

As the century advanced, armies grew in numbers and became more permanent. By 1630, the Spanish army reached a total of almost 300,000 troops although by no means all were native Spaniards. In 1648 at the end of the Thirty Years' War, the French army numbered almost 150,000, the Swedish army over 100,000, and the Dutch Republic about 60,000. By the 1690s the French wartime army had expanded to well over 400,000 troops.

There are still many questions debated today among historians about exactly what factors drove these changes and what sort of, if any, military revolution occurred. If the major issues related to linear tactics and improved firearms, were the more traditionally inclined Spaniards able to adjust their own infantry formations (the *tercios*) to meet the new challenges? Or were they overly conservative and slow to thin out their deep infantry squares and pikemen to adopt additional musketeers and light artillery capable of working in direct support of frontline units? In all armies, were too many troops wasted in penny packet assignments to sedentary garrison duties in towns and fortresses protected by complex modern defense works and bastions of the trace Italienne? And what were the roles of the great sieges that bogged down armies, consumed national treasure, and offered certain graves to thousands of soldiers?

Although much of the raw brutality of earlier conflicts between Catholics and Protestants diminished over the century, this was not at all the case on the frontiers of eastern Europe and in the Mediterranean world, where Islam and Christianity clashed. The Turkish-Habsburg conflicts involving the Austrians, the Spaniards, and other nations produced reports of refined atrocities and cruel barbarism that Europeans circulated in different forms and are still repeated today. The abortive 1683 Turkish siege of Vienna led by Kara Mustafa, by far the most famous collision of the period between armies of the two religions, illustrated pathological hatreds on both sides that blackened human compassion and gave rise to abnormal cruelties.

In Vienna during July 1683, for example, the ten to twelve thousand defending troops and irregular civilian fighters were certain a Turkish fifth column functioned in their midst. Several men who looked foreign suffered horrible deaths as suspected saboteurs. Avenging mobs tore their bodies to pieces and in one case looked on while some persons skinned the corpse of a victim. During the prolonged and bitter siege, the Turks beheaded and otherwise executed thousands of Christian prisoners. At the town of Perchtoldsdorf, Turkish soldiers massacred the surrendered garrison with their sabers, slaughtered noncombatant civilians, and then incinerated a church and tower packed with women and children. The Viennese responded by impaling severed Turkish heads in full view of their trenches and later flayed live captives. In brutal hand-to-hand trench warfare opposing soldiers were in such close proximity that they were able to grab and stab at each other. They fought nasty underground skirmishes in suffocating tunnels and exploded so many gunpowder mines that the stench of rotting flesh and decomposing bodies pervaded the battle zone. Although Austrian armies supported by Poles and Germans drove off the Islamic attackers, the memories of these events remained fresh among Christians who wished to expel the Turks from Hungary and the Balkans.

Overseas, Europeans exported their bellicosity and penchant for internecine violence around the globe. Often minor wars and armed raids disrupted the peace of the Caribbean or the Indian Ocean even when

European powers were more or less at peace. Before the Twelve Year Truce expired, monopolistic joint-stock trading companies such as the Dutch East India Company (1602) and the Dutch West India Company (1621) enlisted their own navies and armies, built fortresses, and projected war against Portuguese and Spanish territories. The companies operated on a truly grand scale with authorization to make war or peace with native peoples. The West India Company received a monopoly over Dutch trade and navigation between the Americas and west Africa. Planning economic projects backed by fleets and soldiers, the major targets included the silver production of New Spain and Peru, the sugar of Brazil, and the gold, ivory, and slaves of Portuguese West Africa. The goal was to deny Spain the enormous treasure needed to operate and finance major military operations in Flanders, Germany, and elsewhere.

In 1628 the capture by Admiral Piet Heyn of the entire Mexican silver fleet of fifteen ships commanded by Captain General Juan de Benavides at Matanzas Bay, Cuba, underscored not only the successes of world warfare but its remarkable potential for attaining spectacular windfall profits for those who invested in war against the Spanish empire. As well as providing a rich dividend to stock holders, Heyn's Spanish treasure of eleven million guilders was sufficient to fund two-thirds of the annual cost of the entire Dutch army. For the magnitude of his defeat, Benavides, a blue-blood aristocrat suffered the ignominy of public execution by having his throat slashed. That year King Philip IV of Spain experienced difficulties paying his far-flung European armies and navies. In addition, he had to contemplate significant expenditures to bolster the naval defenses and to fully modernize major port fortifications of the Americas. Beginning in 1624 the Dutch also attacked and temporarily occupied much of Portuguese Brazil and Angola. Backed by military power, by midcentury the United Provinces dominated commercial trade in the Atlantic world.

Within its even greater domain, the East India Company crushed Portuguese control in the Moluccas, Malaya, Ceylon, and India (Goa 1638–44) but failed against the Spaniards in the Philippines (1647–48). Back in European waters, Admiral Maarten Tromp won a magnificent victory at the Battle of the Downs (1639), commanding a fleet of ninety-six warships, two-thirds of which were leased, over the revitalized Spanish battle fleet commanded by Admiral Antonio de Oquendo, one hundred vessels including sixty-seven purpose built warships. This naval victory proclaimed the dominance of the Netherlands in European waters and encouraged the Dutch to support Portugal with arms, shot, and supplies of gunpowder during the 1640 revolt against Spanish rule. At the same time, however, the successes of the Dutch recipe of making economic war backed by the power of their fleets aroused the cupidity of the English and French who viewed themselves as the natural successors of Spain for world dominance.

For pessimists, it was easy to write off Spain, the great power of the sixteenth century, as hopelessly overburdened by a multiplicity of missions and insoluble problems that would negate any central role in seventeenth-century military affairs. From the perspectives of strategy, tactics, logistics, economics, and technology, the Spaniards faced remarkable challenges that were much beyond the capacities of any contemporary power. In 1621 with the end of the truce in the Netherlands, Philip IV's military command confronted the difficult prospect of rebuilding forces and dispatching elite Spanish and Italian units northward over the military corridor known as the "Spanish Road" through Savoy, Franche-Comté, and Lorraine east of the French frontier. A force of almost seventy thousand troops, mostly foreigners, served Spain in the Netherlands and were paid, fed, and lodged at the expense of the local people. The safety of the transportation and supply corridor depended on French good will or internal civil disorders—factors that changed to the detriment of Spanish interests as the century progressed. In 1635 war broke out between Spain and France merging in 1640 with major revolts in Catalonia and Portugal. Finally, because of the geographic situation of the northern possessions and the Hapsburg family's connections with the emperors of the Holy Roman Empire, Spanish and Spanish-Italian officers participated heavily in the exhausting campaigns of the Thirty Years' War.

In Italy and the Mediterranean, Spain controlled Milan, Naples, Sicily, Sardinia, and the Balearic Islands. All of these possessions had to be garrisoned against possible Ottoman or North African raiders, and Spain had to maintain powerful naval squadrons to keep Algerian and Moroccan pirates in check. In the Atlantic, naval squadrons were assigned to escort treasure fleets and to patrol the Caribbean Sea against pirates and English, Dutch, and French contrabandists who sometimes engaged in piratical raiding on the side. Moreover, foreign interlopers promoted by the Dutch had begun to settle the North and South American littoral and on islands that Spain had agreed in treaties that it could not effectively occupy. At the same time that they faced these daunting problems requiring expenditures on fortress construction and naval squadrons, Spanish naval strategists recognized that they had to rebuild a modern battle fleet to match Dutch and sometimes French sea power in the English Channel and Baltic Sea. The crushing naval defeat in 1639 at the Battle of the Downs against the Dutch came as a heavy blow. Between 1621 and 1640, the Spanish treasury spent almost half of its total annual income on military expenditures.

Spanish infantry forces of the seventeenth century often are viewed as conservative in their organization and dependent upon deep squares of pikemen supported by wings of musketeers and cavalry. While it is correct that the *tercios* possessed grand traditions that extended back for well over a century, they did evolve smaller more flexible formations to employ arquebuses and muskets that earlier had been regarded as secondary to the heavy squares or rectangles of pikemen. Seventeenth-century Spanish pikemen now deployed in looser formations that permitted the musketeers to fall back through their ranks for protection. With technological improvements in muskets and firepower, all army commanders had to reorganize their forces to take into account improved rates of fire, accuracy, and the striking power of bullets. Nevertheless, older organizational deployments of forces on some occasions defeated more modern systems.

In 1634 at the Battle of Nördlingen during the Thirty Years' War, new style Swedish formations collapsed in the face of heavy infantry squares. In any battle, there were many variables to account for such as the weather, the topography and condition of the ground, the morale and health of the troops on both sides, and all important logistical support. No general or commander for most of the seventeenth century could be absolutely certain that artillery and musketry possessed sufficient striking force to win the day—that is without taking into consideration the essential assistance of pikemen and cavalry. Until the 1680s and 1690s, those who disparaged the "prince of weapons" (the pikes) risked possible disasters.

Sir James Turner, an Englishman who fought for Denmark and Sweden beginning in the 1630s, stated the case for armored pikemen who, if properly commanded, could present an impenetrable "iron wall" to enemy cavalry. With the added protection of five- or six-foot-long wooden stakes with iron points called Swedish Feathers set into the ground just at the right height to tear into the breasts of onrushing horses, good pikemen resisted cavalry. The use of caltrops (a spiked device designed to cut into horses' hooves formed much like the jacks used in the children's game), deep ditches, and even ferocious war dogs trained to leap up to bite horses' nostrils, all these provided the infantry with additional protection. Turner criticized commanders in contemporary armies who permitted pikemen to take on cavalry without adequate protection. Typically, cavalry troops executed a maneuver called the "caracole" in which they rushed forward at full gallop in deep linear formations toward the enemy infantry, fired their muskets or carbines at close range, and then wheeled about and rode to the rear to reload while the succeeding ranks fired and followed the same maneuver. If the heads, backs, and chests of pikemen were not adequately protected by armor, their formations could be discomfited by cavalry fire.

The objective of the horsemen was to get in among the infantry to exploit breaches and to wield their sabers at close quarters. To prevent this dangerous eventuality, Turner recommended that all pikemen should be issued helmets, back- and belly-pieces, *taslets* for their thighs, and greaves for their arms. The helmet and breast and belly armor had to be tested carbine proof and the back-piece at least pistol proof. Turner recognized that some commanders disparaged the pikemen and failed to recognize that the strongest, tallest, and largest men should be assigned to carry pikes rather than muskets. Against those military reformers who pressed for musketeers to replace pikemen—arguing that gunners sent "messengers of death" (bullets) as well as receiving them—Turner insisted that if musketeers stood their ground and took a volley or two, the push of the opposition pikemen inevitably would overwhelm them. He pointed out the flexibility of pikemen who during sieges labored on defensive works and trenches with shovels and mattocks. During assaults they met enemy attackers with stones, grenades, two-handed swords, morning stars, or wielded their pikes. In a word, unlike musketeers these soldiers served in a variety of different duties as pioneers, sentinels, escorts, or wherever necessary.

Another chronicler, Raimondo Montecuccoli, an Italian cavalry officer who served first with the Spaniards in the Netherlands, later with the imperial armies during the Thirty Years' War, and finally in the wars against the French, also lauded the pike as the weapon that had no equal to ward off cavalry attacks. Montecuccoli noted the extensive use of cavalry in the devastated regions of Germany in the Thirty Years' War, concluding that a military force without pikemen was completely disjoined, "like arms and legs lacking a torso." The pike battalion provided "a wall, the stability of which permits the army to stand its ground. It holds a foe at bay thus facilitating the junction of the cavalry and the musketry in its rear." While Montecuccoli advised against heavy pike squares in which soldiers in the center of the formation could not wield their weapons efficiently and the advantage of numbers might be lost, he argued in favor of battalions arranged in six to seven ranks armed with eighteen-foot pikes. With three feet of the pike occupied by the hands of the soldiers, an almost impenetrable pike forest formation took shape as the lines of soldiers extended their weapons fifteen feet for the first rank down to about three feet for the fifth rank. The points of the sixth rank just barely protruded from the front of the formation. Any additional ranks in the rear could not employ their arms effectively and were useless except as reserves to fill gaps caused by casualties in combat.

In the Netherlands, battlefield tactics were mainly a theoretical matter since sieges, maneuver, and small unit operations were the general rule. During the 1621–48 war both the Spanish and the Dutch sides deployed as many as thirty thousand troops simply to garrison the fortresses, towns, and other strategic points such as dikes, ports, and river crossings. It was in this theater of operations that Prince Maurice of Nassau (1567–1625) reorganized his Protestant Dutch army formations in response to his own view that the firepower of muskets had become the decisive factor replacing the element of shock delivered by heavy squares of pikes. Employing Roman-style tactics and drill learned from republished classical works by Aelian and Vegetius, Maurice adopted linear formations of musketeers ten deep who learned to fire simultaneously from the front line and then to wheel about to the rear of their file to reload, move forward, and fire again. The result in theory at least was to present continuous fire to distress enemy infantry and cavalry. The major role of the reduced number of pikemen was now to protect the infantry from cavalry attacks. Although the "walking citadels," or squares of massed infantrymen armed with pikes, did not fit into Maurice's thinking, there were few large battles in the Netherlands fought on open fields.

Opposing Maurice, General Ambrosio Spínola, Marqués de las Balbases, son of a leading banking family of Genoa, arrived in the Netherlands in 1602 with an expeditionary force of nine thousand Lombard soldiers. In 1604 Spínola recaptured the city of Ostend and was named commander of the Spanish forces of Flanders based at Brussels, a post that he held for over two decades. While Maurice became much better known for his military innovations, Spínola gained wide acclaim as one of the most effective commanders of his age. Indeed, Maurice recognized the talents of his opponent whom he described as second in ability only to himself. Spínola understood the economic factors that underlay successful military actions, and his realistic advice to King Philip IV and his chief minister the count-duke of Olivares, head of the enormous Spanish war machine of ministers and provisioners, was not always appreciated. Indeed, after 1621 Spanish war planners experienced difficulty finding new troops for the army of Flanders, and some observers complained that recruiters in Spain were depopulating the country of young men.

After the outbreak of the Thirty Years' War with Spanish troops already serving in central Europe, the French under the aggressive policies of Cardinal Richelieu increased military pressures upon their eastern frontiers. Spínola with only limited forces had to maintain the corridor from Milan to Brussels, dominate the strategic Rhine Valley, and confront the Dutch Protestants. Beyond these demands, the Spaniards received pleas for reinforcements to increase the garrisons at strategic North African, Philippine, and American fortresses. Much of Europe, including France, England, Denmark, Sweden, Venice, Savoy, the Palatinate, the German Protestant princes, and the Dutch, opposed Spain. Although Olivares argued a "domino theory" and insisted that it was best to fight enemies abroad rather than at home, leading military commanders such as Spínola recognized that total exhaustion and defeat were on the horizon.

Almost as an echo of the earlier glories of Spanish arms, in 1625 Philip IV's overstretched and under financed armies and navies produced a Miraculous Year. In June 1624 Spínola besieged the North Brabant garrison town of Breda, encircling the town with sophisticated fortifications that contemporary military observers described as brilliantly planned and executed. Rather than attempting assaults on breaches, Spínola flooded the countryside to cut off Dutch efforts to raise the siege and then waited nine months without even using much artillery bombardment until May 1625 when the town garrison surrendered due to advancing starvation. Maurice of Nassau died in late April and last minute efforts to relieve Breda had been driven off with heavy casualties. On May 27, Governor Justin of Nassau capitulated under honorable terms and marched out of the fortress with thirty-five hundred men who turned out to be in much better condition than the twenty-two thousand hungry Spanish army besiegers.

Although the great triumph at Breda bolstered Spanish morale, it accomplished little in terms of the wider struggle. However, the euphoria had not faded when news arrived in July of the Dutch surrender at Bahia, Brazil, to an expeditionary force commanded by Don Fadrique de Toledo. Added to these victories, Spanish land and maritime forces successfully defended Genoa against France and Savoy and repelled a Dutch assault against the Caribbean Island of Puerto Rico. Finally, in November 1625, the Spaniards were surprised when an Anglo-Dutch fleet of ninety ships under Sir Edward Cecil appeared at Cádiz and immediately commenced an assault on the city. Although Olivares feared major implications and named himself general of the Spanish cavalry, the invading troops succeeded only in liberating large wine supplies that turned them into an intoxicated and helpless rabble. Not only was the amphibious attack on Cádiz a total debacle, but the English fleet also failed to intercept the Spanish treasure ships.

In recognition of the 1625 feats of Spanish arms, Lope de Vega produced a new play titled "Brazil Restored" and Pedro Calderón de la Barca presented an even more famous play glorifying Spanish heroism called "The Siege of Breda." To preserve the memory of the victories, Philip IV commissioned a series of heroic battle paintings including Diego de Velázquez's "Surrender of Breda" that with considerable artistic license portrayed Spínola and his hungry soldiers as plump, well clothed, and content. Instead of sitting on horseback to receive the surrender of the Dutch commander, Velázquez had Spínola dismount to prevent his former foe from kneeling to present the keys of Breda. In fact, Spínola's magnanimous act of granting generous terms was not unusual in the Netherlands where general rules of war existed to terminate sieges prior to desperate assaults that produced heavy loss of life and often led to uncontrolled looting and atrocities against civilians. Velázquez's memorable portrayal of Spanish honor—adjusted though it was to capture the heroism of the victorious general—served to illustrate the existence of a spirit of human civility even between old enemies.

The year of victories of 1625 soon faded as Spanish military and civilian bureaucrats recognized that exhaustion and lack of funding would scuttle many of the ambitious projects supported by Olivares. Indeed, dispatches from every theater for troops and funding arriving at Madrid produced a confusing cacophony of demands. Spínola's urgent request

Fig. 7.1. *The Surrender of Breda (Las Lanzas)*, by Diego Rodriguez de Silva y Velázquez. Prado Museum, Madrid.

for seventy thousand troops in the Netherlands could not be met. In 1628 Piet Heyn captured the treasure fleet and with it funding designated for military projects. The outbreak of the Mantuan War in Italy (1628–31) was a disastrous affair that even Spínola could not resolve before his death in 1630. War against France (1635–59), the Dutch destruction of the Spanish fleet in 1639, and the revolts of Catalonia and Portugal in 1640 overloaded Spain's military system. Soldiers billeted on the populations of Extremadura and Castile were said to cause as much ruin as the Portuguese rebels.

In addition to these purely military disasters, Spain suffered a succession of terrible epidemics, loss of morale, the rise of unfettered immorality among the ruling classes, and the growth of intolerant piety among the general population. In the first decades of the century much of Iberia suffered from a series of epidemics of plague, malaria, and contagious fevers that swept away up to half a million people. At the same time, bad weather and crop failures produced hunger that uprooted some populations and exposed many to disease. By midcentury, a new epidemic produced rumors that French agents were scattering maleficent powders that caused illnesses designed to devastate the population. In Madrid, the urban authorities passed laws to enumerate all French residents and visitors to the city. In Andalusia, Málaga, Valencia, and Cádiz, an epidemic of fevers killed inhabitants so quickly that bodies had to be burned and in Murcia there were reports of dogs eating corpses in the streets. At Seville in the 1670s and 1680s, some districts near the Guadalquivir River were so badly hit that local militia assemblies ceased for several years.

Despite significant population losses during the century of well over one million Spaniards, army recruiters and forced levies continued to draw young men out of the country to serve in Italy, Flanders, Germany, and in many other locations. Very few of these soldiers ever returned to their homeland. Indeed, James Turner noted his shock while visiting Antwerp where he observed destitute Spanish soldiers who were entrusted with the defense of the city begging alms in the streets. Even in Iberia, forced conscription, pillaging, and devastation marked the revolts in Catalonia and Portugal. Although Spain did begin to recover economically prior to the end of the seventeenth century, its dominant military power in Europe could not be restored. In many respects, warfare and imperial pretensions bankrupted Spain and the demands for troops bled the country of young men and drove many others to emigrate to the New World beyond the reach of recruiters and forced levies.

Even in decline, however, the Spaniards clung to their European possessions. On some occasions their forces and tactics continued to win victories. In 1638, for example, a Spanish army commanded by the governor of Antwerp, Felipe de Silva, met a force of six thousand Dutch, German, and Scottish troops from Voorme. The battle continued for several days before the Spaniards punched through the dikes to overwhelm the Dutch in a fierce night engagement. The Spaniards had almost three hundred killed and eight thousand wounded, but the Dutch army collapsed, with hundreds killed and twenty-five thousand men captured, including two colonels. However, the tables turned at the Battle of Rocroi in Flanders in 1643, where a French army of twenty-three thousand troops defeated a Spanish force of twenty-seven thousand cavalry and infantry. After the French shattered the Spanish cavalry, the *tercios* formed defensive squares for a last stand. They managed to repel three French cavalry attacks before their formations of pikemen collapsed and a massacre ensued. The Spaniards had as many as seven thousand killed and six thousand captured compared to French losses of approximately four thousand killed and wounded. This victory, while by no means as definitive as some historians have suggested, foreshadowed the onset of French military preeminence.

The sieges, maneuvers, and battles in the Netherlands and Flanders made army commanders on both sides aware of changes in military tactics and equipment. Gradual improvements in the quality of matchlock muskets, cavalry carbines, and pistols led to the adoption of linear formations and to an increase in the ratio of musketeers to pikemen. However, the pikes often continued to offer the best defense against cavalry attacks. The musketeers frequently carried swords and under duress in confused melees, they defended themselves by wielding their heavy matchlocks as primitive bludgeons. By the 1640s some musketeers recognized the benefits of sticking knives about a foot long by the haft into the bore of their muskets to create a defensive weapon much like a half pike. Although the knives often became jammed making muskets useless for their primary purpose, the plug bayonet became the forerunner of more sophisticated ring bayonets developed in the 1680s and socket bayonets of the 1690s that did not interrupt firing. The development of the much more effective and lighter flintlock muskets made for better systems of attaching bayonets so that by the 1670s pikemen began to disappear as a complement to infantry musketeers. The flintlock musket was adopted by the Austrians in 1684, the British in 1685, and the Swedes in 1690. By the eighteenth century, pikemen were obsolete in most armies and the debates about their defensive and offensive effectiveness altered to focus on the merits of attack or defense by infantrymen with fixed bayonets.

Many of these changes in military technology and tactics emerged from the conflicts of the Netherlands and from the Thirty Years' War (1618–48) centered in Bohemia and Germany, which either directly or indirectly involved most countries and jurisdictions of the Continent. The complex series of struggles in central Europe involved religious, dynastic, political, strategic, and economic issues. Eventually the original causes became blurred by conflicts between competing military forces that devastated societies, destroyed economies, and at times reduced war to primitive barbarism. Famines and disease epidemics of typhoid, plague, dysentery, and the ubiquitous venereal diseases spread by marauding armies produced significant population declines. Nevertheless, most historians today have modified earlier cataclysmic interpretations of demographic disaster reported in the propaganda of contemporary observers. Yet there were many examples of cultural desolation and moral degradation and even some incidents of cannibalism in regions affected by pillaging, successive crop failures, and starvation. The long wars destroyed libraries and archives, killed off productive segments of the populations, and severely damaged industrial and economic endeavors. There were many great battles, sieges, and thousands of now forgotten skirmishes between armed forces that ravaged or totally destroyed villages, castles, and towns. Peasants lost animals and seed, townspeople feared rapine and looting by conquering armies, and in general civilians came to hate soldiers.

The war began in Bohemia over old religious issues, but it soon spread to involve Denmark, Sweden, and, after 1635, France. Although much of the fighting took place in greater Germany and Austria and there were many elements of civil war, behind the regional issues of the struggle continued the old conflicts for dominance between the Hapsburgs and the Bourbons. On the Habsburg side, Spain and its possessions in Italy, Flanders, and elsewhere supported the Holy Roman Emperor with armies and highly skilled officers such as Ambrosio Spínola, Raimondo Montecuccoli, and Ottavio Piccolomini. Moving beyond the old religious divisions, Catholic France under Cardinal Richelieu fought alongside the German Protestant princes and the Protestant Swedes who also opposed the Holy Roman Emperor. In the first phase beginning in 1618, the Protestant Bohemians (Czechs) at Prague opened the violence when they tossed two emissaries of the Habsburg emperor out of a window. Following this incident, called the "defenestration" of Prague, Catholic forces including fifteen companies of Spanish Walloon troops from the Netherlands mobilized to overwhelm the Protestants. In 1620 Spínola marched with thirty-one companies, mostly Italian, from Milan and other units were sent from Naples and Spain. Almost half of the infantry available to the emperor were soldiers of Spanish origin.

Three years of indecisive fighting, guerrilla warfare, and maneuver culminated in November 1620 at the Battle of the White Mountain in Bohemia about five kilometers west of Prague. The Bohemians assembled a large force including among their own units Austrians, Moravians, Silesians, Netherlanders, and Hungarians, with some financial support from the Protestant Dutch and even the English. Although the Protestants had the numbers, they lacked sufficient cohesion and leadership to capture Vienna. The emperor received financial assistance from the pope and troop reinforcements from the Spanish Habsburgs and the

Poles. At the White Mountain, about twenty-eight thousand imperial troops, including Germans, Spaniards, Italians, Walloons, and Poles, faced twenty-one thousand on the Bohemian side.

As both sides prepared for battle, the Catholics launched a punishing raid on the Hungarian contingent that reduced their zeal for further combat. Protestant forces deployed their infantry units alternated with cavalry squadrons in formations placed along a broad front. In the battle that commenced about noon and lasted only about two hours, the Catholic side which possessed superior manpower deployed along a shorter front that allowed for greater depth of units. Both sides formed five large infantry squares of musketeers and pikemen that advanced toward the opposition with cavalry squadrons between and behind them. After a short period of ineffective artillery and musket fire at long range, the Bohemian cavalry managed to break into and disrupt one of the imperial infantry pike squares. Nevertheless, the larger Catholic cavalry squadrons and supporting infantry squares maintained their cohesion and advanced. Recognizing that they were in trouble, some Bohemian regiments lost their forward initiative and pulled back leaving their flanks exposed to attack from all sides. Before long they were pursued by saber-wielding imperial cavalrymen and cut down during a precipitous rout. In many respects, the Battle of the White Mountain illustrated a more traditional style of tactical combat practiced successfully by the *tercios* in which pikemen played significant roles supported by cavalry, musketeers, and artillery.

With the Protestants in disarray and Catholic power extending to the Baltic Sea where Dutch, Danish, and Swedish strategic interests were threatened, in 1616 the King of Denmark intervened with an army of thirty thousand troops. Without a much stronger anti-Habsburg alliance, however, the Danes were no match for the forces of two outstanding imperial generals, Johan Tzerclaes, the count of Tilly, and Albrecht von Wallenstein, duke of Friedland and Mecklenburg. Like the Spanish General Spínola and Prince Maurice of Nassau in the Netherlands, Wallenstein put into place some important pieces of the military organizational puzzle that were to advance armies of the early modern era. A highly intelligent, ambitious, ruthless, and sometimes pitiless soldier, Wallenstein's unique strength lay in his managerial brilliance and his understanding of entrepreneurship directed toward the preservation and maintenance of armies. While he was not a truly brilliant general or tactician, he mastered the technical and logistical sides of supplying an army that allowed him to achieve remarkable successes as a contractor able to raise and to maintain very large forces. In addition, as a soldier Wallenstein learned from his contemporaries and emulated the systems of the Swedish king Gustavus Adolphus.

Appointed in 1618 to command an infantry regiment of three thousand troops, Wallenstein quickly recognized the long-term destructiveness of looting and plundering practiced by imperial troops such as the Spanish Walloons. Instead of the pillaging that destroyed future productivity, Wallenstein insisted upon the organized exploitation of the resources of captured towns and districts, harnessing economic potential to serve his military needs. In 1621 Wallenstein became commander of Prague and all of Bohemia and in 1623 the emperor promoted him to lieutenant general. Although he used his troops to control peasant populations by force, Wallenstein garnered land holdings and resources that in 1625 permitted him to raise twenty-one cavalry regiments and six infantry regiments or an army of almost thirty thousand men. In productive regions and districts, rural tenants and urban craftsmen supplied and supported the army and paid their taxes. By these means, weapons, munitions, food, billets, clothing, medical care, cavalry horses, transport, and military equipment were made available. On a smaller scale, many other military contractors raised and commanded forces to support the different factions.

Before Wallenstein's emergence, Spínola and many other commanders had argued that an army of thirty thousand troops was about the maximum limit for operational parameters governed by supply, logistics, housing, and pay. In 1627 Wallenstein proved them wrong when he raised an army of one hundred thousand soldiers supported from the base of his Bohemian and Silesian magazines. No other European monarch or general ever had commanded such a force. Now the equal in power of dynastic princes, Wallenstein had to deal with a multitude of enemies on both sides of the war who wanted to destroy him. At his apogee of power, however, he moved into Jutland and occupied Mecklenburg and Pomerania, stimulating a dream project of Count Duke Olivares of Spain that a dominant shipping and military-commercial alliance could be organized to link Spain, the Spanish Netherlands, the Hansa towns, and Poland. The emperor rewarded Wallenstein by appointing him general of the Imperial Armada and admiral of the Atlantic and Baltic Seas. In 1629, when the Danes accepted moderate terms to abandon the war, the Swedes and Dutch were convinced that their monopoly of the Baltic was threatened. At this point, France helped to negotiate a peace between Poland and Sweden that opened the way for Gustavus Adolphus to intervene in the empire. In the meantime, Wallenstein's mercurial career continued until 1634 when assassins invaded his bedroom and stabbed him to death after he had been charged with treason against the emperor. Many of his close associates and senior commanders were massacred during a banquet by hired Scottish, Irish, English, and German soldier-assassins.

The intervention in Germany of Gustavus Adolphus in 1630 with a small Swedish army of thirteen thousand troops marked a second stage of the Thirty Years' War. A powerful advocate of the Protestant cause, Gustavus also responded to economic threats contained in the aggressive Hapsburg strategies directed toward the Swedish sphere of influence in the Baltic. Often called the father of modern warfare, Gustavus was well tutored in military classics including the works of Caesar and Vegetius, and he understood the organizational reforms introduced by Maurice of Nassau and other exemplary commanders of the age. Just as important for a military reformer, Gustavus enjoyed an almost unparalleled firsthand understanding of the battlefield and of weapons. As a commander, he often led from the vanguard and had been wounded in the hip and shoulder by bullets during earlier campaigns against the Poles and Russians. His reforms touched almost every area of military science from weapons to tactics, conditions of service, education, and doctrine. Although many of the changes adopted in the Swedish army represented continuity with innovations introduced previously elsewhere, Gustavus Adolphus was the first to create a national standing army based on conscription for the infantry and on close linkages between the regular forces and militia units raised for home defense. In this process, the Swedish king possessed the special advantage of drawing on a small but homogeneous population. Most other armies were heterogeneous amalgams involving numerous mercenaries of different nationalities and diverse ethnic groups.

While the Swedes also used mercenary forces to supplement numbers, unlike most other armies of the epoch they were able to preserve a national character that often enhanced their fighting abilities. In this area, they acted much like Spanish soldiers of the sixteenth century. Once involved in Germany, however, the Swedes required additional troops to fight the enormous Habsburg formations and they had no alternative other than to hire mercenaries. In 1631 just over half of

Gustavus's soldiers at the Battle of Breitenfeld were Swedes. However, Swedish commanders made efforts to reduce the great number of camp followers including gamblers, prostitutes, and noncombatant family members who interfered with the efficiency of soldiers on the move or in garrisons and winter cantonments.

In his tactics, Gustavus followed Maurice of Nassau in employing linear formations against the unwieldy infantry *tercios* used by the Imperialists. Gustavus increased the number of musketeers and reduced the combat line to six ranks rather than the accustomed ten. The Swedes discarded older arquebuses and replaced them with improved matchlock muskets that they fired from a forked rest. Later, lighter muskets were introduced that could be fired from the shoulder without the need for a rest. For efficiency, Gustavus introduced packaged paper cartridges containing gunpowder and a ball. Soldiers bit off the end of the cartridge, poured a small quantity into the firing pan and rammed the remainder into the barrel with the ramrod. This system saved many steps where powder had to be measured under less than perfect battlefield conditions or in poor weather. Each musketeer now wore a bandoleer across his chest or a belt containing ten to fifteen cartridges ready for immediate use.

In battle, Swedish musketeers aimed for horses and were taught not to bother with the riders who were almost useless anyway once thrown on the ground into a maelstrom of flailing wounded animals and the charges of their mounted comrades. If they did hit the cavalryman, even if the large-caliber soft-lead balls did not penetrate his cuirass, the blow of a bullet was sufficient to stun or knock almost any rider to the ground or at least to disable him as an effective fighter. Notwithstanding his attention to firearms, Gustavus recognized pikemen as essential to protect musketeers against cavalry assaults. Despite opposition from some of his commanders, he argued that the pike was a battle-winning weapon that served to drive the enemy from the field. However, Swedish pikemen were not as heavily armored as their opponents and most were protected only by an iron helmet. It was said that Gustavus discarded armor himself because it chaffed against the scars of his earlier wounds. Equipping the Swedish troops with warm clothing—often made of blue or gray homespun—they stood out for their simplicity compared to the showy regalia and colorful individual attire adopted by many of the Imperial troops. Nevertheless, the highly disciplined Swedish soldiers maintained high morale and unity of purpose. Backed by strong religious commitment, especially during their first years in Germany, they were difficult to beat.

Gustavus's reforms centered on working out tactical problems concerned with attack upon enemy infantry squares and heavy lines that presented a solid front or pike-hedge wall. The Swedish musketeers were trained to fire by salvo or volley of ranks so that continuous fire could be maintained. In preparation to receive an enemy charge, the six ranks of musketeers formed up with the front line kneeling so that they could fire a simultaneous heavy volley. Once the opposition troops wavered, Gustavus sent in his pikemen and cavalry. Rather than simply firing off their pistols and retreating to reload in the caracole method, Swedish mounted troops followed Polish techniques and pressed home their attacks with their sabers using speed and shock as they hit the enemy lines. To add flexibility to these assaults dragoons or mounted infantrymen served either as trained infantry musketeers or as cavalry capable of charging in ranks with swords or lances.

The final element needed to pierce enemy lines came with the Swedish reforms in the field of artillery. An expert in gunnery, Gustavus reduced the calibers of his heavy guns to twenty-four-, twelve-, and six-pounders. To make these guns more mobile, he used lighter gun carriages, shortened gun barrels, and reduced the thickness of metal employed in the artillery tubes. These changes required technical improvements in the areas of design, casting, and metallurgy. Foreign specialists who settled in Sweden worked on these problems and also brought gunpowder to a much better standard of quality. In addition to these reforms, Gustavus experimented with light fast-firing regimental three-pound guns mounted on carriages that could be moved by a horse or two or three men. These wire-wrapped leather-sheathed pieces were highly mobile, but they tended to overheat and were replaced by light bronze guns assigned two each to the infantry regiments. The light field pieces functioned in direct support of infantry and cavalry operations. For the first time, artillery that had been a separate craft became a regular branch of the army.

For about fifteen months after landing on the Pomeranean coast, Gustavus threw up fieldworks to hold the vulnerable beachhead while he sought allies. Some Protestants joined the Swedes and Gustavus obtained financial subsidies from Cardinal Richelieu that helped him to hire mercenaries. When the city of Magdeburg to the south rose up against Imperial rule in favor of the Protestants, Gustavus was still too weak to march to its rescue. The forces of Count Tilly besieged the city before assaulting, plundering, and burning the stronghold. Unpaid Catholic troops ran amuck, looting, raping, and killing as many as twenty thousand residents. For many weeks, hacked corpses filled the Elbe River. This atrocity aroused Protestant anger everywhere and caused the Dutch to pledge financial subsidies to support Gustavus and to plan diversionary attacks against Catholic Flanders. In the meantime, the Swedes consolidated their positions and declined to engage in battle until they could recruit sufficient allies in Brandenburg and Saxony. On the Imperial side, Count Tilly awaited reinforcements from Italy, where they had been fighting France over the Duchy of Mantua.

The great drama of battlefield confrontations that military historians often have portrayed as a struggle between the old system of the *tercios* versus a new age of shock and firepower, represented by the reforms of Gustavus Adolphus, produced three epic confrontations: the Battle of Breitenfeld (see the case study), September 17, 1631; the Battle of Lützen, November 16, 1632; and the Battle of Nördlingen, September 6, 1634. The Swedish-Saxon army won a great victory at Breitenfeld, a most famous battle often viewed by historians with the Battle of Rocroi in 1643 as illustrating the emergence of firepower and new tactics and the decline of the heavy infantry squares. The Swedes won again at Lützen against Wallenstein, but on this occasion chance rather than brilliance on the part of the commanders won the day which was almost a draw. In the short time since Breitenfeld, Wallenstein altered his tactics and adopted the light artillery used by the Swedes. The Imperialists had twelve thousand troops killed, wounded, and prisoners compared to Swedish losses of about ten thousand troops. The battle was costly for the Imperialists particularly when Count Gottfried Pappenheim suffered a mortal wound from a cannonball. For the Swedes, the victory was even more bittersweet since Gustavus Adolphus in a typically impulsive act became separated from his guards while he was at the front line with his cavalry. First shot in the arm by an Imperial musketeer and then in the back by a horseman, the king fell from his horse mortally wounded. Final shots in the back of his head as he lay face down in the mud supplied the coup de grace while other Imperialist soldiers stabbed and stripped the corpse. Gustavus's leather jerkin became a war trophy in Vienna until the end of World War I when it was returned to the Swedes for display in Stockholm's Nordic Museum.

For the Swedish army there was worse to come. At the Battle of Nördlingen, all of the technical and tactical advances taught by Gustavus were insufficient to overcome the fact that Imperial forces outnumbered them by as many as forty thousand to twenty-five thousand troops. The Swedes and their allies lost ten thousand to twelve thousand troops killed and four thousand taken prisoner, including Field Marshal Gustav Horn. For the Protestants in Germany, the subdivision of operational forces to look after a multitude of garrison duties and other commitments left insufficient troops available to fight a major battle. Although the Swedes recovered to win victories at Wittstock in 1636, Jankov in 1645, and in many smaller engagements, by this time their friends and foes alike had emulated the new ideas, tactics, and equipment of Gustavus Adolphus.

Case Study: The Battle of Breitenfeld

At the Battle of Breitenfeld, Gustavus seconded by Field Marshal Johan Banér commanded an army of forty-two thousand troops (twenty-four thousand Swedes and eighteen thousand Saxons and other allies) against Count Tilly's army of thirty-five thousand Imperial troops. In addition to numerical advantage, the Swedish cavalry outnumbered the Imperialist horse and Gustavus had about seventy-five cannon for only twenty-six distributed among Tilly's forces. Facing each other on level ground outside the village of Breitenfeld the Swedish side approached in formation against the Imperialists who already had taken up an advantageous position on the open plain. Martial music, artillery fire, and skirmishing by advanced light forces preceded the general engagement. In the main force, Tilly employed traditional formations of heavy pike squares and musketeers in *tercio* form with his cavalry deployed to the right and left to protect the flanks. As the battle approached, he formed his infantry in a deep compact line. The Swedish-Saxon army advanced in a linear arrangement that extended their flanks on both sides beyond Tilly's more tightly packed forces. Gustavus interspersed musketeer detachments and light artillery pieces with the pike companies. Over a broad front of four to five kilometers, both armies deployed their infantry in the center and their cavalry forces on the flanks.

Although somewhat outnumbered, Tilly depended on the quality of his veteran troops—especially against the Saxons who were mostly green levies lacking combat experience. The battle opened with a precipitous but unauthorized assault by Count Gottfried Pappenheim's famous black cuirassier cavalry by caracole firing wheel-lock pistols against the

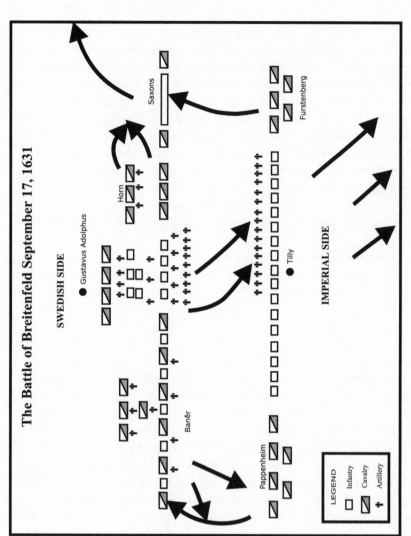

The Battle of Breitenfeld September 17, 1631

SWEDISH SIDE

● Gustavus Adolphus

Horn

Banér

Saxons

Pappenheim

Furstenberg

● Tilly

IMPERIAL SIDE

LEGEND

☐ Infantry

▨ Cavalry

✝ Artillery

Map 7.1

front and flank of the Swedish right wing. The Swedish infantry and cavalry held their fire until the cuirassiers drew near and then unleashed withering volleys of musketry and light artillery fire followed up by cavalry rushes with drawn sabers that overran the Imperial cavalry with their velocity and shock. At first undeterred by the repulse, Pappenheim ordered seven attacks before exhaustion and heavy casualties prevented further offensive action in that sector.

While these actions took place on the Imperial left wing, the main infantry battle lines did not meet except through exchanges of artillery fire that temporarily opened ragged holes in the opposing formations of troops. Since the more numerous Swedish-Saxon artillery caused greater carnage among the Imperial troops, Tilly decided to send his right flank to envelop the less experienced Saxons. Moving four heavy infantry formations from the Imperial center with the cavalry of that flank Tilly drove the Saxons from the battlefield and exposed the left flank of the Swedes. With the Saxons out of the way, the Imperial forces now enjoyed a numerical advantage. In response, the Swedish commander of that sector, Gustav Horn, hastily called up reserves to resist the four ponderous imperial infantry formations that were reorganizing after having crushed the Saxons. Unleashing volleys of musketry, light artillery fire and attacks by cavalry supported by musketeers, the Swedes first successfully repelled the Imperial cavalry as they had done earlier with Pappenheim on their opposite flank. In the smoke and dust of the battlefield, once deprived of cavalry the separated infantry squares lost communications and could not support each other effectively when they came under attack on all sides. Musketry, light artillery fire, and even cannonades fired by the Swedes from captured Imperial batteries wreaked terrible havoc among the tightly packed infantrymen. Tilly suffered several wounds and almost fell into the hands of the Swedes.

Although the figures may be a little inaccurate, the Imperial side suffered almost twenty thousand casualties at the Battle of Breitenfeld including seventy-six hundred killed and many others cut down as they fled by Swedish cavalry or by angry peasants bent on revenge and pillage. As was customary, the nine thousand captured Imperial prisoners joined the Swedish forces and bolstered their numbers. The Swedes and Saxons lost twenty-one hundred men killed and wounded. On the surface, Gustavus's victory at Breitenfeld illustrated mobility and flexibility involving linear tactics, maneuver, firepower, shock, and collaboration between the different branches of the army. The use of sheer weight of numbers and heavy *tercios* of the Spanish army appeared to be over. On the other hand, depending on a variety of conditions, the vagaries of command, and the sometimes impenetrable fog of battle, more traditional troop deployments sometimes won the day. The preponderance of artillery enjoyed by the Swedish-Saxon forces that shattered many Imperial regiments before they could enter combat in the future would be countered by strengthening the artillery. In any battle, enemy heavy batteries had to be attacked by cavalry and counterbattery fire. Once under active fire, artillery crews often became erratic, immobile, and even ran for cover if they suffered casualties.

The Thirty Years' War dragged on almost beyond the point of exhaustion until the Peace of Westphalia in 1648. Many of the military reforms became obscured by logistical problems, sieges, difficulties garrisoning defended towns and fortresses and by the loss of cohesion in operational forces. In Germany, armies preyed upon civilians, ravaged provinces, and mutinied when governments failed to pay their troops. In some cases, gangs of soldiers became bandits with little if any allegiance to any legitimate cause. By midcentury, Spain had suffered grievous losses caused by its own civil wars, the effort to support the Habsburgs, the continuing struggle in the Spanish Netherlands, and in the war against France. Spain and its empire presented a perfect example of a great power overcommitted to strategic and military causes beyond its human and financial capacity. In France, Richelieu's death, internal opposition to war and internal strife offset any euphoria from the great victory of 1643 at Rocroi. The Swedes complained bitterly about the high costs of war and lamented the loss of so many young men that few if any remained in many villages and towns. Conscription to fight German wars no longer produced great victories and the small population demanded peace. In England, the outbreak of the civil war in 1642 brought with it many of the accompanying horrors of seventeenth-century warfare. With the creation of Cromwell's quite professional New Model Army— twenty-one thousand troops divided into six thousand cavalry, one thousand dragoons, and fourteen thousand infantry—some of the reforms of Gustavus Adolphus took root. Both the Royalists and Round Heads hired soldiers who had fought on the Continent and were familiar with Spanish, French, Swedish, and Imperial tactical systems.

By the middle decades of the seventeenth century, the Habsburgs lost their military preeminence as France and the House of Bourbon took the initiative. With a large population of over twenty million and the economic potential to build and maintain powerful armies and fleets, France possessed all of the potential resources for military power. Earlier beset by a series of disruptive regencies and minorities, struggles for power between the monarchy and the great nobles, and the debilitating civil disorders of the Fronde (1648–53), for some time France had not been able to take its place as successor to the Habsburgs. The French produced some of the truly great army commanders of the age including Henri de Bourbon, future Prince of Condé (1621–86) and Henri de la Tour d'Auvergne, viscomte de Turenne (1611–75). At Rocroi, Condé first exhibited his fighting skills, audacity, and decisiveness as a cavalry commander that showed he was an apt pupil of Gustavus in the use of combined arms on the battlefield. Turenne served with French armies in Germany during the 1630s where he learned in hard campaigns to become a thoughtful, careful, and thorough commander. As a young officer in Germany, Turenne fed his troops by selling off his own family pewter and extending his personal credit to purchase supplies and provisions.

During the struggles of the Fronde, Condé took the side of the rebels against the policies of Cardinal Mazarin, chief minister of the French Crown, while Turenne served the monarchy. Both officers fought tenaciously against each other during the rebellions and they met in combat in 1658 at the Battle of the Dunes on the Channel Coast where Turenne prevailed. By this time Condé had changed sides temporarily and joined Spain and the army of the Spanish Netherlands. Turenne commanded a powerful army and was ready to roll through the Spanish Netherlands, but in 1659 Spain signed the Peace of the Pyrenees. With the Treaties of Westphalia and the Pyrenees in place, France set about asserting its military power.

Once the French crown managed to gain control over its rebellious provinces, haughty aristocrats, corrupt administrators, and chaotic finances, a nation that had been a second rate military power soon dominated Europe and competed with England, the Netherlands, and Spain for world dominance. In many respects, France's rise to power rested on its army and the implementation of a complex military system involving strategies, tactics, and finance that had evolved first with sixteenth-century Spain and then with Maurice of Nassau, Count Wallenstein, Gustavus Adolphus, and many other reformers. The process was evolutionary rather than revolutionary. Nevertheless, few observers of the period could have imagined that King Louis XIV (1643–1715), who came to power in 1661, would construct a military machine that rapidly became the wonder of the age. It was obvious, for example from the Dutch, Swedish, and even from the English Parliamentary forces that many of the abuses of armies—attacks on civilians, looting, extortion, protection rackets, mutinies, and other corrupt and criminal practices—had to be brought under control if any force was to retain its effectiveness. Moreover, something had to be done about high disease rates and desertion levels that eroded armed forces at a time when nations wanted to increase or stabilize their military structures.

In France, Louis XIV centralized the state which was the only agency with sufficient power to entrench military reforms. The chaos of the Fronde was lesson enough for the king and his gifted bureaucrats in the war department, Michel le Tellier (1643–66) who was followed by his son François Michel le Tellier, Marquis de Louvois. Although their work was never complete, these officials tamed the nobles within the officer corps and created a centralized military administrative system capable of raising large armies, moving them to areas of contention and supporting them for as long as was necessary to achieve strategic goals. Around Louvois as minister of war a full, departmentalized government office took shape. By 1680 five bureaus had been established, each headed by a *chef de bureau* and a full staff of assistants.

The development of a more effective centralized civil administration in many respects put an end to the inefficient often corrupt contractors who had raised and maintained military forces. In the Spanish system for example, captains or colonels had recruited companies within their home provinces. As private contractors they purchased arms, munitions, and clothing before transporting the new soldiers to distant theaters of war. Once on station, other contractors provided soldiers with inferior rations and services while the civilian population suffered from having to furnish billets. In France during Richelieu's administration, officials called *Intendants d'armées* supervised the dealings of military contractors. Provincial Intendants represented the crown in the regions where they held broad judicial powers and appointed *commissaires* who watched over recruitment, militias, barracks, military pay, equipment, supply, and taxation to support military units.

Under Louvois, the state moved to exercise direct controls over areas that had been handled by senior officers and contractors. State arsenals and magazines took up the responsibilities to supply military forces, factories produced standardized arms and munitions, and new roads were built to meet military and strategic needs—particularly when Louis XIV commenced a series of wars to expand his frontiers. Uniforms that had appeared earlier in some specialized situations now became the rule since the state provided garments to its soldiers. Intendants inspected garrisons to check bookkeeping, barracks, hospital provisions, and especially muster rolls of troops actually present for duty. In 1675 the French revised their system of military ranks along Spanish lines and in the *Ordre du Tableau* defined the duties and privileges of each rank and outlined the exact requirements for promotion. Since seniority and dates of commission became important, the army and its officers took vital interest in record keeping and archiving service records. The construction of barracks removed French army units from negative contacts with society at large and in theory created an atmosphere in which the disciplined lifestyle of the new soldier could be developed. For veterans—particularly disabled soldiers—the creation in 1670 of the Hôtel des Invalides established care for disabled ex-soldiers and at the same time kept them off the streets and away from lives of crime.

The implementation of these reforms made the French army much more stable and permanent. Indeed, the need for garrison forces in France's great bastioned fortresses guarding potential invasion routes and for disciplined field armies drilled in linear tactics, made the standing army an absolute necessity. Officers and noncommissioned officers drilled their troops to develop group morale and the discipline needed to fire volleys into enemy forces at point blank range. The appointment of Jean Martinet as inspector-general of infantry, brought to power a man intensely disliked by the soldiers for his strict enforcement of rigorous discipline and parade square drill. He gave his name to perpetuity as one bound by rigid adherence to rules and regulations. By this time, the matchlock musket had been improved to the point that the rest was no longer necessary to steady the barrel during firing. Other technological changes of the seventeenth century solidified these reforms. Many of the weaknesses of the matchlock were overcome by the development of the flintlock, which used a piece of flint held between the jaws of the cock to ignite the gunpowder in the pan. A simple pull of the trigger struck sparks from steel to fire the musket. Adopted by most armies during the 1680s and 1690s, the flintlock or fusil increased the rate of fire by reducing the length of time and number of steps required for reloading. And with the adoption of the flintlock, the plug bayonet, which had been around since the 1640s for use with the matchlock could be adapted. The ring and socket bayonets of the 1680s and 1690s allowed the attachment of the bayonet over the barrel leaving the musket free to fire. In the 1660s, France's great military engineer Sébastien Le Prestre de Vauban (1633–1707) became a strong advocate of the flintlock and designer of an effective bayonet. With these developments all soldiers became firearm users and except for ceremonial uses the now obsolete pikemen disappeared. The full ramifications of these changes became evident in eighteenth-century warfare.

The late-seventeenth-century wars of supremacy directed by Louis XIV against Spain, the Dutch Republic, and other allies required more than purely military reforms. If Louvois set the direction for an effective regular army, Minister of Finance Jean-Baptiste Colbert developed the French economy and advocated financial security through expanding trade, industry, and the construction of fleets to extend the overseas empire. France's aggression began with mercantilist policies and the nearly insatiable appetite of Louis XIV for the territories and resources of his weaker neighbors. By the 1690s the allies that had assisted France in defeating Spain united to check Louis XIV's expansionism. The Nine Years' War, also known as the War of the League of Augsburg and the War of the Grand Alliance (1688–97), brought together England, Holland, Austria, Spain, Savoy, Sweden, and the German states. Forced to fight a coalition that could deploy large armies against France by land and in amphibious raids on the coasts, the French army reached a wartime total strength of almost four hundred thousand troops.

Most French aggression during this epoch was directed toward the Spanish Netherlands and other eastern border regions including Luxembourg, Alsace, the Palatinate, Franche-Comté, and northern Italy. In the Spanish Netherlands, once again the cockpit of Europe, France pressed for territorial gains in a region of considerable wealth and prosperity. Already fought over in many previous wars, fortified towns and new frontier fortresses made for a war of sieges rather than pitched battles. Indeed, where battles did occur, they took place in association with relief of a besieged town or fortress. In the brief War of Devolution (1667–68), Vauban distinguished himself as a master of siege craft and other aspects of military engineering during the French attacks on the Spanish Netherlands. Successful at applying the science of siege craft, Vauban was also a military architect who gained long-term fame for the design of his fortresses that employed complex variations of the well-known bastioned trace. Through the wars of the period, he convinced

Louis XIV to authorize the construction of a series of heavily defended fortresses along the French borders designed to deny any enemy entry to France and to serve as launching points for offensive thrusts against neighboring countries.

Vauban's much admired system for the attack of fortresses took shape in 1673 during the siege of Maastricht and at the siege of Luxembourg in 1684. In fact, many of his approaches simply drew together and perfected ideas developed during the Eighty Years' War between the Dutch and Spaniards. Following a formalized and quite leisurely procedure, the besiegers began by accumulating troops, sappers, and siege equipment out of the range of defending fire. The sappers then dug a deep trench toward the fortification to a point that a parallel trench was extended at right angles to the approach trench and facing the section of the walls selected for eventual attack. Called the "first parallel," this trench became the base for men, equipment, and artillery batteries. In addition to firing on a direct trajectory to knock enemy guns off their carriages, Vauban fired his heavy cannon and howitzers at high elevation and extreme range so that the balls would drift toward the end of their flight and ricochet through the defenses leaving no corner safe for the defenders. From the first parallel trench, zigzag approaches moved the besiegers forward to a second and finally third parallel usually within pistol range close to the foot of the glacis. At this point, the attackers threw up earthworks and a parapet from which they could fire or hurl grenades at the defenders. Heavy siege artillery from protected positions in the second parallel and sometimes gunpowder mines dug under the fortifications were used to breach the defenses.

In an age of growing moderation in warfare, the commander of a besieged fortress or town communicated with his opponent and often surrendered when summoned to do so if he recognized that there was a practicable breach to assault. Only occasionally did infantrymen, called the "Forlorn Hopes," have to attack the breach. Usually this followed a third and final summons to surrender under terms. Fortified by alcohol and shouting their battle cries to suppress fear, the attackers rushed forward to drive the defenders from cover. In such cases, victorious assault troops often received permission for a period of pillage that opened the way to abuses and wide-scale atrocities against noncombatants.

Despite the improvements introduced by Louvois and other reformers, the lives of seventeenth-century soldiers tended to be brutish and short. Toward the end of the century even with some improvements in hygiene, soldiers lived in fetid conditions in barracks that observers described as worse than pig sties. Vauban lamented that French troops were "housed like swine, half-naked, dying of hunger." Indeed, the effort to separate soldiers from civilians by terminating the system of billeting exposed men to diseases of crowded conditions such as typhus (known as ship fever aboard warships), typhoid, dysentery, food poisoning, and many skin diseases such as mange and scabies. During the 1625 Anglo-Dutch expedition against Cádiz, for example, in a twenty-one-day voyage there were almost five thousand casualties from typhus. Bad diet caused scurvy, which disabled many soldiers in garrisons and on active duty. Lice and other parasites flourished among men who lived closely packed and without washing water or changes of clothing. Not only were barracks filthy unventilated places, but officers ordered them closed up tight at night to deter desertions. Lack of facilities sometimes forced men to sleep two or more to a bed. In camps and cantonments, exposure to the climate and especially to constant damp prevented soldiers from drying their feet and clothing. These conditions exposed them to colds, influenza, pulmonary pneumonia, rheumatism, gout, hernias, and sores. As might be expected with the numbers of camp followers and dislocations caused by warfare, armies were like vectors that communicated syphilis and other venereal diseases. On the move, regiments of three thousand troops were often followed by four thousand or more non-combatants on foot or riding in carts. In 1648 a Bavarian army of forty thousand troops was said to drag a tail of almost one hundred thousand camp followers including soldiers' wives and families, prostitutes, servants, sutlers, gamblers, and a variety of hucksters who lived off the soldiers.

Although Gustavus Adolphus made attempts to keep women camp followers far from his soldiers and the French implemented similar orders late in the century, most efforts of this sort failed shortly after implementation. Even in the reformed armies of Louis XIV, French garrisons often went without adequate provisions and soldiers were described as being half-naked or dressed in rags. The fact was that no seventeenth-century government possessed the level of organization needed to care for its troops. Soldiers garrisoned in the Netherlands, Germany, Italy, and elsewhere insisted that women were essential to look after sewing, washing, spinning, nursing, and dealing with the sale of old clothing and other items. Some women built up small businesses selling tobacco and pipes, alcoholic drinks, fresh produce that they collected, and participating in illegal gambling games. Others were outright prostitutes who despite regulations to ban their presence sold sex to a willing clientele. In the French army, laws enacted in the 1680s to halt the spread of venereal diseases, proclaimed that any prostitute discovered within two leagues of a military camp was to suffer the draconian punishment of having her nose and ears split. Needless to say, even with these threats, syphilis continued to be a major medical problem.

Many women followed their husbands who served foreign armies far from their homelands. English, Irish, Scottish, and Italian women ended up in Spain, the Netherlands, Germany, or in other distant theaters of war. In addition, Spanish soldiers—including Italians, Irishmen, and many other nationalities garrisoned in the Netherlands—married Walloon women, settled down to raise families, and seldom returned to their homeland. When their men died or suffered capture, women sometimes found themselves abandoned in foreign lands and reduced to begging for survival. Although the women of common soldiers possessed little recourse, some officers' wives were able to obtain subsidies and small army pensions.

Given the fact military service was almost tantamount to a death sentence through the seventeenth century, it might seem strange that most soldiers actually volunteered for duty. Except for the Swedish army that conscripted infantrymen from village populations, there were certain common features in most other military forces. All armies including the Swedes hired contingents of foreign mercenaries such as the Irish, Scottish, Swiss, English, Italian, and Croatians. Officers were mostly members of the nobility (of the rank of seigneurs or hidalgos for France and Spain). Many were second and third sons who recognized that under laws of primogeniture they had little hope of inheriting family lands and properties. Some families in all countries had traditions of sending sons into martial careers and there were often lucrative opportunities as contractors, who enlisted, equipped, trained, and led their men into service. Generals, colonels, and captains received royal commissions to recruit forces with the intention of making money and furthering their own private interests. The name of Wallenstein comes to mind as the truly great military entrepreneur of the period, but Bernard of Saxe-Weimar was also a great enterpriser in this field and there were many others.

A senior officer, such as a colonel, first sold off company commands or captaincies. The recruits often came from the home districts of their commanders. Some joined because of financial hardship, pending criminal charges, hope for betterment, or simply to fulfill personal expectations of glory and adventure. Posted to the bloody battlefields of Germany during the Thirty Years' War, to garrison towns during the hardships of sieges in the Netherlands, or to the defense of Vienna in 1683 against the implacable Turks, these same men must have wondered what momentary insanity had taken possession of them when they took the oath to serve their general or flag and listened to the penalties for crimes, such as desertion, outlined in the articles of war.

Seventeenth-century soldiers faced a variety of punishments for indiscipline, desertion, and other crimes. On occasion, officers and soldiers received death sentences by hanging or firing squads for cowardice in the face of the enemy. Lesser punishments for gambling, excessive drunkenness, brawling, and cursing were frequent and varied. The Swedes condemned delinquent soldiers to a period of time riding the wooden horse—a saw horse like contraption that they straddled with their feet off the ground and heavy muskets added to increase the pain. Another punishment called "the Swedish drink" involved pouring human excrement down a victim's throat. In the armies of France and Spain, convicted soldiers had to run the gauntlet a number of times between files of their comrades who whacked them hard with their ramrods. Other punishments included the rack, whipping, and the strappado (where the victim, secured by the hands, was raised and then let fall until brought up smartly by a taut rope). If these punishments did not fit the crime, courts-martial simply sentenced offenders to additional years in the army. About the only crime that armies of the period did not take too seriously for common soldiers was the accepted practice of going over to serve the enemy if captured in combat or after a siege.

New recruits received a bounty from the royal treasury or from the jurisdiction that hired them and their senior officers paid wages after deducting the costs of food, equipment, and clothing. By the 1620s, the Swedish army adopted standard forms of dress for regiments. By the 1640s, the Imperial armies often wore pearl gray and in 1645 the New Model Army in England adopted the distinctive red coats of the later British army. Despite these examples, uniforms in national colors did not appear in most armies until later in the century.

Most recruits received weapons, munitions, equipment, and a loose fitting suit of clothing—a coat, shirt, breeches, stockings, and shoes (possibly the first pair they had owned for men of some regions). Many contractors provided poor-quality garments and chiseled their men wherever possible to earn better profits. If soldiers received the opportunities to plunder or to strip dead enemies and prisoners, or they had money for distinctive dress, they added feathers, colorful sashes, medallions, and other individual flourishes to their outfits that gave them the appearance of showy dandies.

To identify themselves to their comrades, soldiers wore hat bands, sashes, or tokens—red for the Habsburgs, blue and yellow for the Swedes, orange for the Dutch. Regiments carried banners that identified units on battlefields and became important trophies if captured that can be seen today in military museums—red for Spain, orange for Holland, white for France, and the black double-headed eagle for the Austrians and Germans. Under Louvois, the French were the first to issue full uniforms—using different colors at first before they settled on white coats. In addition, Louis XIV renewed the old and inexpensive tradition of issuing medals and service ribbons to honor longevity and distinguished service.

Considering the number of wars, the growth in the size of armies, and the wider distribution of firearms, military medicine did not progress fast enough to keep pace with ghastly wounds caused by bullets or cures for the many illnesses suffered by soldiers. Confounded by infection that killed most patients, physicians developed a variety of spurious treatments involving some harmful preparations. Military medical chests of the period contained a variety of different surgical instruments and a pharmacopoeia of remedies that included less harmful natural plant materials such as rhubarb, palm juice, and powdered sandalwood, and much more dangerous and disgusting preparations such as mummy dust, oil of vipers, earwigs, human and dog fat, excrement, crabs' eyes, mercury, and opium. Bloodletting was widely practiced as were purges and enemas using many different preparations. In the treatment of wounds, amputation was the best hope but the advances made by Ambroise Paré in the area of ligature for example appear to have been forgotten. Hospitals operated by civilian contractors and religious orders provided primitive care at best and often with a total absence of good hygiene. There were improvements in the French army under Louvois and by the 1690s, the Dutch provided wagons for field ambulances, field hospitals, and permanent military hospitals in major centers. At the same time, wounded British soldiers serving in the Netherlands received almost no hospital care and on some occasions they had to endure barge and boat trips back to London for treatment.

By the first decade of the seventeenth century it was evident that Spain had lost its pretensions to dominate the oceans. Dutch commanders smashed Spanish and Portuguese fleets in the Atlantic, Indian, and Pacific Oceans, grabbing territories and extending the range and power of their merchant marine. They showed the Spaniards in the Netherlands that trade, aggression at sea, and global economic power based on the marine preeminence of the Dutch East India Company and Dutch West India Company were excellent solutions to defeating Spain's land power on the European continent. The Dutch broke Spain's stranglehold on the Caribbean and there were schemes in Amsterdam during the 1620s to overthrow Spanish rule in Chile, to occupy the Straits of Magellan, and even to launch an overland invasion of Spanish Peru.

At midcentury, Dutch admirals flouted English pretensions in the Channel and protected their seaborne commerce, whaling, fishing fleets, and other activities around the world. At the same time, however, it is noteworthy to recall that the Dutch failed to hold Brazil, most of their African conquests, and that possession of their North American holding of New Amsterdam was not pursued with vigor. Unable to become an imperial power like Spain or England, because Dutch people did not emigrate in sufficient numbers, their control over the oceans and trade of the world attracted hostility from England that culminated in the Navigation Act of 1651 and aggressive rivalries that led to the outbreak of three Anglo-Dutch Wars (1652–54, 1665–67, and 1672–74). The ubiquitous presence and power of the Dutch around the world led one frustrated English observer to comment, "the Devil shits Dutchmen."

For their own part, the English were equally aggressive in their efforts to control the seas between their own coastline and the Continent. English warships demanded "the honor of the flag" which meant that foreign vessels were to lower their topsails and strike flags in recognition of the supremacy of the King of England (or the Commonwealth). The succeeding naval struggles between England and the Netherlands involved France and other countries in a much larger future conflict for world commercial domination in the eighteenth century.

Although fighting ships with heavy broadside capabilities were not the inventions of the seventeenth century, this was the seed time for naval tactics and strategies and for getting the most out of ships and guns. The Spaniards and the Portuguese had learned a great deal about navigating and dominating the seas and continental littorals that the Dutch, English, and French put into practice in their own projects to dominate their immediate coastal seas, the Mediterranean, and the oceans of the world.

The purpose built warship or "great ship" emerged by the mid-seventeenth century as a decisive weapon. As early as the 1630s, three deckers such as England's *Prince Royal* and *Sovereign of the Seas* armed with one hundred heavy guns pointed to the future directions of naval war. A nation that engaged in the business of naval war and the application of sea power required ready access to resources for shipbuilding and naval stores, a professional corps of experienced officers and ratings who could sail and fight their ships, and a complex infrastructure of shipyards, naval architects, ordnance specialists, and sustained government support to maintain budgets. Enormous quantities of timber, cordage, and pitch were needed along with a skilled workforce to build and maintain specialized warships. In the logistical sense, a navy placed heavier demands on a country than an army. It is remarkable that a fleet of the period possessed much more heavy weaponry and firepower than an army. One large warship of the 1670s had more cannon aboard than a contemporary field army and it expended more powder as well as other resources. Indeed, one fully armed great ship cost about the same as a fortress built of stone, brick, and earth, but the vessel could founder in minutes during a storm, be consumed by marine borers in tropical seas in a matter of weeks, or be sunk in battle in a few hours.

Despite the widespread opinion that the Dutch were the preeminent sea power, at the outbreak of the first Anglo-Dutch war in 1652, Admiral Maarten Tromp discovered that English ships armed with over fifty heavy guns were capable of defending themselves effectively against a much larger number of lighter gunned and smaller Dutch warships. Both sides experimented since there had been no fleet action since the 1588 Armada campaign. Unlike the English who relied on gunnery alone, the Dutch used boarding and fireships—attacking effectively in the Thames River and raiding ports but unable to match broadsides on the high seas. For the second war, the Dutch built almost an entirely new fleet of large seventy to eighty gun warships—using thirty-six-pounders, twenty-four-pounders, and eighteen-pounders. In the Four Day Fight of 1666, Admiral Michiel de Ruyter belatedly imitated the English tactic of fighting in line-ahead formation. In reply, the English built seven 94- to 100-gun behemoths armed with forty-two-pound guns (each of these weighed over three tons and required a crew of twelve men) in their batteries and other vessels with 64 to 70 guns. In rough seas, the lower

Fig. 7.2. *The Seventeenth-Century Anglo-Dutch Naval Wars.* From *The Four Days' Battle, June 1666* by Abraham Storck. National Maritime Museum, London. Courtesy of Compagnie Royale D'Artillerie, La Prairie, Quebec.

gun ports could not be opened, making the heaviest caliber guns useless. The French built four 120-gun three-deckers at Brest and Toulon, but like earlier experiments with very large ships these deep draught battleships were cumbersome and unable to fight effectively in shallow waters. In the third war, the English and French allied against the outnumbered Dutch who opened their dikes to halt a French invasion and under De Ruyter and Tromp fought courageously against mutually suspicious allies who did not work well together.

Almost purely naval conflicts, the three costly Anglo-Dutch wars established the dominance of great ships armed with heavy guns fighting in line formation as required by the Fighting Instructions first issued by the Commonwealth navy. The dominance of the line-ahead formation and of artillery duels almost completely ended the melee and boarding style of earlier times. In 1691 the *English Fighting Instructions* codified an approach to naval battle that would endure and formalize (some critics would say fossilize) naval war for almost a century. Solidly constructed capital ships—two or three deckers—now formed the main battle line. Serving them and acting as eyes and ears for the fleet were frigates, speedy yachts, and supply ships.

There were seldom sufficient volunteers in any country willing to serve their country aboard naval ships. As a result, press gangs in port towns and aboard merchant ships rounded up seafaring men who appeared healthy enough to do the job. Often, the dragnets of taverns, gambling dens, and brothels swept up agricultural laborers and other landmen who found themselves compelled to take on naval duties. They were right to fear the navy and nearly all of the rumors they heard about hardships were true. Scurvy in northern waters caused by a lack of ascorbic acid in the diet of biscuit and salt meat or fish hampered the ability of sailors' bodies to renew connective tissues. The symptoms of gradual breakdown were dark spots covering the body caused by minor hemorrhages, swollen joints, bleeding gums, and loss of teeth. Cuts and wounds did not heal and as the disease progressed old injuries reopened and knitted bones broke once again. Eventually seamen simply could not stand up and any exertion to do so could produce internal bleeding and heart failure. In tropical waters, seamen suffered from fevers, constipation and dysentery. Sometimes when they opened or pumped out the ship's bilges men fell ill or even passed out from breathing the poisonous vapors emitted from the hold. Fleas, lice, bedbugs, and cockroaches abounded and rats ruined food, damaged equipment, and fouled living spaces aboard the ship. Venereal and pulmonary diseases spread among the tightly packed crews, and the heavy consumption of liquor (since water was usually bad) caused many accidents and falls. Discipline and punishments by arbitrary officers—especially with whips and lashes—left many men permanently scarred or disabled. Even without combat and injuries caused by the impact of cannonballs and splinters that tore into human flesh, the naval surgeon was as helpless as his regimental colleagues ashore in treating most ailments and wounds.

In terms of technological adaptations, strategy, tactics, logistics, and the governance of military forces, the seventeenth century was a pivotal period in military affairs. Looking back from the 1690s, one can trace a line of constant growth of armed forces. For the second half of the century, France set the standard and drew into its orbit many of the next generation of military commanders, technologists, strategists, and thinkers. One young officer who served Turenne was the Englishman John Churchill, later the duke of Marlborough. Military developments followed a line of evolution rather than revolution. Firearms became more efficient permitting the development of linear tactics. With the addition of bayonets, pikemen disappeared. Artillery entered the battlefield as well as serving in key roles during the countless sieges of the century. Fortress development continued to evolve as did better methods of defense and offense. Indeed, sieges in the Netherlands, Flanders, and Germany were more frequent than battles fought on open fields. At sea, Europeans developed powerful fighting ships and appetites for world domination that would continue uninterrupted for the next two and a half centuries.

In certain periods, during the conflicts of the Netherlands, in Germany during the Thirty Years' War, and on the frontier between Christianity and Islam, war did seem capable of mobilizing the potential resources of a region and then of so ravaging societies and economies that the term "war desert" has been used. Fortunately, the demographic disasters identified by earlier historians did not have enduring impact. In the case of France and some other nations, the military served the cause of centralism against recalcitrant nobles and regions. And as for total war, it appeared by the end of the century that many Europeans wished to back away from the barbarism that had characterized earlier conflicts. Although the so-called limited wars of the next century would be bloody affairs, in many regions society would be spared direct participation.

Suggested Reading

The topic of military revolution has continued to be a major subject of debate for the seventeenth century. See Michael Roberts, *The Military Revolution, 1560–1660* (Belfast, 1956); Christopher M. Duffy, *The Military Revolution and the State, 1500–1808* (Exeter, 1980); Geoffrey Parker, *The Military Revolution: Military Innovation and the Rise of the West, 1500–1800* (Cambridge, 1988); Jeremy Black, *A Military Revolution? Military Change and European Society, 1550–1808* (Atlantic Highlands, 1991); Jeremy Black, *European Warfare, 1660–1815* (New Haven, 1994); John A. Lynn, "The *Trace Italienne* and the Growth of Armies: The French Case," *The Journal of Military History* 55:3 (1991): 297–330; Mahinder S. Kingra, "The *Trace Italienne* and the Military Revolution during the Eighty Years' War, 1567–1648," *The Journal of Military History* 57:3 (1993): 431–46; and Clifford Rogers, ed., *The Military Revolution Debate: Readings on the Military Transformation of Early Modern Europe* (Boulder CO, 1995).

Students interested in broad surveys treating arms, strategy, military medicine and society should see M. S. Anderson, *War and Society in Europe of the Old Regime, 1618–1789* (New York, 1988); David G. Chandler, *Atlas of Military Strategy: The Art, Theory and Practice of War, 1618–1878* (Don Mills, 1980); John Childs, *Armies and Warfare in Europe, 1648–1789* (Manchester, 1982); André

Corvisier, *Armies and Societies in Europe, 1494–1789* (Bloomington IN, 1979); Hans Delbrück, *The Dawn of Modern Warfare*, vol. 4 (Lincoln NE, 1990); Robert A. Doughty and Ira D. Gruber et al., *Warfare in the Western World*, vol. 1 (Lexington, 1996); Christopher Duffy, *Siege Warfare: The Fortress in the Early Modern World, 1494–1660* (London, 1979); Richard Gabriel and Karen S. Metz, *A History of Military Medicine* II, (New York, 1992); Michael Howard, *War in European History* (New York, 1976); B. P. Hughes, *Firepower: Weapons Effectiveness on the Battlefield, 1630–1850* (London, 1974); Archer Jones, *The Art of War in the Western World* (Urbana IL, 1987); John A. Lynn, *Feeding Mars: Logistics in Western Warfare from the Middle Ages to the Present* (Boulder CO, 1993); William H. McNeill, *The Pursuit of Power* (Chicago, 1984); H. B. C. Pollard, *A History of Firearms* (New York, 1973); Friedrich Prinzing, *Epidemics Resulting from Wars* (Oxford, 1916); and Sir James Turner, *Military Essays of the Ancient Grecian, Roman, and Modern Art of War: Written in the Years 1670 and 1671* (New York, 1968).

For works on the wars of Spain, France, and the Netherlands, see Charles R. Boxer, *The Dutch Seaborne Empire* (New York, 1965); Jonathan Brown and J. H. Elliott, *A Palace for a King: The Buen Retiro and the Court of Philip IV* (New Haven, 1985); John H. Elliott, *Imperial Spain, 1469–1713* (London, 1970); John H. Elliott, *The Count-Duke of Olivares: The Statesman in an Age of Decline* (New Haven, 1986); Pieter Geyl, *The Netherlands in the Seventeenth Century, 1609–1648* (New York, 1961); Henry Gráinne, *The Irish Military Community in Spanish Flanders, 1586–1621* (Dublin, 1992); Jonathan I. Israel, *The Dutch Republic and the Hispanic World, 1606–1661* (Oxford, 1982); Henry Kamen, *Spain in the Later Seventeenth Century, 1665–1700* (London, 1980); John A. Lynn, *Giant of the Grand Siècle: The French Army, 1610–1715* (Cambridge, 1997); Geoffrey Parker, *The Army of Flanders and the Spanish Road, 1567–1659* (Cambridge, 1972); Geoffrey Parker, *The Dutch Revolt* (London, 1977); Geoffrey Parker, *Spain and the Netherlands, 1559–1660: Ten Studies* (London, 1979); John H. Parry, *The Spanish Seaborne Empire* (New York, 1966); Carla R. Phillips, *Six Galleons for the King of Spain: Imperial Defense in the Early Seventeenth Century* (Baltimore, 1986); N. A. M. Rodger, *The Safeguard at Sea: A Navel History of Britain, 660–1649* (London, 1997); R. A. Stradling, *The Armada of Flanders: Spanish Policy and European War, 1568–1688* (Cambridge, 1992); and I. A. A. Thompson, *War and Government in Habsburg Spain, 1560–1620* (London, 1976).

For studies on the Thirty Years' War, see Thomas M. Barker, *The Military Intellectual and Battle: Raimondo Montecuccoli and the Thirty Years War* (Albany, 1975); Herbert Langer, *The Thirty Years' War* (Poole, 1980); Stephen J. Lee, *The Thirty Years' War* (London, 1991); Golo Mann, *Wallenstein; His Life Narrated* (New York, 1976); Peter Limm, *The Thirty Years' War* (New York, 1984); Geoffrey Parker, *Europe in Crisis, 1598–1648* (London, 1979); Geoffrey Parker, *The Thirty Years' War* (London, 1987); J. V. Polisensky, *The Thirty Years' War*

(Berkeley, 1971); J. V. Polisensky, *War and Society in Europe, 1618–1648* (Cambridge, 1978); Michael Roberts, *Gustavus Adolphus and the Rise of Sweden* (London, 1973); Michael Roberts, *Gustavus Adolphus: A History of Sweden, 1611–1632,* 2 vols. (London, 1953–58); S. H. Steinberg, *The Thirty Years' War and the Conflict for European Hegemony, 1600–1660* (London, 1960); and C. V. Wedgwood, *The Thirty Years' War* (London, 1938).

For studies on land conflicts and naval history of the late seventeenth century, see Thomas M. Barker, *Double Eagle and Crescent: Vienna's Second Turkish Siege and Its Historical Setting* (Albany, 1967); Reginald Bloomfield, *Sebastien le Prestre de Vauban, 1633–1707* (New York, 1971); Charles R. Boxer, *The Anglo-Dutch Wars of the Seventeenth Century* (London, 1974); Peter T. Bradley, *The Lure of Peru: Maritime Intrusion into the South Sea, 1598–1701* (London, 1989); John Childs, *The Nine Years, War and the British Army, 1688–1697: The Operations in the Low Countries* (Manchester, 1991); J. R. Jones, *The Anglo-Dutch Wars of the Seventeenth Century* (London, 1996); Brian Lavery, ed., *Deane's Doctrine of Naval Architecture, 1670* (London, 1981); John A. Lynn, "The Growth of the French Army during the Seventeenth Century," *Armed Forces and Society* 6 (1980): 568–85; O. H. K. Spate, *Monopolists and Freebooters* (Minneapolis, 1983); Geoffrey Symcox, *The Crisis of French Sea Power, 1688–1697* (The Hague, 1974); John B. Wolf, *Louis XIV* (New York, 1968).

8. ABSOLUTISM AND WAR
The Eighteenth Century

Bring your firelock to your left side!
Unfix your bayonet!
Return your bayonet!
Poise your firelock!
March! – Regulations for the Prussian Infantry, 1759

Eyewitness reports, dispatches, diaries, and heroic paintings give us a glimpse of the drama and carnage of the eighteenth-century battle-field. Armies of highly disciplined and sometimes splendidly uniformed infantrymen—grenadiers and fusiliers in their companies, battalions, and regiments—march through complex evolutions. They wheel from advancing columns into linear formations stretched out in three or more ranks across open ground. Their flintlock muskets, called "fusils" or "firelocks," with glistening bayonets attached, reflect danger into the eyes of the enemy. The weapon is both a firearm and an effective short pike. In the distance, the formations of blue-coated Prussians or Swedes; red-coated British, Hanoverian, or Danish forces; white-coated French, Austrians, or Spaniards; or green-coated Russians appear more suitably attired for formal inspections or grand balls than for mortal combat. They march under regimental and battalion colors in lockstep cadence advancing toward inevitable clash like automatons heedless of their fate.

A closer inspection would show most men ashen in color, their visages frozen by fear and determination, the vile smell of their unwashed sweating bodies hangs in the air after they have passed. Some issued fiery alcoholic drinks to stimulate their ardor exhibit reckless bravado, while most appear numb contemplating their fate. Officers on horseback urge them on with huzzahs, waves of their hats, and invocations for God to damn the enemy. As the battle opens, cannonballs from batteries of two-, four-, and six-pounders shriek back and forth overhead and ricochet about the battlefield. Gunners soon find their range and elevation—decapitating soldiers and cavalry horses, tearing off limbs, cleaving appalling wounds, and splattering uninjured survivors with blood, flesh, and fragments of bone.

The thunder of artillery, the beat of drums, the invocation of fifes, bagpipes, and bugles heighten emotions. Blood-curdling battle cries and war songs from both sides mix with the shrieks of wounded men and animals. Soldiers face a sensory nightmare and cacophony that some observers recall as the look and din of Hell. Cavalry formations hang ominously at the rear and flanks waiting for signs of weakness. The two forces converge at a measured pace, neither side seeming to want to unleash the first fusillade. Soldiers stare blankly into the faces of their enemies. Fifty meters apart—sometimes a little more or less—one side halts, presents, and fires a thunderous salvo that cracks the air as if from one gun. This is followed by murderous rolling barrages from companies along the battle line. The impact rocks the enemy lines before they reply in kind. No one attempts to aim at specific targets. The object, as all soldiers know, is rapid fire by salvo meant to fell whole clumps of enemy troops.

Repelled by the ghastliness of bloody carnage, even battle-hardened veterans sometimes lose their forward momentum, waver, or turn to withdraw. Enemy musket salvos and light artillery firing balls, canister, and grapeshot tear larger breaches in the lines. Gradually, the officers lose direct control as companies flounder in the impenetrable smoke. Some soldiers shot through the body by large-caliber soft-lead musket balls perish instantly, still facing the enemy. Others lie gasping and writhing on the ground. Injured men cry out for assistance as they struggle to staunch the flow of blood from ghastly wounds. In minutes, hours, sometimes stretching to days, they lie in wretched misery without medical assistance or water. Their lives slowly ebb away. A few drag themselves slowly and laboriously across the battlefield—some men clutching or dragging nearly severed limbs others using their muskets as crutches.

Despite the confusion, well-disciplined professionals reload their sturdy flintlock muskets and fire two or three rounds per minute—probably more if they are well-trained Prussians. Even the confusion of battle fails to blur drills beaten into them during training. However, many shots in succession overheat the musket barrels and make them unstable and likely to explode. Muskets become clogged with powder residues so that even with iron ramrods, fresh cartridges are difficult to ram into place. Repeated fire blunts the flints that with each snap of the trigger produce weaker spark. Rainfall and high humidity multiply misfires making the bayonet the weapon of choice. Notwithstanding the enthusiasm of theoretical tacticians for the bayonet, soldiers dread hand-to-hand combat with cold steel—particularly against a foe of equal resolve and training. Everything changes though should the resolve of the enemy evaporate and in panic they break to flee. Unless exhausted, the infantry and cavalry of the now victorious army chase them in near frenzy to stab, to bludgeon, and to hack down those who only minutes earlier threatened their lives. For a time until they are satiated and without energy to continue, the pursuers sometimes neglect to offer quarter.

Despite the frequency of wars during the eighteenth century, sieges, minor engagements, and skirmishes were much more prevalent than general battles. Most generals—mediocre or talented—preferred the prospect of a controlled siege to the uncertainties of battle. Recognizing that combat sometimes took twists that tore the best planning to shreds and that the science of war was at best an imperfect study, most commanders avoided the gamble. Armies were expensive to raise, took years to train, and could be lost almost in an instant. French marshal duc de Villars underscored the element of chance in a conversation with Marshal Hermann-Maurice, comte de Saxe (1696–1750), author of the authoritative *Mes Rêveries* (1732). Villars stated that French infantry forces he commanded routed Imperialist troops and chased them through a wood. On the other side, two unidentified cavalry squadrons—possibly even French—appeared in the distance. Seeing them, a French soldier yelled, "We are cut off!" In an instant, the victorious troops turned tail and fled in panic plunging through the wood and continuing their flight beyond the original battle lines. Villars attempted to rally them, but the same soldiers who had been cool in victory, in a moment collapsed becoming little more than a cowardly mob. Saxe used the example in his study to point out that war was and is an "obscure and imperfect" science that cannot be reduced to certainties and rules that will grant absolute advantages.

Soldiers who served under John Churchill, duke of Marlborough, of Great Britain, and Prince Eugene of Savoy at the beginning of the War of the Spanish Succession (1701–13) fought with weapons similar to those used one hundred years later in the armies of Napoleon or the duke of Wellington. For example, the English "Brown Bess" musket came into service about 1715 based upon an earlier model. After 130 years of manufacture, 7.8 million had been made and were in use around the world. There were some changes and alterations in battlefield tactics, deployment of artillery, communications, and logistics recommended by Saxe, Frederick the Great, Jean Baptiste Gribeauval, Count Jacques Antoine Guibert, and other writers, but these modifications simply refined a system of war based upon the flintlock musket, bayonet, and smooth-bore artillery. This technology and thinking spread European systems of warfare around the world.

The eighteenth-century age of absolutism, rationalism, and enlight-ened despotism in some respects moderated the vicious enmities of ear-lier monarchs, generals, and admirals. Curiosity about the world and the scientific impulses of the Enlightenment diminished religious hatreds and cracked open the closed minds of the past. In the 1780s, for exam-ple, the British, French, and Anglo-Americans recognized that the state of war between their nations should not interrupt the scientific explo-rations of Captain James Cook to the Pacific Ocean on his third voyage (1776–80).

The somewhat confusing and misunderstood term "limited war" is often used referring to the period extending from the decades following the Thirty Years' War in the seventeenth century up to the 1790s and the onset of the French revolutionary wars. Except in the Balkan region where the animosities between Christianity and Islam still burned and in conflicts between European and non-European peoples overseas, the re-ligious hatreds, bloody atrocities, massacres, and barbarities that marked the Thirty Years' War tended to fade. As much as possible, Europeans sought to insulate military forces and the actions of war from the gen-eral populace. Soldiers paid and maintained by the different states were to live in barracks under rigorous regulations outlined in military ordi-nances. On the move, armies were to supply themselves from magazines and to forgo foraging, plundering, and billeting in civilian lodgings.

Even so, this was not to say that the battlefield would be a safer place. One musket volley fired at close range could kill and wound 20 to 30 percent of the opposition troops. In large armies of fifty to sixty thou-sand troops, death rates would include those killed outright and many of the wounded who later perished from exposure, infection, and dis-ease. The same was true at sea in protracted engagements involving broadsides fired at point-blank range between opposing ships-of-the-line. Moreover, atrocities committed by soldiers in wartime did not en-

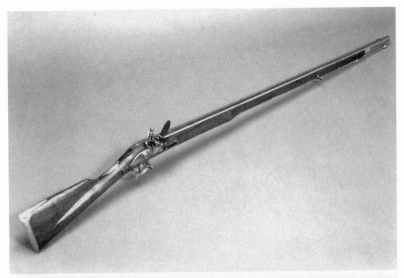

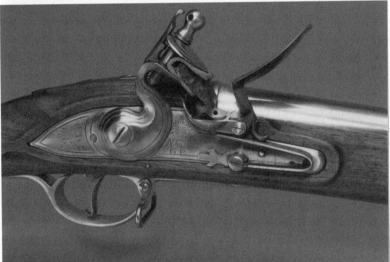

Fig. 8.1. French flintlock musket (two views). Courtesy of Compagnie Royale D'Artillerie, La Prairie, Quebec.

tirely disappear. In 1712, for example, Marlborough's troops massacred four hundred French villagers at Molain for firing on foragers and defending themselves behind temporary barricades. The soldiers locked up the people in the local church, burned the building to the ground, and plundered and torched the village.

With the reforms of Louis XIV, the centralized state was able to pay and train armies of professional soldiers supported by tax revenues. By the first decade of the century, the French army had grown to almost 380,000 troops. Of course, it is important to note that total figures for eighteenth-century armies very often reflected theoretical rather than effective strengths. Units reported soldiers who were not available, officers sometimes collected pay for fictitious troops, and even with full disclosure of manpower at any time many soldiers were sick, imprisoned, or detached from their companies for other duties. Enlistments of eight to twelve years and longer permitted the rigorous disciplining and training of soldiers. Standardized uniforms and equipment, the military code, and, in many nations, special separate judicial treatment detached the soldier from the remainder of society and made him identifiable. Years of training men in the complex evolutions and formations needed to fight battles with smoothbore flintlock muskets compelled regimes to recognize and to protect the value of their investments. Held under rigid—and sometimes tyrannical—discipline in barracks and fortresses, soldiers were less able to abuse the citizenry. Military forces of the eighteenth century assigned army engineers to build roads and bridges, to establish supply magazines and fortresses, and to plan cantonments. In the protracted sieges of the Netherlands, Flanders, and Germany that were part of almost every major conflict, commanders usually negotiated surrender terms. Once siege parallels, zigzag trenches, and artillery bombardments opened a practicable breach, it made good sense to avoid the bloody assaults and retribution that followed. In the Age of Reason, negotiation was to replace the effusion of blood, abuse of civilians, the plundering of properties, and the destruction of productive industry and commerce.

Military campaigns in Europe and elsewhere in the Northern Hemisphere almost always took place in the months from April to October. During the winter months, transportation—difficult under the best of circumstances in Europe and almost impossible overseas—bogged down in water, mud, and cold. Cart and wagon wheels cut deeply into dirt roads, marching regiments and battalions waded through seas of mud, and even the strongest gun carriages broke axles and other parts. The mobility or lack thereof in many armies of the century can be evaluated by examining the state of gun carriages and ammunition carts. No intelligent general contemplated moving his force without sufficient wheelwrights, blacksmiths, and specialized carpenters. Even under normal conditions, Marshal Saxe warned that a single campaign reduced an army by a third and sometimes by half of its original strength. This was in addition to old age, disease, and desertion that depleted armies of 20 percent of their strength each year. Cavalry horses were so exhausted and run down by October, that this arm was almost useless.

In addition to maintaining thousands of cavalry and artillery horses and mules, armies of the period required enormous numbers of draft animals to pull wagons and carts that conveyed munitions, supplies, tents, bedding, hospital utensils, and medical and pharmacy supplies. Sundry equipment included stoves, firewood, cooking pots, kettles, lanterns, candles, fireplace equipment, axes, water bottles, haversacks, casks of spirits or wine, and the personal belongings of the officers. Without green forage that was available only in the summer months, each working horse required at least twenty pounds of good hay daily and about nine pounds of oats or other grain. An army of sixty thousand troops required at least forty-nine thousand horses. Officers insisted on having a number of good chargers and as noblemen they expected to convey sundry furniture, clothing, equipment, and many luxury items.

At the Battle of Blenheim (1704), Brigadier General Count de Mérode-Westerloo complained that during the battle several of his horses were shot down and later he lost another ninety-seven to a disease called "the German sickness." In addition, he traveled with two dozen mules that conveyed his "most vital possessions"—including field furniture, chairs, tables, beds, utensils, and field ovens. With the enormous numbers of animals and humans crowded into encampments or on the march, it is little wonder that soldiers complained that they lived in a sea of horse manure and human excrement.

If soldiers were not to live off the land, the army commissary had to provide bread, biscuit, meat or fish, and other food items. While diet reflected regional and national characteristics, a common portion per day for a man was one pound of bread and a pound of beef or nine ounces of pork or mutton, sometimes supplemented by weekly allowances of cheese. As available the commissary supplied dried peas, sometimes rice, sauerkraut, and seasonal fresh vegetables. In the British army, senior commanders most certainly supported enthusiastically by soldiers believed that rum was essential as a reward for arduous duty and also as a water purifier and body strengthener. Issued in the field at a quart per day for each six men under the supervision of their sergeants, soldiers often mixed the rum with water in their canteens. Before the discovery of cures for scurvy, British and some German troops were given a quart of porter (dark beer) daily during the winter months as a preventative. Soldier's wives and camp followers sold additional alcohol to any who wished to supplement the amounts provided. French and Spanish soldiers consumed great quantities of wine and cognac. Outside of their homelands or overseas, soldiers replaced their own traditional alcoholic drinks with almost any other rough fermented beverages or distilled spirits made from sugarcane and fruit. In northern forces, spruce beer manufactured from old biscuit, sugar, and spruce tips was thought to ward off scurvy. As a result, many soldiers passed their time in a semidrunken haze and alcoholism was a major problem.

During active combat duty or in winter quarters, armies required warehouse workers, agents, packers, coopers, bakers, clerks, muleteers, thousands of laborers, and if situated close to the sea, a fleet of small cargo ships, docks, and other port facilities. An army of fifty to sixty thousand troops needed to operate sixty bread ovens managed by a large staff of bakers and laborers. Bricks for ovens, mills to grind grain, fuel for cooking, and supplies of flour had to be transported. On the march, most armies issued soldiers with rations for about four days. This meant that on the fourth day the army had to halt to bake bread and to gather forage for the cavalry horses and pack animals. For maintenance and general upkeep, an eighteenth-century army needed numerous gunsmiths, tailors, embroiderers, servants, carpenters, wagon makers, wheelwrights, saddle makers, harness makers, blacksmiths, and stablemen. Women, wives, and relatives of soldiers held many of these noncombatant posts and as in the past accompanied most armies. Strident proclamations that fulminated against evil "camp followers" had limited impact.

If the commissary system failed or did not exist, an army on the march or in winter quarters soon lost efficiency or dissolved into an angry mob. At Valley Forge in 1776, for example, Washington's soldiers grumbled about having to eat horseflesh for their meat, and when that ran out they had nothing but "firecake" (a mixture of flour and water burned on a grill). Desertions increased and the camp rang with cries of "No Meat! No Meat!" and with soldiers mimicking the calls and hoots of crows and owls. Food supplied by private contractors was of inferior quality and quantity. To alleviate this chronic problem for all armies, the French used their regional intendants and appointed *commissaires de guerre* to supervise provisioning and to guarantee good quality. Spain adopted the effective French army administrative system and exported it with other reforms to the American empire.

Unfortunately, soldiers continued to suffer from malnourishment, food poisoning, and many other illnesses. Abysmal sanitation, endemic and epidemic diseases, and filthy hospitals were a much greater threat to the lives of soldiers than combat duty. In many armies, low pay, poor food, inferior lodgings, and draconian punishments produced desertions, poor morale, and even mutinies. Eighteenth-century soldiers stationed overseas in colonial fortresses or condemned to duty in frontier wars were not far from the truth when they complained that they had been abandoned into "permanent involuntary servitude." Separated and forgotten, they wore tattered rags of uniforms and often supplied their own food and necessities. Tropical diseases such as malaria and yellow fever sometimes wiped out entire regiments. During the American Revolution, German soldiers from Hesse-Cassel complained of unbearable heat, sunstroke, impaired reason, constant perspiration, ear worm, and skin eruptions caused by "billions" of biting insects. Captain Johann Ewald reported that the heat and bad water "decomposed" German blood and caused a disease he called "land fever." He lamented: "To this must be added that all medicines are lacking, and that we have already resorted to using earth mixed with sugar to deceive the poor invalids, which is given to them as an emetic. When they are bled, the blood of everyone is vermilion, and it does not take long before the land fever turns into putrid fever."

The campaigns involving France, Austria, the German states, and Russia were fought mostly in the Netherlands, Flanders, Germany, central Europe, and northern Italy. As in previous periods, these strategic regions formed conduits between eastern and northern France and the German plain and in the south between France and Austria. Large populations, complex political divisions, valuable resources, and agricultural output combined with developed river, canal, road, and seaborne systems of transport to make these regions magnets for military operations. Ambitious states viewed neighboring jurisdictions as sources of new wealth and territory open to conquest. In addition, combatants in continental Europe held captured lands as bargaining chips in the international peace negotiations that followed each major war. Europe was now only one theater in conflicts that developed into world wars in which tropical islands, much sought after commodities such as sugar and slaves and commercial dominance, were at stake.

When armies moved quickly under a bold inventive general such as Marlborough or Frederick the Great and when soldiers operated in far-flung territories beyond the reach of normal constraints, marauding and foraging soon reappeared. In the overseas campaigns of the Americas involving Britain and Bourbon France and Spain, the addition of aboriginal fighters and of guerrilla-style tactics made atrocities and unrestrained barbarism more frequent. In India, Africa, and elsewhere beyond Europe, soldiers sometimes felt few restraints. These were different times in terms of racial attitudes and slavery was legal almost everywhere. However, the recipients or victims of European military power would not have comprehended the meaning of limited war. Violence, rape, kidnapping, and plundering marked the routes of European armed forces in the broader world. Even overseas, officers of competing nations who were from noble blood behaved in a gentle manner toward each other—accepting surrenders with honor, paroling prisoners of war, and accepting flags of truce. Indigenous soldiers and civilians could not expect similar treatment.

War dominated the eighteenth century and absorbed the resources of all protagonists. The European Enlightenment took place with a backdrop of conflict that often intruded upon and influenced the work of the great philosophers, scientists, writers, musicians, and artists. The century opened with two major conflicts. The first, the Great Northern War (1700–1718) involved Sweden under King Charles XII in what many historians have described as campaigns that were throwbacks to a previous age against Poland, Russia, and Denmark. Although the Swedish army performed near miracles, the campaign against Russia commencing in 1707 offered graphic lessons for future would-be conquerors. To achieve success, invaders would need large reserves of manpower and logistical support prior to plunging into the almost limitless Russian territories. On June 28, 1709, the Swedish army suffered catastrophic defeat at the Battle of Poltava near Kharkov. Charles XII and the remnants of his army fled south to seek sanctuary in Turkey. Although Charles returned to Sweden, the military ascendancy of his nation was lost. Russia under Peter the Great emerged as a major military factor. Small powers such as Sweden and the Netherlands ceased to be major military players in the alliances and wars of the century.

The other major conflict, the War of the Spanish Succession (1701–13) encompassed much more than a struggle between Habsburgs, Bourbons, and their respective allies. The stakes were much larger involving a continental competition for power within Europe with major campaigns in Flanders, Germany, Italy, and Spain, and strategic struggles for dominance in the Mediterranean Sea, the Atlantic, and the Indian Ocean. While non-Europeans often were victims more than belligerents, this struggle foreshadowed a series of wars in which Europeans utilized naval power to project their military prowess and advanced weaponry overseas. Amphibious warfare, large-scale naval clashes in the Caribbean, invasions directed against settled colonies, and attacks on isolated and inhospitable outposts such as the French raids against the fur trading posts of Hudson's Bay, illustrated that eighteenth-century war would be global in its scope.

Even before the death of King Carlos II of Spain (1665–1700), Britain and other powers maneuvered to prevent Louis XIV from placing his grandson Philip of Anjou on the Spanish throne. The French were successful in this regard, but they fared poorly against the armies of Marlborough and Prince Eugene. Prussia emerged for the first time as a significant military power, and even after the war, unsettled Franco-German grievances threatened European peace. France lost territory in North America to Britain, and it was clear that its possession of Canada would lead to further conflict. Principally a maritime power, Britain subsidized the German states so as to hold the Bourbon powers in check. A key element in British strategic policy was to keep France and Spain involved in wars on land and in the Mediterranean Basin. The objective was to deter French cross-channel invasion projects and to free the Royal Navy to blockade European ports or to extend its power overseas.

On the Continent, Marlborough's successful 1704 campaign with Prince Eugene against the French and Bavarians reached from the Low Countries to the Danube Basin. Viewed as a brilliantly planned operation in its day, Marlborough's mission was to relieve Vienna from imminent danger of invasion. At Bleinheim on the Danube River, Marlborough's allied army of fifty-six thousand troops unleashed combined infantry and cavalry assaults against the larger Franco-Bavarian forces totaling about sixty thousand soldiers. As the battle evolved, large numbers of French infantry and dragoons became hopelessly packed into the town. Many died as the result of friendly fire from their own units while others were burnt alive when the town erupted in flames. When they retreated, French soldiers fled toward the Danube River where many drowned as they attempted to swim to safety on the other side. The French lost over thirty-five thousand troops killed, wounded, drowned, deserted, or taken prisoner. In the army of Marborough and Eugene, six thousand died and eight thousand suffered wounds. The victors captured 103 guns, 14 mortars, 129 colors, 110 standards, and a mass of assorted equipment. The booty included thirty-four coaches, twenty-four barrels of silver, and thirty mules laden with the silver plate and baggage of the French officers.

Marlborough returned to Flanders, where over the next several years he conducted successful sieges and won battles against the French at Ramilles (1706), Oudenarde (1708), and Malplaquet (1709). He was a master tactician and logistician who also possessed the diplomatic skills needed to work with coalition partners. Although the French were on the defensive during much of this period and morale sagged following their defeats, they performed much better at Malplaquet. Marshal Villars dug in his troops and prepared well-sited artillery batteries. His troops decimated Dutch attackers at the center of the attacking line where observers insisted that the fighting was as obstinate and bloody as they had ever witnessed. Although shot in the knee and in great pain, Villars refused to leave the battlefield. Eventually Marlborough prevailed but the victory was costly. The Dutch condemned him for having squandered the lives of so many of their brave young men. In victory, the Allies lost twenty-four thousand killed and wounded while the French lost half of this number. In total casualties, Malplaquet was the most costly modern European battle until the epoch of Napoleon.

In 1702, Admiral Sir George Rooke, commander of an Anglo-Dutch naval force dispatched to capture Cádiz found the Spanish port well prepared for attack. As something of an afterthought, Rooke decided to take the minor fortress of Gibraltar near Algeciras that was garrisoned by only eighty troops. In 1708, British forces conquered the Island of Minorca in the Balearic Islands. Through these fortuitous conquests, Britain gained preeminence in the western Mediterranean. Of even greater importance for the long term, the Royal Navy was able to observe French naval movements at Toulon and other ports. With accurate intelligence, British commanders could intercept the fleets of France and Spain and prevent them from coalescing their Mediterranean and Atlantic fleets to undertake large combined campaigns. These projects included the invasion of Great Britain and attacks directed against the West Indian or North American colonies. In Spain, frustration over the loss of Gibraltar and Minorca spurred naval reforms and preoccupied the nation.

In 1713, the Treaty of Utrecht ended the long conflict. Spain lost Gibraltar and Minorca, the Spanish Netherlands, its Italian possessions, and Sardinia. In addition, Madrid conceded permission for the entry of one British merchant ship at Portobelo in Panama thus cracking the centuries of Spanish monopoly over legal trade with the American colonies. In addition, Britain won the *asiento*, the contract to deliver African slaves for sale in Spanish America. This became a war aim of the naval powers in the subsequent wars of the century. The theory beyond the incentives of profit was that the trans-Atlantic slave trade was a nursery for training sailors for naval service. In fact, many thousands of young seamen perished from diseases such as malaria and yellow fever on the African coast or during the trans-Atlantic crossing. The disadvantages of this abominable business greatly offset any positive factors. For the French who had a poor war record, the country emerged intact and Philip V succeeded to the Spanish throne. This paved the way for the Family Pact, a close military and naval alliance between France and Spain that would endure until the French Revolution.

In the aftermath of the War of the Spanish Succession and the Great Northern War, unsettled issues provoked a series of conflicts. With Britain occupying Gibraltar and Minorca, Spain used almost any pretext to lure France into a new military alliance. In 1727, Spanish forces attacked Gibraltar unsuccessfully for the third time. Spain also used the confused conflict known as the War of the Polish Succession (1733–35) to join France and Savoy against Austria in Italy. In 1735, the Hapsburgs surrendered control of Naples and Sicily to Don Carlos of Spain who in 1759 was to become king of Spain and its overseas empire. During the 1730s, the Bourbon alliance emerged as a major factor in the European strategic situation. For Britain, this danger threatened the global as well as the European balance of power on land and sea. As future crises unfolded, the British concentrated their own major efforts on sea power and turned to the German states and sometimes to Austria, Russia, and smaller powers for continental allies.

In 1739, Britain declared war on Spain. On the surface, the conflict called the War of Jenkins' Ear developed from rather trivial incidents in the Caribbean where heavy-handed Spanish coast guards (*guardacostas*) captured and condemned British merchant vessels in prize courts for contraband trading. Robert Jenkins, an English merchant captain, appeared on the floor of the House of Commons with the story that not only had his ship been boarded, but a brutal Spanish officer had sliced off his ear. Jenkins produced a bottle containing an ear preserved in alcohol. Merchants, politicians, and the British public believed the worst about so-called Spanish barbarities based mostly upon old legends and rivalries that dated back to the sixteenth century. London merchants and pamphleteers drummed up latent anti-Spanish sentiments and supported the view that Spanish America was ripe for revolution against the repressive rule of Spain.

While the British had not evolved specific strategic plans to achieve world maritime hegemony, during the struggle with Spain that soon merged with the wider War of Austrian Succession (1740–47), two projects foreshadowed grander naval and military projects for the future. First, the British conceived a plan to send an expeditionary force to conquer heavily fortified Havana, Panama, and Cartagena. Second, a fleet of eight ships commanded by Commodore George Anson was to open a new theater of formal European war in the Pacific Ocean. The fleet included the *Centurion* with sixty guns, the *Gloucester* with fifty guns, the *Severn* with forty guns, the *Wager*, an East Indiaman of twenty guns, a small five gun sloop *Tryal*, and two supply vessels. The plan was to attack the Spanish-American ports on the Pacific Ocean side of the American continents, to intercept the fabled Manila galleon off Acapulco, and even to capture the Philippine Islands. The latter project was part of a plan to grant British merchants and traders advantageous bases in the China seas. This project was more ambitious in scope than earlier raids into the Pacific by buccaneers and privateers. However, when the government made available only five hundred marines, the expedition became more of a traditional plundering raid along Elizabethan lines. Anson did receive instructions to convoke a council of war off Callao, Peru, to decide if the port could be captured, and to determine if the British could incite a general Indian rebellion against Spanish rule. One intelligence report advised that the garrison at the Callao fortress would not resist even one night due to inactivity and "a life of sloth and ease." To support an indigenous rebellion, the expedition carried five hundred extra muskets, some field artillery, mortars, shells, powder, tents, pick axes, shovels, and sandbags.

In the meantime, in 1740 the British government authorized a powerful expedition of 176 warships and troop transports, commanded by Vice-Admiral Edward Vernon and army brigadier general Thomas Wentworth. The fleet included eight eighty-gun ships-of-the-line, five seventy-gun ships, fifteen fifty-gun ships, and smaller warships including fast frigates, fire ships, and bomb vessels. This squadron escorted eighty-five merchant ships that transported six marine regiments (meaning soldiers who served afloat and abroad), artillery, munitions, and a great quantity of supplies needed to undertake protracted sieges. While some of the troops were satisfactory, for want of volunteers the marine units recruited young boys, run-down veterans, criminals, and other disreputable elements. An observer described a regiment of about three thousand men raised in the North American colonies as a useless rabble, "Blacksmiths, Tailors, Barbers, Shoemakers, and all the Banditry the colonies afford."

Well before the expeditionary force arrived off Cartagena, dreadful conditions aboard the crowded transports spread diseases that killed many soldiers and left others debilitated. These ailments included scurvy, typhoid, typhus, smallpox, malaria, yellow fever, dysentery, mange, heat stroke, and venereal diseases. Combat deaths and injuries killed about one thousand men—rather insignificant numbers compared with the prodigious losses to disease. After being repulsed at Cartagena by a much more energetic and capable Spanish defense than the British had anticipated, Vernon made unsuccessful attacks on Puerto Bello at Panama and Guantanamo, Cuba. By 1742 the expeditionary army had withered to the point that it almost ceased to exist. Of a total of 14,195 soldiers who sailed with the expedition, 10,126 men died and others deserted to save their lives.

Anson's more modest fleet did not depart from Portsmouth until September 1740, about eight months after the king approved the expedition. With the outbreak of the War of Austrian Succession, the Admiralty lacked sufficient manpower, provisions, and supplies. Anson received truly wretched sailors—some impressed landlubbers of no maritime experience and a mixture of vagrants and petty criminals who were also victims of the press-gangs. Anson described his soldiers as "a pitiful procession of army pensioners from Chelsea Hospital." The marine force was a mixture of raw recruits, disabled hospital convalescents, and men beset with chronic illnesses who were completely incapable of active infantry duty. Many of these soldiers were found to be in their sixties and several were over seventy years of age. Not one of these poor victims survived the voyage.

Even before the squadron sailed, Anson's surgeons complained that the men were covered with lice and the vessels swarmed with rats. During the Atlantic crossing, overcrowding, lack of ventilation, and contaminated water caused epidemic dysentery and an outbreak of typhus. In Brazilian waters, malaria and fevers contributed to the general debilitation. Aboard the *Centurion* and the *Severn*, seventy-five of the pensioners, marines, and some sailors died. Anson did not know that Spanish spies in England had informed Madrid about British designs upon their Pacific possessions. The Spanish navy dispatched a powerful squadron of six warships and a crack infantry regiment under the command of Admiral José Pizarro to intercept Anson and to reinforce coastal garrisons along the west coast of South America. Off the coast of Patagonia, Pizarro's flagship actually sighted and chased one of Anson's supply vessels that had separated from the squadron.

By this point the British expedition encountered even greater miseries. The passage around Cape Horn through a procession of dreadful storms and mountainous seas dismasted some ships and compelled the *Severn* and a supply ship to turn back into the Atlantic. With most officers and crewmen suffering from advanced scurvy, the *Wager* ran hard aground on the Patagonian coast and was wrecked with the loss of the field guns, mortars, and other equipment required for land operations. Thirty-seven wretched men suffered unspeakable hardships and an open boat odyssey before the survivors made it back to England. Only the *Centurion*, *Gloucester*, and *Tryal* reached safe harbor on Juan Fernández Island off the Chilean coast with 335 pitiful survivors. Scurvy ravaged these men covering them with discolored spots and producing luxuriant growths of fungus that could not be treated. They all suffered swelled legs, rotten gums, loose teeth, stinking breath, ghastly ulcers, and such lassitude that most could not be aroused to perform minimal duties. On some men, old wounds healed for years reopened and long healed bones refractured. Later during the Pacific crossing, scurvy reappeared to further reduce the band of survivors. Lieutenant Davis recorded: "Our men by this time died like rotten sheep, tossing overboard six, eight, ten or twelve in a day."

Sailors knew that they could restore their health if they could get ashore to consume fresh provisions and greens. Despite this knowledge, the navy was slow to learn how to avoid scurvy on long voyages. In 1747, John Lind recognized the efficacy of lemon juice, but later experiments conducted by Captain James Cook during his voyages of exploration in the 1770s confused the issue. It was not until the 1790s that the Royal Navy recognized that bottled lemon juice would do the trick. For Anson's men and for many other seamen and soldiers on lengthy cruises and in winter quarters where there were no fresh provisions, there was no effective cure.

About the only good news for Anson's survivors was that the vicious storms dispersed Pizarro's pursuit squadron and compelled the survivors to turn back into the Atlantic Ocean. Only the flagship returned to Spain with about one hundred alive of three thousand men dispatched to intercept the British expedition. Despite the losses of men and ships, Anson's depleted force raided the coasts of Chile and Peru where there were no defensive preparations. At Panama, the British learned of the defeat of Vernon at Cartagena and continued north to lay off Acapulco hoping to capture the outgoing Manila galleon. When this vessel did not leave port, Anson decided to sail for the Philippine Islands. He sank several Spanish prizes, released most prisoners and kept 108 mulatto and Indian seamen to help work his ships. The Pacific crossing brought renewed scurvy, dysentery, and fevers that further reduced Anson's complement. Now short of seamen, he burned the *Gloucester* just prior to making landfall in the Mariana Islands.

His fleet reduced to one ship, the *Centurion*, Anson put into Macao for repairs and then sailed to the Philippines where he intercepted and defeated the Manila galleon *Nuestra Señora de Covadonga*. Burdened by an enormous captured treasure, the expedition returned in triumph to England by way of the Cape of Good Hope. Of the 1,955 men who set sail in 1740, 1,050 were lost and only 155 men completed the circumnavigation. A wartime hero who had demonstrated spectacular leadership qualities, Anson later became first lord of the admiralty and a powerful naval reformer. He played a major role in improving the quality of shipbuilding and introduced new regulations for hygiene and victualing. With Anson as First Lord, by midcentury Britain was ready to take on all comers for maritime dominance.

Like the previous wars, the War of the Austrian Succession related to dynastic issues and territorial ambitions. The deaths of Frederick William I of Prussia and Emperor Charles VI of Austria were catalysts for what soon became a major conflagration that spread all over Europe and overseas to India, Canada, and the Caribbean. In 1740, Frederick II (later known as Frederick the Great) seized neighboring Silesia without warning. At the Battle of Mollwitz on April 10, 1741, Frederick exercised personal command. Although the Austrian cavalry performed a rapid envelopment maneuver and almost captured Frederick, in the end the green Austrian infantrymen armed with muskets that still used outdated wooden ramrods collapsed before the Prussian onslaught. Despite this setback and her inheritance difficulties with the heterogeneous Habsburg dominions, Maria Theresa, the heir of Charles VI, proved to be a redoubtable warrior. Nevertheless, Austria's military preoccupations with the Turks and the French impeded concentration upon the Prussian invaders. In July 1743, Frederick signed a peace agreement with Austria. By December 1745, he recommenced his belligerency so that he could exploit new advantages and establish a balance of power that would keep Austria in check.

The Peace of Aix-la-Chapelle ending the war in 1748 was in fact little more than a truce. Despite the Spanish successes against Admiral Vernon at Cartagena and in the Caribbean, the war pointed out basic flaws in the strategic and military capacities of the Bourbons. In 1743 France and Spain signed the Second Family pact, which foreshadowed grander designs. In 1745 when France captured Brussels, the British feared the possibility of a new cross-channel invasion attempt. Although preparations were made to assemble an invasion flotilla, France directed its naval resources to *guerre de course* or attacks against British trade and shipping rather than following through with the invasion project.

In North America, Admiral Sir Peter Warren assembled an expeditionary force including Anglo-American colonial militias and privateers that captured France's great fortress at Louisbourg. In one stroke, the British removed a clear danger to New England, won control over the mouth of the St. Lawrence River, and dominated the valuable Newfoundland fisheries. Halifax in Nova Scotia emerged as a major British naval base guarding the western North Atlantic. In 1747, Admiral Anson intercepted a French convoy off Cape Finnesterre with troops and supplies for India, and the same year Admiral Edward Hawke destroyed a French convoy for the West Indies. By 1748, the Royal Navy was able to interdict French commerce and communications, to assist military operations on land, and to undermine the economies and finances of the Bourbon powers.

The Seven Years' War (1756–63) opened with France and Austria allied against Prussia. Fortunately for King Frederick, Britain subsidized Prussia to maintain some semblance of military balance on the continent and to renew the attacks against the Bourbon powers. As was his custom, in 1757 Frederick grabbed the initiative and advanced into Bohemia to defeat an Austrian army and to besiege the city of Prague. Unwilling to lose such a prize, Field Marshal Count Leopold Daun led an army of over forty thousand men and 150 guns to lift the siege. With only thirty-two thousand troops, Frederick had to abandon the siege and to fight the Austrian army. At the Battle of Kolin, the Prussians found themselves bogged down in a frontal battle of attrition against superior numbers. The Austrians employed their artillery effectively and harassed the Prussians with light infantry. Frederick withdrew in defeat having lost over ten thousand men dead and giving up five thousand prisoners.

Although the Prussian cause appeared bleak, Frederick's soldiers managed to repel the Austrians at the gates of Berlin. Following this victory, Frederick led an army of twenty-one thousand that at the Battle of Rossbach defeated a much larger Franco-Austrian army of forty-one thousand men. First Prussian cavalry attacked and turned the main allied force as it advanced in five heavy columns. Later in the battle, the Prussian horsemen fell upon the Franco-Austrian infantry just as their bayonet attack ran out of forward velocity. Surprised, exhausted, and with their morale flagging, the allied troops lost their momentum and some men turned to withdraw. In an instant, Prussian cavalry hacked at their backs turning an ordered retreat into a pitiful flight. The allies lost 10,000 dead for only 550 casualties on the Prussian side.

There was no time for celebration by the Prussians since Marshal Daun's army of over sixty-five thousand troops blocked the road to Breslau and threatened all of Silesia. On December 5, 1757, Frederick with almost thirty-six thousand troops rushed to engage the enemy at Leuthen. Surprise, high velocity, and the use of attack in "oblique order" that was a tactic of the Ancient Greeks made the Battle of Leuthen a classic confrontation that officers of many different armies wished to emulate. The key element in this tactic was to mass forces against one section of the enemy line in order to overwhelm it completely while at the same time holding fast at other parts of the line. Using feints and skirmishes to occupy the Austrian right, Frederick marched his main force in two columns along the reverse slope of a ridge out of sight on the enemy and toward the left flank of the Austrian battle line. Caught by surprise, the Austrians attempted to turn, but artillery fire and assaults by the Prussian cavalry and infantry broke their morale and rolled up the flank—piling up the Austrian troops in heaps. They retreated, losing twenty-one thousand soldiers to sixty-four hundred on the Prussian side.

After 1757 Frederick confronted the danger of a two-front war. With an alliance between Austria and Russia, the Prussians feared that they would be overwhelmed. However, Frederick's aggressiveness and willingness to engage in offensive battles tested the resolve of his enemies. He was able to deter more cautious generals from pressing their initiative. Despite some significant reverses and outright defeats, Frederick continued to mobilize forces for the battlefield. However, the quality of Prussian troops declined as combat and fatigue consumed their reserves of trained soldiers who were replaced by green recruits. Austrian light infantry units attacked the Prussian supply system and strengthened the defensive to blunt Frederick's offensives. The Russians who the Prussians held in great contempt proved at the battles of Zorndorf (1758) and Kunersdorf (1759) that they had learned the science of offensive and defensive warfare. During the final years of the Seven Years' War, Frederick who truly loved the offensive confronted the larger Russian and Austrian armies with fortified dug in positions that were most difficult to assault. Although the Prussians lost over 180,000 soldiers during the war years, Frederick's methods and theories, as well as the discipline of the Prussians, were admired almost universally by soldiers of every army.

The Anglo-French conflict during the Seven Years' War confirmed that Britain rather than France had conceived a strategy for a global maritime dominance. Nevertheless, this was not immediately evident in the first years of the conflict. In 1756 the British dispatched a fleet commanded by Admiral John Byng to resist a French invasion directed against Minorca. When Byng arrived, he discovered that the French had anticipated him and already commenced a siege backed by a more powerful fleet than that of the British. After an inconclusive engagement, Byng sailed for Gibraltar leaving the French to continue their siege. For his indecisiveness and for embarrassing the navy, Byng faced outrage from an aroused British public. Mobs burned him in effigy and made his name synonymous with cowardice. The government edited Byng's dispatches so as to conceal any suspicion that the Royal Navy fleet sent to relieve Minorca was too weak and to make the poor admiral appear personally culpable. A highly controversial court-martial sentenced Byng to death. Although many thought that the execution would be commuted, Byng was hanged on the quarterdeck of his own flagship. This conclusion that resulted from inflexible regulations and government pandering to demands of the crowd, shocked many European intellectuals. Voltaire noted in *Candide* that the English "find it pays to shoot an admiral from time to time to encourage the others."

During 1757 the British also failed in an amphibious raid against Rochefort. In North America the French made significant gains in an invasion of New York. In India, Prince Siraj-ud-Daula who had taken over Bengal and the city of Calcutta before being expelled by the forces of Robert Clive, sought the aid of the French to march against Madras. In the Battle of Plassey, June 23, 1757, Clive's small army of 850 British troops, twenty-one hundred sepoys, and twelve guns defeated an enormous Indian force of over fifty thousand men supported by about two hundred French auxiliaries and fifty-three guns. This spectacular victory illustrated the superiority of European troops and organization over enormous untrained and ill-equipped indigenous masses. Bengal fell under British control. In Europe, however, British coastal raids against France failed to divert French armies that concentrated to attack Hanover and Prussia. British blunders and mismanagement ended when Prime Minister Sir William Pitt selected strategic targets for attack and appointed capable commanders to undertake the missions. In North America, General James Abercrombie pushed up the Hudson River valley and across Lake George to threaten the French in Montreal and Québec. France's great fortress of Louisbourg returned in the 1748 peace accord fell once again this time to the forces of General Jeffrey Amherst backed by the fleet of Admiral Edward Boscawen.

In European waters, the British had to exercise care in assigning limited numbers of warships. The Prussians wanted a squadron in the Baltic and commanders in the Mediterranean begged for reinforcements. The Western Squadron on blockade duty off Brest and other ports in the Bay of Biscay needed additional ships. Most important of all, the English Channel fleet had to be kept powerful enough to protect against yet another French invasion attempt. The British knew that French troopships required for an invasion attempt were being readied at ports such as Bordeaux and Nantes.

Gradually, the British naval strategies began to turn the tide. Admiral Hawke's blockade forces destroyed or disabled many of the French warships and transports assigned to reinforce Canada. Pitt dispatched an expedition to the Caribbean that in January 1759, captured the Island of Guadalupe. Admiral Boscawen chased the French fleet based at Toulon commanded by the Marquis de la Clue as it departed the Mediterranean to join the Brest fleet. These movements formed part of the French plan to launch an invasion force against Britain. Boscawen's fleet engaged the French off Lagos on the Portuguese Coast, destroyed two ships, captured three, and blockaded the rest in the Tagus River at Lisbon where they were of no use to the French. In North America, British forces captured French forts at Niagara, Ticonderoga, and Crown Point that gave them naval control of the Great Lakes. The invasion route by way of Lake Champlain into French Canada now lay open as well.

The year 1759 is known in British history as "the Year of Victories" or the "Glorious year." This was a year not to be French since remarkable good luck further enhanced British good management and brilliantly conceived operations. In May 1759, the British assembled a fleet of twenty-two ships-of-the-line, twelve frigates, and an expeditionary army of fourteen thousand troops at Louisbourg for the invasion of Québec. General James Wolfe, only thirty-two years of age, had his work cut out to control his own subordinate commanders. Suffering chronic poor health, he had to conceive a plan to crack the defenses at Québec under the command of the Marquis de Montcalm. The French in Canada were by no means an easy target. The British had to complete the conquest before the fleet withdrew prior to the freeze up of the St. Lawrence River. The French unleashed fire ships down the river into the advancing British squadron but ignited them prematurely so that they could be fended off with little trouble. During July and August, the British bombarded French positions, landed troops to skirmish with the more numerous defenders, and tested the defenses of Québec City. Since little had been accomplished at the end of August, Wolfe decided to attempt a surprise night attack from the rear or upstream from the French defenses. By 4:00 A.M. on September 13 the British had scaled the 175-foot cliffs, overcome minor resistance, and opened the way to the Plains of Abraham leading to the city. By dawn, the British had 4,500 troops on the field arrayed for combat.

A surprised Montcalm decided to fight before the British had time to land additional troops and artillery needed to commence a formal siege. Dispatching light infantrymen and Indian marksmen to harass the invaders, at 10:00 A.M. Montcalm attacked with a force of about 4,250 troops. The British troops opened fire with light artillery and unleashed a murderous musket volley only forty yards from the French. Following up with a bayonet attack, the British overwhelmed the French, killing 500 soldiers, capturing 350, and wounding Montcalm, who died after he had been carried back to the city. The British lost 58 killed, including Wolfe, who was shot three times, and 600 wounded. French reinforcements that arriving during the battle under the comte de Bougainville, were too late to turn the tide. On September 18, Québec City surrendered. While Montreal remained under French control and the British occupation force spent an uncomfortable winter, the issue of which side would win was settled by the arrival of British rather than French warships at spring breakup. The French province of Québec with the Great Lakes, the Ohio country, and the Mississippi Valley to the north of the Province of Louisiana now fell under British dominion.

As the fall of Québec illustrated, the British navy was now dominant in the Atlantic Ocean. The French counterstrategy called for a bold project to dispatch a fleet up the west coast of Ireland and to land an invasion force in Scotland. The idea was to divert British attention and to rekindle the embers of Scottish rebellion. The key to this plan required the French navy to break the British blockade of Brest so that transports could be assembled from Nantes, Bordeaux, and other ports. Although Admiral Marquis de Conflans managed to evade the blockade, Admiral Hawke pursued the French into Quiberon Bay where they sought refuge from an Atlantic storm. On November 20, 1759, the battle commenced despite the existence of uncharted rocks and shoals. The struggle became a general melee in which ships-of-the-line engaged in close-quarter slugging matches. When night fell, British commanders warped their three-deckers into position close to French vessels so that the gunners could concentrate their deadly broadsides. Many of the French warships sought refuge in the Vilaine River where some ran hard aground and broke their keels in shallow water. The defeat at Quiberon Bay not only terminated French invasion schemes but left Britain as the undisputed ruler of the oceans.

From this point forward, Britain blockaded the French navy in Brest, Rochefort, and Toulon. In 1761 the Spanish crown unwisely declared war on Britain to assist its fading Bourbon partner. By this time having attacked many French possessions, the British rejoiced at the prospect of new targets. In 1762 a successful amphibious attack led to the occupation of Havana, known by the Spaniards as "the key to the Caribbean." This operation illustrated that the British had learned lessons in former expeditions and increased the effectiveness of their strategies. Lord Albermarle's fleet of twenty-two ships-of-the-line and thirty transports conveyed 11,351 troops from Britain and the American colonies. After a siege of seventy days, the citadel of El Morro capitulated soon followed by the surrender of the city of Havana and of much of Spain's Caribbean naval force. As a grand finale to the war, a British squadron commanded by Rear Admiral Sir Samuel Cornish occupied Manila from the East Indies. This last conquest followed the negotiation of the Peace of Paris (1763) so that Britain did not receive compensation.

Through these lopsided victories, Britain acquired permanent enemies and fueled Bourbon desires for revenge. The Spanish province of Florida became British in exchange for Havana that Spain simply could not afford to relinquish. Much to the opposition of some observers, Canada was kept while Martinique returned to France. For its part, France handed over the province of Louisiana to Spain now that it was no longer linked to a dream of continental domination. This backhanded gift added some unwilling new Spanish subjects and an indefensible frontier with the truculent British North Americans. Although Britain was at the apogee of its eighteenth-century power, Spain, France, and some other Continental powers waited for any signs of weakness.

Spain confronted the disasters of its short participation in the Seven Years' War by undertaking thorough administrative and military reforms. Dependence in the Americas upon small garrisons and strong defensive fortifications at ports such as Havana, Cartagena, Veracruz, and Pensacola no longer worked. After a series of contentious debates in Madrid about colonial defense, the imperial government agreed to raise colonial armies in Cuba and in other possessions. These would be composed of some European regular units on rotation, local regular regiments fixed to their territories, and a broad system of militias designed to assist the regular forces. Each of the new American units would receive a training cadre of European officers and NCOs. While some observers recognized the incipient dangers of arming colonial peoples, the loss of Havana left no other alternative. In this way, the basic military system of Frederick the Great—modified somewhat to meet Spanish requirements—reached into many parts of the Americas. Also, the Spanish navy undertook major new building programs in Spain and in shipyards of the New World. Of 227 ships-of-the-line constructed by Spain in the eighteenth century, 74 were built at the Havana shipyard. In 1769 the Havana yard launched the *Santíssima Trinidad*, the largest warship of the century and one of many Spanish ships sunk in 1805 at Trafalgar by Admiral Nelson's fleet.

As might be expected, in 1775 there was considerable interest in France when British troops fired on Anglo-American militias and rapidly became mired in an expanding struggle. From the beginning, the American Revolution (1775–83) exhibited elements of a civil war and wide-

Fig. 8.2. Eighteenth-century Spanish American cavalryman. España. Ministerio de Educación, Cultura y Deporte, Archivo General de Indias.

Fig. 8.3. Eighteenth-century infantryman of New Spain. España. Ministerio de
Educación, Cultura y Deporte, Archivo General de Indias.

spread insurgent uprising as well as a more conventional conflict following the European model of warfare. If Britain's initial torment was sweet revenge of a sort, at first France, Spain, and the Netherlands offered little more than clandestine aid. After all, support for colonial revolt might provide examples for all colonial peoples—including those of France and Spain. In 1777 the surrender of a British army under General John Burgoyne at the Battle of Saratoga convinced France and Spain that the rebels might actually win. After signing a secret accord promising a military alliance on August 2, 1778, France declared war against Britain. This time, France avoided military entanglements in Europe. Britain was isolated—even the Dutch were against them—and the Germans were unwilling to join the war. For the first time in the eighteenth century, except for the great siege of Gibraltar that followed Spain's entry into the war in 1779, there would be little fighting in Europe.

Notwithstanding their opportunities, the Bourbons failed to take advantage of their temporary maritime superiority. In 1779 a Franco-Spanish fleet of sixty-six ships cruised the English Channel with impunity and there were new plans for an invasion of Britain. As always, the window of opportunity soon slammed shut. Accidents including fires put some French warships out of action and three new ships-of-the-line proved to be so top-heavy after launching that they threatened to capsize in calm seas. To make matters worse, a French raid on the Channel Islands failed miserably. Accentuating these reverses, due in large part to British patrols and blockades, France experienced a severe shortage of lumber, masts, spars, hemp, tar, and other Baltic naval stores. Chronic shortages of experienced sailors and shipyard workers further decreased the efficiency and fighting capacity of the French fleet. A deadly epidemic felled the marine population at Brest. Even the winds that year kept the French fleet in port and prevented offensive action. In spite of superior number of warships, the Bourbon allies failed to assume maritime supremacy and did not even test the Royal Navy squadrons that defended the British coasts.

The American Revolutionary War that opened as a conflict between Britain and its American colonies soon became a new global struggle. Prior to the actual outbreak of war with France in July 1778, Admiral Augustus Keppel engaged a French fleet off Brest in an inconclusive but bloody and costly battle. Like Byng before him, Keppel faced a court-martial that had political overtones. The charge was that Keppel failed to keep his battle line ahead as demanded in the still sacrosanct *Perma-*

nent Fighting Instructions. Keppel's highly popular exoneration seemed to indicate that depending upon the circumstances admirals might develop their own tactics. This was important and in part foreshadowed Admiral George Rodney's victory over Admiral Comte de Grasse in the Caribbean at the Battle of the Saints (1782). However, Rodney's victory also resulted from a change in the wind direction. The British captured five French ships-of-the-line, took Admiral de Grasse prisoner, and probably saved Jamaica from a French invasion. The victory was particularly sweet since for the first time the Franco-Spanish combined fleet outnumbered and outgunned the British.

For Spain, in addition to unofficially supporting the Anglo-American revolutionaries and organizing campaigns to regain Florida and other gulf coast territories, the war provided a opportunity to retake Gibraltar. Beginning on July 11, 1779, a small Spanish naval force assaulted the Gibraltar fortress. When the attack failed, the Spanish navy established a formal blockade to starve the garrison and commenced shelling from the sea. To maximize the impact of heavy bombardment, the Spaniards constructed ten newly designed heavy floating artillery platforms or battering ships purpose built to fire at the British fortifications from one heavily armored side of the vessel. To protect the gun crews from British fire, builders interspersed layers of wet sand between three to six feet of green timber. The defensive wall was bolted together with heavy iron and covered with cork and rawhide. The surface was soaked constantly with water so that the vessels could absorb cannonballs and exploding shells without endangering the gun crews. In addition, overhanging roofs of heavy cordage covered by hides and wood set at an angle deflected shells into the sea. These vessels anchored half a cannon shot or about twelve hundred meters off the fortifications moored by heavy iron chains.

On September 12, 1782, the Franco-Spanish combined fleet attacked with forty-seven, two- and three-decker ships-of-the-line and three hundred troop transports with the ten battering ships and a flotilla of fire ships, bomb ketches, mortar boats, and cannon launches. They opened fire at point-blank range and at first appeared impervious to the solid shot of British thirty-two-pounder guns. With approximately two-hundred heavy guns firing from the battering ships and answering fire from the fortress, the exchange involved well over four hundred siege-type guns and many mortars, howitzers, and lighter guns. As anticipated, the British shells deflected harmlessly from the angled roofs and the round-shot of the thirty-two-pounders made no impression upon the fortified vessels.

Unfortunately for their cause, the Franco-Spanish engineers and technicians had failed to consider the possibility of red-hot shot. On September 13 the British set up furnaces and loaded their guns with waddings of clay and damp hay or cotton between the cartridges and the red-hot balls that the artillerymen called "roasted potatoes." Although the procedure was extremely dangerous and the gun had to be fired quickly to prevent explosions within the chamber, the impact upon the Spanish battering ships was spectacular or horrible depending upon one's side. Firing point-blank, the red-hot balls penetrated the armor of the battering ships, smoldered for a time, and then caught fire. Six of the vessels erupted in fire and had to be abandoned. Two others disappeared instantaneously in spectacular explosions when sparks or flame penetrated their magazines. The attack collapsed with heavy loss of life among the Franco-Spanish gun crews and sailors and only light casualties among the British defenders. Despite Spain's massive investment of resources and manpower, in the four years of shelling from land and sea only 330 British soldiers died from combat. A total of 717 troops died from sicknesses such as dysentery, yellow fever, scurvy, and other illnesses.

In 1783 mutual exhaustion brought the American and Bourbon war to an end. Both sides were eager for peace. In America, following the British defeat at the Battle of Yorktown (1781), both sides recognized that Britain had lost the war and there was little additional fighting. The French and Spanish enjoyed some revenge for losses in earlier wars, but they failed to match Britain at sea. Shortages of naval supplies, of trained shipyard artisans, of well-equipped dockyards, and most of all of experienced seamen simply could not be overcome during wartime crises. Nevertheless, Britain lost the thirteen colonies, Minorca, and Florida. Spain regained territories as a result of the successful campaigns of Bernardo de Gálvez in Florida and Alabama, but Britain held on to the strategic fortress of Gibraltar. The Dutch won control over Ceylon and the French took Senegal and the Caribbean islands of St. Lucia, St. Vincent, and Grenada.

As well as examining the nature of the wars we have discussed, military historians often study the theory of war in the eighteenth century as a means to understand how Napoleon Bonaparte developed his thinking. Most educated officers were of noble blood and they spoke and read French, which was the language of military tracts and treatises as well as culture. Formal military education became possible at the Prussian Cadet Corps (1717), the Dutch Artillery School (1735), Woolwich Engineering and Military Academy (1741), the Ecole Militaire, Paris (1749), and at many other schools. However, most young men of noble blood went to their regiments as cadets where they learned on the job as apprentice-officers. In many countries, their families purchased the post when the boys were very young so that they could begin to acquire seniority that commenced with the date of first enlistment.

As in the past, most educated officers studied ancient warfare and searched for precedents. It will be recalled that King Frederick's "oblique order" came from his reading about the ancient Greeks. Many writers recalled the debate between the phalanx and the legion—proposing revivals of the phalanx and use of heavy columns equipped with muskets and bayonets. At the siege of the great French fortress of Louisbourg in 1758, when one of General James Wolfe's officers remarked about his use of light infantry, he responded, "I had it from Xenophon, but our friends here are astonished at what I have done because they have read nothing."

Eighteenth-century students of strategy and tactics had to work within the constraints of the available weapons. They considered the existence of powerful fortresses, the bad roads away from coasts and canals, and the absence of transportation networks required to move armed forces. If challenged, an army could simply sit tight behind its fortified parapets and at worst face a lengthy siege. On active campaigns, given the primitive nature of intelligence gathering and the lack of accurate maps, most generals either could not locate the enemy or marched away from battles that in most cases required both sides to play.

Battlefield commanders had to decide whether to exploit shock and the use of the *ordre profond* (heavy columns of infantry, cold steel or the bayonet, and heavy cavalry); the *ordre mince* (combat in linear form and the use of the firepower of the musket); or a combination of the above. The Spanish writer the marqués de Santa Cruz adopted the latter approach in his work *Reflexiones Militares* (1724–30), which was translated into French and widely read in many countries. Santa Cruz employed two battle lines each four soldiers deep and interspersed heavy columns of infantry and cavalry. The *ordre profond* had many supporters in France, including the influential Jean-Charles de Folard, who wrote *Nouvelles*

Découvertes sur la Guerre (1724). Folard served in the Italian campaigns of the War of the Spanish Succession, with Charles XII of Sweden, and he was wounded at the Battle of Malplaquet. Folard advocated the use of heavy columns and attack employing the bayonet as the primary weapon of shock rather than fire. Many French commanders feared that their troops were not sufficiently disciplined to employ the *ordre mince*, but supporters of this formation argued that the thin linear system emphasized fire but was also adequate enough for shock.

Although some historians today find the debates between French tacticians to be a little arid, most of these writers were soldiers with considerable combat experience. Marshal Saxe in *Mes Rêveries* picked his way through the different deployments and views of his time, appearing modern in many respects and old fashioned in some others. Like Frederick who followed him, Saxe stressed that discipline "is the soul of all armies" for otherwise they became "contemptible heaps of rabble . . . more dangerous to the very state that maintains them, than even its declared enemies." He concluded: "Those armies which have been subject to the severest discipline, have always performed the greatest things." Nevertheless, discipline had to be tempered with "great tenderness and moderation" displayed by senior officers. Saxe opposed the death penalty for marauders who might be guilty only of attempting to satisfy their hunger. He rejected the branding of deserters and was highly critical of the brutal and ignominious punishment of running the gauntlet. Soldiers were sentenced to a specific number of runs between two files of soldiers from their regiment who had to beat them with their ramrods or with hardwood staffs. To prevent the victim from running too fast, he was preceded by a sergeant who walked backwards slowly pointing a musket and bayonet. Many soldiers received permanent injuries, some died, and the act following the punishment of passing the regimental colors over the victim's head to reduce the ignominy did nothing to end the pain or the social stigma. Saxe noted that soldiers shared this form of punishment with whores, rogues, and offenders who fell under the jurisdiction of the hangman.

On the battlefield, Saxe stressed that victories were won by the "legs" of his soldiers—a statement that Napoleon would adopt. He proposed the use of legions composed of four infantry regiments, cavalry squadrons, and light artillery or 3,582 troops under the command of a legionary general. The importance of this idea was that it made battlefield flexibility possible and foreshadowed the division that would be capable of moving and acting independently. Against an enemy force, the legion would present a formidable appearance and pose difficulties for any enemy. Saxe's legion formed up four lines deep with the two front lines armed with muskets and the two rear lines with iron-pointed thirteen-foot-long half pikes and muskets on their shoulders. With their pikes leveled, the tips would extend six or seven feet in front of the first two ranks. The idea was to protect the front line gunners so that they could aim their weapons. Light rapid-firing long-barreled artillery pieces called *amusettes* operated by three man crews were to be assigned to the legion. Employed individually or in batteries, they would gall the enemy at ranges up to three thousand paces.

In addition, Saxe proposed the use of light infantry armed with ri-fled breech-loading fusils similar to fowling pieces. These troops were to be physically fit and able to run and to fire accurately at three hun-dred paces from the enemy lines and to continue firing until the enemy troops were only fifty paces away. Then they were to fall back into the general infantry formation. The cavalry troopers were to be armed with breech-loading rifled carbines, swords, and the front ranks with twelve-foot lances. Finally, Saxe proposed to protect his troops with cuirasses weighing thirty pounds—employing his own design of fixing iron plates upon hide that were proof against sword and pike thrusts but not in-tended to stop a musket ball fired point-blank. With the addition of Ro-man style helmets, Saxe's ideal soldiers were an interesting blend of the old and the new. An army would consist of ten legions, eight cavalry reg-iments, and sixteen dragoon regiments—thirty-four thousand infantry and twelve thousand horse for a total of forty-six thousand troops. Of great interest considering the difficulties with recruitment and the gen-erally low opinion of soldiers as the refuse of society, Saxe proposed that all young men should serve their king in military duty for five years.

As Saxe illustrated, by the 1750s there were many tactical combi-nations possible. In military circles, the debates were influenced sig-nificantly by the successes of the Prussian army under King Frederick William I (1713–40) and then under his successor, Frederick the Great. Until 1740 the Prussian infantry used tightly packed formations four ranks deep. Although Prussia had a population of just over two-and-a-half million inhabitants, Frederick inherited an army of eighty-three thousand troops that was recognized as the best disciplined in Europe. In the Silesian wars (1740–42 and 1744–45) and then the Seven Years' War (1756–63), Austria, France, Russia, and other opponents and allies attempted to emulate Prussian tactics and methods. The Prussian infantry regiment of two battalions each composed of a grenadier company and five companies of fusiliers for a total of 1,629 men became the model for many other armies. British companies listed 60 men; the French, 50; and the Prussians, 114.

Under Frederick, the Prussians perfected traditional methods through years of meticulous drill and careful planning. They attained the highest rate of fire with their fusils and a level of performance on the battlefield that could not be duplicated by any other army. Under the best conditions, Prussian soldiers fired four rounds per minute and up to five or six rounds with new model muskets introduced during Frederick's reign. Grenadiers selected for their reliability and strong constitutions and not so much for their size could be formed into battalions separate from their normal regiments. Prussian troops took up their battle lines by a spectacularly executed maneuver from the order of march. They deployed from two or three open columns by rapid simultaneous wheels—thus presenting a surprised and much less organized enemy army with a well-dressed line of battle. They marched at 75 steps per minute and could increase this pace to 120 steps per minute during their evolutions. In 1740, Frederick reduced the number of Prussian battlefield ranks to three and during the Seven Years' War when manpower was in short supply sometimes to only two lines. Though Frederick was not comparable to Marshal Saxe as a creative military thinker, discipline, efficiency, and iron resolve served in most cases to get the job accomplished.

While the Prussians were effective in their use of rapid platoon firing to maintain continuous volleys, for a long while Frederick advocated the bayonet over firepower. He backed the assault with platoons and regiments of cavalry cuirassiers. They wore iron breastplates and used powerful horses to crush the flanks of enemy armies and to smash their cavalry. Reverses and defeats in the Seven Years' War pushed Frederick toward greater advocacy of firepower. Against Austrian and particularly Croatian light infantry and hussars (light cavalry) trained to harass close-order formations, the Prussians developed the light infantry Feldjäger-Corps. Unlike ordinary infantrymen who were never completely trusted for fear that they would desert if permitted too much freedom, the *jägers* were loyal men capable of fighting in dispersed formations. They wore green coats and carried heavy rifled carbines that permitted them to aim at enemy targets at longer ranges.

During the Seven Years' War, army commanders on all sides had a number of different models to consider for their tactical dispositions. They had to consider mass formations, thin lines, light infantry skirmishers, light battalion guns, and organization around what would become the divisional system. The French who did rather poorly in the war recognized that their troops were not sufficiently disciplined to engage Prussian or British infantry using three ranks. Some French commanders replied that the ardor of their soldiers had to be harnessed through the use of bayonet charges. This led to various proposals for attacks by column supported by a deployed line or an *ordre mixte* that would incorporate the strengths of the *ordre mince* and the *ordre profond*. Others such as Marshal Charles de Belle-Isle turned to artillery. In addition to field batteries of standardized four-pounders and eight-pounders, Belle-Isle recommended that one or two rapid-firing light guns and mounted mortars could be assigned to battalions and accompany the infantry on the attack. As might be expected, there were opponents to such ideas who argued against the dispersal of artillery along the battle line.

The outcome of what was a scholarly international debate depended eventually upon the test of the battlefield. This of course involved a multitude of human and environmental questions as well as good tactical thinking. No battle took place under controlled conditions and victory did not necessarily provide a model suitable for general adoption. Following the Seven Years' War, there was sufficient theory and accumulated practical experience for Comte Jacques Guibert (1743–90) and other writers to devise systems of tactics that formed the basis for the mobile warfare of the French Revolution and of Napoleon. Guibert was only twenty-nine when he published his famous *Essai général de tactique* (1772), that would appear in many editions and translations including one in Persian. He grew up in a military family and as a boy played war games with his father involving armies represented by wooden blocks. Guibert served in the Seven Years' War and emerged thereafter as an ambitious military *philosophe* who desired fame as a literary figure as well as a soldier. Unlike other writers who concentrated on the infantry, Guibert emphasized artillery and the coordination of the three branches—infantry, cavalry, and artillery.

More than most military thinkers before him, Guibert suspected that phalanx-like heavy columns were left over from the days when pikes required density for survival. If so, overdependence on them by some eighteenth-century tacticians and the creation of the cult of the bayonet represented yet another archaic holdover from the past. Guibert concluded that advances in the lethality of firepower and range of muskets and artillery threatened continued advocacy of shock tactics and the deep formations of the Ancients. Reflecting the influence of Marshal Saxe, Guibert proposed that the male youth of the country should undergo military training. He argued that the complex training in drill and speed of fire at the expense of accuracy as stressed by the Prussians produced a great noise but few casualties on the enemy side. Guibert proposed greater attention to practice shooting and exercises in fencing with the bayonet that were almost unknown. In fact, soldiers in most armies fired few live shots during training exercises. Guibert concluded that three ranks of infantrymen were sufficient and proposed an increase in the rate of step so that French forces could get at the enemy and deliver fire quickly before being obliterated or disabled. While bullets fired by fusils carried about 400 yards, the effective killing or disabling range was only about 175 yards.

Guibert's tactics emphasized mobility and firepower. He proposed the replacement of convoluted parade square drill with field training in more difficult topography where soldiers would learn to deal with obstacles such as ravines, streams, and heights. Soldiers were to maneuver at double step and to practice triple step to envelop an enemy flank or to charge. Because all of the troops were to be trained in skirmishing and scouting, Guibert opposed the use of light infantry. His drill book reduced evolutions to only four: doubling ranks (against cavalry attack), wheeling (essential to form the line), forming column, and arranging the order of battle. Attack was by three files with the front rank firing straight at the enemy, the second rank over the right shoulders of the first, and the rear rank firing over the left shoulders of the leading rank. There would be no firing on the advance by rolling volleys (*feu de change*) in the Prussian manner. French troops were to fire from stationary positions so that they could aim their weapons and cause greater slaughter. In the open, Guibert recommended that soldiers should be permitted to fire at will when they felt that they could hit specific targets. Guibert proposed the use of columns for attack against an enemy force that lay behind a parapet or in an entrenched position. Different than the proposals of Saxe, Guibert recommended that cavalry be armed with carbine and pistols designed for speed and shock. He expressed no regard for armor or the heavy cuirass.

In his advocacy of attack to keep an enemy off balance, Guibert recommended flexible columns that were capable of different combinations depending upon the situation. They were to move rapidly and to sever their ties with the cumbersome magazines that stultified warfare. He argued that in hostile territory, the army should forage and live at enemy expense. While many advocates of "limited war" found such ideas dangerous and even close to anathema, Napoleon recognized Guibert as one of his primary inspirations.

By the time of Guibert, the artillery employed by any of the major European armies had changed since the early decades of the century. During the War of the Spanish Succession, the massive artillery pieces were still difficult to transport and to deploy effectively on the battlefield. Even within one army, a confusion of different calibers and types of gun reduced efficiency and made munitioning and training a nightmare. All but the lightest regimental guns used a horse-pulled limber or *avant-train* that was a pair of wheels on an axle. The rear trail of the cannon carriage lifted up to attach with the limber—producing a four-wheeled vehicle. In 1732, a French artillery officer, Jean-Florent de Vallière reformed the system of artillery that was codified in a royal ordinance of October 7, 1732. Henceforth, there were to be five types of French artillery—twenty-four-, sixteen-, twelve-, eight-, and four-pounders. While this change was important, the guns continued to be very heavy. A twelve-pounder weighed 3,200 pounds and its carriage added another 4,966 pounds. Even the light four-pounder weighed 1,150 pounds on a carriage that weighed 2,438 pounds. Although there were efforts to reduce the size of French guns, up to this point both the Prussians and the Austrians were more successful.

Guibert found help in the field of artillery from the brilliant General Jean-Baptiste Gribeauval (1715–89), who reformed French artillery and created the authoritative Gribeauval system. After visits to Prussia and inspection trips to Austria, Gribeauval introduced significant changes that altered all aspects of French artillery. Making a distinction between field and siege artillery, Gribeauval restricted twelve-, eight-, and four-pounders and a six-and-one-half-pounder howitzer for field uses. For siege work, he retained the eight-, twelve-, sixteen-, and twenty-four-pounders. Gribeauval's guns were cast solid in bronze and then drilled to the required bore which permitted reductions of weight without loss of strength. Stronger but lighter construction allowed for reduced powder charges and increased diameter of balls to reduce windage (the space between the interior of the barrel and the projectile). The four-pounder field gun barrel now weighed just over six hundred pounds.

Of high importance, Gribeauval totally redesigned gun carriages and set an ammunition box on top of the limber of the field guns. French gun carriages became much stronger and less prone to chronic breakdowns that slowed the advance of every army. Even more significant, Gribeauval introduced standardized construction and interchangeable parts for field gun carriages and wheels. He added a brass screw to elevate or depress the muzzle and a simple sight screw to improve rapidity and accuracy of fire. Finally, Gribeauval reorganized French artillery by regiment and company. In combat, an artillery company manned a division of eight guns. Under this system, artillery became a recognized arm equal with infantry and cavalry. Although a great controversy raged over the efficacy of the reform system, Gribeauval's appointment in 1774 to the post of inspector-general of artillery set in place an effective mobile system that would carry France through the wars of the revolution and empire. After centuries of use as an adjunct to battle, artillery was now a flexible, effective, and devastating weapon for use on the battlefield.

The reputation of eighteenth-century soldiers deserves further consideration. For most readers familiar with the literature of the period, descriptions often include such terms as "scum," "refuse," "*banditti*," "corrupt," "immoral," "lazy," and "violent." Frederick of Prussia left an indelible impression with his critical comments describing his own army as "for the most part composed of the dregs of society—sluggards, rakes, debauchees, rioters, undutiful sons, and the like who have as little attachment to their masters or concern about them as do foreigners." In Frederick's view, soldiers had to be made to fear their officers who would lead them into battle. Soldiers of all contemporary armies were well known for their violent behavior, chronic drunkenness, debauchery, danger to respectable women, and addictions to illegal card games, cock fights, horse races, and games of chance.

Few parents hoped that their sons would seek military careers. Many appealed to the authorities when their boys volunteered or were conscripted for eight or more years. Their arguments often rested upon their low esteem for the army and its recruits. A common refrain was, "My son is neither a criminal nor a vagabond." When civilians had to put up with troops billeted in their homes, they expressed outrage at the damages committed by their house guests to furniture, doors, windows, and other property. Soldiers sometimes kindled fires with books and documents—and by mistake set fire to their lodgings. Writing in June 1728 from Gibraltar, a British soldier reported: "Here is nothing to do nor any news, all things being dormant and in suspense, with the harmless diversions of drinking, dancing, reveling, whoring, gaming and other innocent debaucheries to pass the time—and really, to speak my own opinion I think and believe that Sodom and Gomorrah were not half so wicked and profane as this worthy city and garrison of Gibraltar." In New York during the American Revolution, the inhabitants expressed outrage at the behavior of the Hessians who "once a month go to head-quarters for their rations including spirits, and then for three days they are for the most part given up to intoxication, and we have trying and grievous scenes to go through; fighting brawls, drumming and fifing, and dancing the night long, card and dice playing, and every abomination going on under our very roofs." Civilians feared that their houses would be burned down around them and where possible protected their women and daughters by nailing shut the doors to parts of the house occupied by the Germans. Also in New York, British soldiers behaved with symbolic barbarism when they impaled little girls' dolls on the points of their bayonets.

While most officers in all of the major armies came from noble families, or at least the respectable classes, common soldiers entered army life from a variety of different backgrounds and with diverse motivations. Some volunteered to seek advancement to NCO, to escape from the hardships of village life, or to find camaraderie and adventure as promised by recruiting parties. Others in dire need joined up for the cash bounty and through desperate need to support themselves and their dependents. On some occasions, if foreign invaders threatened their lands, men enlisted for patriotic reasons. The Prussians conscripted their own young men and hired foreigners. The French, British, and Spanish sometimes drafted militiamen to strengthen depleted regular army units during wartime. Militiamen burdened by large numbers of dependents sometimes mutinied against mobilizations that threatened to move them from their home districts. In England during 1757, farmers and laborers insulted justices of the peace and rioted in some towns for fear that they would be sent abroad. The Russians simply rounded up peasants and forced them into the army almost for life.

In most armies, many soldiers entered military service through different forms of hard and soft compulsion. Debtors, vagabonds, and criminals even including murderers who committed crimes of passion such as killing a friend in a tavern brawl, received the alternative of enlistment as opposed to much worse penalties. Naive country boys who made the mistake of spending an evening drinking and carousing with soldiers woke up hung over and in irons to discover that they had taken the oath and made their mark in lieu of a signature to serve their monarch. Others, blinded by soldiers' tales of glory, fine uniforms, sexual conquests, and other adventures, suffered momentary lapses and signed up for eight years or more. Once men agreed to serve, there was no return. Before they could flee or seek assistance from their families, the NCOs marched them off to distant barracks and new lives. Kept under lock and key, they mustered to hear read the military ordinances and learned the draconian punishments for talking back, striking a NCO, theft, negligence of duty, and most of all about the abominable crime of desertion from the army in peace and in war. They faced corporal punishment for almost any breach of discipline and death sentences for a long list of more serious crimes. Most soldiers had little contact with their officers except in disciplinary matters and they spent their time in company with sergeants, corporals, and other soldiers.

In all eighteenth-century armies, military regulations outlined a multitude of rules and listed severe punishments for crimes and misdemeanors. Depending upon the army, corporal punishment included liberal applications of the cat-o'-nine-tails, riding the wooden horse, branding for theft, and running the gauntlet for many offenses including sale of uniform parts, equipment, and weapons. For more serious crimes soldiers could expect penalties of fifteen years at the oars in Marseilles or in other Mediterranean galleys, forced labor in arsenals (very harmful to the health), sentence to overseas military duty in the colonies, and execution by hanging or firing squad. Minor offenders suffered reduction of rank, a short period of confinement in the guardhouse, and added nighttime police and patrol duty. Mutiny, plundering, and fighting for the enemy were the most likely crimes to result in executions.

In the Prussian army, however, cruel punishments were more common. For first offense of absence from camp without permission, a soldier had to run the gauntlet ten times between two files of two hundred comrades who lashed him with wet hazel wands. The perpetrator also received an additional eight years added on to his military enlistment. Drummers beat a ruffle to cover the screams of the victim and the regimental major observed to make certain that the punishment detail lay on properly. Spanish soldiers used their ramrods to punish offenders who sometimes suffered permanent injuries. In wartime, Prussian soldiers found outside their advanced posts were hanged or shot as deserters.

Desertion was the crime that armies could neither condone nor contain. Since so many soldiers served through compulsion or were petty delinquents in their previous careers, they could be expected to flee if given the opportunity. During the Seven Years' War, eighty thousand Prussians, seventy thousand French, and sixty-two thousand Austrians deserted. To prevent escapes, sentinels at barracks and camps served two-way guard duty to protect the perimeter against enemy intruders and to stop the flight of deserters. According to the Prussian Infantry Regulations of 1759, soldiers whether volunteers or not were to be hanged without mercy for desertion. Civil and police authorities rang alarm bells ordering searches of districts near army camps and commanders offered cash rewards to those who made apprehensions. The penalty for any civilian who assisted a deserter was death. In Spain, the military authorities assigned trustworthy light-infantry squads and cavalry detachments to patrol roads and paid bounties for those who tracked down and returned escaped soldiers. Elsewhere, professional bounty hunters did the same job.

Soldiers deserted for many reasons beyond mere delinquency. Young men who had never been away from their home districts suffered homesickness as well as depression when they learned about the restrictions and rigors of their new lives. Those conscripted who had families to support or seasonal deadlines for planting and harvests often risked everything to escape. Even without considering aversion to the danger of combat, soldiers who witnessed the devastating impact and high death rates of yellow fever or other epidemics among their comrades, deserted in panic to save their own lives. Because of the high incidence of desertion and chronic shortages of trained soldiers, courts-martial were loath to apply the letter of the law. Instead, offenders received public lashings of fifty or more stripes of the cat-o'-nine-tails. Tied to a post called "the adjutant's daughter" and in the presence of their comrades as an object lesson, they had their backs turned to bloody jelly. Even in the Continental army, American soldiers received thirty lashes for being drunk on guard duty, forty lashes for begging money from civilians, and eighty lashes for stealing a watch. For those guilty of re-incidence of desertion or other serious offenses, the sentence of the court-martial—hanging or shooting by firing squad—followed a prescribed form. Guarded by his fully armed comrades, the condemned man was escorted to the gallows or placed before a firing squad. The regimental adjutant read the sentence, the chaplain addressed those assembled, and the condemned man was blindfolded. While the completely traumatized man quivered in mortal fear expecting certain death, instead the adjutant read a letter of reprieve!

In his journal, Jeremiah Greenman, a common soldier during the American Revolution, summed up the sorts of penalties handed down by courts-martial on the revolutionary side. He wrote: "This day set on General Court Martial of which Major E. Flag was President. Tried Jack Champlin for Stealing, Benjamin Buffington for Desertion and Mathew Henly, Cornilius Driskill, Charles Stevens, and James Singleton, all which plead Guilty and was sentenced to receive 100 lashes. Tried Cuff Roberts for Stealing and was sentenced to receive 100 lashes. Nathan Gale was tried by the same Court for repeat'd Desertion plead Guilty and threw himself on the Mercy of ye Court. The Court having considered the Prisoner's General Character in the Regiment do sentence him to Suffer Death." There was no indication whether or not Gale made a successful appeal or received a last-minute pardon issued by his commander.

The basic uniform for European and colonial soldiers consisted of a bright-colored frock coat, a long waistcoat, shirt, knee breeches, gaiters, stockings, buckled shoes, and either tricorn hats or brass-fronted caps. In addition to their muskets, each soldier wore cross belts, a cartridge pouch, and a bayonet in a scabbard and carried a knapsack for equipment, spare clothing, tent pegs, and food preparation implements. Although there were some exceptions, the uniforms were tight and uncomfortable, made for appearance rather than for normal service or combat duty. Some grenadier shakos (helmets) were so heavy that men had to wear metal chin straps and to walk with their heads bent forward. Their hair took hours to dress and powder in military style. Bald men were not better off since they had to purchase and wear wigs. In wet weather these became sodden, heavy, and in some cases caused hypothermia and other hazards to the health.

The lapels and turnbacks on some military frock coats were cut so narrow that they would not fold over in cold weather to cover the soldier's chest. Underpants had not been invented so the soldier tucked the tails of his shirt under the buttocks. In some units, the knee beeches were so tight that soldiers simply could not bend down to pick up objects on the ground. White breeches and gaiters that looked elegant on the pa-

Fig. 8.4. Soldiers of the War of American Independence. Library of Congress, Washington DC.

rade square soon became dirty and were almost impossible to keep clean during campaign duty. The gaiters were tight and the rows of buttons sometimes took hours to do up with a special iron hook. Garters used to hold up stockings often cut off circulation at the knee. The Germans wore woolen stockings that crippled many men with blisters, ulcers, and inflammation. Shoes were a perennial problem because they wore out, disintegrated after a short time in rough terrain, or did not fit the soldiers' feet in the first place. On marches, soldiers wrapped their feet with rags soaked in tallow to prevent blisters. The grease also excluded moisture and kept the leather of their shoes more supple.

No matter how much time soldiers spent with pipe clay to whiten their leather belts or caring for their uniforms, wet weather, constant use, and lack of spare garments and equipment soon left soldiers dressed in little more than patched rags. The Prussians replaced uniforms annually, the French every three years, but sometimes longer, and the Spanish every six years. Duty in tropical climates rotted cloth and dyes that were not fixed with proper mordents often ran. Spanish soldiers embarrassed to appear in public went barefoot and complained that their tattered uniforms no longer covered their nakedness. Sometimes, soldiers created their own problems by selling off newer uniform parts in markets and keeping only their oldest coats and beeches. In more rigorous climates, soldiers had to sew their own overcoats. The Austrians and Russians issued heavy cloaks and waterproof boots. In North America, British troops often developed fatigue-style uniforms to respond to backwoods conditions. They cut the tails off their coats, trimmed their hair short, wore comfortable woolen caps, and toned down their red coats to a more brownish hue.

In all armies of the period, living conditions were difficult and barracks crowded. NCOs and grenadiers slept two to a bed while privates sometimes had to endure three to as many as five to a bed. Soldiers who unlocked the barracks in the morning commented on the stench that emanated out of the doors. Under such conditions, sickness and epidemic diseases killed and disabled many more soldiers than perished in combat. In some garrisons, well over half of the troops suffered from syphilis and gonorrhea. Open latrines attracted swarms of flies and the odor so repelled many men who then declined to use them and instead relieved themselves wherever they could find a spot. Army camps and cantonments reeked of wood smoke, gunpowder, urine, feces, and animal offal.

Without women present to clean clothing and to maintain good hygiene, some soldiers were very dirty in their habits and in their appearance. In North America, after the Seven Years' War, British officers made their men bathe in streams and wash their clothing regularly to prevent the spread of a skin disease called "the Itch." The ailment caused by poor hygiene and from sleeping on the ground left some men entirely covered with scabs and unfit for duty. Soldiers who suffered the disease were "ointed" with hog's lard or pine tar and brimstone—a treatment that made "the Devil of a stink." General George Washington ordered his soldiers to bathe regularly no matter what the weather and if possible to use soap. The men took to the water with enthusiasm, splashing about and showing off stark naked before ladies "of the first fashion."

Many soldiers who contracted diseases or suffered injuries resisted hospitalization until they could no longer function. Although military medical care improved in major hospitals, overcrowding, lack of ventilation, filth, unsanitary practices, poor food, soiled bedding, and polluted water supplies made these institutions terrible places for the sick and wounded. Dysentery or bloody flux as it was called because of blood in the stool—"the constant and fatal epidemic of camps"—turned hospital wards into open privies. Sick men often lay on straw pallets in ankle deep excrement. Sir John Pringle, author of the authoritative and much published study *Observations on the Diseases of the Army* (1752), recommended frequent bleeding, constant opiates, emetics, vomiting, and purges. For coughs he bled his patients and treated them with opium and laudanum. For venereal diseases, physicians applied a number of cures involving mercury. From the beginning of the century, France created a system of eighty-five military hospitals watched over by medical inspectors and advisory surgeons. They also led the way in creating companies of soldier invalids who performed guard duties and other minor roles.

Battlefield medicine had not improved markedly since the seventeenth century, and casualties still lay on the field for hours or days before they saw a surgeon. Working in barns, basements, and sheds under the most primitive conditions, surgeons seldom took care with cleanliness and spread infection from one patient to another. They amputated injured arms and legs and probed wounds for bullets. Dr. John Hunter (1728–93) who served during the Seven Years' War improved treatment of gunshot wounds and became an opponent of bleeding. Pierre-Joseph Desault (1744–95) of France, who coined the term "debridement," like Hunter opposed the enlargement of bullet wounds and improved methods to remove foreign matter from deep penetration injuries. While some surgeons received better instruments including forceps and screw tourniquets that allowed for thigh amputations, most made do with primitive equipment. In surgery cases, tetanus often caused death.

As we have seen earlier in this chapter, the impact of European wars of the eighteenth century was felt in much of the world. Larger and more seaworthy ships carried warfare to the littoral of the populated continents and transported soldiers and their weaponry. The technology of smoothbore gunpowder weapons and wood reinforced construction dictated the ways of warfare at sea. As the unfortunate career of the great Havana-built 120-gun Spanish warship *Santíssima Trinidad* (later expanded to a four-decker with 140 guns) illustrated, a ship had to be manageable in all conditions as well as to carry as much ordnance as possible into battle. The two- and three-decker ship-of-the-line—the battleship of the period—was arguably the highest concentration of skilled technology and artisanship until the Industrial Age. The ship was a flexible means to gain domination abroad and both an offensive and defensive tool of war that made the seas and oceans extensions of land battlefields. Through the century, the British Royal Navy served as the decisive force in turning back invasion attempts in 1708, 1744–46, 1759, and again in 1805.

At the same time, a warship that fired smoothbore cannon had to position most heavy guns along its sides and not at the bow and stern. This factor dictated that the only obvious tactical formation to fully maximize the broadside armament of warships of this type was line-ahead formation. By as early as the 1660s, *Permanent Fighting Instructions* called for the deployment of warships in this form so that the vulnerable bows and sterns of ships were protected and the annihilating fire of the broadside could be brought to bear. Of course, as in the case of infantry armed with smoothbore muskets deployed in linear formations, both sides had to agree to play by certain rules. In naval war even more than on land, combat became both formalized and hidebound. Until the 1780s when the British introduced gun-training tackles into the ships-of-the-line, warships fired at each other virtually at right angles.

Since line-ahead formations were both offensive and defensive in nature, opposing admirals found limited opportunities for innovation. In May 1747, Anson's success in running down an entire French squadron and eighteen merchantmen led to an adjustment in the fighting instructions. If the enemy turned tail and ran, British warships could break the line to engage in a general chase. Until 1783, British commanders were ordered not to stray from the *Permanent Fighting Instructions*. If possible, they approached from windward or with the weather gage to take on the full enemy battle line. With primitive ship to ship communications, inadequate signals, and differing sailing abilities depending upon the warship, admirals often experienced problems simply getting their fleet into line-ahead formation. There was to be no pursuit unless the main body of enemy fleet attempted to flee.

As a result of these constraints, the opposing lines approached and passed each majestically much like heavy trucks on a divided highway. Even at close range—and some ships actually touched as they blasted away at each other—damage and casualties did not mean that a vessel was in danger of foundering. It was often said that British vessels fired at the hull to deal death and destruction to enemy gunners and the frame of ships while the French and Spanish shot at rigging and sails to slow down or to disable the opposition. In fact, stronger squadrons fired at hulls while weaker forces sought to disable in case they needed to flee. Also, British battle-winning abilities were legendary so that morale was a factor in how different fleets engaged in battle. For most of the century, line-ahead tactics under by these rules usually produced indecisive and quite unproductive duels. From 1700 to 1782 with the Battle of the Saints, there were no truly decisive naval battles on the high seas.

In April 1782, a British battle fleet under Admiral George Rodney, a capable but contentious commander, pursued and engaged a French fleet commanded by Admiral Comte François de Grasse. The battle took place between Martinique and Guadalupe Islands in the Caribbean where Franco-Spanish forces had begun to mobilize for an invasion of Jamaica. The British had the advantage of the larger and more powerful fleet—thirty-six three-decker battleships ranging from sixty-four-, seventy-four-, and a few ninety-gun ships-of-the-line and requisite reconnaissance frigates. Many of the British ships were faster than French warships because they were copper-sheathed to avoid fouling and to ward off the effect of tropical *terridos* (marine borers) that made short work of wooden ships.

Because of variable winds, rather than innovative planning, gaps appeared in the French line ahead. Without a specific plan, Rodney's ships broke through. The impact of broadsides and of new light-weight short-barreled guns called carronades (also called smashers) wrought terrible effect upon the French ships at short range. As was often the case, the better trained British gun crews were able to fire almost twice as fast as the French. De Grasse's flagship *Ville de Paris* was surrounded by British warships that swept it with fire. After several hours, De Grasse had lost almost all of his officers, and he struck his flag. When the British boarded the *Ville de Paris* they found the decks covered with blood and the mangled limbs of the dead and dying. Over 400 French seamen and gunners died and even more suffered wounds. Aboard the warship *Glorieux*, thirteen officers and 489 men died, and forty-eight officers and 1,563 men suffered wounds. In the battle, the British captured five French ships-of-the-line. Six French captains died, and the total French killed, wounded, and captured totaled almost 14,000 men. The British who lost 272 killed and 853 wounded had won a spectacular victory. With better morale and gunnery, the pell-mell battle came into its own during the 1790s and under more aggressive admirals such as Horatio Nelson.

Although the Royal Navy pared down its size following every war and ships were put in "rotten row" until the next crisis unfolded, British governments recognized the importance of maintaining naval supremacy. Until midcentury, the British navy was stronger than the combined French and Spanish fleets. This "two-power standard" ended when both Bourbon powers rebuilt their fleets with well-designed modern vessels. While British ship designs were sometimes quite conservative, captures of fine French and Spanish vessels provided ships for the Royal Navy and templates for naval construction. In the 1740s for example, British officers waxed eloquent about the captured Spanish warship *Princessa* (formerly *Princesa*) that they described as "a glorious ship" or "a magnificent ship." However, the two-decker British-designed seventy-four-gun ship-of-the-line was well constructed, heavily armed, and very seaworthy. As we have seen, Admiral Anson who gained fame for his own exploits, as first sea lord reformed the British dockyards, adopted new designs and ratings for ships, modified the *Permanent Fighting Instructions*, and introduced the naval officer's uniform.

Following Britain's overwhelming victories in the Seven Years' War, in a few years naval dominance was lost. Some ships-of-the-line that should have been in service during the 1780s turned out to have been constructed of unseasoned wood. Many of these vessels grew a profusion of toadstools while anchored in the Thames River and there were some spectacular tragedies such as the loss of the *Royal George* with all hands. Until it was too late, Britain's political and military leadership slashed budgets and failed to respond to changing demands. Cursed with patronage appointments, admirals such as Richard Kempenfelt and George Rodney while competent enough were neither brilliant nor innovative. They became more rule bound and conservative often emulating the French whom the British had so often defeated.

By 1779, the French had prepared for revenge with eighty excellent ships of the line backed by new dockyards and a system of naval conscription. Spain weighed in with its own naval reforms that made available another sixty capital ships for the Bourbon alliance. Without allies, against this danger Britain could no longer maintain its accustomed maritime mastery. To cover the strategic points—the English Channel, Gibraltar, the West Indies, and the American seaboard—Britain embarked late upon a period of intense naval building. Through the use of naval blockades and victories in combat based in part upon moral superiority and the tradition of victory, in the end Britain throttled the Bourbon powers and denied them adequate access to timber, masts, and other vital naval stores.

Unlike armies where noble and wealthy families often purchased places for their sons as cadets well before they were of an age to serve, most naval forces took young men and trained them without cost. Well-connected boys of thirteen or fourteen who had a thirst for adventure and travel could go to sea as an officer's servant and later become midshipmen. Although officer recruitment and training differed from country to country, naval careers provided talented and ambitious young men with possibilities for social and economic ascension. Although most young officers were second and third sons from elite families who were not required at home to run estates, there were some cases of common seamen who became sea officers. They joined the navy as common seamen, moved up to petty officer, and finally earned commissions as lieutenants. Finally, some merchant seamen such as Captain James Cook commenced their careers in merchant service and transferred to the navy.

In all of the major navies, promotion up the ladder from lieutenant to command of capital ships depended upon patronage connections. Young officers followed the careers of a successful senior naval patron and hoped that he would advance their careers along with his own. Nepotism, favoritism, often vicious competitiveness, and special interests made the politics of all naval services both turbulent and dirty. No young officer wished to be posted too long in colonial duty or on overseas missions where they would lose touch with their mentors in London, Paris, Madrid, or in the great naval ports such as Brest, Portsmouth, or Cádiz. Admiral Anson received criticism for favoring the men who accompanied him on his expedition of global circumnavigation. However, during the Seven Years' War, Anson was known for his impartiality in seeking out the most talented captains and admirals who could win victories at sea.

There were practical reasons that made naval service popular with officers that had nothing to do with sea battles, blockade duty, convoy service, or any of the other missions on large and small naval ships. During wartime, there was the possibility of significant prize money earned from conducting war against enemy merchant shipping. The interception of a merchant convoy rekindled the sort of dreams in British naval officers that had driven the Elizabethan sea dogs. Through pursuit of *guerre de course*, French and Spanish warships intercepted British commerce. For Spain, a record of failure in larger fleet engagements could be offset at least partially by raiding British merchant shipping and in single vessel duels involving ships-of-the-line and well-armed frigates. Every officer hoped for assignment to a lucrative station in wartime. In what was outright freedom to loot, each naval power granted its naval commanders and armed privateers the right to enemy property captured at sea. There was no similar parallel that sanctioned systematic legal pillaging in warfare on land.

There were three ways for naval commanders to make money well in excess of their naval pay. In prize courts that condemned captured vessels, captains in Britain's Royal Navy received no less than three-eighths of the proceeds of the sale of cargo and the enemy vessel. Flag officers who commanded the station received one-eighth. Lieutenants and ship's masters divided another eighth and the remaining two- to three-eighths was distributed among the seamen of the lower deck. Since senior officers could accumulate great fortunes through captures, captains fought to be posted to the best "cruising stations" in major shipping lanes and off important ports. Again, patronage was the key since an admiral could advance the fortunes of his favorites and thereby increase his own wealth. Less lucrative, British captains who captured enemy warships received five pounds "head money" for each enemy crewman taken alive. These funds were distributed much like prize money. Finally, in peace and war, flag officers and captains received "freight money" for carrying bullion or coin that ranged from half a percent in peacetime upward to one-and-one-half percent in wartime conditions. In the 1750s, a British captain in Mediterranean duty could earn as much as £1,000 in addition to his naval pay of about £110 per year. Little wonder that there was a great deal of squabbling over freight among commanders who often degenerated into a band of angry brokers.

The situation on the lower deck provided the real test of eighteenth-century naval planners. The offer of adventure and travel were seldom sufficient to attract adequate numbers of volunteers. It was difficult to hide the fact that harsh naval discipline, arbitrary punishments, and diseases such as scurvy, typhus (ship fever), and dysentery (bloody flux) deterred possible recruits such as merchant sailors, fishermen, and all those with lives connected with the sea. France, Spain, and other nations might build the finest warships, but without experienced crews many of these vessels either could not raise anchor or keep proper place in a line of war. In addition to competent officers, proficient petty officers and seamen were essential to working and fighting any warship. Captain Augustus Hervey of the Royal Navy told a story about a Spanish fleet at Cádiz in 1731 that was being readied to convey Prince Don Carlos to take possession of the Duchies of Parma and Piacenza in Italy. Confronted with the complexities of working warships, the crews were so green having been put aboard in such haste that they had no idea which ropes to pull. The officers attached playing cards to the different ropes so the men were ordered to "Pull away the Ace of Spades. Make fast the King of Hearts and so on."

While this story may have been apocryphal, or at least blown out of proportion by British superiority, it underscored chronic difficulties faced by all of the major navies. The manning of fleets during wartime produced intractable difficulties. It seems strange that in spite all of the well-known abuses caused by impressment, Britain was more successful at finding naval crews than its enemies. Given the widespread stories about kidnapping of country boys and the transfer of criminals into naval service, it is important to stress that some men did volunteer for naval duty. Living conditions aboard a warship may have been difficult, but considering the lives experienced by many poor men in Britain and Europe, naval service relieved starvation with plentiful food if not a well-balanced diet. Seamen received other basics of life that they may not have enjoyed otherwise. Volunteers—both seamen and landsmen—received a cash bounty for enlisting and even some of those impressed were able to "volunteer" at the last moment so as to collect the bounty. Also, naval impressment and conscription were not unpopular with urban port authorities who rid their towns of gamblers, petty criminals, and a variety of other miscreants unwanted in society.

Some modern historians have reevaluated the abuses, grievances, and cruelties of naval life on the lower deck portrayed through popular literature and other sources. Obviously, naval captains could not operate and fight their warships simply through vicious cruelty and harsh discipline. Even with impressment, during all of the eighteenth-century wars, British ships usually fought better than those of the Bourbon powers. However, wartime naval impressment remained a smoldering issue in British ports. Press-gangs authorized to scour ports for seamen sometimes grabbed those who had no connections with the sea. Naval boats stopped inbound East India vessels in the English Channel to impress men who had been at sea for months and needed time ashore to recover their health. In the 1740s there were several bloody incidents at sea in which incoming crews fought back, killing some men, wounding others. Fights, riots, and brawls broke out in port cities and some maritime populations of fishermen and whalers were well known as tenacious defenders against press-gangs. Women in groups sometimes attacked the gangs to protect their men. Naval lieutenants commanding these operations feared for their lives and some suffered stabbing and bludgeoning injuries. When the wartime demand for men became desperate, the use of embargo and "the hot press" produced sweeps of port cities following secret Admiralty orders and compelled merchant captains to surrender part of their crews. During the years of the American Revolution, talk of rights and liberties left out the third to half of the sailors in Royal Navy crews who had been compelled by force to do their duty.

Case Study: The American Revolutionary War

Upon arrival at an army camp near Philadelphia in 1778, the Chevalier de Pontgibaud, a French volunteer with the American forces viewed what he termed "an armed mob." Quite taken aback he wrote: "My imagination had pictured an army with uniforms, the glitter of arms, standards, etc., in short military pomp of all sorts. Instead of the imposing spectacle I expected, I saw grouped together or standing alone, a few militiamen poorly clad, and for the most part without shoes; many of them badly armed, but all well supplied with provisions, and I noticed that tea and sugar formed part of their rations." Marylander recruits who did not receive army shirts instead wore blankets "elegantly turned around them." Some shoes imported from France were of such poor quality that they wore out after a one-day march. At Valley Forge, the Marquis de Lafayette wrote, "The unfortunate soldiers were in want of everything; they had neither coats, nor hats, nor shirts, nor shoes. Their feet and legs froze till they grew black, and it was often necessary to amputate them."

Foreign observers who otherwise expressed admiration for the general health and appearance of Americans—"a slender and well-formed people"—had great difficulty understanding their ill-disciplined ways and lack of respect for social niceties. Spanish observers could not believe that following exercises American militia officers and soldiers fraternized and even drank punch together at taverns. Foreigners serving with Americans reported much random firing of muskets in American camps. The soldiers used muskets to start fires, snapped their flintlocks at each other in fun sometimes forgetting that they were loaded, and they blasted away at wild geese or other birds flying overhead. When men felt that they were needed in the fields at home, they deserted without apparent remorse.

European officers who admired the discipline and formations of Frederick the Great found little to appreciate with American soldiers who wore tattered clothing patched with different colored cloth and only the lid of their hats. During the Seven Years' War, General Wolfe had described American soldiers as "the dirtiest, most contemptible, cowardly dogs you can conceive. There is no depending upon them in action." Little wonder that many British officers were contemptuous of the Americans and expected to crush the rebels without much difficulty. They failed to note that these troops had pride enough to keep their muskets clean and shiny and powdered their hair with provisioning flour to look better on parade. The rural militiamen who were dangerous marksmen actually took pride in their wild appearance and sometimes dressed like Indians.

For the first twenty months of the war, the Continental army suffered a succession of defeats. Beginning with the basis of the old provincial militias, the Americans found themselves on a steep learning curve. At first, Congress failed to provide sufficient provisions, arms, munitions, clothing, food, and equipment. The British were better organized, experienced in maintaining overseas forces from the Seven Years' War, and certainly capable from their background in Scotland and Ireland of heavy-handed policies to suppress rebellion. Like many insurgents after them, the Americans believed at first that they could fight a conventional war. In September 1775, they launched an ambitious expedition to make Canada the fourteenth state. By June 1776 combat, starvation, disease, distance, and the climate defeated the invasion force with the loss of almost five thousand men. In 1776, the rebels suffered defeats that drove them off Long Island and cost them control of New York City. In close-quarter combat where training and discipline counted, the revolutionary soldiers often collapsed and in their flight threw away precious muskets and equipment. With experience and better training—in part by foreign experts such as Baron Friedrich von Stueben who came to instill order and discipline following the approaches of King Frederick—the Continental soldiers learned to hold ground and even to advance against British veterans. The militias were a different story, but they could be deployed in other ways to harass and gall the British troops.

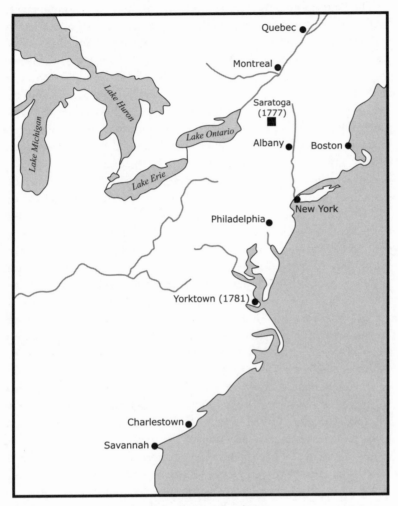

Map. 8.1. Theaters of Combat in the American Revolution

The British found themselves in a war that they were ill-equipped to fight and even less so to win. On the political side, some senior military and naval commanders wanted nothing to do with a campaign to suppress the Anglo-Americans. Admiral Keppel, who was happy to take on the French, refused to accept any commission that would involve him against the Americans. Without allies and lacking sufficient troops, the British government hired foreign mercenaries and hoped for the assistance of loyalist (Tory) militias that would look after counterinsurgency in the rural districts. After failing to obtain 20,000 Russian troops, the British turned to old allies in Germany. In the end, a total of 29,867 German troops—indiscriminately described by the Americans as Hessians since many originated in Hesse-Cassel—arrived in America to bolster British forces as the hired enforcers of colonial rule. Many of these Germans—weavers, shoemakers, laborers, and agricultural workers—volunteered or were conscripted, impressed, and shipped off by force. Bitter about their fate, some suffered low morale, abused the American populace (especially with their habit of pillaging civilian property), and they were less than completely dedicated to the British cause.

Accompanying the German forces were elite *Jäger* rifle companies drawn from among foresters, hunters, and others experts at shooting. Like some French *chasseurs*, they carried rifled muskets with hexagonal bores and better sights than smoothbore weapons. They did not use bayonets and instead wore hunting swords for use in close combat. They wore green coats with carmine collars, cuffs, and lapels, and green vests trimmed with gold. Called "greencoats" in America, these soldiers were to be used mounted and dismounted for reconnaissance, patrols, and to guard foragers. They often led the vanguard or guarded the rear of British and Hessian forces, picked off enemy artillerymen during sieges, and were effective in ambushes and in other counterinsurgency or antiguerrilla operations or what both sides called "partisan warfare." The *Jägers* were feared by the Americans for their accurate fire. In a word, these troops played the same roles as the legendary American riflemen armed with Pennsylvania rifles who were the scourge of British forces.

Once the Americans were able to show that a sufficient percentage of the population supported republicanism, the British had almost no chance of victory. The war in America was in many respects a land conflict that could be influenced but not won through the application of sea power. The British forces that numbered usually about thirty-five thousand troops with some loyalist militias, ran headlong into the conundrum of all counterinsurgents—they could not hold the vast territories of America, garrison the towns and cities, and still have sufficient forces left over to form operational armies. As a result, much of the countryside with its production was left in enemy hands. All too often when British forces and loyalist units entered the countryside, they did so as plunderers and pillagers who ran off livestock, desecrated and burned churches, and sometimes molested women. In Pennsylvania, Hessian troops met German settlers who wanted nothing to do with them. In 1777 an old woman expressed her view: "What harm have we people done to you, that you Germans come over here to suck us dry and drive us out of house and home? We have heard enough of your murderous burning. Will you do the same here as in New York and in the Jerseys? You shall get your pay yet!"

The British pinned their hopes on a climactic battle, but when one occurred at Saratoga, New York, on October 7, 1777, the result was not at all what they had in mind. Counterinsurgents might not control the rural countryside, but they could not afford to lose a major set-piece battle. General John Burgoyne (known as Gentleman Johnny) led an army of six thousand regulars (half foreign mercenaries) south from Montreal with the plan to join up with the New York garrison and sever rebel communications between New England and rebel bases in Pennsylvania and further to the south. Prepared for a conventional battle involving linear tactics, Burgoyne's army escorted a large artillery train, many baggage carts, and a large number of women and children. Burgoyne's own baggage including his wardrobe, library, liquor, and dogs, filled thirty carts. From the outset, the army bogged down on the wilderness trails and the troops had to confront a thoroughly hostile populace along the route. The Americans practiced guerrilla tricks—felling trees, digging pits, and flooding the trails to slow enemy progress. They burned off the grass, destroyed stocks of grain, killed all livestock and practiced scorched-earth tactics to weaken the British. From the woods and treetops, American riflemen picked off the British and German soldiers.

Following an inconclusive first battle at Saratoga, Burgoyne had his soldiers dig trenches and build redoubts. Cut off from provisions and forage, the British troops were on short rations of flour and salt pork and without forage the horses began to starve. Militiamen deserted and all units suffered harassing rebel fire. Some officers recommended a retreat back to Canada, but Burgoyne demurred. Instead, the British advanced toward the rebel forces in three columns and wheeled into line, and then halted to rest. The Americans attacked from the woods at the British flanks with such ferocity the British were thrown into confusion. The British line collapsed leaving Burgoyne's army surrounded and without provisions. Without other options, Burgoyne surrendered 5,721 troops and seven generals and handed over twenty-seven guns and five thousand stand of arms. Burgoyne and his army marched to Boston for the ignominious repatriation to Britain. On the basis of this victory, France, Spain, and Holland joined the war. From this point forward, French arms, munitions, uniforms, and supplies helped rebel forces to attain some parity with the British. By 1780, almost 12,000 French soldiers and sailors arrived to support the American Revolution.

When the war shifted to the South in 1779, British troops who hoped for stronger loyalist support again found themselves surrounded by a hostile population. While for a time they had the firepower to move through Georgia and the Carolinas, they did so almost as a plague that scoured the land. They confiscated crops, wagons, coaches, implements, furniture, bedding, and clothing. They destroyed rebel property, plundered houses, and used black slaves to drive off cattle, horses, mules, sheep, and even chickens. What they could not remove they smashed—including windows, mills, forges, and agricultural equipment. Women and children, who were the only ones left in some districts, usually received fairly good treatment though it was well known that their husbands and sons were under arms. Many women carried messages and supplies. At Pleasant Ford on the Catawba River, one loyalist officer noted: "This settlement is composed of the most violent Rebels I ever saw, particularly the young ladies."

Civil war and skirmishes between revolutionaries and loyalists supported by British armies left the South devastated and its farmlands destroyed. The British won battles at Savannah (1778), Augusta (1779), Charleston (1780), and Camden (1780). On the revolutionary side, the impressment of men and foraging for supplies also led to pillaging that eroded the support of neutrals and even some sympathetic Americans. Some rejoined the loyalists. Captain Johann Ewald on the British side expressed surprise at the coercive power exerted by Congress. He declared, "In no monarchy in the world is levying done more forcibly than in this country, where it is said without distinction or position, 'Serve or provide your man, else you lose your goods and chattels.'" State and local authorities feared such power in the hands of the Continental army and the clear danger of militarism. Regional and local officials and jurisdictions acted to protect the citizens of their state, county, town or village.

In January 1781 Lord Cornwallis entered North Carolina with a small British army and the belief that loyalist forces would increase his numbers. From the beginning, the campaign failed to produce the results desired. On January 17, 1781, at Hannah's Cowpens, the American militiamen stood firm against British infantry assault—aiming specifically at the officers and sergeants and firing devastating volleys before they withdrew. As the British advance became ragged, the American cavalry fell upon them followed by the infantry. In what was an unusual tactical defeat, at the Battle of the Cowpens the British lost eight hundred troops and officers taken prisoner and over one hundred killed and wounded. Cornwallis continued his march southward in pursuit of the American army of General Nathanial Greene. The next engagement at Guilford, North Carolina, called the Battle of Guilford Courthouse, was a bloody affair narrowly won by the British who could not afford to take heavy casualties. By now, about one-third of Cornwallis's army had been killed or wounded. With few loyalists coming forward and many committed rebels willing to fight, each skirmish or battle reduced the ability of the British force to pursue the war.

As Cornwallis's dwindling army of operations lurched from place to place without any clear objectives, his marauding soldiers won few friends. Captain Ewald described the army as "similar to a wandering Arabian or Tartar horde." The officers gathered horses and took black slaves to look after their new property and women to cook and mend. The soldiers' own women who accompanied the army also had black servants and many soldiers had personal servants who carried their provisions and booty. For a time, over four thousand black men, women, and children followed the British baggage train. While the British encouraged slave desertion to damage the economy of the South and made vague promises of protection and freedom, few blacks bore arms during the war. Most who hoped for emancipation labored in the construction of fortifications, dug latrines, and served in military hospitals.

With the countryside in rebel hands except where British forces actually held territory, the war was all but lost. Without fresh troops from Europe and with constant bickering between Cornwallis and Clinton, the war might have become stalemated for some years. On their own, the American forces continued to experience problems in equipping, arming, and paying an army large enough for General Washington to eliminate the British in New York or in other ports that could be supported from the sea. By 1781, however, French troops, money, and equipment backed by the navy had begun to make a difference. While many Americans disliked the French monarchists and there were even fights at Newport involving French soldiers and Americans, foreign military aid helped to tip the balance. When Cornwallis fortified Yorktown, Virginia, on Chesapeake Bay, the Americans and French organized an army of 20,000 troops including 7,800 French soldiers to besiege the British and Hessian force of 9,750 men. With the fleet of Admiral de Grasse blockading Chesapeake Bay, Washington and the comte de Rochambeau commenced the final event. After a European-style siege with zigzag approach trenches and parallels and an awesome bombardment of the town and fortifications, Cornwallis capitulated. A British relief force from New York under General Clinton arrived too late. Although the war dragged on for two more years, there was little fighting. The Americans had won their independence.

At the time, relatively few direct military lessons were learned from the American Revolutionary War. Soldiers then as well as now despise messy insurgency struggles and the British lacked sufficient loyalist support to organize effective counterinsurgency militias. The use of light infantry and rifle companies of *chasseurs*, *Jägers*, and American riflemen had limited impact in European armies that already experimented with such troops. Loose order skirmishing and the employment of marksmen may have influenced some British army officers. For the British, the lessons were more strategic than tactical. The temporary loss of maritime preeminence provided sufficient warning. The debilitating internecine struggle between motherland and colonies could not be won and would not be tried again. The Spanish allies who assisted the Americans and fought so well in Florida and in the Mississippi Basin like so many others in the future learned nothing from the Anglo-American rebels. Years later they fought their own ruinous wars to suppress revolution in Spanish America.

Suggested Reading

There is an extensive bibliography of published works treating many aspects of eighteenth-century warfare from technology to biography and including rich social, economic, and cultural studies that treat almost every theme imaginable. Historians and the writers of good historical fiction take particular delight in writing about naval clashes, battles involving linear formations and the clash of empires, invasion plots directed against Britain, naval expeditions to far-off and romantic locations, and biographies of the fascinating characters who inhabit the century. Because of the Enlightenment and the expanded curiosity of contemporary observers, good journals, diaries, logbooks, and memoirs present the views of the participants. In cities such as London, Paris, and Amsterdam, major figures published broadsides and presented their interpretations of military and naval events. Some wrote to explain defeats or other peculiar transactions, to curry favor with political interests, or simply to meet the demands of a growing market enthusiasm for stories about adventure and foreign places. Many kept private diaries that in many cases have been printed and are available in good libraries today.

Beginning with general overviews, students should examine M. S. Anderson, *War and Society in Europe of the Old Regime* (New York, 1988); Jeremy Black, *European Warfare, 1660–1815* (New Haven, 1994), and *A Military Revolution? Military Change and European Society, 1550–1808* (Atlantic Highlands, 1991); David G. Chandler, *Atlas of Military Strategy: The Art, Theory and Practice of War, 1618–1878* (Don Mills, 1980); John Childs, *Armies and Warfare in Europe, 1648–1789* (Manchester, 1982); André Corvisier, *Armies and Societies in Europe, 1494–1789* (Bloomington IN, 1979); Hans Delbrück, *History of the Art of War*, vol. 4, *The Dawn of Modern Warfare* (Lincoln NE, 1990); Archer Jones, *The Art of War in the Western World* (Urbana IL, 1987); William McNeill, *The Pursuit of Power: Technology, Armed Force, and Society since A.D. 1000* (Chicago, 1982); David Marley, *Wars of the Americas: A Chronology of Armed Conflict in the New World, 1492 to the Present* (Santa Barbara, 1998); and Geoffrey Parker, *the Military Revolution: Military Innovation and the Rise of the West, 1500–1800* (Cambridge, 1988).

For an introduction to broad medical questions, see Richard A. Gabriel and Karen S. Metz, *A History of Military Medicine*, vol. 2, *From the Renaissance Through Modern Times* (New York, 1992), and Peter Mathias, "Swords and Ploughshares: The Armed Forces, Medicine and Public Health in the Late Eighteenth Century," in J. M. Winter, ed., *War and Economic Development: Essays in Memory of David Joslin* (Cambridge, 1975). On the question of alcohol and armed forces, see Paul E. Kopperman, " 'The Cheapest Pay': Alcohol Abuse in the Eighteenth-Century British Army," *The Journal of Military History* 60:3 (1996): 445–70. For a contemporary view in many different editions, see Sir John Pringle, *Observations on the Diseases of the Army* (Philadelphia, 1810).

Moving to the eighteenth century specifically, for a good overview see Christopher Duffy, *The Military Experience in the Age of Reason* (London, 1987); Liddel Hart, *The Ghost of Napoleon* (Westport CT, 1980); and Robert S. Quinby, *The Background of Napoleonic Warfare: The Theory of Military Tactics in Eighteenth Century France* (New York, 1968).

As might be expected, there are many studies on different aspects of the War of the Spanish Succession, including biographies of most major participants. See David Chandler, *Robert Parker and Comte de Mérode-Westerloo: The Marlborough Wars* (London, 1969), and *The Art of War in the Age of Marlborough* (London, 1976); David Francis, *The First Peninsular War, 1702–1713* (London, 1975); Henry Kamen, *The War of Succession in Spain, . 1700–15* (London, 1969); and John A. Lynn, *Giant of the Grand Siècle: The French Army, 1610–1715* (Cambridge, 1997).

Moving to the epoch of the War of Austrian Succession, the Seven Years' War, and of Frederick the Great, see Christon I. Archer, *The Army in Bourbon Mexico, 1760–1810* (Albuquerque NM, 1977); Gordon Craig, *The Politics of the Prussian Army, 1640–1945* (New York, 1964); Christopher Duffy, *The Army of Frederick the Great* (London, 1974); J. L. Keep, *Soldiers of the Tsar. Army and Society in Russia, 1462–1874* (Oxford, 1985); Lee Kennett, *The French Armies in the Seven Years' War: A Study in Military Organization and Administration* (Durham NC, 1967); Jay Luvass, *Frederick the Great and the Art of War* (New York, 1966); *Regulations for the Prussian Infantry* (New York, 1968); Richard Pares, *War and Trade in the West Indies, 1739–1763* (London, 1963); Gerhard Ritter, *Frederick the Great* (Berkeley, 1968); and Field Marshal Count Saxe, *Reveries, or Memoirs upon the Art of War* (New York, 1976).

The bibliography on eighteenth-century naval war is quite exhaustive. For an introduction to the field, see Jeremy Black and Philip Woodfine, eds., *The British Navy and the Use of Naval Power in the Eighteenth Century* (Atlantic Highlands, 1987); Julian D. Corbett, *Fighting Instructions, 1513–1816* (London, 1905); James Dodds and James Moore, *Building the Wooden Fighting Ship* (New York, 1984); Jonathan R. Dull, *The French Navy and American Independence: A Study of Arms and Diplomacy, 1774–1787* (Princeton, 1975); David Erskine, ed., *Augustus Hervey's Journal: Being the Intimate Account of the Life of a Captain in the Royal Navy Ashore and Afloat, 1746–1759* (London, 1954); Alan Frost, *Voyage of the Endeavour: Captain Cook and the Discovery of the Pacific* (St. Leonards, New South Wales, 1998); John Harland, *Seamanship in the Age of Sail* (Annapolis, 1984); R. J. Hill, *The Oxford Illustrated History of the Royal Navy* (Oxford, 1995); W. Johnson, "The Siege of Gibraltar: Mostly relating to the Shooting of Hot Shot and Setting Fire to a Besieging Fleet," *International Journal of Impact Engineering* 6:3 (1987): 175–210; Paul M. Kennedy, *The Rise and Fall of British Naval Mastery* (London, 1976); Brian Lavery, *Nelson's Navy: The Ships, Men and Organization, 1793–1815* (London, 1989); Charles L. Lewis, *Admiral De Grasse and American Independence* (Annapolis, 1948); Nicholas A. M. Rodger, *The Wooden World: An Anatomy of the Georgian Navy* (London, 1986); Nicholas Rogers, *Crowds, Culture and Politics in Georgian Britain* (Oxford, 1998); and Glyndwr Williams, ed., *Documents Relating to Anson's Voyage Round the World, 1740–44* (London, 1967).

Finally, the American Revolution has been studied from almost every perspective. Strangely, however, the military history of the war has not attracted as much attention as other areas. For an introduction to the field, see R. Arthur Bowler, *Logistics and the Failure of the British Army in America, 1775–1783* (Princeton, 1975); E. Wayne Carp, *To Starve the Army at Pleasure: Continental Army Administration and American Political Culture, 1775–1783* (Chapel Hill NC, 1984); Louis Clinton Hatch, *The Administration of the American Revolutionary Army* (New York, 1970); Don Higgenbotham, *The War of American Independence: Military Attitudes, Policies and Practice, 1763–11789* (Bloomington IN, 1971); Christopher Hibbert, *Redcoats and Rebels: The American Revolution Through British Eyes* (New York, 1990); Lee Kennett, *The French Forces in America, 1780–1783* (Westport CT, 1977); Charles Royster, *A Revolutionary People at War: The Continental Army and American Character, 1775–1783* (Chapel Hill NC, 1979); Sylvia R. Frey, *The British Soldier in America: A Social History of Military Life in the Revolutionary Period* (Austin TX, 1981); Joseph P. Tustin, trans., *Diary of the American War: A Hessian Journal by Captain Johann Ewald* (New Haven, 1979); and W. J. Wood, *Battles of the Revolutionary War, 1775–1781* (New York, 1995).

9. THE REVOLUTIONARY ERA

Napoleon Bonaparte, ranked by Carl von Clausewitz as a true genius at the operational art of war (that is, the actual deployment of combat forces), enjoyed a truly meteoric rise to power: army commander at age twenty-seven, ruler of France at thirty, and emperor at thirty-five. David Chandler, a leading scholar of the Napoleonic wars, argues that in the field Napoleon displayed "a fertile imagination (for adapting plans to particular situations), and intuitive sense (to divine the enemy's intentions), indomitable will power(to get his way no matter what opposition he faced), and firmness of soul (or his refusal to allow his main purpose to be diverted or blunted by the wear and tear of minor accidents and complications)."

For generations to follow, the name of Napoleon was synonymous with French revolutionary warfare. Mobilization of the nation's manpower and material resources for war, an emphasis on morale and élan, concentration of forces at the decisive point, rapidity of movement, ruthless pursuit of a beaten foe—all these Napoleonic traits became accepted axioms of nineteenth-century warfare. Henri Jomini immortalized Napoleon's campaigns as an exact science in his *Precis of the Art of War*. Even Queen Victoria enhanced the Napoleonic legend when on a state visit to France she forced the future King Edward VII to "kneel down before the tomb of the great Napoleon" at the Invalides shrine. Nor was Bonaparte's widely recognized genius limited to Europe. Dennis Hart Mahan brought Napoleon to West Point by way of Jomini: French was the only foreign language taught at the academy, a Napoleon Club was started to familiarize the cadets with the great captain, and the academy's library was imported from France. Dennis Hart Mahan's son, Alfred Thayer Mahan, eventually honored all three men by naming his dog "Jomini."

But how much of this is hyperbole and how much reality? Where is the dividing line between fact and fiction in the Napoleonic legacy? Put differently, what changed under Napoleon in terms of some of the major subthemes of this book—the idea of war, the impact of civilian as well as military technological innovation on warfare, the nature of armies, and the experience of the soldier? This chapter will suggest that much in the way of "revolutionary warfare" was in place by the time that Napoleon arrived on the scene and that he was both inheritor and benefactor of this revolution in the art of war. Through a combination of meticulous planning and flexible execution, Bonaparte raised French revolutionary warfare to a level that both terrified and mystified his contemporaries. In short, the Revolution created the political, social, and economic conditions that enabled France to become a superpower and Napoleon a potential hegemon.

Eighteenth-century armies, as was shown in the previous chapter, were severely limited both in size and mobility. While Gustavus Adolphus in Sweden had organized an army of 70,000 men and the French had 400,000 men under arms during the War of Spanish Succession, the overall strength of field armies generally had been deemed optimal at 50,000 men by commanders such as Maurice de Saxe and John of Nassau. In fact, the field strength of Gustavus Adolphus's armies hovered between 16,000 soldiers when he first arrived on the Continent in 1630 and 30,000 at the height of his campaigns in the German states. But the French Revolution and the Napoleonic Empire changed that calculus drastically. Universal male conscription, the greater administrative power of the French state, nationalism, technology, and the early industrial revolution affected the size and killing power of the modern army. At the battles of Wagram (1809) and Borodino (1812), for example, Napoleon commanded about 250,000 combatants; the paper strength of his armed forces, in fact, had approached 1 million men. The Battle of Nations at Leipzig in 1813 became a milestone of sorts as Bonaparte marshaled 460,000 soldiers on the field that day. But before Bonaparte, European *ancien régime* armies tended to be limited both in size and in operation.

Transportation was a major impediment to military deployment. Roads were generally poor, and carriage gauges varied greatly, with the result that not even ruts in the soft sand were standard. Water transport likewise was an inhibitor. While vast numbers of draft animals were required to pull rafts and floats up river from shore, these same rafts were usually disbanded when coming downstream and their logs sold to sawmills. Maps were both scarce and grossly inaccurate. What one to-day calls cartographic infrastructure was almost nonexistent. Maps were in fact regarded as state secrets, not for distribution. F. W. Schelton's topographical atlas of Prussia in 1780, for example, was immediately secluded in the archives upon completion for fear that it could fall into hostile hands. While one could on occasion rely upon captured en-emy maps—such as Frederick II of Prussia's use of Austrian maps of Silesia—local guides were usually the most reliable source of informa-tion (and were greatly exploited by Napoleon's marshals). Finally, there existed more than a dozen different "miles" (*Meilen*) in central Europe alone; the metric system came into use only during and after the French Revolution.

What went for long-range military intelligence usually consisted of basic information gleaned from travel books, merchants, diplomats, and travelers. For tactical information during wartime, armies resorted to spies, scouts, enemy deserters, prisoners of war, and local inhabitants. News traveled at best at the rate of sixty to ninety kilometers per day. During the Seven Years' War, French commanders east of the Rhine River often had to wait two weeks for orders from Versailles. Fifty years later, news of the Battle of Waterloo reached London only by means of a private homing-pigeon service operated by the House of Rothschild. While Napoleon eventually used clocks to time his operations, his mar-shals still preferred terms such as "at the crack of dawn" and regularly neglected to note the time of major actions or battles in their dispatches to the emperor. Again, highly variable local time militated against the effective use of synchronized clocks.

Supply was perhaps the most critical issue. Even the highly disciplined armies of Frederick II of Prussia could march but for ten days before be-ing forced to halt so that new supplies and bake ovens could be brought up from rear echelon depots. Horses were always in short supply and only France and Prussia were able to maintain regular fodder maga-zines. Armies routinely halted to gather foodstuffs every four days or so. They could scarcely "live off the land" since food was abundant only during the harvest season and since requisitioning detachments had the unfortunate habit of using the opportunity to desert. Hence Sir Arthur Wellesley, the duke of Wellington's, famous description of the troops as "the scum of the earth, enlisted for drink."

The lack of reliable data further limited military endeavors. National census taking was almost unknown and only Prussia maintained rudimentary statistics on economic production and population in the famous *Acta Borussica*. Contemporary demographic estimates were often as much as 50 percent off. Most governments simply multiplied the annual number of births (when these were known) by a magical factor of twenty-four or twenty-five (or any other regional guess on the proportion of births to the general population) in order to arrive at population size. The first proper national statistical office was created in France during the Revolution under Antoine L. Lavoisier.

Military technology also had remained rather stagnant. Neither Gustavus Adolphus nor Maurice de Saxe had enjoyed decided technological advantages over their adversaries, and Napoleon likewise possessed no distinct, clear-cut technological superiority. But there was at least one advantage to this lack of technological superiority: Frederick II and Napoleon, especially, were able to incorporate entire captured armies and arsenals into their own forces.

To be sure, some technological advances had taken place. The reliability and rate of fire of flintlock muskets had been enhanced through improvements in locks, the replacement of wooden ramrods with iron ones, and the invention of the paper cartridge containing powder, wad, and ball in a single package. The immediate result of enhanced small-arms firepower was a spreading out of infantry. Maurice of Nassau's eight-rank formation had yielded to Gustavus Adolphus's standard six-man line of attack, and this, in turn, was reduced to an infantry line that was first four, then three, and finally two deep. The latter on the eve of the French Revolution featured one line firing, the other loading.

Vast spreading out of infantry complicated command and control. Tactical control was effectively limited to the battalion level (300 to 600 soldiers). Eighteenth-century armies, already renowned for their rigid discipline, were subjected to iron (indeed brutal) discipline unknown since the days of Rome. Through incessant rigid drill, Frederick the Great's soldiers were turned almost into automatons. In France, Colonel Jean Martinet's iron treatment of his soldiers added a new word to the English military dictionary. But rigid discipline allowed eighteenth-century commanders greater operational freedom. Units could now change fronts or direction in an orderly fashion, readily shift from marching column or line into battle formation, advance in orderly fashion over broken or hilly terrain, and fire by platoon rather than by linear formation. This added mobility, as manifested in Frederick's oblique order, could produce maximum fire and shock value by being massed at a chosen spot on the battlefield.

The rifle, originally used purely as a hunting weapon in the Rhineland, came into use by the end of the eighteenth century and had a further impact upon infantry tactics. Its grooved barrel imparted a twist to the fired bullet, thereby affording better accuracy and range than the smoothbore musket. The rifle was used primarily by special units called *Jäger* (hunters) in Austria and Germany. It came to North America via Pennsylvania (the so-called Kentucky rifle), where it was adapted for woodsmen in a lighter and longer-barreled version. "Light" or "rifle" regiments were used as skirmishers both by the British and by the American revolutionary armies.

Artisanal production was a final inhibiting factor on eighteenth-century warfare by keeping armaments production low. In terms of cost outlays, Frederick II of Prussia spent less than 1 percent of military expenditures on muskets, powder, and lead and about 13 percent on materials and supplies. The bulk of military outlays went for food, horses, fodder, and transport. Indeed, wars had to be kept limited in scope for economic and social reasons. Peasants were sorely needed to produce food, maintain roads and waterways, and provision armies that passed through their lands. Townsmen were needed to provide cash for the royal treasury. Thus, any attempt to expand the war effort would seriously jeopardize the state's fiscal security and endanger its agrarian-social order. Nor did rulers overlook the obvious danger inherent in permanently arming and training a sizeable portion of their population. War was designed to remain the sport of kings.

Defeat often drives reform. The French debacles at Rossbach (1757) and Minden (1759) during the Seven Years' War (1756–63), in which France joined Austria and Russia against Prussia, provided the necessary impetus for military reform down to the Revolution of 1789. The French became the great innovators in the military revolution of the late eighteenth century largely because their abysmal performance against the Frederican armies of Prussia allowed no other alternative.

At the administrative level, the French after 1763 divided their armies into self-contained, permanent strategic units for the first time since the Roman Empire. In 1776 the War Ministry partitioned France into sixteen (later eighteen) territorial military divisions and created permanent infantry brigades. These units were the first modern combined arms formations, each with its own headquarters and communications, designed to conduct independent operations for a limited time. Additionally, the French army, heeding the advice of Marshal F. M. de Broglie, by 1787 or 1788 had been arranged along divisional lines. Each division of up to twelve thousand men was established as an independent fighting unit, either complete in itself or combined with others. France also introduced the first general staffs designed as a superior headquarters to coordinate the movements of the various divisions within the army. A logical next step—finalized under Napoleon Bonaparte—was to gather divisions into individual corps, or *corps d'armée*. These were each a miniature army able to operate as much as fifty to one hundred kilometers (or several days' distance) from army headquarters. Decentralization of the main army into independent corps greatly increased the chance of an unexpected encounter with the enemy and hence the numbers of battles.

The increase in size of armies as well as their growing complexity cried out for more efficient and centralized staffs. In time, armies developed a rigorous administrative infrastructure. The replacement of military-feudal service with cash payment (*scutagium*) led to written records, receipts, pay-books, rosters, and the like. The arrival of paper from the East, the discovery of movable type and printing, Italian double-entry bookkeeping, the replacement of Roman with Arabic numerals, William Napier's discovery of logarithms, and Simon Stevin's decimal system for recording fractions—all these innovations greatly compounded the need for highly trained staff to administer military forces. In the course of the eighteenth century, military staff began to use standardized printed forms and to carry portable printing presses into campaigns with them. But while a printed general order might be issued before a battle, thereafter commands were disseminated mainly by dispatch rider. Overall command and control rested with the commander, surveying the five- to seven-kilometer-wide battlefield through a telescope, usually from a hill some distance to the rear.

Enhanced training was required for the emerging staff. Generally speaking, military academies for staff officers (*écoles militaires*) were established at Berlin, Munich, Paris, St. Petersburg, Wiener Neustadt, and Woolwich, while naval colleges were created at Brest, Dartmouth, Le Havre, and Toulon. Junior academies were founded at Potsdam and at Brienne le Château, which graduated Napoleon. By 1787 France had even established a school to teach noncommissioned officers how to read and write. And whereas Maximilien Robespierre's experimental *École de Mars* eventually failed, the Revolution was highly successful with its new engineer officer training academy (*École polytechnique*) as well as its advanced gunnery instruction at Châlons and its military engineering school at Metz. Napoleon's *École speciale militaire*, founded at Fontainebleu in 1803 and moved to Saint Cyr five years later, especially, flourished and was later copied on the shores of the Hudson River in New York. War became such a serious science that at the end of the revolutionary era a special advanced "war academy" (*Kriegsschule*) was established at Berlin.

A host of innovations in special arms development accompanied these administrative reforms. At first content merely to copy existing Prussian field manuals, the French in time turned to more sweeping reform. As early as 1765, Pierre Bourçet set up schools to train aides-de-camp in the new art of drawing up battle plans from maps (Napoleon is reputed to have used Bourçet's *Principles de la Guerre des Montagnes* to cross the Alps in 1797). Moreover, Bourçet called for the use of separate formations. An army, he argued, should march in separate divisions, using different roads, and then concentrate at the site of battle in order to ease supply problems, to enhance mobility, and to confound the enemy. With the help of Mesnil Durand, Bourçet's column tactics were incorporated into French regulations in 1787 and 1788. A standard French field manual, stressing the deployment of combinations of lines and columns, was issued for all troops in August 1791.

Undoubtedly the greatest technological reform came in the field artillery. Previously, guns had been cast in individual molds and hence been much too heavy to drag across battlefields. Gustavus Adolphus, for example, had preferred massed light artillery, with individual pieces bound together by leather (hence the term "leather cannon"). The secret to enhanced use of cannon lay in greater mobility, that is, reduced weight. Jean Maritz in Switzerland and Benjamin Robins as well as John Wilkinson in England in the 1740s devised a system whereby the gun was cast as a solid piece of metal and its barrel then bored out afterward. The result was a true bore and thinner walls—in short, a safer, lighter, more maneuverable artillery piece. Closer fit between gun tube and ball resulted in less windage and meant that smaller charges and shorter barrels could be used without reducing effect. The new field artillery soon developed an effective range five to six times that of muskets.

In France, as highlighted in the previous chapter, Jean Baptiste Vacqueville de Gribeauval between 1763 and 1767 radically reformed French field artillery. Gribeauval adapted a new screw device with an adjustable hairline and reduced gun calibers to four (four-, eight-, and twelve-pounders) plus a six-inch howitzer. Standardized parts were designed for all pieces. Shot and powder were combined in a single, prepackaged round, thereby doubling the rate of fire. In terms of administration, Gribeauval removed artillery from the hands of civilian contractors and placed it in those of the regular gun crews. The upshot was the creation of a truly mobile field artillery that could bombard targets up to one thousand yards. On the eve of the Revolution, France possessed thirteen hundred field and eighty-five hundred siege and fortress guns of Gribeauval design. The prerevolutionary ratio of one cannon per four hundred men would be cut in half by Napoleon. Gribeauval's artillery remained standard to 1829; major technological change would come only in the 1850s with the advent of breech-loaders. Gribeauval's twelve-pounder gun, later dubbed the "Napoleon" in honor of Napoleon III, dominated the battlefields of the world.

The Chevalier Jean du Teil next developed new tactics to enable the field artillery to play a more decisive role in combat. Mobile field artillery, he argued, should "concentrate the greatest quantity of fire on the principal points and on the weak spots that are most threatened"; in short, on the enemy's infantry. Du Teil's brother commanded not only a regiment but also taught the chevalier's methods at an artillery school, where his students included a young Corsican destined to become Europe's foremost artillery-man. Under Napoleon, guns would be rushed across a battlefield and then concentrated in the open against enemy infantry in order to tear gaping holes in its ranks. These would then be exploited first by infantry advancing with bayonets fixed and thereafter by heavy cavalry hacking away at the shattered formations.

In 1784 Lieutenant Henry Shrapnel of the Royal Artillery in England had developed a new artillery shell that would bear his name. Shrapnel filled a hollow iron ball with lead bullets surrounded by a bursting charge and fuse; the shell was designed to explode in the air, raining a shower of anywhere between 27 and 170 musket balls over an extended area. As the shells were prone to explode prematurely in flight due to friction heat, shrapnel came into its own only after 1852 when Captain E. M. Boxer devised a reliable fuse. Shrapnel was extremely lethal to troops moving over open ground. In 1880 at Ahmed Kheyl, Sir Donald Stewart's force of only seven thousand men held off an entire Afghan army by shattering its charge at close range with shrapnel. "The ground before the guns was covered with heaps of torn and mutilated dead and dying." Four years later at Tamai, a British battery of four guns firing shrapnel mowed down on-rushing Sudanese dervishes who had broken into the British square.

Cavalry, for its part, saw little in the way of major reform. Throughout much of Europe, horsemen armed with light muskets and pistols were deployed alongside infantry, firing their weapons as they advanced. Only in France and Sweden was cavalry assigned shock action with sabers. Frederick II of Prussia by the 1760s had restored cavalry to its traditional roles of reconnaissance and shock action. With the exception of dragoons, who were heavily armed with swords, shortened muskets, bayonets, and pistols and who were trained to fight on foot as well as on horseback, Prussian cavalry was denied firearms and retrained to use the saber. It was deployed independent of infantry and instructed to charge at full gallop in lines of three and later two rows deep. Generally speaking, European cavalry by 1800 constituted from one-fourth to one-sixth of most armies. Heavy body armor had largely been abandoned: at Waterloo, only the cuirassier's helmet and breastplate remained from former times. Cavalry's functions remained screening, reconnaissance, and pursuit. For hostile infantry, it definitely retained its tremendous shock value. New was "light cavalry." First developed in Austria during the Seven Years' War as skirmishers modeled upon the Croatian units defending the border with Turkey, these forces were deployed as sharpshooters or as special units to interfere with enemy convoys and generally to harass the enemy's rear.

Infantry remained the queen of battle. It changed little in terms of technology. As previously noted, the standard weapon was the smooth-bore flintlock musket and ring bayonet. The French pattern 1777 muzzle-loader, which remained in use until 1815, had an effective range of about one hundred yards. Twelve separate motions were required to load and fire the weapon, and a good infantryman could repeat this cycle two or three times a minute. Experiments with breech-loading muskets after 1768 had not proved successful. Musket fire was most effective when massed at point-blank range and inflicted casualty rates of 10 to 15 percent per volley. It was not uncommon even for victorious armies to sustain 40 percent casualty rates. In 1798 Eli Whitney, the inventor of the cotton gin, introduced the manufacture of muskets with interchangeable parts, thereby forecasting the mass production of guns. The cold steel of the bayonet remained a highly feared weapon, yet Napoleon's surgeon, D. J. B. Larrey, estimated that his staff treated one hundred small arms or artillery wounds for every bayonet wound.

The crux of the revolution in military affairs that took place during the French Revolution was not technological but political. Especially the Revolution's ability to combine hardware, training, doctrine, organization, and patriotic fervor into a decisive whole forever changed the nature of combat. Before the Revolution, war had been the concern solely of the monarch and his advisers. The king's agents recruited soldiers for fixed terms and fixed pay, which came from the sovereign's treasury. The nobility supplied the vast majority of officers. While the highest ranks were dominated by leading aristocrats with court connections (*noblesse presentée*), lesser noblemen filled the lower commissioned ranks. The Segur Law of 1781, requiring four generations of aristocratic lineage for entry into the officer corps, not surprisingly antagonized many French middle class and newly ennobled aspirants. The purchase of commissions gradually was phased out (and abolished in February 1790) in France, while royal rules of promotion were not only made uniform but also public. In 1790 it was decreed that commissions could be garnered only by competitive examination and that peacetime promotion up to the rank of colonel would be based on seniority rather than patronage.

Enlisted personnel for France's *ancien régime* army was drawn from society's lower orders. Many joined to escape a dull village life or as an alternative to imprisonment. Wine, false promises, deception, and the use of force were customary devices to "persuade" young men to take up soldiering. Desertion, which in the relatively peaceful 1780s ran at about 3,000 men a year, made it virtually impossible to maintain a ready reserve. The Bourbon monarchy maintained 198,000 men at a cost of 115 million livres annually on the eve of the Revolution.

Royal finances dictated the nature of warfare. As Cicero had already observed concerning the never-ending cost of war in the days of Rome, *pecuniam infinitam*. In France the absence of credit institutions, the incoherent taxation system, and the aristocratic resistance to tax reform militated against mobilization of the nation's military potential. Yet even in this most sensitive of reform areas, the French had been surprisingly daring. In 1772 Comte J.-A. H. de Guibert had published his famous *Essai genéral de Tactique*, in which he advocated not only a synthesis of line and column (*l'ordre mixte*) and greater strategic mobility, but even the development of a citizen militia. Guibert had also suggested that such an army could subsist on its enemy's resources. Undoubtedly recognizing that his proposals presupposed a social revolution, the comte later apologized for his temerity.

Indeed, the social and economic restraints of the Old Regime precluded dramatic innovations in the French army. Few, if any, of Guibert's contemporaries could have guessed that just over the horizon lay the mobilization of the full range of the nation's resources or that its people would become full participants in war. Fewer still could have imagined that Europe was about to plunge into more than two decades of almost uninterrupted warfare. Prime Minister William Pitt (the Younger), introducing the budget of 1792 in Britain, happily assured the House of Commons that "there never was a time in the history of this country, when, from the situation in Europe, we might more reasonably expect fifteen years of peace than we may at the present moment."

The truly revolutionary nature of the new relationship between the French nation and the art of war came out perhaps most clearly in the Convention's *levée en masse* decree of August 23, 1793. In April 1792 the French Legislative Assembly, believing that the Revolution could never be secure at home unless it spread to the rest of Europe, had declared war ("War of the First Coalition," 1792–97) against the monarchs of the Old Regime. The so-called second revolution of August 1792 brought about the National Convention and the Terror. The Convention's decree of the *levée en masse* is worth citing at length: "Article I. From this moment until that in which our enemies shall have been driven from the territory of the Republic, all Frenchmen are permanently requisitioned for service in the armies. Young men will go forth to battle; married men will forge weapons and transport munitions; women will make tents and clothing and serve in hospitals; children will make lint from old linen; and old men will be brought to the public squares to arouse the courage of the soldiers, while preaching the unity of the Republic and hatred against kings." Therewith, the nature of modern warfare had entered a new phase, one in which total effort was demanded of the populace regardless of age, gender, race, or creed.

The decree, which had been passed partially owing to the efforts of Lazare Carnot, the fabled "organizer of victory," called to arms all unmarried men between eighteen and twenty-five years of age. While execution of the decree lagged far behind intent, revolutionary France nevertheless managed to marshal for its field armies five hundred thousand men by the end of the year. Most importantly, subjects now became citizens with a personal stake in the Republic's survival. And having won the loyalty of the vast majority of Frenchmen, the Republic could with confidence place arms in their hands.

The most radical characteristic of the *levée en masse* was its call to mobilize the manpower and material resources of the entire nation for war. By the time that King Louis XVI attempted to flee the country in 1791, almost half of the officer corps was in exile; an additional six thousand officers left France between 1791 and 1796. The assembly tackled the resulting acute shortage in two ways. The National Guard was greatly expanded and its officers (at least to April 1795) elected in each district and a volunteer army drafted men by lot, initially for six months service but by 1792 for twelve months. In January 1794 the assembly decreed the amalgamation of both regulars and volunteers. Loyalty to the nation, a desire to protect the gains of the Revolution, fear of punishment, peer as well as public pressure, and economic calamities (poor harvests, catastrophic inflation, unemployment) generally assured the assembly of sufficient recruits. Not even the general mobilization between 1793 and 1794, which made enlistment indefinite, kept young men from serving the Republic. And when shortages did occur as a result of years of almost uninterrupted warfare, they were easily compensated by forced call-ups in the "liberated" lands. Napoleon's 611,000-man *Grande Armée* in 1812, for example, included only 230,000 men from "old France."

In the six years following the recruitment legislation of 1792, France lost the service of 600,000 men in battle. Consequently, during the "War of the Second Coalition" (1798–1801), in which Bonaparte hoped to strike at England's possessions in India indirectly by way of invading Egypt, the Directory in 1798 passed the Loi Jourdan. "Every Frenchman," it decreed, "is a soldier and owes himself to the defense of the *patrie*." All males between the ages of twenty and twenty-five were to report for medical exams and registration. The legislature annually was to decide how many men to impress, the Ministry of War would assign quotas to each *département*, and local authorities would choose recruits from the lists, starting with the youngest. By 1799 it became legal to choose substitutes, thereby effectively negating the Revolutionary principle of equality. But the new conscription act served Napoleon well. Approximately 1.3 million conscripts, or 41 percent of France's eligible males, were enrolled through the Ministry of War between 1800 and

1812. Modern armies thus not only radically enhanced their size and killing power by way of conscription, centralized state power, nationalism, and early industrial output, but also their ability to take punishment. The Loi Jourdan basically remained in effect until 1871.

The material needs of the revolutionary armies were satisfied surprisingly easily. While French arsenals had been depleted as a result of the American War of Independence—France had sent the rebellious colonies no fewer than 100,000 muskets—stocks had been replenished to 245,500 muskets by 1791. The number of Gribeauval artillery pieces doubled from 1,300 in 1789 to more than 2,600 in 1795. The former royal weapons factories at Maubeuge, Charleville, and Saint Étienne were augmented by additional facilities at Autun, Clermont-Ferrand, Montauban, and Paris. Once again, Napoleon was the chief benefactor of the Revolution's efforts. Production of iron cannon under the empire increased from nine hundred to thirteen thousand per annum. Seventeen new foundries added fourteen thousand bronze pieces a year to the total. With regard to small arms, France between 1805 and 1815 produced 3.9 million muskets, rifles, carbines, and pistols—almost one million more than Britain. In short, revolution and empire greatly enhanced both the quantitative and qualitative supply of men and weapons for modern warfare.

The revolutionary government also actively recruited the best scientific and engineering minds of the day, including Prieur de la Côte d'Or and Gaspar Monge, to supervise the nation's mobilization for war. Over time, 258 new public workshops employed five thousand men to produce 750 muskets a day. When war cut off the supply of saltpeter from Turkey and when scrapings from stables and latrines no longer met the national requirement, chemists devised a way of synthetically manufacturing this critical ingredient of gunpowder. The copper required for bronze cannon was found by requisitioning church bells. The need for iron likewise was met through "nationalizing" wrought-iron fences and gates. Private blast furnaces as well as confiscated churches and chapels were converted into cannon foundries, mass producing series of artillery pieces of similar caliber. New networks of roads, canals, and bridges enhanced the movement of artillery and supplies to the point where eighteen days' stock of food became the norm for the army. Each soldier carried three days worth of food, the bread wagons of each company hauled a further six days' supply, and flour wagons of the commissary were responsible for the remaining nine days' supply. But total mobilization of the nation's resources still lay beyond the ability of the state due to lack of data concerning its overall material and manpower reserves. The Revolution was thus forced to rely on a combination of compulsion, exhortation, and payment at fixed prices (Law of the Maximum) to meet its needs. Finally, it resorted to large-scale plundering on foreign soil (Belgium, Germany, Italy) to pay for the massive war effort.

France's revolutionary armies also experimented with new technology. A semaphore telegram developed by Claude Chappe linked Paris to the front, and a research center at Meudon conducted tests with pyrotechnics and experimental weaponry. The Revolution's arsenal also included Montgolfier hot-air balloons, and a pioneering company of *aerostatiers* was formed in April 1794. First battlefield use of balloons came in June 1794 at Fleurus. Napoleon experimented with observation balloons during the Italian campaign in 1796 and two years later took a balloon company to Egypt (where it fell into the hands of the Royal Navy). Yet, in the final analysis, the *aerostatiers* proved to be of little military value. The time required to inflate—often as much as forty-eight hours—was too great to benefit ground commanders; balloons flew too high to be effective; and crews usually were too inexperienced to make accurate observations. There was also the problem of communicating with the ground: flag signals routinely were missed or misread and pigeons used to send messages to the ground often lost their way and some were captured and eaten by the enemy.

Neither the revolutionary nor the Napoleonic regime managed successfully to address the deplorable state of military medicine. While the Convention established three new National Schools of Health and the Committee of Public Safety made physicians, surgeons, and pharmacists liable for military service, "abandonment and disdain of the wounded" remained the rule in the French army. There were, of course, no anesthetics or antiseptics (save vinegar) and the wounded were often left on the field for hours or even days, by which time sepsis, peritonitis, and dehydration took their toll. Eventually, two reformers did have an impact upon military medicine. Dominique-Jean Larrey and Pierre-François Percy became convinced that the wounded should be treated during, not after, battle and to this end designed casualty evacuation vehicles and "flying hospitals" (*ambulances volantes*).

Surgery remained primitive. Its practitioners continued to be popularly associated with barbers, and their tools of trade were limited to knives, scalpels, saws, forceps, sponges, and pins, augmented by a little opium and canteens of spirits. After the Battle of Vimeiro in 1808, for example, a British private recalled the surgeons "with their sleeves turned up, and their hands and arms covered with blood looking like butchers in the shambles." Diseases were almost untreatable in the field. Typhus, typhoid, dysentery, and enteric fever ravaged the French Grand Army in Russia. According to one estimate, Napoleon lost 219,000 soldiers during his invasion of Russia in 1812 through disease—as compared to 105,000 through combat.

The future of revolutionary France, of course, would depend upon its ability to survive in the monarchical concert of Europe. On April 20, 1792, as stated above, France had declared war on Austria and Prussia largely in an attempt to shore up its power and to resolve domestic problems. How well would the new armies perform in the field? Would the citizen recruits bolt at the first smell of gunpowder? And could the hastily promoted 593 new generals shoulder the responsibility of command?

The so-called cannonade of Valmy in September 1792 was the baptism of fire for the revolutionary armies. About 36,000 French soldiers faced 34,000 Prussians; the French lost 300 officers and men and the Prussians, 184. A cold, drizzling rain convinced the Prussian commander, Karl Wilhelm, duke of Brunswick, not to engage the French. "We will not fight here." But the very fact that the French recruits had not panicked during the artillery duel—which on the French side had included forty Gribeauval pieces—gave the Revolution a much needed propaganda victory. The German poet, Johann Wolfgang von Goethe, an observer that September 20, immortalized the "battle" in his memoirs: "From this place and from this day forth commences a new era in the world's history and you can all say that you were present at its birth."

Goethe's hyperbole notwithstanding, the French army had stood its ground. But the leaders of the Convention fully realized that wars were not won by standoffs or moral victories. Hence, they busied themselves honing especially command and control over the armies in the field. In April 1793 the Convention created a Committee of Public Safety to energize the war effort. Two decrees in October and December empowered the Committee to nominate generals and to conduct diplomacy. The Convention's military section under Carnot over time came to dominate the national war effort through its small staff (*Bureau topographique*) in the Tuileries. It sent no less than sixty generals to the guillotine for the unpardonable crime of having lost a battle. Battlefield success as well as political reliability rather than social standing and seniority were critical for promotion—indeed, survival—in the armed forces of the Republic.

The Convention's most radical innovation was the appointment in April 1793 of special "representatives of the people" (*représentant en mission*) "to each and every army of the Republic." The Representatives on Mission were to speed up conscription, secure weapons and supplies, and keep Paris informed of developments at the front. In effect, they assured civilian control over the military. They would be copied in the twentieth century by totalitarian regimes in the Soviet Union, Germany, and China. At their most extreme, the representatives could conduct summary executions of front commanders in the name of the people.

The Convention also refined the army's organization. In 1794 after experimenting with Austrian (Wurtz) "flying batteries" of horse artillery featuring light caissons, the Convention created an independent corps of "Light Artillery." That same year Carnot refined Bourçet's divisional system: by integrating infantry, cavalry, and artillery into single divisions, Carnot rendered them capable of operating independently in the field. Moreover, each line battalion joined two conscript battalions in a new formation, the demibrigade of 2,437 men. Two demibrigades were then combined in a brigade and two or more brigades formed a division, commanded by a general of division (lieutenant general). Divisional strengths varied widely, ranging from 7,800 to 13,400 men. When combined with cavalry, field artillery, service troops, and a small staff, the multiarms division attained the character that it would maintain until the First World War. The corps structure became a permanent feature of the French Army only by 1804.

This plethora of reforms finally came to fruition in revolutionary field tactics. By 1793 and 1794, formal tactics had been abandoned in favor of what Louis Antoine de Saint Just termed "shock tactics." The "natural combativeness of a highly politicized army" shaped the nature of the battlefield. In February 1794 Carnot translated Saint Just's order into his famous "general instructions," wherein he admonished his generals "always to maneuver in mass and offensively; to maintain strict, but not overly meticulous discipline . . . and to use the bayonet on every occasion." Indeed, Carnot had already devised his own revolutionary recipe for victory at Wattignies in the previous autumn: speed of march, concentration at the strategic point, aggressive tactics, use of skirmishers, and patriotic fervor expressed by singing revolutionary songs. Such "horde tactics" were denounced by one French Royalist officer as a process whereby "fifty savage beasts foaming at the mouth like cannibals hurl themselves at top speed upon soldiers whose courage has been excited by no passion." In the case of domestic opposition, as occurred in the royalist Vendée, the Convention's search and destroy columns (*colonnes inferneles*) turned the area into "heaps of ashes, death, and famine." The precise order of the eighteenth century had yielded to the unbridled passion of the nineteenth.

By the time of Napoleon Bonaparte's famous "whiff of grapeshot" (in reality, canister) in 1799, much of the reform work had been accomplished. The "little Corsican" inherited large conscript armies endowed with revolutionary ardor, led by ambitious and tested commanders, and accustomed to a mobile, offensive, and ruthless way of war. Living off the land had become a national policy and plunder a French tradition. Napoleon added to this raw material his own genius in the art of war and his tremendous ability to inspire fierce loyalty in his troops but also his paranoid obsession with total security.

Napoleon introduced few fundamental changes in the army's organization and tactics before 1808. He retained the three battalion demibrigade (renamed regiment in 1803) as the basic infantry unit. He continued to use the division (composed of three, four, or five regiments) and only after 1804 organized them into multiarms corps. The latter, first tried in 1800 when General Jean Victor Moreau grouped the eleven divisions of the Army of the Rhine into four corps, varied in size and composition mainly in order to baffle enemy intelligence. Marshal Michel Ney's VI Corps, composed of three infantry divisions and one of cavalry (24,000 soldiers in all) perhaps was typical.

Napoleon inherited the so-called attack column from the Revolution. Carnot had developed the column as the standard infantry formation in large measure to compensate for the poorly trained hordes that were created by the *levée en masse*. It took incredibly brave and well trained soldiers to man the thin linear system of most European armies and Carnot could hardly expect the Revolution to provide him with such troops. Instead, he deployed a number of linear battalions in depth to provide cohesion and security for the raw recruits. Under Napoleon, the attack column, which should not be confused with the phalanx or the Spanish square, provided flexibility and versatility. Trained by the hard master of war, French infantry columns could easily march over broken terrain and deploy in numerous formations. Above all, the use of columns allowed Napoleon to bring his infantry in close order and rapidly to the front—usually in time to exploit holes blasted in enemy formations by French artillery.

Napoleon abolished regimental artillery both to enhance infantry's mobility and to provide greater firepower at higher command echelons, most notably the Army Artillery Reserve. By 1805, this branch boasted over eighty-three hundred howitzers, seventeen hundred mortars, forty-five hundred heavy guns, and seventy-three hundred medium guns—a ratio of about three guns per thousand troops. "Great battles," Napoleon once remarked, "are won by artillery." His favorite stratagem was to mass his artillery into a *grande batterie* designed to support his efforts at the critical sector of the battlefield and literally to blast holes into his adversary's line, which could then be exploited by the infantry.

Cavalry was used principally as a shock force. Napoleon not only concentrated his cavalry during battle but supplied it with horse artillery. His favorite tactic was to unleash the cavalry against hostile infantry already shaken by massive artillery bombardment. French cavalry was superb at exploiting initial successes through lightning pursuit of disorganized enemy units. In terms of organization, Napoleon removed cavalry from divisional command and reorganized it into a separate Army Cavalry Reserve.

Napoleon's perhaps most successful stratagem was to carry on the Revolution's policy of basing promotion primarily upon merit. "The career open to talent" (*la carrière ouvert aux talents*), a revolutionary concept that had made possible Napoleon's own rise to power, became a byword for the Napoleonic meritocracy. Moreover, officers continued to be recruited and promoted from the ranks (nearly 50 percent of the corps by 1805) on the basis of meritorious service. Defeat at the hands of Napoleon would force many European powers—most notably Prussia—to adopt similar policies. But victory also produced nepotism: Napoleon's brother Jérôme became king of Westphalia, Joseph became king of Naples and Spain, and Louis became king of Holland. The emperor's marshals in time behaved less like revolutionary representatives and more like Oriental potentates. The ranks continued to be recruited under the Loi Jourdan of 1798: no fewer than 1.3 million Frenchmen were called to serve the emperor between 1800 and 1812. But even here, the customary eighteenth-century brutal discipline gave way to regimental pride, patriotism, and plain élan.

Fig. 9.1. *The Great Captain: Napoleon at the Battle of Austerlitz, 1805.*

Napoleon was the master at the operational art of war. He customarily began a battle by using maneuver to gain a strategic advantage. Thereafter, he sought a general battle in order to destroy the enemy's army. Tactically, the emperor often directed his main blow against the adversary's flank while concurrently assaulting his center. At other times, he pressed for a decision both by breaking through the hostile center and by simultaneously enveloping the hostile flank. In both cases, Napoleon supported his advancing infantry attack columns with massed artillery fire; divisions whose flanks were exposed could be assured of protection from French cavalry. The enemy's political and strategic centers concerned Napoleon only after this initial operational success.

Combining forethought with flexibility, Napoleon always sought to strike boldly and decisively in order to throw his adversary off balance and to impose his will upon that of the enemy commander. The emperor typically struck at his enemies with deep, rapid, slashing blows and thereafter sought to retain the initiative in order to deny his adversary a chance to regroup his shattered forces. "The loss of time," he once suggested, was "irreparable in war." Relentless pursuit of the demoralized enemy became the norm. In 1806 the Grand Army (as it had been designated the year before) marched from Bavaria to the Baltic Sea in thirty-three days, killing or wounding forty-five thousand Prussians and taking 140,000 prisoners along with one thousand cannon. "I see only one thing, namely the enemy's main body," Napoleon crowed. "I try to crush it."

Napoleon's strategic deployments were carefully planned to bring about the desired decisive battle. When the Grand Army moved, swarms of light cavalry screened its line of advance, secured its communications, and gathered information on the whereabouts of the enemy. The multiarms corps marched along separate routes—the strategic net often covered as much as two hundred to three hundred miles—and united again only when the main body of the enemy had been located. Napoleon thereupon deployed his forces in a loosely quadrilateral formation (*bataillon carrée*), with his corps at best a day's march apart. Final concentration usually came only at the very moment that battle was commenced.

Why, then, did "the God of War," as Carl von Clausewitz dubbed Napoleon, eventually lose the war? A host of cogent explanations have been put forth. The emperor began to underestimate his enemies as a result of his brilliant tactical masterpieces. As well, he failed to appreciate that they were reforming their forces along French revolutionary lines even as he inflicted defeat after defeat on them. Moreover, Napoleon particularly misjudged the temper of the Spanish people, with the result that instead of unconditional surrender after he had defeated the Spanish regular army, he faced a massive guerrilla campaign during the Peninsular War in Spain from 1808 to 1813. Typically, Napoleon in 1808 deserted his army in Spain never to return. His marshals were left to cope with the rising tide of guerrilla warfare, augmented by the presence of a British army under the duke of Wellington. The "Spanish ulcer" continued to drain thousands of well-trained French veterans, badly needed elsewhere, from the Imperial Army.

Tactically, British infantry eventually was able to stand up to Napoleon. Wellington maintained the two-deep line but deployed his light infantry, armed with rifles or light muskets, either individually or in close order. He combined accurate fire with a steady line. His infantry, especially when in square formation, was able to fend off French infantry as well as cavalry. Most importantly, Wellington as well as other British commanders had learned from past experience both in North America and on the Iberian Peninsula. They no longer exposed infantry to the devastating fire of French artillery until the battle had opened by placing it, wherever possible, on reverse slopes. Second, they did their utmost to protect infantry against skirmishers by building up their own light troops. And finally, British commanders used natural obstacles or their own cavalry to secure the infantry's flanks at all times.

On a deeper level, Napoleon ignored revolutionary ideology. By assuming the imperial dignity and by placing members of his family on the new thrones in Europe, he assumed the role of military conqueror and thus lost the prorevolutionary sentiment that dominated many of the states and principalities of central and south Europe. Even in Russia, it never occurred to Napoleon to rally Poles, Lithuanians, and other minorities to his cause. Nor did the emperor's indiscriminate looting and plundering—the small state of Prussia, for example, was assessed a war "contribution" of 160 million francs in 1806—endear him to the conquered peoples of Europe.

With regard to the army, Napoleon's one-man rule ultimately constrained the capabilities of his forces. During the period of the "Grand Empire" (1804–14), he became not only chief of state and supreme commander of the armed forces, but also his own foreign minister and operations officer. His staff did not generate plans and never developed independent judgment. Likewise, his twenty-six marshals (*les gros bonnets*), while excellent tactical commanders, were never instructed in his art of warfare. Near the end, the army became too large and cumbersome even for Napoleon to control personally. Mesmerized by the search for a decisive battle, he failed to see that in both Spain and Russia military solutions could not deal with what basically were political issues. Finally, Napoleon had to learn the bitter lesson that the instrument with which one conducts war tends to wear down in proportion to the duration of the conflict. Whereas at Valmy in 1792 the French had left about three hundred dead on the field of battle, by the time of the Battle of Nations in 1813 that figure had risen to sixty thousand.

Above all, Napoleon never appreciated the tenacity of the British and failed to comprehend the influence of sea power on the strategic balance. For, while the Royal Navy alone could never have defeated Napoleon, sea power in conjunction with Britain's wealth and strategic insight guaranteed a protracted war. Safe from invasion—as First Lord of the Admiralty Sir John Jervis (Earl of St. Vincent), memorably put it, "I do not say that the French cannot come. I only say they cannot come by sea"—and with its lines of commerce and communications secure, Britain was free to organize and finance (to the tune of £65 million) no fewer than seven coalitions against the French. Control of the seas further accorded the British the luxury of inserting—and, if need be, extracting—what the historian Sir Julian Corbett would later call a "disposal force" on the French periphery, be it in Portugal or Spain. The experience of the American War of Independence—the case study in the preceding chapter—had endowed Britain with a seaborne supply system capable of succoring these very forces.

In fact, war at sea had not changed dramatically during the eighteenth century. After 1750 English naval architects had abandoned lofty and ornate sterns in order to design a better-armed, more effective fighting vessel. Copper sheathing for ships' bottoms and short-barreled, large caliber guns (carronades) were introduced at the time of the French Revolution. But the customary battles of attrition (Beachy Head 1690, Malaga 1704, Toulon 1744) had yielded meager results, while the shape and strength of oak timbers limited the size of warships. Naval battles normally took place in coastal waters as one fleet prepared to enter or leave a port. Victory meant that one's own convoys sailed in safety, while those of the vanquished were swept from the sea. Yet command of what the naval theorist Alfred Thayer Mahan would later call the main "thoroughways" of maritime commerce was seldom complete: isolated raiders and merchantmen usually slipped through even a close blockade.

Life aboard ship was harsh by any standard. Admiral Horatio Nelson's sailors faced the elements without waterproof gear and went barefoot on timbered decks. They lived in cramped, damp quarters and consumed miserable food and drink. Scurvy took its toll, as did the vicissitudes of battle on board wooden vessels raked by cannon fire. A British midshipman aboard the *Neptune* at the Battle of Cape Trafalgar (1805) gave a vivid description of what a vanquished enemy vessel looked like. "She had between three and four hundred killed and wounded, her beams were covered with Blood, Brains and pieces of Flesh, and the after part of her Decks with wounded, some without legs and some without an Arm." Trust was a scarce commodity: Nelson's men were not even issued metal cutlery. Winston Churchill's later comment that rum, sodomy, and the lash constituted the traditions of the Royal Navy was not all that far off the mark for Nelson's day.

Two tactical schools of thought had emerged in England by the late seventeenth century. Both agreed on entering battle with the line-ahead formation but disagreed on how to conduct the battle once joined. The "formal" school, which dominated down to Nelson's day, argued that it was crucial to adhere to the line-ahead formation ("the parallel, conterminous, inviolable Line") at any cost. Each ship would follow in the wake of the preceding vessel and train its guns on the enemy unit closest to it. This would let the admiral of the fleet know where each ship was at any given time, assure him that each ship was pounding its hostile counterpart, and permit him to break the battle off should the need arise. The "melee" school, on the other hand, argued that, should the occasion arise, the admiral of the fleet should be able to release individual commanders to move out of the line and join in mass attacks against the enemy. This tactic, the meleeists insisted, brought to bear the traditional fighting spirit of the Royal Navy while concurrently rewarding individual initiative and daring.

Whatever the school, the Royal Navy favored the offensive. If at all possible, British commanders chose to have the wind at their backs (the weather gage) in order to bear down upon the enemy. The French, for their part, preferred the lee gage, with the wind in their faces, prepared if need be to effect a hasty escape. As a result, British guns faced down toward French hulls, while French cannon faced up into the wind, against British sails, masts, and rigging. And while the British relied heavily upon artillery, the French still placed great weight on small-arms fire. It was French marines in riggings that killed Nelson at Cape Trafalgar. Still, what the historian Colin Gray has called "the generally moderate spirit of the age" (before Nelson) was a factor for restraint. Battles of annihilation were unlikely as most admirals were content simply to "win." Admiral George Rodney with a fleet of thirty-six ships at the Saints in 1782, for example, was content with a victory that destroyed only five French ships out of a fleet of thirty.

Amphibious operations were usually restricted to desolate stretches of beach. Against fortified positions, even the best ships were unable to carry sufficient heavy guns or ammunition for a major assault; covering fire tended to be highly inaccurate; and ships' hulls were more vulnerable to shells and fire than were stone forts. Nevertheless, the British in the Peninsular War effectively used "limited interference in unlimited war." The duke of Wellington was clear that his "disposal force" in 1813 posed a threat out of all proportion to the intrinsic strength employed or the positive results that it could give. Above all, he appreciated that "our maritime superiority gives me the power of maintaining my army while the enemy are unable to do so." Such "strength in limited war" constituted what Corbett termed the true genius of the British way of war.

While Britain possessed a surfeit of talented naval leaders—St. Vincent, Duncan, Cornwallis, Keith, Collingwood, Howe, and Hood, to name but a few—Lord Nelson towers above them all by his unique combination of intelligence, eagerness for victory, tactical genius, and leadership. Nelson was the champion of the "melee" school. He understood that given the inaccuracy of the guns of his day, it was critical to close to within a few hundred yards of the enemy, to concentrate one's vessels and fire on a section of the enemy line of ships, to break up the hostile formation, and to isolate and then annihilate his scattered forces. Rapidity of fire (three broadsides every four minutes) counted far more than sheer numbers of ships. Moreover, Nelson had the Napoleonic touch when it came to rallying his troops: "England confides that every man will do his duty." And he shrewdly evaluated the psychology of the nation: "It is . . . annihilation that the country wants—not merely a splendid victory." Nelson got the chance to implement his proposals during the "War of the Third Coalition" (1803–05).

On October 21, 1805, off Cape Trafalgar, Nelson's twenty-seven ships of the line faced a Franco-Spanish fleet of thirty-three ships of the line under Admiral Pierre de Villeneuve—*un misérable*, as Napoleon later called him. In clear, simple terms, Nelson presented his captains with the plan of battle (the so-called Secret Memorandum), giving them latitude for independence of action within the overall concept. Flaunting the prevailing *Permanent Fighting Instructions* that called for massing his ships, Nelson instead divided his fleet into three divisions, with the fastest one held in reserve. The other two divisions proceeded according to the general directive worked out beforehand at Merton Place, Surrey: "I would go at them at once, if I can, about one-third of their line from the leading ship. . . . I think it will surprise and confound the Enemy. They won't know what I am about. It will bring forward a pell-mell Battle, and that is what I want." Accordingly, the English concentrated their ships with their high rate of fire to overwhelm more than half of the Franco-Spanish fleet before the head of their line could turn and come to its aid. The results were spectacular. In five hours, eighteen enemy ships were taken and eleven fled the scene of battle. About fourteen thousand officers and men—tenfold Nelson's losses—were left behind. Not a single English ship was lost. French and Spanish naval power had been broken and Britannia reaffirmed as mistress of the seas.

The French for the remainder of the war were to learn the bitter lesson that there was no substitute for sea duty. While years of blockade of French ports were hardly uplifting for British morale, the French were thereby denied even the most rudimentary training. Huddled idle in port and with numerous officers and men taken off the ships to serve with the Grand Army, the French Navy was reduced to floating hulks—a fleet-in-being, at best. The seventy ships of the line that the empire built after the Battle of Trafalgar attested mainly to the diligence of French naval yards. They did not affect British sea control.

The Revolutionary and Napoleonic wars changed the nature of warfare forever. The older traditions of dynastic wars with limited participation and limited aims were a thing of the past. By a canny combination of patriotic fervor, massive conscription, enhanced mobility, and industrial-scientific effort, the armies of revolutionary France swept the forces of the *ancien régime* from the field. Multiarms corps fighting in columns and skirmish lines, supported by massed batteries of mobile field artillery, now became the universally emulated standard in Austria, Prussia, and Russia.

Above all, the political aspects of warfare had been totally revolutionized. The old regime subject now became an active citizen, one who owed the nation military service. In return, the nation trusted the *citoyen* sufficiently to place arms in his hands. No longer afraid of desertions, the nation's military was able to divide its forces during long marches, to create special requisitioning troops, and to maneuver through woods and on foreign soil. While the broader implications of the 1793 *levée en masse* decree, designed to mobilize both male and female, young and old, remained a distant theoretical aspiration, the nation's ability between 1800 and 1815 to muster 2.5 million young men was a major achievement. And while the Convention's efforts to mobilize the nation's material resources lay beyond the physical capabilities even of the French state of the 1790s, its engineers and mathematicians, especially, were capably harnessed to the war effort. Was this a harbinger of things to come? Ironically, in 1813 Comte Henri de Saint-Simon, a man who was later to put his entire faith in science to solve modern civilization's problems, expressed his fears concerning the role of scientists in "modern" warfare. "All Europe is cutting its throat. What are you doing to stop this butchery? Nothing. What am I saying? It is you who perfect the means of destruction, you who direct their use in all the armies."

Eighteenth-century commanders such as Marlborough, Maurice de Saxe, and Frederick the Great had understood that "rapidity of movement, security of movement, ease of manoeuvre, and efficient supply were the primary conditions for victory." Unfortunately for them, they had lacked the physical means to translate their theories into reality. The Revolution was the transitional phase that created the weapon with which Napoleon terrorized Europe. But it should also be pointed out that the revolutionary and Napoleonic armies left a less savory legacy. In the Vendée and on the Iberian Peninsula, opposition to French revolutionary rule produced an escalating spiral of murder, torture, atrocities, and reprisals. In the German and Italian states, the introduction of French laws and administration quickly degenerated into an orgy of state-planned looting and plundering. The antiforeign sentiment associated with the Revolution eventually produced the bloodbath of the Terror. The ultimate legacy of the Revolution and empire was more than two decades of bloody conflict from Lisbon to Moscow and from Aboukir to Copenhagen.

Many of the states that had embraced French military reforms under Napoleon eventually returned to the spirit and forms of the eighteenth century. Artillery soon was neglected in favor of long lines of tightly packed and brightly clad infantry and glittering columns of cavalry, wheeling in precision on Europe's parade squares. The Revolution's flirtation with scientific and technological developments earned the distrust of most commanders. General staffs likewise were considered too "cerebral" by the men of the sword. Emperor Francis Joseph I of Austria summed up the feelings of many commanders when he asserted that the quality of his army "does not depend on learned officers but on brave and chivalrous men."

Finally, there was little progress in military theory after Napoleon. The great captain's legend sufficed to stifle debate. Especially Jomini's elaborate ten major maxims and three general combinations emphasizing mass, mobility, and pressure against the decisive strategic point became sacrosanct readings in military academies such as Saint Cyr and West Point. Clausewitz's *On War*, with its specific rejection of rigid formulae and schematic expositions, although translated into French in 1849 and English in 1873, had only limited impact. Above all, it was the military revolution at the operational level brought about by cheap repercussion rifle-muskets, breech-loaders, rifled artillery, dense railroad and telegraph networks, and the general staff of Helmuth von

Moltke (which first realized the forces unleashed by the industrial revolution) that transformed Napoleonic warfare by the 1860s and 1870.

Case Study: The Battle of Austerlitz

Napoleon's genius for war perhaps can best be demonstrated by the Battle of Austerlitz, fought on December 2, 1805, during the "War of the Third Coalition." Having failed in his bid to re-create a French empire in America through defeat in Haiti and the sale of Louisiana to the United States, in May 1804 Napoleon crowned himself emperor of the French. Austria thereupon signed an alliance first with England and then with Russia, and in 1805 invaded Bavaria. Napoleon, smarting from his naval defeat at Trafalgar, decided at once to eliminate the potential threat of the Third Coalition. In a bold political move he abandoned Hanover and southern Italy. Militarily, the emperor marched his army five hundred miles from northern France across Central Europe to Ulm, Vienna, and Austerlitz. It was an incomparable feat: two hundred thousand soldiers maintained an average of nearly twenty-four kilometers per day for five weeks. Along the way, they inflicted defeats upon the Austrians and their Russian allies at Ulm, Maria Zell, and Vienna. Still seeking *the* decisive battle, Napoleon advanced into Bohemia. Leaving Marshal Louis Davout with twenty-two thousand men to garrison Vienna, the emperor moved his remaining forces of sixty-five thousand men to Brünn. Aligned against him were eighteen thousand enemy soldiers under Archduke Ferdinand at Prague and ninety thousand under Emperors Alexander I of Russia and Francis I of Austria at Olmütz. Concurrently, the Austrian archdukes Charles and John struggled to bring their eighty thousand-man forces up from south of the Alps. Obviously, the Allies' strategy was to unite their numerically superior forces, circle Napoleon's right flank, and sever his lines of communications. The logical move for Napoleon would have been to retreat, reorganize, rest, and reinforce his army.

Napoleon did nothing of the sort. He correctly anticipated the Allied strategy and decided to force a decisive battle. To redress the numerical imbalance, he summoned Davout from Vienna and Marshal J. P. Bernadotte from Iglau. In a forced march, General Louis Friant's division of Davout's III Corps covered one hundred kilometers in just over thirty-six hours. Napoleon next deliberately pulled his forces off the Pratzen Heights onto low ground and over-extended his right wing by two miles. The Austro-Russian commanders took the bait: they decided

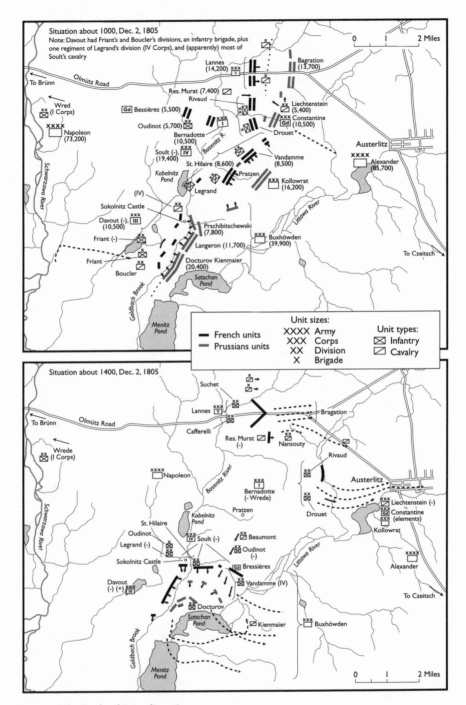

Map 9.1. The Battle of Austerlitz, 1805

to crush the exposed division and to drive a wedge between Napoleon and Vienna. In the process, they weakened their center.

On December 2 the Allies with total commitment struck the reinforced French right (8,000 additional men from Vienna). Davout had the honor of holding the "right of the line" and with the aid of Friant's exhausted division stabilized the French right flank, despite unfavorable odds of four to one. In fact, through repeated jarring local counterattacks, Davout threw the enemy assault off balance by 10:00 A.M. that morning. Thereupon Napoleon sprung his trap. Marshal Nicolas de Soult's corps stormed the Pratzen Heights, splitting the Allied front, and then wheeled south against the Austro-Russian left wing. By nightfall the Allied army had ceased to exist. Only the December darkness and falling snow prevented an even more vigorous pursuit of the enemy armies. French losses of nine thousand men measured up against Austro-Russian losses of twenty-six thousand. Tsar Alexander I escaped capture by Davout and retreated to Russia. Emperor Francis I agreed to an unconditional surrender. Six weeks after the naval disaster off Cape Trafalgar, Napoleon was master of central Europe.

The Battle of Austerlitz, fought on the first anniversary of the founding of Napoleon's empire, had shown the "little Corsican" at his innovative best. Speed, mass, and aggressive maneuver accentuated his campaign in 1805. From Ulm to Austerlitz, Napoleon had doggedly pursued his foes until a decisive battle had been fought. "Never allow any rest to either the conquerors or to the conquered," was one of his favorite maxims. Austerlitz firmly welded soldiers and standards: regiments were now allowed to add battle honors to their flags and the city of Paris donated gold laurel leaves to regimental standards to honor their role in this epic battle. A recent scholar of Napoleonic warfare has presciently observed that Austerlitz constituted the "shotgun marriage of Royal Army theory with Revolutionary improvisation."

Suggested Reading

Two useful overviews of the French army of the Revolution and empire are Gunther E. Rothenberg, *The Art of Warfare in the Age of Napoleon* (Bloomington IN, 1980), and Hew Strachan, *European Armies and the Conduct of War* (London, 1983). Three more general, philosophical works on armed forces and society have been offered by Alfred Vagts, *A History of Militarism* (New York, 1937); John U. Nef, *War and Human Progress* (Cambridge MA, 1950); and, more specifically with regard to the Prussian-German case, by Emilio Willems, *A Way of Life and Death: Three Centuries of Prussian-German Militarism. An Anthropological Approach* (Nashville, 1986). The general topic of technology and armed forces can be pursued in William H. McNeill, *The Pursuit of Power: Technology, Armed Force, and Society since A.D. 1000* (Chicago, 1982), and Martin van Creveld, *Technology and War: From 2000 B.C. to the Present* (New York, 1989). Moreover, Martin van Creveld's *Supplying War: Logistics from Wallenstein to Patton* (Cambridge, 1977), contains an interesting chapter on Napoleonic warfare ("An army marches on its stomach!").

The reform period prior to the French Revolution has been admirably investigated by Samuel F. Scott, *The Response of the Royal Army to the French Revolution, 1787–1793* (New York, 1978). The older work by Henry S. Wilkinson, *The French Army before Napoleon* (Oxford, 1915), is still worth reading. The evolution of English warfare before the French Revolution is detailed by David C. Chandler, *The Art of War in the Age of Marlborough* (New York, 1976). French tactics prior to 1789 are handled by Robert A. Quimby, *The Background of Napoleonic Warfare: The Theory of Military Tactics in 18th Century France* (New York, 1957), while those of the Revolution are tackled capably by John A. Lynn, *The Bayonets of the Republic: Motivation and Tactics in the Army of Revolutionary France, 1791–94* (Urbana IL, 1984).

For Napoleon, the student should consult the splendid works of David G. Chandler, *The Campaigns of Napoleon* (New York, 1966), and *Napoleon's Marshals* (New York, 1987). A brief evaluation of the "little Corsican" can be gleaned from Peter Paret, "Napoleon and the Revolution in War," in Peter Paret, ed., *Makers of Modern Strategy from Machiavelli to the Nuclear Age* (Princeton, 1986). Baron Jomini's writings on Napoleon are analyzed by John Shy, "Jomini," in the same volume. Most recently, John R. Elting has provided an excellent account of the Grand Army: *Swords Around a Throne: Napoleon's Grande Armée* (New York, 1988).

The experience of the rank and file in warfare has been examined by T. McGuffie, *Rank and File: The Common Soldier in Peace and War, 1642–1914* (Hutchinson, 1964), and the effect of artillery upon the battlefield is presented by B. P. Hughes, *Firepower Weapons' Effectiveness on the Battlefield 1630–1850* (London, 1974). The development of military medicine can be researched in J. Laffin, *Surgeons in the Field* (Dent, 1970). Finally, readings in naval warfare should start with Julian S. Corbett, *Some Principles of Maritime Strategy* (Annapolis, 1988), and Colin S. Gray, *The Leverage of Sea Power: The Strategic Advantage of Navies in War* (New York, 1992). Tom Pocock, *Horatio Nelson* (New York, 1988), is a most recent, highly readable study of the renowned British naval leader. A general account of the Anglo-French naval wars is in Alfred T. Mahan, *The Influence of Sea Power upon the French Revolution and Empire*, 2 vols. (Boston, 1892).

10. THE BEGINNINGS OF INDUSTRIAL WARFARE

Conservatism and orthodoxy were the hallmarks of post-Napoleonic warfare. Reform schemes for both weaponry and manpower collected dust in military archives as parsimonious bureaucrats were reluctant to dole out monies for innovative proposals. Commanders distrusted the French Revolution's flirtation with science and technology as well as its emphasis on mass conscript armies. The development in Prussia of a "cerebral" General Staff likewise aroused the suspicion of men of the sword. Nor did tactics change much after 1815. Artillery was neglected in favor of tightly massed infantry and brightly clad cavalry columns wheeling in precision on Europe's parade squares. And with regard to theory, Baron Henri Jomini's distillation of Napoleon's art of warfare into firm laws and procedures sufficed to stifle further debate.

But reforms came about by midcentury mainly as a result of the industrial revolution. Steam power, railroads, electric telegraph, and cables had impacts on national planning in terms of both strategy and tactics. Railroads became a major logistical weapon, permitting commanders to concentrate their forces at great speed and thereafter to resupply them. Telegraphs allowed governments to maintain constant communication with field commanders and war correspondents to keep their readership informed of daily events.

In short, the idea of war, the experience of "total" war, the impact of both civilian and military technological innovation on warfare and the nature of armies—four subthemes of this book—underwent major transformation during the beginning of industrial warfare.

After 1815 European states tried as quickly as possible to put the Napoleonic legacy of *la grande guerre* behind them. Once again, war became the sport of kings. So-called cabinet wars, controlled by the ruling elite, took the place of peoples' struggles as in the French Revolution and the Napoleonic aftermath. The notion of the nation in arms was anathema to most dynasts. Monarchs preferred small forces made up of long-serving regular troops (*l'armée de métier*), recruited from the conservative peasantry (64 percent in the Prussian army) and officered by landowning aristocrats. Such a politically reliable standing army seemed the best guarantee against radical liberal reformers, nationalists of every ilk, and socialist revolutionary insurgents. Not surprisingly, in 1815 a "Holy Alliance" was established to suppress revolutionary movements. Eight years later, French forces under Duke Louis d'Angoulême invaded Spain and crushed the reform movement of Colonel Rafael del Riego y Núñez. In 1831 Russian and Prussian forces jointly suppressed the Polish rebellion, and in 1848 Prussian formations helped stamp out liberal uprisings in Baden and Saxony.

But planners realized that such expeditionary forces were militarily ineffective for power projection. Moreover, commanding officers were fully aware that the population of Europe was growing by leaps and bounds: from 187 million in 1800 to 266 million in 1850 and to 401 million in 1900. And yet armed forces remained quantitatively static after 1815. In Prussia, for example, by the early 1850s, twenty-eight thousand young men out of an age group of sixty-six thousand escaped service annually. How could armies fulfill their roles—both as "schools of the nation" and as instruments of statecraft—if such a large part of the youth was not required to serve with the colors? Thus, it came as no surprise that Austria, France, Germany, and Italy increased the size of their standing armies from about two hundred thousand men before 1850 to eight hundred thousand by 1914. Yet in western Europe the better-off classes could still purchase substitutes or pay a special "blood tax" to avoid military service. Much the same practice was enshrined in the U.S. Conscription Act of March 1863, whereby a drafted man could provide a substitute or pay a three-hundred-dollar commutation fee. In Russia conscripts served for life.

Ironically, the conservative Prussian state was most resolute in clinging to the principle of universal male conscription for short service. Theoretically, each soldier spent two years with the regular army, five in the reserves, and eleven in the militia (*Landwehr*). At optimal strength, the Prussian army could mobilize seven annual intakes—plus the militia. Yet even in Prussia, the system was not without problems. Armies cost vast amounts of money, and legislatures were loath to provide these sums without acquiring at least fiscal control over the dynast's armed forces. The king, for his part, adamantly refused to surrender control over his "royal corps."

The result of this military conservatism was stagnation of doctrine and an initial unwillingness to adapt technology to warfare. Communication on the battlefield continued to rely on lamps and flags as well as on mounted messengers. When the electromagnetic telegraph was developed, its application to the battlefield was restricted because it lacked mobility, could easily be disrupted, and was susceptible to tapping. Even the progressive Prussians used it only to link headquarters to Berlin rather than to field armies or forward units. Cavalry and infantry likewise remained in a military coma. The former continued to be the socially and militarily favored arm. All armies stressed the shock effect of mounted mass cuirassiers, Cossacks, or Uhlans. Cavalry could be effectively deployed against urban radicals, offered employment for the scions of an atavistic warrior class, and provided much-needed income for horse breeders. Even the twenty-five-pound cuirass worn around 1850 remained an ocular symbol of the connection between medieval knight and modern cavalryman. The only reform for this branch consisted in lengthening the distance of the final charge from one hundred to eight hundred yards in order to counter massed musket fire.

Still, a major evolution in cavalry tactics came about, however briefly, during the American Civil War. The Confederate cavalry of General Jeb Stuart proved highly adept not only at reconnaissance but also at screening and raiding. At Chancellorsville in 1863, Stuart's force skillfully screened the advance of General Thomas J. "Stonewall" Jackson's corps from Union forces, thereby allowing Jackson to launch a devastating surprise attack. Using a detached column for raiding, Stuart ranged fast, deep, and far into hostile territory, hitting the enemy's supply and communications centers and then, equally swiftly, withdrawing. On the Union side, General Philip H. Sheridan recognized that improved small-arms fire had altered cavalry's tools of trade from lance and saber to carbine and pistol. Sheridan's dragoons, fighting either mounted or dismounted, interdicted supply lines and destroyed Confederate depots, thereby depriving General Robert E. Lee of bases of operations.

But the greatest "revolution in military affairs" came about by the 1850s as industrial mass production techniques were applied to the gun trade. The "Bessemer system" produced a higher quality of steel and

Fig. 10.1. Austrian and Prussian cavalry clash at Streseti, 1866 (*Reiterkampf bei Strezetic, 1866*), by Václav Sochor. Heeresgeschichtliches Museum, Vienna, BI 18.800.

the "American system of manufacture"—so-called because it had largely been developed at Springfield, Massachusetts, and in the Connecticut River valley—used automatic and semiautomatic machines to cut component parts for guns to prescribed shapes. Standardization and interchangeability of parts as well as mass production became the hallmarks of weapons production. Whereas in the late 1840s it would have taken Nikolaus von Dreyse thirty years of artisanal production to equip the 320,000 men of the Prussian army with his new "needle-gun," Antoine Alphonse Chassepot after 1866 was able in four years to produce one million of his famous breechloaders for the French army. In short, industrialization revolutionized warfare.

Muzzle-loading artillery was replaced with breech-loading guns firing armor-piercing shells and smoothbore cannon yielded to rifled guns. Cannon recoil was buffered by new controlled springs; hydraulic absorption (recoil) methods were on the drawing boards. Shells were streamlined and elongated, fixed with explosive charges and detonated by improved fuses. Smokeless powder, trench mortars, and hand grenades were in the experimental stage by the 1860s. Artillery became more mobile and more deadly as a result of these technological advances.

Perhaps the greatest revolution came in small-arms fire as the Minié ball gave way to elongated conical bullets and the single-shot muzzle-loader to repeating magazine rifles. Range, accuracy, and volume of fire increased dramatically. As a result, frontal attack by cavalry and infantry became almost suicidal—which is not to say uncommon. The character of warfare was transformed: the battlefield was spread out and troops dispersed; maneuver was stressed to take the place of frontal assaults; trench warfare emerged owing to man's natural inclination to dig in to avoid the deadly hail of iron and lead; and cavalry shock action gradually yielded in favor of screening and reconnaissance. The midcentury wars in Europe and North America reflected these changes in the nature of battle.

The American Civil War once again proved to be the pacesetter in the changing nature of warfare. In a particularly brutal application of "total war"—that is, a process whereby the sharp demarcation line between combatant and civilian was blurred if not entirely eliminated—U.S. general Ulysses S. Grant in September 1864 ordered General Sheridan to follow General Jubal Early's Confederate forces down the Shenandoah Valley "to the death." According to Grant's instructions, Sheridan was to "eat out Virginia clear and clean" and to turn the Shenandoah Valley into such a "barren waste" that even crows would have to pack their "provender" in order to fly over it after Sheridan had finished raiding it. And Sheridan did not disappoint. By mid-October, he reported, "I have destroyed over 2,000 barns filled with wheat, hay and farming implements; over seventy mills, filled with flour and wheat; have driven in front of the army over 4,000 head of stock, and have killed and issued to the troops not less than 30,000 sheep." It was a hard war.

But European armies by and large blissfully ignored these developments. In October 1854, during the Battle of Balaclava in the Crimean War, Lord Cardigan's British Light Cavalry Brigade charged up (and back down) a narrow "Valley of Death" enfiladed by Russian field batteries. In twenty minutes, the British lost 247 men (37 percent of the brigade) and 497 horses. Not to be outdone in gallantry, the Fourth French Chasseurs d'Afrique likewise charged the Russian artillery. French general Pierre Bosquet aptly commented: "It is magnificent but it is not war." And in July 1866, during the Battle of Königgrätz in the Austro-Prussian War, both Austrian and Prussian cavalry with lance and saber charged massed infantry armed with rifles and muskets. Finally, in 1870 during the Franco-Prussian War, which will be discussed as a case study later in the chapter, nearly one hundred thousand cavalrymen were likewise armed and deployed. In short, the shock tactics of the charge en masse had lost none of their fatal attraction for European cavalry since the Battle of Waterloo in 1815.

The primary function of infantry massed in attack columns also remained that of shock effect. The military theorist Jomini continued to tout battalion columns as the desired infantry formation. General Helmuth von Moltke, chief of the General Staff of the Prussian army, favored columnar deployment in which he believed the real power of decision rested. While the Prussian regulations of 1847 and 1861 stressed the desirability of maneuvering into the open, they offered no suggestion as to how this could be achieved. Command and control, concentration, and rapidity of movement, the argument ran, could be accomplished only in closed formations. In all armies there was an extreme reluctance to accept the new supremacy of small-arms fire on the battlefield. Moltke in particular warned company commanders not to allow their tight formations to deteriorate into unmanageable clusters of skirmishers; the latter, he suggested, were suitable only to deliver the bayonet charge. Indeed, the case for the bayonet was perhaps best put by Sir Hough Gough during the first Sikh war (1845–46), when, upon learning that his artillery had expended its ammunition, he cheerily replied: "Thank God! Then I'll be at them with the bayonet."

The futility of frontal assaults was demonstrated conclusively both in the Crimean War and the American Civil War. In November 1854 the Russian commander, Prince A. S. Menshikov, sacrificed twelve thousand infantrymen during an all-day assault on British positions at Inkerman. Menshikov's successor, Prince Michael Gorchkov, in a five-hour charge against French and Sardinian forces at Traktir Ridge in August 1855 lost nearly ten thousand men. The Allies likewise suffered horrendous casualties at Kerch in May and at Redan in June 1855 by hurling infantry against fortified Russian positions.

During the American Civil War, Confederate general Lee, who along with about three hundred Confederate officers had learned tactics at West Point from the writings of Jomini as distilled by Dennis Hart Mahan, launched a frontal assault at Malvern Hill in July 1862. Lee lost five thousand men in less than two hours. Undaunted, Lee repeated the maneuver precisely one year later at Gettysburg, where General George E. Pickett's "charge" cost the Confederates seventy-five hundred brave men in less than an hour. Union commanders, 750 of whom likewise had learned their tactics at West Point, were no better. In June 1864 General Grant mounted a columnar assault against dug-in Confederate positions at Cold Harbor and promptly lost seven thousand men in less than an hour. At Kennesaw Mountain that same month, General William Tecumseh Sherman's forces sustained three thousand casualties in yet another frontal assault; Confederate general Joseph E. Johnston, defending the mountain, lost only eight hundred men.

Few in Europe took these lessons to heart. Europe's soldiers decried the American Civil War as unprofessional, as a tribal affair fought between civilian warriors. They argued that American battles were sloppy and confused and deplored the lack of both a hereditary warrior class endowed with the ability to command and a distinct military tradition, or American way of war. Politically dominated volunteers hardly were designed to impress professional soldiers. Europe's military establishment nurtured a general feeling of superiority over anything American. The scale and intensity of the American Civil War left them unimpressed.

As did its "total war" rhetoric. The escalation of verbal violence during the American Civil War was perhaps best encapsulated by Union general Sherman's curt instruction to the mayor of Atlanta in September 1864: "War is cruelty and you cannot refine it. . . . We are not only fighting hostile armies, but a hostile people, and must make old and young, rich and poor, feel the hard hand of war." Or, as one of Sherman's men put it during the general's sixty-mile-wide swath of destruction through Georgia later that November, "[W]e had a gay old campaign. Destroyed all we could not eat, stole their niggers, burned their cotton & gins, spilled their sorghum, burned & twisted their R. Roads and raised Hell generally."

In terms of European warfare, it is necessary to go back to the Crimean War (1853–56) in order to detect the genesis of reform. That confused struggle among Britain, France, and Russia, in fact, was a watershed. Not only did it end the concert of Europe created at Vienna in 1815, but it revealed all the problems engendered by the stagnation of warfare since then. Inadequate stores of muskets, tediously slow supply systems, utter lack of medical facilities, and antiquated guns and ships unleashed a public outcry, which, in turn, encouraged a technological-industrial revolution. Whereas under the French Republic and Napoleon Bonaparte radical reforms had come in the areas of social and political institutions rather than in technology, this situation would be reversed in the mid-nineteenth century. For the first time, military engineering surged ahead of its civilian counterpart in innovation and production.

At sea the British emerged supreme from the wars against Napoleon. The Royal Navy in 1815 comprised 214 ships-of-the-line and 792 cruisers of all kinds. Without the threat of France and given that many of these vessels were dilapidated and antiquated, the British between 1814 and 1820 either sold or scrapped 550 ships. They could well afford to do so as there were no serious rivals at sea. The last major exchange of broadsides by wooden ships of the line occurred on October 20, 1827, at the Battle of Navarino. It was a strange affair. A combined Anglo-French-Russian force under the command of Admiral Sir Edward Codrington almost by accident exchanged volleys with a Turco-Egyptian fleet under Tahir Pasha. Both fleets were at anchor, and before the day was out, Codrington had destroyed three-fourths of the enemy fleet consisting of three ships-of-the-line, fifteen frigates, and more than fifty smaller craft. Thereafter the Royal Navy ruled supreme.

With regard to the principal sea powers, defeat drove reform once more. The French, no doubt hoping to erase Britain's naval dominance through technology, pioneered nautical innovations. In 1822 Henri Joseph Paixhans published a book entitled *Nouvelle force maritime*, in which he demanded the construction of ships protected by armor plate and mounting large-caliber guns capable of firing explosive shells. His vision eventually became reality. In 1850 France launched the *Napoleon*, capable of steaming at thirteen knots. Eight years later it unveiled *La Gloire*, a vessel protected by four-and-one-half-inch iron plates. Following France's lead, the Russians in 1853 used explosive shells to demolish a Turkish Flotilla at Sinope in the Black Sea in less than six hours. Moreover, steam power began to supplant sail and propellers replaced cumbersome paddle wheels.

Naval developments proceeded abreast in North America as well. On March 8, 1862, the Confederate ironclad *Merrimack* (css *Virginia*), sallying from Norfolk, Virginia, successfully destroyed the *Cumberland* and the *Congress*. The following day, the world's first encounter between ironclads took place in the famous, albeit indecisive, encounter in Hampton Roads between the armor-plated *Merrimack* and the uss *Monitor*, thereby inaugurating the age of armor-plated turret ships (*Monitor*). By the end of the American Civil War, the U.S. Navy was the world's largest, with 671 ships including 236 steam vessels built during the war. In terms of operations, while the line-ahead strategy still dominated most navies, a few radicals were toying with the notion of "crossing the T," that is, using superior speed to allow a fleet in single file to concentrate its fire on the lead ships of the hostile's slower line.

Even the tradition-bound British Royal Navy followed suit. It met every foreign technological challenge with one of its own. Naval engineers radically redesigned ordnance. The new guns required to puncture armor were too ponderous to be mounted in rows along a warship's side. Instead, they had to be mounted amidships, thereby necessitating the removal of masts and sails in order to create a clear field of fire. Engineers also introduced armored turrets to protect gunners from hostile fire. And since the turrets had to revolve in order to fire in various directions, they devised new hydraulic machinery and electrical ignition.

Britain's superior industrial capacity assured the country continued maritime dominance. In fact, the nascent Anglo-French naval arms race set in motion a spiral that would become familiar to later generations. Security against more powerful guns and explosive shells called for enhanced armor protection and this extra weight, in turn, demanded more powerful steam propulsion plants to drive the ship. And greater steam engines translated into greater displacement.

By the 1890s European navies were building battleships of around ten-thousand-ton displacement, powered by 10,000-horse-power reciprocal engines, mounting main batteries of four to six twelve-inch guns, and possessing best speeds of around sixteen knots. Series production of homogeneous types began in Britain in 1893. The pinnacle of this stage of naval construction was reached in 1905 with the "all-big-gun, one-caliber battleship." HMS *Dreadnought* was a seventeen-thousand-ton warship powered by 27,500-horse-power steam turbines with a main armament of ten twelve-inch guns and best speed of twenty-one knots. The vessel's arrangement of five twin turrets (one fore, two aft, two side) gave it the firing-power equivalent of three predreadnoughts firing ahead. A range finder in a tripod guided the entire broadside (6,800 lbs. metal weight). Long-range artillery duels replaced the hallowed Nelsonian "hail of fire" approach to naval gunnery.

With regard to land warfare, reform was also in order. The lackluster British performance in the Crimean War, combined with the experiences garnered from the Austro-Prussian War in 1866, caused many in Britain to reassess military practice. There were calls to end the division of responsibility between the field commander appointed by the Crown and the secretary of state for war and colonies. Others demanded that the militia, yeomanry, and volunteers be removed from the home office and likewise be placed under the secretary of state for war. Still others cried out that both the brutalizing conditions of service among lower ranks and the system of purchasing commissions and promotions in the army be ended.

The issue of reform fell on State Secretary for War Lord Edward Cardwell. His reforms were both deep and controversial. Cardwell reduced regular enlistment to twelve years, half of which could be with the reserve, and introduced the linked-battalion system whereby regiments kept one battalion at home as a recruiting and training cadre to support the battalion stationed overseas. Next, he expanded the single home battalion to three battalions of militia, both to train and to use as a reservoir of volunteers in time of war. In 1872 he abolished the purchase system and based promotion, at least in theory, on seniority and merit. In time, most officers entering service came via the Royal Military College at Sandhurst (cavalry and infantry) or the "Shop" at Woolwich (artillery and engineering). Cardwell also subordinated field commanders to the secretary of state for war, deprived lords-lieutenants of the landed gentry of their power to appoint officers in the militia, and abolished flogging. Finally, a musketry school was established at Hythe and Fleetwood and a gunnery school at Shoeburyness.

On the Continent, nothing less than a triple revolution occurred in military affairs: improved transport, small-arms fire, and artillery. Railroads offered commanders the prospect of moving men, weapons, and supplies on an unprecedented scale. In addition to rapidity of concentration—as much as fifteen times as fast as marching speed—railroads allowed troops to arrive fresh rather than exhausted from weeks of marching. By simplifying the problem of supplying a large force in the field, railroads accorded armies greater mobility. Theoretically at least, armies of hundreds of thousands of men could operate in the field for years, hundreds of miles from manufacturing centers and depots. The problem of supply beyond the railhead, however, continued to vex military planners.

Although Europe's soldiers generally discounted the lessons of the American Civil War, they nevertheless appreciated the role that railroads had played in that struggle. In a war theater the size of Europe, both Union and Confederacy had swiftly shuttled huge armies from one center of operations to another and on occasion deployed straight from railroad cars. The Union army as early as 1862 had appointed a military director and superintendent of U.S. military railroads. Daniel C.

McCallum possessed at times as many as twelve thousand troops under his command and was responsible for the maintenance of twenty-three thousand miles of track; later in the war, the Union added a further four thousand miles of new lines and maintained about two thousand miles of captured Confederate lines as well. The Prussian army between 1861 and 1866 also developed a railway department with its own staff and troops. One of the three major branches of its General Staff in Berlin was given responsibility for railroads and supplies. General Staffers later recalled that the great Moltke never made a military plan without first consulting the Prussian railroad timetable.

The range and rate of small-arms fire increased tenfold between 1840 and 1900. The front-loading, smoothbore musket had been the weapon of choice from Turenne to Napoleon. The duke of Wellington, in fact, had argued that the Brown Bess (or Tower) musket could not be improved. This notwithstanding, Captain Claude Minié in France developed a rifled gun barrel as well as a "cylindro-conoidal-shaped bullet" that enhanced range and accuracy of infantry fire. In fact, Sir William Napier in England complained bitterly that Minié's inventions would transform infantry into "long-range assassins." At least American soldiers had witnessed from their civil war the deadly nature of massed small-arms fire. Over 90 percent of all wounds inflicted during this conflict resulted from musket or rifle fire. The chief surgeon of the Army of the Potomac reported that in a few days in May 1864 his doctors had treated 1 wound from a sword, 14 inflicted by bayonets, 749 by artillery shells, and a staggering 8,218 by rifle bullets. And U.S. private firms, which in 1860 had produced a mere fifty thousand rifles, during the Civil War provided the Union army with no fewer than 2.5 million rifles.

The real revolution, however, was yet to come. In Germany Dreyse developed a breech-loading rifle that permitted its user to fire crouching or lying down, rather than standing erect as with the musket. The Prussian army in 1866 was fully equipped with the so-called needle-gun, which gave it six-to-one superiority in rate of fire over the Austrians. In France, Chassepot that same year came out with a superior version: by using a rubber ring to seal the breech, the *chassepot* allowed less gas to escape, permitting the gun to be sighted up to sixteen hundred yards, one thousand yards more than Dreyse's *Zündnadelgewehr*. Its impact on the battlefield was dramatic. In August 1870 at Gravelotte-St. Privat, one Prussian regiment sustained 68 percent casualties in less than thirty minutes charging French infantry armed with the *chassepot*.

The French also developed a rudimentary gun-carriage-mounted machine gun, the *mitrailleuse*. Like the U.S. Gatling gun, its twenty-five barrels were detonated by turning a handle; the weapon had a range of nearly two thousand yards and a rate of fire of 150 rounds per minute. The French army kept the gun so secret that troops were not allowed to train with it before 1870. Moreover, the French viewed the *mitrailleuse* as an artillery piece and failed to grasp its primary function as close infantry support.

Over time the machine gun became a most efficient and deadly weapon. By the mid-1880s, Hiram Maxim had developed a light, single-barreled, water-cooled weapon that could fire ten rounds per second and that used the force of the recoil to operate the loading, firing, and rejection mechanism. Britain, Germany, and Russia adopted the Maxim, while France and Japan opted for a Hotchkiss model that used the gases released on firing to operate its mechanism. However, no clear doctrine emerged on how to use the machine gun; most planners feared that it would lead mainly to exorbitant waste of ammunition. The U.S. Army as late as 1911 still viewed the machine gun as a "weapon of emergency." The British, on the other hand, termed it a "weapon of opportunity."

Artillery became the decisive branch of warfare. While the British stuck with wrought iron and the Austrians and French with traditional bronze muzzle-loading guns, Prussia was once again the pioneer. Driven by the negative battlefield experience with Austrian artillery in 1866, the Prussian army endorsed radical change. Alfried Krupp at Essen had already experimented with steel guns, whose advantages were that they were light, mobile, and able to take rifling as well as breech-loading. Moreover, their greater muzzle velocities meant increase in caliber. Whereas smoothbore field artillery had a range of one thousand yards and a rate of fire of two rounds per minute, Krupp's steel guns were sighted at two to three miles and fired ten rounds per minute. A special Gunnery School was established in Prussia to familiarize the troops with the new weapons.

And the technological revolution surged on. Metallic cartridges enhanced the loading and firing of guns. Alfred Nobel's discovery of nitroglycerin led to smokeless powder, which meant that the battlefield was no longer obscured by smoke, thus again enhancing range and effectiveness of artillery fire. Wille in Germany and Langlois in France even experimented with recoiled barrels—whose obvious advantage was that fire could be maintained uninterruptedly because there no longer existed the need to run the gun back up and relay it after each round. And when infantry entrenched in order to escape lateral fire, the artillery responded with the howitzer, which fired at high angles in order to reach targets that were protected to the front of the gun.

These technological-industrial innovations brought a hellish din to the battlefield. The experience of the common soldier in combat—the fifth subtheme of this book—was accurately reflected by one veteran of the Austro-Prussian War of 1866. Recalling his first encounter with modern artillery fire, the soldier, camped in a small village, later wrote: "We looked for cover, but where was one to find it in this kind of fire! The bombshells crashed through the clay walls as if through cardboard; and, finally, raking fire set the village on fire." Even a hasty retreat into a nearby wood offered no protection: "Jagged hunks of wood and big tree splinters flew around our heads. . . . Inside of ten seconds, four bombshells and one shrapnel shell exploded right in front of us. . . . We all felt we were in God's hand." When a member of the Order of the Knights of St. John rode over the battlefield the next day, he observed that "the grain fields and the great stretches of sugar beets were trampled and covered with the dead." Modern warfare had been further brutalized by the industrial revolution.

But help was on the way. Once more, the Crimean War had been the catalyst for reform. Cholera, typhus, dysentery, and scurvy had caused the British army to sustain the highest losses from disease in any war. In addition, the army had gone to battle woefully unprepared: a mere ten litters were assigned to each regiment, no winter clothing was provided for the men, no shelter tents, and only an ineffective corps of male nurses conscripted from the line. An outcry in the press, the public, and Parliament resulted in the well-known dispatch of Florence Nightingale and her corps of thirty-two trained nurses. Modern nursing was born as sanitary conditions improved immensely, wooden huts were built to house the wounded, and distinguished chefs supervised diets. Additionally, an official eight-volume medical and surgical history of the war was the first of its kind.

The Austro-Italian War of 1859 brought additional relief. Henri Dunant, a Swiss volunteer, came upon forty thousand dead or dying men at the Battle of Solferino on June 24. There existed no adequate medical care and the churches, homes, and schools of the nearby town of Castiglione already were filled with the wounded. Dunant organized local housewives, priests, and travelers to bind wounds and to comfort and

Fig. 10.2. Battery of the Dead, 1866 (*Batterie der Toten, 1866*), by Václav Sochor. Heeresgeschichtliches Museum, Vienna, BI 18.799.

feed the victims of war. In 1862 he published his graphic description of the battlefield as *Un Souvenir de Solférino* and the following year formed a committee, later to become the International Committee of the Red Cross, to formulate rules for care of those injured in combat. In 1864 the representatives of a dozen nations met at Geneva and drew up the first international treaty—in fact the first Geneva convention—whereby governments agreed to care for both friendly and hostile wounded of war. A red cross on a white field became the new symbol of care.

The American Civil War also furthered the way for reform in military medicine. The large-scale slaughter of 1862 appalled many leaders on both sides. Men who had escaped the customary camp diseases, such as dysentery, malaria, and typhoid fever thereafter, in the graphic words of historians Allan R. Millett and Peter Maslowski, were "blasted into shapeless masses of purple gore. In warm weather the bodies and parts of bodies bloated, turned black, and putrefied rapidly, filling the air with a pungent stench." Joshua Chamberlain, commander of the 20th Maine Volunteers, described the scene at Fredericksburg in December 1862: "A smothered moan . . . seemed to come from distances beyond the reach of the natural sense, a wail so far and deep and wide, as if a thousand discords were flowing together into a key-note weird, unearthly, terrible to hear and bear, yet startling with its nearness; the writhing concord broken by cries for help, pierced with shrieks of paroxysm . . .

and underneath, all the time, that deep bass note from closed lips too hopeless or too heroic to articulate their agony."

In order to provide medical succor, the Union army's surgeon-general, William Hammond, in 1862 appointed Jonathan K. Letterman medical director of the Army of the Potomac. Letterman immediately instituted three critical reforms: he established a trained ambulance corps for each army corps; he recreated mobile field hospitals of the kind that D. J. Larrey had pioneered during the Napoleonic wars; and by judicious selection of medicines and supplies, he cut by half the number of supply wagons that had to be dragged to every front. Still, the butchery of midcentury combat remained staggeringly high: U.S. combat deaths of 578,000 men in World War I, World War II, and Korea combined did not reach the Civil War total of 620,000.

In Prussia the war with Austria revealed not only the shortcomings of the army's artillery but also the sanitary inefficiency of its medical service. At the advice of army surgeon G. F. F. Loeffler, King William I called a conference of leading surgeons; the upshot was a complete reorganization of the medical service, including expansion of voluntary medical aid units. In the Franco-Prussian War between 1870 and 1871 surgeons were put in charge of each unit from battalion to regiment, division to corps, and a chief surgeon was appointed for the entire army. The wounded were expeditiously evacuated via field ambulances to dressing stations and field hospitals, while the more serious cases graduated to evacuation hospitals and finally to base hospitals. Indeed, the war between 1870 and 1871 was novel insofar as it was the first major conflict in which mortality from battle casualties exceeded that from disease (typhus, dysentery, and smallpox). Part of the answer lies in the fact that Prussian soldiers, unlike their French counterparts, had received Jennerian vaccination against smallpox. The immediate result was that the Prussians suffered only 4,835 cases of smallpox; the French, on the other hand, sustained 14,178 smallpox infections.

Surgery was on the threshold of legitimacy. Sepsis, wound infection, gangrene, tetanus, and erysipelas had ravaged all armies before 1850, when surgeons were primarily barbers and blood-letters. A scientific revolution transformed military medicine. Ether and chloroform for anesthesia came about in 1847, surgical antisepsis followed in 1867, steam sterilization of surgical instruments was practiced by 1886, and X-rays appeared on the scene in 1895. Even venereal disease was reduced to manageable proportions. While no cure existed, the Prussian army in

1835 ordered that all infected prostitutes report to and register with the police. England followed this example in 1866 with the Contagious Diseases Act. During the American Civil War, the Union army cleared up such pestholes as Nashville and Memphis by likewise forcing prostitutes to register with military authorities.

This flood of reforms in military affairs needed but one vital ingredient in order to transform the nature of warfare: a central nerve center staffed by a cadre of specially trained officers to coordinate its application to war. Again it was Prussia, where General Gerhard von Scharnhorst had established just such an institution in the Prussian General Staff in 1806, that was best situated to deal with the strategical, operational, and tactical significance of the technological revolution.

The Prussian General Staff, as we know it, was the work of Helmuth von Moltke (chief of the General Staff, 1857–88). Three principles guided him. First, Moltke took only the brightest. Competitive examinations, promotion according to merit rather than birth or seniority, rigorous training through staff rides and war games, flexibility, initiative, and iron self-discipline were demanded of all staff officers. Second, Moltke insisted that the new command-and-control system adhere to a common combat doctrine and to common operational procedures. He accomplished this by selecting annually the best graduates of the War Academy (*Kriegsakademie*) in Berlin, and thereafter by rotating staff appointments with line duty. This not only made certain that Moltke's ideas were disseminated throughout the entire army but gave the chief of the General Staff what amounted to personal representatives with each divisional and corps command. Finally, aware that most officers would never experience the complete range of operational situations, Moltke reached back to Carl von Clausewitz: the study of military history would acquaint his pupils with the many possible contingencies of armed conflict. Staff officers remained on probation throughout their tenure at the General Staff, and those who failed to meet Moltke's high standards were returned to regimental duty. In time, Moltke created three main branches of the General Staff—movements, railroads and supply, and intelligence—which were entrusted with preparing war plans and overseeing their execution, studying past campaigns, and correcting errors committed.

Moltke, by the sheer power of his intellect and personality, elevated the General Staff to a position of almost unquestioned primacy. He liberated the General Staff from subservience to the Ministry of War, acquired the right of direct communication with troop commanders, and even gained the privilege of direct access to the monarch. The brilliant victories at Königgrätz in 1866 and Sedan in 1870 prompted numerous foreign lands to emulate the Prussian staff system. Austria-Hungary followed in 1871, France in 1883, the United States in 1903, Britain and Russia in 1906, and most of Latin America by 1914.

But the Prussian General Staff system also carried within it the seeds of its eventual demise. Removed from parliamentary control, responsible for its actions only to the monarch and thus able to plan in isolation, the General Staff threatened to become quarantined from both army and nation. Even its distinct dark burgundy pants stripes tended to set its members apart from those of regular formations. Chancellor Otto von Bismarck later bitterly complained about what he called the "demigods" of the General Staff. Above all, its almost exclusive concentration on the technical side of war planning nurtured a blinkered professionalism that all too readily prompted its members to view war abstractly, as a theoretical exercise, rather than as merely one component of the national polity. But no one could argue with its phenomenal success under Moltke. The query of a bewildered divisional commander at Königgrätz in 1866 upon receiving an order from the chief of the General Staff— "but who *is* General von Moltke"—would not be repeated.

The ready recourse to arms on the part of Austria, Britain, France, Germany, Italy, Russia, and the United States in the two decades after 1850 prompted the men of the sword to ponder anew the meaning of war. What had been "normal": the short "cabinet" wars of Bismarck or the long peoples' struggle in the United States; the envelopmental strategy of Sedan or the trench warfare of Cold Harbor? Up for debate was the very essence of national strategy in an age of beginning industrial warfare.

On one side of the discussion stood the apostles of what would later be termed "total war." During the American Civil War, the Union had mobilized two million men, with its forces reaching their maximum complement of one million late in the war; conversely, the Confederacy had drafted 900,000 men, and its armed forces reached their zenith with 465,500 soldiers late in 1863. That same year, General Sherman of the Union army offered perhaps the most pungent exposition of the new style of warfare as applied to the Confederate states: "The government of the United States has . . . any and all rights which they choose to enforce in war, to take their lives, their houses, their lands, their everything, because they cannot deny that war exists there, and war is simply power unrestrained by constitution or compact. If they want eternal warfare, well and good."

In Germany, War Minister General Julius von Verdy du Vernois, a General Staff branch chief during the Franco-Prussian War, likewise wrestled with the nature of future warfare. While not as radical in his views as Sherman, Verdy du Vernois nevertheless demanded full implementation of the draft, which thirty to forty thousand young men annually escaped due to lack of funds. Verdy du Vernois coined the term "nation in arms" (*Volk in Waffen*) to define his theoretical concept. But the normally mercurial Emperor William II demurred, stating that he preferred a small, well-disciplined, and politically reliable "corps royal" to a mass conscript army. The alleged "red menace," the monarch argued, allowed no other course. In the end, German planners arrived at a compromise between the extreme poles of a domestic Praetorian guard and a revolutionary citizens' army. Bismarck's "iron law" of 1867, whereby the nation strove to maintain one percent of the populace under arms, remained in effect.

The second debate, aside from the size and the nature of armies, concerned the conduct of modern warfare. How would command and control function in an army of perhaps a million men or more? What sort of armed conflict was possible in the age of the industrial revolution? And what ends could combat serve? Again, the German example after 1871 perhaps best illustrates the nature of the debate.

General Helmuth von Moltke returned from the Franco-Prussian War a wiser soldier. A liberal humanist by temperament—as a General Staff aspirant he had translated the six volumes of Edward Gibbon's *The Decline and Fall of the Roman Empire*—Moltke developed a keen appreciation of Clausewitz's unsettling notion of warfare (escalation, friction, fog of war, and interaction). Moreover, the chief of the General Staff came to appreciate the interrelationship between war and politics. As he struggled to find a solution to the problem of a possible two-front war with France and Russia after 1871, Moltke came to the sobering conclusion that "diplomacy" in the end would have to resolve the issue. And in a series of position papers he questioned the very nature and efficacy of warfare.

Mobilization and concentration of armies, what the Germans called the *Aufmarsch*, would be all-decisive in modern warfare. "An error in the

original concentration of armies," Moltke warned, "can hardly be cor-
rected during the whole course of a campaign." Thus, the commander's
primary responsibility was to marshal his forces for the initial campaign
in superior numbers and at the critical point. Thereafter, strategy would
be reduced to a system of expedients: "No plan of operations can look
with any certainty beyond the first meeting with the major forces of the
enemy." In case General Staff officers missed the point, Moltke put the
issue more bluntly still: "No plan of operations survives the first collision with the main enemy body." What Clausewitz termed the intangibles of war would force commanders in the field to reach decisions on
the spot "on the basis of situations that cannot be predicted." Once the
main armies engaged, "all consecutive acts of war" would no longer be
"actions of a premeditated plan, but spontaneous actions, directed by
military tact." Reliance on the Napoleonic coup d'oeil was dangerous.
"Genius," Moltke reminded his General Staff, "is work." In simple, yet
powerful terms, the elder Moltke encapsulated the art of war in the modern era: "The problem is to grasp in innumerable special cases the actual
situation that is covered by the mist of uncertainty, to appraise the facts
correctly and to guess the unknown elements, to reach a decision quickly
and then to carry it out forcefully and relentlessly." Above all, Moltke
cautioned that "war cannot be conducted from a work desk."

General Alfred von Schlieffen (chief of the General Staff, 1891–
1905), by contrast, championed precisely such managing of war "from
a work desk." An austere, solitary man educated in the spirit of Prussian Pietism, Schlieffen became the best-known and most controversial
strategist of the times. A pure technician of war, he is alleged to have
brusquely commented, when an adjutant pointed out the beauty of the
Pregal Valley in its spring flower: "An insignificant obstacle."

In 1908, shortly after his retirement as chief of the General Staff,
Schlieffen published a highly interesting article on "Contemporary
War," which sharply differentiated his concept of modern conflict from
that espoused by Moltke. In the tract, Schlieffen rejected a strategy of
attrition as being "impossible," if maintaining millions of troops would
cost billions of Marks. Instead, he championed an elite strategy designed to allow Germany to conduct warfare in an age of the industrial
masses—without, however, resorting to Verdy du Vernois's concept of
the "nation in arms." The secret, Schlieffen argued, lay in a controlled
system of strategy, the *manoeuvre à priori*. Its hallmarks were preplanning
and centralized command.

In "Contemporary War," which Kaiser William II deemed sufficiently important to have read aloud at the New Year's gathering of Commanding Generals in 1909, Schlieffen envisaged the war of the future. Mobilization and concentration would take place long before the first clash with the enemy. Each soldier would know beforehand the streets, ways, and direction as well as daily objectives of the *Aufmarsch*. "Deployment for battle begins as soon as the troops have left the train." From the frontier train depots, divisions and corps would march to their designated areas of concentration in the precise order in which they were to proceed into battle. Each corps would have exactly 25,000 rifles and 144 field guns. And although battlefronts were now three times as extended than during the Franco-Prussian War, each corps would nevertheless have to attack, hold seized ground, sustain casualties of up to 50 percent, and still be able to muster the decisive "final charge." Dirigibles would undertake reconnaissance and cavalry would seek out the enemy rear for massed assault. Each branch of the service would duel with its opposite before a decision could be reached. "More or less, artillery will be pitted against artillery, cavalry against cavalry, dirigibles against dirigibles, before all combined could assist infantry to final victory."

And whereas Moltke had assumed a minimalist stance, Schlieffen championed a highly centralized role for the modern Alexander. The *Feldherr* would be situated farther behind the front than in the days of Napoleon, "in a house with spacious orderly-rooms, where electric and wireless telegraphs, telephone and signaling apparatuses are readily at hand." Platoons of motorcars and motorcycles, "outfitted for even the most distant of journeys," would stand by to dispatch orders. "The modern Napoleon, seated in a comfortable chair before a wide table, the entire battlefield on a map before him" would be ready to receive a flood of reports from "army and corps commanders, from dirigibles and tethered balloons, which observed the enemy's movements and guarded his position along the entire expanse of his lines." The commander, for his part, would send out "stirring words" via his network of telephones.

Schlieffen's visionary article contained not a word concerning the role of the emperor, his chancellor, or his diplomats. Nor about logistics or chance. It was robotic warfare concocted in a cocoon. Forgotten or ignored were not only the intangibles of war but above all Clausewitz's dictum that while war admittedly had its own "grammar," it did not possess "its own logic," which could be supplied only by politics. Schlieffen was content to become a "superb grammarian."

Yet Schlieffen became *the* master for the generation of German soldiers prior to 1914, relegating Clausewitz to the dustbin. Some future senior commanders (Helmuth von Moltke the Younger, Wilhelm Groener, and Leo Geyr von Schweppenburg, for example) saw no value in reading "books on high strategy." Still others (Colmar von der Goltz, Paul von Hindenburg, and Alfred Kraus come to mind) patently turned Clausewitz on his head and argued that Scharnhorst's chief of staff had upheld the primacy of military considerations. Perhaps nothing better demonstrates the perversion of Clausewitz by German soldiers than the fact that all editions of *On War* after 1853 falsified one of its cardinal tenets. Whereas Clausewitz had stated in the original text that the commander in chief should be included in cabinet sessions so that he could participate in the political deliberations, the altered version asserted that the general should be made a member of the cabinet so that he could participate actively in decision making.

Not surprisingly, Schlieffen's pupils avoided deeper analyses of statecraft and historical forces. They worshipped the goddess "efficiency" as the logical culmination of nineteenth-century rationalism and positivism. Theirs became a narrow world of technical marvels: cartography, communications, railroads, weapons systems, and the like. They mastered statistical tables, devised intricate mobilization schedules, and formulated complicated military responses to every conceivable political contingency. Long before the advent of the computer age, they reduced the art of warfare to an exact algebra.

Whether that would suffice for the war of the future was the crux of the matter. In Germany two such disparate personalities as Helmuth von Moltke (the Elder) and Friedrich Engels contested Schlieffen's vision of a clockwork war. In his farewell speech to the Reichstag in 1890, Moltke, the victor of Königgrätz and Sedan, warned his countrymen that the next war could turn into a seven, even a thirty years' war. "Woe betide him who sets Europe ablaze." Engels at about the same time predicted a war in which "eight to ten million soldiers will strangle each other and in the process decimate Europe as no swarm of locusts ever did." Hunger, pests, and the barbarization of entire peoples would ensue. Trade, industry, and banking would wither. The old states of Europe would be swept away. Dozens of crowns would roll in the streets, without takers. "The ravages of the Thirty Years' War will be telescoped into three or four years and extended to the entire Continent."

Little wonder, then, that when Helmuth von Moltke (the Younger) succeeded Schlieffen as chief of the General Staff in 1906, he did so with grave reservations. "Whether it is at all possible to control by unified command the mass armies we are setting up, and how it is to be done, nobody can know in advance." The answer would come eight years later.

Case Study: The Franco-Prussian War

The selection of a case study for nearly a century of warfare in Europe and North America, in particular, is not an easy matter. The obvious choice among many possibilities is the American Civil War. There, conscript armies fought long and hard in a conflict that approached the modern notion of "total war." Decimating small-arms fire and massed artillery showed the war of the future—as did the extensive use of railroads, the first signs of trench warfare, and the first naval battles between armored vessels. But this is precisely the problem: a case study needs to reflect more the customary patterns of war of the period (beginning industrial warfare) than to be the harbinger of things to come. Thus, the Franco-Prussian War (1870–71) seems to offer perhaps more representative insights into both the nature of nineteenth-century warfare and into several of the major subthemes of this book—the idea of war, the impact of technological innovation, the nature of armies, and the experience of the soldier.

On the surface, and as contemporary observers noted, the Franco-Prussian War should not have been much of a contest. The French army recently had defeated both Russia and Austria, was led by another Napoleon, and alone deemed itself capable of commanders possessing the Napoleonic coup d'oeil. Surely, the fury of the Imperial French Army (*furia francese*) would prove an easy match for what French experts derided as the Prussian army of "lawyers and oculists." In fact, the war quickly revealed that superiority in mobilization, leadership, and artillery dominated the new style of warfare.

The Prussian General Staff, consisting of a total of eleven officers, estimated in 1870 that six rail lines in three weeks could bring 484,000 troops to the Rhineland. In reality, in eighteen days, 1,183,000 regular and reserve troops passed through German barracks and 462,000 soldiers were expedited to the French frontier. Rail transport had been decentralized down to the corps level and each unit knew the precise day and hour when it would leave the barracks and head for the concentration area. Not since the legendary armies of the Persian Emperor Xerxes, one French historian remarked, had such a force been put in the field.

The opening battles of the war established a pattern: initial superiority in numbers was decisive; broad deployment was conducive to envelopmental tactics; rifle fire was extremely effective in halting frontal assaults; and artillery easily overcame rifle fire. German tactics (*Auftragstaktik*) were simple but effective. Front-line commanders were given leeway within the general strategic design to march to the sound of the guns, which indicated the decisive pressure point. Moltke's strategic genius lay in his ability to adjust to conditions as they presented themselves, rather than in readjusting his armies to fit into a prearranged plan; in short, in his brilliant opportunism.

Infantry quickly learned that advancing in close-order company columns was suicidal against breech-loading rifles. Units rapidly disintegrated under the withering fire into a ragged skirmishing line. At Spichern on August 8, 1871, roughly 12 percent of the forty-two thousand Prussians engaged were killed or wounded in a twelve-hour period—mainly by point-blank rifle fire and artillery fire at deadly ranges. The General Staff would later analyze the Battle of Spichern to construct mathematical casualty tables. Ten days later at Gravelotte-St. Privat, Prince Augustus of Württemberg ordered the prestigious Guard Corps to undertake a frontal assault in close-order columns, without artillery support, up a slope against entrenched French infantry, with regimental bugles and drums blaring. The result was a massacre. In twenty minutes, the guard lost over 25 percent of total strength—eight thousand officers and men. It came no closer than six hundred yards to the French line. The action foreshadowed the worst of what was to come forty years later.

But the Prussian army learned from its experience at Gravelotte-St. Privat. First, at Sedan on September 1 it withheld its infantry and left the main work to the artillery—with the result that German losses in this major battle were a mere 850 more than at the relatively minor skirmish at Gravelotte-St. Privat. Second, on October 30 German infantry deployed around Paris devised new tactics. The guard counterattacked not in company columns but in loose lines of widely-spaced soldiers, making use of cover, offering small targets, advancing by bands, and covering each advance by fire. Only in 1917 did the German army return to this practice with the deployment of "storm troops."

Cavalry was still regarded as the premier branch of the service. The Franco-Prussian War would reveal its basic choice to be between suicide and idleness. On August 5, 1870, French general A. E. Michel's cuirassier brigade charged down a slope against Prussian infantry at Morsbronn: nine of its squadrons were destroyed, apparently without the loss of a single Prussian soldier. Nine days later, the cuirassiers of the Imperial French Guard regiment were sacrificed at Rezonville in a suicidal charge against Prussian infantry. And at Sedan on September 1, French cavalry commanded by General Jean A. Margueritte repeatedly charged German infantry. While this piece of gallantry earned from Kaiser William I the admiring comment, "*Ah! Les braves gens!*" it also constituted suicide. German infantrymen reverently saluted as they allowed the last remnants of Margueritte's shattered cavalry to pass through their lines unmolested.

But the obvious lesson was not drawn. Future commanders simply ignored the actions at Morsbronn, Rezonville, and Sedan. Instead, they preferred to point out that during the Battle of Vionville on August 16, six squadrons of German cavalry had overrun the French gun line and therewith had saved infantry units hard-pressed by a hailstorm of *chassepot* fire. General Adalbert von Bredow's so-called death ride, probably the last massed boot-to-boot cavalry charge in European warfare, thus preserved the reputation of this branch of the armed forces for another war. In reconnaissance and in raids against enemy supply lines, cavalry alone served a useful purpose.

Artillery certainly helped to win the war. Krupp's breech-loading steel guns, with their percussion fuses that exploded upon impact and their high degree of accuracy in fire, ushered in a new age of applied technology. The Battle of Sedan proved the superiority of artillery. In the Bois de la Garenne, for example, ten German batteries massacred French forces. Each battery took a different section of the wood under fire and each gun in the battery fired at a different elevation. The entire wood was blanketed with artillery fire. French units that sought to leave the cover of trees were driven back into them by fresh artillery fire. Entire French battalions simply piled up their arms and surrendered. The Germans inspected their artillery's handiwork and were suitably impressed: "In the large heaps of ruins . . . the defenders . . . lay all around, fearfully torn and mutilated by the German shell; limbs and bodies were blown from thirty to fifty paces apart, and the stones and sand were here and there covered with pools of blood. . . . All around there lay rifles

Fig. 10.3. Sedan, 1870: The Saxon Regiment. Friedrich August storms three French *mitrailleuse*. Bundesarchiv-Militärarchiv, Freiburg.

and swords, knapsacks and cartridges, the remains of limbers which had been blown up, broken gun-carriages and wheels, and a large number of hideously torn and mangled horses."

Sedan also revealed the sang-froid of German leaders. Chancellor Otto von Bismarck prepared the way diplomatically by instructing the Belgian government that if it did not disarm Marshal Patrice MacMahon's army of Châlons (should it try to cross into Belgium), the Germans reserved the right to pursue it. Moltke, secure in the knowledge that he thus had the French in a "mousetrap," casually joined Kaiser William I, Bismarck, the various German princes, and a host of foreign military observers, including General Sheridan of the U.S. Army, on the heights above Frénois to watch the turkey shoot. The Battle of Sedan in fact cemented the German operational art of the *Kesselschlacht*: a planned battle of encirclement and annihilation, using first strategic maneuver to encircle large hostile forces, and thereafter the tactical defensive to allow firepower to smash the enemy as it tried to break out of the ring.

For the French, Sedan drove home the Clausewitzean notion of "friction." Units could not be found. Messengers lost their way. Commanders without maps took wrong turns. Burning wagons and dead horses blocked choke points. Troops moving in contrary direction collided. It was Murphy's Law applied to combat. But the Battle of Sedan also

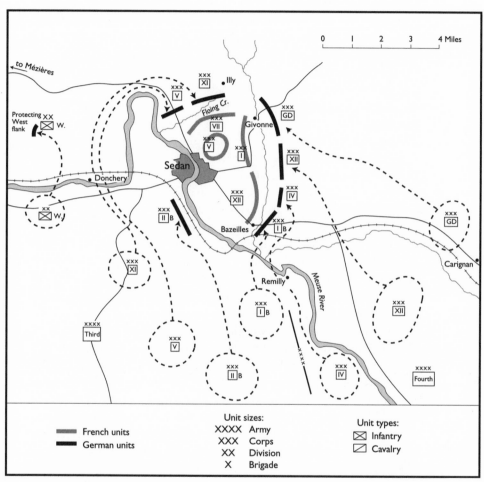

0   1   2   3   4 Miles

to Mézières

XXX
XI   • Illy

XXX
V

Floing Cr.

XXX
VII   XXX
                        GD
             • Givonne

Protecting
West   XX
flank   ⊠ W.

XXX
V

XXX
I   XXX
                 XII

Sedan

XX   XXX
⊠ W.   • Donchery   IV

XXX   XXX
II B   XII   XXX
                                GD
                   • Bazeilles
                          XXX
                          I B   • Carignan

XXX
XI

                   • Remilly

XXXX   Meuse River
Third   XXX
                   I B   XXX
                                        XII

XXX
V

XXX   XXX   XXXX
II B   IV   Fourth

Unit sizes: Unit types:

▬▬ French units   XXXX Army   ⊠ Infantry
━━ German units   XXX   Corps   ⊡ Cavalry
                      XX   Division
                      X   Brigade

Map 10.1. The Battle of Sedan, 1870

brought home to the Germans Clausewitz's emphasis upon "escalation." The French nation refused to accept the defeat of the Imperial French armies of Napoleon III. Under the leadership of Léon Gambetta and Charles de Freycinet, it demanded *la guerre à outrance*. The ideas of 1793 resurfaced: censorship of the press, compulsory patriotic readings, requisitioning of supplies, conscription of engineers, doctors, architects, and scientists, abolition of restrictions on promotions, calls to resurrect both the *levée en masse* and the Committee of Public Safety—in short, the notion of the nation in arms. Naval supremacy alone permitted France to import a bewildering array of Enfields, Remingtons, Scharps, Sniders, Spencers, Springfields, and Winchesters from Britain and the United States.

Above all, emulating the example of the Spanish against Napoleon I, the French turned to guerrilla warfare. Special *franc-tireur* units were created to block roads, harass German supply columns, detonate charges at bridges, tunnels, and along rail lines. Even the gout-ridden Italian revolutionary Giuseppe Garibaldi arrived to assist in such "scorched earth" endeavors. The line between soldier and civilian quickly became blurred.

The Prussian reaction to the French recourse to guerrilla warfare was surprisingly moderate. Guerrillas were generally denied status as combatants and when the French complained of this to Bismarck, the latter coldly replied that "our trees still bear the marks where your generals hanged our people on them" during the French occupation of Prussia between 1806 and 1814. But there were no large-scale executions of French civilians or razing of French villages. U.S. general Sheridan obviously was puzzled by such a tame reaction. Undoubtedly remembering his words during the Shenandoah Valley campaign of 1864, Sheridan informed German headquarters that "the proper strategy" for Prussia consisted "in causing the inhabitants so much suffering that they must long for peace, and force the government to demand it." Sheridan apprised the Prussians of the American way of war: "The people must be left nothing but their eyes to weep with over the war."

The French *sortie en masse* was crushed by German regular units at Orléans and Le Mans. Reduced to exhausted, hungry, and mutinous hordes, the French sued for peace. General von Moltke, for his part, was quite prepared to pursue French forces down the Loire River and to the Spanish frontier. Above all, he recognized that a basic decision was at hand: "the question of which is preferable, a trained army or a militia. . . . If the French succeed in throwing us out of France, all the

Powers will introduce a militia system, and if we remain the victors, then every State will imitate us with universal service in a standing army."

Finally, Paris—for some the queen of Europe, for others the modern Babylon—became the center of gravity (*Schwerpunkt*) of the war. On the French side, Gambetta raised his citizen armies not in order to defeat the German forces in the field but rather to relieve Paris. The Germans, in turn, decided to reduce the city as if it were one of Sebastian de Vauban's seventeenth-century fortresses. Strategy, after all, is not a matter of geometry but one of politics, and the latter is a matter of tradition and sentiment. The great city underwent shelling by fifteen-centimeter siege guns and twenty-one-centimeter mortars. Between two and three hundred shells per day landed in its perimeter. Parisians tried to maintain contact with the outside world in a variety of ways. A cable laid on the bed of the Seine River was quickly dredged up by the Germans when they failed to break its coded messages. An attempt to float messages down the Seine in hollow zinc globes was likewise thwarted. Microscopic messages sent by carrier pigeons often went astray. Balloons, fired by the new coal gas, proved most effective. Roughly sixty-five balloons eventually carried twenty-three thousand pounds of messages out of the city and only a few either wafted out to sea or fell into German hands.

The siege was directed against civilian morale rather than against combatants. Lower-middle class women and children suffered most because of a shortage of milk and fresh vegetables. Pillage and robbery increased dramatically. Dog and cat butchers did a brisk business in the meaner streets of Paris. But the famous menus featuring buffalo, camel, elephant, wapiti, yak, and zebra meat from the Jardin d'Acclimatation were more publicity than reality. Above all, the siege was a harbinger of things to come for civilians in major metropolitan areas.

The war revealed the friction inherent in coordinating such a massive undertaking. While Bismarck complained bitterly that he was purposely being kept ignorant of military affairs by the generals, Moltke remonstrated that Bismarck constantly interfered in purely military matters. The issue struck at the heart of modern warfare. For Bismarck, war was but an extension of politics by other means and political considerations remained supreme. For Moltke, even "total" war against the French nation in arms was "only" a military matter. Kaiser William I's failure to rule on this basic question was to haunt German planners, both civilian and military, for the next half century.

The Franco-Prussian War unleashed the full fury of nationalism and xenophobia in both lands. The public radicalization of war emerged as perhaps the most sinister problem of modern national war, from which the great catastrophes of more recent German history developed and from which the Germans foundered twice in the twentieth century.

Suggested Reading

Detailed accounts of the art of warfare in the early industrial age are provided by Hew Strachan, *European Armies and the Conduct of War* (London, 1983); Larry H. Addington, *The Patterns of War since the Eighteenth Century* (Bloomington IN, 1984); William McElwee, *The Art of War: Waterloo to Mons* (Bloomington IN, 1974); and Archer Jones, *The Art of War in the Western World* (New York, 1987).

The nuts and bolts of the technological revolution, both on land and at sea, are offered by William H. McNeill, *The Pursuit of Power: Technology, Armed Force, and Society since A.D. 1000* (Chicago, 1982). Martin van Creveld, *Supplying War: Logistics From Wallenstein to Patton* (Cambridge, 1977), offers comments on the logistical side of war and especially on the use of railroads. Dennis E. Showalter, *Railroads and Rifles: Soldiers, Technology, and the Unification of Germany* (Hamden CT, 1975), is good on the technical side of the Austro-Prussian War of 1866. F. H. Garrison, *Notes on the History of Military Medicine* (Hildesheim, 1970), and Richard A. Gabriel and Karen S. Metz, *A History of Military Medicine* 2 vols. (New York, 1992), offer a succinct synopses on the medical reforms after the Crimean War.

Warfare at sea in this period is the story of the Royal Navy. A brief overview can be gleaned from Paul M. Kennedy, *The Rise and Fall of British Naval Mastery* (New York, 1976). The period of British naval dominance after Napoleon is detailed by C. J. Bartlett, *Great Britain and Sea Power 1815–1853* (Oxford, 1963); the later years are covered by C. Barnett, *The Collapse of British Power* (London, 1972). Especially valuable is Donald M. Schurman, *The Education of a Navy: The Development of British Naval Strategic Thought 1867–1914* (London, 1965). For the French, the standard remains Theodore Ropp, *The Development of a Modern Navy: French Naval Policy 1871–1904* (Annapolis, 1987). Finally, the genesis and course of the Anglo-German naval arms race after 1900 can be garnered from Arthur J. Marder, *From the Dreadnought to Scapa Flow: The Royal Navy in the Fisher Era, 1904–1919*, vol. 1, *The Road to War, 1904–1914* (London, 1961), and Holger H. Herwig, *"Luxury" Fleet: The Imperial German Navy 1888–1918* (London, 1987).

The Prussian way of war was first analyzed by Gordon A. Craig, *The Politics of the Prussian Army 1640–1945* (Oxford, 1955). Craig also penned a stirring account of *The Battle of Königgrätz: Prussia's Victory over Austria, 1866* (Westport CT, 1964). Two selections from Peter Paret, ed., *Makers of Modern Strategy from Machiavelli to the Nuclear Age* (Princeton, 1986), are highly recommended: Hajo Holborn's original piece on "The Prusso-German School: Moltke and the Rise of the General Staff" and Gunther E. Rothenberg's new appraisal of "Moltke, Schlieffen, and the Doctrine of Strategic Envelopment." More recent, on the other hand, is Arden Bucholz, *Moltke, Schlieffen and Prussian War Planning* (New York, 1991).

The case study of the Franco-Prussian War of 1870 relied heavily on what is perhaps Michael Howard's best work, *The Franco-Prussian War: The German Invasion of France, 1870–1871* (London, 1961 and 1979). The influence of Clausewitz on the German generals has been examined by Jehuda L. Wallach, *The Dogma of the Battle of Annihilation: The Theories of Clausewitz and Schlieffen and Their Impact on the German Conduct of Two World Wars* (Westport CT, 1986). Jay Luvaas has analyzed the interrelationship between the U.S. and European ways of war during this period in *The Military Legacy of the Civil War: The European Inheritance* (Chicago, 1959). The discussion of the Civil War was taken mainly from James M. McPherson, *Battle Cry of Freedom: The Civil War Era* (New York, 1988).

11. THE WEST CONQUERS THE WORLD
War and Society in the Age of European
Imperialism, 1757–1914

Between 1757 and 1914 the West took over the world. This, the greatest conquest in history, had many sources, but one was the most fundamental of them all: Western armies crushed the others, making imperialism so cheap that minor causes sparked great conquests. Ultimately, the greatest cause of imperialism was not profound political and economic factors but simply the military ease with which it could be accomplished. European armies were superior in technology, tactics, and organization because for centuries their states had regularly fought major wars against each other. Only the strongest survived in a constant competition to produce armies and to improve them. State finances were honed to this end, as were administration and politics. Compromises between monarchs and nobles produced things unique to Europe: states that routinely maintained the largest and best armies they could afford, which gave authority over them to a technically competent but politically loyal officer corps. European states became the most militarized and militarily effective on earth. By 1750, conversely, military competition characterized only one other part of the old world, south Asia, where states were also unusually quick to assimilate Western tactics. The armies of other Asian states were ossified. When struck they collapsed and then blocked the path to progress. Old armies often had to be destroyed before good ones could begin. Meanwhile, if they wished to match the administrative and political foundations of Western power, non-Western states had to undergo a revolution. European countries could maintain large armies without threatening their existence and become militarily stronger simply by raising more revenues and regiments. For non-European states, to raise taxes was to create crises, to strengthen armies was to weaken the state. Still, this process did not happen overnight. Mastery by Western armies took generations to rise in the theaters where they most frequently fought non-Western forces between 1700 and 1850, Ukraine, India, and Ohio.

The conquest of the non-Western world began in eastern Europe. In 1700, Turkish defenses against Russia rested on the desolation of Ukraine, the cavalry of the Crimean Tatars, forts on the rivers flowing south to the Black Sea, and a navy. Elements of the system were mutually dependent—Tatars made Ukraine a desert but needed Turkey to keep Russia on the other side. In order to penetrate this system anywhere, Russians had to overcome all its strengths at once. Huge armies had to cross a desert and besiege great forts, as horse raided supplies and disease stalked men—in the Russo-Turkish War (1735–39), sixty-thousand Russian soldiers died of hunger or sickness. Turkish armies were mediocre but so were Russian, and Turks fought only when they wanted to, when the conditions were favorable. So long as the system as a whole stood, even major Russian gains—ravaging the Crimean peninsula, destroying a fort or an army—were fruitless. From the 1750s, however, this system unraveled. Ottoman military organization entered a fatal slump. The central government lost control over its territories and its revenues slipped, crippling the ability to form and feed armies. Janissary infantry and feudal cavalry ceased to be effective or loyal but became an armed mob, a terror to their master but not his enemies. Turkey fielded a large army, but a bad one, three hundred thousand men lagging in morale, discipline, technology, and tactics. Many Janissaries had no military training. Their large and clumsy units could not form line or column and would not hold bayonets on their antique muskets, ostensibly because they were "infidel weapons," in reality because to adopt bayonets and fight in line and column would force Janissaries to change their tactics or, even worse, to train seriously. They could not maneuver or deliver effective fire, and they fought at close quarters as swordsmen jammed together shoulder to shoulder. Even worse, the Janissaries were still the Ottoman elite. Most other Turkish forces were armed irregulars without standard training or weapons. One senior Turkish officer complained that in 1768, "The pashas from Anatolia recruited thieves and the homeless and then were held captive by them—at every hamlet or bridge-crossing, the men demanded salaries and bonuses, a tyranny completely contrary to custom." Turkish command became amateurish, the plaything of politics. At the start of the war between 1768 and 1774, an ailing civilian became commander of the field army. Mehmed Emin asked his generals, "When we cross the Danube, which

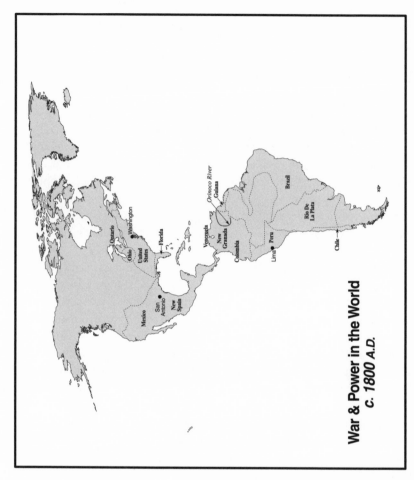

War & Power in the World
C. 1800 A.D.

Map 11.1

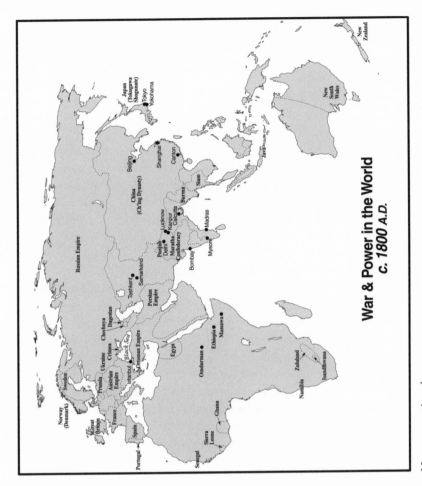

War & Power in the World
C. 1800 A.D.

Map 11.1 continued

way shall we go? . . . As I am unfamiliar with the region and have not been on a campaign, in these matters I should be accounted among the ignorant."

Meanwhile, Russia developed a good logistical base in Ukraine, food stored in magazines for shipments down rivers along with small but effective armies that could be supplied and win. As one Russian commander, Petr Aleksandrovich Rumyantsev, wrote, the Russian army "does not ask how big the enemy is, it only wants to find out where he is." It had excellent generals, good officers, disciplined and determined soldiers, and tactics unlike those of western Europe, especially designed to break huge but undisciplined Turkish armies—fast forced marches, often through woods, night attacks, and bayonet charges, preferably launched by surprise, to exploit Turkish weakness at shock warfare. Disciplined forces thrust bayonets seven feet from their bodies into packed masses of swordsmen, who were unable to wield their weapons with effect. Muskets were subordinate to bayonets, though Russians could also bring withering firepower to bear. The great Russian commander Aleksandr Vasililevich Suvarov wrote, "The bullet is a fool, but the bayonet is terrific," yet also that "he who accurately levels his musket at the chest or the guts will always shoot his man." Russians rejected movement in lines because this was slow and left outnumbered forces vulnerable to envelopment. Instead, they found a solution like that which the Imperial Roman Army had used against a similar problem—wedge tactics. The Russians advanced in a razor-edged checkerboard formation of battalions in squares, units cutting forward with crossfire, some pinning unwieldy Turkish masses from the front, others striking in the flank. Russians preferred aimed fire to volleys so that small armies with dubious supply would make every shot count, assisted by the rapid deployment of light guns on the battlefield. Stronger logistics let Russians mount better sieges despite their crude techniques, and their soldiers were more successful at storm. In two wars between 1768 and 1792, Russia rolled up vital elements of Turkish frontier defenses, forcing the Ottoman army to stand and be smashed even it was when four times larger, as was often the case. At Kagul on July 21, 1770, for example, 35,000 Russians defeated perhaps 150,000 Turks, killing or capturing 20,000 of them for 1,000 Russians dead. Russia broke Turkey's defense system, seized Crimea, made Ukraine a breadbasket, producing a new and permanent threat to Istanbul, while sparking political and financial crises that weakened Turkey still more.

By 1757 Western-style infantry proved better in battle than any other forces in India, while new techniques of siege and storm broke a fundamental rule of warfare in the subcontinent: that fortresses fell slowly. This suited Britain, able to afford the largest effective army in India, which ultimately reached forty-five thousand British and two hundred thousand native soldiers, or sepoys. It also had a unified command system, good officers, shrewd politics, and local support—Robert Clive won the Battle of Plassey in 1757, which made Britain the dominant military power on the subcontinent, largely because Indian allies financed him to bribe enemy generals, and with an army consisting primarily of sepoys. Response to this menace was hard—in 1757 Indian armies centered on cavalry and none had Western-style infantry, who were expensive to maintain. Still, several Indian powers adapted to this menace and did so more effectively than any other non-Western states would do until 1890. Between 1767 and 1799, Britain fought four wars against two kings of Mysore. Haider Ali and Tipu Sultan used twenty thousand disciplined but not westernized infantry and eighteen thousand cavalry to pursue a sophisticated strategy. Men and guns held walled cities while cavalry slashed the supply of British besiegers, smashed columns on the move, raided British controlled territories, and seized major towns. For decades, this approach worked. Britain won only through superior resources and the aid of allied Mahratta horse to check Mysore's cavalry.

Then, in the second Anglo-Mahratta war (1803–5), British forces smashed the Mahrattas, who had good light cavalry and westernized infantry and artillery in large numbers, fielding fifty-six thousand regular soldiers to Britain's thirty-seven thousand. The Mahratta army had weaknesses: it could not coordinate cavalry with infantry, its leaders were divided, and their forces fought in fragments, while the commanders of infantry battalions and brigades, European mercenaries, deserted their men. Even so, Mahratta strategy and siege craft were good and they fought well. In battles against them, British commanders concluded that their own forces would lose a pounding match of firepower and won through desperate bayonet assaults. The British general Lake said that Mahratta infantry "fought like devils, or rather heroes" while their artillery were better than British and "as well served as they can possibly be, the gunners standing by their guns until killed by the bayonet." Decades later, when asked to name his "best" battle, the duke of Wellington said "Assaye," fought against Marathas in 1803. Both rated Maratha infantry equal to British-led sepoys, and victory was costly: sixteen hundred of

Wellington's forty-five hundred men at Assaye were casualties. Finally, in the 1840s the British engaged the Sikh kingdom of the Punjab, with the largest Western-style army in Asia and the first national one, having sixty-five thousand Sikh officers and men and guns to match the British. Again, British victory rested on exploitation of the political confusion within its enemies—even so, it required the two hardest British battles fought between 1815 and 1914. One should not distort the quality of Sikhs and Mahrattas—they were beaten despite possessing superior strength, but they were better far than any contemporary Asian forces, and the Sikhs were comparable in quality to many European armies.

American Indian resistance to Anglo-American forces in the eighteenth century was terrific. Both sides had similar weapons and strength, with forces usually between 25 to 250 men, rarely 1,500. When joined in confederacies, American Indians smashed larger Anglo-American armies, ambushing slow columns of infantry in the wilderness and cutting them up on the forest floor as they fled, isolating forts and ravaging border settlements. They made shrewd use of terror, leaving mutilated corpses or scalps nailed on trees to frighten settlers and soldiers. As one British commander, Colonel Henry Bosenquet, said, Native forces were so fast that they "fight only when they think they have the advantage" and "elude the most eager pursuit." British regulars were trained for European conditions, colonial troops were not trained at all, both tied to long supply columns and bad roads. In 1755, General Braddock's column, five miles long, moved six miles per day on its path to destruction. Native generalship surpassed their enemies' and their politics were shrewd, using the locally weaker Western power to hold off the stronger, French against British, English against Americans. Yet Native forces had flaws. They won battles but did not use them—they could not take forts or fight for long. Loosely knit warbands fighting to prove manhood and the power of spirits fled after defeat and returned home after victory with wounded, prisoners and loot. Anglo-American victories were rarer but more fruitful, used to seize land and build forts. Even more, so long as they did not lose, Americans won. American Indian populations were small and American settlers drove westward, steadily reducing Native lands.

Most settlers could not match Native forces and lost thousands of lives and square miles of frontier during major conflicts. From 1760, however, backwoodsmen—"Big Knives," American Indians called them, after their favorite weapons—moving from Virginia adapted to fight effectively. Like American Indians, backwoodsmen fought on foot as skirmishers and sharpshooters, using tomahawks and knives at close quarters; unlike American Indians, French, or British, they used horses to strike over distances and to charge at close quarters. For seventy years, Native and backwoods warriors struggled to master Ohio by murder—burning settlements, ripping open women's bellies, and torturing prisoners to death. American Indian warfare had always been terrible, but most peoples had adopted many captives; the backwoodsmen killed them all. Meanwhile, isolated tribes were easily defeated, Native unity was hard to establish and during long conflicts they needed a Western power to provide gunpowder and to feed families. This aid failed them. Throughout the Seven Years' War, a French and Native alliance mastered Ohio, yet Britain conquered it by victories elsewhere. Between 1783 and 1815, Native fortunes hinged on Britain. Before the American Revolution, the British could not restrain backwoodsman. During it, American Indians preferred neutrality, but constant American attacks forced them to join Britain. An American Indian confederacy with small British assistance smashed larger American forces and ravaged the frontier. Afterward, however, British aid fell while Native confederacies eroded. Against this, American military power was tiny—rarely more than 850 men stood on the Ohio frontier, whom the U.S. adjutant general called "the offscourings of large towns and Cities;-enervated by idleness, Debaucheries and every species of Vice." Battles were rare and American Indians were outnumbered, but still they won twice, most notably annihilating six hundred of General St. Clair's army of fourteen hundred in 1793, suffering in return one major defeat, Fallen Timbers (1794), and one minor one, Tippecanoe (1810). The backwoodsmen, however, wrecked the Native economy and society. In the last stand of the eastern American Indians, the war of 1812, small British and Native armies smashed two large American forces but lost one battle, Thames River in 1814, and with it the nations of the Ohio country were broken. The United States lost the War of 1812 to Britain and Canada but won it against the American Indians, in the process conquering 33 percent of the modern American Midwest and South.

As these accounts show, Western superiority over other military systems emerged around 1750 and quickly overwhelmed incompetent foes, while growing gradually against enemies who adapted well. Initially, its main roots were the greater wealth and population of Western states and their army organization. Western forces had better discipline, endurance, and ability to move and feed armies on the field than most non-Western foes. They also had the ability to operate despite heavy casualties and two unique attributes—officer corps of skill and self-sacrifice and the socket bayonet, which let European infantry alone on earth move instantly from fire to shock. In 1879 even Zulus trained for close combat with shields and spears (*assegais*) feared bayonets. It is no coincidence that the two non-Western armies that best adapted to European warfare by 1900, the Turkish and Japanese, also became famous for bayonet fighting. Beyond the bayonet, technology was irrelevant—if Turkish weapons were worse than Russian, Indian artillery was better than British. Until 1830 Western military superiority was limited and produced limited gains—Britain dominated India, Russia annexed southern Ukraine, and the Caucasus and the United States took much of eight states—and only after great effort. Good non-Western armies matched Western ones. During the mid-1820s by using stockades and natural cover, Ashanti armies in Ghana stalled a British expedition of two thousand men with rockets, while ten thousand Anglo-Indian soldiers backed by a steam gunboat barely beat Burmans. Popular guerrilla movements stalemated all major European armies. The standard Western approach of line, column, and volley failed outside Europe. British and Russians defeated non-Western armies only by fundamentally altering their systems to fit the local environment and by abandoning western European styles of war, to downplay fire and emphasize shock. On thinly populated frontiers, the best Western forces were warrior societies that adapted local styles of warfare, like Cossacks or "big knives."

From 1830, however, Western superiority grew in scale and significance—British conquered India, Russians campaigned to Istanbul, European armies dominated east Asia and seized southeast Asia, central Asia, and almost all of Africa, and the United States and Canada annexed North America. These conquests were easier than before, often made by a few thousand men in a few years. European armies had less need to adapt their tactics to those of local armies. They maintained their earlier advantages, massively multiplied by technological superiority. Western sea power provided crushing support in coastal regions and inland—naval brigades, composed of sailors serving as gunners and infantry, provided key reinforcements to many British imperial armies while the French navy dominated the conquest of Indochina. Granted, Western superiority was not always absolute. Throughout the later nineteenth century, the Turkish and Japanese armies matched European developments. In 1876, no country had better military equipment than Egypt, and Turkey had the third largest modern fleet at sea, while Peru owned the world's best warship. Still, from 1870 quick-firing artillery, repeating rifles, and machine guns firing five to eleven rounds per second provided edges against most non-Western peoples, for whom Western armies reserved the deadliest of weapons. One French officer described the effect of expanding bullets on African soldiers: "a bullet in the head takes off the skull, a bullet in the chest makes a hole the size of a plate in the victim's back, the limbs are crushed and the bones broken in a horrible manner."

Non-Western armies had two choices: either adapt to this challenge or fail. Few passed this test. In the 1860s, after sharp lessons demonstrated that they would lose stand up battles against the British, Maori forces in New Zealand altered their tactical system to minimize their weaknesses and exploit British ones. Maori riflemen stood behind elaborate trench and bunker forts, *pa*, often organized in systems thousands of yards long or deep and able to withstand bombardment by the most advanced firepower of the day. *Pa* were designed to lead attackers into prepared killing zones where they were pinned by obstacles and massacred by Maoris with old muskets but good discipline. British veterans commented, "you might as well drive a lot of men into a sheep pen and shoot them down as let them assault a place like that." These means let Maoris defeat forces ten times stronger than their own, kill far more enemy than they lost, and shelter their own civilians. Maoris avoided guerrilla warfare, which would let raiders wreck their societies. Instead, they established *pa* on the edge of British camps, far from their own civilians, luring the enemy to suffer heavy losses assaulting powerful defenses without strategic significance. Meanwhile, constant attacks on supply lines paralyzed the enemy's ability to penetrate Maori territory. This approach worked as well as was possible. Ultimately Anglo-New Zealand forces won campaigns only because of great superiority in strength—eighteen thousand men to four thousand between 1863 and 1865—and did not take everything. The Maoris won a better peace and saved more of their land than did any other indigenous people of Australasia or the Americas.

On the northwest frontier of India even between 1897 and 1898, Pathan snipers, often veterans of the Indian army with excellent rifles, fought fifty-nine thousand British and Indian soldiers to a standstill, ambushing units and picking off officers. Such triumphs, however, were possible only for peoples with disciplined warriors, flexible armies, and intelligent commanders able to abandon their own preference for stand up fights and to adopt novel tactics that combined disciplined fire and shrewd use of ground, with attacks on the most vulnerable part of any imperial army—its line of supply. Few peoples possessed these characteristics. Usually, technology produced a tragic disparity in imperial wars, as small forces suffering tiny casualties and fighting for no particular reason annihilated foes fighting total wars of self-defense. Consider how a British sergeant described the Battle of Omdurman of 1898, where fourteen thousand British soldiers engaged fifty thousand Sudanese armed with spears, swords, and bows:

> We laid down again and had another snatch of sleep and about 4.15 A.M. reveille we had some Tea and biscuits then took up position . . . again and the Lancers went out, we waited some time and bye and bye it went round they're coming and sure enough we could see the Lancers slowly retiring and hear them shooting, about 6 or 6.30 we could see them swarming over the hills in front there were thousands with their banners flying and covering the same extent of ground that we did, they waited until they got some way down the hill then the guns next to us started firing, they started with one shot to find the range and all the Officers were watching with their glasses . . . then they all opened fire and if anyone had to face a hail of lead these Dervishes did, but still they came on and as they got closer the shells simply made lanes and empty spaces in their ranks where a minute before they were as thick as bees, then the Infantry opened fire, and what a din, but no smoke . . . gradually the fire got less and less and then we could see them in scattered groups and bodies making for the hills . . . the big guns still worrying them whenever a body got together, everybody then had a breather and they went around and got a list of the casualties . . . there is no doubt about it the Dervishes are very brave to stick it like they did was wonderful, we saw one case during the fight, some of the Dervishes were under cover halted under a small rising in the ground but four a few paces apart came on carrying a banner, first one dropped, then the fellow carrying the flag, another picked it up and still came on, when the two left almost dropped together, they marched straight to death right enough. The Maxims too did awful execution. . . . I heard the Captain saw steady now men, cease fire and wait till they come over the rise, pointing it about 650 or 750 yards away as they came over he said now, traversing fire commence and as the guns went from right to left they simply fell down in a line, just the same as if they had been told to lie down, some of the bodies

they saw afterwards had been hit with bullets five and six times in a line across their bodies before they fell.

What surprised me most was the behaviour of our own troops but it seemed just as if we were on a Field day at Aldershot, everyone cool, talking, and when not firing having a smoke, and the officers had to tell them to lie down because they would stand or kneel to see what was going on, the firing, volleys, were splendid, they fired one rank at a time and when the rifles got very hot and the men tired they relieved each other and the fellows just finished would clean out their rifles and sit down and have a few whiffs until they were wanted again.

The pattern of imperial war varied by continent. The roots for the greatest of these conflicts, the Latin American wars of independence, were the alienation of the native-born "criollo" white population from Spanish rule and Napoleon's conquest of Spain in 1808. These sparked wars of independence in Spain and its colonies—when their armies were whipped, Spaniards refused to surrender, creating juntas to fight on for king and country. Criollos followed the Spanish example, which destroyed political legitimacy and stability in Spanish America: juntas took over local military forces and became autonomous in fact, while many declared themselves independent republics. These ideological and political developments, combined with rivalries between juntas, led to civil wars against royalists, a coalition of Spaniards, criollos and some Indians, thought the processes varied widely by region. Spanish rule vanished in much of the Americas. Spain could restore it only by smashing its own colonial defenses and reconquering its people. Invasion and civil strife at home prevented Spain from doing so. Not until 1812 did the first peninsular soldiers reach the Americas. Only around thirty thousand ever arrived, most of them divided between Mexico and Colombia, better trained than patriots but not much stronger, their strength eroded by disease and distance. Neither royalists nor patriots had much manpower or firepower—in 1824, both sides in Peru together had barely ten guns in the field—and few means to replace weapons. They had to import worn out muskets from merchants or manufacture their own arms, poor ones—swords so brittle that they snapped in the scabbard and cannon that shattered when fired. The fate of campaigns turned on the loss of a few thousand muskets in battle or their purchase from abroad. Spanish regulars and patriot mercenaries used the conventional linear tactics of Europe, but battles turned less on firepower and casualties than on shock and speed thrown against lack of training and nerve. Both sides produced sound and innovative generals; Spanish officers, trained in Fredrician tactics, formulated sophisticated strategies of counterinsurgency that let a few thousand soldiers control Mexico against a deeply rooted guerrilla movement for a decade or create armies of Indians able to ambush and destroy superior enemy forces in the highlands of Peru. Some patriot commanders, military amateurs, demonstrated boldness, judgment, and the ability to take a few thousand men across the Andes and overturn the fate of a continent. As in all civil wars, politics had profound military consequences—frequently it disrupted patriot preparations, and ultimately it cost Spain the war. Patriot governments often would not cooperate with each other, and their generals intrigued against and sometimes executed one another. Service in the Americas was unpopular among Spanish soldiers, who deserted wherever possible. In 1820 rather than be sent abroad, the last Spanish expeditionary force gathered to reconquer the Americas instead launched a liberal coup at home and the new regime denounced royalist military finance abroad, splintering political cohesion among royalists in Colombia, Mexico, and Peru, though the last grim Spanish captain surrendered only in 1826, after a two-year siege in Peru.

The wars had three huge theaters, with different characteristics. In Mexico, the elite fought the people; in northern and southern South America, the elite fought itself, with the people bystanders or conscripts. The rising of a huge millenarian and social revolutionary movement of peasants led by Father Hidalgo in 1810 drove events in Mexico; when its leadership slipped from the hands of criollos, they feared that it might be turned against them and elected to become loyalists. Hidalgo's horde of seventy thousand men, women, and children could not fight effectively. It surged from town to town, sometimes headed by terrified Spanish hostages to symbolize victory and deter shooting. However, the movement broke before a whiff of grapeshot from a few thousand disciplined royalists. Hidalgo was executed and his movement atomized, but his soul marched on. His men, aware that they lacked the arms and discipline needed for conventional battles, turned to guerrilla warfare and found local leaders—many were bandits and others priests. They besieged towns and harassed loyalists from isolated bases, disrupting administration and the economy, in bands that ranged from gangs of robbers to armies of five thousand men with many guns. Initially, royalists met this threat by terrorizing civilians, but this caused many people

to flee and join the rebels. Then, royalists militarized the people, forming local militias to free regulars for operations against insurgents, but
still the need for garrisons left few men for the field. Royalists did defend
towns, seize rebel bases, and crush their armies, but their strength and
morale slid in a small but permanent war of pinpricks and exhaustion.
From 1816 royalists stayed in their forts rather than chase rebels. Guerrillas controlled the countryside and royalists the cities, each increasingly
tired of the war and of the political causes they defended. The stalemate
broke in 1821 when loyalist and rebel armies ended the war by rejecting
their political masters and combining to form an independent state,
which they ruled.

In South America, the war took a different form than in Mexico—
though soldiers wore ragged uniforms or Indian clothing, campaigns
were more conventional, forces more balanced, and the struggle blood-
ier. Spain had fewer friends and more territory to reconquer. Its navy
could not stop patriot fleets, often led by British veterans, from dominating the seas and landing arms or men in new theaters. The patriot
leader in Colombia, Simon Bolivar, proclaimed a "War to the Death,"
execution for any Spaniard who did not join the rebel cause; royalists
responded in kind. This produced regular massacres of prisoners. Both
sides used terror to control civilians and to seize money and supplies.
Armies were small, usually three thousand to six thousand men, rarely
reaching ten thousand even in the battles that broke the Spanish empire,
like Carabobo in Colombia during 1821 and Ayacucho in Peru during
1824. Losses were high—sickness, desertion, and battle often claimed 50
percent of strength every few months during campaigns—replacements
were rare and those were inexperienced with discipline or weapons. By
1819 twelve thousand of the fifteen thousand Spaniards sent to Colombia since 1814 had died or deserted, and most of its soldiers had been
recruited locally. Armies found it hard to garner even three thousand
recruits during a campaign and thus shrank rapidly. Forcibly conscripted
Indians and freed slaves ultimately formed most of their soldiers. In these
key areas the patriots gained because their leaders were more willing
than royalists ones to free slaves, trust criollos, and reduce racially based
laws on Indians and mulattos. The best forces fought for pay or plunder,
not for ideology. One thousand motivated veterans—Spanish regulars,
irregular Indian cavalry (*llaneros*), Irish mercenaries—were worth their
weight in bayonets, while conscript masses usually were cannon fodder.
As Bolivar once wrote, "any losses suffered by my army will be irrepara-

ble. Its strength depends upon quality, not quantity, and for this reason I am very sensitive of any losses. The others can replace recruits with recruits, but here there are no veterans to replace veterans." One small blow could break the bones of armies so fragile and sometimes their backs. Military-administrative machines constantly broke or jammed. Notably, the great patriot successes (the seizure of Chile in 1818, southern Colombia in 1819, and Lima in 1821) came in surges, followed by one or two years of rebuilding for the next step.

In 1814 patriots ruled Colombia and Venezuela, but weakly and with little support among the rural population, with *llaneros* and royalist guerrillas attacking from peripheral regions. Then an expeditionary force of ten thousand Spaniards, led by the skilled General Morillo, swept the patriots away and conquered a territory twice the size of Spain, taking every town, though by siege. Spaniards lacked the firepower and manpower for storm, and even the 106-day-long siege of Cartagena led to the loss through death and desertion of three thousand of Morillo's men. However, sickness and the need for garrisons weakened Spanish forces during four years of occupation while their attempts to rebuild a stable royalist order created many enemies, especially among *llaneros*, royalist guerrillas, and their leaders, disease resistant allies whom the Spanish treated as potential enemies precisely because they were local popular forces. For this reason, Morillo wished to send most of his criollo units away from Venezuela to Peru. He soon realized that the war could not be won: local populations were hostile to Spain and his irregular allies unreliable, while the more battles the government won, the worse its position: "if the rebels lose territory, they reconcentrate and are stronger at the point they attack, while we are really weaker." *Llaneros*, including many former supporters of the royalists, turned against them. Bolivar found a small fleet and a new front on the Orinoco River in eastern Venezuela and built an army of five thousand *llaneros* riding for booty, with one thousand European infantry mounted as dragoons. In 1819 they drove six hundred miles across the southern highlands of Venezuela and the Andes into the interior of Colombia, playing his strengths against the enemy's weaknesses. This assault caught the enemy by surprise and smashed several dispersed forces. Additionally, it brought new popular support to the patriots and, gradually, many of Morillo's irregular allies and criollo troops deserted to the patriots. It established a new patriot base in Colombia that royalists could not assault except by exposing their weaknesses to Bolivar's strengths; yet neither could he take towns nor win major conventional battles. *Llaneros* were masters of the plains and royalist infantry were kings of the mountains, and Morillo, a better commander on the field, smashed two attempts by Bolivar to break through. Bolivar took two agonizing years to overcome this weakness: "I must have 10,000 muskets . . . or I shall go mad" he wrote, only to receive weapons that were useless without major repairs and raw recruits who had never seen guns before. He advocated freedom for slaves primarily so that they could serve as soldiers. "Is it not proper that the slaves should acquire their rights on the battlefield and that their dangerous numbers should be lessened by a process both just and effective?" Ultimately, Bolivar formed a good army, with conscript infantry trained by European soldiers able to hold a front and *llanero* lancers and a storm battalion of one thousand British mercenaries to launch a murderous close-quarter assault and pursuit. Meanwhile, political division in Spain caused dissension among royalist ranks—many of their best officers, including Morillo, retired to Spain. As Bolivar's men became better organized, the royalists slipped in quality and resilience, and half its men melted away. When Bolivar's army won but one major victory during 1821, throwing mercenaries and *llaneros* together in an overwhelming flank assault, bayonet by lance head, royalist forces in northern South America were broken.

Spain never had the strength even to counterattack in southern Latin America. The war in that region was fought between its viceroyalties—La Plata, based on Buenos Aires, for the patriots and Peru, resting on Lima, for the royalists. Between 1810 and 1821 Peru fought rebels around the Andes, while La Plata suppressed or suborned local rivals and spread revolution. Its last stroke came in 1818 when it sent fifty-five hundred men across the Andes that, cooperating with local patriots, destroyed royalist forces in Chile. Then from north and south, patriots poured into Peru, the last bastion of royalist strength and a three-year struggle that wrecked the Spanish empire. Initially, patriots wished to avoid battle with the larger royalists but instead to starve them from Lima, which they did, helped by a patriot naval blockade. Royalists withdrew to the highlands and became more dangerous than before, smashing expeditions of eight thousand patriots in several pitched battles. Meanwhile, the patriot assault faltered as civil war engulfed La Plata, the government in Colombia lost interest, and the commanders of the northern and southern armies, Bolivar and San Martin, fell out. The belligerents rarely had ten thousand men, frequently halved overnight, and little firepower, which its men misused—at Ayacucho, royalist artillery outnumbered the rebels ten guns to one, yet killed virtually no patriots. Ninety percent of royalist forces and 50 percent of patriots were Indian conscripts, often held in chains until the day of battle. Ultimately, the royalists lost because their cohesion was fragile: in 1824 the commander of one-third their forces revolted against the rest, while at two battles their infantry broke before they fought, routed by the sight of a cavalry charge at Reyes and an hour's bombardment from one patriot gun at Ayacucho.

The wars of independence had grave consequences for Latin America. They devastated economies and populations and dissolved political stability. Spain's empire broke into fifteen successors, politically fragile and militarily impotent. For two centuries, Latin America had been the base for world power, providing resources that were projected deep into wars in North America and Europe, invulnerable to foreign attack. As one world power set in the Americas, another rose.

Warfare in North America was dominated by the power of the United States and its limits. American statesmen wished to master the continent, but British strength tempered their dreams. Anglo-Canadian forces broke American attempts to conquer Canada between 1812 and 1815, wrecking several large armies, though these did win some battles and ravage Ontario. These failures occurred because American organization was bad and their enemy's was good. Between 1812 and 1813, the United States raised 450,000 soldiers, against 17,000 British regulars and Canadian militiamen and 3,500 allied American Indians but did not often deploy even 10,000 in Canada. It rarely maintained field forces larger than the enemy, which usually lost when they did. American transport could not move its soldiers nor its logistics feed them. Its militia routinely refused to serve outside their state boundaries, even when friendly forces were dying just a few hours away. Its main commanders were incompetents who halted at the slightest opposition. With the fall of Napoleon, Britain used its power to teach, smashing American maritime trade and bombarding its ports and burning Washington. It also discovered that Americans fought better defending their own land than attacking another's. These lessons were learned on both sides—until 1892 Americans spent more on coastal defense than a navy; each country avoided challenges to the other and for generations stood poised like scorpions, ready to strike but fearing to do so, one to invade Canada, the other to flatten American coastal cities, until the reasons for war seeped away.

Meanwhile, Britain ceased to dispute American expansion to the Pacific over the ruins of the American Indian nations. These wars were struggles between two peoples for one land, marked by ruthlessness: the main commander on the Plains during the 1870s, General Philip Sheridan, held that campaigns must aim for "annihilation, obliteration and complete destruction. . . . We must act with vindictive earnestness against the Sioux, even to their extermination, men, women and children." Sheridan rarely deployed five thousand soldiers in any campaign, but that equaled the warrior population of the Dakota and Cheyenne nations combined. He used his men with ability, striking one nation at a time and during winter when American Indian supplies were low, to force starvation or surrender, and, at their camps and civilians, to make resistance fatal. The Great Plains nations fought with courage, but they were outnumbered, outgunned, and mediocre strategists, unable to pursue long and systematic campaigns or to strike at enemy weaknesses, like its supply system. Only incompetence and bad luck could produce a serious American defeat, as at Little Big Horn.

The United States also expanded to the south, because its neighbor was weaker. Mexico inherited borders that only the combined power of Latin America and Spain could have sustained, and perhaps not even then. In 1835 the American population in Texas revolted against Mexico. Their situation was less desperate than legend has it, because Mexico was ill-prepared for war while Texan forces were motivated and included many mobile sharpshooters who knew the land. President Santa Anna improvised an army of six thousand troops, little larger than Texan forces and less armed, mostly using Brown Bess muskets. Without adequate transport and medical care, they advanced across desert and mountain to a theater six hundred miles from Mexico City, suffering from dysentery and their leader. Santa Anna, a bold general but overconfident and careless, attacked the advanced Texan outpost, the fortified compound of the Alamo at San Antonio, with linear formations and no finesse; nor had he brought the strength in guns needed to make storm a cheap affair. His men, ravaged by grapeshot and marksmen, retaliated by giving no quarter when the compound finally fell. Though the Alamo is remembered as a deliberate death stand by men who gave themselves to buy time for Texas, it actually stemmed from miscalculations on both sides—Texans assumed that the enemy would never arrive at all or else could easily be checked, and Mexicans assumed that their regulars could smash this foe as easily as it had done guerrilla bands a generation earlier. Soldiers on both sides fought with courage, but it was costly for the Mexicans, as a surprise Texan attack soon smashed in their camp as they advanced. Santa Anna was captured and ceded independence to Texas.

A better general might have won this campaign, which, while difficult, was fought against Texan irregulars in equal strength. In the next clash, Mexico had less chance. In 1846 the United States annexed Texas and indicated an intention to seize all Mexican provinces north of the Rio Grande to the Pacific. Mexico declared war. Its army of twenty thousand men was little better than it had been in 1836. Its men were brave and its officers as competent as their enemy's, but they were handicapped by chaotic politics and a preference for decisive battle rather than for the strategy of evasion and irregular war that wore down Spain by 1821, the French invasion between 1862 and 1867, and the American "punitive expedition" of 1916. They also had no idea of how deadly modern artillery could be against infantry. The U.S. Army of eighty-five hundred men was good, its strength multiplied by thirty-five thousand new recruits and seventy-three thousand volunteers. Its infantry and cavalry units were no better than the enemy and not much larger, while both armies used the same Napoleonic tactics. However, the United States had a devastating edge in artillery, with scores of guns that ripped Mexican forces apart at distances their smoothbore cannon could not reach. American columns surged to California and across the Rio Grande, where superior firepower broke several Mexican forces and their strongest fortifications. Santa Anna retaliated like a gambler, throwing the main Mexican force of fifteen thousand northward through hundreds of miles of mountains in a surprise attack against one American column that he knew to be isolated. Between February 22 and 23, 1847, his exhausted men attacked five thousand green American soldiers at the Battle of Angostura/Buena Vista. They came close to victory but broke on the rock of American guns, without which, General Wool said, his men would not have stood "for a single hour." The Mexicans lost twenty-five hundred killed, wounded, and missing, about five times the enemy's casualties. Meanwhile, the United States feared that a deep advance into Mexico from the north would leave its supply lines exposed to irregular attack— its great concern throughout the war. Instead, it landed at Veracruz and marched inland along the short route to Mexico City, aiming to make the enemy surrender and end the war quickly. Though the loss of Mexico's northernmost territories was unavoidable, still a strategy of evasion, combining the threat of a conventional army with guerrilla attacks on supplies, which were carried by mule trains over mountain trails, might have defeated this American objective. This, however, would have forced a total war and a popular war, which neither American nor Mexican leaders wished to risk. Instead, Mexican forces stood, fought, and lost several engagements and the war and accepted American terms, the loss of all Mexican territory north of the Rio Grande—half of its land, 25 percent of that of the present United States.

In Asia, Western military supremacy rested on firepower. Until 1770 forts and cavalry checked Western forces in India and the Balkans. Then their power declined, though forts retained some strength for decades. In 1836, 8,700 French soldiers failed to capture the walled Algerian town of Constantine, losing 1,000 men killed in the assault and withdrawal; 20,400 Frenchmen were needed to take it in 1837. The future French marshal Achille de Saint-Arnaud wrote that the Algerian gunners "defended themselves with desperate courage. They fired and we killed them while they were reloading: what admirable soldiers! Our bayonets did not leave one alive. We did not take prisoners." More characteristically, between 1827 and 1829 Russians troops seized the strongest of Turkish and Iranian forts, while in 1840 a few British warships and marines seized the Lebanese port of Acre and forced Egypt into a hard peace that slashed its armed strength. By 1864 a few thousand Russians stormed fabled cities like Tashkent and Samarkand after sieges of a few days, and by 1882 they easily annihilated the last of the great nomadic hordes, the Tekke Turkomans, just east of the Caspian Sea.

Between 1838 and 1868 Western sea power, siege trains, and tiny forces of storm troops crushed the strongest forts of China and Japan and reshaped east Asia. The Opium War (1840–42) forced Chinese subordination to the Western economic system. Chinese leaders believed that they could win simply by refusing to trade tea and rhubarb, which they thought essential to Western digestion. They distorted the power of obsolete guns and forts, marines with bows and spears, and "water-braves" able to swim below Western ships and bore holes in their bottoms. "The foreign ships," wrote the Chinese viceroy at Canton, Commissioner Lin, "only have confidence when they are in open waters on the high seas, where they can maneuver at will. Once inside a river-mouth they are like fish in a cauldron; they can at once be captured and destroyed." In fact, Chinese guns and water-braves were useless while seasickness and corruption incapacitated the marines. China was able to deploy no more soldiers to the theater than Britain could. The Ch'ing army was small and bad, half its men "ghost soldiers," existing only on paper while officers pocketed their pay. When Lin suggested that 10 percent of the revenues derived from Canton be used to finance coastal defenses and warships, the Emperor retorted, "a pack of nonsense!" A few British frigates and steam gunboats with four hundred guns and three thousand men entered the Pearl River and bombarded Canton, where local authority collapsed—according to a Chinese account, "Since the army crouched in one quarter, conducting halfway measures and not marshaling to meet the enemy, the people clamoured like rushing waters, saying that the soldiers were not to be depended upon. The city would certainly be destroyed, and the barbarians would enter to burn and loot." Then, the British moved up the coast, wrecking forts of 175 to 200 guns and stopping food shipments to Beijing until the Ch'ing government surrendered. Twenty years later, another conflict prompted Anglo-French forces to force the river route toward Beijing and to burn the Imperial Palace, solely in order to signal their power over China.

Such events destabilized the regime and contributed to a political crisis, the revolt of a millenarian peasant movement throughout half of central China, the Tai'ping rebellion, where again Western forces were central. Between 1861 and 1864, on behalf of Western and Ch'ing interests, the "Ever-Victorious Army" assaulted Tai'ping forces around Shanghai. This army of sixty siege guns and five thousand Chinese stormtroops led by Western mercenaries, often using steamers to strike down channels of the Yellow River Delta, broke the deadlock. It focused on assaulting walled cities, which was fatal to the Tai'ping rebels, whose power centered on cities which Ch'ing forces could not take. The Tai'ping general Li Hsiu-Ch'eng, wrote, "the onslaught of the devil soldiers upon a city was very fierce." They "usually accomplished their work in ten or twelve hours if no help came from outside within that time. Their guns were exceedingly powerful, and every one of their shots took effect, thus destroying our city wall. After destroying the city wall, they would again open fire along their lines and then under cover of this would make a bold dash for the city."

Similarly, in 1853 an American flotilla entered Tokyo Bay, forcing the Shogunate to abandon its policy of isolationism and creating a fifteen-year crisis in Japan. The Shogun's political enemies demanded that he honor his title of "barbarian subduing general" and act on the slogan *Sonno Joi*, "honor the Emperor, expel the barbarian": his officials realized that this was impossible—the samurai had lost their edge. In 1864, the most antiforeign clans, Chosun and Satsuma, attacked westerners. In retaliation, British, French, American, and Dutch warships smashed their coastal fortifications in one of the most influential bombardments in history, while a few thousand Western soldiers routed the Chosun army. British forces occupied Yokohama while Western diplomats played crucial roles in the civil war. *Sonno Joi* withered away. The Chosun and Satsuma clans learned the hard lesson of Western superiority and the need to account for it. By 1868, various Japanese authorities had imported fifty thousand Enfield rifles and hundreds of artillery pieces. Chosun and other clans westernized part of their forces and formed mixed units of samurai and peasants, armed with rifles and swords. Some of these forces were trained by Western units stationed in Japan, others followed the instructions in translated Dutch and British drill books. They approached their enemy in European style lines and fired rapid volleys, but then dropped their rifles and surged into the enemy with swords—at this time, Japanese forces found rifles with bayonets too large and heavy to use. This military and social challenge to the Tokugawa system eroded its military superiority. The Shogun hastily tried to westernize his own forces, but too late—in 1868, twenty thousand of his men were smashed by four thousand of his foes, only some of whom were westernized. The Imperial House, Chosun and Satsuma abolished the Shogunate and brought about the Meiji restoration, aiming to learn from the West so to save Japan from it.

Western armies were unsuccessful in sub-Saharan Africa before 1860—sizable expeditions were rare and unsuccessful, with one portentous exception. On December 16, 1838, 460 Boers in an excellent defensive position at Blood River in South Africa, riflemen behind wagons, killed three thousand of twelve thousand Zulu attackers packed into a small front that they could not penetrate. African armies often were well-organized national forces with conscription, reserve systems, twenty to thirty thousand regular soldiers with good tactics, brave men, and able officers, but, as one European cynic, Hilaire Belloc, wrote, "Thank God! That we have got, The Maxim gun and they have not." African armies relied on spears, shields, bows, and flintlocks. European expeditions rarely exceeded fifteen hundred soldiers, but from 1860 they had decisive advantages in weaponry. Zulu, Mahdist, Sokoto, Matabele, Ashanti, and Tukalor armies were the proud forces of conquest states, used to fighting decisive battles, who often underestimated the effect of firepower. King Cetshwayo told his men before the Anglo-Zulu War of 1879, "There will only be one day of fighting, it will all be over in one day." African armies deployed their usual tactics against Western ones and were annihilated at frightful cost. The few exceptions stemmed from the incompetence of overconfident forces, as at Massawa where, on March 1, 1896, an extraordinarily botched night attack scattered eighteen thousand Italians and their African soldiers in fragments over twenty-five square miles of mountains. Ten thousand of them were killed or captured by human wave assaults of one hundred thousand Ethiopian soldiers, who lost seven thousand slain.

The Zulu system was better suited to fight Europeans than were the cumbersome phalanxes more common in Africa. They had a national army of twenty-five thousand men equipped with cowhide shields, assegais, and clubs. Though they used throwing spears and rifles, a Zulu warrior, Mangwanana Mcunu, expressed a common view—"a gun is a coward's weapon and a man has to be a man to fight with assegais. If a man is a man he will fight at close quarters." Zulus moved as fast as cavalry across rough country, in columns covered by skirmishers. They attacked in a classic formation, the "beasts' horns"—the "chest" hit the front, backed by a reserve, the "loins," while two "horns" struck the flanks, exploiting concealment to gain surprise. This drill provided ample opportunity for breakthrough and envelopment. Against Western forces, Zulus advanced in open lines, using cover against rifles, and charged at close quarters, firing guns and throwing spears to disrupt the enemy, hoping that surprise and speed would bring them into the enemy before rifles, machine guns, and artillery cut them down. This was difficult to achieve even under lucky circumstances. On January 23, 1879, a British column marched unknowingly into an area where the main Zulu army lay hidden and divided in two parts. The Zulus annihilated one half of them—killing one thousand of thirteen hundred British and native soldiers—in an undefended camp at Isandlwana, unable to establish formation before being forced into battle. The other half of the column, despite reports of fighting, did not believe that meant danger—"How very amusing! Actually attacking our camp! Most amusing," one staff officer said. Even so, the Zulus suffered far heavier casualties than the defenders and won only because the British ammunition resupply system collapsed. The first Zulu charges were broken. Their men lay down, taking forty thousand rounds for an hour, before British fire slackened. Then, spurred by regimental pride, in the words of one Zulu, uMhoti, "like a flame the whole Zulu force sprang to its feet and darted upon them." Subsequently, Zulus won other minor engagements but were smashed in two battles, Khambula and Ulundi, the latter almost a suicide stand by twenty thousand men who knew they could not win but refused to yield. Another Zulu, Zimena, described the experience of charging into fire:

> we heard one of our men shout with pain as he was shot, and saw him fall. We rushed into battle . . . they brought out their "by and by " [artillery] and we heard what we thought was a long pipe [rocket] coming through the air towards us. We never got closer than 50 paces to the English, and although we tried to climb over our fallen brothers we could not get very far ahead because the white men were firing heavily close to the ground into our front ranks , while the "by and by" was firing over our heads into the regiments behind us . . . Some of our men had their arms torn right off by [shells]. The battle was so fierce that we had to wipe the blood and the brains of the killed and wounded from our heads, faces, arms, legs and shields after the fighting.

Nor was this an ordeal just of fire—vengeful pursuit demolished fleeing Zulus after their great defeats. In 1879 Zulus killed fifteen hundred of ten thousand attackers but lost 40 percent of their soldiers and their freedom.

Europeans found it more difficult to fight Africans using guerrilla tactics. By 1898, for example, British taxation sparked a popular revolt in Sierra Leone. Before the "Hut Tax" war began, insurgents acquired better firearms, built stockades around villages and roads, and seized all water transport. During it, British flying columns had to attack one stockaded town after another, ambushed constantly by guerrillas who focused their fire on officers and porters. The British suppressed the revolt, but at a greater cost than they suffered to smash thirty thousand Sokoto regulars in Nigeria. Again, in 1885, Samori Toure, master of a Malian empire with thirty-five thousand regular soldiers, fought France and learned the need for new forces and tactics. He acquired modern single shot rifles and sent men into French forces to learn how to repair and to use them. When France attacked between 1891 and 1893, Toure refused to send large forces to their slaughter. Instead, he deployed riflemen behind small defenses across roads, making the French fight for each one, while guerrillas harassed their communications and denied them food. Toure adapted effectively to European forces, yet still he lost the war and his territory. Ten of his men died for every French soldier killed or wounded. In differing ways, Zulus and Toure show the quality of African soldiers and strategy in the heyday of imperialism and how hopeless the effort was.

More generally, until the 1860s popular movements using guerrilla tactics regularly defeated small European forces—between 1838 and 1842, for example, Afghans defeated ninety-five hundred British and Indian soldiers and six thousand irregular allies, ultimately killing half of them and thousands of their followers in a pitiless rout through drifts of snow down the Khyber Pass—and stalled large ones. Armies could defeat determined armed societies only through prolonged and ruthless campaigns. The great Russian conqueror General M. D. Skobelov espoused the "principle that, in Asia the duration of peace is in direct proportion to the slaughter you inflict on the enemy. The harder you hit them, the longer they will remain quiet afterwards." Counterinsurgency was always harsh and sometimes approached genocide. Germany, for example, suppressed the Namibian rebellion of 1904 and 1905 by driving the rebellious Herrero and Nama peoples into the Kalarai desert to die, where 66 percent of them did.

Yet, peoples whose organization beyond the clan or village was loose could not easily mount prolonged guerrilla campaigns. In order to do so, elites and people needed to perceive a deadly threat to their way of life and to possess some bodies able to serve as the sociopolitical backbone for resistance. These were hard to find and often fragile: in 1865 a great Maori warband collapsed because its leader slept with a woman, wrecking both his ritual status and military organization; though Hidalgo headed a genuinely mass movement, its political organization splintered under elementary pressure and was never restored. He rallied peasants by claiming that the uprising was in defense of the faith and the Virgin of Guadalupe—his forces carried her image on banners and badges; many of his men claimed to act on behalf of the Spanish king, who they claimed actually accompanied their army hidden in a black coach. In the nineteenth century, religious bodies usually were the only sociopolitical means available to rally a guerrilla movement. Masters of guerrilla warfare supported by Sufi Muslim brotherhoods, for example, led the two greatest struggles against Western conquest of the mid-nineteenth century. In Algeria during 1834, religious fraternities appointed Abd el-Qadir, a prominent Qadiriyya sufi, to lead resistance against France's invasion of Algeria. This movement checked one hundred thousand French soldiers for fifteen years. Initially, French forces were divided between blockhouses or field forces unable to fight the Algerians unless they chose to stand. As Governor Thomas Bugeaud said in 1837, "You drag thousands of wagons and heavy artillery with you which slows your movements. Rather than surprise the Arabs with rapid, offensive marches, you stay on the defensive, marching slowly. Your enemies follow you and attack at their convenience. All this is going to change! . . . no more heavy artillery, no more of these heavy wagons, no more of these enormous forage trains. . . . The convoys will be on mule back and the only cannons permitted will be light ones." This approach could defeat large forces which stood to fight, but not a popular insurrection without capital city or regular army. Against that, Bugeaud used classic counterinsurgent tactics, systematically clearing one district after another, raiding villages, devastating crops, killing all male insurgents but sparing women and children, continually pursuing a fleeing foe but accepting the surrender of a beaten one. His soldiers complained that they needed "the thighs of a buck, the heart of a lion and the stomach of an ant."

Similarly, between 1834 and 1859, Inam Shamyl led Chechen and Daghestani guerrillas, who were rallied by the Naqshbandiyya-Khallidiyya sect, which preached social revolution alongside the defense of faith and culture. They tied down fifty to two hundred thousand Russian soldiers in Caucasia, where tens of thousands of them died. Shamyl was aided by the declining quality of the Russian army, focused on beautiful drill rather than warlike arts, and by the incompetence of its command. For a decade, Russians were thrown into blockhouses in the wilderness, often huts of reed and mud, disease-ridden, irrelevant, and overwhelmed. Shamyl coordinated resistance and established conscription and taxation systems among hundreds of thousands of people. When Russians destroyed the crops of one village, others fed its women and children until the next harvest. When massive Russian forces drove deep into the forested mountains of Chechnya, guerrillas evaded them, withdrew until the Russians retreated, ambushed their columns in narrow passes, and smashed tired and divided soldiers. Between 1842 and 1847, Shamyl's men overran the Russian fortification system in Chechnya, broke two field forces of a size that had smashed the main armies of Turkey or Iran just a decade before, and crippled several others. The Russians finally won only through a slow process of military, political, and ecological warfare, consolidating one district after another. Protected by soldiers, Russian axemen cut down forests and established effective forts deep in Chechen valleys, from which garrisons provided stable rule to villages that surrendered and fire to those that resisted.

These counterinsurgents of the nineteenth century knew all of the tricks used in the twentieth and had more success with them, while guerrillas had weaker means of political organization and less foreign help against their masters. In this context, the rise of Western superiority in firepower from 1880 wrecked the ability of guerrilla forces to withstand determined efforts at conquest. This situation changed only after 1945, when guerrilla forces were bolstered by better firepower and more effective sociopolitical organization.

Indigenous resistance to European conquests was remarkable, but so was local cooperation with it. That shaped the politics of imperialism in the nineteenth century and of decolonization after 1945. European colonial armies were weak in strength and poor in reputation. One commander of French forces in Senegal described his men as "drunkards and marauders, disturbed and profoundly vicious men"; another claimed that, unless restrained, French soldiers in Africa "would be drunk from morning to night and would die of dysentery. Drunkenness here is the cause of death for half the white soldiers"—not surprising, as 70 percent of them were there as a military penal punishment. Combat and sickness had a phenomenal impact on European colonial forces. In 1827 and 1828, 45 percent of European troops in Java died; between 1828 and 1858, Russians stationed in Caucasian forts lived three to six years on average. A permanent manpower crisis gripped colonial armies. Russia solved this problem by using national units. The maritime empires did so by creating imperial forces, manned by mercenaries from Europe and especially from indigenous groups. The latter usually but not always were ethnic minorities—imperialists knew that an army raised from the dominant local nationality might become loyal to it and challenge European rule. Indigenous personnel served because this offered them advantages. Virtually all of their officers were European, though a few natives became junior officers in French forces; however, relationships between European officers and colonial soldiers often rested on human ties rather than racial hierarchy. Britain centered its professional army, which the duke of Wellington called "the scum of the earth enlisted for drink," around imperial work, augmented by the Indian army. Forty percent of European recruits for Dutch forces in Indonesia (nicknamed "the sewer of Europe") were mercenaries, the rest Dutchman joining from poverty. Until 1890, the Dutch recruited fewer native forces than the British or French but ultimately Eurasians and native Christians provided 60 percent of Dutch strength. This small army, rarely more than thirty thousand men, conquered Indonesia only with great bloodshed and after eighty years.

The French Imperial Army, "La Coloniale," was larger than this and drawn from more sources. It included the "Armee d'Afrique," recruited from white settlers in North Africa and the Foreign Legion, famed for discipline, desertion, self-sacrifice, and alcoholism. Often these characteristics were combined. At the siege of Dien Bien Phu in 1954, dehydrated wine was airdropped so that the Legion could celebrate its regimental holiday, "Camerone Day," named after a famous disaster in Mexico, when a force of legionnaires died to the last man. When the shipment accidentally fell behind enemy lines, the Legion called for volunteers to recover it—there was no shortage. Legionnaires stormed hundreds of yards, broke through enemy trenches, and returned with the vital elixir. "La Coloniale" also recruited "Tirailleurs" (sharpshooters) from many of its subject peoples in Africa. One of these forces, the "Tirailleurs Senegalais," stemmed from Senegal around 1820, when France formed armed companies of slaves. Even in 1900 half its men were originally slaves. Given their low pay, the Tirailleurs Senegalais had to be recruited from men who wished to join, and an obvious source were the slave and free soldiers of African states conquered by France. Sons of defeated ruling classes, including those of Samori Toure, dominated the native officer ranks of the Tiralleurs Senegalais. It steadily grew from 750 men in 1854 to eighty-five hundred in 1900, as France used some Africans to conquer others. In order to maintain unit cohesion, France encouraged stable families for its soldiers, who chose wives from captured slaves; women of the regiment served as the support echelon on campaign. Soldiers lived tolerably well, with families, slaves, and the chance for booty. Subsequently, French statesmen came to see the Tirailleurs Senegalais as a means to tap the reservoir of African manhood for the power of France. By 1912 selective conscription was adopted to man the Tirailleurs Senegalais and between 1914 and 1918, 170,000 Senegalese served on the western front. Thirty thousand were killed. They developed pride in their status and loyalty to France, reinforced by awards of pensions, medical care, education for their children, and status. Most "Free French" soldiers between 1940 and 1944 were Africans. In order to overcome this embarrassment, in 1944 the Free French "whitened" their most famous divisions—

transferring African troops out, keeping the name, and filling the units with new personnel who could take credit for the work of the old ones. After 1960 the native officer corps of British and French colonial forces became the government of many newly independent African states.

Case Study: The Indian "Mutiny"

In 1857 a revolt by a peasant army almost broke a European empire. The Indian "mutiny" had social roots. British rule in India rested on its military dominance and on indigenous soldiers organized in three separate armies. The officers of the most important of these forces, the Bengal army, deliberately recruited their men from high caste rural groups, whom they believed would provide the best soldiers and also most solidify British rule in the countryside. In turn, members of social groups whose economic or Brahminical status was marginal used the British connection to bolster themselves. Most sepoys of the Bengal army were drawn from a few high caste groups with a fragile economic status, particularly smallholders of an independent state allied to Britain, Awadh. Employment as sepoys was essential to the economic and social status of these men, yet in the decades before 1857 the British put this at risk. They concluded that the privileges of the sepoys were eroding their value—sepoys deserted and mutinied if made to take any action that compromised their caste status, such as crossing the sea—and wished to make the Bengal army less pampered and more professional. They recruited sepoys from new social groups who competed with old ones for scarce jobs. After decades of encouraging soldiers to claim high caste status, even ensuring that Brahmin prostitutes alone serviced their men, the British imposed new forms of discipline that challenged sepoys' status and labor conditions. They pursued aggressive policies that violated Indian concepts of justice, annexing allied states and challenging property rights and increasing taxes. The British deposed the king of Awadh, to whom many sepoys and peasants owed feudal loyalty, eroded the economic status of the communities from which sepoys came, and threatened their livelihoods. Sepoys came to fear that Britain wished to destroy their social and religious status. They remembered that the British suppressed military dissent ruthlessly, often forming up mutinous units on parade and then shooting them down. Rumor multiplied fear. When new Enfield rifles were issued to sepoys, stories spread that their bullets were coated with pork and cow fat, anathema to Muslims and Hindus, deliberately so, in order to achieve Britain's true aim, which was to break the religion of sepoys or to drive them from the army.

All this sparked a conspiracy among sepoys. Their initial aims are uncertain—many may have intended merely to strike over labor conditions, a practice common among them, but members of a conspiracy within the conspiracy pursued darker aims. From the first outbreak on May 10, 1857, some sepoys massacred British officers and their families and committed the rest to desperate stakes. The mutineers marched to Delhi and announced loyalty to the Mughal empire. When they were not immediately crushed, mutiny spread like a string of firecrackers. Most regiments of the Bengal army mutinied, the rest were mostly disbanded by force—only one came through loyal and intact. Though units were in contact with others, each made its own decision through barrack room debates. Some sepoys remained loyal, including many whom British units forced away from mistrust, while others deserted. Most sepoys, however, followed their comrades—many on leave returned to their mutinous regiments.

Two things crippled the mutiny from the start. It remained limited to units of the Bengal army. Though Britain could not use the Bombay and Madras Armies to suppress the mutiny, they did not join it. Again, British authorities believed that most of India was ready to explode. This did not happen because the mutiny imploded. The mutineers started without a military strategy and never found one. As General Wilson, the first British commander before Delhi noted, "Luckily the enemy have no head and no method." The mutineers' great hope was to spread the revolt far and fast. Initially the British could not have blocked such moves, which might have spread revolt throughout India and mutiny into the Madras and Bombay armies. Instead, the mutineers rallied on Delhi and Lucknow, the capitals of the Mughul empire and Awadh, concentrating at the center of the rebellion rather than on expanding it.

The mutiny sparked many revolts but no national revolution. This was from lack not of desire but of nation. The sepoys, recruited from many regions and religions, were a corporate body with pan-Indian views. As some policemen noted, "All black men are one. It is a matter of religion. Why should we lose our religion." The mutineers turned for legitimacy to Mughal and Mahratta princes, to nobles and notables, and made them leaders. Hindu and Muslim mutineers and nobles played to religious sentiments and pursued a common front against the British, but they failed to create one or even to form effective local governments among the 30 million people free of British rule. This vacuum was filled by local movements. In Awadh and some economically marginal areas, peasant insurgents launched a popular war against the British. In other places, local groups immediately began to fight each other, while most regions remained quiet. Large armies of independent Indian princes who might have turned the tide stood uncertain for months, and then attacked the British only after the sepoys had been smashed. The British would have lost without support from Indians. Allied Gurkha and new Sikh and Pathan units provided half of their field forces, while Sikh peasants attacked sepoys who had conquered them a bare generation before.

Mutiny led to atrocity. Mutineers sometimes escorted British officers and their families to safety, but generally someone killed them. Few mutineers were murderers, but many paid for it. Most notoriously, Indian forces led by a Mahratta noble, Nana Sahib, offered safe passage to British soldiers and civilians trapped at Kanpur but then slaughtered them in a public spectacle watched by thousands of Indian civilians. Yet weeks later, sepoys refused Nana Sahib's order to kill the surviving European women and children in the room where they were held, the Bibighar—his servants had to do the deed by secret. Again, hundreds of British women were murdered, but none were raped, though fear of this fate fuelled the rage of British soldiers. For their part, Britons believed that their rule rested on fear and that only a demonstration of terror could stop the mutiny and avenge the murders. The march to Kanpur was marked by British atrocities, triggered by the slightest sign of disrespect; they rose after the Bibighar was found. A routine was established: soldiers moving upcountry were taken to the Bibighar, where white women's blood stained the walls, and unleashed on sepoy and civilian. This sparked deadly oaths—the future Field Marshal Garnett Wolseley took the vow "most soldiers made there—of vengeance and of having blood for blood, not drop for drop, but barrels and barrels of the filth which flows in these niggers' veins for every drop of blood which marked the floors and walls of that fearful house." British soldiers murdered perhaps one hundred Indian civilians for every European killed. This became counterproductive as they wished to restore order—one commander near Agra noted in late 1857, "We have established such a terror, that it is impossible to get any one to come in." While British anger toward civilians ebbed, they remained pitiless toward sepoys. Many captured mutineers were taken to the Bibighar, made to lick out blood, and hung; others were tied alive across cannon muzzles and their bodies blown apart.

At various stages in 1857, seventy thousand sepoys were in revolt, joined by as many members of princely armies and more guerillas. British resources were scant—forty-five thousand white troops in India, eight thousand more within easy reach. Seventy-five percent of these men were needed to watch the Bengal and Madras armies, to cover the peripheries of the revolt, to disband Bengal army units, and to control three hundred million Indians. The remainder could not be used rationally. The purely military response was to hold a ring, to wait for reinforcements, and to strike with power concentrated and coordinated. Commanders correctly believed that if they did not move fast, the revolt would spread; nor could they abandon white civilians in isolated garrisons. Small British forces immediately drove to save civilians besieged in Lucknow and Kanpur, and to retake Delhi, reinforcements dribbling behind as they arrived. By July 1857 five thousand British and allied troops stood before Delhi, held by thirty thousand mutineers, while another fifteen hundred moved on Lucknow, against thirteen thousand enemies. They could be reinforced only with difficulty, leaving four thousand British soldiers to garrison twenty-five million Punjabis. Even so, in September 1857 barely eight thousand men, including just twenty-three hundred white infantry, were available to assault Delhi. Reinforcements rose steadily, however—thirty thousand British and Indian soldiers took Lucknow in March 1858—while sepoy numbers shrank.

The sepoys had numbers but no officers. Few mutineers had commanded two hundred men in battle before, none more. Within small units they fought well, but they failed in higher tasks like maneuvering units on the battlefield or coordinating infantry, artillery, and cavalry. They wasted their strength and lost the war. In June and July 1857, mutineers outnumbered British at Delhi six to one. They never used their forces to crush the enemy or to cut its communications. Instead, to prove its loyalty, as each body of mutineers reached Delhi, it marched in front of prepared British positions and artillery, stopped in the open, exchanged fire for hours, and withdrew without charging the defender. Casualties were devastating and one-sided. The British command system was unimpaired and able to control new Indian allies. Its men and officers fought with fanaticism and overwhelming superiority in open combat. Several times on the road to Lucknow, British artillery and riflemen cut up superior numbers of sepoys in line, bayonet charges smashed their flanks, and cavalry completed the slaughter. More effectively, Awadi soldiers forced the British into costly assaults against strongpoints on the roads, held by snipers. By September 1857 mutineer losses through combat and desertion were enormous. Units were at half strength and demoralized. One group of captured sepoys later said, "Sahib, it has all been the work of fate. After what we had done, we never could fight. No matter whether your troops were black or white, native or European, we could not stand against them; *our salt choked us.*" Yet British losses in street fighting were huge, their morale cracking and victory in assaults on walled towns was uncertain. The first force reaching Lucknow on September 25, 1857, was so weak that it just left a few reinforcements and withdrew to escort civilians to safety. On September 14 the British attacked Delhi with even numerical odds. The walls were shattered but so was the army—33 percent of assaulting British infantry and 50 percent of their officers were casualties. Discipline collapsed, men refused orders, falling drunk while penned along the wall, their commander killed in a desperate attempt to rally his forces. A resolute enemy could have won the battle, but the mutineers collapsed, and with them the mutiny.

After the reconquest of Delhi, scattered bodies of mutineers fought on while princely armies raised minor revolts for some months. Peasant insurgency subsided with one exception, Awadh. The British took Lucknow as a boot kicks a firepit, scattering sparks into the undergrowth— its garrison of fifteen thousand sepoys and fifty thousand irregulars simply withdrew. The British commander wrote that "the enemy is as formidable after he has been beaten as he was before." British officials estimated that 75 percent of Awadi males fought in a "general, almost universal" revolt against them. Sepoys proved easier to defeat than guerrillas, large in numbers, high in morale, and fighting in jungles dotted with forts. As one insurgent leader, Khan Bahadur Khan, said, "Do not attempt to meet the regular columns of the infidels, because they are superior to you in discipline and bunderbust [organization], and have big guns; but watch their movements, guard all their ghauts on the rivers, intercept their communications, stop their supplies, cut up their daks and posts, and keep constantly hanging about their camps; give them no rest." Ultimately, only constant military pressure combined with an amnesty to irregulars, and an effort to redress the socio-economic causes for the rebellion in Awadh, suppressed the guerrillas. To the sepoys, the British offered nothing but death, and they honored that promise.

Western armies reshaped the world during the nineteenth century through influence as well as conquest. They forced other states to westernize their armies or die. The road to military westernization was hard. It led not just to minor changes in offices or weapons but to a revolution—the abandonment of indigenous systems of organization, recruitment, and tactics and their replacement with Western ones. States had to create military industries, large armies, and officer corps, which were technically competent but politically loyal, and pay for all of these institutions and to control them. Failure to get every one of these reforms right at the right time could wreck a policy that was otherwise good. Meanwhile, to westernize an army was to change power within a state and the people who controlled it. Military revolutions produced political ones, while even inefficient moves toward westernization had great unintended consequences.

The first state outside India that tried to westernize its army was Egypt, a feudatory of the Ottoman Empire. Its governor, Mehmet Ali, witnessed French and British armies fighting in Egypt in 1801 and wished to make himself independent and powerful. He raised revenues tenfold, half going to the military, and tried to discipline his army and to westernize it. When his army rejected both options, Ali created a new one. Its men were peasants, recruited through a brutal conscription system and marched off in chains for life. Its officers were drawn from the old Mamluk ruling class of Egypt and new slaves purchased from the Caucasus, all trained by French personnel. Egypt was one of the most militarized societies on earth—2 percent of its adult males were soldiers and its economy focused on the maintenance of an arsenal. Mehmet Ali procured modern firearms and sent men to Europe for industrial training: Egypt could produce three thousand muskets per month, artillery, and sail-of-the-line. This effort led to disaster. By 1839 it produced economic and political crises, which forced Mehmet Ali into war with Turkey and a disastrous clash with Britain. His army, while the best in the Middle East, was far below European standards of quality. After 1840 the Egyptian army declined in scale as did its military industries. Still, Egypt purchased and produced leading weapons—Colt revolvers, Krupp artillery, Minié rifles—in large numbers. Between 1869 and 1880 its army was as well equipped as any on earth and launched campaigns of conquest far down the Nile River. This effort again caused disaster. Sudanese forces smashed the overstretched Egyptian empire on the Nile. These policies bankrupted Egypt and produced a militaristic nationalism that linked upper and lower classes. A popular movement embodied in the army and led by an officer, Colonel Urabi, overturned the government. That sparked the British conquest of 1882—when Egyptian troops were well equipped but whipped. The identification of army with nation, however, remained fundamental in Egypt. It helped to destroy British rule in the 1950s and to shape Egyptian politics for decades afterward.

The Ottoman Empire took decades to address its military problems and until 1840, only divisions among foreign powers saved it. Sultan Selim III sought just to discipline his army: this so angered the Janisaries that in 1807 they killed him and his new soldiers. His successor, Mahmud II, achieved Selim's aims. In 1826, when the Janissaries again preferred revolt to reform, he slaughtered them. Mahmud created a new army and used it to finance itself by reestablishing direct control over Turkish territories in Anatolia and part of the Balkans. He devoted 70 percent of his revenues to the military but he did not westernize it. His army was larger and better disciplined, able to overawe all internal dissent, but it remained poor against external foes—smashed by Russia in 1829, by Egypt in 1832 and 1839. Mahmud distrusted foreign advisors. He made unqualified favorites or privates into officers and did not train them or their units well. The command system was weak. In 1839, the leaders of a Turkish army near the frontier with Egypt wished to evacuate a poor position but feared this would make the army disintegrate. Instead, that army stood, fought and was smashed, though it significantly outnumbered the Egyptians.

Despite these failures, Mahmud legitimized the improvement of the army and integrated its leadership into the Ottoman elite. Soon Turkey established a respectable army of the second class, equal in quality to the Russian and fighting in a similar fashion. In 1770, Russian armies won despite great numerical inferiority; by 1877, only through substantial superiority. With an effective and socially accepted system of conscription and reserve units, Turkish strength rose from twenty-seven thousand men in 1828 to seven hundred thousand by 1914, fairly well trained and equipped, the infantry famed for self-sacrifice and ferocity at close range. Problems were plenty. The officers corps was below the European standard—even in 1914, 33 percent of them were illiterate—

though it always contained able men. Support services were poor as were many reserve units. Yet the Turkish army did well against Russia in the Crimean War and in the war of 1877 and against half a million Russian and British combat soldiers between 1914 and 1918. Between 1919 and 1923 it defied the victorious allies and saved Turkey.

This was the best record of any non-Western army in the heyday of European imperialism, but it came at a cost. The Turkish army created a nation by subverting an empire. In order to westernize, the army developed a thick network of schools and arsenals and became a self-contained corporation, the strongest in the Ottoman Empire. It was the nursery of the Turkish nation and of a political faction. Officers developed their own political ideology, tinged by secularization, Turkish nationalism, and a demand for the rapid pursuit of radical ends. Such doctrines destabilized a conservative multinational empire. In 1876 officers revolted against one Sultan, and in 1908 against another, this time successfully. Politicization crippled Turkey and its army. Between 1879 and 1908 Sultan Abdulhamid II refused to let his troops maneuver or train with their modern weapons, for fear this would facilitate another mutiny. He left his expensive and well-equipped fleet, which bombarded Istanbul during the abortive coup of 1876, to rot. The officers who seized power in Istanbul during 1908 drove their empire to ruin by 1918 in pursuit of greater Turkey, especially by antagonizing non-Turkish nationalities and by taking a costly part in the First World War. They bequeathed a problematic relationship between army and state in Turkey that persisted throughout the twentieth century.

One non-Western country reformed its armies better than the rest because it began with advantages. In 1868, Japan already was a nation-state, the only one outside the West, with a strong central government, a high level of literacy, and a well-integrated national economy. Even then, Britain believed that a far larger army would be required to defeat Japan than China. Japanese leaders learned the right lessons from their brush with Western power and acted on them with rare foresight and determination. They pursued a "Rich Nation, Strong Army"—a modern military-industrial base for a westernized army and navy to defend Japan from attack and to expand its power in Asia. They pursued this end through a revolution from above. Government leaders were samurai, but they broke the exclusive role of their class as warriors, banned the wearing of swords, and stopped the subsidies that many samurai needed to maintain their status. The government replaced them with an army of peasant conscripts, officers drawn primarily from samurai of the Chosun and Satsuma clans, faithful to the government, all indoctrinated with a version of bushido and shintoism intended to inculcate loyalty to the new regime. This created a large but loyal army and also several samurai revolts, most notably one of twenty-five thousand in 1877. These swordsmen lost every battle they fought against forty-five thousand peasant conscripts with rifles, and died virtually to a man, but they were defeated only when another twenty thousand samurai loyal to the state joined the fray, and only after six months of combat and killing sixty-three hundred of their foes. This showed the success of the first decade of military reform but also its limits.

However, Japan brought in training missions from the world's best forces, the German army and the Royal Navy. Members of these missions had a free hand on the technical side of military reform but no executive authority. They worked effectively and transmitted their own organizational system and styles of war to their Japanese counterparts. Japanese forces adopted Western uniforms and traditions—the officer training school of the Imperial Japanese Navy, Etijima, was an exact duplicate of its British model, Dartmouth, built of red bricks imported from England, centered on a shrine built around a glass casket containing a lock of Nelson's hair—but they never became slaves to one foreign military and bought equipment from many countries. By 1900 Japan possessed a solid army, well equipped with modern weapons, and one of the best second-class fleets in the world—the first good navy that any non-Western state had produced in three hundred years. Soon Japan smashed Russia in a major war, became a great power, and began to carve an empire from its neighbors. Meanwhile, the government created a statist and militarist economy. It taxed peasants heavily and deployed half its revenues to the military. It used much of the rest to encourage industries linked to military power. The government supported that effort through the acquisition of technology, by purchasing foreign equipment, copying the best designs, and establishing firms able to make copies and then to manufacture designs of their own. By 1900 Japan became the first non-Western nation with a great industrial base, able to produce modern warships—the most complicated machinery of the day. By 1939 it had the sixth strongest economy on earth. It became an air power precisely as it had become a sea power—acquiring French and British training missions, purchasing foreign equipment and copying it, developing firms able to produce copies and then original designs, and massively subsidizing the industry. These military reforms met their aims—Japan defended itself and created an empire but at a price. Ultimately, the new army destabilized the state and promoted a spirit of militaristic nationalism that drove Japan into the disasters of the Pacific war.

Two abortive attempts to import the European army show how hard the road was. After 1885 Chile hired thirty-six German instructors, led by Captain Emil Körner, to modernize its antiquated army. Körner did so by pouring Chilean wine into German bottles. Chile became known as "the Prussia of the Pacific." Its soldiers wore Prussian spiked helmets, goose stepped to Prussian tunes played on German-made bugles, and used German weapons, regulations for cavalry, infantry, and artillery and systems of military organization and conscription. Körner modeled Chilean training schools after Prussian ones, using translated German manuals, and created an *Academia de Guerra* and *Estado Mayor Jeneral* copied from Prussian models. By 1914, 25 percent of Chilean officers had been trained in Germany. The Prussian General Staff deemed the Chilean army of twenty-six thousand regulars "the best in South America."

But appearances were deceiving: Chilean wine went sour in German bottles. Prussian forms worked well only if the content was suitable—the state effective, autocratic, and militaristic, the people educated but obedient. Chile was not Prussia nor Chileans Japanese. Its government was unwilling to make the financial sacrifices needed to modernize its military, its economy was unable to bear the burden, while its people were poor servants. Only 30 percent of Chileans were literate, while the affluent evaded the draft, aided by doctors and lawyers. Many Chilean officers failed the War Academy—unthinkable in Prussia and indicating problems of competence. The Chilean army remained an organizational nightmare, worsened by Körner's repeated tinkering, without effective infrastructure. Barracks were squalid, troops ill-fed, supply and medical systems primitive, and equipment expensive but poorly maintained. Meanwhile, the mission betrayed its trust. During the revolution of 1891, Körner joined the insurgents, turning the Chilean army against the government that had hired him. He used this position to further his aims and German ones at Chile's expense. Körner purchased rifles and artillery exclusively from specific German firms and corruption by him, German purveyors and Chilean purchasers was substantial. Chile created a big army for which it had little use, which distorted its development throughout the twentieth century.

The process of military westernization was even more traumatic in China. From 1838, defeat by Western powers showed the need to reform Chinese armies. By 1862 the Tai'ping rebellion made it unavoidable. The only forces able to halt that revolt were provincial armies, loyal to their officers rather than the state. In order to keep their forces supplied and able to fight, generals became governors, controlling civil administration and garrisons. Initially, the dangers of this trend were avoided because generals were loyal to Confucian ideals, but increasingly they pursued self-interest. So long as officers were Confucians, they were politically loyal but technically mediocre; the development of a military education system to provide qualified officers sapped Confucian ideals and politicized the army. As the central government failed to create and control effective military forces, its power waned. The Chinese army became regionalized and politicized, while the government played each faction against the other. Intrigue determined the appointment of officers, the allocation of resources, and the pursuit of military policies, damaging the army and its country. The army could not protect China from external threat but posed an internal one, culminating after 1916 in the division of China between provincial warlords, the degradation of the people and impotence against a devastating invasion by Japan. In Turkey, the army captured the state but saved the people; in China, the army destroyed the state and weakened the nation. By 1864 a leading Ch'ing commander against Tai'ping forces, Li Hung-Chang, concluded that Chinese armies "cannot measure up to" Western ones. "I daily exhort my officers and soldiers to be of unprejudiced mind and to stand prepared to study some of the methods of the westerners, so that we may add what they have and use it in battle." For the next thirty years he pursued a policy of "self-strengthening." Li trained troops on Western lines though he trusted foreign advisors less than the Japanese and misunderstood the need to train a technically qualified officer corps. He established large arsenals and civilian firms with Western technology because "to rely on foreigners for our supplies is suicide." Yet between 1894 and 1895, Japan smashed all of his forces. Li failed because China faced more problems and enemies than Japan did but primarily for this reason: "Although I have desired reforms and self-strengthening, without talented men, without funds, without supporters, what can we do?" The Japanese pursued these aims systematically and with all of their resources. Li could do so only with resources under his control, perhaps 15 percent of Chinese state finances, while many officials wished him to fail—in 1894–95 they threw his forces against the Japanese while saving their own.

Asian states westernized their armies only when they made that aim fundamental and survived the political crises that it inevitably caused. Even then, bad westernized armies were easy to produce. Foreign training missions provided the easiest access to expertise, but, from fear of the political consequences, many states rejected this idea while missions routinely proved incompetent or abused their positions. Modern equipment was necessary to match Western firepower, but few states could pay for it, and many of those never used these weapons effectively. Meanwhile, the westernization of armies strained the financial, economic, and administrative systems of states that pursued the aim. This could fail if it did not proceed far and fast: more powerful rivals often smashed westernizing armies before the task was done, as Britain did to Mahrattas, Sikhs, and Egyptians, Japan did to China, and Russia and Egypt almost did to Turkey.

The greatest problem lay with the creation of an officer corps, which linked the problems of military and political command. Westernization must fail unless it produced a large and competent officer corps with real control of armed forces; yet such a corps might overthrow its political masters. In every case of westernization, for long periods officer corps proved incompetent, disloyal, or both, with one exception—Japan, where westernization followed a revolution and officers were selected for loyalty to a regime and its policies. Sooner or later, every westernizing officer corps overthrew the regime that created it, including the Japanese military in the 1930s. The greatest technical difficulty faced by westernizing military forces was how to produce officers with a uniform and good level of quality. The westernization of military institutions always provoked political crises—revolts by old armies, coups by new ones. It increased the power of states over society. It created institutions that revolutionized their countries. It produced wars, for westernized armies immediately attacked their neighbors, and, by spreading Western military techniques across the globe, it eroded Western military hegemony.

In some ways, the power of Western armies rose after 1914. During the 1930s, ten thousand British soldiers and 150 aircraft dominated the Middle East, while in Ethiopia Italian armored cars and poison gas avenged Massawa. Still, the roots of European superiority were withering. Several non-Western powers had created westernized armies and nation-states, which could compete on fairly equal terms in their own territories and neighboring ones with Western powers. Over coming years other countries followed these models, which raised their military power and overturned their politics: Egyptian and Turkish patterns of military intervention in politics, for example, became characteristic of states in the Islamic world. New forms of political organization proved better able to sustain wars of national liberation against foreign conquest, while after 1945 guerrillas received more foreign support than any of the nineteenth century had been able to acquire. Western conquest was no longer cheap. As it became more expensive, it became less common. Western armies remained more powerful than most non-Western ones but attacked them less often. Even more than this, during the century of Western military dominance, wars between Western states were rare. In 1914 and 1939, however, European states began total wars against each other that destroyed their power against the world.

Suggested Reading

In terms of method, three recent works are central to the understanding of military relations between Western and non-Western powers in the period under review. Richard White, *The Middle Ground, Indians, Empires and Republics in the Great Lakes region, 1650–1815* (Cambridge, 1991); Matthew Headrick, *The Tools of Empire: Technology and European Imperialism in the Nineteenth Century* (Oxford, 1981); and James Belich, *The New Zealand Wars and the Victorian Interpretation of Racial Conflict* (Auckland, 1986). Douglas Peers, ed., *Warfare and Empires, Contact and Conflict Between European and Non-European military and maritime forces and cultures, An Expanding World, vol. 24* (Ashgate, 1997), is a useful reader on the topic.

There is a large literature on the armies of imperialism. For the Russian side of the Russo-Turkish wars and the conquest of the Caucasus, see William Fuller, *Strategy and Power in Russia, 1600–1914* (New York, 1992), and John Curtiss, *The Russian Army Under Nicholas 1, 1825–1855* (Durham NC, 1965). Russell Weigley, *The American Way of War, A History of United States Military Strategy and Policy* (Bloomington IN, 1973), and Maurice Matloff, *Army Historical Series, American Military History* (West Point 1969). K. Jack Bauer, *The Mexican War, 1846–1848,* (Lincoln NE, 1974), and Francis Paul Prucha, *The Sword of the Republic, The United States Army on the Frontier, 1783–1846* (London, 1969) offer useful accounts of the American wars in the Ohio country and on the plains, with Britain and Canada between 1812 and 1914 and against Mexico between 1845 1848. Christon Archer, ed., *The Wars of Independence in Spanish America* (Wilmington DE, 2000), is an excellent study of that topic. Good studies of two elements of the French colonial army are Douglas Porch, *The French Foreign*

Legion, A Complete History of the Legendary Fighting Force (New York, 1991), and Myron Echenberg, *Colonial Conscripts, The Tiralleurs Senegalais in French West Africa, 1857–1960* (Portsmouth NH, 1991).

For the case study, two recent works are important to understanding the sociopolitical and organizational background to the Indian Army: Douglas M. Peers, *Between Mars and Mammon, Colonial Armies and the Garrison State in Early Nineteenth Century India* (London, 1995), and Seema Alavi, *The Sepoy and the Company, Tradition and Transition in Northern India, 1770–1830* (Delhi, 1995). The two fundamental accounts of the "mutiny" are Eric Stokes, *The Peasant Armed, The Indian Rebellion of 1857* (Oxford, 1986), and Rudrangshu Mukherjee, *Awadh in Revolt, 1857–1858, A Study of Popular Resistance* (Delhi, 1984). Christopher Hibbert, *The Great Mutiny, India 1857* (London, 1978), is a readable and thoroughly researched collection, though its analysis is questionable.

Belich offers the standard account of the New Zealand wars. Important accounts of wars, battles, and military systems in India are Randolf G. S. Cooper, "Wellington and the Marathas in 1803," and John Pemble, "Resources and Techniques in the Second Maratha War," in Peers, *Warfare and Empires*. For war and military institutions in China, Peter Ward Fay, *The Opium War, Barbarians in the Celestial Empire in the Early Part of the Nineteenth Century and the War by Which They Forced Her Gates Ajar* (Chapel Hill NC, 1975); Philip A. Kuhn, *Rebellion and its Enemies in Late Imperial China* (Cambridge MA, 1970); Stanley Spector, *Li Hung-Chang and the Huai Army, A Study in Nineteenth-Century Chinese Regionalism* (Seattle, 1964); and, a useful contemporary account, Andrew Wilson, *The Ever-Victorious Army, A History of the Chinese Campaign under LieutenantColonel C. G. Gordon, CB, RE, and of the Suppression of the Tai-Ping rebellion* (London, 1991). Interesting Chinese accounts of such wars may be found in E. H. Parker, *Chinese Account of the Opium War* (Wilmington DE, 1970), and Arthur Waley, *The Opium War Through Chinese Eyes* (Stanford, 1958).

Useful accounts of indigenous African military systems and resistance to European conquest may be found in Joseph P. Smaldone, *Warfare in the Sokoto Caliphate, Historical and Sociological Perspectives* (Cambridge, 1977); Ian Knight, *The Anatomy of the Zulu Army, from Shaka to Cetshwayo, 1818–1879* (London, 1995); and two collections, especially Michael Crowther, *West African Resistance* (New York, 1972), and, to a lesser degree, Bethwell A. Ogot, ed., *War and Society in Africa, Ten Studies* (London, 1972). Some of the many useful and readable accounts of such wars from the European side include Donald R. Morris, *The Washing of the Spears, The Rise and Fall of the Zulu Nation* (New York, 1966); Frank Emery, *Marching over Africa, Letters from Victorian Soldiers* (London, 1986); and Thomas Pakenham, *The Scramble for Africa, 1876–1912* (New York, 1991).

David B. Ralston, *Importing the European Army, The Introduction of European Military Techniques and Institutions into the Extra-European World, 1600–1914* (Chicago, 1990), provides a basic introduction to the issue of the impact of

Western military institutions on non-Western countries. There is a small but useful literature on specific aspects of this issue: for Chile, see Holger Herwig and William F. Sater, *The Grand Illusion: The Prussianization of the Chilean Army* (Lincoln NE, 1999); for Japan, see Richard J. Samuels, *"Rich Nation, Strong Army," National Security and the Technological Transformation of Japan* (Ithaca, 1994), Ernst Presseisen, *Before Aggression, Europeans Prepare the Japanese Army* (Tucson, 1965), and John Ferris, "A British 'Unofficial' Aviation Mission and Japanese Naval Developments, 1919–1929," *The Journal of Strategic Studies*, 10:3, September 1982.

12. TWENTIETH-CENTURY MILITARISMS AND TECHNOLOGICAL WARFARE

The First World War

The First World War has generated much controversy and a very large literature. But most historians agree that initially there was a good deal of enthusiasm for the war among combatants, who expected the conflict to be short. The high casualties of the war then began to produce disillusionment, cynicism, and criticism, especially after the western front battles of 1916. By 1918 most participants were fatalistic and anxious for the war to end. Undoubtedly the war had an indelible impact on the societies involved, with postwar discussions of a lost generation. Numerous war memoirs also produced considerable criticism of the way the war was conducted by the relevant high commands and a sense of pessimism. In regard to technology and technical change, it is clear that World War I unleashed an unprecedented application of technology to the battlefield, resulting in the high casualties of the war. Because of this, the experience of the average soldier was often at the limit of human endurance, especially in the battles of 1916 and 1917. All in all, the First World War marked a distinct and terrifying break from the warfare of the past.

The problem of the origins of the First World War has produced considerable debate and argument, but the immediate spark was certainly the murder of Archduke Franz Ferdinand by Bosnian Serb nationalists in Sarajevo on June 28, 1914. Ferdinand was the heir to Franz Joseph of Austria-Hungary, who had annexed Bosnia Herzegovina in 1908. In reaction, Serbian military intelligence inspired and supported the assassination, and thus Serbia must bear much responsibility for this precipitating event. Next, Austria-Hungary deliberately set out to launch a Balkan war to retain control over Serbia and at the same time appealed to its ally, Germany. Berlin then opted for war on the basis of a sense of diplomatic encirclement and the fear of Russian rearmament, which would threaten Germany's place in Europe. The feeling in Germany was that it was better to strike now rather than later, when the odds would be worse. In turn, France supported its ally, Russia, while Britain prepared to go to war on the basis of the violation of Belgian neutrality as well as the belief that Germany would become far too powerful on the continent should it prove victorious. Thus, by the first days of August 1914, the die was cast and the greatest conflict of the early twentieth century was underway.

However, war requires mobilization and there the manpower abilities of the different armies revealed considerable differences. In Germany, despite increases to the peacetime army through government bills increasing reservists in 1912 and 1913, German manpower strength was still only 748,000 compared to the Russian and French peacetime armies, which had a total strength of 2,170,000. However, at full wartime strength in 1914 the German army was able to mobilize 2.15 million men, plus around 1.3 million Austro-Hungarian troops. On the other hand, Russia had 3.4 million wartime soldiers in 1914, and France had 1.8 million men. The weakest of the major powers in 1914 in terms of manpower was Britain, who, largely for reasons of financial economy, only had seven regular army divisions, one of which was cavalry. There was also a Territorial army force of part-time reserve soldiers in Britain, but these were not fit for battle until later in the war. However, Lord Kitchener, the secretary of state for war, issued a call for volunteers in 1914 and some 2.5 million men did volunteer, producing about seventy divisions. Even this was not enough, and conscription was introduced in 1916. Belgium was also poorly prepared, and in 1914 could only mobilize 200,000 men. In France, benefiting from the 1913 Three Years Law of compulsory military service, a higher percentage of the population (2.29 percent) was under arms in 1914 than in any other nation.

To summarize, in 1914 the Central Powers could field just under 3.5 million troops, while the Entente and its allies could produce 5.7 million men. Hence, in 1914 as war started on the western front, Anglo-French-Belgian forces numbered ninety-two divisions and 2.38 million men against seventy-three German divisions of 1.8 million men, thus ensuring that Germany would not have an easy time during the initial German Schlieffen offensive.

The numbers of men that each major country could put into the field were impressive, but were these men eager to serve? This is a controversial subject, especially because among all nations involved there was a belief that the war would be short, probably over by Christmas 1914, so there was a rush to join up before it was too late. Thus, there was an initial euphoria, especially among the patriotic middle and upper classes, although the working classes were less enthusiastic. Hence, in Germany students and the upper middle class were keen to join up, and these produced about 308,000 volunteers between 1914 and 1915, formed into twenty-two divisions. In Britain the middle and upper classes joined up in record numbers so that of 539 boys who left the exclusive public (private) school Winchester between 1909 and 1915, only 8 boys did not volunteer. Among other groups, economic motives and peer pressure certainly played a part as reasons for enlistment. In France, despite considerable patriotic teaching in the schools, there does not appear to have been much enthusiasm for the war, and it is known that around 700,000 civilians fled Paris by September 1914, including the government and the whole civil service. On the other hand, there was no resistance to mobilization but only a resigned acceptance: "France did not want war; she was attacked; we will do our duty." Only in Russia was there was physical resistance to mobilization by some peasants, because the outbreak of war took place on the eve of the harvest.

The actual process of mobilization was a complicated matter. For example, in Germany there was a seven-stage mobilization plan; the first four stages alerted and called up the troops. Stage five was the actual military travel plan, where the railroads played a crucial role. Germany's west army, initially composed of 1.6 million men, moved across the Rhine bridges at a rate of 560 trains per day and at the unusually fast speed of twenty miles per hour. In the east, approximately nine German divisions moved into place by August 22, using the less extensive east Prussian railroad network. Altogether, the German General Staff mobilized their entire army, including 600,000 horses, in 312 hours, using 11,000 trains. Stage six concentrated the troops, and stage seven brought the troops into contact with the enemy. It was a remarkable performance.

Turning to strategy, in the west, Germany planned a sweeping envelopment of France through Belgium and northern France, called the Schlieffen Plan after Graf Schlieffen, chief of the German General Staff from 1891 to 1906. The right wheel, pivoting on Metz-Thionville, required fifty-three divisions, backed up by Landwehr and Ersatz units, while the left flank defended Germany with eight divisions, and ten divisions held the Russians in check.

Schlieffen's successor, Von Moltke the Younger, weakened the plan's right wing and strengthened the left flank, but criticisms of Moltke cannot disguise the fact that the Schlieffen Plan was very much a long shot in the days before motorized transport became available. However, the French army obliged by mounting useless attacks into Lorraine and Alsace and only gradually understood the intent of the Schlieffen Plan. Joffre, in charge of the French forces, belatedly realized the danger he was in and on August 25 issued a new battle plan whereby French troops were deployed from the south to the center to protect Paris and strengthen his left wing. Meanwhile on the far left of the French line stood an initially small British Expeditionary Force (BEF) of four divisions of infantry and five brigades of cavalry.

Through August the German army advanced in its wide sweep but met increasing resistance. This was called the "Battle of the Frontiers," in which France suffered over three hundred thousand casualties, while the small British Expeditionary Force fought a series of battles in retreat at Mons and Le Cateau. But now the German commander in chief amended the right wheel so that the German First Army aimed to pass to the east of Paris instead of to the west, which meant that a true envelopment was even less likely. Then on September 5, 1914, Joffre launched a counter attack, which developed into the Battle of the Marne, that halted the German advance and recaptured a considerable amount of French territory. Then began an attempt by each side to outflank the other until the sea was reached, and when this happened both sides commenced to dig in and construct defensive lines. These were first rifle pits, which were then joined up to become continuous trenches. Thus, around October 1914, in the absence of movement, trench warfare started. However, at the Battle of First Ypres in October and November 1914, there took place a determined attempt by the German army to rapidly reach Calais, but the power of modern weapons, including the magazine rifle, the machine gun, and the quick firing guns of the artillery (75s for the French, 18-pounders for the British), proved difficult, if not impossible, to overcome.

In fact, the power of the rifle, the machine gun, and the artillery piece drove both sides to shelter in trenches, which favored the defense, since sheltered defenders could fire at attackers, who were above the ground, with relative impunity. The fire power of the machine gun and artillery in particular produced a fire-swept zone across which it was extremely dangerous to advance unless one's own artillery made it possible. As armies learned the new style of warfare, it was discovered that artillery could make an advance possible across this fire-swept zone if the artillery preparatory barrage destroyed the trenches of the enemy and if the artillery then produced a moving barrage behind which the infantry might advance through the enemy defensive zone. To assist this advance it was also necessary for the artillery to knock out enemy machine guns, which was difficult because they were hard to locate, and also enemy artillery pieces (counterbattery fire). If all of this worked well, an advance might be successful. But the necessary technical skills and the technology (including aerial spotting of enemy guns and targets) for such attacks to succeed in a reliable way did not really emerge until 1917. So it was that modern weapons really created a defense dominated style of warfare, a trench deadlock. This was actually foreshadowed in the Boer War (1899–1902) and in the Russo-Japanese War (1904–5). Thus, the rifle, the artillery piece, and the machine gun became masters of the battlefield on the western front, and this remained true, with a few exceptions such as the development of the tank, until late in the war.

On the western front, after failure in the Ypres offensive, the German army went on to the defensive in 1915, while going on the offensive on the eastern front (see below). On the other hand, the French and the British armies on the western front tried several methods in 1915 of breaking the trench deadlock. Among these methods were the surprise breakthrough (Neuve Chapelle); the mass attack (Champagne); new weapons (gas at Loos); reliance on the artillery (the method favored by the French corps commander Philipe Pétain); the "more and more" system (whereby if an attack failed, the number of men, artillery, and amount of munitions were simply doubled, for example, at Artois); prolongation of the offensive, hoping the enemy would eventually break (just about everywhere); and the diversion of attacks away from the western front (the Gallipoli campaign). But Allied breakthroughs simply did not happen because of the overwhelming power of the defense, the lack of heavy artillery, and the inexperience of the attackers. Meanwhile all armies began to run out of artillery shells in 1915 due to the unprecedented demand, and at the same time the search for appropriate trench warfare weapons became intensive. Hence armies stressed the production of bombs, grenades, light machine guns, mortars, and, above all, the need for heavier artillery to destroy enemy defenses.

In 1916 the German commander in the west, Falkenhayn, decided to bleed the French army, and perhaps cause a moral collapse, by attacking a place that was symbolically important for the French to defend to the last, Verdun. Thus, the strategy of the German army remaining on the defensive in the west was reversed. Falkenhayn expected to defeat the French by relying on massive amounts of artillery, but although an early success occurred with the capture of Fort Douaumont on February 25, due to French carelessness, the German army was drawn into an attrition battle. Falkenhayn believed he could use up the French reserves and thus in the end capture Verdun, but unfortunately this also required using up too many of his own troops. There were German advances, such as the capture of Fort Vaux on June 7 and an advance to the outworks of Verdun on June 23, caused by the surprise deployment of a new gas, phosgene, delivered by the new, more accurate method of artillery shells. Yet the offensive failed to capture Verdun and became so bogged down that the Germans were unwillingly drawn into an attrition battle. Perhaps if the local German commander had risked everything on phosgene, success might have followed, but he did not. The Verdun campaign was also derailed by the joint Franco-British Somme offensive, which commenced in late June 1916 with a massive artillery bombardment. Although Verdun continued until December 1916, because of the Somme offensive, no new German divisions arrived at Verdun. Nevertheless, Verdun casualties were horrific, some 377,000 French and 337,000 Germans killed, wounded, and missing over the ten-month period. Falkenhayn's gamble had failed, and he was dismissed in August 1916.

Case Study: The Somme, July 1, 1916

By now the German army faced a major offensive astride the Somme River. Fourteen British and five French divisions actually attacked on July 1, 1916, and as far as the British were concerned, the day was a major disaster. There were 57,470 British casualties, including 19,240 killed on July 1 alone. Moreover, except in the southern part of the attack, the British divisions gained very little ground. The central cause of this disaster was the British artillery, which was not capable of cutting the German barbed wire defenses properly, which could not deal with the deep German dug outs, and which could not silence the German guns and machine guns. Another important cause of failure was that the artillery barrage, which the British infantry followed and which was supposed to take them through the German first and second line of trenches, advanced too quickly, and so the infantry fell behind. This made them vulnerable to the German defenders' fire because the artillery barrage passed over the German trenches some time before the British infantry reached them, allowing the German defenders time to get out of their deep dug outs and man their trenches with rifles and machine guns before the British infantry arrived.

Curiously enough, the British commander in charge of the Somme offensive, Rawlinson, knew about this problem from the previous year. In a letter written on June 21, 1915, and referring to a 1915 British attack, Rawlinson noted that "our artillery preparation . . . had not the desired effect on the enemy, and on the majority of the front he was able to man his parapets before the infantry could deliver their assault." In the same letter, Rawlinson repeated his analysis: "Into these cellars [deep dugouts] the [enemy] garrison withdrew during the bombardment so that when the moment came for the assault they were able to rush out & line their trenches without having suffered to any serious extent from the hellish bombardment we had given them. This was I think the chief cause of failure." Why then did neither Rawlinson nor his superior, Douglas Haig, the British commander in chief, learn from their previous experience? There seem to be two possible answers: first, Haig and Rawlinson were slow learners. And second, ironically, the British artillery bombardment at the Somme was much heavier and more impressive than in 1915. Thus, during the week before the actual attack, 2,207 guns fired 1.7 million shells, and on July 1, 1916, the first day of the Somme, 1,513 guns fired 600,000 rounds in the barrage for the assault. It must have seemed to Haig and Rawlinson that this enormous weight of shells would undoubtedly enable the attack to succeed. However, as so often in World War I, the ability of the defenders to burrow deep into the ground to avoid shelling, the problem of the inaccuracy of the artillery, inexperience in mounting offensives, and the difficulty of closely coordinating the infantry assault with the artillery barrage all spelled failure.

What was it like to be involved in the mass warfare of the battle on July 1, 1916? Above the battlefield the British pilot Cecil Lewis was flying a contact patrol thirty minutes before the attack. "Half an hour to go! The whole salient, from Beaumont Hamel to the marshes of the Somme, covered to a depth of several hundred yards with the coverlet of white wool—smoking shell bursts! It was the greatest bombardment of the war, the greatest in the history of the world. The clock hands crept on, the thrumming of the shells took on a higher note. It was now a continuous vibration, as if Wotan . . . were using the hollow world as a drum and under his beat the crust of it was shaking. Nothing could live under that rain of splintering steel." Thus far Cecil Lewis's account supports the idea that Haig and Rawlinson, too, were simply overimpressed with the visual impact of the bombardment. But Lewis went on to quote from his logbook the same day: "From our point of view an entire failure. . . . Many active [German] batteries seen and though all information was wirelessed . . . our batteries did not reply on the co-ordinates given. There must be colossal lack of organisation somewhere." Lewis was right, for the important British counter battery work (the destruction of enemy batteries) that day was not nearly effective enough.

Partly as a result of artillery failure but mostly because of the artillery barrage moving too fast for the infantry, leaving the German defenders free to man their parapets and destroy the attack, there occurred many such scenes as Henry Williamson recalled. He was a junior officer with 8 Division, attacking toward Ovillers on July 1, 1916:

> I see men arising and walking forward; and I go forward with them, in a glassy delirium wherein some seem to pause, with bowed heads, and sink carefully to their knees, and roll slowly over, and lie still. Others roll and roll, and scream, and grip my legs in uttermost fear, and I have to struggle to break away, while the dust and earth on my tunic changes from grey to red.
>
> And I go on with aching feet, up and down across ground like a huge honey comb, and my wave melts away, and the second wave comes up, and also melts away, and then the third wave merges into the ruins of the first and second, and after a while the fourth blunders into the remnants of the others, and we begin to run forward to catch up with the barrage, gasping and sweating, in bunches, anyhow, every bit of the months of drill and rehearsal forgotten, for who could have imagined that the "Big Push" was going to be like this?

Williamson's account points out the infantry wave system of attack and the difficulty of keeping up with the barrage as well as the many casualties occurring. On the other side of the battle, the German defenders of Ovillers, actually the German 108 Regiment, saw the attack from a different perspective:

At 7:30 A.M. the hurricane of shells ceased as suddenly as it had begun. Our men at once clambered up the steep shafts leading up from the dugouts. . . . The machine guns were pulled out of the dugouts and hurriedly placed in position, their crews dragging the heavy ammunition boxes up the steps and out to the guns. . . . As soon as the men were in position, a series of extended lines were seen moving forward from the British trenches. The first line appeared to continue without end to right and left. It was quickly followed by a second, then a third and fourth. They came on at a steady pace as if expecting to find nothing alive in our front trenches. . . . A few minutes later, when the leading British line was within a few hundred yards, the rattle of machine gun and rifle fire broke out along the whole line of shell holes. Some fired kneeling so as to get a better target over the broken ground, while others, in the excitement of the moment, stood up regardless of their own safety, to fire into the crowd of men in front of them. Red rockets sped up into the blue sky as a signal to the artillery, and immediately afterwards a mass of shells tore through the air and burst among the advancing lines. Whole sections seemed to fall . . . the advance rapidly crumbled under this hail of shells and bullets. All along the line men could be seen throwing up their arms and collapsing, never to move again. Badly wounded rolled about in their agony, and others, less severely injured, crawled to the nearest shell hole for shelter.

This German account shows how both the British barrage and counter battery work failed on July 1, 1916, and, at the same time, how the German defenders took advantage of shell holes in front of their trenches to avoid shelling. Also the German defenders found the British wave system of attack offered good targets for their artillery, machine guns, and rifles. Yet strangely enough, the French in the south of the Somme offensive fared much better than the British, so much better in fact that the French obtained all their objectives, while the British only gained their objectives in the southern section of the line. At the same time, the British suffered over 4,000 casualties per division, while the French only sustained 450 per division. How was this incredible disparity possible? The answer is primarily that the French had overwhelming artillery superiority; for example, south of the Somme River, the French deployed eighty-five heavy batteries against eight German heavy batteries. The French also used the experience gained from the Verdun campaign in designing tactics that emphasized firepower rather than manpower so that if a village such as Curlu offered stern resistance, instead of wasting lives in continuously attacking, the French artillery reduced the village to splinters before the French reassaulted. Similarly the French used small groups rushing forward under covering fire instead of the steady waves of the British. Other advantages included attacking two hours later than the British south of the Somme and the fact that the country south of the Somme was flat rather than the ridges the British faced. But it was the artillery advantage that really made the difference for the French.

The experience of war for the individual soldier, whether on the western front, or elsewhere, was a brutal one. Yet most soldiers afterward spoke of the continuing misery of the trenches rather than the moments of terror during offensives. Soldiers complained of mud and cold and lack of sleep. In the trenches, many suffered from trench foot, caused by standing in water for long periods; trench fever, caused by parasites; the constant attention of lice; and there was always diarrhea and dysentery, caused by unsanitary conditions. Perhaps as many as one quarter of all combatants suffered at one time or another from what was then called "shell shock" but is now labeled "posttraumatic stress disorder." For some this led to shaking and weeping, or worse, to loss of speech or a fugue state, meaning physical paralysis. Nor were these problems easily curable, as witnessed by the large number of cases that continued throughout the postwar period.

And yet, there were medical advances in World War I that saved lives. Initially, doctors applied conservative treatments to wounds, 70 percent of which were caused by the artillery. This treatment consisted primarily of closing up the wound and bandaging it, but this led to high rates of infection, partly because of the manure contaminated soil of Europe, which led to gas gangrene and subsequent death (wound mortality was 28 percent in 1915). There was also too much amputation of limbs, perhaps as high as 40 percent. Consequently, doctors experimented and discovered that wounds should be thoroughly cleaned and then kept open to drain, using sodium hypochlorite to assist the process. By the end of the war, wound mortality had been reduced to 8 percent, which also decreased the amputation rate. Prosthetic devices and an emphasis on rehabilitation, together with the development of plastic surgery by Britain and the United States, helped the badly wounded to face the postwar world. Another major advance occurred with the growing use of blood transfusion, using sodium citrate to prevent coagulation, plus greater understanding of blood typing. Finally, vaccines were developed that reduced tetanus from around 30 percent of the wounded in 1914 to almost zero by 1918. Other vaccines helped to offset typhoid, small pox, and cholera. The war did produce 7 million dead and 19 million wounded, but chances of survival for the wounded and the diseased improved dramatically between 1914 and 1918.

Returning to the Somme campaign, after July 1, 1916, the British (and the French) continued a series of generally small-scale offensives that used up manpower, without ever being able to attack faster than the German army was able to build further lines of defense. By the time the Somme campaign halted in November 1916, there were approximately 420,000 British casualties and another 200,000 for the French, while the German army had about 500,000 casualties. Although the Somme was obviously very costly for the Franco-British forces, the new German high command of Hindenburg and Ludendorff also sought to reduce their own casualties by reasserting the German defensive policy on the western front and approved a new defense in depth scheme in late 1916. This scheme cancelled the old tactic of defending a line at all costs and instead thought of defending an area. Moreover, by sharply extending the depth of the area defended and dividing up the defense into three zones—outpost zone, battle zone, and rear counterattack zone—this ensured that when the Allied offensive did penetrate the main battle zone, their artillery would be out of range and the attacking troops exhausted by the distance they had covered. Furthermore, the battle zone was covered by machine gun nests with interlocking zones of fire ("rocks in a stream"), which made any advance very difficult, and the fresh counterattack units in the rear zone, together with artillery in range now of the attackers, completed the task of recapturing any ground lost.

However, 1917 saw several Allied attempts to break through these new German defensive systems. The first was the large French offensive of April along the Chemin des Dames, launched by General Nivelle and supported by the British Arras offensive. Nivelle relied on a lengthy preparatory bombardment followed by the rapid advance of his forces. However, the German army fell back in March to the strongly constructed Hindenburg Line, which undercut much of Nivelle's plan. In any case, the Nivelle offensive failed against powerful defenses and, worse than this, produced a major mutiny in the French army. On May 3, the Second Colonial Division mutinied, and soon other French units followed suit, bleating like lambs going to the slaughter as they went to the front. The troops declared "We will defend the trenches, but we won't attack," and, "We are not so stupid as to march against undamaged machine guns!" All but two divisions in the Champagne area were unreliable, and there were 21,174 French deserters in 1917. Pétain was appointed to replace Nivelle in May, and he toured the front to listen to complaints. As a result, tactics were changed to focus on firepower rather than manpower, leaves were increased, rest camps improved, and tours of duty in the front trenches equalized. Pétain also executed twenty-three men and exiled more than one hundred of the ringleaders to the colonies. In this way, order was slowly restored, but it was clear that the BEF would be required to do much of the fighting for the rest of 1917 and probably into 1918.

Already in April 1917, the supporting Arras offensive resulted in good initial gains, but as the battle continued, heavy losses mounted in familiar fashion. One exception was the Canadian Corps capture of Vimy Ridge on April 9. This latter operation was carefully prepared and owed much of its success to three factors. The first was the excellent Canadian artillery preparation, counter battery work, and attack barrage. The second factor related to the old-fashioned German defensive system, which either could not or would not adapt to the new defense-in-depth concept. Thus, the German counterattack units, instead of being readily available, were a six-hours march away. The third factor was the élan of the attacking troops, supported by open order offensive tactics, plus greater firepower weapons among the infantry platoons, such as Lewis guns.

Another successful Allied operation followed Vimy, when the BEF sprang an extensive mine operation at Messines in June. Nineteen large mines were exploded, followed by a well-timed barrage and then the infantry. Within an hour, the German front lines were taken. Although not easily repeatable, Messines showed what a well-planned limited objective operation could achieve.

However, at the end of July 1917, Haig launched his long-desired offensive at Ypres, known as Passchendaele. Fewer divisions were involved than at the Somme, twelve in all, but British artillery dominated the German defenses, largely because of their number—3,091 guns, of which one-third were heavy pieces. These guns fired a preparatory bombardment of ten days' duration, and on the day of the assault, July 31, 1917, the BEF divisions advanced well on the left, almost two miles, but were held up on the right. Then rain fell, and the offensive began to bog

Fig. 12.1. British soldiers and an officer hauling an eighteen-pound artillery piece out of the mud near Zillebeke, August 9, 1917, during the Battle of Passchendaele. The picture gives a good idea of the conditions of this western-front battlefield. Imperial War Museum, London, Q 6236.

down. Now it became apparent that Haig had chosen a poor battlefield: there was good German artillery observation, the defensive strength of the ridge was significant, the water-logged ground prevented movement, and not all of the ridge was included in the attack plans because Second Army on the right did little to help. Despite useful Allied advances in September and early October, the rains then fell in earnest and turned Passchendaele into a quagmire. The campaign continued longer than it should have, with no particular strategic objective in view, and only careful preparation enabled the Canadian Corps to eventually take the symbolic village of Passchendaele by November 10, 1917, with the loss of 16,000 men. Altogether Passchendaele had cost 275,000 BEF casualties, and perhaps German casualties came close to this. Again, Passchendaele, like the Somme, cannot be seen as an Allied victory, but it is also certain that the German army could less "afford" this rate of casualties.

"Mud and blood" has come to symbolize the static trench warfare experience of World War I, and although this disguises continuous and extensive tactical and technical changes, there is much truth to the phrase. Each campaign and offensive produced its own deadly truth, yet perhaps the Battle of Passchendaele in 1917 revealed the greatest depth of despair. One of the strongest statements comes from the diary of Edwin Vaughan, a junior Second Lieutenant in the Royal Warwickshire Regiment. Part of his diary records the attack of his platoon at Passchendaele on August 16, 1917:

> Dully I hoisted myself out of the mud and gave the signal to advance, which was answered by every man rising and stepping unhesitatingly into the [enemy] barrage. The effect was so striking that I felt no more that awful dread of the shellfire, but followed them calmly into the crashing, spitting hell until we were surrounded by bursting shells and singing fragments, while above us a stream of bullets added their whining to the general pandemonium. The men were wonderful! And it was astounding that although no one ran or ducked, whilst many were blown over by shells bursting at our very feet no one was touched until we were through the thickest part of the barrage and making for the little ridge in front.
>
> Then I saw fellows drop lifeless while others began to stagger and limp; the fragments were getting us and in front was a belt of wire. At this moment I felt my feet sink and though I struggled to get on, I was dragged down to the waist in sticky clay. The others passed on, not noticing my plight until by yelling and firing my revolver into the air I attracted the attention of Sergeant Gunn, who returned and dragged me out. I caught up the troops who were passing through a gap in the wire, and I was following Corporal Breeze when a shell burst at his feet. As I was blown backwards I saw him thrown into the air to land at my feet, a crumpled heap of torn flesh.

A few moments later, Vaughan noticed that

> from the heap of flesh that had been Breeze, I saw the stump of an arm raised an inch or two. Others saw it too and before I needed to tell them, the stretcher bearers were on their way to him. Very gently they brought him in to where I was sitting. He was terribly mutilated, both his feet had gone and one arm, his legs and trunk were torn to ribbons and his face was dreadful. But he was conscious and as I bent over him I saw in his remaining eye a gleam of mingled recognition and terror. His feeble hand clutched my equipment, and then the light faded from his eye. The shells continued to pour in but we gave poor Breezy a burial in a shell hole and the padre read a hurried prayer.

Was the terrible scene that Vaughan describes "total war"? Not in the sense of a war that involves whole societies as World War II did, but in the sense of the very depth and tragedy of what war could be like, it is. World War I was a total war because it seemed as if Armageddon had arrived and engulfed the participants in a brutal dance of death.

Toward the end of 1917, on November 20, the BEF launched its celebrated Cambrai offensive, celebrated because it employed two innovations—476 tanks of all kinds and predicting artillery fire (i.e., firing off the map without previous registration). Which of these was the more important is disputed, but the net result was genuine surprise because there was no need for a preparatory bombardment and the tanks could take over the wire-cutting exercise of the artillery. Above the battlefield fourteen squadrons of the Royal Flying Corps (RFC) operated to observe, bomb, and strafe the German forces, and behind the tanks came six divisions of infantry, many in single-file, or "worm," formation. This looked like, and was, a new form of warfare. It was not blitzkrieg yet, but it foreshadowed future developments. The Cambrai attack gained six miles of the Hindenburg line, to a maximum depth of four and a half miles, at a cost of only four thousand casualties. But as so often happened, the attack was pushed for too long, in fact a week, and on November 30 a German counterattack recovered all and more of the territory lost. However, what was significant about this German counterattack, and what the BEF failed to notice, was the manner of it, for the German assault used a new infiltration system in which small, fast-moving groups bypassed strong areas, infiltrated through open areas, and moved swiftly on to attack the artillery supports.

The new German offensive system went undetected by the French and British, although not by Russia and Italy where it had already been employed. This was important because in early 1918 German policy changed again to an offensive doctrine on the western front, partly because the Russian Revolution of 1917 relieved pressure on the eastern front and partly because of the entry into the war of the United States. The latter country entered the war in April 1917, primarily because of the German announcement of an unlimited U-boat (submarine) campaign against merchant shipping. Therefore, Germany now realized that the industrial and manpower potential of the United States was such that an all or nothing offensive campaign in the west was essential before the United States exerted sufficient force to win the war, either in 1918 or certainly in 1919. Hence, Germany prepared for a massive series of

"Peace Offensives" on the western front and launched the first on March 21, 1918, under the direction of Colonel Bruchmuller, the artillery specialist. This offensive aimed at the BEF's Third and Fifth Armies, particularly the latter, since it was the point of juncture with the French army.

Operations began with the massing of guns for the offensive, plus the stockpiling of ammunition. This was no small task since of the three armies involved, Eighteenth Army in the south possessed 1,568 light artillery, 1,028 heavy guns, 27 super-heavy guns, and 1,257 mortars. Seventeenth Army in the north came in at a slightly lower total: 1,408 light artillery, 801 heavy guns, 25 super-heavy guns, and 1,197 trench mortars. Second Army in the center produced an equivalent number of guns. The first objective was to drench the front to be attacked from March 9 to March 19 with Yellow Cross (mustard gas) shells. On March 19 this shifted to a bombardment of Blue Cross (a mixture of 75 percent high explosive and 25 percent diphenylchlorasine) and Green Cross (phosgene) gas shells along the broad track the attack was to follow, with more mustard gas along the flanks of the operation. On March 21 at 4:40 A.M., the use of Blue and Green Cross shells increased, while some heavy guns fired at targets in the British rear. Then exactly five hours later, the infantry barrage commenced, using light field guns and mortars firing Blue Cross plus more high explosive. These guns had all been preregistered behind the lines and fired off maps that were very accurate because the areas the Germans were attacking had been the rear of the German position from 1914 to 1917. At 9:40 A.M. the offensive commenced, with storm troopers following the barrage. These troops, trucked into the area just before the attack, were armed with machine guns, trench mortars, flamethrowers, and infantry weapons. Avoiding strong points, they were instructed to push ahead as far as possible, regardless of the situation on the flanks. The storm troops were immediately followed by infantry regiments, also well armed, even including light field guns.

Essentially, the German attack was flexible enough to make deep inroads into the British defensive system, especially Eighteenth Army operating against the BEF's Fifth Army. The BEF failed to defend successfully because it was unused to the defensive role; because mist shielded the attackers during most of the morning of March 21; because the Fifth Army in particular held a lengthy line and neglected to properly defend the Oise marsh area; and because British HQ's began to panic and created a snowball effect in retreat. Most important to the success of the German offensive, however, was the BEF's attempt to adopt the defense-in-depth system, which it did not understand and which it did not actually deploy in some areas, for example, the Fifth Army's area generally. The net result was a German penetration along a front of eighty kilometers and losses to the BEF of 90,000 prisoners, 1,300 guns, and 200,000 killed and wounded. On the other hand, the German artillery failed to keep pace with the German advance, BEF reserves and indirect artillery and machine gun fire slowed the advance, and exhaustion set in by March 30. Moreover, German losses of their best assault division troops was also high, at about 240,000, so that by April 5 Ludendorff was forced to call off the offensive, codenamed Michael.

Three more "Peace Offensives" were tried, but each met the same fate of great initial success followed by gradual slowing down and exhaustion. Then it was the Allies turn to attack, now under the overall command of Marshal Foch. On July 18, with the benefit of good intelligence, the French launched a massive counterattack on the Marne, with twenty-four divisions (four from the United States), and 750 tanks against eleven indifferent German divisions. This gained four miles of territory and gave the German High Command a nasty shock. Only one more minor "Peace Offensive" was attempted, on August 4, which lasted only four days. Instead, the German army now went on the defensive and remained so until the end of the war. This situation was hammered home by the BEF's Amiens offensive of August 8, 1918. This was to be a surprise, mass assault by more than five hundred tanks, eight hundred planes, two thousand guns, and eight divisions of the Australian and Canadian Corps, plus flanking attacks by the BEF's III Corps and French IX Corps. All went well, surprise was largely achieved, mist and smoke helped the attack, and the offensive penetrated to a depth of six miles and more on an eleven-mile front. Ludendorff called August 8 the "black day of the German army" because of German losses of twenty-seven thousand as against BEF casualties of nine thousand and because the large number of German prisoners showed that morale was slipping dangerously.

From now on, for the BEF and the French on the western front, it was a matter of mounting attacks all along the German line, not to break through but to crumble the line. By the end of September, the Hindenburg Line was breached using the largest expenditure of artillery shells in the war (945,000 shells fired between September 28 and 29) plus massive amounts of men and technology. After this, the German army simply retreated from one defensive line to the next but inflicted heavy casualties on the attackers. Thus, while the BEF suffered around 275,000 casualties during the Passchendaele offensive (July 31 to mid-November 1917), for the comparable period from August 7 to November 11, 1918, incomplete BEF figures show 314,200 casualties. Canadian Corps statistics are even more striking—29,725 casualties during Passchendaele but 49,152 for August to November 1918 inclusive. The reason for the higher casualties in the last one hundred days is that the BEF and French forces were attacking more continuously than in 1917, while the German army was defending stubbornly with artillery and machine guns rather than with sheer manpower. And yet, by July and August 1918, the German army had clearly shot its bolt, the "Peace Offensives" had failed, and morale had sunk beyond recovery. German Official History figures show that between July 18, 1918, and November 11, 1918, the German army on the western front lost 420,000 dead and wounded, plus 340,000 prisoners of war. Another 750,000 to 1 million may have deserted or refused to serve in addition to the 1 million casualties during the offensives from March to July 1918. Hence, the German army may have suffered some 2,760,000 casualties and deserters during 1918. And while there were still ninety-eight fully "fit" German divisions on August 1, 1918, that number had fallen to forty-seven on September 1 and to only four by the Armistice. Thus, the German army literally ran out of men on the western front during 1918.

What then caused the collapse of the German army on the western front in 1918? First was the cumulative effect of the attrition warfare of previous years, especially between 1916 and 1918. Second, the failure of the "Peace Offensives" really marked the end of Germany's chances on the western front, quite apart from the losses suffered by the last of the elite troops of the German assault divisions. Third, the Allies built up overwhelming superiority of manpower and technology in 1918; by the end of the war the United States had landed some 2 million men and would have added another 2 million in 1919. Fourth, Germany retained too many of its men and resources on the eastern front (see below), which certainly produced victory over Russia but did not prevent a collapse on the western front. Fifth, the Allies developed by 1918 a more efficient system of combined arms tactics of artillery, tanks, air, and infantry plus the use of mobile infantry weapons such as light mortars, Lewis guns, and rifle grenades. Technical skills also improved and enabled surprise attacks such as at Cambrai, while the 106 contact fuse, in use since 1917, improved artillery effectiveness, and the tank represented a formidable new weapon when properly used. Sixth, and in the long run a decisive factor, the resources of Germany and her allies were simply not sufficient in the long run to deal with the combined resources of Britain, France, Russia, the United States, Italy, and other minor allies. According to the historian Paul Kennedy, war expenditures over the period 1914 to 1919, at 1913 prices in billions of dollars, equaled 57.7 for the Allies as against only 24.7 for the Central Powers of Germany, Austria-Hungary, Bulgaria, and Turkey. Similarly, total mobilized forces for the Allies over this period amounted to 40.7 million, as against the much smaller 25.1 million for the Central Powers. These six factors are quite sufficient to account for the Allied victory in the west in 1918.

Indeed, the wonder is that Germany and her allies survived so long before crumbling. The Hindenburg program of 1916, designed to meet the country's needs for total war, could not achieve its fantastic goals, for example doubling munitions production and trebling machine gun output, although production advances were made. But the program required the massive withdrawal of skilled workers from the battle fronts and paid insufficient attention to the vital agriculture sector, although perhaps the program did prolong the war. Other reasons for the longevity of the Central Powers are varied and include the fact that the nature of warfare in the First World War precluded a simple victory. Breakthroughs on the western front simply did not happen on a large scale until 1918, and after 1914 Germany remained on the defensive for much of the war when the defensive was much the stronger form of warfare. Germany also enjoyed internal lines of communication, which permitted easier transfers of troops from west to east or vice-versa or simply between armies on one front by a network of railway lines. Then the economic and material strength of the Allies could only be slowly built up and applied against the Central Powers, especially since the United States only entered the war in 1917. The same applies to naval strength, as Allied superiority in maritime affairs, including a maritime blockade of Germany, could only work slowly against the Central Powers.

The reference to maritime warfare draws attention to the major naval battle of the war, Jutland, fought between May 31 and June 1, 1916. Despite the prominent arrival of the Dreadnought class of battleships before the war and the feverish naval race between Germany and Britain, neither side was anxious to risk their high-priced battleships in unfavorable circumstances on the high seas. Britain could theoretically lose the war in an afternoon if a naval defeat gave Germany control over supplies and men crossing the Channel, while Germany feared to lose their High Seas Fleet to the larger British Grand Fleet. This stalemate was all the more awkward because of the vulnerability of the mighty battleship to the humble mine and the torpedo, whether delivered by U-Boat or destroyer. The British navy was ridiculously unprepared for such warfare, so for example, U-Boat 9 managed to sink three British cruisers in September 1914. Then HMS *Audacious* was lost to a mine in October 1914, when there were a grand total of six minesweepers available. As for actions at sea, only minor engagements took place, such as raids and the inconclusive battles of the Falklands (1914) and of the Dogger Bank (1915).

However, in early 1916 a more aggressive German naval commander in chief was appointed, Admiral Scheer. He decided to defeat the British fleet in detail by sending out a bait of battle cruisers and then luring the British ships onto a line of U-Boats and the main High Seas Fleet. The trap was laid on May 31, 1916, but when Beatty's six battle cruisers and four super-Dreadnoughts and Jellicoe's twenty-four Dreadnoughts set forth, the U-Boats failed to make any impression on the fleet. Ultimately, the British fleet at sea comprised twenty-eight Dreadnoughts, nine battle cruisers, thirty-four light cruisers, and seventy-eight destroyers. The German Grand Fleet deployed fewer ships, sixteen Dreadnoughts and six pre-Dreadnoughts, five battle cruisers, eleven light cruisers, and sixty-one destroyers. Yet, when the fleets blundered into each other over the course of the afternoon and evening, it was the British ships that suffered most. HMS *Lion* nearly foundered after a hit on Q turret, due to a cordite flash down the loading system of the turret. The heroic efforts of the dying Major Harvey, who despite having both legs blown off ordered the flooding of the magazines, saved the ship. Not so fortunate were HMS *Indefatigable* and HMS *Queen Mary*, who both blew up around 4:00 P.M., followed later by HMS *Invincible* at 6:30 P.M. Nevertheless, Jellicoe managed to "cross the T" twice over and so brought the majority of the guns of his battleships to bear on the bows of the German battleships. Moreover, Jellicoe's main fleet now cut off the German High Seas Fleet from their harbor. But darkness, confusion, inattention to intelligence messages, lack of initiative, and poor performance at night firing all enabled Scheer to slip behind the British fleet and regain the safety of harbor the next morning via a passage through the heavily mined Horns Reef.

The score card of the battle was in favor of the German fleet, since fourteen British ships were sunk, as against eleven German ships. But the German High Seas Fleet rarely ventured forth again, and the net result was therefore a strategic victory for the British Grand Fleet. As a consequence, Britain continued to blockade Germany, while Germany pushed forward its U-Boat campaign. This campaign went into high gear with the declaration of unrestricted submarine warfare on February 1, 1917. German calculations required the loss of 600,000 tons of British, Allied, and neutral shipping per month. At first this seemed feasible, for in May 1917, 600,000 Allied and neutral tons of shipping went to the bottom, followed by 680,000 tons in June, and 540,000 tons in July. But by May 1917 the convoy system was introduced and gradually spread through the various shipping routes. Even if 2.25 million tons of shipping was sunk between August 1917 and January 1918, this was not enough, at an average of 375,000 tons per month. Thus, the U-Boat (and surface raider) campaign did not succeed.

Thus far, the war in the west has been emphasized. However, in the British Cabinet there was always a lively interest in the fate of British interests overseas as well as a school of thought which favored an Eastern policy. This latter group, led by Lloyd George, came to be known as the easterners, in contrast to the westerners, who believed in putting the main stress on the western front. Both groups understood the need to support all theaters of war, but it was a question of where the emphasis should be placed. The easterners, among others, supported overseas campaigns such as Gallipoli, Salonika, Egypt and Palestine, Mesopotamia, Italy, and east Africa. Many of these campaigns involved the Ottoman Turks, who proved to be excellent soldiers. In particular, the Franco-British forces in Gallipoli during 1915 were never able to outfight or outmaneuver the Ottoman Turks, who were directed by the able German commander Liman von Sanders. An attempt was made in March 1915 by British and French ships to run the Straits, enter the Sea of Marmora, and bombard Constantinople, in order to compel the Ottoman Turks to surrender. But Allied mine sweepers were driven off by shore-based Ottoman batteries, while Allied naval gunfire could not destroy these batteries. On March 18 the Allied fleet tried a new tactic by closing in on the shore batteries in the Straits, but six battleships hit mines in an unswept area and the attempt was a miserable failure. The campaign then turned to a land offensive on Gallipoli, with the idea of capturing the high ground that would permit artillery protection of the ships as they ran the Straits on their way to the Sea of Marmora and the bombardment of Constantinople. But although British (including Australian and New Zealand) and French forces landed on April 25, suffering considerable losses in the process, further progress against Ottoman trenches, machine guns, and artillery was not possible. A major offensive in the Anzac area and a landing at Suvla in early August followed, but this also bogged down, due partly to an overambitious though ingenious plan, poor Allied commanders, and the initiative and hard-driving command style of the Ottoman commander, Mustafa Kemal (later Ataturk, the leader of modern Turkey). Gallipoli was then judged a stalemate and was evacuated in late 1915 and early 1916. The basic causes of this Allied failure were poor British leadership (by Sir Ian Hamilton, Major General Hunter-Weston, Major General Stopford, and other senior officers), inexperience, the sheer technical difficulty of the campaign, lack of men and material at critical times, problems of naval-military cooperation, and dogged defensive fighting by the tough Ottoman Turks. However, the other campaigns mentioned eventually resulted in Allied successes, mainly because of the development of numerical superiority in men and material and through more effective leadership, for example, the hard driving General Allenby in the Palestine campaign.

The mention of Allenby leads to a brief consideration of the campaign in the Middle East. Much of the Arab world was Ottoman territory, and this imperial and geographic fact threatened the important communications link provided by the Suez Canal. Hence, British policy emphasized defense of the canal, so a large British force guarded the canal zone. But in 1916 the British commander General Sir Archibald Murray moved to a more offensive stance. In 1916 his forces built a pipeline and a railway across the Sinai and then tried to capture Gaza in March 1917 with three infantry and two cavalry divisions. The plan was well conceived, but overcaution by the British HQ produced an unnecessary withdrawal. A second attempt against Gaza in April failed because the Ottoman forces were now well prepared. Murray was recalled and replaced by Allenby. A failure on the western front, Allenby was in his element in the Middle East, where he galvanized the British, Indian, and Australian troops and also received reinforcements giving him ten divisions, plus air superiority, and thus a considerable advantage over the enemy. A third attack on Gaza succeeded in October 1917, partly due to a thrilling cavalry charge by the Australian light horse. Allenby followed up relentlessly, and Jerusalem fell in December 1917. Meanwhile, a romantic figure,

T. E. Lawrence, gained fame in fomenting an Arab revolt against the Ottomans in the Hejaz region. Lawrence launched long-range desert raids against the Ottoman Hejaz railway and also succeeded in capturing the port of Aqaba in mid-1917 after a two-month journey of six hundred miles. After a quiet few months in 1918, Allenby launched a major offensive up the coast, aiming eventually for Damascus. Using deception, careful planning, air power, and the sweeping cavalry movements of the Desert Mounted Corps under the Australian Chauvel, Damascus fell on October 1, 1918. By the end of October, the Ottomans capitulated.

World War I also spread over vast areas of eastern Europe, generally known as the eastern front. Here battles raged among the wide plains, rivers, swamps, and forests of Russia, including Poland, as a kind of forward defensive zone and in a number of other areas such as the huge empire of Austria Hungary, in the lakes and forests of East Prussia, in the late-entering and soon-to-be-defeated Romania, in the Baltic area, on the Serbian front, and in the Ukraine. These almost limitless perspectives thus produced a very different kind of war. There was always a low ratio of force to space; for example, over the winter of 1916 and 1917, German divisions in the east held sectors twenty to thirty kilometers wide, which on the western front might be filled with six to eight divisions. Thus, there was much greater scope for maneuver, large scale victories, and for massive disasters, unknown in the west.

One such disaster for the Russian army, and a corresponding success for the German army, was Tannenberg. The Russian army at the beginning of the war was beset by many problems, among them poor officers with little sympathy for the men they led, a largely untrained mass of soldiers, rudimentary or nonexistent tactics, usually relying on simple mass advances, a shaky logistics and transportation system, an artillery corps that had no wish to cooperate with the infantry, and a geriatric high command of uncommonly low intelligence. In fact, it is surprising that the Russian army survived and even achieved victories, such as the Brusilov offensive of 1916, before dissolving in 1917. The Austro-Hungarian army was not far behind the Russians in lack of competence, being badly led and poorly armed. The most efficient army on the eastern front was the German army, although its weakness was the long running argument in the German high command whether to try for a decision on the eastern or the western front.

Because of the vast sweep of events on the eastern front it will be possible to only focus on one or two campaigns. Early in August 1914, under pressure from their allies the French, the Russian army mobilized and mounted an invasion of East Prussia. The plan was for the northern army (First Army, commanded by Rennenkampf) to attack first, draw the German forces in that direction, and then for the southern army (Second Army, commanded by Samsonov) to move across the German rear and envelop whatever German forces could be cut off. Initially the plan seemed to work, for in the north the German riposte to the Russian advance was a frontal attack that left the German XVII Corps with sharp losses. Both sides remained cautious, contemplating retirement, in fact the German overall commander, Prittwitz, lost his nerve on August 20 and actually telephoned the German high command to say that he was retiring behind the Vistula River. He was relieved of his command and replaced by the fateful pair of Hindenburg and Ludendorff.

However, the Russian plan contained a flaw, namely, the fact that the Masurian Lakes provided a barrier between the Russian northern and southern armies, and it was in the south that the Russian Second Army was to need help. As the offensive developed, the two armies drew even further apart. Then, poor intelligence from the overall Russian commander, Zhilinski, and an overoptimistic attitude by Samsonov led Samsonov to drive his army forward into what became a trap for his several corps. Some delays in attacking by the German I Corps on August 25 and 26 helped to draw the Russians even further into an encirclement. Ludendorff had not really planned on this, but chance presented him with a great opportunity. By August 29 Samsonov's army was cut off, and approximately ninety-two thousand Russians surrendered, to go along with the fifty thousand dead and wounded. With an eye on a nearby location where the Teutonic Knights had been routed in 1410, this German victory was named Tannenberg. Although this success only represented the loss of a small fraction of the Russian army, the Russian Stavka (high command) lost confidence and during most of the rest of the war, failed to discover any way of breaking through. Instead the Russian system relied on piling up large superiorities of men, artillery, and shells at the point of attack and then launching narrow frontal assaults, hoping that sheer mass would do the trick.

It was left to a Russian general named Brusilov to demonstrate in 1916 that there was another way besides the bludgeon-style attack. Brusilov decided to attack the Austro-Hungarian army in June 1916 on a wide front, at four separate locations, between Czernovitz and the Pripyat marshes.

The Russian artillery operated close to the enemy lines, within two kilometers, and dovetailed its plans with the infantry. Tunnels were dug close to the enemy trenches, and reserves were located nearby in dugouts so that they could follow the initial attack immediately. Wire was cut effectively, and the opening bombardment smashed the Austro-Hungarian front lines, where two-thirds of their soldiers were located. The artillery barrage, which the troops followed closely, was composed of smoke, gas, and high explosive and sufficiently covered the advance. Finally, surprise was obtained, perhaps as important as any other factor in the success of the whole offensive. Altogether Brusilov achieved the capture of 193,000 prisoners, 216 guns, 645 machine guns, and 196 heavy mortars. Together with killed and wounded, the Austro-Hungarians lost more than half of their forces in the east.

Yet Brusilov could not duplicate this feat, and by 1917 the stress of war, huge casualties, demoralization, loss of faith in the officers and in the high command of the army, severe agricultural shortages, starvation, inflation, economic decline, lack of supplies for the troops, and indeed the failure of the whole Russian system led to the 1917 February/March revolution and then the October/November 1917 Bolshevik revolution. Despite the efforts of the Russian provisional government to continue the war in 1917, the army voted with its feet, and the Bolsheviks were forced to sign the highly unfavorable Brest-Litovsk Treaty with Germany in March 1918. The German army on the eastern front had succeeded, perhaps as much through Russian errors as German cleverness. However, there were significant German advances in the art of war in the east, for example Gorlice Tarnow in 1915, and the capture of Riga in 1917, under the direction of the artillery specialist Bruchmuller, with his combination of gas shells, intense three-hour bombardment, and suppression fire from massed trench mortars. But German focus on the east may have cost Germany the war, since it maintained over 1 million men to control the empire there, soldiers that may have made the difference in the west. As Falkenhayn once justly remarked: "The East gives nothing back," a comment that a later German leader would have done well to heed.

Germany's partner in the east, Austria-Hungary, also faced the daunting prospect of a two-front war in 1914: against Serbia in the south and against Russia in southern Poland. General Franz Conrad von Hötzendorf, chief of the General Staff, resolved this predicament by dividing his army into three separate parts. The largest formation,

A-Staffel, was to deploy against the Russians in Galicia; Minimalgruppe Balkan was detailed for operations against Serbia; and a strategic reserve (B-Staffel) would act as a swing force, to be sent against Russia or Serbia, depending on the needs of the moment.

But Conrad's visceral hatred of "dog" Serbia prompted him in August 1914 to send his strategic reserve immediately against Serbia, without waiting for Russian mobilization. The Austro-Hungarian forces, led by the incompetent courtier Oskar von Potiorek, were defeated by Serbian general Radomir Putnik at Jadar on August 16 and along the Drina River between September 8 and 18. Panic-stricken by the unexpectedly rapid advance of Russian units in Galicia, Conrad hurriedly recalled his strategic reserve, now reconstituted as the Second Army, from Serbia. Instead of waiting for this force to arrive, Conrad engaged the Russians in a series of heavy engagements southwest of the Pripet Marshes. On September 1, the Russian cavalry discovered a sixty-mile gap between the Austro-Hungarian First and Fourth Armies near Lemberg (Lvov) and massed infantry exploited this gap and drove a wedge between Conrad's two armies. Chaos ensued. The Austro-Hungarian railway system collapsed while the Fourth Army lost 50 percent of its officers and 25 percent of its rank and file. In the words of Winston Churchill, Conrad's strategic reserve was recalled from General Potiorek "before it could win him a victory" and was returned to Conrad in Galicia "in time to participate in his defeat."

On September 11, Conrad ordered a general withdrawal behind the San River, abandoning 150 miles of territory in Galicia and the Bukovina. The great belt fortress of Przemysl and its fifteen-thousand-man garrison was besieged by the Russians. In the first three weeks of the war, Conrad had lost one-third of his combat effectives, about 250,000 dead and wounded and 100,000 prisoners of war, including most of his regular junior officers and experienced noncommissioned officers. Conrad compared his situation in the fall of 1914 to that of Frederick the Great of Prussia in 1759.

The spring of 1915 was no kinder to Conrad von Hötzendorf. On January 23, in deep snow and bitter cold, he attacked out of the Carpathians in the direction of Czernowitz and suffered ninety thousand casualties. Undeterred, Conrad renewed the attack on February 27, with the same results. The official history of the war spoke of the Habsburg Army as a "militia army" after this time. On March 23 the fortress of Przemysl, along with 120,000 officers and men, surrendered to the Russians. Habsburg fortunes were saved only by General August von Mackensen's successful Gorlice-Tarnow offensive in May 1915 that drove the Russians behind the San River.

That same month, Italy declared war on Austria-Hungary, adding a third front for Conrad's staff. Of the eleven battles that followed in the howling wilderness of stone that was the Isonzo River valley, neither Austria nor Italy were able to gain the upper hand. On this deadly front, each battle cost each side about one hundred thousand casualties.

The final blows to Austro-Hungarian military power came in May and June 1916. On May 15, Conrad mounted his so-called punitive expedition against the Italian "snake" out of the high plain of Lavarone-Folgaria. After some minor initial gains, the offensive ground to a halt due to lack of surprise, ammunition, and resupply. Then on June 4, General A. A. Brusilov launched a major assault against the Austrians at Lutsk along the Styr River. Archduke Joseph Ferdinand's Fourth Army caved in on the first day of the offensive. Chaos ensued as Austrian units deserted their trenches and guns. Seven hundred fifty thousand men (including 380,000 taken prisoner) were lost. The Germans rushed five divisions to Lutsk and managed to stabilize the front—Brusilov, for his part, lost 1 million soldiers.

The war in the east had taken on a certain routine: as each of Conrad's grandiose offensives were shattered, German reinforcements rushed to plug the holes in the front. Habsburg and Hohenzollern divisions, corps, and armies became mixed. German NCOs and officers (so-called corset staves) were inserted into Austrian units along with artillery, trench mortars, and gas to stiffen them. Politically, the Germans set the tone in the direction of war aims and operations. Thus, it was largely General Otto von Below's Fourteenth Army that was instrumental in smashing the Italian Second Army at Caporetto in October 1917, inflicting more than 350,000 casualties on General Luigi Cadorna's army.

On June 6, 1918, Conrad launched Austria-Hungary's last major offensive out of the Tyrol. It broke in less than two weeks against determined British and French as well as Italian resistance. It was the last straw. Morale plummeted, desertions increased dramatically, and "green cadres" of bandits roamed the countryside at will. Soldiers were down to 120 pounds average weight, possessed no new equipment or uniforms, and sought only an end to the war. Ethnic Slav units, and even Hungarian forces, simply deserted their posts and trickled home. On November 3, 1918, Austria-Hungary signed an armistice at the Villa near Padua.

Thereafter the Italian army took the offensive and scored the "victory" of Vittorio Veneto against an army leaderless and in dissolution.

Austria-Hungary had mobilized about 8 million men. Of these, 1 million had been killed, 2 million were wounded, and 1.7 million taken prisoner.

In summary, Germany and its allies had two chances to win the war in the west, once in 1914 with the Schlieffen Plan, and once in early 1918 with the so-called spring and summer peace offensives. The Schlieffen Plan was well conceived but overoptimistic in its possibilities. However, the early 1918 period marked a second real opportunity for the Central Powers because of the earlier French mutinies in 1917, the Italian defeat at Caporetto in late 1917, low British morale following Passchendaele in late 1917, the Russian collapse in 1917, and the early successes of the U-Boat campaign. These conditions favored the Central Powers. Indeed, the German offensive in March 1918 nearly succeeded and almost separated the French and British armies. Had this happened, the British would have been forced to evacuate from the Channel Ports, as in another war in 1940. But the relatively slow-moving nature of 1918 warfare prevented the German army from achieving a strategic breakthrough in March, while greater Allied resources eventually guaranteed victory on the western front by November 1918. On the eastern front, the Russian collapse led to success by the Central Powers, which, however, proved to be a pyrrhic victory. On the other hand, the Austro-Hungarian war effort was ineffective, partly due to Conrad's poor leadership and strategy. Ultimately, the superior industrial economies of the Allies and the larger numbers of men and material gradually deployed by them on the western front (and against the Ottoman Turks) was always likely to win the war in the west, unless Germany had been able to exploit its two chances of victory.

Apart from the results of the war, the First World War was also significant because it marked the transition from a largely human-centered battlefield to a more technology-oriented battlefield. No longer were moral qualities sufficient to win; now it was necessary as never before to integrate technology in the form of various weapon systems into the operations of war. Technology could more easily defeat technology, rather than relying on courage and discipline to overcome machine guns and artillery. Senior commanders often found this a difficult transition to make and sometimes organized offensives without regard to utilizing weapons in the best possible way. Only from 1917 onward did a better understanding of weapons and technology emerge among senior staff and commanders. On the other hand, tactical change did occur quite rapidly, usually due to middle and junior level officers and staff who were willing to innovate. The First World War was also unusual, at least on the western front, for the stalemate that resulted from trench warfare and produced relative immobility for four years. Yet a great many technical and tactical changes were underway during this period of stalemate, and so it is a mistake to interpret lack of geographical change with lack of tactical, strategic, and technical change. In fact, the distant origins of blitzkrieg warfare can be seen in the use of tanks, planes, and light infantry weapons by the Allies coupled with the artillery and "storm troop" tactics developed by the German army.

Because the First World War was a transitional war and because of the horrors and heavy casualties of trench war endured by a relatively innocent and naive generation, the war shocked the consciousness of the Western world. This then produced a remarkable outpouring of literature, poetry, music, painting, and films of high quality. Focusing only on literature, much of it autobiographical, some works still remain classics. For example, Henri Barbusse, *Under Fire* (1917); Erich Maria Remarque, *All Quiet on the Western Front* (1929), Ernst Jünger, *Storm of Steel* (1931); Robert Graves, *Goodbye to All That* (1929); Siegfried Sassoon, *Memoirs of an Infantry Officer* (1930); and Vera Brittain, *Testament of Youth* (1933). However, it would be wrong to think of the First World War as creating a whole new way of thinking that was reflected in the arts. Rather, the war hastened changes that were already underway before the war began and that came to fruition in the 1920s and 1930s.

Nevertheless, the tragedy of the First World War was that it did not solve the problems that caused the conflict. Despite a horrifying collective death total of some thirteen million, the war only provided fertile ground for the outbreak of another and more devastating world conflict.

The Second World War

The two world wars are often seen as polar opposites, with blood and mud and stalemate contrasted to the heady days of blitzkrieg. This view is mistaken. These struggles were identical in nature—prolonged and total wars of attrition fought among armed forces and entire industrialized societies—and the second was far more destructive than the first. Twenty-eight million soldiers served in the Red Army, 10 million died there; 4.5 million German soldiers died and 8 million were wounded, which equaled 75 percent of its total force and almost half its adult male population of 1939. Between 1941 and 1945 the USSR built ninety-eight thousand tanks. It lost ninety-six thousand. Economic and demographic power and technological, scientific, and administrative effectiveness were each as necessary to victory as skill in military operations. Failure in the factories often negated success on the battlefield. In order to triumph, the belligerents had to maximize their military power and, in particular, to exploit their economic and demographic capacities in unprecedented ways. This usually meant cutting civilian consumption to the bone. Only the United States and the British dominions escaped this rule, increasing their production both of civilian goods and armaments.

The Second World War was fought between two alliances. The Axis powers—Germany, Italy, and Japan—were inferior in economic and demographic power. Between 1939 and 1942, however, Germany was militarily superior on land, as Japan was at sea for the first period of the Pacific war, and the economically inferior side almost won before the conflict became a prolonged struggle of attrition. By 1942 the tide turned. The Allies—the British Commonwealth, Soviet Russia, and the United States—finally brought their resources to bear and overcame their military inferiority. The stronger coalition then produced twice as many tons of steel as the weaker side, four times as many aircraft and tanks, and seven times as many artillery pieces and machine guns. Not surprisingly, it also won the war.

The discrepancy between Japanese and U.S. industrial output decided the outcome of the Pacific war by itself. Admiral Yamamoto Isoruku, architect of the brilliant attack on Pearl Harbor, warned his masters that "anyone who has seen the auto factories and the oil fields in Texas knows that Japan lacks the national power" to challenge the United States. "If we are ordered to do it, then I guarantee to put up a tough fight for the first six months, but I have absolutely no confidence in what would happen if it went on for one or two years." He was right. The United States applied one-third of its industrial capacity to the Pacific war and still produced four times more aircraft and warships than Japan. By January 1943 the Imperial Japanese Navy (IJN) and the U.S. Navy (USN) had each lost half its warship tonnage of 1941. Over the next two and one-half years, the IJN replaced these losses once. The USN did so every six months.

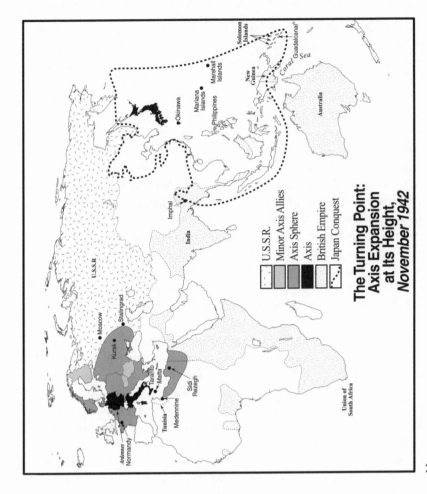

The Turning Point:
Axis Expansion
at Its Height,
November 1942

U.S.S.R.

Minor Axis Allies

Axis Sphere

Axis

British Empire

Japan Conquest

Map 12.1

The balance of power in Europe was more complex. During 1940 and 1942 Germany controlled most of Europe's economic resources and its productive capacity surpassed that of Britain and the USSR combined; indeed, potentially it matched that of the United States. Germany did not exploit this situation—its leaders did not even understand the need to do so. "American war production a menace to Germany?" said Hermann Goering, overlord of the Nazi war economy in 1941, "It is a bluff. They can make cars and refrigerators, not aircraft." During 1940 and 1942 Germany feasted off Europe and failed to establish an efficient war economy. Between September 1940 and May 1941, its production of aircraft declined by 40 percent. Meanwhile, Britain and the USSR left their populations at the bare level of survival and each manufactured twice as many tanks, guns, and aircraft as Germany. Properly organized, Germany should have matched this production; in August 1944 it built as many tanks as it did in the whole of 1941. The opportunity cost was devastating and one of the greatest causes for Germany's defeat. Germany lost far more tanks through economic error than enemy action.

The Second World War featured not merely extensive but intensive tapping of economies. Technology and science were fundamental to military power, and the refinement of just one piece of equipment often revolutionized warfare. Thus, centimetric radar could detect naval movements on the surface at night. When Allied navies acquired this device between 1942 and 1943, it wrecked the tactics of the Japanese and German surface fleets and German U-boats alike in one blow, never to recover. Similarly, the chief of U.S. submarines in the Pacific once complained that if the USN could not give his forces effective torpedoes or guns, it should at least provide boathooks to "rip the plates off the target's sides." The war fostered the production of new technology such as jet aircraft, guided missiles, and the prototype of the computer and forced revolutions in virtually all existing weapon systems. Not one tank model of 1939 was of first line quality by 1942. In the application of science and technology to warfare, the Allies outstripped the Axis. Germany developed impressive weapon systems, but few of the famous secret weapons ever saw combat. Germany could not match the Allies in technological innovation, in turning ideas into weapons. Germany's physicists never overcame the elementary problems involved in developing atomic weapons, its code breakers never penetrated machine cipher systems, its enemies did both. The Allies had the only secret weapons that mattered.

Meanwhile, strategic coordination between the Axis powers was virtually nonexistent. In 1941 Germany attacked the USSR and Japan attacked the United States without informing their allies in advance and, with absurd overconfidence, assuming that victory was assured because race and spirit must make German and Japanese warriors superior to Slavic or U.S. soldiers. The Anglo-American blockade prevented the Axis from coordinating their economic resources, from trading raw materials under Japanese control for German technology—oil for radar sets. Coordination even within the Axis countries was surprisingly lax. The Nazi state rested on organizational confusion and bureaucratic infighting, which wasted German resources. In 1943 the German army desperately needed men and weapons to stand Soviet punishment, but Germany gave this institution only half the resources it sent to the eastern front. It siphoned off its best men and weapons to form a separate Nazi army, the *Waffen SS*, which at least provided effective forces at exorbitant cost; even worse, it formed surplus ground crews into *Luftwaffe* Field Divisions, which collapsed under serious pressure. The Japanese army and navy fought separate wars and lied to each other on crucial matters. After the disaster at Midway in 1942, when one-third of Japan's aircraft carriers sank in an hour, the Imperial Japanese Navy (IJN) hosted victory parties for army officers. Similarly, in 1944 the IJN entered the Battle of the Marianas expecting to receive support from the army air force, which had already been annihilated. The IJN did not learn this fact until its own air force too was smashed.

Coordination within and between the Allies was far from perfect— excluding the simultaneous attacks on Normandy and Belorussia in the summer of 1944, the western Allies and the USSR conducted uncoordinated but parallel campaigns, while on the field of battle Unites States and Commonwealth forces often fought independent wars against the same enemy. During 1944, Mark Clark, the U.S. commander in Italy, threatened to fire on British forces if they tried to race him to Rome. Nonetheless, Allied performance exceeded that of the Axis—at least they cooperated sometimes. Without the supply of 450,000 trucks from the United States—twice as many as Germany produced—the Red Army could not so handily have crushed the *Wehrmacht* beneath its wheels during 1943 and 1945. The western Allies coordinated their resources and strategy more thoroughly than any previous coalition in history. They had joint commands, staffed by officers of both nationalities, and they shared technology and intelligence and integrated war production in an unheard of fashion.

The Allies had greater resources than the Axis, and they used them more effectively and in a synergistic way. Soviet forces engaged and destroyed the bulk of German military manpower, inflicting 80 percent of its military casualties. This let Anglo-American forces fight a capital-intensive war against a fraction of the foe, using firepower and high technology to smash a numerically smaller enemy at the minimum possible cost and also to engage and destroy the *Luftwaffe* and half of the firepower available to the German army. This forced Germany to fight a labor-intensive and low-technology war in the east, where the western allies divided German firepower and multiplied Soviet striking power. That helped the Red Army, superior both in numbers and technology, to engage and destroy most German military manpower, the point where the equation began.

The military importance of economics, technology, and administration is best seen in the case of airpower. Loss rates during air combat were staggeringly high—by 1943 the *Luftwaffe* lost 30 percent of its combat strength every month while strategic bombers sometimes lost fifty to one hundred aircraft and five hundred to one thousand aircrew in a single raid, 3 to 5 percent of their total establishment. Meanwhile, important new types of equipment were developed virtually every month. Air forces that could not manage these factors suffered no matter their pilots' skill and courage. Those that could not replace one thousand trained aircrew lost every month entered a never-ending spiral to oblivion in which the quality of personnel fell while losses rose. The U.S. air forces and the Royal Air Force (RAF) overcame these problems by making training a first priority. Even in the worst days of the Battle of Britain the RAF declined to degrade its training schedule or to send half-trained pilots into the fray. By 1944 the United States was producing more pilots than it could use. A failure to adopt this approach was central to the collapse of the Japanese and German air forces under the strain of total war.

These forces began at a high level of quality. In 1941 the IJN had the finest naval aviation pilots and aircraft in the world. Within a year, however, the United States had developed better aircraft that turned the Zero fighter into a flying coffin. Japan never replaced the Zero—even worse, it barely produced enough of them to replace its losses. Again, the IJN entered the war with a program to train just 2,750 finely crafted new pilots a year—far too small a number to match either the wastage of war or mass production in the United States of good aircrew. This problem was exacerbated because whereas the USN made every effort to rescue pilots shot down at sea, the IJN left its own to drown, losing large numbers of high-quality personnel in exchange for poorly trained replacements. Eighteen months after the war began the IJN's air force was weaker than in 1941, its aircraft were outclassed and the quality of its aircrew was collapsing. By 1944 Japanese pilots received only one tenth the flying training of Unites States officers. Japan adopted *Shimpu* (often called "Kamikaze") tactics largely because its poorly trained pilots offered an easy target to U.S. aircraft but could still crash-dive into warships.

Similarly, in 1940 the personnel and equipment of the RAF and the *Luftwaffe* were roughly equal in quality and ahead of the United States and the USSR. Soon, however, Germany was fighting three states with larger air forces, two of which were better. The United States and Britain pulled far ahead of Germany in quantity and quality and stayed there. Incompetent management dogged the *Luftwaffe*'s research and development program: it produced dozens of prototypes but put few new models in service. In 1939 Germany tested a prototype jet fighter, eighteen months ahead of Britain, but the RAF had them in service long before the *Luftwaffe*. In June 1941, the *Luftwaffe*'s combat strength was merely fifty aircraft larger than twelve months before. During 1942 it produced just 30 percent more aircraft than in 1939, while British and Soviet production had tripled. Since German maintenance was poor, 40 to 70 percent of its aircraft were grounded at any one time, two to three times the British and U.S. rate. For the *Luftwaffe*, the training of aircrew was always the last priority. At the outbreak of war half its personnel were only half-trained, and in 1940 it lost almost two-thirds of its pilots. By 1941 the *Luftwaffe* routinely sent partly trained pilots to squadrons, just to keep numbers up. Then, during late 1942 and early 1943, precisely as its casualties and need for training skyrocketed, the *Luftwaffe* closed its training establishment for several months and threw most of it away in costly and unsuccessful attempts to resupply by air garrisons encircled at Stalingrad and Tunisia. These losses permanently crippled the *Luftwaffe* and its training command, which also took the lion's share of cuts in the allocation of aviation fuel. By 1944 Allied pilots received three times more hours of training before combat than German ones. The latter died in droves, at their own hands as well as the enemy's. Throughout the war almost half of the *Luftwaffe's* losses happened through accidents, three times the British and American level, taking 33 percent of German combat aircraft with them.

National cohesion was also fundamental to military power. Only the shield of a solid home front could withstand the crushing blows every belligerent received. By 1939 and 1940 social classes in France and Italy distrusted each other and their governments to an extraordinary degree. Many French conservatives preferred Nazi Germany to French socialists while French communists applauded Germany's capture of Paris as a worker's victory. Italy's military performance was far worse between 1940 and 1943 than in 1915 and 1918, largely because few Italians cared to die for Benito Mussolini. Such social fragility did not inevitably produce defeat. It did mean that when defeats occurred Frenchmen and Italians would not rally and let France and Italy fight on. In 1941 so hated was the Soviet regime that many of its citizens actively supported Germany as soon as they had the chance. When Nazi troops first passed their villages, even Jews rejoiced and offered bread and salt, a traditional sign of political submission. Had Germans not behaved like Mongols, they might have acquired the support of most Soviet citizens and the aid of millions of soldiers. Social fragility could have smashed the USSR fifty years before it finally collapsed. Precisely this happened when Japan overran the European colonies of southeast Asia. Local populations offered little support to their masters and many voluntarily assisted Japan. They, and many Arabs and Europeans, viewed the Axis as liberators.

The national willpower of the other major belligerents and many of the minor ones was greater. In 1940 the British population declined to surrender in the face of a nearly hopeless position; five years later Germany had to be overrun and its armies smashed before Germans gave up the fight. Powerful resistance movements thrived in Yugoslavia, China, and Poland despite (perhaps because of) the fact that millions of their people died at the occupier's hands. The Second World War demonstrated that modern nation-states were tough and hungry animals. They could make millions of their people die for them. In order to achieve national cohesion, states had to overcome the political rivalries of peacetime and harness the most powerful of existing social structures to the war effort. In the USSR Joseph Stalin married Russian nationalism to socialist internationalism, and two old enemies, the Orthodox Church and the Communist Party, joined arms against a common foe. Together they rallied most ethnic Russians (although not every group in the USSR) to total war after Germany treated all Slavs with savagery. Winston Churchill's government rested on an alliance between the British state and the two most powerful institutions in its society, the Conservative Party and the trade union movement. Given this political unanimity, the class system produced tens of thousands of upper-class men ready to command and millions of working-class males prepared to grumble and obey.

National cohesion had limits everywhere—in Britain and the United States, for example, a legacy of bad relations between workers and bosses led to coal strikes during the war—and like any political accommodation it came at a cost. In particular, shortages of labor crippled arms production in most countries. Few, however, augmented their limited manpower through a maximum use of womanpower. Such a policy would have challenged socially accepted views about the role of women and the interests of male workers. If women could replace skilled workmen during the war, why not after it? And, if so, why should movements of workmen, with bitter memories of the Great Depression, commit economic suicide in order to win a war for their bosses? This was a powerful argument in most countries. No Western state employed nearly as many women in economic production as was possible. For ideological reasons, Germany did not actively follow such a policy at all. Comparatively, twice as many British and U.S. women per capita worked in the war economy, but powerful obstacles stood before female labor. Women were welcome as clerical and unskilled labor but few were engaged in skilled industrial work. The real symbol of female war work was not "Rosie the Riveter," the poster image of woman with kerchief, lipstick, and jackhammer, but the "Land Girls," British women who pulled up potatoes by hand as agricultural laborers. Women workers were paid about one-third less than their male counterparts. They were constantly reminded that they were there only for the duration of the war, after which servicemen must return to their jobs. The dictates of national cohesion and the war economy directly conflicted regarding female labor, and most countries used their womanpower with remarkable inefficiency. Only in the USSR, suffering the most savage loss of manpower, did women routinely work in heavy industry—indeed, millions of them served in the front line, primarily in support roles, but hundreds of thousands of them also fought in combat.

Civilians were not merely part of military power. Far more than in the First World War, they were also its target. Hurting enemy civilians, it was hoped, might erode their will to fight and their industrial output. The slow starvation of blockade was augmented by sudden death from the air. During this period any bombing of urban centers had to produce heavy civilian casualties—strategic bombing was by definition terror bombing. What Germany did sporadically against Warsaw, Rotterdam, London, and Belgrade, the western Allies did systematically against every city in Germany and Japan, killing millions of Axis civilians. Japan and Germany used terror to control the vast territories that they could overrun but not administer. When the Chinese Communist Party claimed that guerrillas were the fish and the people the ocean, Japanese occupiers responded with a program of "draining the ocean"—if one just killed enough peasants, the survivors would not dare harbor guerrillas. As a result, as many civilians were killed in China, well over twenty million of them, as in all of Europe.

The Axis powers met resistance with massacre. They enslaved millions of civilians to serve their military machines, as forced laborers in Germany and Japan, as "comfort girls" for Japanese fighting forces. Beyond this stood the "final solution," the genocide of six million Jews. Nazi Germany also killed two million Polish, five hundred thousand Gypsy, and several million Russian civilians; the German army shot out of hand all Jews and commissars it captured from the Red Army and starved at least 3.3 million Soviet prisoners of war to death in German camps. All this was merely a first step. Germany planned to execute tens of millions more Slavs and to enslave the remainder forever. Genocide was a German war aim for which it made military and economic sacrifices. Not surprisingly, Soviet troops took revenge on German civilians and prisoners at the end of the war, although they killed perhaps only one defenseless German for every five Soviets murdered by Germans. All this made the Second World War the most costly conflict ever known. Yet the attacks on civilians had mixed results. They did weaken the morale of all their victims and perhaps they broke the nerve of peoples whose national cohesion was low, but they did not destroy any enemy whose will to fight was strong.

The war opened with a run of brilliant Axis successes. Between 1939 and 1941 Germany overran Europe between Dunkirk and Moscow, killing or capturing twice as many soldiers as it possessed itself and forcing Britain and the USSR to the wall. In the first months of the Pacific war, Japan smashed its British and U.S. enemies and stood master over east and southeast Asia. Yet however successful these operations, they rested on irrational strategy. German and Japanese leaders grossly underestimated their enemies, stretched their own forces to the breaking point, and deliberately forced stronger powers to fight them. Germany, in particular, started a second front against the USSR at a time when Britain still fought and almost immediately afterward, following the attack on Pearl Harbor, declared war on the United States, which otherwise might not have joined the European campaign.

Then the war entered its decisive phase. Every belligerent was like a battered boxer, half-blind and staggering, desperately throwing his last energy into knock-out blows that he was too tired to aim or his enemy to avoid. They fought in isolated places, far from their centers of power—in November 1942 Germany was throwing all its strength toward the Caspian Sea, Tunisia, and the North Atlantic, the United States into North Africa and New Guinea. Attritional struggles, high in intensity and casualties, occurred on every front between 1940 and 1942. The Royal Navy fought across the Mediterranean Sea just off the shores of southern Europe, desperately thrusting convoys through a powerful Italian fleet and thousands of German and Italian aircraft to relieve the garrison of Malta or to evacuate that of Crete and to hammer the enemy whenever it could. This campaign cost Britain two battleships, two carriers, thirteen cruisers, and fifty-six destroyers, almost 15 percent of its warship tonnage of 1939, but it broke the Italian navy and made Malta into a razor that slashed the arteries of Axis power in the Mediterranean. Meanwhile, Germany threw four hundred tanks and fifty thousand men into four square miles of buildings in the city of Stalingrad, three thousand miles from home, where Soviet defenders took 90 percent losses— taking greater casualties than suffered by the entire United States between 1941 and 1945—and still fought on.

When the dust of these collisions had settled, everywhere there was a winner and a loser. In the Pacific war, for example, the period between August 1942 and September 1943 was one of equilibrium and attrition between forces roughly equal in quantity, quality, and initiative. The buildup of U.S. and Australian strength in New Guinea and the Solomon Islands turned the forward edge of Japanese conquest into the central battlefield of the Pacific war. Here the bulk of the U.S. and Japanese navies and their airpower in the Pacific smashed head-on for a year of constant combat, swirling around large land battles on the Solomon Islands and New Guinea. On the floor of Ironbottom Sound, the ten-mile-long and eight-mile-wide channel north of Guadalcanal, rested two battleships, twelve cruisers, and twenty-three destroyers—more tonnage than sunk at Jutland. The operations in these areas cost Japan more than the United States. Japan was less able to replace losses, because its casualties in aircraft, pilots, transport vessels, and soldiers substantially exceeded those of the Allies, while the latter used their forces with greater economy and effect. Initially, U.S. forces were less good than Japanese ones yet they learned fast, their strategy was shrewd and bold, and their taste for aggressive attack against the enemy's strength suited the circumstances. As General Douglas MacArthur wrote, "The only way to beat him is to fight him incessantly. Combat must not be avoided but must be sought so that the ultimate policy of attrition can at once become effective. No matter what the theoretical odds may be against us, if we fight him we will beat him." Even more fortunately for the Americans, Japanese commanders held similar views but with less justification.

In this campaign, the sources and targets of military power were armed men and the means to keep them armed. Both sides strove to maintain large forces in some of the least developed places between the poles, twenty-five hundred miles from Tokyo and eight thousand miles from San Francisco, where no logistical infrastructure existed. In such a war and such an environment, the United States held the strongest cards. Nowhere could it more thoroughly outmatch Japan than in creating an entirely new system of military logistics and in fighting a war of material attrition. Japan had expanded until it could go no further. There, at its level of incompetence, it fought with all its power to the death. The battlefields were simply too large and too far forward to suit its tiny logistical and transport capabilities. Every mile further from its main centers of power the battles were fought, the greater its logistical problems and the more exposed its lines of communication. Japan was fighting precisely the war that least suited its material resources, a prolonged and costly battle of attrition beyond easy reach of its supply system.

This drove Japan, as a matter of routine, to take great, and often costly, risks, such as shipping divisions to the most forward ports under its control or onto islands held by the enemy and into the maw of enemy air and naval strength or operating hundreds of aircraft from the same base, all vulnerable to one massive onslaught. Japan's fighting and logistical services entered a vicious circle, which progressively weakened their ability to fight anywhere at all. For as both sides strained their muscles to strangle the other in New Guinea and the Solomon Islands, U.S. forces began to slash the exposed limbs of Japanese logistics. The southwest Pacific witnessed a terrible campaign of maritime interdiction, rendered even more deadly and one-sided by Japan's failure to retaliate in kind and its incompetence in convoy escort. These engagements eroded still further the relative ability of Japanese logistics to support a prolonged war of attrition. They also directly shaped operations—the Battle of the Bismarck Sea, where in April 1943 U.S. air forces smashed a Japanese transport fleet, drowned not merely a division but any hope for Japanese strategic initiative in New Guinea. Similarly, preemptive air strikes wrecked Japan's forward airbases on that island and destroyed most of its air forces on the ground, largely because it failed to develop an effective early warning system for air defense or to use properly its few radar sets. This crippled Japan's air performance and increased the scale of its aircraft losses. By early 1944, exactly as Japan adopted a strategy of human (though not material) attrition, these campaigns had destroyed the naval and air strength needed to brace its forward line against the U.S. sledgehammer.

Then, after eighteen months of bitter resistance where the Allies paid heavily in time and blood for every inch advanced, Japanese air and naval strength crumbled and its forward perimeter suddenly cracked in two places at once, New Guinea and the Marshal Islands. This opened a one-thousand-mile line of sea room for a dazzling campaign of maneuver toward the Philippines. With a few sharp blows in a few short months, the U.S. sledgehammer stove in both the outer and inner defenses of the Japanese empire, in the process demolishing what remained of its navy and air force and rendering useless every soldier and ton of supplies elsewhere on the forward line at a tiny cost.

During these bitter campaigns of 1942 and 1943, Allied strategy became better than its enemies. British and American decision makers favored different strategies for victory in the European theater, but by hammering out their differences they blended the best of their approaches. This process weeded out bad ideas and left both partners to pursue good ones with determination and skill. The British, for example, were less enthusiastic than the United States for the assault on Normandy in 1944, but once that decision was made, they dominated the planning that made that operation a success. Some might argue that Anglo-American strategy in Europe could have been better, but none can call it bad. The Allies made a rational, and often bold, use of force—few military moves in history have been as daring as "Torch," by which in November 1942 half a million Anglo-American soldiers in Britain and the United States were thrown into a large-scale amphibious attack on North Africa, crossing the Atlantic with entire safety and surprise during the height of the U-boat campaign and overturning the military balance in Europe. Even the much criticized Italian campaign tied down more Nazi resources than Allied in Italy and the Balkans, the rough equivalent in strength of German forces in France on D-Day or an army group on the eastern front, leaving them vulnerable to the kill in other theaters. The Allies deployed their forces with more resolution and effect than the Axis, constantly catching them off balance, throwing their strengths against the enemy's weaknesses, and exploiting greater skill in intelligence and deception.

In the Pacific war, code-breaking continually betrayed Japanese intentions and capabilities to the United States, which then used its resources with maximum effect. During 1942 the USN in the Pacific was heavily outnumbered by a qualitatively superior enemy, but excellent intelligence and command thrice let it concentrate its entire strength against fractions of the IJN. The first produced the ambush at the Coral Sea (May 7–8, 1942) where losses were equal. The second produced the Battle of Midway (June 5, 1942) and the exchange of four Japanese for one American carrier, after which the USN was no longer outnumbered. The third produced the American seizure of Guadalcanal (August 7, 1942) and the eighteen-month-long Solomon Islands campaign, where the IJN crumbled. Then, in 1944, the American "island hopping" strategy, which broke the back of Japanese defenses in the Pacific during 1944 at a remarkably cheap price, was possible only because intelligence showed how to strike where the enemy was weakest.

Between 1942 and 1945 British code-breaking provided an almost letter-perfect grasp of the location and strength of German forces. This let Allied commanders use their strategic resources against Germany efficiently. No military operation is more difficult to conduct than an amphibious assault against enemy defenses. Due to superior intelligence, however, every major Allied amphibious operation between 1942 and 1944 hit the enemy at weak points and caught it by surprise. This occurred because German intelligence was incompetent and its command was manipulated by British deception. German authorities believed that the western Allies possessed twice as many divisions as they actually had. Germany allocated between 33 percent and 66 percent of its scarce divisions in southern Europe and France to guard against dangers that could be real only if these formations were. But they were illusions, so ghosts removed Germans from the battle. Similarly, until the autumn of 1944 the Red Army rarely outnumbered the Germans and their allies on the eastern front by even two to one, yet it routinely outmatched them in breakthrough sectors by ten to one—again, incompetent intelligence led directly to German disasters.

In June 1944 Allied deception led the Germans to annihilation in both west and east. Germany expected a Soviet attack only in southern Poland, where it concentrated all its reserves. It missed the redeployment of four hundred thousand Russian soldiers and four thousand tanks one thousand miles to Belorussia in the north, where they launched an assault that demolished the German army on the entire eastern front in six weeks. Meanwhile, the Germans believed that the attack on Normandy was merely a feint to cover a real invasion one hundred miles north. Only 33 percent of its divisions in France were within five days' march of Normandy when the invasion began, and Germany left another 33 percent of them at the wrong place for the first month of the battle. East and west, every Allied division was at the right place.

In the Second World War, sea power had greater importance than in any other conflict since 1815. The struggle between the large and good navies of Britain, Germany, Japan, and the United States and the big and mediocre Italian fleet determined the outcome of the Pacific war and shaped the war in Europe. Britain and Japan lived and died by sea power. The United States could only reach the theaters of war by sea, while the German and Italian navies could win the European war by strangling Great Britain or by preventing an Anglo-American invasion of the continent. The war featured extraordinary activity in every form of sea power—fleet engagements, small ship fights, commerce raiding, and convoy escort—and in no other conflict have amphibious operations played so central a role.

This war is often seen as the birthplace of a new era of sea power, where airplanes replaced guns. That view is wrong. In fact, surface ships fought each other with guns far more often in the Second World War than they had done in the First, and with effect. Every carrier that came within range of enemy guns was sunk, and especially at night, they were helpless without surface escorts. Immediately after their victory at Midway, U.S. carriers ran straight for Hawaii, away from Japanese cruisers. Aircraft carriers remained subsidiary in the narrow waters of Europe, because they were too vulnerable to submarines, surface warships, and the *Luftwaffe*; instead, battleships, Britannia, and land-based aviation ruled the waves. Even in the Pacific during 1942, surface ships were as important as aircraft carriers. If carriers determined the battles of Midway and Coral Sea, the Solomon Islands campaign was fought as much by guns as airplanes. Although carriers dominated the Pacific war from 1943, they always required the support of surface warships. As late as autumn 1944, when the IJN attacked U.S. transports at Leyte Gulf during the start of the invasion of the Philippines, battleships were still in a position to strike heavy blows. They were also the only warships that could survive major air strikes. A dozen dive bombers could sink a cruiser or carrier, but scores or hundreds were required to sink a battleship. Few battleships at sea were destroyed by aircraft—just as many carriers were destroyed by surface warships and submarines. The naval revolution happened after the war, not during it.

There was not one typical pattern of naval battle during the Second World War but several of them. In European waters, and often in the Pacific, engagements were fought between fleets of two to fifteen warships armed with heavy guns. Sometimes squadrons moved like chessmen in the Arctic or Adriatic seas, firing under tight control at targets ten to twenty miles away. Sometimes wild melees occurred, a dozen ships charging about a five-square-mile area, each gun crew firing individually and instantaneously at point-blank range toward flashes in the dark. Here the IJN, the master of night fighting, held a major advantage until the onset of centimetric radar. Through this means, during the Solomon Islands campaign it inflicted the heaviest defeats ever suffered by the USN at sea, including the Battle of Savo Island, August 8, 1942. In the Pacific, equally often fleets of three to forty warships, hundreds of miles apart, felt for each other through aerial reconnaissance and then struck with hundreds of dive-bombers and torpedo-bombers. The first blow might be the deathblow. Defensive fighters could rarely stop all attacking aircraft, and anything but complete success could be utter disaster. Of the first two waves of U.S. aircraft at Midway, for example, 90 percent missed their targets, 40 percent were shot down, yet 24 dive-bombers sank three Japanese carriers within five minutes. Finally, surprise air attacks twice caught a main fleet in port, sinking one-third of the battleships of Italy at Taranto in December 1940 and the United

States at Pearl Harbor in December 1941 for virtually no loss; similarly, in December 1941 a few Italian frogmen sank one British battleship in Alexandria harbor and disabled another.

Generally, since the 1500s, main fleet engagements have been rare and losses in naval combat low. Navies could not easily find or cripple each other. Both sides rarely sought battle at the same time; generally one or both were trying to avoid it. The four good fleets of the Second World War, however, had all imbibed the Nelsonian tradition of seeking decisive battle, while their ordnance could inflict deadly damage on men of war. Consequently, naval battles were unusually common and their costs extraordinarily high. By the end of 1942 almost half of the world's warship tonnage of 1939 was sunk or undergoing massive repair, and the war at sea was dying through exhaustion. Half of Britain's battleships were sunk or temporarily out of action, and every one of its carriers of 1939 destroyed; only 33 percent of heavy German warships were operational; battle damage and lack of nerve immobilized the Italian navy; every U.S. carrier in the Pacific was destroyed or undergoing massive repair, while 80 percent of the IJN's pilots of December 1941 were dead.

Since losses had been so high, victory turned on the ability to replace the losses. While both sides had strong right hooks, one had a glass jaw. The western Allies possessed 75 percent of the world's shipbuilding capacity. Britain completed almost as much warship tonnage as the Axis combined and the United States more than the rest of the world put together, producing a revolution in power—the United States replaced Britain as master of the waves. During 1940 and 1942 the war at sea was nearly done, but by 1943 the Anglo-American navies had more than replaced their losses. The Axis powers could not and their navies became irrelevant. Italy surrendered, Germany scrapped its heavy surface fleet, and the IJN suffered massive and one-sided losses whenever it came within reach of the USN. By 1944 the Allies had larger navies than they could use. The war at sea began with a bang. It ended with a whimper.

Warfare on land was revolutionized by the rise of firepower that could not only kill but move, for tanks, trucks, aircraft, and radio gave armies unheard of mobility and destructive capacity. This change should not be exaggerated. Most German and Soviet soldiers moved by foot and horse-drawn cart; artillery and machine guns remained the biggest killers on the battlefield and infantry the largest arm. More tanks fought in the Yom Kippur war of 1973 than the Battle of Kursk of 1943. The precision and the power of artillery and machine guns, those weapons that had defined the western front, increased dramatically. The German MG-42 machine gun fired twelve hundred rounds per minute; under the British "time on target" procedure, the artillery rounds fired by 250 guns scattered over a forty-square-mile area would explode over the same one hundred square yards in the space of a single second. Many battles fought between 1942 and 1945 were slugging matches reminiscent of the western front. Nonetheless, armies could more easily fight battles of maneuver than twenty-five years before and, in particular, they could find a means to sidestep attrition and to achieve quick, cheap, and decisive victory—blitzkrieg. Here massive but mobile firepower was used not to hit the enemy's arms but to blow out its brains—to stave in a narrow sector of the front and drive into the enemy's rear areas, slashing its communications and command and shattering its army. The German army was the first to apply this technique. This was to some extent an accident—between 1919 and 1939 German commanders were not enamored of armor, and in 1940 their tanks were technically less well suited for a main battle than British, French, or Soviet ones. The *Wehrmacht* stumbled into blitzkrieg but mastered the art with rapidity. It was quick to learn the value of combined arms, that tanks could most profitably be engaged by antitank guns, artillery and antitank guns by infantry, and infantry by armor and just as quick to use this approach in defense as attack. Its army and officers were better than its enemies, and for several years the discrepancy grew as it destroyed the best large armies of Europe and engaged hastily raised and untrained replacements. During 1939 and 1942 it smashed far larger enemies as a matter of routine.

In a classic blitzkrieg attack, one hundred tanks followed closely by several thousand infantryman on foot struck a front one mile wide, preferably by surprise. Bullets bounced off armor while machine guns, artillery, and dive-bombers pinned the defenders down. Within a moment of coming into the open, the attackers were on top of their enemy, crushing defenses under their treads and shooting soldiers in the back as they fled in panic. Tanks and motorized infantry then drove into the enemy's rear, up to one hundred miles per day, dicing armies like vegetables before their commanders could respond. Such attacks rarely featured complex fire support or sophisticated tactics. When attacking Commonwealth infantry and artillery at Sidi Rezeg airfield in Libya during November 1941, the Afrika Korps simply formed a long single line of tanks and trucks abreast and charged, capturing the position and losing 40 percent of its vehicles. Such primitive tactics were characteristic of the German style of blitzkrieg during its heyday, and they were feasible for one reason only: the relative invulnerability of the tank. During 1939 and 1941 only Germans and Soviets had effective antitank weapons, and not in great numbers. Even so, just a handful of these weapons could paralyze or wreck any frontal assault. In virtually every other case, unless the defender had tanks or artillery at the point of contact, any armored assault could rupture any front. Then a war of maneuver would follow where decisions had to be made in minutes, not days, something that the commanders and communication systems of no army except the *Wehrmacht* could do until late 1942.

Thus, in 1940 the British and French intended to fight as in 1918. Their commanders were scattered in chalets across the countryside and communicated through the French civil telephone network, which was notoriously inefficient: telephone operators often disconnected generals during emergencies. The highest French headquarters did not possess a single radio set and sometimes had just one telephone to coordinate half a million men. No action could occur until several commands were consulted—if communication with just one failed, the Allies could not coordinate any actions. In order to counter a German thrust into Belgium and to man the defenses of the Maginot Line, the French allocated only a few third-line units in the Ardennes at the center of the front— precisely where the main German attack was launched. This was a risky operation, for three good French divisions with artillery could easily have blocked this small area of few roads and allowed Allied air forces a field day against a stalled and massive column behind. That did not occur. When the head of the German column passed through the Ardennes it was forced to launch a frontal assault across the Meuse River. Here, panicked by dive-bomber attacks, French artillerymen fled and nothing remained to stop German tanks from crossing the Meuse and driving to the Atlantic. At precisely this moment, Allied communications and command collapsed. Commanders could not contact each other; every counterattack took several days to be organized, so few were launched; the Allied armies simply disintegrated. In six weeks, for forty-five thousand dead, Germany killed or captured 2.75 million French and Belgian soldiers, forced half a million English ones to flee the continent, and mastered western Europe.

Much the same was true on a titanic scale for the USSR. Had the Red Army been mobilized on the western frontier in June 1941, it would have outnumbered the enemy by two to one. Its forces, however, were scattered across two continents and caught by surprise and their command cracked. Over the first four months of the war the *Wehrmacht* advanced rapidly, smashing each echelon of the Red Army as it appeared: Axis strength always massed at the point of decision, and the Soviets were often outnumbered. By May 1942, 4.5 million Soviet soldiers, most of its trained personnel, were prisoners or dead and 21,500 tanks were destroyed. The Red Army had to be rebuilt from the start.

By 1942 Germany occupied Europe from Spain to Stalingrad. Here its luck changed. If Germany could not win quickly it could not win at all, because it could not sustain a prolonged war of attrition. Yet Germany failed to smash Britain or Russia before the United States turned the military balance in favor of the Allies. Instead, it grew weaker while its enemies grew stronger.

Every number tells the story. Between June 1941 and April 1942, the *Wehrmacht* lost six hundred thousand men dead and permanently disabled on the eastern front, while five hundred thousand more suffered serious wounds. It received five hundred thousand replacements. Germany never recovered its strength of 1941. In 1942 it rebuilt half its armored divisions and one third of its infantry, but the rest of its forces held long, thin fronts with 66 percent of their establishment in manpower and firepower. Though the USSR suffered far greater losses, it replaced all its casualties and built forty-five hundred tanks, three thousand aircraft, and fourteen thousand guns—twice as many as Germany. Despite the slaughter of Soviet forces, by June 1942 they still outnumbered Germany and its minor Axis allies by 1.5 to 1 (5.3 million men to 3.7 million). Only if Germany again killed Soviet soldiers as it had done in 1941 before new ones were trained and others raised could it survive its encounter with the colossus. Adolf Hitler knew that 1942 would decide the war, and his actions decided that it would go to the enemy. He threw German weaknesses against Soviet strengths. In 1942 the *Wehrmacht* drove to the east, doubling the length of its front but killing few of the enemy, who received nine precious months to train, and then entered a bloody pointless battle at Stalingrad. Here, Soviet forces surged back. In a year of staggering losses between May 1942 and April 1943, 1 million Germans and 600,000 Axis allies were killed, captured, or permanently disabled, while 2.5 million Soviet soldiers died.

For the last time Germany replaced these losses, but the tide was turning fast. One million western Allied soldiers stood ready to invade Europe from Tunisia and another million from Britain. Between November 1942 and May 1943 they killed or captured 100,000 German and 300,000 Italian soldiers in Africa and destroyed 2,422 aircraft, 40 percent of the *Luftwaffe's* combat strength. In 1943 the Allies made Italy and its 1.5 million soldiers surrender. They also tied down the *Luftwaffe*, half the German gun barrels, which could destroy Soviet armor, and as many men (1.5 million) as Germany sent as replacements to the eastern front. Meanwhile, the Red Army more than replaced its losses. By May 1943 on the eastern front, 3 million German soldiers, 1,400 tanks, 6,400 guns, and 600,000 allies faced 5.8 million Soviet soldiers, 6,000 tanks, and 20,000 guns. From this point, Germany increased its firepower in the east despite catastrophic losses almost every month, but manpower could never be replaced. Between July and September 1943, the German army suffered 650,000 casualties on the eastern front and received 280,000 replacements: its infantry strength there fell by another 35 percent; its Axis allies, once 25 percent of its numerical strength on the eastern front, melted away and Soviet superiority rose. The weaker Germany was, the more Germans were lost. Between November 1943 and June 1944, 1.5 million German soldiers were killed or captured on all fronts, another 1.4 million between June and November 1944—far heavier losses than their enemies suffered. Only about sixty (or 20 percent) of German divisions were well-equipped and effective formations, though these were numerically equal to the Commonwealth and U.S. armies in Europe. The remainder, withered from losses or incompetence, inferior to every western Allied unit and half the Soviet ones, often crumpled at one blow.

Yet numbers do not tell the whole story. After 1942 Allied military quality improved remarkably. Several Allied generals became the equal of German ones, the *Wehrmacht* became just another army, and the German form of blitzkrieg died on its feet. While no army ever quite matched the Germans at mobile operations, the *Wehrmacht* fell behind in crucial areas, especially the use of firepower. Its artillery arm was weaker in quality and quantity than those of its enemies, and even its old superiority in armor declined. During the Battle of Kursk on July 12, 1943, eight hundred Soviet and well over four hundred German tanks charged into each other near the town of Prokhorovka. In a day long melee both suffered high and virtually identical losses, 400 Soviet and over 320 German armored fighting vehicles (AFVS). At Medennine in Tunisia on March 6, 1943, in one of the last major German attacks thrown against the western Allies, the Afrika Korps launched yet another cavalry charge, tank tread to tank tread. Half its strength was blown apart in half an hour. The British lost four tanks. If Germany could not win such battles, it could not win the war.

Meanwhile, every army came to terms with blitzkrieg. They learned to make calm and quick decisions over radio; they adjusted to the new tempo of battle. If a defender's nerve could not be broken, breakthrough could not be exploited far, nor was it easy to achieve. From the summer of 1942, blitzkrieg became increasingly less effective. This did not stem from Allied incompetence—German attacks were even less successful—but from another revolution in military operations. Effective antitank weapons, ranging from high-velocity guns to hand-held infantry weapons like bazookas, became widespread. By 1942 infantry battalions of eight hundred men had as much antitank firepower as had divisions of sixteen thousand in 1940: by 1944 platoons of thirty-five men posed more danger to armor than brigades of thirty-five hundred had done five years before. A tank charge against infantry no longer produced breakthrough, just suicide, as Germans discovered every time they tried it against western forces. During 1940 and 1942 infantry followed tanks into battle; by 1943 tanks moved behind infantry. Land operations from 1943 to 1945 were more like 1918 than 1940. The pace of warfare slowed; defensive systems became elaborate and killing zones deeper and deadlier, with layers of antitank weapons, machine guns, artillery, and bunkers; the lowly mine, scattered in the millions, paralyzed mobility, as tankmen feared for their treads and infantry for their genitals. Thus, at Kursk 1.5 million Soviet soldiers, forty-seven hundred tanks, and nineteen thousand guns manned a fortified region containing eight defensive lines, 200 miles wide and 120 miles thick, with twenty-one hundred mines per mile of front. The strongest attack ever launched by any German army in history, including half its total tank strength (three thousand), barely dented this position—for the loss of seventy thousand crack troops and one thousand AFVs.

Such systems were rare on the eastern front; hence, the Red Army launched blitzkrieg successfully until the autumn of 1944. German strength varied dramatically from one eastern place to another. Wherever the *Wehrmacht* deployed its main force, two thousand AFVs, twenty-five hundred antitank guns, and five hundred thousand crack soldiers could bolster one hundred thousand men holding a front two hundred miles long. These concentrations were impervious to blitzkrieg—they smashed many great Soviet attempts at it. Elsewhere, sixty thousand Germans might hold a two-hundred-mile sector, their front line consisting of minefields watched by one thousand soldiers in three man outposts two hundred yards apart, backed four miles behind by two thousand men and twenty antitank weapons every ten miles in sketchy defenses; supported, finally, by a sector reserve of thirty thousand men, one hundred antitank guns, and fifty tanks fifty miles to the rear. The Red Army could penetrate such sectors like a lever and use that advantage to unhinge the entire German front.

It did so by selecting a weak area for attack while threatening several others to divert main German forces. This was helped by the *Wehrmacht's* propensity to launch deep counter-attacks against Soviet assaults in one place, which deprived it of the reserves needed to parry another four hundred miles away. Soviet blitzkrieg began with heavy infantry and armor attacks against several parts of a weak German front, clearing minefields, wrecking local defenses, and absorbing sector reserves, aiming to cut deep and narrow channels through to open country. Then, artillery barrages and aircraft strikes paralyzed all adjacent German defenses, reserves, and command; tank corps of two hundred AFVs and 15,000 men surged through these channels and turned fifty miles behind to encircle the sector; task forces of 5,000 men in trucks and sixty tanks seized places vital for deep penetration and led tank armies of four hundred AFVs and 60,000 mechanized infantry hundreds of miles to the rear, aiming to encircle 25 percent of the German army in the east. This approach did not always work—when tank armies were unleashed against intact German defenses, they were butchered in the killing zone. But between 1943 and 1944 Soviet blitzkrieg often did succeed and when it did the Red Army captured hundreds of thousands of German troops and square miles of territory at a small cost. Thus, in the summer of 1944, the Soviet attack in Belorussia destroyed 500,000 German soldiers and two thousand tanks and pinned another 600,000 men on the Baltic coast in return for the loss of 250,000 Soviet men and forty-three hundred tanks. Meanwhile, for a price of 100,000 men the Red Army killed or captured 400,000 German and Axis soldiers in Rumania and forced 400,000 Finns out of the war.

Soviet blitzkrieg worked by avoiding German concentrations. This the western Allies could not do. Deep defensive systems were routine along the narrow fronts of the west, while force to space ratios were high—more German men and guns stood on every average mile in the west than in their strongest defenses to the east. Moreover, the Allies, forced to launch seaborne assaults against heavily defended positions, could not leave beachheads until their strength had built up, by which time the *Wehrmacht* had surrounded them in a powerful ring. Thus, at Normandy, the Anglo-Canadian part of the invasion forces cut through the most deadly prepared defenses of the war virtually without a scratch and then drove straight off the shore into a killing zone twenty miles deep and twenty-five miles long, held by ninety thousand crack German soldiers, forty thousand decent ones, one thousand AFVs, over one thousand effective antitank guns, and millions of mines. Neither German nor Soviet styles of blitzkrieg could have walked through these sort of defenses. They could be broken only at cost and through slow and controlled set-piece battles. Fortunately, Germans fought this sort of war no better than the Allies and were far less able to sustain it.

In set-piece battles, a continual series of limited infantry and armored attacks ground down German strength. Since these attacks were thrown against prepared defenses, they often failed and were costly, but no other armies could assault prepared defenses with this effect, ingenuity, and economy. Firepower of unprecedented power and precision hammered the enemy. With utter command of the air and aircraft always overhead, the western Allies established the "cab rank" system. When commanders requested immediate support against any target of opportunity, one airplane immediately peeled off to strike while another moved up ready to serve the next client. Aircraft lurking behind German lines shot up troops, commanders, and supplies, while one thousand heavy bombers could support any single ground attack. Every Allied gun could switch at a moment's notice from separate operations to a single combined and smashing shoot. A platoon could call for help and within thirty seconds have thousands of rounds fall precisely on a German attack two thousand yards ahead. Allied power broke any but elite German divisions and crippled even their nerve and material power.

When the enemy was sufficiently weakened, the coup de grace was delivered exactly as Napoleon would have done—artillery and aircraft smashed everything in sight along a narrow corridor, and tanks and mechanized infantry drove through the ruins into the enemy's rear. Under both the German and Soviet forms of blitzkrieg, breakthrough avoided attrition. In set-piece battles, breakthrough followed attrition. Such operations were often poorly handled. Rapid advances could be paralyzed because massive firepower devastated terrain or because immense and uncontrolled numbers of Allied vehicles produced a traffic jam. Yet when handled effectively, as in Tunisia during 1943, Normandy in 1944, and the Roer Forest in 1945, this approach smashed large forces in powerful positions at a cheap price. Neither German nor Soviet forces between 1942 and 1945 could break through such defensive systems and suffered far greater casualties in their failures than the western Allies did in their successes.

Land operations in the Pacific theater were different in nature. They were fought in wildernesses without roads where force to space ratios were lower than in Europe, while the army of Japan fought like no other on earth. It followed a style of warfare, adopted by many nonindustrialized countries in Asia during the twentieth century, like Turkey and Vietnam, that was shaped to trump the Western strong suits of firepower and technology. This style of war was marked by an unusual emphasis on maneuver and rapid attack and away from prepared firepower. Where this approach failed to achieve quick victory, the exponents of this style of war moved to a strategy of grinding attrition, willing to accept far higher casualties than the foe so long as its losses too were heavy, in the hope of destroying its will to fight. This style has often defeated rich but irresolute powers, but it has always failed against determined enemies able to transfer high force-to-space ratios to Asia.

When on the defense, the Japanese army established thick and deep positions, resting on the well-hidden strongpoints of foxholes, communication trenches, and bunkers, on high ground and in rough terrain. Camouflaged machine guns were sited to mow down attackers from the flank at point-blank range and to cover positions hundreds of yards away down prepared lanes of fire. At their most elaborate, as on Okinawa in 1945, such defenses rested on a two-hundred-square-mile system of tunnels, where one hundred thousand soldiers hid underground. When attacking such positions, poorly trained forces were stalled by weeds and wire, stunned by fire, struck by showers of grenades, and smashed by counterattacks at bayonet point. Between 1942 and 1943 Japanese companies in defensive positions often stalled enemy divisions for weeks, despite being outnumbered literally seventy-five men to one. Only carefully trained and controlled troops using proper techniques of fire and movement and supported by precise and heavy weaponry, especially tanks equipped with heavy guns or flamethrowers, could take these positions, and then only by destroying all defenses and every defender, because they were the only soldiers on earth who literally and invariably fought to the death. As the officer who destroyed more Japanese armies than any other Western commander, the British general William Slim wrote, "All armies talk about fighting to the last man and the last cartridge. The Japanese actually did it." Even more: when Japanese units committed suicide, Japanese civilians attached to them in the area did so as well. At the end of the Battle of Saipan (June 1944), dozens of Japanese girls, black hair flying loose over white kimonos, threw themselves over cliffs onto rocky shores hundreds of feet below.

On the attack Japanese forces trusted far less in firepower. The Japanese answered Western superiority in firepower, which Anglo-American armies expected to be their strong suit, by evading it. Meanwhile, their low technology solution, the use of easily deployable mortars, light machine guns, and pack artillery, provided great support in areas of rough terrain and poorly developed transport systems, where massive centralized firepower would be impotent. By maneuvering as they preferred, Japanese units automatically had superior firepower where they chose to fight. Once located, an enemy force was immediately attacked, often by the bayonet, and pinned, while the main body moved across country to strike simultaneously at both flanks and the rear. Such daring and unrelenting attacks broke numerically superior but inexperienced troops, whether British, American, or Chinese. In the Malayan campaign between 1941 and 1942, Japanese forces were outnumbered by two to one but killed or captured 132,000 British troops for a total cost of 3,500 Japanese soldiers slain. Even Australian troops, the first Western soldiers of the Pacific war to master Japanese tactics, broke when they initially met the enemy on New Guinea—"they ran like rabbits," scoffed their commander. Yet Japanese commanders often were addicted to reckless attacks and their tactics were suicidal against determined troops well supported by firepower: Soviets at Khalkin-Ghol in 1939 , U.S. forces at Guadalcanal and Australians in New Guinea in 1942, and British and Indians at Imphal-Kohima in 1944. They often degenerated into human wave assaults against machine guns. During 1944 and 1945 Allied divisions had five times the firepower of Japanese ones and the Japanese sometimes lost ten to twenty times more men in battle than their enemies. Japan was beaten because its enemies were willing to take heavy losses without giving up, while it simply could not match their weight of fire.

The clash between military forces that regarded the other as inhuman, each with radically different cultural roots and styles of fighting, made the Pacific war a savage war. While generally similar to Western armies, the Japanese military was unique in a few important areas. It used offensive tactics that made the attacker's death absolutely certain (instead of, say, highly likely); these tactics were selected for that precise reason, and these were not rare and individual acts but routine and collective ones. This stemmed from the culture of Japan and its fighting forces. Its military had adopted a bastardized version of Bushido as an institutional ethic. In the process it forced a social revolution, making all Japanese behave as only samurai had done before. Soldiers and civilians were expected to die rather than surrender, and they did. When in hopeless positions Japanese units routinely launched assaults with the literal aim of *gyokusai*, or honorable death, while senior Japanese officers committed *seppuku*, or individual suicide. This ideology was enforced on soldiers through harsh discipline and a military system of "spiritual training." This linked regimental tradition and nationalist education to the Japanese variant of Confucianism—the belief that everyone owed and must repay a debt of life to family and society. While all this had Western counterparts, other elements of spiritual training were uniquely Japanese. Both Bushido and a popular cult of the tragic hero preached that death was a meaningful—the only meaningful—response to defeat, through which one's spirit could surmount annihilation. At the center of spiritual training was this tradition, linked to a Shinto cult that held that Japan was the land of gods, the center of value in the universe. Self-sacrifice for Japan would make one a god, part of the collective and eternal spirit of the ancestral dead, to be worshipped forever at the Yakusuni shrine—as millions of Japanese do today. U.S. citizens were portrayed as pitiless demons who wished only to smash Japan with fire and iron, who could be defeated only by superiority in spirit, as symbolized by the willing self-sacrifice of the individual for the whole, embodied by the emperor.

From this stemmed an obsession with suicide forces. Their use was not simply irrational. Human power alone could surmount Japan's desperate industrial weaknesses. Defeat could be avoided only by making the enemy pay heavier losses than it could bear, by convincing it that Japanese spirit was a material factor, nor was this strategy entirely wrong. When U.S. forces attacked large Japanese forces in defensive positions, casualties were worryingly heavy, and by late 1944, once U.S. forces had entered the Philippines, tough fighting could no longer be avoided since strong garrisons held each position in the heart of Japanese defenses. A strategy of island hopping rendered most of Japan's strengths irrelevant and exploited all of its weaknesses. Once bypassing was abandoned, Japan's strategy of delay and attrition crippled U.S. manpower and willpower.

While honorable death was often counterproductive, sometimes it did achieve its aim. In the Battle of Okinawa (May–June 1945), ten times as many Japanese soldiers as U.S. soldiers were killed. Yet when sick and wounded are added to the toll, this heavily outnumbered Japanese garrison took U.S. soldiers out of the battle one to one, and many of these incapacitated personnel were unavailable to invade Japan several months later. Japanese forces in the Philippines had the same effect. Similarly, by 1944 only through *Shimpu* attacks could Japanese aircraft damage enemy naval forces, but then with surprising effect. Some five thousand *Shimpu* pilots and aircraft were destroyed between 1944 and 1945. They killed far more than five thousand U.S. sailors and wounded just as many. About 15 percent of *Shimpu* aircraft damaged U.S. warships, and 1.5 percent of them sank their targets, a tolerably cost-efficient tally. Ironically, since Japan surrendered before most *Shimpu* personnel launched their death flights, their survival rates were identical to those of the aircrew of British or U.S. strategic bombers.

The cultural roots of suicide forces, however, were more powerful than their strategic ones. Ultimately, they were adopted for their own sake, to embody Japanese spirit and wield it against the enemy. The *Shimpu*, or "divine wind," forces, for example, were named after the legendary typhoons by which the gods of Japan had wrecked Mongol invasions in 1274 and 1281. *Shimpu* pilots went to battle as if to their funeral. They wore scarves of white, the color associated with death in Japanese culture, and white samurai-style headcloths decorated with emblems of Japan. Their units and operations were named after celebrated events in the history of Bushido. *Shimpu* aircraft were called *oka*, or "cherry-blossoms," a traditional Japanese symbol of purity, death, and the triumph of spirit over annihilation. Admiral Onishi, the founder of the *Shimpu* program, told his men as they readied for their first action, "You are already gods, without earthly desires. . . . I shall watch your efforts to the end, and report your deeds to the Throne." When he knew the war was lost, Onishi himself committed *seppuku*.

All this had mixed effects on Japanese soldiers. Some fought to the death of their own will. Most *Shimpu* pilots were university students, who sometimes applied for admission with letters written in their own blood to prove the purity of their motives. Some soldiers believed in the teachings of the military-religious cult; others—including many *Shimpu* pilots—were agnostic liberals who questioned Shintoism and the Japanese system of government but acted from a sense of duty and the need to defend their people against a deadly foe. Still others fought to the death only because of the pressure of an intensely disciplined society and army or from lack of other choice. Either their officers would kill them or the enemy would. Sometimes, a collective spirit of exaltation held Japanese units together under punishment that would have smashed any other army. In other cases, the only bond that held them together was fear; morale was low and officers despised, with reason. In January 1945 the Japanese air commander of the Philippines, General Tominaga Kyogi, ordered all his surviving airmen to become *Shimpu* and then immediately flew away to safety. A startling number of the few Japanese servicemen who were captured helped the Allies—on the condition that their families not be informed that they were alive. Having betrayed themselves through capture, nothing restrained Japanese prisoners from betraying their country.

For their part, before December 1941 British and U.S. citizens viewed the Japanese as racially inferior. Then, shocked by the successful attacks on Pearl Harbor and Singapore, the savage Japanese treatment of prisoners, their refusal to surrender, their frightening suicide attacks and deadly defenses, they saw Japanese as inhuman—in Slim's words, as "man-sized soldier ants." Meanwhile, Allied forces applied horrific tactics against the Japanese—not from racial hatred but military necessity. U.S., Australian, British, and Indian forces did not want to adopt these tactics, because to do so was inconvenient. They wished to fight Japanese as they did Germans or Italians, particularly by using massive but not overly precise firepower to smash formations or seize ground. Quickly, they discovered that this was impossible. When their formations were shattered, individual Germans and Italians fled or surrendered, but Japanese fought and died, complicating Allied advances and inflicting heavy casualties. Allied forces found that they could not win by smashing Japanese divisions, but only by killing every Japanese soldier. This was hard to do. Allied forces had to recalibrate every way they fought—instead of moving evenly spaced lines of men behind steady barrages that aimed to neutralize the entire defensive zone, for example, they had to throw killing fire and sharp attacks against one stronghold after another; the value of firepower had to be gauged by its precision rather than by its weight. As Slim put it, "the plan which will kill Japs is the only one which will succeed and . . . the men who are well trained and out to kill the Japs are the only ones who will work out the plan. Japanese determination to fight to the last necessitates the concentration of overwhelming force against him. . . . All plans must be regarded from the aspect of their potential for killing Japs rather than from the angle of attaining tactical objectives." Similarly, Admiral William "Bull" Halsey defined USN aims against the Japanese as "kill, kill, kill." Allied forces ceased trying to take prisoners and instead adopted tactics that made Japanese surrender impossible. U.S. forces used the atomic bomb against Japan because they believed that otherwise the Japanese people literally would fight to the death and take hundreds of thousands of Allied soldiers with them, which probably is what would have happened had the Allies invaded the Japanese home islands. The combination of Japanese and Western tactics spelled death for every Japanese person caught in the combat zone.

Case Study: Economic Warfare

Military forces attacked economies as well as armies. Their aim was to sidestep attrition and to cut an enemy's throat or else to make it pay disproportionately in withstanding such attacks. The success of economic warfare can be gauged only by economic criteria, by determining (*a*) the absolute cost required to launch and to absorb these operations and (*b*) their "cost effectiveness," or their relative effect on attacker and defender. When applied to events, these criteria produce surprising conclusions. Between 1942 and 1945, for example, Germany devoted industrial resources that would have produced twenty-four thousand fighters (doubling its output of such aircraft) to the V-1 and V-2 guided missile projects. Less than one thousand Spitfires, which would have been tied down in Britain in any case, parried the V-1s while both projects together killed just a few thousand civilians and scarcely affected war production at all. This was not a smart way to fight a war. Again, simply because a campaign halved a country's productive capacity does not necessarily mean that this halved its military production—such damage could be overcome by learning to use fewer resources more efficiently. Above all, economic warfare worked not merely by destroying production but also by forcing the enemy's decision makers to solve new and complex problems. The Allies won the battle of the Atlantic because they were inefficient but very fat; the Germans lost the battle of Germany because they were fat and very inefficient.

In the major forms of economic warfare—the submarine and strategic bombing campaigns—attackers and defenders had to locate the enemy and control forces scattered over vast areas. Otherwise aircraft and warships would meander across sea and sky in search of targets, wasting time, fuel, and opportunity. Only sophisticated command systems could overcome these problems, and they were available. Radar, aircraft reconnaissance, and signals intelligence detected enemy forces with surprising accuracy and in time for commanders to respond, fostering both the economy and the concentration of force. British and U.S. submarines often knew the location of every Italian and Japanese merchant ship at sea and sometimes even their precise cargos and hence exactly which ships in a convoy should first be sunk. Similarly, during much of 1941 Britain knew exactly where German wolf packs were located in the Atlantic and rerouted its convoys away from them, halving both the tonnage sunk per U-boat and their military effect. While Germany rarely reached this standard of perfection, its U-boats still received excellent intelligence. In strategic bombing, intelligence gave any defender a great edge, normally detecting the height, airspeed, direction, and number of attacking bombers long before they reached one's territory. Once such intelligence was collected, commanders had to collate it and allocate their forces instantly and immediately. The leaders of the best of these command systems knew with complete accuracy the military situation over the skies of western Europe or the surface of the North Atlantic or the western Pacific in real time and dispatched their forces against the enemy with near perfect efficiency. Never had commanders been better informed or warfare so much like chess instead of poker.

In submarine warfare, the advantage lay with the hunter if it could find the prey. Individual submarines could easily sink single merchant ships or those in poorly escorted convoys. Since Japanese mercantile convoys had weak escorts—the IJN regarded this as a defensive and dishonorable task, although battleships sometimes escorted troop transports—the small fleet of U.S. submarines could pick off as many targets as they had torpedoes; meanwhile, intelligence guided them into the most cheap, cost-efficient, and successful campaign of economic warfare ever mounted. Between July 1943 and August 1945 they sank the entire Japanese merchant fleet.

In the Atlantic the Allies took convoy seriously, but even so, between 1940 and 1941 only two or three warships escorted any of their convoys, while German wolf packs had five to twenty submarines. Wolf packs were strung out in a patrol line up to two hundred miles long, which no convoy could cross without detection. Once a convoy was located the wolves stalked their prey on the surface at day, which allowed submarines to redeploy more rapidly and massively increased the numbers that could attack and then struck in mass at night, again on the surface. During the peak month of German success, March 1943, some convoys lost 50 percent of their merchant ships, while over 10 percent of Allied mercantile tonnage on the Atlantic was lost: by that stage 30 percent of the western Allies' merchant marine of 1939 had been sunk.

That was a cost-effective and successful campaign, yet even this success was a kind of failure. It destroyed much Allied material but they had material to burn. The Allies controlled 70 percent of the world's merchant tonnage and by 1943 they produced over one million new tons of shipping per month, without much cost to other sectors of the war economy. At best, Germany sank fewer tons per month than Allied shipyards built, and whenever losses threatened to become a problem, the Allies overcame it simply by increasing their efficiency of usage, such as hastening turn-around times in port. The British population survived on half its prewar tonnage of imports—the U-boats forced them to diet but not to die. The Allies feared that they would lose the battle of the Atlantic and thus the war, but they never had less tonnage than they required. Germany lacked the strength to destroy Britain when that possibility existed and it vanished once the United States entered the war.

The battle of the Atlantic was won in the shipyards, not in naval battles, by cost accountants rather than naval captains, and the Allies merely forced a stalemate at sea. By 1943 eighty long-range aircraft covered the North Atlantic—thus preventing U-boats from moving on the surface and gutting the redeployment capability that was the heart of the wolf pack strategy. This step alone reduced the power of the U-boats by 75 percent. Now they needed four submarines to do the work that one had done before, and that work became harder. Every convoy received twice as many escorts, close air support, centimetric radar, and sometimes the aid of a dozen destroyers during emergencies, which demolished the fighting superiority of wolf packs. Until then wolf packs invariably and massively outnumbered convoy escorts while Allied warships could rarely sink submarines—no longer. In several convoy battles between May and July 1943, German submarines failed to sink any merchant ships at all while suffering heavy losses in a one-to-one ratio with escorts. Aircraft patrols around convoys forced U-boats down or sank them; centimetric radar led destroyers straight for the kill; the nerve of submarine crews broke, and their campaign collapsed. For the last two years of the war, U-boats sank few merchant vessels. Yet they absorbed an asset for which Germany had little other use—shipbuilding resources—and only eight thousand men at any one time. Against this, the Allies maintained one hundred thousand men in convoy escort while the need to make all ships sail in convoy instead of at their maximum speed reduced their shipping capacity by 10 percent. Even without sinking one merchant ship in convoy, the last phase of the U-boat campaign was a rational investment, but the return was too small to matter.

The military balance in the strategic bombing campaign was very different. Bombers had to reach targets hundreds of miles from their base, often flying one thousand miles in hostile airspace, survive enemy fighters, and find, hit, and damage their target. None of these tasks was easy. No air force, for example, was prepared to handle night navigation. In 1940 the *Luftwaffe* relied on radio beams for this purpose; when Britain discovered and jammed them, navigation and bombing both collapsed. In 1941 the navigators on British night bombers determined their locations by opening their cockpits in subzero weather and taking a dead reckoning from the stars with a sextant. No air force could deliver its bombs with accuracy while bombers were simple to locate and highly vulnerable to fighters controlled by contemporary air defense systems. Numerically inferior defenders savaged their enemies. Fifty percent of the *Luftwaffe* was destroyed in four months during the battle of Britain, 1,700 German aircraft for 787 British. During 1943, the U.S. Army Air Force (USAAF) sometimes lost 16 percent of its bombers on daylight raids while the RAF calculated that 90 percent of airmen forced to fly one hundred missions would be shot down. These losses nearly wrecked the Allies' Combined Bomber Offensive (CBO). It was only saved when USAAF fighters escorted bombers to the target, in the process burning the *Luftwaffe* to cinders.

Even so, strategic bombing was not cost effective because there was no cheap and simple way to break the enemy's economy or morale. In 1940 the Germans never adopted any rational targeting policy, nor did the Allies do much better. RAF "area bombing" at night killed German civilians and eroded their morale and production but completely destroyed neither, nor was American "precision bombing" successful. The USAAF never found a target that would wreck the German economy: if ball bearing plants were destroyed, Germany merely increased its imports from Sweden. The Allies did not systematically attack the critical and vulnerable German railway net, the veins of its war economy, until August 1944 and ignored Germany's Achille's heel, its electrical power grid. Nor did they actually achieve the aims of their targeting strategies. Most U.S. bombs fell on civilians, since "industrial" targets were usually located in urban centers, while precision bombing was anything but precise—British area bombers at night placed their bombs with more accuracy than USAF precision bombers at day. Meanwhile, the same proportion of British bombs accidentally hit economic targets as U.S. bombs ones did intentionally.

The CBO absorbed two million of the best-educated men of the western Allies—equal in number to the combat strength of their armies in Europe—and 25 percent of the production of their war economies, even more in high-technology sectors. In return it killed a million and a half German civilians and ground down enemy morale and war production. It is impossible to calculate precisely how strategic bombing shaped victory or how it affected the economic balance, that is, how many more munitions not only Germany but Britain and the United States would have produced in its absence, and how many soldiers would have been freed for other purposes, and how this would have mattered. Some factors, however, are indicative.

By 1943 strategic bombing forced Germany to place most of the *Luftwaffe* and nine hundred thousand soldiers and twenty-two thousand antiaircraft guns (devastatingly effective against tanks) at home instead of the front and to keep them there. This crippled the *Wehrmacht*. Only 15 percent of the 19,713 dual-purpose 88-milimeter and 128-milimeter antitank and antiaircraft guns produced between 1942 and 1944 went to the army, the remainder to German cities. Germany allocated as many tank-killing gun barrels against the CBO as it did against the Red Army. Allied bombing knocked out some armament plants for several months, dislocated the production of complex weapons, and tied up 1 million Germans in cleaning up bomb damage. Meanwhile, British terror bombing had great unanticipated consequences. In 1943 Hitler, enraged that anyone but Germans would dare kill civilians, made several sensationally bad decisions. Despite pleas from the *Luftwaffe* to focus resources on maximizing fighter production, Hitler ordered a new offensive. This stripped what remained of the *Luftwaffe*'s bombers from other fronts and frittered them away in hopeless attacks on Britain. Hitler also pursued the inefficient V-1 and V-2 programs and for two years prevented air authorities from building a jet fighter, instead ordering them to focus on a vengeance jet bomber.

The gains were significant though costly. By 1943 the CBO removed half of Germany's potential combat firepower from the eastern front, in return for halving the potential number of Anglo-American soldiers in the west. At the cost of 25 percent of Anglo-American war production, the CBO absorbed roughly the same part of German economic resources, by pinning and smashing German air production. This was not achieved in a cost efficient fashion: in absolute terms this success of 1943 may have cost the western Allies three times more than it did the enemy, but then they could afford this loss much better than Germany. This clearly slowed the growth of German war production, and delayed its progress toward maximum munitions output. Even if the CBO did no more than slow this rate of growth by 10 percent, that might easily have cost Germany three thousand tanks and twenty-five hundred guns, or its average material strength on the eastern front in 1943 and 1944. During this period, however, Germany could also afford to lose much industrial plant without affecting armament production, since there was so much slack in its economy. Ironically, the gross inefficiency in Germany's war economy between 1939 and 1942 proved to be its greatest shield against the strategic bombing campaign. While bombing did reduce German industrial capacity, its production of munitions skyrocketed.

From August 1944, however, Germany's war economy rapidly fell apart, primarily because of strategic bombing but also as an indirect consequence of defeats on land, the loss of raw materials, and the need to turn workers into soldiers. Between August and October 1944, German oil production vanished, rail shipments halved, steel plants received just 33 percent the coal they needed to function, their output fell by 75 percent, and the Reich Minister for Equipment and War Production calculated that "on account of destruction of traffic installations and lack of power, from 30 to 50 percent of all works in west Germany were at a standstill." Though munition firms held enough reserve stock to produce substantial numbers of weapons, subcontractors could not deliver vital parts while the destruction and dislocation caused by the CBO hampered the use of those munitions that were produced. Half of German fighters produced were destroyed on the ground, either in factories or airfields; of the 1,800 ME 262 jet fighters constructed, 500 were destroyed in factories and only 100 saw active service; 33 percent of tanks never made it to front line units and half of these that did were crippled from lack of fuel. In the last year of the war, the CBO was cost effective, and it matched the Red Army in delivering the Allies' absolutely heaviest blows on Germany.

The verdict on the CBO across the board from 1941 to 1945 is mixed. In absolute terms it cost the western Allies substantially more to mount than it did the enemy, but still it tied down a vast amount of Nazi resources and a greater proportion of them. The western Allies, moreover, were not Germany's only enemy: the most significant indicator of the CBO's success is its effect on the eastern front. Here, the CBO halved the firepower that Germany could otherwise have deployed and reduced its potential manpower there by perhaps 10 percent, where they engaged 100 percent of Soviet power (multiplied by western aid). Through the CBO, the western Allies played to their strong suit and to Germany's weak one, inflicting the heaviest damage of any campaign of economic warfare ever waged. However inefficient and costly, this was a good investment for the Allies. Compared to this, the submarine campaigns fought by Germany and Britain in European waters and the United States in the Pacific were far more cost-effective but far less significant. None of them defeated the enemy by themselves. The U.S. and British campaigns finished off the Italian and Japanese mercantile marines, but by the time they did so those countries were bleeding from so many fatal wounds that another one was of limited value. Germany's submarine campaign was cost effective but too small to matter.

Above all, no form of economic warfare quickly and cheaply cut the throat of any enemy. Advocates of economic warfare had argued that it would succeed because the morale of enemy civilians and the structures of industrialized economies were fragile—instead, they proved solid. While each campaign helped one side against the other, none definitively turned the tide of attrition in anyone's favor. Theorists had promoted economic warfare precisely as a means to sidestep attrition. This did not happen: instead it became the most attritional aspect of the war. The western front was reborn in the skies over Europe and on the waves of the Atlantic Ocean.

Suggested Reading

The literature on World War I is vast, but the extensive bibliography contained in Hew Strachan, ed., *The Oxford Illustrated History of the First World War* (Oxford, 1998), is a reliable place to start. For mobilization and enthusiasm but not for war, see John Horne, ed., *State, Society and Mobilization during the First World War* (Cambridge, 1997). A recent overview of the war, emphasizing political, economic, and social history, is Niall Ferguson, *The Pity of War* (New York, 1999). On the Central Powers, an excellent source is Holger Herwig, *The First World War: Germany and Austria-Hungary, 1914–1918* (London, 1997). German tactics are discussed in Bruce Gudmundsson, *Stormtroop Tactics: Innovation in the German Army, 1914–1918* (New York, 1989). A useful look at the German World War I artillery innovator occurs in David Zabecki, *Steel Wind: Colonel Georg Bruchmüller and the Birth of Modern Artillery* (Westport CT, 1994). An interesting comparison is Martin Samuels, *Command or Control? Command, Training and Tactics in the British and German Armies, 1888–1918* (London, 1995). For France, there is Jean Jacques Becker, *The Great War and the French People* (Leamington, 1985), which, as the title implies, deals with social history. A stimulating analysis of a French division is Leonard Smith, *Between Mutiny and Obedience: The Case of the French Fifth Infantry Division During World War I* (Princeton, 1994). A brief overview is undertaken by I. Sumner, *The French Army, 1914–1918* (London, 1995). In regard to Britain, a large number of books exist, but a very selective list would include Denis Winter, *Death's Men: Soldiers of the Great War* (London, 1978); Trevor Wilson, *The Myriad Faces of War* (Cambridge, 1986); Robin Prior and Trevor Wilson, *Command on the Western Front: The Military Career of Sir Henry Rawlinson, 1914–1918* (Oxford, 1992); Robin Prior and Trevor Wilson, *Passchendaele: The Untold Story* (New Haven CT, 1996); Tim Travers, *The Killing Ground: The British Army, the Western Front, and the Emergence of Modern Warfare, 1900–1918* (London, 1987); and an extensive overview of the war in Hugh Cecil and Peter Liddle, eds., *Facing Armageddon* (London, 1996). Other classic accounts not mentioned in the text include, for the air, Cecil Lewis, *Sagittarius Rising* (1936), and, for the land, Edwin Vaughan, *Some Desperate Glory* (1981). The literature of the war is brilliantly discussed in Paul Fussell, *The Great War and Modern Memory* (Oxford, 1975).

The literature on the Second World War is huge but flawed because disproportionate attention has been paid to material in the English language, compared to those of all other foreign languages and to the memoirs of generals (especially German ones).

This bibliography will refer only to the best books on major topics. The best introduction to the Second World War is Peter Calvocoressi and Guy Wint, *Total War, Causes and Courses of the Second World War* (London, 1972), while the best analytical account is Richard Overy, *Why the Allies Won* (London, 1995). Mark Harrison's *Accounting for War, Soviet Production, Employment, and the Defence Burden, 1940–1945* (London, 1996), is the best study of any military-economic aspect of the war.

The best studies of the eastern front are John Erickson, *The Road to Stalingrad: Stalin's War with Germany*, vol. 1 (London, 1979), and *The Road to Berlin* (Boulder CO, 1983); David M. Glantz and Jonathon House, *When Titan's Clashed, How the Red Army Stopped Hitler* (Lawrence KS, 1995); and Omer Bartov, *The Eastern Front 1941–1945, German Troops and the Barbarisation of Warfare* (New York, 1985), and *Hitler's Army* (New York, 1992). The best overall account of the war in east Asia and the Pacific is Ronald Spector, *Eagle Against the Sun: The American War with Japan* (New York, 1985), and the official histories of Great Britain, the United States, and Australia. Excellent studies of more detailed aspects of that war include Louis Allen, *Burma, The Longest War, 1941–45* (London, 1984). There is a vast literature on the military campaigns in North Africa and western Europe. The best studies of the desert war are the two South African official histories of the 1950s, Agar-Hamilton and J. C. F. Turner, *The Sidi Rezeg Battles* (Cape Town, 1957), and *Crisis in the Desert* (Cape Town, 1954). Perhaps the best accounts of Allied operations in Italy and Normandy are by Carlo D'Este: *Decision in Normandy* (New York, 1983), *Bitter Victory: The Battle for Sicily, 1943* (New York, 1988), *World War II in the Mediterranean* (New York, 1990), and *Fatal Decision, Anzio and the battle for Rome* (New York, 1994). Other useful works include Dominick Graham and Shelford Bidwell, *Tug of War: The Battle for Italy, 1943–45* (New York, 1986).

There are a host of useful studies of socio-military life at the front: for good examples, see Mark Wells, *Courage and Air Warfare* (London, 1995); Terry Copp and William McAndrew, *Battle Exhaustion* (Montreal, 1990); Charles B. Mac-Donald, *Company Commander* (New York, 1947); Gerald F. Linderman, *The World Within War, America's Combat Experience in World War II* (New York, 1997); Paul Fussell, *Wartime, Understanding and Behaviour in the Second World War* (New York, 1989); John Ellis, *The Sharp End of War* (London, 1980); and many of the pieces in Paul Addison and Angus Calder, eds., *Time to Kill, The Soldier's experience of War in the West, 1939–1945* (Edinborough, 1997). Two good compilations of oral accounts of the war, taken decades after the event, are Studs Terkel, *The Good War, An Oral History of World War Two* (New York, 1984), and Barry Broadfoot, *Six War Years, 1939–1945: Memories of Canadians at Home and Abroad* (Don Mills, 1974). For the social and cultural dynamics of the Pacific War, two useful studies are John Dower, *War Without Mercy, Race and Power in the Pacific War* (New York, 1986), and Ivan Morris, *The Nobility of Failure: Tragic Heroes in the History of Japan* (London, 1976).

13. THIRD WORLD WARS
War and Society during the Cold War and After

The two central political developments in the world after 1945 were the Cold War, the division of the industrialized states into two loose and antagonistic camps, and decolonization, the destruction of the European empires in Asia and Africa. The Cold War reordered relations among the industrialized powers; decolonization altered relations between them and rest of the world; together they brought new players into the game of politics and revolutionized its structure. Europe ceased to be the center of world politics and nothing took its place. No longer did power on one continent determine power everywhere on earth. Local power had to be struggled for in each region, and success in one region did not determine events in another. The USSR and the United States were far more powerful than any other powers in history, but neither of them picked up the pieces of European imperialism. They simply established ties with the regional successor states. While some of these countries depended utterly on their protector and collapsed when external aid ceased, most were far more than satellites of the superpowers. Often the tail wagged the dog—during much of the 1970s and 1980s, Israel and Syria dictated the terms of their alliances with the United States and the USSR. In local issues, regional powers like India and Egypt often defied the superpowers with success, and after decolonization world politics consisted of nothing but regional issues. These factors determined the nature of war and the role of force on earth.

Under the Cold War the strongest states on earth formed remarkably stable alliances and devoted an unprecedented part of their wealth to defense. Between 1950 and 1989, military expenditure averaged 9 percent of the U.S gross domestic product (GDP) compared to 1 percent between 1919 and 1939. The USSR devoted even more to its military, perhaps even 33 percent of its GDP, which triggered its economic decline and political collapse. These alliances possessed the deadliest weapons and waged the greatest arms races ever known to mankind, particularly regarding weapons of mass destruction. Atomic, nuclear, chemical, and bacteriological weapons revolutionized the nature and the value of military power. A total war between states possessing them carried the risk of total suicide, which imposed a new upper limit on the rationality of force. Simultaneously, the range and the destructive power of conventional weapons were more frequently revolutionized during the forty years following 1945 than in the previous four centuries, and such changes have revolutionized campaigns. When provided with simple and effective surface-to-air missiles in the 1980s, for example, Afghani *fedeyin* were immediately able to drive Soviet helicopters from the skies and to wreck the Soviet campaign in Afghanistan. This increase in military power shaped world politics, and in a surprising way. The industrialized alliances of the Cold War spent unparalleled amounts of money on weapons that they never used in anger. Each treated the other as a threat, but they never went to war for fear that nuclear weapons would render "victory" meaningless. Thus, each alliance negated the other's power. The industrialized states possessed far greater military strength than in 1939 but their influence in the world declined sharply.

The Gulf War of 1991 demonstrated the overwhelming power that modern armies could bring to bear when they had complete freedom to act, but such freedom was rare between 1945 and 1990, and it has not been more common with the end of the Cold War. Had these industrialized alliances fought one another, they might have engaged in yet another total war to the death, using the most advanced weapons of the day. But this has not been the pattern of warfare since 1945. The industrialized states have not fought each other nor, excepting the guerrilla wars that accompanied decolonization, frequently fought anyone at all. The center of world power was not the center of world war—Asia and Africa, where movements and governments first fought European imperialism and then each other. Rarely have these states possessed the economic or administrative capabilities needed to fight total wars or to win quick, cheap, and decisive victories. Rarely has anyone achieved the classic goal of annihilating the enemy's army and dictating terms of peace in its captured capital. States in Asia and Africa have responded to this situation in different ways.

In Asia, regimes have feared that prolonged wars might be a form of suicide; hence, they have preferred to fight for limited aims and with lim-

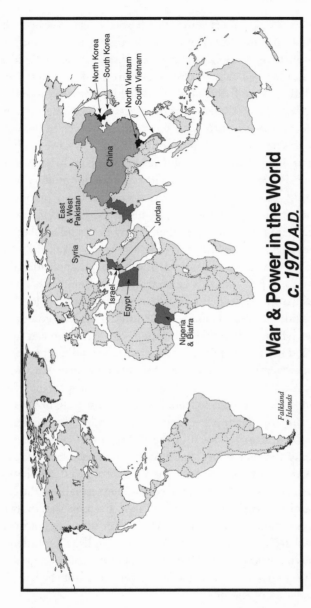

North Korea
South Korea
North Vietnam
South Vietnam

China

East
& West
Pakistan

Jordan

Syria

Israel

Egypt

Nigeria
& Biafra

Falkland
Islands

War & Power in the World
C. 1970 A.D.

Map 13.1

ited means. Since 1945 most conventional wars in Asia have been short in duration and small in effect. While some of them have been long, costly, and total wars fought by weak states, more often than not both sides have called a halt long before their resources were totally exploited and the butcher's bill paid in full or decisive battlefield victories achieved. In Asia there have been many six-day or three-week wars costing thousands of lives but few three- or thirty-year wars with hundreds of thousands of dead. Conversely, the wars fought continually in Africa since the 1960s have been prolonged, indecisive, and destructive, largely because in each case neither side could effectively tap its resources for military purposes. Between 1967 and 1970 Nigeria, the richest and most populous state in black Africa with fifty million people under the federal government's control, could not maintain more than eighty thousand combat soldiers against the rebel regime of Biafra. Nigeria simply blockaded Biafra until its economy and willpower collapsed and its people surrendered rather than starve to death. Nigeria's generals put the country back together with statesmanship, but their performance on the battlefield was poor. Nigeria could not even maintain an air force of its own to destroy the lumbering civilian aircraft that flew supplies to Biafra and had to rely on Egyptian and mercenary pilots. The Egyptians could not find their targets; the mercenaries would not destroy them, because that would end the war and their pay. At one stage a seventy-four-year-old Swede— Count von Rosen, a renegade from the Red Cross to fight for Biafra— flew a civilian propeller airplane arranged for combat, dominating the air over Nigeria, destroying much of the federal air force on the ground, and bombing the capital city. Because the state has been weak in sub-Saharan Africa, its wars have been the most prolonged and devastating anywhere since 1945, killing more civilians than virtually all the conflicts in the rest of the world combined, and have been marked by two central features—stalemate and terror. As a matter of routine, armies have not attacked each other but have instead raped, pillaged, murdered, and starved the enemy's civilians. That has become even more common since the Cold War ended, culminating in the genocide launched against the Tutsi population of Rwanda in 1994.

In the conventional wars fought outside of the industrialized world, military prowess has not been determined simply by a state's numerical strength in men and tanks or by the most modern of weapons. Numbers and technology have mattered but not enough to win every war by themselves. A belligerent willing to take heavy losses without surrendering has often beaten one with high technology and low willpower, while able military forces with no technological edge have often whipped much larger enemies. This is particularly true of war in the air. Between the 1960s and the 1980s, the Israeli air force routinely defeated twice its number of Arab aircraft. In 1982 it destroyed ninety Syrian jets for two Israeli losses. In 1965 the Pakistani air force, outnumbered four to one by Indian aircraft, dominated the battlefield. During the Falkland Islands war of 1982, British Harrier fighters, outnumbered ten to one by the Argentinean air force, lost not a single jet to enemy action while destroying more than their own strength in Argentinean airplanes and winning the war in the air.

Many governments have possessed the leading weapons of the day but few have used them with full effect. Indeed, modern technology has often been a handicap. Increases in quality cost money and reduce quantity. Between 1945 and 1970, fighter aircraft became one hundred times more expensive in constant dollars, and most air forces declined dramatically in size. Between 1955 and 1985, the inventory of American fighters fell from eighteen to seven thousand. While increases in complexity and cost have sometimes justified the decline in numbers, this has frequently not been the case. The more sophisticated the equipment, moreover, the larger the number of parts that can fail, and one minor but irreparable breakdown may produce military humiliation. During the 1970s, for example, the Iranian armed forces adopted a computerized data-retrieval system that could locate every single spare part they held for all of their weapons. They also ceased to keep their written accounts in order. In 1979 following the Islamic revolution and Iran's alienation of the rest of the world, U.S. technicians withdrew. The system immediately collapsed. During the war with Iraq that followed, Iran could only locate spare parts by establishing elite teams of quartermaster commandos who every week received lists of specific items to find and then ransacked every supply base in Iran looking for them. Not surprisingly, mechanical breakdowns crippled Iran's military performance. During the last years of the war its fighter aircraft possessed weapons able to destroy enemy targets one hundred miles away that were useless because of tiny malfunctions in their guidance systems. This has not been simply a third world phenomenon. During the Vietnam War half of the U.S. Army's Sheridan tanks were frequently out of action awaiting attention by one of only four qualified technicians in the theater, while a two-year backlog of damaged Phantom jets waited for repair.

What has really governed military power has been the ability of countries to tap their economic and demographic resources for strategic purposes—the relative efficiency of their administrative and military institutions. The secret of Israel's battlefield success has been the fact that it possesses Western military administrative techniques like universal conscription and a mass, efficient, and quickly mobilized military reserve while its neighbors do not. The Jews of Israel are outnumbered twenty to one by the populations of Egypt, Syria, and Jordan, but, unlike them, Israel can tap most of its entire population and economy to fight a total war for about a week. Its neighbors have never outnumbered Israel's mobilized army by three to one even on paper. In fact, largely because of its hair-trigger readiness to start wars whenever it regards itself in peril, Israel has usually possessed a larger army on the battlefield than its adversaries. Only once in its five wars—in 1973—has Israel actually been outnumbered on the front, and as often as not it initiated the hostilities. Superior educational standards have ensured that Israelis handle modern weapons more effectively than Arabs. Israel's military is a national and professional force, with one task only—winning wars for the Jews of Israel, who have believed that defeat might produce another holocaust. Against this, Arab armies have been intensely politicized. Their fundamental aim has been not to serve a people or to win wars but to keep a regime in power. They have tapped the resources of only part of their population, the politically reliable part. Thus, virtually all Syrian officers come from the Alawite sect, only 10 percent of Syria's population. This gravely limits the power of their armies. Most Arab resources have never been used in war, while most Israeli resources have. Arab regimes have often preferred to lose a war rather than lose their army, for that may destroy their control over their populations and cause their political, and physical, extinction. Not that such a strategy is always foolish, which explains why Saddam Hussein's regime in Iraq survived the loss of the Gulf War.

Given the wide range of this administrative and technological capacity, wars since 1945 have featured military styles ranging from the Space Age to the Stone Age. Some campaigns have been slower and costlier than the Somme, others quicker and cheaper than the fall of France. On occasion human wave assaults have beaten mechanized armies. The Iran-Iraq war was a rerun of the western front, fought with the most modern weapons of the 1980s: in Zaire during 1963 and Uganda in 1986, tribesmen armed with spears, shields, and prophecies attacked machine guns mounted on jeeps; 1991 witnessed the most perfect marriage yet seen between fire and movement. Since 1945 there has been no single dominant style of warfare because there has been no single dominant set of military conditions and styles well suited for one set have failed in others.

The Korean War between 1950 and 1953 illustrates this process clearly. In this seesaw campaign, armies swept three times from one end of the Korean peninsula to the other and older styles of war increasingly replaced newer ones. In its opening phase, the tactics and equipment of the North Korean army were based on the Soviet model of 1945. It concentrated on a narrow sector, achieving a ten-to-one superiority in men and firepower and attacking by surprise. The South Korean army, a paramilitary force with few heavy weapons, was smashed by artillery, overrun by tanks and mechanized infantry, and 1940 was repeated. South Korea quickly fell except for an area around the port of Pusan, where U.S. troops applied the defensive tactics and equipment of western Europe in 1944. These once again put blitzkrieg in check. In the second phase of the war, U.S. forces launched a riposte that combined the offensive styles of the Second World War in the Pacific and Europe. An amphibious assault captured the Port of Inchon while blitzkrieg into North Korea crushed the old enemy. It also brought a new enemy into the fight, and the Chinese People's Liberation Army (PLA) countered the tactics of George S. Patton with those of Stonewall Jackson. In the third phase, Chinese light infantry with few heavy weapons moved rapidly through the mountainous countryside in the dead of winter, cutting up better-equipped, numerically equal but roadbound and divided U.S. forces. The U.S. Army, outthought, outfought, and softened from years of garrison and geishas in Japan, collapsed. The only Allied troops to fight effectively during the rout, like the American marines and the British Brigade, did so through a series of controlled and phased light infantry withdrawals, which would have been conventional in 1914. A Turkish battalion broke through Chinese encirclement with a mass bayonet charge such as their forefathers had launched against Russian forces one hundred years before. Until this moment both sides had been fighting for complete victory throughout all Korea. In the spring of 1951, however, the allies decided against attempting more than the reestablishment of South Korea at roughly its prewar border. They chose to fight for a stalemate at a low rate of Allied casualties in an efficient but surprising way: they returned to the training manuals of 1918. They formed a deep and continuous line of prepared positions supported by massive firepower across the Korean peninsula. Chinese tactics of infiltration and maneuver became ineffective because the Allied line had no holes and no open flanks; nor could the Communist forces match the United Nations (UN) in firepower. As the PLA commander Peng Duhuai noted, "The enemy forces are so closely knit together that there exists no gap and tactically they advance and retreat steadily and entrench themselves at every step." Since their political leadership refused to end the war, however, Chinese generals turned to human wave assaults. Not only were these tactics costly, they were useless against good troops. At Kap Yong in April 1951, when assaulted by superior Chinese forces, a Canadian battalion held its foxholes, called massive artillery fire directly in front and on top of itself, and then counterattacked, killing eight hundred Chinese soldiers in eight minutes for twenty of their own. This pattern was repeated for two more bloody years of stalemate, producing the loss of tens of thousands of Allied and hundreds of thousands of Chinese lives, until China finally negotiated a ceasefire in 1953.

Since 1945, the industrialized states have rarely fought in these conventional wars but they have routinely supported one side or the other. Such support usually followed the pattern of Cold War alignments, but not always. During the Nigerian civil war, Britain, the United States, the USSR, and several Arab governments all helped the federal government— each to increase its influence in Africa—while Biafra was supported by France, China, and Israel, all simply to embarrass one or another of Nigeria's allies. Similarly, during the Iran-Iraq war, Iraq acquired weapons from virtually everyone on earth, while Iran could not regularly purchase arms from anyone—a key cause for its eventual defeat. The nature of such external help has varied and so has its importance. Given the weakness of postcolonial Africa, outside powers have often kept their friends alive for years merely by supplying small amounts of arms and a few military trainers. In Africa, France has been a superpower, while the intervention of a few thousand Cuban, South African, or mercenary soldiers has revolutionized campaigns. Even private humanitarian aid has had major military consequences, often contributing to a destructive stalemate. From the 1960s onward, food and medical supplies dispatched to end the famines caused by wars in Africa have prolonged the wars that created the famines. Such aid has been used to supply soldiers or else has freed regimes from the need to feed their population and enabled them to throw all of their energies into war. By the 1970s, conversely, it became very expensive even for the superpowers to buy friends or influence enemies in the Middle East because they had driven the market up so far. This was one of the most heavily armed areas on earth—several of its states possessed more soldiers, tanks, and aircraft than West Germany—because oil-rich countries could buy the most modern of weapons, while the United States and the USSR gave them away to important but impoverished allies. The supply of arms was the most obvious way to help a friend but not the only one. An ally with a veto at the Security Council could delay the timing of a UN ceasefire and hence shape how, when, and where a conventional war would end and who would win it. In 1967 and 1971, the ability of a superpower ally to delay a ceasefire ensured the strategic success of Israel and India. In 1973 the U.S. refusal to delay a ceasefire prevented Israel from smashing an Egyptian army that was otherwise at its mercy.

War and diplomacy have been linked in an unusual way. During the conflicts in Korea and Indochina, armistice negotiations continued for years alongside bloody battles. Combat and diplomacy became interchangeable means to wear down the enemy and achieve victory. In the public negotiations at Panjummong during the Korean War, Chinese officials once denied that U.S. forces held a particular hill—which they immediately captured simply to embarrass U.S. diplomats. Entire wars were fought just to achieve specific diplomatic ends. Thus, by 1973 the president of Egypt wished to end the war with Israel and to regain the territory lost in 1967. Anwar el-Sadat could not do so through negotiations because no one respected Egyptian military prowess enough to bargain with him. The purpose of war was to show that Egypt could not be ignored and thus to improve its bargaining position. Sadat achieved this aim even though his army was broken—that is, military defeat produced diplomatic victory. Here, as in many limited wars since 1945, the relationship between victory on the field of battle and success at the table of peace was complex. Force was intended to achieve precise political objectives. Even the most brilliant of operations may not do so unless diplomatic circumstances are favorable, while with a strong political wind at its back, even a mediocre military performance may produce strategic success.

For the winners in the three most sensational campaigns since 1945— Israel in 1967, Britain in 1982, and the UN coalition in 1991—victory was better by far than defeat and produced substantial, but limited, gains. In 1967 Israel seized adjacent territories but neither forced the Arab states to accept the status quo nor smashed their power. Rather the opposite—by 1973 Arab armies were more dangerous to Israel than before and over the next twenty years the gains of 1967 were slowly whittled away. Military power alone could not achieve Israeli aims. In 1982 Britain recovered prestige, the Falkland Islands, and an expensive new commitment populated by two thousand people and two million sheep. While the victory of 1991 liberated Kuwait and crippled Iraqi military capacity, it did not destroy the Iraqi regime or prevent its recovery. Through politics, Saddam Hussein transformed defeat into draw and then waged a new war through covert means against his enemies.

The two most consequential wars since 1945 demonstrate how politics can transform power. By August 1945, after decades of internal strife and Japanese attack, China was divided between two armed political movements. On paper, the military balance in the Chinese civil war was unequal. The Chinese Nationalist Party, or Kuomintang (KMT), controlled the cities with an army of 2.6 million men, 500,000 of whom were trained and equipped like U.S. forces. The Chinese Communist Party (CCP) controlled far less territory, but this included 40 million people. Only half of the PLA's 475,000 regular soldiers even had rifles, though about 100,000 of them were well trained and equipped. The KMT, however, was corrupt and incompetent. Its armies belonged to rival factions who routinely betrayed each other in battle; the more people the KMT ruled, the less it was liked. Although the CCP was ruthless, able, and popular, it did not win the war; the KMT lost it. Between 1945 and 1946, the KMT scattered its army to garrison all the cities and railway lines of China, its forces incapable of mutual support, alienating urban populations and never controlling the peasantry. The best KMT troops fought well, but most were bad, unwilling to engage a tough foe in rough country; many hated their masters more than their enemy. The CCP's leader, Mao Zhe Dung, used guerrillas to stretch his foe but concentrated on conventional operations: "Make wiping out the enemy's effective strength our main objective; do not make holding or seizing a place our main objective. . . . In every battle, concentrate an absolutely superior force, encircle the enemy forces completely, strive to wipe them out thoroughly and do not let any escape from the net." In this war, small bodies of men charged across large spaces, though heavy battles between large forces were common. The PLA grew steadily larger and better, characterized by speed, maneuver, concentration, and light infantry making good use of small firepower. It exploited its enemy's fragmentation and immobility by trapping KMT troops in cities, cutting the rail lines that the enemy needed to move men and supplies, and annihilating divisions as they moved cross country. The KMT could not replace its losses, especially among its best units. Meanwhile, between August 1945 and August 1947 the PLA quadrupled in size, to two million, because the CCP effectively tapped the resources of the increasingly large population under its control and defeated Nationalist soldiers routinely joined the PLA. These new soldiers were equipped with captured arms—between 1945 and 1949 the PLA took three million rifles and two hundred thousand machine guns. In 1947, after two years of battle, the KMT burst like a balloon. Several sharp blows by three hundred thousand to five hundred thousand PLA soldiers wrecked KMT forces of equal strength; rather than abandon hopeless positions, the KMT threw its best units there, to be surrounded and annihilated, often after months of resistance; instead of combining against the enemy, each faction of the KMT sold the others out. Defeat became rout, and with the CCP's victory in 1949, China became a great power for the first time in a century.

The Indo-Pakistani war of 1971 was a shorter and less bloody conflict but no less significant. It shows how force combined with diplomacy can achieve victory. Pakistani power in the subcontinent hinged on the union between its eastern and western halves. By 1971 the Pakistani army's savage suppression of East Pakistan left the Bengali population longing for liberation from the unified state. It also limited the value of Pakistan's superpower allies. When opinion in the United States and the world turned against these well-publicized atrocities, the U.S. government could not block an Indian attack limited to East Pakistan. Nor did China, although both warned India to leave West Pakistan be. India's decision to ally with the USSR further checked Pakistan's allies and also provided a means to delay the passage of a ceasefire resolution at the UN. Thus, India received the political opportunity to smash its only rival in the subcontinent—if it could defeat Pakistani forces in East Pakistan. Not only were these forces small, they were also deployed to control the local population rather than to withstand a conventional attack. The operations of the Indian army in 1971 were creditable but not brilliant; yet they had the greatest strategic consequences of any short conventional war since 1945. They created Indian hegemony throughout southern Asia and broke Pakistan in two.

Since 1945 conventional wars have been a central tool of politics in Asia and Africa. They have created regional powers and determined what regimes would succeed the European empires, but equally important have been guerrilla wars. This phenomenon is much misunderstood. It is often supposed that guerrilla movements invariably win their wars. In fact, most are strangled in their cradle and few ever defeat their foe. Nor is there just one kind of guerrilla war. Some are wars of national liberation against foreign occupation; others are civil wars fought between different factions in a country, each supported by a minority of the population. The bulk of the guerrilla movements that achieved spectacular success after 1945 were fighting wars of national liberation where the guerrillas had much active support from the population and the government little or none. Most of these successes occurred between 1945 and 1963 in the European empires overseas: their main strategic consequence was to hasten the end of European colonialism. Since then, circumstances have changed. Guerrilla struggles have generally been a form of civil war, often dragging on inconclusively for years. Guerrillas have won spectacular success in civil wars only against unusually corrupt and incompetent regimes. In Cuba during the late 1950s, one thousand guerrillas with the military expertise of a troop of Boy Scouts smashed fifty thousand well-equipped soldiers, not because guerrillas are intrinsically powerful but because the regime was hopelessly rotten.

Many of these misconceptions stem from the fact that the prevailing definitions of guerrilla war are themselves highly politicized. In the liberal tradition and the influential theories of Mao Zhe Dung, guerrillas are seen as representatives of "the people" as a whole in a struggle against oppression by a few. While people are real, "the people" is an idea, and abstractions do not fight wars. There is no such thing as "the people" with one universal set of aims and grievances, nor do people necessarily behave as liberals or Maoists think "the people" should. The people of any country are often profoundly divided on religious, ethnic, cultural, social, and economic grounds. They do not fight primarily, or at all, for the lofty ideals of liberal democratic nationalism or Maoist social revolution but for more parochial and particular concerns. Liberal and Maoist principles have attracted non-European peoples less than religious sentiments or a tradition of patriotic pride and prejudice. These were the forces, in the form of jihad, that fuelled the deadliest guerrillas of the 1980s—the Shi'ites of Lebanon, who killed more Israeli soldiers than had the entire Arab world in 1967, and the Afghanis, who broke the Russian army. Above all else, success or failure in a guerrilla war is shaped by the sociology of the local population. Guerrillas, like any political movement, must favor specific groups of people against others, and gaining one group as supporters often turns another just down the road into an enemy. Many people remain neutral. In guerrilla wars two armed minorities are generally trying to bully a reluctant majority. Nor does the fashionable jargon of Maoists or liberal counterinsurgency theorists explain guerrilla wars in practice. Their theories work only when people behave like Maoists or liberals. Neither explains how to make them do so. Both theories assume that all guerrilla wars are won or lost through the application of the same universal principles and techniques. Both theories are wrong: guerrilla wars must always be seen in the particular.

Consider the classic example of success in counterinsurgency—the British campaign against the Malayan Communist Party (MCP) during the 1950s. For some years MCP guerrillas controlled much of this British colony, but they failed in one key area. Malaya was a country of many nationalities, of whom only 15 percent were Chinese. That community was divided on social and economic lines; it was feared by the rest of the population, yet the MCP's membership was almost entirely Chinese. Its support came primarily from just 20 percent of the Chinese population, three hundred thousand landless squatters in the interior. The British counterattacked in many ways but always by exploiting specific circumstances. They bought off existing political elites and parties, gave them administrative power, and finally granted independence. Thus, the British acquired support from every community, including, ultimately, the Chinese one. Chinese businessmen had little to gain from Maoist revolution. The British also removed the squatters from the guerrillas' control by resettling them in "controlled villages." Before doing so, they identified and arrested supporters of the guerrillas and then moved the villagers to new locations, where, despite some hardships, their standard of living soon rose. They were given housing, electrical power, medical care, secure leases on farmland, and a definite status as citizens. The British armed villages of any nationality that proved their loyalty to the government so that they could fight off the guerrillas themselves. All of this increase in British control at the grass roots was possible because the civil administration in Malaya was tolerably honest and efficient and useful because it addressed the social roots of insurgency. These actions destroyed the guerrillas' base of supplies and recruits and left them isolated deep in the bush, where they fought on their own terms. The British hunted the guerrillas with small forces of light infantry, which were often out on patrol—"jungle-bashing"—for weeks on end, far from their base. This was feasible because the MCP, unable to acquire large supplies of arms from outside, could never stand up even to tiny British forces. So simple an approach could never have worked in Indochina. The British systematically cleared the country district by district, pushing the guerrillas from the population. When its forces located the enemy, British aircraft paradropped reinforcements and bombed the guerrillas, thus bringing massive but precise firepower down on the enemy while reducing civilian deaths to a minimum. Ultimately, the guerrillas fled to the far north of the country, where they became irrelevant.

These techniques worked in Malaya but not everywhere. Agricultural and political reform and the winning of hearts and minds are the universal panaceas of liberal counterinsurgency theory. These lay at the heart of British success, but they were possible only because a limited degree of social and economic reform in Malaya did not bother authorities in London. Britain was also willing to sacrifice political power so to defend its economic interests in Malaya. Generally, however, third-world governments are fighting to keep power. They will not give it away. Since their aim is to avoid wide-ranging and thorough reform, they cannot use such a policy as a tactic. A government that did so would alienate its own supporters and weaken instead of strengthen its position against the guerrillas. At most, this tactic may be used to end a localized insurrection among relatively small numbers of peasants, as in Malaya and the Philippines during the 1950s. In the third world, social and political reform are good things in themselves, but they are of small practical value as tools of counterinsurgency. And when used by an inefficient or corrupt government, all the classic principles and techniques of counterinsurgency can backfire.

During the 1950s and 1960s, the more the South Vietnamese government's power swelled at the grass roots, the more unpopular it became. It used that power to benefit its supporters at the expense of the population, robbing from the poor to give to the rich. It strengthened the hold of landlords over their tenants in a country where 72 percent of the population owned only 15 percent of agricultural land. It made peasants pay several years of back rent all at once or return property to their landlords. The administration was controlled by Catholic refugees from North Vietnam, who used it for their own parochial interests. They expropriated land from Buddhists and gave it to Catholics, they outlawed Buddhist marriage customs, they destroyed Buddhist temples, and they killed Buddhists on religious holidays. Whereas in Malaya just 6 percent of the population was moved to "controlled villages," in South Vietnam the government tried to relocate almost half the population, because every controlled village offered a new opportunity to embezzle U.S. funds provided for the program. Most villagers hated "population resettlement" because this cost them their land, wrecked their standard of living, and destroyed the central religious and social cult of ancestor worship. In any case, since Viet Cong cadres were not removed from the relocated population, this policy spread the guerrillas instead of smashing them. In this context, to strengthen the army was to weaken the state. The more firepower possessed by the Army of the Republic of Vietnam (ARVN), the more it could force unpopular policies on the peasantry and the greater the support they gave the guerrillas. Moreover, in 1961 the Viet Cong had few automatic weapons and could not engage ARVN in battle. However, the United States provided automatic weapons to militias in controlled villages without ensuring that these forces were loyal or could defend themselves. These militias immediately became the first target for attack and infiltration by the Viet Cong. It quickly seized these weapons and, by 1963, began to smash ARVN to pieces in battle after battle.

In practice, guerrillas always face substantial problems. The surprising thing is not that they succeed so rarely but that they ever do. They begin as tiny and poorly armed movements without military experience. They have to operate in isolated areas of a country: otherwise they will be destroyed. They usually acquire arms only by seizing them from the government's army. Even if a neighboring country offers assistance, the guerrillas' strength is small while their aims are vast—simultaneously to create an army and an administration and defeat those the government already possesses and to take over an entire country. The guerrillas' target is as much the civil administration as the army. The assassination or subversion of local officials often damages a government more than attacks on soldiers. It is also safer. Similarly, governments can break the guerrillas' ability to draw support from the population simply by strengthening their own administrative control in the countryside. Guerrilla wars are fought simultaneously on three levels—at the administrative plane, in the struggle for grass-roots influence among the population; at the dimension of high politics, or the creation of movements that can create or coordinate general support from the population; and on the purely military plane. Nothing forces any side to fight effectively on all of these levels. Both can treat the population with brutality, leaving it to bow not to the more liked but the more feared faction. But if one side declines to fight on all three of these levels, it concedes a crucial opportunity to its enemy—an uncontested victory that may decide a war. Defeat at any of these levels can be fatal. If one destroys the popular support of a guerrilla movement, one need not even annihilate its army but merely drive it into the wilderness. A powerful, ruthless, and hated army alone can keep a popular guerrilla movement from victory for decades on end.

Guerrillas were so successful against the colonial regimes precisely because the Europeans could not easily compete on all of these levels. Their rule had rested on a few white soldiers and administrators, much prestige, and the political disorganization of the colonized peoples. After 1945 these conditions vanished—first of all in southeast Asia, where the Japanese occupiers deliberately broke European power and prestige and fostered armed national forces. After the defeat of Japan, the local elites and populations did not wish to be colonized again—they would no longer consent to European rule—while the usual discrepancy between the power of guerrilla and government was reversed. The Europeans had to rebuild their armies and administrations from the beginning, while those of the guerrillas were already in place. In 1946 the Viet Minh controlled every town in Vietnam—the French had to drive them out before they could even begin to reestablish their rule. The Dutch failed to reconquer Indonesia because they could not smash the nationalist army fostered by Japan. The British did not even try to do so in Burma. One guerrilla success, meanwhile, spawned another. Some leading Algerian revolutionaries had prior experience with guerrilla wars—they had served as soldiers of France against the Viet Minh, who provided a lesson in how to defeat colonialism. Several Algerian soldiers captured at Dien Bien Phu, for example, were ordered to pass a minefield across the bodies on dead Viet Minh soldiers. When they came to a dying soldier, his lips still moving, the senior Viet Minh officer said, "Get going. You can step on him. He has done his duty for the Democratic Republic of Vietnam." One of these prisoners years later, by then a senior Algerian officer, recalled, "You know, me and the other Algerians—we were very impressed." With the end of the era of colonial wars, the situation changed. Guerrilla wars have been endemic in Asia, Africa, and Latin America since the 1960s, but wars of national liberation have been rare. Governments with little popular support or outside help—as in

Rhodesia and Nicaragua during the 1960s and 1970s—fought guerril-las more resolutely and effectively than the colonial or the superpowers ever did, because they had no other choice. Defeat meant exile, impov-erishment, or death. In guerrilla wars willpower counts for as much as firepower.

Guerrilla conflicts have been total wars fought within individual so-cieties. They have been longer, more nasty, and more brutal than most conventional wars fought since 1945, and the use of terror against civil-ians has been virtually universal. Many guerrilla movements, whether in Vietnam or Peru, have routinely tortured and executed civilians in front of their neighbors. Nothing quite illustrates the impotence of the state better than the public castration of a village chief followed by the massacre of his family. Nothing better exploits the economic and so-cial tensions in peasant societies than the Chinese communist tactic of having the population of entire villages beat its landlords to death with sticks, and nothing better burns peasants' bridges to the state. Many governments—whether France, Britain, the United States, the USSR, or Israel—have used torture to acquire intelligence, assassination teams to kill enemy politicians in neutral countries, and death squads to terrorize civilians; they have devastated the economy and massacred the popu-lation of the countryside through air strikes. Such horrific tactics are sometimes successful and sometimes not. Throughout the thirty-year war in Vietnam, communist forces murdered tens of thousands of un-armed civilians, members of other political parties, and government of-ficials. This crippled its rivals for power although it also created dan-gerous local enemies. Conversely, the brutality of Israel's occupation of Lebanon during the 1980s, combined with a tradition of martyrdom in the Shi'ite faith, sparked the creation of the suicide bombers who forced Israel to withdraw.

Between 1880 and 1914 revolutionary groups assassinated public figures, including one U.S. president, one Russian tsar, and dozens of members of royalty or government officials, and exploded bombs across Europe and the United States in pursuit of "propaganda by the deed"— the idea that a sensational attack on a state or its servants, if witnessed by people and reported in the media, would sap the government and strengthen the revolution. Between the 1960s and 1980s "New Left" groups emulated such actions across the Western world. Frequently, terrorist groups have been allied to or the tools of states that search for hidden means to strike a neighbor. The "Black Hand," a secret society that was an unofficial arm of the Serbian military, organized the assassination of Crown Prince Francis Ferdinand of Austria, which sparked the outbreak of the First World War. However, after 1945 attacks by nonstate groups on civilians flourished as never before in modern history, under many ideological banners—nationalism, Marxism, fascism, anarchism, and jihad. The nature, size, and effect of such groups has varied widely; as a rule, the longer their name, the less they matter. States routinely supported such movements as a means to strike their enemies (e.g., East Germany with the Red Army Faction against West Germany; Syria, Iraq, and Iran with anti-Israeli organizations of Lebanese and Palestinians). Groups in dozens of Western countries attacked their states and countrymen, sparking some insurgencies that lasted for decades, killing tens of thousands of people, and destabilizing governments across Europe and Latin America. In pursuit of "propaganda by the deed" on television, they aimed for sensational actions, such as hijacking airliners or blowing them up in the skies. Some of these actions were sophisticated and devastating. In September 1970, the Popular Front for the Liberation of Palestine organized the simultaneous hijacking of four airliners, their flight to Cairo and Amman, and their destruction in front of international cameras after the passengers were evacuated. On September 11, 2001, commercial airliners, transformed into flying suicide bombs, smashed the twin towers of Manhattan, killing three thousand people and ravaging the U.S. economy, the arc of their death flights immortalized on television. "Terrorism" was bidding to remain one of the characteristic forms of war and society during the twenty-first century.

Since 1945 military forces have shaped the world even when not fighting. While the alliances of the Cold War never fought a world war, they did create a structure for world power. During the late 1940s, the United States was the dominant economic power on earth and became the military protector of Japan and western Europe. By the 1980s its economic power had declined to a par with that of western Europe or Japan, yet it retained a loose leadership over them, largely because of its military alliances. While U.S. citizens often complained that their allies were unwilling to defend themselves, this was a necessary cause for their political dominance. Had Japan doubled its defense expenditure, as President Reagan's administration demanded, it might quickly have become the United States's greatest security problem in the Pacific. Military strength was of even greater moment to the USSR. Its economy failing, its political attraction waning, its military alone allowed the Soviet Union to remain so powerful in the world for so long. The alliance system of the Warsaw Pact left the USSR dominant in eastern Europe until 1989, while its ability to provide good weapons for free and to neutralize the United States gave it much influence in the world.

Simultaneously, military technology and production became a more important component of the world's economy than ever before in peacetime. The spin-offs from such activity often had critical significance—the technology used by the civilian airline industry is parasitical on the military sector, while until the late 1970s the development of the computer was shaped primarily by military requirements for ballistics and code breaking. Since the major states preferred to maintain indigenous sources of military equipment, while few could buy enough of their own production to keep these industries afloat, the international arms trade became a key export sector. The competition for markets spread modern weaponry across the world, at a heavy cost. In economic terms, expenditure on armed forces is spending that does not produce goods—literally the equivalent of welfare. Even allowing for spin-offs, investments in the research, development, and production of weapons are not the optimum means to improve one's GNP. These investments, however, have been substantial. By the 1980s, 30 percent of the engineers in the United States worked in defense related industries, while civilian firms suffered from shortages of such personnel. It is not coincidental that those industrialized states with the lowest per capita expenditure on defense between 1970 and 1990, like Japan, Germany, and Canada, had higher rates of economic growth than those with the highest rates of defense expenditure—the United States and Great Britain. The latter spent two to three times more of their GNP on defense than their allies. They paid to defend their allies, who repaid the favor with heightened economic competition.

Since 1945 the relationship between war and society has also changed drastically in the Western world. Consider simply two issues, military recruitment systems and public attitudes toward war. The spread of universal male conscription for military service was one of the crucial events of nineteenth-century Europe. It increased the armed strength of governments and the damage inflicted by war and the power of states over their societies. In the eighteenth century few European governments could even tax their populations. A century later many could make all of their male citizens fight and risk death for them. The spread of conscription was related to the development of mass nationalism, universal literacy, and improved public health—armies could not be effective unless conscripts could read instruction manuals, carry heavy equipment, and regard themselves as expendable tools of the nation-state, to follow their country right or wrong and to the death. In the process militarism, the fetishizing of the values and behavior of soldiers and warriors, became a central ideology throughout the Western world. As an important English publicist of airpower, C. G. Grey, put it in 1918, "The human animal is a fighting animal, and the fighting man is still, as in all the world's history, the finest type of humanity." In the eyes of the liberal nationalists of France, the army was the school of the nation; in Imperial Germany, army officers had greater prestige than any civilian profession; the writings and speeches of Joseph Stalin and all of his successors until the 1980s were laced with military metaphors.

In the United States since 1945, military institutions have acquired greater influence in government policy, but the opposite has been true in most Western countries. Militarism survives in the public fascination with military technology and elite forces or the popularity of the Rambo films. In the Star Trek television series of the 1960s the future literally was a military institution and plot lines centered on a captain's fantasies about the joys of sex with a starship. Since 1945, nonetheless, compared to the century before 1939, the power of the militaristic tradition has declined, and a liberal view, antimilitaristic and often antimilitary in tone, has achieved a limited victory in the Western world as a whole. The public no longer regards war as good in itself but at best a necessary evil, while pacifist views are more powerful than in the nineteenth century. Nowhere are these things more true than in Germany and Japan, which possessed the most militaristic cultures on earth in 1939 and the most antimilitaristic of any since 1945. By the 1970s in western Europe, the home of the mass conscript army, public opinion forced governments to decrease the period of compulsory military service and to increase opportunities for conscientious objection. By the 1980s U.S. political candidates no longer suffered painfully for having avoided active service during their country's wars. Western populations remain willing to defend themselves against aggression and to support external wars— the cheaper the war, the greater the support. Still, to an unprecedented degree, sizable elements of Western populations have openly opposed the wars of their own countries while these were still being fought. The opponents of war have usually been a minority but a sizable one. The domestic opposition in Britain, France, and the United States to the Suez affair and to the wars in Algeria and Vietnam, in Germany and Japan to the Gulf War of 1991, and in Israel to the 1982 invasion of Lebanon all reveal the existence of new limits to the military freedom of action of liberal democratic governments. Western populations appear less willing than before to be treated as mere tools of state, while the importance of individual conscience against collective patriotism has risen. Many citizens have demanded the freedom to support or oppose a war depending on their own individual assessment of its justice.

Broader social changes affected the organization of all Western military institutions after 1945, and nowhere more than in the United States. Its military services expanded dramatically and permanently in size, from a few hundred thousand in 1941 to several million after 1951. Hence, the officer corps could no longer draw its members just from its old pools of recruitment. It ceased to be the possession of a social elite, isolated from civilian society. Like the United States itself, the officer corps became middle class and dominated by a managerial ethos, more professional and less warlike than before. The organizational model for the U.S. military became General Motors instead of General Grant. Some such changes were perhaps unavoidable and had advantages to offer but at a price. Before 1941 the officer corps was an old-boys network that, despite its amateurism and cronyism, was flexible enough to tolerate able eccentrics and to forgive occasional errors and small enough to give senior officers a personal sense of their subordinates' strengths and weaknesses. By the 1950s the officer corps had become a bureaucracy instead of a club. Officers were promoted on the basis of regular assessments by their superiors; woe betide he or she who ever received any but glowing comments, who committed a major error as a junior officer, or who upset the institutional boat. By official decree, any officer's promotion to general rank hinged in part on assessments of the social skills of his or her spouse. "Blood and Guts" Patton, "Bull" Halsey, and "Billy" Mitchell would each have failed one of these criteria, if not all of them.

Meanwhile, the ethnic composition of the military altered dramatically. Before 1941 nonwhite personnel hardly served in the USN at all, mainly as mess stewards, and the USN increased its use of them during the Second World War primarily as a sop to political pressure. While the army had many black units, including the "buffalo soldiers" of the Old West and Afro-American officers graduated from West Point, between 1900 and 1945 nonwhite personnel rarely served in combat.

Those who did were invariably segregated, as with the Nisei battalion and the Tuskegee airmen of the Second World War; however, the service most opposed to the use of African Americans, the navy, established integrated units because this was preferable to the alternative, which was segregated ships entirely manned and commanded by blacks. During the First World War, the army loaned regular black troops and officers to the French for combat service rather than have them fight alongside white U.S. soldiers. Even in 1945 the army refused the obvious solution to its dire manpower situation, assigning black soldiers to white units. General Marshall, the head of the U.S. Army, rejected integration of black soldiers in white units as being "tantamount to solving a social problem which has perplexed the American people throughout the history of the nation. The army cannot accomplish such a solution, and should not be charged with the undertaking." Yet, that is precisely what happened within the next thirty years, as one southern senator complained that the military was being used "as an instrument for social reform."

In 1949, for moral and political reasons, President Truman ordered the armed forces to abandon legal segregation. Meanwhile, wartime experience convinced many senior officers that the United States must make more effective use of African Americans, who had much to offer their country. In 1951, during the Korean War, unlike the case just six years before, the army solved the problem of replacing heavy losses by integrating black soldiers in white combat units. Soon, as the military adopted conscription in peacetime, a new problem emerged. Unless a large cadre of regular personnel could be maintained, the armed services would decline in quality. Too few white personnel were willing to reenlist to meet that need. An obvious solution was to enlist nonwhite fighting men, and white U.S. citizens were glad to have blacks bear their share of peacetime conscription. Thus, the most conservative institutions of the United States, the armed forces, were the first to abandon legal segregation and to recruit black personnel according to their share of the population. The services took these actions for reasons of self-interest, and their policies varied with the need for conscripts. The USN required the fewest conscripts and, supported by powerful Congressional allies who opposed desegregation in general, took only cosmetic steps in this direction. The army, the service that most needed conscripts, took the most serious steps. For example, between 1949 and 1962 the proportion of African Americans in the army's officer corps doubled, to almost 6 percent. By the late 1950s, the army, and to a lesser extent the other services, was the only large U.S. institution where black men regularly gave orders and white men obeyed. In principle, nonwhite personnel could enter any branch of any service and promotion was to occur by color-blind merit. These principles were not thoroughly followed in practice. Blacks were plentiful in support and combat roles but rarer in technical branches. Promotion to officer and senior noncommissioned ranks was difficult. In the air force and the navy some segregation persisted—one shift crew might be all-black, another all-white—while in many states the national guard remained segregated until 1965. The armed forces had started a social revolution. They had not completed it.

In 1945 most U.S. combat troops were white, recruited on a tolerably equitable social basis from the Caucasian population. The personnel of individual units were often drawn from the same region of the country, neighbors commanded by their bosses; their officers frequently came from local social elites. Units fought together for the duration, allowing experience and mutual confidence to form among all ranks. The fighting services of 1965 were fundamentally different. Personnel were recruited through "selective service," a form of conscription in which some eighteen-year-old males were made to join the military for two years while most were allowed to go free. Local draft boards, composed of respectable citizens of the district, separated the sheep from the goats, and in a notoriously inequitable fashion. Boys of privileged social classes could avoid service through loopholes like college deferments far more easily than boys from other classes. During the Vietnam War, low-income U.S. citizens were twice as likely to serve in combat units as high-income citizens, high school dropouts 50 percent more likely to do so than college graduates. All this affected their casualty rates. Both officers and enlisted men came from different sources than in 1945. Between 1965 and 1966 the proportion of blacks in combat units significantly exceeded their share of the U.S. population, although by 1968 this ceased to be the case. The officers were white college boys, drawn from a wider (and, in social terms, less exclusive) group than in 1945. Officers and men stemmed from different regions of the United States. Few officers were black—only 3 percent of army officers in 1968 and only 0.7 percent of the incoming class of West Point cadets—and they often felt that they were treated with disdain by their white counterparts.

This institutional revolution created social and racial tension. Afro-American nationalists could easily argue that black men were being

forced to fight brown men for the sake of white men, and, as the box-
ing champion Muhammad Ali said when refusing to serve, "I ain't got
nothing against them Viet Cong." These problems were unintention-
ally exacerbated by the army's managerial approach. The army wished
to maximize the number of its junior officers with combat experience;
hence it rotated them through fighting units every six months. During
the Second World War, Dwight Eisenhower told his son, a junior officer, that "really getting to know every single man in (your platoon);
that is the real secret of leadership. . . . Always try to make your whole
platoon look upon you as the 'old man.'" This was hard to do in Vietnam: officers had little chance to acquire experience or to know their
men, who served in combat for longer periods of time. Soldiers were
also continually rotated in and out of units as individuals. The aim was
to equalize the risk among the army. The effect was to weaken the cohesion and morale of combat forces and to increase losses—green soldiers
suffered higher casualties than veterans. Moreover, the army used a
statistical means of management to gauge the progress of a statistical
means of war, attrition. It judged the performance of units by their body
counts—the number of enemy claimed as killed. Any officer who hoped
for a successful career had to better his predecessor's performance or else
raise questions about his competence. This produced a climate of institutional corruption. Nothing was easier than to inflate body counts—dead
children and blood stains could be added to the list at will—and nothing
could more thoroughly wreck the means by which the army determined
its success in the war. All this sapped trust and discipline within units.
Many soldiers came to feel that their officers were amateurs who were
exposing their men to meaningless engagements purely to help their
own careers.

The U.S. Army was in the midst of an institutional revolution, the
traditional social structure of its units was collapsing, and all this during
a long, bloody, and inconclusive war of a sort that has often eroded the
nerve of armies of industrialized states since 1945. Just like the armies
of France during the Algerian war, Israel during its counter-insurgency
campaigns of the 1980s, and the USSR in Afghanistan, by 1969 the U.S.
military in Vietnam was cracking beneath the strain. It faced unprecedented problems of racial strife even in front line units. Race riots broke
out on aircraft carriers and in military prisons. Afro-American sailors
went on strike, raising "black power" salutes for television cameras.
Drug abuse was widespread and discipline collapsed. At least 520 cases

of "fragging," or attempted murder, usually directed against unpopular "lifers"—career officers and noncommissioned officers—by their men, led to eighty-six U.S. deaths.

When, after the Vietnam War, the U.S. forces returned to an all-volunteer system, their reliance on nonwhite servicemen became even more pronounced than before. The proportion of blacks in the services almost doubled between 1970 and 1980 and settled at 20 percent of the whole. This decade witnessed another notable development: the U.S. services solved the social and racial problems that had surfaced in Vietnam, largely because senior officers worked to make it so. Trivial matters can reveal the spirit of any military institution. During the 1920s one British admiral insisted that all of his officers own at least one polo pony, because only a horseman and sportsman could be a true officer. By the early 1970s the head of the USN, Admiral Elmo Zumwalt, was convinced that the USN was "a racist institution." He personally devoted much time to addressing these issues, even to the extent of ensuring that base exchanges were stocked with the brands of makeup used by African American sailors and their families. The armed services became an occupation of choice for many African Americans, and more black recruits had a high school diploma than did white ones. Blacks reached far more senior positions in the military and in far greater numbers than in any comparable business or government organization. Between 1968 and 1988 the proportion of blacks in West Point classes multiplied by ten, to 7 percent. Ten percent of the army's officers were black, as were 5 percent in the U.S. Air Force (USAF) and 3 percent in the USN. By the 1990s one hundred Afro-Americans had reached general or admiral rank, and by 1991 a black man was the most senior U.S. military officer—Colin Powell, the chief of the Joint Chiefs of Staff. The U.S. armed forces and the Democratic Party had become the only genuinely integrated large organizations in the United States. A conservative military institution had fostered a social revolution.

By the 1990s they were entering another revolution, as the tradition that women cannot be warriors and the macho atmosphere of fighting services were challenged by the institutional needs of the U.S. armed forces and the social norms of the United States. During the Second World War, 150,000 women entered the U.S. military in ancillary branches, where, as the surgeon-general of the USN said, "You can fill a man's shoes and still do a woman's work." Afterward, many wished to remain. Allowing them to do so had institutional advantages. Women were paid less than men for the same jobs, while many military personnel performed work that was identified with women. If females were to work in the military, the services preferred that they be under proper discipline. Hence, women were allowed to enter some sections of the military, those that did "women's work," like the nursing or clerical branches. They received lesser benefits than men. They were allowed to occupy only 2 percent of the places in the armed forces and were denied entry to the service academies. By the 1970s changes in social attitudes toward women's work and the difficulties faced in finding enough volunteers led to radical changes in this sphere. The formal principle of equal pay for equal work was adopted. Women were allowed to enter the service academies and most branches of the armed forces, including technical ones from which they had previously been excluded. The only exception were combat units themselves, although many women served in immediate support companies. By 1991, 11 percent of the U.S. military were women, almost half of whom were black. All this occurred against much opposition. Zumwalt noted how critics warned of "unisex showers and floating orgies." He believed that many old navy men were even more reluctant "to give up the notion that their beloved service should be all male than . . . all white."

By the 1990s a debate broke out regarding the culminating point of this process. Some argued that women could and should serve in fighting units, others that they were incapable of performing the function and that any attempt to do so would wreck the camaraderie of men under fire. This debate was soon rendered academic. During the Gulf War, women served as soldiers within the combat zone, and all of the confusion on the topic became plain. It also made headlines. Some women went to war, leaving their children in the care of soldier-husbands who remained stateside. Thousands of U.S. women risked their lives in the combat zone. Some women flew aircraft behind enemy lines, others worked with units in the front line, and five were killed by enemy fire. Some military men thought that the presence of women soldiers had hampered morale, some did not. The Gulf War produced paradoxical results regarding fighting women. On the one hand, the U.S. government steadily moved toward allowing women to enter combat roles. On the other, accounts of sexual harassment in the armed forces became public knowledge. The Pentagon announced that during the Gulf War one woman soldier had been taken prisoner and molested by her captors, while thirty-four others had been sexually assaulted by their U.S. comrades. In 1992 a furor arose when it became known that at a convention of naval aviators and in the presence of top brass, as if to prove Zumwalt right, dozens of drunken male pilots had sexually assaulted many women, including female officers, and that USN authorities had tried to hide the scandal. According to the Pentagon, the admiral in charge of the investigation compared women navy pilots to "hookers." Retired military men with conservative opinions charged publicly that the lives and careers of their wives and daughters, who were members of the services, were routinely suffering from sexual harassment. Again, the U.S. military was serving as a mirror of social change and perhaps as a spur to it, and this pattern was common throughout the Western world.

Since 1945 the relationship between military institutions and societies has been fraught in the non-Western world. India has been blessed by the survival of the British tradition that the army remain a servant of state, not its master, while in Israel universal military service has helped to turn a host of immigrants from half of the world into one people. Elsewhere, most armed forces have become highly politicized and the dominant force in countries where all civilian institutions are weak. In many countries armies have become their own masters. The militias of Lebanon or Somalia are not soldiers but mafiosi. War has ceased to be a tool to achieve a specific end. It has become an end in itself, a business and a way of life: without war, the militias could not exist and therefore they can never voluntarily let it end. Most armed forces in the third world have pursued a policy of military corporatism, where the army controls much of the economy and many civilian political parties, and not only defends the state but defines it. While similar patterns have existed in Western and communist states, there the armed services have been relatively weaker. Military corporatism is the military-industrial complex run wild, as if the USN was the largest shareholder in General Motors and master of the Democratic Party, the U.S. Air Force ran IBM and dominated a major faction of the Republican Party, while the army, in conjunction with Colombian drug dealers, controlled every state government on the southern tier of the United States and the Drug Enforcement Agency. Precisely this pattern persists in countries like Thailand, Uganda, Pakistan, and Brazil and in several continents.

Latin America, for example, was characterized by military politicization and the impact of ideology on the use of force. Its armies had traditions of intervention in politics, seeing themselves watchdogs over constitution and Christianity, and they faced constant insurgencies. Trotskyites, Maoists, Marxist-Leninists, anarcho-syndicalists, Castroists, Peronistas, and liberals pursued distinct brands of guerrilla war, as did drug cartels, regionalists, and Indians. While such insurgencies usually rested on peasants, they also included urban guerrillas, who argued that their approach alone could destroy regimes using modern counterinsurgency techniques and technology. Many of these movements were amateurish; in Bolivia between 1967 and 1968, Ernesto "Che" Guevara launched a classic example of incompetent guerrilla war, ignorant of the people he hoped to mobilize and even of their language. Insurgents won only in Cuba and Nicaragua, but even those that lost had significance. Often they were powerful and popular, and the more so, the more ruthless the state concerned with a material and moral threat, and the more military support it gained from the United States, which viewed such movements as communist. Many of these wars were long and costly stalemates, marked by torture, death squads, air strikes on slums, assassinations of individuals, and slaughters of villages. Though armies generally were the worst offenders, some guerrilla movements, like the Sendero Luminoso (Shining Path) group of Peru, were as murderous as any military and more than most. Hundreds of thousands of civilians died between 1948 and 1956 in "La Violencia" in Colombia and also in the several insurgencies of Central America between 1968 and 1994. Though most guerrilla movements were crushed or contained, their pressure broke political systems throughout Latin America. It heightened military fears of subversion and produced constant military coups. In Uruguay and Argentina during the 1970s, urban guerrilla movements lost but toppled fragile governments and triggered military rule—exactly what they had aimed to do, because their theorists wrongly assumed that this would hasten the revolution. Instead, it killed the revolutionaries. Military regimes became the norm in Latin America, their aims ranging from social-democratic reformism to authoritarian Catholic traditionalism. Many ruled for a long time—the military governed Brazil between 1964 and 1985; all believed their actions for the good; none succeeded; and by 1985 most retreated to their barracks, humiliated by their errors and excesses. They left civilian governments to overcome the bitter memories of civil wars and reconcile army, guerrillas, and people.

Military politicization has had unfortunate consequences for armies and states. Military institutions have not been successful as nation build-ers or as modernizers, while soldiers have rarely been brilliant statesmen. Moreover, the obvious form of politics in a state dominated by an army is a military coup d'état, and once coups become the currency of poli-tics, bad coin drives out good. That is particularly true when any group of officers has reason to fear the wreaking of revenge (or justice) for its deeds (or misdeeds) while in office. This has crippled political stability, not to mention the evolution of a liberal democratic system, in much of the third world. Moreover, the politicization of armies has damaged their combat quality. Many regimes have systematically promoted their own loyalists at the direct cost of military efficiency. During the 1960s, for example, Syrian politics were chaotic and its combat performance abysmal because its military was extremely politicized. Generals dared not risk their commands against Israel because these were their polit-ical power base in Damascus. These political and military weaknesses ended only when one faction finally achieved total victory, annihilated its opponents and created an army that was loyal and able.

The pattern of conflict changed with the end of the Cold War. The USSR ceased to matter militarily, as did regimes dependent on strength borrowed from it. The balance of power fundamentally altered and so did its nature. Initially, Western states assumed they could master the new world order, and not without reason. They were secure against threats, with an edge in military technology as overwhelming as ever in the nineteenth century; the 1991 Gulf War demonstrated that, united and determined, they could smash third world armies. Yet experience soon showed that those conditions were unusual and the West could not easily master the world. Weapons of mass destruction—nuclear, chemi-cal, and bacteriological—were widely disseminated and sometimes used; the risk that they might be deployed on a sizable scale in the West or elsewhere seemed higher than ever. Meanwhile, Western states gener-ally did not use their power against strong non-Western states, which dominated their own regions and acquired weapons of mass destruc-tion. When Western states actively used their power, they did so in an odd way. Their peoples, reluctant to fight except for their own vital in-terests, still sometimes wished one foreign party would cease to bully another and deployed token forces so to achieve that end. However, they remained uncertain whether to use that force and how. The re-sults combined tragedy with force. Any government can easily pursue its interests by using its army unilaterally. Western states were pursuing more difficult ends—international acts of charity through multilateral military means, driven not by reason of state but by public opinion and humanitarianism, aiming not to defeat a foe or to further an interest but to do good and no bad, expecting a mere declaration of war to produce immediate victory, through high technology and low casualties. Such ends were hard to achieve or even to pursue.

Western outrage or troop movements did not make bullies mend their ways. Tiny but ruthless powers defied western Europe and the United States for years, as in ex-Yugoslavia and Somalia, watching them bluster or run when a few U.S. Rangers were massacred in Somalia during 1993 or Belgian paratroops in Rwanda during 1994. Regimes in Iraq and Serbia gained political strength by defying the West, which often was divided, as it faced localized and unlimited wars, marked by ethnic cleansing and mass murder. These wars were fought by militias armed with a mixed bag of weapons—the machete dominated the most terrible of them, the Rwandan genocide of 1994. Their aim was to steal a neighbor's land and to kill its people for an example or its own sake. The West found it hard to help the weak. It did little to protect Bosnian civilians from Serb and Croat militias and nothing for millions of Africans killed in Rwanda, Sudan, and Sierra Leone. This process, however, did encourage weaker groups deliberately to attack the stronger side and its civilians, aiming to escalate the crisis in order to outrage Western opinion and provoke its intervention. Nor could that intervention easily achieve its aims. Sometimes Western powers did arm a weaker side and aid it to survive, as with Rwandan Tutsis, but more often it just helped a lesser evil against a greater one. Thus, in 1995, to end Serb attacks on Bosnian Muslims, the West helped Croatia to attack Serbia and to drive two hundred thousand Serbs from their homes. Nor was this impotence typical just of the NATO powers. Israel, overwhelmingly powerful against its neighbors, abandoned much of the West Bank in response to the *intifada*, or Arab civilian uprising. India's attempts to settle a civil war in Sri Lanka produced heavy losses, a humiliating withdrawal, and the assassination of the Indian prime minister. Expeditionary forces mounted by African countries failed to solve murderous strife in Sierra Leone or Liberia. Islamic suicide bombers inflicted the heaviest blow the United States, the only superpower left standing, had ever suffered in peacetime. Power was not what it once had been. What it would become remained uncertain.

Case Study: The Indochina Wars

The thirty-year conflict in Indochina illustrates all of the characteristic features of war and society during the Cold War. This war began when France decided to reconquer the Asian colonies it had lost to Japan. France intended to avoid another entry on its long list of military humiliations since 1870. Instead, it added another one. This occurred primarily because of a complete failure in the political and administrative dimensions of guerrilla war. France declined to surrender power to national and nationwide political parties for fear that this would subvert French rule. Thus, it acquired no strong allies in Vietnam as a whole. Yet only where France, however reluctantly, did acquire allies could it deny local support to its enemy, most notably in southern Vietnam. Invariably these groups, while powerful in one region, could not pose a nationwide threat to French power, like some non-Vietnamese tribesmen, or "Montagnards," in the mountains, and minority elements of the Vietnamese population like the schismatic Cao Dai and Hoa Hao religions in the Mekong Delta, Catholics in the Red River Delta around Hanoi, and the Binh Xuyen mafia in Saigon. Elsewhere, France simply conceded the battle on the political and administrative levels. This was a disastrous error given the sociology of Vietnam. Ethnic Vietnamese comprised 90 percent of the population, and Vietnamese Buddhists alone made up 75 percent of it, while the leaders of the Viet Minh belonged to the traditional ruling elite of the country. Part of the national leadership of Vietnam was rallying an unusually homogeneous people with a powerful tradition of resistance to foreign oppression in order to serve a patriotic war and a communist revolution. Through terror, armed struggle, systematic agricultural, and social reform within villages, and the fact that they were the only alternative to French rule by 1950 the Viet Minh established political dominance over the population of northern Vietnam. Even in the Red River Delta, the center of French power in the north, where almost half of its army in Indochina was stationed, one French officer described government forces as being just "bread crumbs in the soup." The Viet Minh controlled most villages, barely 10 percent of which paid taxes to the French or had regular contact with its civil administration. Meanwhile, Viet Minh political control spread steadily in central Vietnam.

This political success gave the Viet Minh access to recruits and supplies and set the stage for military victories. These were not easy to acquire, however, because the French were better soldiers than politicians.

The performance of the French military was far from bad, given the limits to its resources, but these resources were limited in the extreme. By 1954 the French possessed just 180 aging combat aircraft in Vietnam. Had this been the only air cover available to U.S. marines in 1968, the besieged firebase of Khe Sanh might have fallen: given the U.S. airpower of 1968, the besieged airbase of Dien Bien Phu might well have survived. France refused to send conscripts to the theater because it feared that heavy casualties might erode the will to fight of the population at home. It was slow to raise a regular army of Vietnamese—such a force might threaten colonial rule. Its army was drawn from regular French soldiers, some Indochinese troops, African colonial forces, and the mercenaries of the Foreign Legion, hence the motley band that stood in the catastrophe at Dien Bien Phu in 1954—French and Vietnamese paratroops, Algerian and Moroccan infantrymen, and former members of the *Waffen SS* dying alongside Spanish anarchists in the ranks of the Foreign Legion. France maintained around 175,000 regular soldiers in Indochina with another 250,000 local, mostly paramilitary, troops. After garrisoning the towns, barely 50,000 regular troops remained free to engage the enemy in the field.

This was a formidable foe. The Viet Minh raised 260,000 guerrillas and, by 1953, with assistance from communist China, a conventional field army that reached 110,000 brave and well-trained men, outnumbering the French field force by two to one in manpower and possessing as much artillery. Its guerrilla and conventional forces posed a two-punch threat to France. To keep guerrillas from completely controlling the population, French forces had to be dispersed; to withstand the divisions, they had to be concentrated: the French lacked the strength to do both these things simultaneously. They could not take the initiative— they could not find the Viet Minh, which fought only when and where it wanted to. The French could not afford even one heavy defeat. They could not defend everything and the Viet Minh struck everywhere, particularly at areas of French weakness. French shock troops fought with élan but no sooner was one threat surmounted than another emerged. When in 1950 French garrisons were scattered along the Chinese frontier, Viet Minh divisions smashed each in isolation from the rest, killing ten thousand regular French soldiers. In 1951, however, French forces, grossly outnumbered in manpower though still amply backed by riverine firepower, armor, and aircraft, crushed infantry assaults against Hanoi, killing perhaps twenty thousand men, 40 percent of the Viet Minh's regular personnel, and incapacitating thousands of others. The Viet Minh recognized that French firepower could smash any attack in open country and turned to a new strategy, attacking the French at their weakest rather than strongest points. It withdrew to adjacent terrain that armor could not enter—permanently pinning the bulk of French regular forces in the defense of Hanoi—while opening a new theater of operations.

In demographic terms, Indochina consisted of several densely populated pockets separated by a series of vast, thinly populated, and roadless highlands. In 1951 the Viet Minh operated in only one of these pockets, northern Vietnam, which allowed France to concentrate most of its assault forces there. Over the next few years, however, the Viet Minh developed a logistical network based on the backs of hundreds of thousands of porters, which allowed tens of thousands of soldiers to move ten miles a day across hundreds of miles of hill and bush and then to fight with full supplies. There the Viet Minh regularly annihilated French troops. They moved more easily and speedily than the enemy through these highlands and struck unexpectedly at all French garrisons and friends. This stretched the flimsy French logistical network ever thinner and tied down more and more of their forces as garrisons—multiplying every French weakness, dividing every strength.

Between 1951 and 1953 the Viet Minh seized military control over the highlands of northern and central Vietnam. By late 1953 its army was poised to strike not only at central Vietnam and the Red River Delta but also at Laos and toward two previously secure pillars of French power—Cambodia and southern Vietnam. In order to check this danger, France occupied a valley in northwestern Vietnam, Dien Bien Phu. This position was intended to serve as a base for guerrillas working against the Viet Minh and block its movement toward Laos or southern Vietnam. The valley was isolated except by air and the fifteen-thousand-man garrison was too weak to hold the hills over its head. French commanders assumed that these problems would be irrelevant because the Viet Minh could not move large forces and heavy equipment to the region; these assumptions proved false. In an extraordinary feat of logistics, strategy, and camouflage, the Viet Minh first launched the assault which Dien Bien Phu was intended to forestall. Thirty thousand Viet Minh regulars stampeded through the highlands of Indochina, simultaneously driving into Laos, threatening Cambodia and southcentral Vietnam, smashing several large French forces, including mechanized units. French reserves scattered throughout Indochina and its logistical

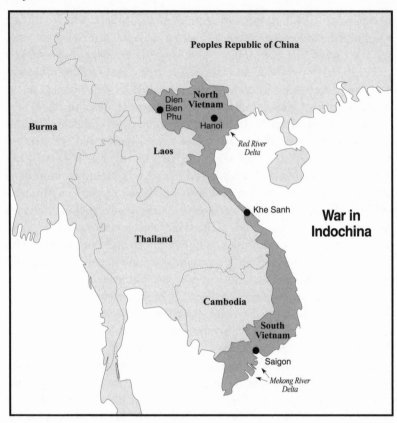

Map 13.2

network was stretched to breaking point. While continuing these offensives, the Viet Minh moved forty-nine thousand men and over two hundred guns to Dien Bien Phu—all in secret. Then massive artillery barrages closed the airstrip; continual human wave assaults eroded French strength and morale; the Viet Minh had vastly superior firepower at hand and dispatched ten thousand replacements for their losses. French casualties could not be flown out and supplies could not be flown in. Although the French dispatched most of their shock troops as reinforcements these could not save the day. The garrison surrendered after an epic siege, and, with half of its scarce elite forces in Indochina destroyed, France's ability to continue the struggle was gone. So was its will. At precisely this moment ten thousand Viet Minh regulars who had infiltrated inside French defenses around the Red River Delta joined hands with local guerrillas and launched a new assault. These French garrisons had to fight their way back to Hanoi.

The war was over, yet these losses were less than those that France frequently had suffered on single days of the First World War. France had too much will to abandon Vietnam but too little to hold it. As the Viet Minh commander, General Giap, had predicted, "The enemy will pass slowly from the offensive to the defensive. The blitzkrieg will transform itself into a war of long duration. Thus, the enemy will be caught in a dilemma: He has to drag out the war in order to win it and does not possess . . . the psychological and political means to fight a long-drawn-out war." Viet Minh casualties at Dien Bien Phu were higher than those of France—25 percent of its regular army was killed—but throughout the Indochina wars the communists were always better able to take casualties and continue fighting than their enemies.

Between 1957 and 1975 the second Indochina War pitted the heirs of the Viet Minh (North Vietnam and the Viet Cong) against South Vietnam and its U.S. ally. The fundamental factor in this war was the weakness of the South Vietnamese state. It provided no political or administrative competition for its terrible but able enemies. The government alienated most Vietnamese and Montagnards and smashed the anticommunist but non-Catholic groups that had cooperated with the French, such as the Cao Dai. In fact, fewer people supported the South Vietnamese government than had backed the French colonialists. Most of the population disliked and despised the government but liked or feared the Viet Cong, which had all of the old policies and strengths of the Viet Minh. Nor could ARVN match its adversaries. Its officers were usually urban Catholics and the enlisted men rural Buddhists. Officers mistreated their men, who were conscripted for life and 30 percent of whom deserted each year. In order to reduce the likelihood of coups, the South Vietnamese government splintered the military command system and promoted loyal incompetents. ARVN was primarily an instrument to loot the peasantry for the benefit of generals. For an officer to fight the Viet Cong was to risk his financial and political strength, to beat the enemy while suffering heavy losses was not to win but to lose. ARVN's combat performance was dismal. It would not move at night. It would not knowingly enter areas under enemy control. It only patrolled places where the enemy was thought to be absent—conducting what frustrated U.S. advisors called "safaris" or "search-and-avoid" missions. By January 1963, in the Battle of Ap Bac, Viet Cong militia with rifles and a few machine guns defeated ten times their number of ARVN troops with helicopters, heavy artillery, and armored cars. During 1964 ARVN commanders used their forces to launch coups against each other rather than to fight the enemy that was overrunning the country. The Viet Cong, guerrillas with surprisingly little outside aid at this point, were on the edge of victory. In 1954 the United States fostered the creation of South Vietnam in order to prevent the communists from establishing a unified Vietnam. By 1965 Washington had to intervene directly to save its creation from collapse. North Vietnam responded in kind.

The events of the next decade exposed every strength and weakness of the U.S. Army. It declined to adapt to local conditions or to fight a guerrilla war. When asked to define the answer to guerrillas, the U.S. commander in Vietnam, General Westmoreland, replied, "Firepower." The army simply transferred to Vietnam the U.S. way of war, with its emphasis on the decisive battle, massive firepower, and high technology, its doctrine of "find, fix, fight and finish." The United States expected the enemy to fight by their rules, but it found itself playing an Asian game. It ruled out an invasion of North Vietnam for fear of sparking Chinese intervention and thus, like France before, lacked the strategic initiative. The enemy tried to lure most U.S. forces into the highlands where they could not challenge communist control over the mass of the population in the lowlands. This is exactly what the U.S. forces did. Less than 10 percent of the 550,000 U.S. soldiers were combatants— the remainder were support personnel—and they were fighting 130,000 communist combat soldiers. The United States could not win the war unless the enemy agreed to stop fighting. It hoped to achieve this end by

grinding down the enemy's strength and will, but this attritional strategy played directly into the strong suits of the enemy's style of war.
Since the issue mattered more to Hanoi than Washington, the enemy
was willing to pay a higher price for victory and U.S. will was easier
to grind down. By 1967, Secretary of Defense Robert McNamara realized that the enemy was retaliating in kind to American policy with
"a strategy of attriting our national will." Communist authorities held
that so long as they did not give up, the United States eventually would.
This view was correct and reflects one great strength of North Vietnamese strategy—its recognition of how the war was linked to politics,
particularly in the United States. Two of its three greatest offensives,
in 1968 and 1972, were launched during presidential election years in
order to shape U.S. policy toward Vietnam. The third great offensive,
which smashed South Vietnam, was timed to exploit the confusion that
the Watergate scandal wreaked on U.S. policy. Moreover, the attritional
strategy could work and high technology and firepower could matter
only if the United States could make the communists stand and fight,
but the enemy determined when battles would occur and how expensive
they would be. One U.S. divisional commander recalled that the enemy
"were more elusive. They controlled the battle better. They were the
ones who decided whether there would be a fight." Certainly, the U.S.
Army could crush the enemy's conventional forces every time they came
out in the open. Generally, however, the enemy did not do so, and when
it did it used tactics like "hugging" or "clinging to the belt"—engaging
U.S. troops so closely that the United States could not use its firepower
without killing its own men. In the end, the U.S. Army could only bring
its firepower to bear and make the enemy fight by offering vulnerable
targets to attack. It sent small patrols into the bush with the aim of being
ambushed, turning infantrymen into live bait to attract the attention of
a shark. As one cynical marine put it, "you have to get ambushed before
you can find the enemy." Not surprisingly, this magnified the social tensions within the army.

During the first two years of active U.S. involvement, it saved South
Vietnam from immediate collapse and strengthened the power (although not the popularity) of its administration but did nothing to
weaken the enemy. Washington's approach to military management
and the prevailing atmosphere of institutional corruption prevented it
from recognizing the fact. Body counts were routinely falsified at every
level of command. U.S. authorities overestimated the enemy's losses

and underestimated its ability to keep fighting and led the U.S. public to think that the war was almost won. When that proved to be false, its will to fight eroded. The enemy finally came into the open during the Tet offensive of 1968 in order to shake the growing power of the South Vietnamese state and in the hope that one all-out push would bring total victory. Tet achieved the first aim but not the second and at a heavy price. U.S. troops and firepower killed ten regular or irregular communist soldiers—between forty to sixty thousand of them—for every U.S. soldier or ARVN dead and smashed for some time the enemy's ability to annihilate South Vietnam. In particular, Viet Cong cadres surfaced during Tet and suffered horrendous losses. The survivors could also be located far more easily than before. This information was exploited through Operation Phoenix, the U.S. and South Vietnamese campaign of political assassination. Most of Phoenix's twenty to fifty thousand victims were innocent civilians, and in some districts the campaign was actually controlled by the enemy, but after the war the North Vietnamese minister of foreign affairs claimed that Phoenix had destroyed the Viet Cong in much of South Vietnam. In any case, after 1968 the Viet Cong ceased to be an independent threat to the government.

Tet was a major U.S. victory but not a total one. During 1951 the French had destroyed a larger proportion of the Viet Minh's army and still lost their war. Tet would be a wasting asset unless the United States could use the breathing space to make South Vietnam able to stand by itself. This the United States failed to do. It could not prevent a resurgence in North Vietnamese strength nor could it bolster the South Vietnamese government because it mishandled the politics of the war. In many ways, the U.S. presence actually weakened its ally. The supply of easy money exacerbated the prevailing corruption in Saigon and led officials to believe that the United States would always pay South Vietnam for the privilege of defending it. They had little incentive to improve their efficiency. Once the United States smashed the Viet Cong, the South Vietnamese government no longer faced internal competition and had no need to gain support from its population. When the enemy again declined to come out in the open, U.S. firepower proved counterproductive. Individual platoons could receive as much fire support as regiments in the Battle of Normandy—usually directed not at soldiers but civilians, particularly because the Viet Cong used villagers as a cover when attacking U.S. troops. Many U.S. soldiers began to see all Asians as enemies, and as their discipline declined, atrocities against civilians rose. Indiscriminate U.S. firepower killed hundreds of thousands of civilians and helped to make almost 30 percent of the population refugees at one time or another between 1964 and 1969. This scarcely fostered gratitude for U.S. forces or support for their allies. Even U.S. forces found their own firepower and high technology counterproductive. In the midst of bitter and confusing firefights, junior commanders on the ground sometimes had several senior officers flying above their heads in helicopters, each simultaneously demanding information and providing different orders. Enemy booby traps and land mines caused 20 percent of U.S. infantry casualties and 80 percent of tank losses. Dud U.S. shells and bombs provided much of the ammunition used for this purpose, up to eight hundred tons of high explosives every month.

By the later 1960s, precisely as Hanoi had calculated, the U.S. public tired of a war that had cost fifty thousand U.S. and two million Vietnamese lives and appeared to have no end and no value. Television turned Tet from a military victory into a political defeat. Pictures in every U.S. living room of devastation on the battlefield, of Viet Cong sappers fighting inside the U.S. embassy in Saigon, of the annihilation of the city of Hue demonstrated that the war was far from won. These changes in opinion helped to bring a new president into office with a new strategy, "Vietnamization." By 1971 President Nixon withdrew all U.S. ground forces from Vietnam, reducing U.S. casualties and North Vietnamese pressure on the home front. Simultaneously, the United States maintained great pressure within Indochina, particularly by giving more fire support to ARVN than any previous army in history had ever known. Whether this strategy could have worked can never be known, since it vanished with Watergate. When this happened, South Vietnam immediately collapsed. The Viet Cong regained some ground in the countryside, tying down 25 percent of ARVN. While the quality of ARVN improved, it could withstand serious attack only with massive U.S. support. Between 1974 and 1975 Congress ended such assistance and the ultimate irony occurred. North Vietnam did not win the war with guerrillas but with blitzkrieg. Its army smashed through South Vietnam; columns of trucks and tanks stretched out for miles along the roads—the target for which the U.S. military had yearned for years but one they could no longer attack. All that U.S. airpower could do was to evacuate its diplomats from their embassy in Saigon. Superior politics and willpower had beaten superior firepower and technology.

Suggested Reading

The literature on war and society since 1945 is spotty in quality—there are many mediocre works but fewer strong ones. The standard account of the nuclear forces and strategies is Lawrence Freedman, *The Evolution of Nuclear Strategy* (New York, 1981), while the best strategic account of the cold war is Norman Friedman, *The Fifty Year War, Conflict and Strategy in the Cold War* (Annapolis, 2000). Patrick Brogan, *The Fighting Never Stopped, A Comprehensive Guide to World Conflict Since 1945* (New York, 1990), is a useful compendium of information about all major wars between 1945 and 1990.

There is a significant literature on guerrilla wars and counter insurgency campaigns after 1945, much of which is excellent in quality. The best introduction to the conceptual issues surrounding these issues is D. Michael Shafer, *Deadly Paradigms, The Failure of U.S. Counterinsurgency Policy* (Princeton, 1988); it also has important comments on the Philippine and Indochinese wars. Oddly, the best of these works are on the French wars of decolonization. The best book on the French campaign in Indochina—and probably the best book written on any battle after 1945—is Bernard Fall, *Hell in a Very Small Place; The Siege of Dien Bien Phu* (Philadelphia, 1967); his other works, such as *Viet Nam Witness, 1953–66* (New York, 1966), are also crucial contributions to studies of the wars in Indochina. Alistair Horne, *A Savage War of Peace, Algeria 1954–1962* (London, 1957), is equally brilliant. Antony Clayton, *The French Wars of Decolonization* (London, 1994), offers a good overview of that topic. John Coates, *Suppressing Insurgency, An Analysis of the Malayan Emergency, 1948–1964* (Boulder CO, 1992), is an excellent introduction to an important campaign. There is a huge literature on the U.S. phase of the Indochina wars. Four good recent accounts, which express a wide range of viewpoints, include Richard A. Hunt, *Pacification, The American Struggle for Vietnam's Hearts and Minds* (Boulder CO, 1995); Andrew F. Krepinevich, *The Army and Vietnam* (Baltimore, 1986); Guenter Lewy, *American in Vietnam* (New York, 1978); and Colonel Harry G. Summers *On Strategy, A Critical Analysis of the Vietnam War* (Novato, 1982).

The literature on conventional wars after 1945 is rather less good. Callum A. MacDonald, *Korea, The War Before Vietnam* (New York, 1986), is the best short introduction to the Korean War; Shu Guang Zhang, *Mao's Military Romantacism: China and the Korean War, 1950–1953* (Lawrence KS, 1995), provides an excellent introduction to the Chinese side of the equation. There is a large literature on the Arab-Israeli wars, most of which is bad; the best introduction to the key issues is Michael I. Handel, "The Evolution of Israeli Strategy: The Psychology of Insecurity and the Quest for Absolute Security," in Williamson Murray, MacGregor Knox, and Alvin Bernstein, *The Making of Strategy; Rulers, Wars and States* (Cambridge, 1994). The best analyses of the conventional wars of the 1970s through 1990 are Anthony H. Cordesman and Abraham Wagner, *The Lessons of Modern War*, vol. 1; *The Arab-Israeli Conflicts, 1973–1989*, vol. 2;

The Iran-Iraq War, vol. 3; *The Afghan and Falklands Conflicts*, vol. 4; *The Gulf War* (Boulder CO, 1990).

Useful material on the role of ethnic minorities in world militaries may be found in Warren L. Young, *Minorities and the Military, A Cross National Study in World Perspective* (Westport CT, 1982), and Bernard C. Malty and Morris J. MacGregor, *Blacks in the Military, Essential Documents* (Wilmington DE, 1981).

EPILOGUE

The Future of War and Peace

It can be argued that violence will always be with us. Thus, the themes of this book can also be projected into the future. There will always be some concept or idea of war. Similarly, there will surely be an experience of total war in the future, whether on a large or small scale. If anything, technology is even more rapidly changing the way that conflict is, and will be, conducted. However they will be, structured armed forces will always exist and have their own nature, usually a reflection of the society of the time. Finally, the experience of the soldier will, of course, also continue into the foreseeable future of warfare.

What, then, will be the future of warfare? According to the United Nations, there have been almost five hundred wars since 1945. Yet at the same time the chance of war between major powers has lessened considerably since the end of the Cold War. There is therefore a measure of optimism for the future. The largest conflict of recent years has been the Desert War (1991), in which the United Nations, supported principally by the United States, achieved a rapid defeat of the forces of Iraq that sought to acquire Kuwait. Besides this, the United Nations and the North Atlantic Treaty Organization have undertaken several police actions in the recent past in order to try and halt aggressive actions by lesser powers. These have not always achieved their desired aims, but there seems to be greater willingness to oppose aggressive military actions around the world. As part of this intent, the North Atlantic Treaty Organization recently announced the creation of a rapid reaction force.

In the future conflict appears less likely from major powers and more likely from lesser powers, especially from groups promoting their own specific aims and rivalries. These conflicts might derive from a number of sources: ethnic struggles; drug wars initiated by drug distributors and/or producers; religious conflict between rival sects and even between major religions; competition for illicit trades, such as the diamond trade; modern piracy, often by groups claiming to represent political movements; the ever present but changing conflicts of guerrilla and terrorist groups; violence produced by criminal organizations; and various kinds of civil war. In particular, the attacks of September 11, 2001, against the United States suggest a prolonged conflict against worldwide terrorist groups who use religious justification for their actions. This situation has the potential to involve a large number of nations through a ripple effect. All this becomes even more feasible in the twenty-first century because power and armaments are no longer the exclusive property of the state but have been seized by such groups to further their aims. There are many parts of the world where such conflicts currently exist— for example, Afghanistan, Indonesia, the Balkans, Sri Lanka, Columbia, the Middle East, and many groups in Africa. Environmental degradation of the globe is also a distinct threat with results that could well produce violence, while the widening gap between rich and poor also has ominous overtones for the future.

Lower-level conflict seems likely to increase, yet, on the whole, there is now more optimism about the future absence of world wars, especially since the period of the twentieth-century wars (1914–53) has apparently come to an end. However, this optimism must always be tinged with skepticism, as the whole history of worldwide warfare described in this book seems to suggest. If nations do not protect themselves, as Clausewitz once argued, "gradually blunting our swords in the name of humanity," then perhaps "sooner or later someone will come along with a sharp sword and hack off our arms."

INDEX